THE LIFE OF CHRIST
VOLUME II

THE LIFE OF CHRIST

A HISTORICAL, CRITICAL, AND APOLOGETIC EXPOSITION

BY

THE VERY REV. L. C. FILLION, S.S.

CONSULTOR OF THE PONTIFICAL BIBLICAL COMMISSION

TRANSLATED BY

THE REV. NEWTON THOMPSON, S.T.D.

VOLUME II

B. HERDER BOOK CO.,

15 & 17 SOUTH BROADWAY, ST. LOUIS, MO.,

AND

33 QUEEN SQUARE, LONDON, W. C.

NIHIL OBSTAT

Sti. Ludovici, die 3. Oct., 1928,

H. Hussmann,

Censor Deputatus

IMPRIMATUR

Sti. Ludovici, die 4. Oct., 1928,

✝ *Joannes J. Glennon,*

Archiepiscopus

Vail-Ballou Press, Inc., Binghamton and New York

CONTENTS

PART IV—THE PUBLIC LIFE OF OUR LORD

INTRODUCTORY CHAPTER

FIRST PERIOD

FROM THE BEGINNING OF THE BAPTIST'S MINISTRY UNTIL HIS IMPRISONMENT

CHAPTER I

CHAPTER II

CHAPTER III

CHAPTER III

CHAPTER IV

CHAPTER V

FOURTH PERIOD

FROM THE THIRD PASCH TO THE FEAST OF DEDICATION

CHAPTER I

CONTENTS

CHAPTER II

APPENDICES

THE LIFE OF CHRIST

PART IV

THE PUBLIC LIFE OF OUR LORD

INTRODUCTORY CHAPTER

The Chronology and Length of Christ's Ministry. The Probable Order of Events

THIS period of the Gospel history occupies a particularly important place in the Savior's life because it is the part which enables us to study His Person and His work most thoroughly. And the sacred writers supply us with a relatively large number of details about this period. Before entering upon the narrative, we must consider a chronological question that offers serious difficulties. It consists of a threefold problem: (1) At precisely what time did our Lord's public ministry begin? (2) How long did it last? (3) What is the order of events composing it?

We ought to say at once that a fully satisfactory reply is impossible on any of these points. The information contained in the Gospels is not sufficient for us to reach conclusions that are beyond doubt; and tradition from the very first has given expression to most varied opinions on the beginning and the length of the public life, as also on the order of its events, with the result that later exegesis, perplexed and partly left to its own resources, came to different, sometimes opposite, conclusions. Happily none of these questions is vital and essential for our Lord's history. Notwithstanding that these problems themselves may be very interesting, they are, after all, only secondary. As Bossuet says: "Whether we must place the date of our Lord's birth a few years earlier or later, and consequently lengthen or shorten His life somewhat, is a problem that arises from uncertainties regarding the dates of secular history as much as regarding those of Christ. However that may be, an attentive reader can see that it nowise affects the sequence and fulfilment of God's designs."[1] We will try at least to approach the truth of the matter as nearly as possible and, although unable to attain mathematical exactness in ascertaining these dates, we can do so approximately.

1. At what time shall we place the beginning of Christ's public life? From St. Luke we know that John the Baptist began his preaching "in the fifteenth year of the reign of Tiberius Cæsar."[2] But, according to the sequence of St. Luke's narrative, as likewise that of the other three Evangelists, there could have elapsed only a brief time, a few months at most, between the precursor's appearance and that of the Messias. St. Luke also informs us that when Jesus "was beginning," that is, at the outset of His public life, He "was about the age of thirty years."[3]

These dates, however, are both rather vague. Besides the fact that we are unable to calculate the exact length of time separating the inauguration of the two ministries, it is hardly possible to decide with certainty just what we are to understand by the fifteenth year of the reign of Tiberius. There are two different methods of computing it, thus giving rise to dates that are two years apart. Some reckon the years of this reign by starting with the death of Augustus, Tiberius' predecessor (August 19, A. U. C. 767, being A. D. 14), with the

---

[1] *Discours sur l'Histoire Universelle*, Part I, Epoch 10 (*Œuvres*, Versailles ed., XXXV, 98 f.).
[2] Luke 3 : 1.
[3] Luke 3 : 23.

result that the fifteenth year would extend from August 19, 781 to August 19, 782 (A. D. 28 to 29). Subtracting from this figure the "about thirty years" of our Savior's age at that time, we would obtain as the date of the Nativity the year 751 or 752. But this result is condemned in advance by the need of placing the first Christmas not later than the beginning of 750, before the death of Herod the Great.[4]

To obviate this very real difficulty, most contemporary exegetes prefer to take as the starting-point of Tiberius' reign, that year when Augustus associated Tiberius with himself in the government of the Empire;[5] this took place A. U. C. 765 (A. D. 12). The fifteenth year would thus extend from 779 to 780 (A. D. 26 to 27) and would coincide with the "about thirty years" of Christ's age, reckoned as starting in 749–750. By the aid of ancient inscriptions and medallions it has been proved that this manner of computing the length of the reign of Roman emperors was more or less in use in the provinces of the East.[6]

Another piece of chronological information, supplied by the Fourth Gospel,[7] enables us to place the beginning of our Lord's public life at this same date. Taking literally Christ's words, "Destroy this temple, and in three days I will raise it up," the Jews said to Him: "Six and forty years was this temple in building; and wilt Thou raise it up in three days?" They were speaking of the second Temple, called Zorobabel's, built on the ruins of Solomon's [8] after the close of the Baby-

---

[4] Vol. I, p. 303.

[5] As *collega imperii.* Cf. Tacitus, *Annales,* I, 3; Velleius Paterculus, II, 12.

[6] Wieseler, *Beiträge zur richtigen Würdigung der Evangelien,* pp. 191–194; Ramsay, *Was Christ Born at Bethlehem?* pp. 197–226. We mentioned above (Vol. I, p. 303) the principal works treating of the chronology of our Lord's life. See also E. Mangenot, *Les Évangiles Synoptiques,* pp. 164–170, and Van Bebber, *Zur Chronologie des Lebens Jesu,* 1898.

[7] John 2: 20.

[8] The Chaldeans under Nabuchodonosor burned it after the taking of Jerusalem in 587 B. C.

Ionian Exile,[9] and restored and magnificently enlarged by King Herod.[10] According to Flavius Josephus,[11] this reconstruction, begun A. U. C. 734 (20 B. C.), was not finished until long after,[12] a few years before its destruction by the Romans.[13] By adding 46 to 734, we thus obtain the year 780 (A. D. 27) for the first Pasch of Christ's public life.

2. Inasmuch as the exact time when Jesus commenced His ministry is not certain, evidently we cannot determine with strict accuracy the length of that period of His life. Three different opinions on this subject were formed in early times.

a) Several ecclesiastical writers of the first centuries interpreted too literally that saying of the prophet Isaias which Christ one day applied to Himself: "The Spirit of the Lord is upon me; because . . . He hath sent me to preach to the meek . . . to proclaim the acceptable year of the Lord," [14] and from it they concluded that Christ exercised His ministry for only one year.[15] The text of Isaias certainly refers to the Messias; but the expression "the acceptable year of the Lord" is quite

---

[9] Esdras, chaps. 3–6; Aggeus 2 : 1–10, etc.

[10] Vol. I, pp. 164 ff.

[11] *Ant.*, XV, xi, 1.

[12] While Albinus was governor of Judea (A. D. 62–64).

[13] A. D. 70. Schürer, *Geschichte des jüdischen Volkes im Zeitalter Jesu Christi*, 3d ed., I, 392.

[14] Is. 61 : 1–2; Luke 4 : 18–19.

[15] Such was the view held by several Gnostic sects (the Basilidians, according to Clement of Alexandria, *Stromata*, I, xxi, 146; the Valentinians, according to St. Irenaeus, *Adv. Haer.*, I, ii, 3; xx, 1; XXII, i, 3; II, xxii 1, 5, and St. Epiphanius, *Haer.*, LI, 28; probably also the Docetae, the Aloges, and Marcion, according to W. Bauer, *Das Leben Jesu nach den neutestamentlichen Apokryphen*, p. 281), the author of the *pseudo-Clementine Homilies* (*Hom.*, I, 7; XVII, 19; *Recogn.*, IV, 35), Clement of Alexandria (*Stromata*, I, xxi, 143; V, vi, 37; VI, xi), Julius Africanus (cfr. Bauer, *op. cit.*, p. 282), Tertullian (*Adv. Jud.*, 15), and Lactantius (*Divin. Instit.*, IV, x, 18 and xiv, 11; *De Morte Persecut.*, II, i, 2). Origen expresses two different views: in one place he favors a period of about one year (*Hom. in Luc.*, 32; *De Princip.*, IV, 5: "One year and some months"); in another place he favors "three years and three months" (*Contra Celsum*, II, 12; *Comment. in Matth.*, *Serm.* 40). The same is true of St. Hippolytus (Bauer, *op. cit.*, pp. 288 f.).

general, referring especially to the Israelites' jubilee year and the choice blessings it brought them from Heaven.[16]

A large number of modern commentators, belonging to the most opposite schools, have adopted this theory of one year, though basing their conclusion on other grounds.[17] They allege particularly the fact that the Synoptics mention only a single Pasch in Christ's public life—the Pasch that witnessed His Passion and death.[18]

But this argument is valueless, either because the first three Evangelists, who did not purpose relating the Savior's entire history, considerably abridge His public life and condense its events,[19] or because their accounts really suppose several Paschal solemnities during our Lord's ministry. The incident of the Apostles one day gathering some ears of wheat as they passed through a field,[20] shows that it was then the period of the Pasch, since one of the most interesting ceremonies of that feast consisted in offering the firstfruits of grain to God in the Temple.[21] The chronological place to which the three Evangelists assign this incident proves that a considerable period of time separated it from the beginning and from the close of the public life.[22]

Furthermore, St. Matthew and St. Mark, in agreement with St. John,[23] a little later, giving an account of the first multiplication of the loaves, show us the multitude that accom-

[16] Lev. 25: 1-55.

[17] Notably, in the ranks of Rationalist critics, Th. Keim, *Geschichte Jesu*, I, 493–496; P. W. Schmidt, *Die Geschichte Jesu erläutert*, II, 127–133; H. von Soden, in the *Encyclopædia Britannica*, art. "Chronology." Among Catholics, J. Belser, in the *Biblische Zeitschrift*, 1903, pp. 55–63, 160–174, etc.; L. Fendt, *Die Dauer der öffentlichen Wirksamkeit Jesu*, 1906.

[18] Matt. 26: 2, 17; Mark 14: 1, 12; Luke 22: 1, 7.

[19] See Vol. I, pp. 79.

[20] Matt. 12: 1; Mark 2: 23; Luke 6: 1.

[21] Vol. I, p. 381.

[22] The date indicated by St. Luke, "the second first Sabbath," probably designated the first Sabbath that followed the second day of the Paschal octave. See Fillion, *L'Évangile de S. Luc*, p. 134.

[23] Matt. 14: 19; Mark 6: 39; John 6: 10.

panied our Lord sitting down on the grass. It was, therefore, springtime, and the Pasch was near at hand.[24]

Lastly, if we take into account only the Synoptics, we are easily convinced that "it is materially impossible to embrace within a single year the great number of events which accumulate in their pages, those journeys through the cities and villages of Galilee, those prolonged sojourns at Capharnaum, those excursions into the neighboring regions, . . . those retreats to the mountain and other solitary places, in short, all that going and coming which the Synoptics connect together by transitions that are lacking in precise indications, 'in those days, then, many days after, then it came to pass,' etc. When we try to condense all this mass of events great and small, giving the least possible time to each, so as not to exceed the duration of a single year, we obtain absurd results. There are details that stubbornly refuse to be treated thus." [25]

b) This same author concludes that "it is therefore wiser to return to tradition." But tradition, considered as a whole, always reckoned the length of Christ's public life at about three years. St. Irenaeus vigorously protested against the one-year theory and insisted that it flagrantly contradicts the Gospels, especially several passages of St. John, which we will now examine.[26]

The Fourth Gospel supplements the Synoptics and throws

[24] In 1914, a few days after Easter, we gazed upon the luxuriant beauty of the fields to the north of Lake Tiberias, in the very region where Christ performed this great miracle.

[25] A. Réville, *Jésus de Nazareth*, II, 228 f. Cf. Beyschlag, *Das Leben Jesu*, 4th ed., I, 137; E. Levesque, *Nos Quatre Évangiles, leur Composition et leur Position Respective*, 1917, pp. 85–90.

[26] *Adv. Haer.*, II, xxiii, 3; III, xviii, 7. It is true that the learned Bishop of Lyons falls into another exaggeration when, on the basis of the Jews' reply to Jesus, "Thou art not yet fifty years old, and hast thou seen Abraham?" (John 8:57), he says that our Lord was then almost of that age (*Adv. Haer.*, II, xxii, 6). But this error does not weaken the force of his condemnation of the one-year theory. He extends the length of the Savior's life solely for a mystical reason, with a view to having all ages of human life sanctified by our Lord.

much light on the question in dispute by pointing out a whole series of religious feasts, placed at intervals throughout Christ's public life and requiring for the latter a period of three years and more. The following is a list of these feasts: (1) the first Pasch (John 2: 13); (2) a "festival day of the Jews," the nature of which we shall have to determine (John 5: 1); (3) another Pasch (John 6: 2); (4) the Feast of Tabernacles following this Pasch (John 7: 2); (5) the Feast of the Dedication (John 10: 22); (6) the last Pasch (John 12: 1; cf. 3: 1).

This list clearly designates three Paschs: the first, at the very beginning of Christ's preparatory ministry and shortly after His baptism; the second, about the time of the first multiplication of the loaves; the third, that of our Lord's Passion and death.[27] Yet, according to the early and weighty testimony of St. Irenaeus,[28] to these three Paschs must very probably be added a fourth, that which we place as the second feast in the above list and which is called simply a "festival day of the Jews." [29] Between the first and fourth of these feasts, therefore, three full years elapsed and, as we shall note shortly,

[27] Attempts have been made at times to suppress the second of these Paschal solemnities, namely, that of John 6: 4, on the fallacious pretext that the original text contained only ἦν δὲ ἐγγὺς ἡ ἑορτὴ τῶν Ἰουδαίων ("The festival day of the Jews was near at hand"), instead of ἦν δὲ ἐγγὺς τὸ πάσχα, ἡ ἑορτή . . . The words τὸ πάσχα ("the Pasch") would thus have been added afterwards. For this view, see a lengthy note in Westcott and Hort, *The New Testament in the Original Greek,* II, pp. 77–81 of the Appendix. But these two words unquestionably belong here, because they are to be found in all the manuscripts and all the versions.

[28] *Adv. Haer.,* II, xxii, 3.

[29] For centuries commentators have discussed this passage (John 5: 1) but have been unable to agree on its interpretation. The discussion concerns two distinct points: (1) Should we read ἑορτή without the article, "a festival," or ἡ ἑορτή, with the article, "*the* festival"? (2) What festival was this? For reasons which we have set forth in our commentary, *L'Évangile de S. Jean,* pp. 91–93, we prefer the reading ἡ ἑορτή, "*the* festival," and we believe it refers to the Pasch, which was the Jews' festival *par excellence.* All the religious festivals of Judaism have been advanced by exegetes, as corresponding to this text of St. John. The question is important for determining the length of our Lord's public life.

since Christ's ministry was begun some little time—doubtless several months—before the first Pasch, it lasted about three years and a half. Such was the view of St. Epiphanius,[30] St. Jerome,[31] Eusebius of Caesarea,[32] and many others following them.[33]

c) We have only one remark to make about the intermediate opinion, according to which Jesus preached the gospel for two full years, or even two years and a half. As may readily be seen, this allows only three Paschs in the course of His public life, thus at once reducing its length by one year.[34]

If the first of the three Paschs, according to our previous calculations, fell in the first days of April, A. U. C. 780 (A. D. 27), the fourth would have been that of 783 (A. D. 30.) [35]

3. The preceding pages, especially those concerning the chronological indications in the Fourth Gospel, also enable us to fix upon a few salient points, by the aid of which our Lord's public life becomes divided into regular periods, so as to facilitate the task of arranging the likely sequence of events. In short, they are the very same acts and even sayings of Christ which are related by the Synoptics and with the same progression.

St. Matthew and St. Mark, the former even more so than

---

[30] *Haer.*, LI, 23–26.

[31] *Comment. in Is.*, LXI, 1–2.

[32] *Hist. Eccl.*, I, 10, "not quite four years"; *Demonstr. Evang.*, VIII.

[33] In our own times, among others: J. B. Nisius, *Zur Kontroverse über die Dauer der öffentlichen Wirksamkeit Jesu*, in the *Zeitschrift für kathol. Theologie*, XXXVIII, 457–504; W. Homanner, *Die Dauer der öffentlichen Wirksamkeit Jesu, eine patristisch-exegetische Studie*, 1908; E. Levesque, *Nos Quatre Évangiles*, 1917, pp. 78–150.

[34] Among those holding this view, it will suffice to mention K. Hase, *Geschichte Jesu*, 2d ed., sec. 36 and 76; Bousset, *Jesus*, pp. 6 f.; C. Guignebert, *Manuel d'Histoire Ancienne du Christianisme*, p. 181; W. Sanday, in Hastings' *Dictionary of the Bible*, II, 610; J. M. Pfättisch, *Die Dauer der Lehrtätigkeit Jesu nach dem Evang. des heil. Johannes*, 1911.

[35] We may say, however, that the various authors, even those adopting the hypothesis of three years and a half, are far from being in accord when it is a question of designating the exact dates to which these years correspond.

the latter, are less concerned, in the matter of details, with the chronological order. But St. Luke generally is very faithful to the promise he makes in his prologue,[36] to conform to the real sequence of events. Several times, too, he mentions synchronous dates, which are valuable for us as guide-posts.[37] And then, in what at first sight would seem to be an account of Christ's last journey to Jerusalem,[38] he three times [39] indicates different departures, the last two of which bring the divine traveler back at once. Under these circumstances this detail evidently supposes that the Savior did not go only once to the Holy City, as one might be tempted to believe upon taking St. Matthew's and St. Mark's narratives too literally.

As we have seen, St. John renders us a still greater service in the matter of the chronological order of events, by taking pains to mention the religious feasts that divide Christ's ministry into several sections, and thus enables us to combine the four Gospel accounts harmoniously. These festivals are therefore a veritable guiding thread for us, or, to use another figure, a series of milestones set along our path.

Every Christian is naturally eager to follow the Divine Master as closely as possible through the incidents of His life as missionary, preacher of the gospel, and founder of the Church. Let us endeavor, at this point, to orientate the reader by sketching the order of events which we have thought well to adopt.[40] But at the very start it is proper to make an important reservation. We will say in the words of a recent Life of our Lord that, "against any harmony which can be devised, some plausible objections could be urged. On this subject no two writers have ever been exactly agreed, and this alone is

---

[36] Luke 1:3; καθεξῆς . . . γράψαι; Vulg.: *ex ordine . . . scribere.*

[37] Luke 2:1 f.; 3:1 f.

[38] Luke 9:52——19:58.

[39] Luke 9:52; 13:22; 17:11. See E. Levesque, *Nos Quatre Évangiles,* pp. 63–77.

[40] It will usually be that which we followed, after a deep study of the question, in our *Synopsis Evangelica,* first published in 1882, and reëdited several times since.

sufficient to prove that the Gospels' notices of chronology are too incomplete to render certainty attainable." [41] This is why we are careful not to present our arrangement of events as altogether beyond question. It is merely a possible order and may appear to some to be the probable one.

The earthly existence of the Lord Jesus may be compared to a drama or sublime tragedy which unfolds itself in three acts: the childhood and the hidden life, which we studied at some length in the previous volume, the public life, and the Passion. The whole is preceded by a short prologue and followed by a triumphant epilogue, that of the Savior's Resurrection and Ascension.

The prelude is composed of two parts. In our Lord's life there is first what we might call the prehistoric period, corresponding to the eternal existence of the Word in the bosom of the Father.[42] From that mysterious period we pass to the historical period, properly so called. But not yet does Christ appear in person. We merely have an indirect glimpse of Him, either in the testimony of the ancient prophets or in His ancestors, whose names we learn from His genealogy.[43]

We will not go back over the details of the first act. It is the second act with its different phases that now especially invites our attention. This we will divide into three periods, corresponding approximately to the three years between the first and the fourth Pasch of Christ's public life. To each of these years has been given a name fairly well summing up its general character. There is the year of obscurity, the year of public favor, and the year of opposition. This last leads directly to Calvary.

The first period also has its preamble in the fruitful activity of John the Baptist. The four sacred narratives clearly set

[41] W. Farrar, *Life of Christ*, 23d ed., I, xvii.
[42] John 1 : 1-18. See Vol. I, pp. 205-208.
[43] Vol. I, pp. 209 ff., 310 ff. Matt. 1 : 1-17; Luke 3 : 23-38.

forth his holiness, his preaching, his baptizing, and the testimony he so loyally renders to the Messias. Jesus, too, makes His appearance, but without ado, and is prepared for His divine office by the double consecration of His baptism and His threefold victory over Satan. A few disciples then join Him, at first in a transient way, and soon they witness His first miracle, which He performs at the wedding feast of Cana. Shortly after, we find Him at Jerusalem for the first Pasch, and there He inaugurates His Messianic ministry by driving the sellers from the Temple and performing miracles which win Him a number of followers. Nicodemus, a member of the Sanhedrin, being impressed by these manifestations so plainly denoting a mission from on high, comes to Jesus to ask for certain explanations. But he comes secretly, for it is evident that a feeling of hostility has already laid hold on the religious leaders of Judaism, against Him in whom they foresee a powerful rival. Then Jesus withdraws from Jerusalem and retires to an obscure corner of Judea, followed by His first disciples, who begin to administer a baptism like that of the precursor. It seems that at this period Jesus Himself did not yet exercise any important ministry. After a few months of this silent retreat, He sets out for Galilee, crossing Samaria, where, at the foot of Mount Gerizim, occurs the celebrated meeting with a woman who had strayed from the path of virtue. John the Baptist's imprisonment by the tetrarch Herod Antipas closes this period of preparation, which, in the case of Christ as also of the precursor, has its chief scene of action in the province of Judea.[44]

At the opening of the second period, we see our Lord, who until then has played only an obscure part, suddenly attracting the attention of the multitudes and stirring up a movement of lively enthusiasm in Galilee, by zealously preaching the coming of the Kingdom of God, by performing numerous mir-

[44] See our *Synopsis Evangelica,* pp. 9–16.

acles, by journeying through the countryside in all directions, and by proving in every way that He was truly the Messias.

But let us proceed in order and cite at least the principal events. Jesus is repulsed at Nazareth, which, because of its retired location, was ill-suited for the center of His ministry. He then makes His residence at Capharnaum, on the thickly populated shore of Lake Tiberias. Previously He performed a second miracle at Cana, curing the son of one of Antipas' officers. A little while later, He definitely attaches to Himself four disciples—Peter, Andrew, and the two sons of Zebedee —following a miraculous draught of fishes. To give us a more complete idea of the Savior's activity, the Synoptics here describe in detail one full day of His life (the curing of a demoniac in the synagogue at Capharnaum, the curing of St. Peter's mother-in-law and of numerous other sick persons).

These various deeds form the first section in the period we are studying. The second opens with an evangelizing journey which Jesus, accompanied by His disciples, made through the Galilean villages. But the Evangelists have left us only a brief summary of it. As is their custom, they choose rather to cite a few isolated and particularly remarkable incidents which took place about this time: among others, the healing of a leper and that of a paralytic who was let down through the roof to our Lord's side, then the calling of Levi the publican. St. John is silent on all these events which the Synoptics depict in such realistic colors and which occurred between the precursor's imprisonment and the second Pasch of the public life.[45]

That same Pasch—if we suppose the author of the Fourth Gospel really means the Paschal solemnity when he refers to "a festival day of the Jews"—marks the beginning of a third period, extending to the third Pasch, a period of which

[45] *Ibid.*, pp. 17-23.

our four Evangelists have together preserved many details.[46] The better to describe it, we will divide this period likewise into several sections. For a considerable time, the feeling that dominates the multitudes is still a friendly one; but as our Lord refuses to lend Himself to their Messianic preconceptions and as His enemies, daily growing in number, spread the most odious calumnies about Him, the populace partly withdraws from Him and little by little abandons Him.

First section: from the second Pasch until the choosing of the Apostles.—It begins at Jerusalem with the curing of another paralytic, on the Sabbath. Some time afterwards, we find Jesus in Galilee, where again on a Sabbath there take place the incident of the ears of wheat and the curing of a man with a withered hand. Christ's adversaries profit by these three occasions to renew their attack upon Him. Then He retires to the lake shore, where He is at once rejoined by crowds eager to see and hear Him and to be present at His miracles.

Second section: from the choosing of the Apostles to the anointing by the sinful woman.—The time is come for the Divine Master permanently to attach to His person the twelve chosen disciples who are to constitute the Apostolic College and who, when He shall have ascended into Heaven, will continue His work on earth. After choosing them, He promulgates in their presence and that of other hearers gathered about Him in large numbers, what has been rightly called the great charter of the Kingdom of Heaven, in the form of the Sermon on the Mount. Upon returning to Capharnaum, He cures the centurion's servant; at Naim He restores life to the widow's son. It is then that John the Baptist, from the depth of his prison cell, delegates two of his disciples to go to Jesus and ask whether He is truly the Messias. This question the Savior answers with the eloquent voice of deeds, by per-

---

[46] *Ibid.,* pp. 24–55.

forming several miracles, and also by a discourse in which He highly eulogizes the Baptist, declaring that John was verily a herald sent by God to prepare the way for His Christ. Following this discourse, terrible maledictions are pronounced against the unbelieving cities on the lake shore, and the infinitely sweet invitation: "Come to me . . . ," addressed to all the afflicted. Having been invited to dine in a Pharisee's house, Jesus grants a generous pardon to a sinful woman who gave manifest proofs of repentance.

Third section: between the second and third of our Lord's pastoral journeys through Galilee.—At His setting out we see Him accompanied this time, not only by His Apostles, but also by some devoted women, who provide for His needs. This journey is scarcely begun when the Pharisees, having witnessed a miraculous cure by Christ, dare openly to charge Him before the multitude with accomplishing His prodigies by connivance with the prince of devils. With an eloquence at once calm and powerful, He refutes this atrocious calumny and thereupon takes the offensive, uttering words of menace against His enemies and against the whole unbelieving part of the Jewish nation. He then receives a visit from His mother and relatives. It is immediately after this incident that the Evangelists show us the Savior beginning a new method of preaching, proclaiming His parables of the Kingdom of Heaven. Several miracles then follow: the calming of the tempest on the lake, the curing of the demoniacs of Gerasa, the healing of the woman with a flow of blood, the raising to life of Jairus' daughter, the curing of two blind men and a dumb demoniac. But another visit by the Savior to Nazareth is scarcely less fruitless than the preceding one.

Fourth section: from Christ's third pastoral tour in Galilee to the third Pasch of the public life.—For this preaching tour the Savior has the Apostles associated with Him, sending them ahead two by two to announce the coming of the

Kingdom of God. We possess the text of His instructions given to predispose them for this exalted rôle, which they had not heretofore filled. The Synoptics relate on this occasion, as a rather recent event, the martyrdom of John the Baptist. The first multiplication of the loaves, Christ's walking on the stormy waters of the lake, His miracles in the plain of Genesareth, the discourse in which He promises to institute the Eucharist, a discourse which ill disposed a considerable portion of His hearers and even of His disciples towards Him: these are the chief events that terminate the third period of the public life.

Fourth period: between the third and the fourth Pasch. This period is likewise rich in events; but, in character, it differs greatly from the previous one and still more from the second. The coldness and indifference of the great number succeed the public favor; declared enemies feel themselves more powerful and become bolder. Christ often keeps Himself apart. His miracles become rarer and He is principally engaged in training the Twelve. Yet this last year of the Savior's life on earth is not lacking in glorious deeds.[47]

First section: the long journey of our Lord into the Phenician country and Upper Galilee.—It is a significant feature that from the outset Jesus is in conflict with the Scribes and Pharisees on the subject of the numerous and often superstitious ablutions which "the tradition of the ancients" prescribed. He then undertakes a considerable journey, which leads Him from Lower Galilee, where He usually resided, westward to the districts of Tyre and Sidon. There He cures the daughter of the Chanaanitish woman. After crossing Upper Galilee, He turns south and reaches Decapolis, on the shore of Lake Tiberias. Several cures, the second multiplication of the loaves, and a few incidents of lesser moment also belong to this epoch.

[47] *Synopsis Evangelica*, pp. 59–93.

Second section: the magnificent height of Christ's ministry.—Two resplendent events closely follow each other. Going north as far as Caesarea Philippi, not far from the source of the Jordan, our Lord puts His celebrated question to the Apostles: "Whom do you say that I am?" Simon Peter answers with his momentous "confession," which brings him so superb a reward: "Thou art Peter; and upon this rock I will build my Church . . ." At the same time Jesus deems it timely to inform His followers of His approaching Passion, so as to prepare them for it. Six days later the great mystery of the Transfiguration takes place; then, at the foot of the mountain which was the scene of that mystery, He cures a young demoniac. In the course of another journey in Galilee, Jesus a second time foretells His Passion and death. Returning to Capharnaum, He performs the miracle of the didrachma found in the fish's mouth. Then, more than ever, He devotes Himself to the training of the Apostles, to whom He gives most valuable instructions for their present and future conduct.

Third section: from the Feast of Tabernacles to that of the Dedication.—Christ finally leaves Galilee and goes up to Jerusalem, there to celebrate the very popular Feast of Tabernacles, preceded by the seventy-two disciples, whom He has just formed into a special body and who announce the glad tidings along their route, as the Apostles had previously done. On returning to Him, they are filled with joy as they report the success of their preaching. The parable of the Good Samaritan opens the second series of this charming form of the Savior's teaching. We then find Jesus at Bethania at the home of Martha and Mary. Then unexpectedly He appears in the Temple courts during the Feast of Tabernacles and preaches to the people. St. John has left us a fine summary of His discourses, divided by the episode of the woman

taken in adultery. It is also during the octave of the Dedication that He gives sight to the man born blind, and tells the
allegory of the Good Shepherd. Connected with this same
epoch, at least in a general way, is an important series of lessons given to the disciples and to the multitudes on various
religious subjects, as also the curing of the infirm woman, of
a dropsical man, and of ten lepers, and the continuation of
the second group of parables. Jesus then crosses into the
province of Peraea, which He has already passed through several times, but, as it would seem, without stopping there, and
He there makes a stay of some duration, which the Evangelists mark by a discussion with the Pharisees and the disciples on the question of marriage, by several parables, by the
blessing of little children, and by the sad refusal of the rich
young man to attach himself to the Savior.

Fourth section: from the Feast of the Dedication to the last
Pasch of the public life.—Events are now about to be precipi-
tated. Immediately after the feast, Jesus hastens to leave Jerusalem, where He is no longer safe, so greatly has His enemies' hatred grown. Adhering to His plan of not advancing
the hour fixed by His heavenly Father for the consummation
of His sacrifice, He again seeks temporary asylum in the
tranquillity of Peraea, where He is cordially welcomed. But
after a short stay He leaves Peraea and returns to Bethania
in Judea, to raise His friend Lazarus from the dead. From
there He retires, while awaiting the Pasch, to the little town
of Ephrem, which seems also to have been located in Judea.
On the last days preceding the feast, He starts out for Jerusalem, once more foretelling His death and Resurrection to
His Apostles, whose earthly and ambitious feelings He has to
repress again. At Jericho, whither He has come down, He
invites Himself to the house of Zacheus the publican and
restores sight to two blind men. Lastly, six days before the

Pasch, He is at Bethania, at the home of His friends, who give a great dinner in His honor, during which Mary, Lazarus' sister, anoints His sacred feet.

We beg the reader to excuse the dryness of this summary. It seemed to us that it would be useful to introduce the reader to the public life of the Divine Master and thus facilitate its study.

FIRST PERIOD

FROM THE BEGINNING OF THE BAPTIST'S MINISTRY UNTIL HIS IMPRISONMENT

It is a period of preparation, which we may divide into three parts: John the Baptist's ministry, the Messianic consecration of Jesus, and His first steps in the gospel drama. Almost all the incidents occur in Judea.

CHAPTER I

The Ministry of John the Baptist

LIKE the Savior's hidden life, His public life, too, has its little preface, the elements of which are taken from the history of John the Baptist. The precursor's ministry, which has been well called the "dawn of the gospel history," serves as an introduction, both natural and providential, to that of the Messias. Two of Israel's famous seers, Isaias and Malachias, had clearly announced—one at the most flourishing period of prophecy,[48] the other toward its decline [49]—that the Messias would be preceded by a herald who would proclaim His coming and prepare the way for it.

The four Evangelists apply to the son of Zachary and Elizabeth the following prophecy of Isaias, which possesses great beauty:

"A voice cried out: Prepare in the desert
   The way of the Lord.
Make level in the dry places
   A route for our God.
Let every valley be raised!
   Let every mountain and hill be brought low!
Let the height be changed into a plain
   And the narrow pass into a dale!
Then shall be revealed the glory of the Lord,
   And all flesh without exception shall see it,
   For the mouth of the Lord hath spoken." [50]

[48] Isaias filled his prophetic office all during the second half of the eighth century before Christ.
[49] In the year 433 B. C.
[50] Is. 40: 3–5. Cf. Matt. 3: 3; Mark 1: 3; Luke 3: 4 f.; John 1: 23. We give here

This metaphorical language is easy to understand. "The divinely enlightened prophet contemplates in spirit the future return of the Jews to Palestine after the Babylonian Captivity. Jehovah, their King and Liberator, marches at their head across the Syrian desert, to lead them back in safety to their fatherland. A herald precedes Him, according to the ancient practice of the East, in order to announce His approach and to have the highways put in good condition, for in those remote times no hand ever touched them unless under circumstances of special solemnity." [51]

But in the divine mind Isaias' oracle, after first being fulfilled at the time of the return from exile, was to have a second fulfilment, of a higher order, in Messianic times. Christ also, the royal Savior, must have, in the person of John the Baptist, His precursor, who would march ahead of Him and prepare His way in men's hearts. Malachias' prophecy expresses this same thought in briefer form: "Behold I send My angel [saith the Lord] and he shall prepare the way before My face." [52]

We have already described [53] the chief obstacles which, from the moral point of view, obstructed the Messias' way in Palestine. They could not be better expressed in figure than by those heights to be brought low, those valleys to be filled up, those windings and rough places to be straightened and smoothed in order that Christ the Redeemer, arriving among His people, might find a way worthy of Him. John applies himself whole-heartedly to this work during his short ministry.

a literal translation according to the Hebrew text. The Evangelists quote it somewhat freely, following and more or less abridging the Septuagint Version.

51 Fillion, *L'Évangile de St. Matthieu*, p. 68.

52 Mal. 3 : 1. Cf. Mark 1 : 2; Luke 1 : 17; 7 : 27. On St. Mark's seeming to credit this text to Isaias, see Fillion, *L'Évangile de S. Marc*, p. 24.

53 Vol. I, pp. 177 ff.

I. The Precursor Appears. His Life of Mortification, His Baptizing

Before directing our attention to the powerful voice of Christ's herald St. Luke in particularly solemn terms mentions the time of his appearance. "In the fifteenth year of the reign of Tiberius Caesar, Pontius Pilate being governor of Judea, and Herod being tetrarch of Galilee, and Philip his brother tetrarch of Iturea and the country of Trachonitis, and Lysanias tetrarch of Abilina; under the High Priests Annas and Caiphas, the word of the Lord was made unto John, the son of Zachary, in the desert."

This is a memorable date in sacred annals,[54] a date which marks the entrance of our Lord's life[55] into the general scheme of contemporary history. We would be surprised that the Evangelists do not directly cite either the year of our Savior's birth or that of His death and Resurrection, if we did not bear in mind the extraordinary importance of the office of John the Baptist. This importance had already been pointed out by the prophets; but the Synoptics place it in more apparent relief, whether by presenting the precursor's appearance as "the beginning of the Gospel of Jesus Christ,"[56] or by devoting to the Baptist a relatively large space in their narratives, or especially by later on quoting at great length the glowing tribute which Christ paid to him.[57] Was he not the last prophet of the Old Testament and the link connecting the Jewish theocracy with the Church? More than that, was he not the precursor of the Messias?

But let us return to the synchronous date by which St.

[54] St. Luke is the only one to indicate it, 3:1 f. St. Matthew, 3:1, merely employs the vague phrase, "In those days."
[55] Cf. Luke 1:5, and especially 2:1 f.
[56] Mark 1:1; cf. John 1:6 f.; Acts 1:21 f.; 10:37.
[57] Matt. 11:7–14; Luke 7:24–30.

Luke undertakes to mark the precise time when John the Baptist first appeared on the scene of religious history. The Gospel passage enumerates the names of seven persons who had a more or less direct and active part in the political or religious government of Palestine at that time. We remarked above, when endeavoring to determine the length of our Lord's public life, how difficult it is to say exactly what is to be understood by the fifteenth year of Tiberius. Subject to correction, we accepted the date as corresponding to A. U. C. 779–780 (A. D. 27).

What a depraved name is that of Tiberius Caesar, with which the list opens! Pontius Pilate, who then represented the Emperor in Judea and Samaria in the capacity of pro-curator,[58] was worthy of such a master. We have already characterized his conduct toward his subjects.[59] It was not without good reason that Philo, the Jewish theosophist, re-proached him with "corruption, acts of violence, rapine, ill-treatment, vexations, the execution of many persons without trial, numberless and intolerable cruelties." [60] We shall meet him again at Christ's Passion, where he shows himself ir-resolute, feeble, nay, even lax, coldly unjust, and yet animated by a certain respect for the Divine Victim.

After him the Evangelist names three rulers who at that same period were governing the parts of Palestine not di-rectly subject to the authority of Rome. We likewise made the acquaintance of Herod Antipas in the first volume of this work.[61] The Synoptics several times call our attention to him, always to his discredit, as a ruler of less than light morals,

---

[58] The word *procurante,* by which the Vulgate translates ἡγεμονεύοντος of the primitive text, is very exact. The official title of the governor of Judea was *procurator,* in Greek ἐπίτροπος. Ordinarily the noun ἡγεμών and its derivatives were used to designate a higher dignity, that of proconsul. The Evangelists did not confine themselves to this usage.

[59] Vol. I, pp. 134 f.

[60] *Legatio ad Caium,* 38.

[61] Vol. I, p. 136 f.

sly, weak in character, and at times cruel. His brother Philip
was the best of King Herod's sons. His portion of the paternal
inheritance consisted of several provinces at the northeast of
Palestine. His rule lasted thirty-seven years (4 B. C.–A. D. 33
or 34).

We know but little about Lysanias, tetrarch of Abilina,[62]
who had nothing in common with the family of Herod. His
existence at the date indicated by the Evangelist has been attested in the most positive manner by coins and inscriptions
of the period.[63] We know that after his death the little
province of Abilina became a dependency of Herod Agrippa
I, then of Herod Agrippa II, so that, at the time when St.
Luke wrote his Gospel, it formed to a certain extent part of
what the rabbis proudly called "the Land of Israel." This
is perhaps the reason why it is mentioned here.[64]

The five names that we have just referred to sum up the
political conditions of the Holy Land at the period when
John the Baptist's ministry began. The names of Annas and
Caiphas, which we read next, call to mind the religious conditions. They are likewise significant. Annas [65] had been High
Priest from the year 6 to 15 of our era.[66] He still enjoyed
considerable influence fifteen years after his deposition, at

---

[62] On this province, see Vol. I, p. 113.

[63] Strauss violently attacks St. Luke in the matter of this tetrarch. In his
Nouvelle Vie de Jésus (French trans., II, 20), he writes: "[Luke] thirty years
after the birth of Christ, has a Lysanias governing, who certainly was killed
thirty years before that birth; it is a little error of sixty years." Likewise Keim
(*Geschichte Jesu*, I, 618) and certain others. It is the Rationalist critics who have
committed an error: the existence of two quite distinct Lysanias', that of Strauss,
who governed the province of Chalcis, and that of St. Luke, who was tetrarch of
Abilina, has been proven by ancient monuments. See F. Vigouroux, *Le Nouveau
Testament et les Découvertes Archéologiques Modernes*, 2d ed., pp. 131–141, and
Schürer, *Geschichte des jüdischen Volkes*, 4th ed., I, 707–721.

[64] Zahn, *Das Evangelium des Lucas*, I, 179.

[65] The Greek New Testament calls him Ἅννας (Luke 3:2; John 18:13, 24;
Acts 4:6). Josephus calls him Ἅνανος. This latter spelling is closer to the Hebrew
Hhanan.

[66] Josephus, *Ant.*, XVIII, ii, 1–2; XX, ix, 1; *Bell. Jud.*, V, xii, 2.

the time of our Lord's public life. This is evidently why St. Luke [67] associates him with his son-in-law Joseph, called Caiphas, who was then the official titulary of the high priesthood. It is as an enemy of Christ and of the nascent Church that Annas is presented to us in the New Testament in two other passages where he is mentioned. Caiphas, who was able to retain his high office for about eighteen years (A. D. 17 or 18 to 36 [68]) only because of an uncommon baseness of soul and because of perpetual compliance to Rome, acted even more unworthily with regard to our Savior. He it was who had the Sanhedrin vote a death sentence against Christ, after a semblance of trial in which he took a criminal part. His name, like that of Pilate, will be stigmatized throughout all ages. What a moral decadence of Judaism is implied in the names of these ambitious priests, fond of money, without faith or conscience! [69]

In truth, from every point of view, the country of Jehovah and of the Messias was in great need of regeneration. It was the time when the Christ was hastening to save His people. But behold His precursor suddenly appear,[70] proclaiming that the Liberator would very closely follow him.

---

[67] Here and in the Acts of the Apostles he makes use of very expressive phrases to indicate that, although Caiphas was then High Priest *de jure*, Annas was almost so *de facto*. In the Greek text of the Gospel passage we are considering, we read: ἐπὶ ἀρχιερέως Ἄννα καὶ Καιάφα, "Under the High Priest Annas and Caiphas." The variant ἐπὶ ἀρχιερέων . . . , "Under the high priests" (*sub principibus . . .*) adopted by the Vulgate and several other ancient versions, has in its favor only a very small number of manuscripts; hence it is rather generally rejected as a late correction. In Acts 4: 6, St. Luke expresses a shade of difference when he says: "Ἄννας ὁ ἀρχιερεὺς καὶ Καιάφας, "Annas the High Priest, and Caiphas." These phrases are certainly intentional on the part of the sacred writer, for they well express the reality of the facts; the view that they contain a historical error, is no longer held.

[68] He was deposed by Vitellius.

[69] The personages here named by St. Luke held office throughout our Lord's public life and until some time after His death.

[70] παραγίνεται, says St. Matthew, 3: 1. The use of the present tense indicates a sudden, unexpected appearance.

In fact, as St. Luke says, in that fifteenth year of Tiberius, "the word of the Lord was made unto John, the son of Zachary, in the desert," [71] where the greater part of his life had been passed. This solemn expression, frequently recurring in the Old Testament writings and especially in the prophetical literature,[72] indicates that John did not of his own volition choose the hour when his office of precursor was to begin. It was by virtue of a precise divine communication, like that with which the ancient prophets had been favored, that he left the solitude of his retreat; it was an irresistible power of the Holy Ghost that led him to the region where he was to preach Christ and His Kingdom.

The Evangelists briefly point out the principal scene of his ministry. It is neither cities nor villages; even less is it Jerusalem. This man who grew up in the wilderness, continues to live in the wilderness;[73] but henceforth less for himself than for the Messias and for souls. In several passages the Old Testament books speak of the wilderness of Juda,[74] where, as St. Matthew informs us, John habitually lived at this time. A wild and desolate region it was, bounded on the east by the lower Jordan and the Dead Sea, extending westward almost to the crest of the central plateau of Palestine and northward as far as the ancient boundaries of the tribe of Juda. It is not a sandy desert, like the Sahara, but rather a steppe, uninhabited to-day even as of old, generally uncultivated and hardly tillable, with dry, rocky mountains, numerous valleys and ravines, a wrinkled, dented surface and arid soil. However, in the spring, this desert, a considerable part of which may be seen from the summit of

[71] Luke 3 : 2.

[72] Cf. 4 Kings 17 : 2; Is. 38 : 4; Jer. 1 : 4; Ezech. 1 : 3, etc.

[73] The Synoptics express this idea with slight variations. St. Mark, 1 : 4, says simply: "in the desert." St. Matthew, 3 : 1, is a little more exact: "in the desert of Judea." St. Luke, 3 : 3, is still more so: "into all the country about the Jordan."

[74] Cf. Josue 15 : 61; Judges 1 : 16, etc.

the Mount of Olives, is covered with a little verdure, where the Beduins' sheep and goats come to browse.[75] The northern part, it seems, was where John passed his youth and manhood, until he was about thirty years old; but "the country about the Jordan," where we now find him, was and even now is less wild than the real desert of Juda, although its marlaceous soil barely produces a few briars and other shrubs. Only the immediate vicinity of the river banks is planted with a considerable number of trees. In short, it is the southernmost portion of the Ghor or Jordan valley, a few miles east of Jerusalem and north of the Dead Sea, which was the principal center of the Baptist's activity. The Gospel narrative shows him to us, now on the right bank of the river and now on the left;[76] but we shall also find him "in Ennon near Salim," much farther north.[77]

In obedience to the divine order, John went down to the deep Jordan valley. The Synoptics briefly describe his outer appearance and austere life. He wore a rude, coarse tunic, the material of which was a cloth made of camel's hair.[78] The folds of this heavy garment were gathered about his waist by a leather belt. Thus it was that Elias had been dressed,[79] and the prophets that came after him seem for the most part to have adopted this same costume.[80]

The precursor mortified himself in the matter of food no less than in his dress. The Evangelists mention the two chief articles which composed his nourishment: locusts and wild

[75] See Tristram, *The Land of Israel*, 3d ed., p. 194; A. Stanley, *Sinai and Palestine*, pp. 310–312.

[76] John 1:28; 10:40.

[77] John 3:23.

[78] The Gospel texts do not allow the least doubt on this subject: ἀπὸ τριχῶν καμήλου (Vulg., *de pilis camelorum* or *cameli*. Matt. 3:4; Mark 1:6). Painters and certain commentators are mistaken when they clothe the Baptist in a hairy camel's skin. Even at the present time the poorer Arabs and Beduin nomads wear the same sort of tunic as did the precursor.

[79] 4 Kings 1:8.

[80] Zach. 13:4.

honey, true foods of the wilderness, where they are to be found in abundance. Even in our own times in Arabia, Ethiopia, Palestine, and elsewhere, locusts often serve as food for the poorer classes. The ancient Hebrews, too, knew this article of food,[81] which is not at all unwholesome and which is prepared in a variety of ways.[82] The wild honey is very fragrant, but usually bitter, and is called "wild" by way of contrast with that which is produced by domesticated bees. It has always abounded in Palestine, where it may be found in the trunks of trees and in fissures of the rocks.[83]

It was, then, under such externals that the precursor made his appearance. These details lend significance to the Savior's words when, with gentle irony, He asked the multitude: "What went you out into the desert to see? A man clothed in soft garments" and living delicately?[84] They also help us to understand how certain malicious Pharisees, after saying that "John came neither eating nor drinking," added: "He hath a devil."[85]

II. John the Baptist's Preaching. His First Testimony to Christ

John's preaching was in perfect harmony with his mortified life. "Do penance," he kept crying out, "for the Kingdom of Heaven is at hand."[86] Such words on the lips of such a preacher soon produced the liveliest emotion through the whole region, because their meaning was readily understood.

[81] Cf. Lev. 11 : 22.

[82] The simplest way is to roast the insects over hot coals, after removing the hard portions.

[83] Deut. 32 : 13; 1 Kings 14 : 25–29, etc. Following the example of the Ebionites (St. Epiphanius, *Haer.*, XXX, 13) and of certain exegetes, some writers mistakenly consider this second dish of the precursor to have been a more or less sweet gum which exudes from certain trees, such as the palm, the fig, the tamarisk, etc.

[84] Matt. 11 : 8; Luke 7 : 25.

[85] Matt. 11 : 18; Luke 7 : 33.

[86] Matt. 3 : 2.

They signified that the Messias was soon going to manifest Himself to establish the glorious kingdom which the divine prophecies had so often foretold. And so John was surrounded by large and ever increasing crowds, eager to behold this mysterious prophet at close range and to hear with their own ears the momentous, glad news that he was proclaiming. A religious movement of extraordinary force stirred all Palestine. The mere fact that a prophet was appearing in Israel after several centuries of silence on God's part, could not fail to arouse the enthusiasm of all classes. The people hastened from every district of the Holy Land, as St. Matthew and St. Mark most emphatically say: "Then went out to him Jerusalem and all Judea and all the country about Jordan," [87] and gradually the inhabitants also of Galilee [88] and Peraea. The banks of the Jordan, ordinarily silent and deserted, witnessed a continual stream of thousands of pilgrims for several months.[89] Palestine had seen nothing like it since the far-off days of the Machabees.

We have just cited the general subject and, as it were, the text of the precursor's preaching. To this preaching he joined a symbolic ceremony, a "baptism," whence the name of "Baptist," by which he soon came to be known.[90] This symbolic rite, according to the etymology of the word "baptism," [91] consisted in a complete immersion in the waters of the Jordan. Endeavors have been made to connect its origin with the various kinds of religious ablutions which the Mosaic legislation prescribed for those who had contracted any legal defilement,[92] or with the baptism which proselytes received be-

---

[87] Matt. 3 : 5; Mark 1 : 5.

[88] Several of the Baptist's disciples were Galileans (John 1 : 40–43).

[89] The verb ἐξεπορεύετο (Matthew and Mark) is in the imperfect tense and well expresses this perpetual movement.

[90] Jesus Himself used it at times (Matt. 11 : 11; Luke 7 : 33). Flavius Josephus mentions this title (*Ant.*, XVIII, v. 2) : "John, that was called the Baptist."

[91] βάπτω, "I dip."

[92] Lev. chaps. 11–15; Num. chap. 19, etc. Cf. Mark 7 : 2–4.

fore being enrolled in the ranks of Judaism.[93] But the analogy between it and these two other kinds of lustration is only external. The ceremonial ablutions had to be repeated for each case of defilement, whereas John's baptism was received but once. The baptism of proselytes was received by pagans converted to the Jewish religion; John's was generally administered to Israelites. This rite was, then, really a new one. The precursor's disciples were convinced that it belonged to him and was something special to him; and so we shall see them moved by a feeling of jealousy upon learning that the disciples of Jesus were also beginning to baptize.[94] This detail is significant. What is still more so, is the manner in which the Evangelists take pains to characterize this special baptism and to indicate its nature and purpose. They speak of it as a "baptism of penance, unto remission of sins." [95] As the Baptist himself declared, he had not received from Heaven the power to forgive sins, a power that was reserved exclusively to the Messias. At least, by this symbol, this external washing, he stirred souls to a desire for moral purification, which would lead them to sanctify themselves so as to become worthy to share in the Kingdom of Christ. From all this it follows that John's baptism was really a new and personal institution.

The Greek word which we translate by "penance," conformably to our Latin version, calls for an explanation, because it best expresses the nature of the ceremony of which we are speaking. The noun *metanoia* designates a complete transformation of the soul, a radical change brought about in the inmost feelings, as opposed to a superficial and not very sincere repentance. Consequently there is here meant a total conversion, a generous resolve to sin no more and to expiate

[93] See Edersheim, *Life and Times of Jesus the Messiah*, I, 273 f.; Schürer, *Geschichte des jüdischen Volkes*, 4th ed., III, 130–132.

[94] John 3:26.

[95] That is, with a view to that forgiveness. Mark 1:4; Luke 3:3. Cf. Matt. 3:11.

the faults of the past. Such is the idea at the basis of John's baptizing, which was, therefore, accompanied by a confession,[96] the extent of which we are unable to specify. Perhaps it did not go beyond general expressions of self-accusation, analogous to the Catholic *Confiteor,* or such as we read here and there in the Old Testament [97] and in the Jewish Euchologies.

In the case of Christ's precursor, the herald preceded the baptizer, for it was especially by the details of his preaching that he exercised the extraordinary influence which the Evangelists describe. "I am the voice of one crying," we hear him say in reply to the delegates of the Sanhedrin,[98] applying to himself Isaias' prophecy which we cited above.[99] It was a marvelously eloquent voice, a voice of almost irresistible power, to hear which the people came from all the provinces of the Holy Land—a prophetic voice bearing faithful witness to the Messias on all occasions, a justly stern voice fearlessly and openly rebuking the Jews for their pride and foolish illusions, a voice that could utter words astoundingly practical.

We are led to admire the Baptist's preaching still more by studying it directly in the two specimens which St. Matthew [100] and St. Luke [101] have recorded. The general expressions which the biographers of Christ use, enable us to form a rather definite idea of it. It was a solemn and official proclamation,[102] an evangelization,[103] an urgent exhortation.[104]

[96] Matt. 3:6; Mark 1:5.
[97] Judges 10:10; 1 Kings 7:6; 12:10; 3 Kings 8:47; Esdras 9:6 f.; Judith 7:19; Ps. 105:6; Jer. 3:25; 14:20; Dan. 3:29; 9:5 f., etc.
[98] John 1:23.
[99] Page 21.
[100] Matt. 3:7–12.
[101] Luke 3:7–18.
[102] Mark 1:4, 7, and Luke 3:3; κηρύσσων (Vulg., *praedicans*). The verb κηρύσσω is the New Testament technical term to designate the gospel preaching.
[103] Luke 3:18: εὐηγγελίζετο (Vulg., *evangelizabat*).
[104] Luke 3:18: παρακαλῶν (Vulg., *exhortans*).

The short summary we have of it is so characteristic that it enables us to form a judgment as to the preacher.

The theme that was repeatedly on John's lips was this: "Do penance, for the Kingdom of Heaven is at hand." To explain this pregnant idea, so old and yet so new, which is expressed by the words "the Kingdom of Heaven," we shall wait until we reach that point in our narrative when Jesus, too, uses it at the beginning of His Messianic ministry. But even at this point we know what is to be understood by the penitence which the precursor required and which Christ also required from whosoever aspired to become a subject of the Kingdom of Heaven.[105] It means a complete breaking with the past in whatever was morally evil therein; it is an absolute change of interior dispositions, which one must promptly make conformable to the will of God.

The first of the two fragments which have come down to us of the Baptist's preaching is of a more general sort both in the matter of the thoughts it develops and in the character of the audience to whom it is addressed.[106] In the words of St. Luke, these hearers were "the multitudes that went forth to be baptized by him"; St. Matthew speaks of "many of the Pharisees and Sadducees" coming to John to receive his baptism. The two Evangelists here mutually supplement each other. The common people formed the greater portion of the audience; but a large number of Pharisees and Sadducees were mingled with them, nearly all moved by curiosity or even by a feeling of base jealousy. Their presence, which John readily perceived, gives his address a polemical tone and an accent of severity which were but too well deserved and justified with regard to those proud sceptics, and likewise to those Israelites who subjected themselves to their per-

---

[105] Matt. 3:2: μετανοεῖτε (Vulg., paenitentiam agite).

[106] It is preserved in almost identical terms by St. Matthew, 3:7-10, and by St. Luke, 3:7-9.

verse influence. At times it is needful to strike hardened and haughty sinners with heavy blows to arouse them from their torpidity.

Impelled by burning zeal, John the Baptist said to them: "Ye offspring of vipers, who hath showed you to flee from the wrath to come? Bring forth therefore fruits worthy of penance. And do not begin to say: We have Abraham for our father. For I say unto you, that God is able of these stones to raise up children to Abraham. For now the axe is laid to the root of the trees. Every tree therefore that bringeth not forth good fruit shall be cut down and cast into the fire. . . . But there shall come one . . . whose fan is in His hand, and He will purge His floor and will gather the wheat into His barn; but the chaff He will burn with unquenchable fire." [107]

What vigor of faith is in this language so abounding in figurative expressions, its censures and threats recalling the words of the prophets of old! Twice [108] Jesus brands the Pharisees as a "generation of vipers," which infamous title vividly depicts the low cunning of their conduct and the venom of their doctrines. The dominant idea of this little discourse is that of a divine judgment, of a dread tribunal that will accompany the installing of the Kingdom of Heaven. It is an idea that likewise reëchoes in the ancient prophecies, [109] in the Jewish apocalyptical literature, [110] in the Savior's teaching, [111] and in St. Paul's Epistles. [112] John's hearers were, therefore, not surprised at hearing him announce a near manifestation of divine wrath on the occasion of the Messias' advent. But, as a consequence of the grossest illusion, they

[107] The introductory formula, "He said," which St. Luke, 3 : 7, uses, supposes that the precursor repeated more than once, in the presence of new listeners, the weighty warnings that follow.

[108] Matt. 12 : 34; 23 : 33.

[109] Joel 3 : 1–6; Soph. 1 : 14–18; Mal. 3 : 1–3, etc.

[110] Henoch 90 : 18; 91 : 7; Psalms of Solomon 5 : 20, etc.

[111] Matt. 25 : 31–46, etc.

[112] Rom. 2 : 5; 1 Thess. 1 : 10, etc.

imagined and loudly declared that this wrath and the punishments it would inflict menaced only the pagans. As for
themselves, they had nothing to fear, since the blood of Abraham coursing in their veins would more than suffice to
guarantee their salvation.

The writings of the rabbis contain numerous traces of this
fallacious principle, showing how far the Messianic idea had
been falsified by pride and ignorance and superstition. There
was no extravagance which the Jews of that time did not
commit with reference to the merits of their illustrious ancestor. These merits, joined to those of the other patriarchs
and saints of Israel, formed, they proudly said, a treasure of
incalculable wealth, which belonged in common to all members of the nation and which was amply sufficient to obtain
for each of them pardon for his sins and participation in
eternal happiness. They even represented Abraham as seated
at the entrance to gehenna to liberate immediately such guilty
Israelites as would be condemned to the pains of hell.[113] They
say to Abraham: "Even if your children were bodies without veins and without bones—meaning: if they were dead,
from a moral standpoint—your merits would answer for
them." The words of Isaias, "The morning cometh, also the
night," [114] are thus interpreted by the Talmud: [115] "The night
is reserved for the nations of the world [*i. e.,* for the pagans],
and the morning for Israel." [116] It is not, then, surprising
that John boldly attacked, as Jesus [117] and the Apostle of the
Gentiles [118] did later on, this prejudice which the populace
shared with the Scribes and Pharisees. But participation in

[113] *Bereschith Rabba,* XVIII, 7.

[114] Is. 21 : 12.

[115] *Taanith,* 64, a.

[116] See other curious quotations of the same kind in Weber, *System der altsynagogalen palästinischen Theologie aus Targum, Midrasch und Talmud,* pp.
285–287, and in Edersheim, *Life of Jesus the Messiah,* I, 271 f.

[117] John 8: 33–40.

[118] Rom. 2: 27–29; 9: 6–33.

the Kingdom of Heaven is not a matter of nationality, not a privilege of the Jewish race to the exclusion of other peoples. God's power and liberty are so little restricted by the hereditary rights of the Israelites that He may cast far from Him and condemn without mercy the descendants of Abraham, who possess none of the qualities of their forebear; He may draw forth a new race of true Abrahamites [119] from the hardest and commonest material—"of these stones," said the Baptist, pointing to those which abound in the desert of Juda.

The condemnation with which John threatened his hearers soon burst forth, as is so eloquently expressed by the figures of the axe laid to the root of a barren tree, or the straw and chaff to be burned after the good grain is separated from them.[120] The peril, therefore, was imminent, and no one could escape it except by a genuine conversion, outwardly manifested by acts. This is why the precursor, not wishing to shut anyone out of the Messianic kingdom, interrupted his rebukes and his words of salutary terror with the encouraging admonition: "Bring forth therefore fruits worthy of penance."

Most of his hearers docilely accepted this advice, and signified their good disposition by asking, as on Pentecost those Jews asked who accepted the Christian faith after St. Peter's preaching: [121] "What then shall we do?" [122] St. Luke gives

[119] Cf. Rom. chap. 9; Gal. chap. 3.

[120] "In the country districts of Palestine there were threshing-floors, well beaten down, hard, leveled, and expressly prepared for threshing grain. There the sheaves were gathered and threshed under the feet of horses or oxen, or with large boards to which pieces of iron or stones were fastened and which were dragged over the grain. . . . When the grain was threshed, the straw was removed . . . and kept for fodder. But the powdered straw and the husks were tossed into the air and carried off by the wind, while the good grain fell back on the threshing-floor. When the good grain had been thus sorted and the threshing-floor cleaned, the husks and sweepings were completely burned." Calmet, *Commentaire Litéral sur l'Évangile de S. Matthieu, in hoc loco.* The threshing and winnowing of wheat are still done in this same way in the Biblical East.

[121] Acts 2: 37. Cf. Acts 16: 30; 22: 10.

[122] Luke 3: 10.

us three of John's practical answers to various groups of questioners. They are wonderfully well suited to the circumstances
of each of these categories. It is evident that this solitary, this
man of the desert, had a deep knowledge of human nature
with its needs and defects and was also acquainted with the
moral ailments of his time.

In giving this practical advice, his voice took on a gentler
tone. The terrible preacher became a fatherly counsellor,
whom at first sight we might be tempted to find too accom-
modating. But we would be very much mistaken; if what he
requires appears to be very moderate, in reality it presupposes a veritable *metanoia,* a real conversion. Let us bear in
mind that the Baptist's aim was not to make ascetics like
himself, but to change those who turned to him into upright
men, fearing God and practicing virtue according to their
providential manner of life.

What could have been wiser or more concrete than the
advice he gave day after day? To the multitudes urging him
to mark out the new path upon which they must enter, he
merely repeats the great precept of fraternal charity and
recommends this fundamental virtue so pleasing to God, the
practice of which Christ later made His special commandment. The Baptist says: "He that hath two coats,[123] let him
give to him that hath none; and he that hath meat, let him do
in like manner."

Publicans also came to John to ask the same question as
the multitudes: "Master,[124] what shall we do?" Those who
were called publicans were at that time everywhere detested
because of their unjust exactions and their acts of violence.
These subordinate agents in the service of the Roman knights

---

[123] There is here question of the outer tunic ($\chi i\tau\omega\nu$, in Hebrew *kethoneth*),
which was worn over the shirt ($\sigma\iota\nu\delta\acute{\omega}\nu$).

[124] Commentators note that the publicans are the only ones in this passage who
address the precursor by this honored title, which corresponds to the Hebrew
rabbi.

who farmed the state taxes and grew rich by overtaxing the people, only too well imitated the conduct of their chiefs and openly practiced fraud. In Judea and Palestine, doubly hated were those publicans of Jewish birth who lent their assistance to the abhorred Romans to despoil the people of God and recall their subjection.[125] And so the Talmud [126] ranks them among assassins and robbers, and more than once we shall hear our Lord Himself, in conformity with the ideas of His countrymen,[127] associate their name with what was then the very worst element of society.[128]

How will John deal with them? Will he not require them to give up, as soon as possible, a profession so disreputable and so dangerous from the moral standpoint? No, for it is not intrinsically evil, but he will require that they henceforth conform to this first rule of justice: "Do nothing more than that which is appointed you," i. e., do not exact anything beyond the legal tax.

"And what shall we do?" asked the soldiers whom the precursor's fame prompted to come from their camps to the banks of the Jordan. It is not likely that these were Jews, unless they belonged to the small armed force of Herod Antipas. Rather were they Roman legionaries, from the number of those numerous pagans who were more or less inclined to Judaism [129] and who, like so many others, had been impressed by the Baptist's utterances. "The reputation of sol-

---

[125] The publicans who collected the taxes in Galilee and Peraea in the name of the tetrarch Herod, were subject at least to the general charge of fraudulent extortion.

[126] *Baba bathra,* 113 a.

[127] Matt. 5 : 46; 18 : 17; 21 : 31; Luke 7 : 29; 15 : 1 f.; 18 : 10–14; 19 : 7, etc.

[128] The ancient Greek and Roman authors treat them with no greater respect. Cf. Stobeus, *Serm.,* II, 34; Aristophanes, *Equit.,* 248; Theophrastes, *Charact.,* VI. For further treatment of this subject, see our articles on the publicans in Vigouroux' *Dictionnaire de la Bible,* Vol. V, cols. 858 ff., and Schürer, *Geschichte des jüdischen Volkes,* 4th ed., I, 477–479.

[129] Vol. I, p. 161. The New Testament (Luke 7 : 2–5; Acts 10 : 1 f) refers to two Roman centurions animated by friendly feelings toward the Jewish religion.

diers in that disturbed period was, if possible, even worse than that of publicans. . . . The manner in which armies were recruited was in no small measure accountable for the barbarity of military customs. They were largely composed of adventurers coming from every quarter of the Empire, especially from regions regarded as the rudest (Thrace, Dalmatia, and Germany), insolvent debtors, prodigal sons seeking refuge in the militia, bandits, idlers, and the like. The many recent wars and the freedom which Rome left to her legions in conquered or invaded countries, had developed these evil dispositions to a formidable degree. Thus even the best troops and the most exemplary were to be dreaded." [130] Yet in answer to their question, John simply says: "Do violence to no man; neither calumniate any man; and be content with your pay." Thus did he forbid them to indulge in plundering, marauding, and unjust requisitioning, as also mutiny and revolt, at that time quite frequent in the Roman armies in connection with the matter of pay and food. [131]

By his language, now firm and severe, now full of moderation, John the Baptist touched men's hearts and consciences. What marvelous scenes of conversion the banks of the Jordan witnessed! As our Lord Himself testified, [132] a prodigious enthusiasm, during the months that the precursor's ministry lasted, seized upon a large number of Israelites, who, so to speak, burst into the Kingdom of Heaven. It is a quite similar picture which the Jewish historian Flavius Josephus draws of John and his work: "He was a good man and commanded the Jews to exercise virtue, both as to righteousness towards one another and piety towards God, and so to come to baptism;

[130] Fillion, *L'Évangile de S. Luc*, pp. 96 f.

[131] Several times the emperors were obliged considerably to increase the pay and the rations of the legionaries. The daily *stipendium*, after being 10 asses (a third of a denarius) under Julius Cæsar, was raised by Augustus to 2 denarii, i. e., about 34 cents (Tacitus. *Annales*, V, 17).

[132] Matt. 11:12; Luke 7:29.

for that the washing would be acceptable to God if they made use of it, not in order to the putting away of some sins only, but of all sins. For of what avail would it be to purify the body unless the soul were thoroughly purified beforehand by righteousness? Great numbers gathered around him and the multitudes were eager to hear his words." [133]

The Baptist was not satisfied with continual eloquent appeals to souls to lead them to the practice of justice and good works. While laboring thus to prepare for Christ "a perfect people," [134] he did not fail repeatedly to render personal and direct testimony to Him. The author of the Fourth Gospel, in his sublime prologue,[135] stresses the fact that John the Baptist came to act as a witness to the Messias. The precursor was most faithful in discharging this part of his mission. Throughout his ministry, he was a zealous prophet of the Christ, as our Lord attested later.[136]

In the Gospel narratives we see the Baptist fulfilling his office of witness before three kinds of hearers: the multitudes constantly surrounding him, the delegates of the Sanhedrin, and his own disciples. The Synoptics all set forth the first testimony,[137] which was previous to Christ's baptism, but which John repeated more than once.[138] St. Luke specifically mentions the occasion when it was first given: "As the people were of opinion and all were thinking in their hearts of John, that perhaps he might be the Christ, John answered, saying unto all . . ." The precursor's holiness, his preaching and baptizing, had gradually contributed to embody this popular hypothesis, which, however, spread only with some hesita-

---

[133] *Ant.*, XVIII, v, 2.
[134] Luke 1:17.
[135] John 1:7 f.
[136] Matt. 11:11; Luke 7:28.
[137] Matt. 3:11; Mark 1:6-8; Luke 3:15 f.
[138] This may be inferred from the very nature of the circumstances and also from the little formula by which St. Mark introduces him: ἐκήρυσσεν λέγων (Vulg., *praedicabat dicens*). The use of the imperfect indicates a custom or practice.

tion.[139] But John was not a man who would long tolerate the continued dissemination of so false a notion. Soon, in his deep humility, he protested against the exaggerated esteem of the multitudes and he was able to give his protest all possible publicity.[140] He said:

"I indeed baptize you with water;
  but there shall come one mightier than I,
  the latchet of whose shoes I am not worthy to loose.[141]
He shall baptize you with the Holy Ghost and with fire."

Not only is the language of these lines quite figurative, but it is in rhythm after the Oriental manner, and the parallelism of the parts appears here to emphasize the loftiness and poetical character of the thoughts.[142] To show how inferior he is to the Messias, the precursor uses two expressive antitheses, one referring to the persons, the other to the baptisms. The Messias is represented as being incomparably "mightier," that is, superior, while John by contrast is the weaker, the inferior, unworthy to render this mighty Master the humblest services, ordinarily reserved for the lowest class of slaves, as would be the service of carrying His sandals, and of tying or untying the laces.[143] And there is likewise John's great inferiority from the viewpoint of his baptizing as compared with that of the Messias. His was merely a baptism of water. But water cleanses only the surface; whence it follows that this baptism, although productive of excellent results by stirring up repentance, was incapable of blotting out

[139] We see this from the very words of the Evangelist: μὴ ποτε (ne forte).

[140] The words "saying unto all" are strongly emphatic.

[141] In St. Mark we read this little additional, characteristic detail: "to stoop down and loose."

[142] It is a real strophe. The fourth verse corresponds to the first, the third to the second.

[143] The classical writers of Rome explicitly mention the puelli sandaligeruli and the puellae sandaligerulae.

the stains of the soul. On the contrary, Christ's baptism, with the Holy Ghost and fire as its elements, so to speak, acts to the inmost recesses of man's being, producing wonderful effects of purification and sanctification and even at the very outset bringing about a complete moral regeneration.[144]

[144] Acts 2:33; 10:44, 47; 19:6, etc. Cf. Tertullian, *De Bapt.*, X; St. Cyril of Jerusalem, *Catech.*, XX, 6; St. Thomas Aquinas, *Summa Theol.*, 3a, qu. 38, a. 1. On the utterly false influence which the Rationalists attribute to John the Baptist with regard to Christ, see Appendix I.

CHAPTER II

Christ's Direct Preparation For His High Office

ALTHOUGH His entire life had thus far been a continual preparation for His active rôle as Messias, yet the Savior began the exercise of His Messianic office only after a consecration, which assumed a double aspect. There was first His baptism, which, so to speak, conferred His official titles upon Him; then the temptation, during which He passed through the crucible of trial and proved His fidelity and strength of soul.

I. Jesus is Baptized by John the Baptist [145]

One day, the exact date of which is not given by the Evangelists,[146] John saw coming towards him an Israelite about thirty years of age,[147] whose features and whole bearing reflected a majesty, an intellectual power, a holiness, which greatly impressed him. It was Jesus of Nazareth, who but recently had left His mother, His pleasant solitude, and His calm life at Nazareth, and like so many others, came to the banks of the Jordan on purpose, as St. Matthew explicitly states, to receive baptism at the hands of the precursor.

At first glance this move is most astonishing. What need had the world's Savior, the Incarnate Word, who was purity

---

[145] Matt. 3:13–17; Mark 1:9–11; Luke 3:21 f. Of these three accounts, St. Matthew's is the most complete.

[146] "In those days," is St. Mark's vague indication; that is, at the time when the crowds were coming to John the Baptist from all sides.

[147] Luke 3:23.

43

itself, of a ceremony which implied in those undergoing it the existence of sin and the necessity of conversion? Was not John's baptism a "baptism of penance"? This theological problem received considerable attention at an early date, and at times queer solutions were offered. Thus, in a fragment of the apocryphal Gospel according to the Hebrews, quoted by St. Jerome, we are told that "the mother and brethren [of Jesus] said to Him: John the Baptist is baptizing for the remission of sins; let us go and be baptized by him." [148] This partly heretical legend meets the difficulty in this wise: Jesus did not come to John for baptism for the same reasons as His countrymen; hence it is supposed that of His own accord He had no thought of receiving it. Not within Him, in His moral being, but without, in some external circumstances, must be sought the real motive which led Him to John. So everything is simplified and explained.

John partially solved the difficulty by saying: "That He [the Messias] may be made manifest in Israel, therefore am I come baptizing with water." [149] Christ's baptism was destined to reveal Him solemnly to John, then through John to the whole world, under the circumstances that we will presently consider. St. Justin, while accepting this motive, sets us on the path toward a no less acceptable explanation. He says: "Although Christ was born and although He lived somewhere, He is unknown and possesses no power until Elias consecrates Him by unction." [150] With respect to Jesus, baptism was that which holy anointing was for kings and priests. The Holy Ghost is about to communicate Himself to Him with a new fulness, and God the Father will proclaim Him as

[148] *Adv. Pelag.*, III, 2. Cf. Nestle, *Novi Testamenti Graeci Supplementum,* 1896, pp. 76 f. Another apocryphal writing, the *Praedicatio Pauli,* says that Jesus, "the only man who never sinned, came in spite of Himself, urged by His mother Mary," to receive baptism from John. Cf. Pseudo-Cyprian, *De Rebaptism,* 17.

[149] John 1:31.
[150] *Dial. cum Tryph.,* 88.

His well-beloved Son, so that He will be provided, outwardly as well as inwardly, with full powers to begin His work. He was a private individual before His baptism; after it He will act openly as the Messias. This ceremony was, so to speak, His ordination, His Messianic consecration, the official mark of His office.

Let us rise to a still higher plane in our inquiry. It is true that between the holy, perfect Jesus and the baptism of penance there was a real opposition, even a flagrant contradiction. But did not the Son of God become incarnate to bear and expiate the sins of men? He therefore entered upon His office, when His ministry was about to begin, by taking the appearance and attitude of a penitent sinner, while awaiting the hour when He would become our Victim of propitiation on the cross. To use the Baptist's profound expression, it was as the "Lamb of God," weighted with the crimes of the whole world,[151] that Jesus came to the Jordan to be baptized.[152] Says St. Melito in poetic strain: "Do not the terrestrial sun, the moon, and stars, however pure they may be, bathe in the waters of the ocean?" [153]

Christ's baptism deserves to be viewed as one of the culminating points of His life. Thus we may say that His journey from Nazareth to the Jordan was the most serious step He had taken since that which brought Him from Heaven to Mary's virginal womb. We would like to know the exact spot on the river bank where the precursor stood when Jesus came to him. "A very early tradition, long ago recorded by the Pilgrim of Bordeaux (A. D. 333), indicates as the place of our Lord's baptism a point on the Jordan near the Greek convent of St. John the Baptist (Kasr-el-Yehud, "castle of

---

[151] John 1 : 29.

[152] See St. Justin, *Dial. cum Tryph.*, 88; St. John Chrysostom, *Homil. in Matth.*, XII, 3; St. Thomas, *Summa Theol.*, 3a, qu. 39, a. 1 and 2; Suarez, *Disputationes in III Partem D. Thomae*, disput. XXXIX, 1–2.

[153] Pitra, *Analecta Sacra*, II, 3–5.

the Jews"), which is five Roman miles from the Dead Sea,[154] fifteen minutes' walk from the river. From the fourth to the sixth century it was there that large numbers of catechumens went to be baptized, in honor of the baptism received by Christ." [155] Nevertheless this site is not certain.

What a solemn moment when Jesus, coming to John, asked that he confer his baptism upon Him! Were they then alone on the river bank? A detail mentioned by St. Luke, if interpreted literally, would seem to indicate that they were. St. Luke says that Jesus received baptism "when all the people were baptized." [156] Moreover, none of the Evangelists supposes the presence of other witnesses than John.[157]

Were the two cousins personally acquainted with each other? Or was this the first time they had come face to face? In itself it would not be at all impossible that they had met at Jerusalem with their parents at the time of the pilgrimages prescribed by the Mosaic Law. At any rate the Gospels do not mention any other meeting. If they had seen each other previously, it must have been long before, since the Baptist a few days later says that he did not know Jesus before this meeting.[158]

The short dialogue that took place between them when Jesus presented Himself, proves that John at once recognized Him as the Messias. But this was by virtue of a supernatural intimation which preceded the outward manifestation of the

[154] This is the indication given by the Pilgrim of Bordeaux.

[155] *La Palestine, Guide Historique et Pratique,* by professors of Notre Dame de France à Jerusalem, 2d ed., p. 280.

[156] Luke 3: 21. The correct translation of the words $\dot{\epsilon}\nu\ \tau\tilde{\omega}\ \beta\alpha\pi\tau\iota\sigma\theta\tilde{\eta}\nu\alpha\iota$ is that of St. Ambrose: *cum baptizatus esset omnis populus.* That of the Vulgate, *cum baptizaretur . . . ,* is less exact.

[157] From what is related in John 1: 31-34, it seems right to conclude that the precursor was then alone with Jesus.

[158] John 1: 31. Painters have familiarized us with the gracious idea and their brush has set it forth under most charming forms, namely, that Jesus and John lived near each other in early childhood: but the idea is not true.

Holy Ghost by which (as God had revealed to him) the Messias was to be officially designated to him.

At first John strongly protested and refused to lend himself to the act which Jesus called upon him to perform.[159] At length he said: "I ought to be baptized by Thee, and comest Thou to me?" As his mother had done in Mary's presence on the day of the Visitation,[160] so he humbled himself, proclaimed his unworthiness and the unbecomingness of baptizing Him whose shoes he considered himself not worthy to bear. In a calm and gentle tone Jesus replied: "Suffer it to be so now. For so it becometh us to fulfil all justice." [161] By these words the Savior acknowledged the genuine foundation of John's objection. The Messias was not strictly obliged to receive baptism at the hands of His subordinate. But this ceremony was a preparation for the institution of the Messianic Kingdom and for that reason, although it had not been the object of an explicit order from Heaven, it entered into the divine plan. Later on, Jesus speaks of the precursor's baptizing as a "counsel of God,"—a counsel which the Scribes and Pharisees despised by refusing to submit to it, whereas the common people and even the publicans "justified God" by being baptized by John.[162] It was, then, fitting that the Messias should also submit to this ceremony, however humbling it might be. Therefore John might be assured and might accept this momentary superiority with regard to Christ. The hour was approaching when Jesus would take the place assigned to Him by His office.

This is the second occasion on which the Savior's words

---

[159] St. Matthew's text is significant in this respect. The verb διεκώλυεν (Vulg., *prohibebat*), in the imperfect tense, "he stayed Him," indicates prolonged efforts to dissuade Jesus.

[160] Luke 1 : 40–45.

[161] This is a Hebraism, meaning: all perfection.

[162] Luke 7 : 29 f.

are recorded by the Evangelists.[163] They ended the conflict of humility. In violence to his own feelings, John then proceeded to baptize the Messias. It was the highest point of his noble career. But his ministry was not yet finished, and soon we shall again find him in the full exercise of his office as Christ's herald.

Notwithstanding its importance, the baptism of Jesus is not described by any of His first biographers, who simply make brief mention of the fact. On the other hand, they lay stress upon the phenomena of a superior order that immediately followed the Savior's immersion in the waters of the Jordan. Several times, when describing the most humiliating mysteries of Christ's hidden life, we pointed out the glorious manifestations by which it pleased God for a moment to unveil the greatness of His Chosen One. On the occasion of His baptism, the Messias also received from His heavenly Father a signal testimony. As soon as He stepped forth from the stream, He began to pray,[164] as we shall see Him do in other grave circumstances of His ministry. We may easily surmise the object of the Savior's fervent prayer after His baptism. He generously consecrated Himself to God, put Himself entirely at the disposal of His heavenly Father, and offered Himself to Him as a Victim for all mankind. His Father's answer to this ardent prayer came at once. Jesus and John saw as it were a rent [165] form in the heavens, and from it came forth the Holy Ghost in the form of a dove, descending upon Jesus and remaining over Him for some time,[166] as though

[163] On the first saying, see Vol. I, p. 385.

[164] We owe this precious detail to St. Luke, who, as we have said, likes to mention Christ's prayers.

[165] This is the expression used by St. Mark: "He saw the heavens opened," σχιζομένους. The Latin poet Silius Italicus employs a similar expression (I, 537): *Scisso densa inter nubila caelo.* St. Matthew and St. Luke say merely that "the heavens were opened": a manner of speech that may also be found elsewhere in the Bible, Ezech. 1: 1; Acts 7: 36; Apoc. 4: 1, etc.

[166] This last detail we owe to the Fourth Gospel, John 1: 32.

to establish His abode in Him. Then a voice in the air was heard, saying: "This is My beloved Son, in whom I am well pleased." [167]

A few words in explanation of these marvelous phenomena will not be useless. First of all, let us say that, according to the testimony of the sacred narratives, they possessed an objective, external reality, and did not take place merely in vision in the soul of Christ and of the precursor. The Evangelists' language leaves no doubt about it; and such has also been the constant teaching of the Fathers and of the best Catholic exegetes.[168] Jesus and John saw and heard; the scenes that appeared to their eyes, the sounds that struck their ears were not imaginary, but sensible and external.

At first view it would seem that the descent of the Holy Ghost upon the Messias was superfluous, since the human nature of the Word had been inundated by that Divine Spirit at the very instant when the Word became incarnate in Mary's womb. But we can understand that, when Jesus was about to inaugurate His Messianic office, His humanity received this new effusion of the third Person of the Holy Trinity. This was the unction and consecration which we mentioned above. St. Jerome informs us that, according to the apocryphal Gospel of the Nazarenians, the Holy Ghost, taking possession of Jesus, said to Him: "My Son, I waited for Thee in all the prophets . . . , to rest in Thee, for Thou art My rest." [169] This is certainly a curious addition to the inspired text; and yet it expresses, at bottom, a thought both just and beautiful. At least, it was then that the celebrated prophecies of Isaias were visibly fulfilled: "The spirit of the Lord shall rest upon Him [the Messias]"; "The spirit of

[167] St. Justin, *Dial. cum Tryph.* 88, Tatian's *Diatessaron* (Burkitt, *Evangelion da Mepharreshe*, II, 115), and others add a fourth phenomenon: that of a "great light" accompanying the divine voice.

[168] See Knabenbauer, *Comment. in Evang. sec. Matth.*, I, 147.

[169] In his Commentary on Isaias, 11 : 2.

the Lord is upon Me, because the Lord hath anointed Me." [170]

As to the form [171] under which the Holy Ghost appeared, it is best to explain it by means of the symbolic ideas which the Orientals, more particularly the Israelites, connected with the dove. The dove appears in the story of the Deluge as the figure of faithfulness and peace.[172] The Canticle of Canticles considers it symbolic of innocence and pure love; [173] Jesus Himself extols its candor and simplicity.[174] And the rabbinical writings at times compare it to the Holy Spirit. Thus, to these words of Genesis, "The Spirit of God moved over the waters," [175] one rabbi adds: "like a dove over its little ones." [176] Another rabbi, referring to a passage in the Canticle of Canticles,[177] says that "the voice of the dove is the voice of the Holy Spirit." [178]

The third manifestation, by which the heavenly Father openly recognized Jesus Christ as His Son and Envoy, adds to the second one.[179] It has been questioned whether the words "My Son" must be understood in the broad sense of Messias, which they sometimes have, or in the exact and meta-

---

[170] Is. 11:2 and 61:1.

[171] St. Luke strongly emphasizes the external character of this apparition, saying that it took place ἐν σωματικῷ εἴδει, "in a bodily shape."

[172] Gen. 8:11.

[173] Cant. 1:14; 2:10, 12; 4:1; 5:2; 6:8.

[174] Matt. 10:16.

[175] Gen. 1:2.

[176] *Chagiga*, 15, a.

[177] Cant. 2:12.

[178] *Bammidbar rabba*, 25. Cf. A. Wünsche, *Neue Beiträge zur Erläuterung der Evangelien*, pp. 21 f.

[179] According to the accounts of St. Mark and St. Luke, God addressed Jesus directly: "Thou art My beloved Son . . ." According to St. Matthew, He addressed the Baptist: "This is My beloved Son . . ." These are simple shades of difference, expressing one and the same fact. The direct form is probably the one that was employed. St. Justin, *Dial. cum Tryph.*, 88 and 103, Clement of Alexandria, *Paedag.*, XVI, 25, and some manuscripts erroneously have the variant, "Thou art My Son, this day have I begotten Thee," taken from Ps. 2:7. St. Augustine mentions it (*De Cons. Evangelist.*, II, 14) and says that in his day it did not exist in the most ancient manuscripts.

physical sense, to designate the Son of God, strictly so called. Here again Catholic exegetes and theologians, and with them several Protestant commentators,[180] adopt the latter interpretation, which is required both by the text and by the context. The text, especially in the Greek,[181] is remarkably expressive with its two articles, which accentuate the thought. The context is still clearer, because the preceding accounts of St. Matthew and St. Luke present Jesus to us as engendered by the Holy Ghost and because St. Mark, in his very first line, sums up his whole Gospel in words that are as indicative as possible: "The beginning of the Gospel of Jesus Christ, the Son of God." [182] This divine voice will be heard on two other occasions, glorifying the Savior again: at His Transfiguration,[183] and just a few days before His Passion.[184] On each of these three occasions it utters exquisitely tender words which show the love of God for His only begotten Son, chosen by Him to be the head and Redeemer of all mankind.[185] Here we have the wonderful narratives of the Savior's birth ratified and solemnly authenticated by Heaven itself. Herein, too, we see the double title under which Jesus is now going to begin His work: Messias and Son of God.[186]

II. The Temptation of Christ [187]

Immediately after Jesus was baptized,[188] the Spirit of God, descending upon Him to take more and more complete possession of His sacred humanity, drove Him out into the

---

[180] Among them, Zahn, *Das Evangelium des Matthäus ausgelegt, hoc loco.*
[181] Ὁ υἱός μου, ὁ ἀγαπητός. Literally, *"The* son of me, *the* beloved."
[182] Mark 1 : 1.
[183] Matt. 17 : 5, and the parallel passages in St. Mark and St. Luke.
[184] John 12 : 28–30.
[185] John 12 : 28.
[186] On the critics' interpretation of the baptism of Jesus, see Appendix II.
[187] Matt. 4 : 1–11 ; Mark 1 : 12 f. ; Luke 4 : 1–13.
[188] Here St. Mark makes use of his favorite adverb, "immediately."

desert.[189] St. Matthew tells us the purpose of this sudden move: it was that Christ might "be tempted by the devil."

These words state a mystery which is profound and surprising, though in a different way from the mystery of our Lord's baptism. The Son of God tempted, consequently provoked to do evil; the Son of God in immediate contact with the prince of devils: what a contrast, too, with the manifestations by which He had just been glorified! With the help of St. Paul and the Fathers, Catholic theology has been able to throw some light on this extraordinary incident. In becoming man, the Divine Word accepted all the conditions, all the wretchedness, all the humiliations of our fallen nature. This is why, says the Apostle of the Gentiles, He was "one tempted in all things like as we are." [190] St. Paul goes even farther and does not hesitate to say that "it behoved Him in all things to be made like unto His brethren. . . . For in that, wherein He Himself hath suffered and been tempted, He is able to succor them also that are tempted." [191] Here again there is, on the Savior's part, one of those voluntary abasements which the Epistle to the Philippians describes in such noble language.[192] Moreover, painful though temptation may be, it brings no harm to a soul that successfully withstands it. On the contrary, it shows how far such a soul is steeped in goodness and also increases its merits. With all the more reason may we say that Christ's holiness could not, under like circumstances, suffer the least harm. There was of course between Him and us—and St. Paul is at pains to say this also [193]—this enormous difference, that only too often do we

---

189 This special detail, too, we owe to St. Mark: ἐκβάλλει (Vulg., *expulit*). Literally: the Spirit "drove" Him, *i. e.*, exercised a strong pressure on Him. The other two Synoptics say, with a shade of difference: ἀνήχθη (St. Matthew), "He was led on high" (to a more elevated place); ἤγετο (St. Luke), "He was led."

190 Heb. 4: 15.
191 Heb. 2: 17 f.
192 Phil. 2: 7 f.
193 Heb. 4: 15.

yield to temptation, whereas Jesus remained always "without sin." But the scene that we must now describe and other episodes of the Divine Master's life will show that He could, nevertheless, be stirred to evil, be tempted to fail in duty, His divinity hiding itself, so to speak, for the moment and permitting His human nature to undergo rude trials. From this point of view, the dolorous scene at Gethsemani helps us to understand the temptation in the desert. Even while remaining impeccable, Jesus could, then, be really tempted; but with this other great difference, that in us, in consequence of original sin, there exists a leaven of concupiscence which directly raises up the power of evil, whereas in Jesus, in whom everything was holy and perfect, temptation could come only from without, from Satan or his agents.[194]

The angels were the first to undergo the trial of temptation, and unfortunately many of them succumbed. Adam, too, was tempted, and we know with what desolating results for himself and his posterity. Nor did the second Adam escape the trial of temptation. But what a magnificent victory He wins! Everything considered, to enter upon an open contest with the chief of the empire of darkness and to triumph over him—was not this, for the Head of the Kingdom of Heaven, a worthy beginning of His redemptive activity? In the words of the beloved disciple, "the Son of God appeared, that He might destroy the works of the devil." [195] And St. John Chrysostom, considering Christ's baptism as a strong armor, addresses the Divine Hero thus: "Go forth, then; for if Thou hast taken arms, it is not to seek rest, but to fight." [196]

In the three Gospels setting forth Christ's temptation,[197]

[194] See St. Thomas, *Summa Theol.*, 3a, qu. 41, a. 1–4; Suarez, p. 3, disput. 39, art. 1–4.

[195] John 3 : 8.

[196] *Homil. in Matth.*, XIV.

[197] Since this episode of His life had no witnesses, we owe its account to Christ Himself, who communicated it to His Apostles. The source could not be more reliable.

the place where it took place bears the general name of "desert." It must, therefore, have been part of the wilderness of Juda, which we described above. From the banks of the Jordan, Jesus, led by the Holy Spirit, first traversed the distance of about six miles to Jericho; then, after continuing His journey westward, He stopped, according to St. Matthew's exact indication,[198] in the highest region of the desert. In all likelihood, according to a tradition that goes back at least to the time of the Crusades, this was at the place which to-day bears the name of Djebel Kuruntel or Kuruntul, "Mount of the Quarantania," in memory of the forty days which Christ passed there. It is a particularly frightful district, covered with bare rocks and cut by deep ravines in every direction. The sides of the mountain abound with natural caves, which for many centuries were inhabited by pious hermits desirous of honoring the Savior's temptation on the very site of its occurrence. A detail special to St. Mark suggests its desolate character. He says that Jesus "was with beasts." Even today, in those quite uninhabited quarters, there are many jackals, foxes, hyenas, eagles, vultures, and other beasts of prey.[199]

Christ spent forty days and forty nights in that horrible wilderness, without taking any food.[200] During this long period He lived only the life of the soul, wholly immersed in God, praying for those He had come to save, contemplating in advance the different aspects of His approaching ministry. It was like a continual ecstasy, during which the needs of the body were miraculously suspended. But of a sudden, nature

---

[198] Page 52, note 189.

[199] Tristram, *The Land of Israel,* p. 244; G. A. Smith, *Historical Geography of Palestine,* p. 316.

[200] St. Luke is explicit on this point: "He ate nothing in those days." St. Matthew's expression, "when He had fasted forty days and forty nights," is scarcely less explicit.

imperiously resumed its rights, and the pangs of hunger made themselves felt.

This is the favorable moment for temptation because a human being is then in a weakened condition. Satan took advantage of it to lay his first snare for Christ. The Gospel shows us the prince of devils insidiously coming up to Him, very probably in human form. The various names which the sacred writers here call him are those ordinarily given to him in the other parts of the Bible: "Satan," a Hebrew word meaning "adversary," the "devil" or calumniator, the "tempter." Each of these epithets rightly brands him, emphasizing his particular perfidy. If this enemy of God and man, jealous of both, could but triumph over the Messias, what a victory he would win over both God and man! In his triple assault [211] upon Christ, he displays all his cunning and ability.

The devil, taking Christ's hunger as his starting-point, says to Him: "If Thou be the Son of God, say to this stone that it be made bread." [202] While thus speaking, Satan pointed to, or perhaps even held in his hand, one of the countless

---

[201] In the Second Gospel, the account of the temptation is very much condensed. Without mentioning its three phases, St. Mark limits himself to pointing out briefly four facts. The following is a translation of his narrative according to the Greek text: "[Jesus] passed forty days and forty nights in the desert, tempted by Satan, and He was with the [wild] beasts and the angels ministered to Him." From this summary account, it has sometimes been inferred, following St. Justin, *Dial. cum Tryph.*, 103, the author of the *Clementine Homilies,* XIX, 9, Origen, *Hom. in Luc.*, XXIX, St. Augustine, *De Cons. Evangel.*, II, 16, and certain other early authors, that Christ's temptation was prolonged throughout the forty days; St. Matthew and St. Luke relating only the last phase of it. This opinion seems hardly probable. It has been well said that St. Mark gives only the *torso* of the episode, so abridging his account that it becomes obscure. We must, therefore, explain it by the other two, which are more complete and quite clear. If the last detail, "angels came and ministered to Him," can refer only to the end of the episode, and not to the forty days and nights in their entirety, the words "tempted by Satan" can likewise not be applied to the whole of that same period. Such is the view of most commentators.

[202] We here follow St. Luke's text, which seems the more natural. St. Matthew uses the plural: "Command that these stones be made bread."

stones that covered the surface of the wilderness of the Quarantania. The words, "If Thou be the Son of God," with which he twice prefaced his perfidious suggestions, show that to a certain extent he was aware of Christ's nature and mission.[203] Not long before, at our Lord's baptism, the divine voice had spoken clearly enough to inform him, if it be that he or one of his followers had heard it. At any rate, he might wish to be more certain about the matter. At the same time, those insidious words, "If Thou be . . ." were purposely chosen to touch to the quick the *amour propre* of Him whom he came to tempt and the more easily to obtain the requested miracle.

This first temptation consisted in urging Jesus to use in His personal interest, without any absolute necessity, the gift of performing miracles, a power with which He was certainly vested if He were really the Messias. Why should the Son of God suffer from hunger like a simple mortal in the uninhabited wilderness, when it was so easy for Him to obtain substantial food by a simple word? The suggestion was clever. If Jesus had yielded to it, "He would have subordinated, at least for the moment, His divine nature to the wants of His humanity, placing the human above the divine, changing the divine into a means and the human into an end; He would consequently have reversed the order fixed by God." [204] And so He energetically repelled this first attack.

Disdaining to notice the insinuation contained in the words, "If Thou be the Son of God," He merely replied: "It is written: Not in bread alone doth man live, but in every word that proceedeth from the mouth of God." In triumphing over the devil's assaults, Christ three times takes in hand the keen-

---

[203] The opinion of commentators has always been divided on this point. According to the view of St. John Chrysostom, St. Jerome, St. Augustine, and a considerable number of modern and contemporary authors, the prince of devils really felt some doubt as to Christ's Messianic character.

[204] Fillion, *L'Évangile de S. Matthieu, Introd. Critiq. et Commentaires*, p. 82.

edged, invincible sword of Biblical texts.[205] This first quotation is from Deuteronomy [206] and alludes to the great miracle of the manna. The Israelites, after their exodus from Egypt, were about to be exposed to the peril of hunger during their wanderings through the vast desert of Pharan. But God had just made them His chosen people; and He did not abandon them. By a single word, possessing as it did a creative and almighty power, He supplied them abundantly with a wonderful food that sustained their strength for forty years.[207] Why, then, should Christ, who was in a situation similar to that of the Israelites, perform a miracle on behalf of His own personal needs? God knew them and in His own good time would certainly not fail to provide for them.[208]

Undaunted by this first defeat, the tempter, on the contrary, was stimulated to a new attack, outwardly of quite another sort, which was to move Jesus to make a still more profane abuse of His miraculous powers. The Gospel text says: "The devil took Him up into the Holy City and set Him upon the pinnacle of the Temple." We believe it to be more in conformity with the Evangelists' thought, and with the facts, to take this description literally, as most Catholic interpreters do, and to suppose that the Savior allowed Satan to carry Him rapidly through the air to Jerusalem.[209] At the time of His Passion He lets the traitor Judas deliver Him into the hands of His enemies by a kiss, He permits the servants of the Sanhedrin to strike Him and to spit in His face, Pilate's le-

[205] Cf. Eph. 6:17; Heb. 4:12.

[206] Deut. 8:3. It is taken verbatim, according to the Septuagint.

[207] Ex. 16:1–36; Josue 5:12; Ps. 77:23–25.

[208] Some commentators have distorted the true meaning of Christ's reply by explaining it as if the expression "word of God" here designated, not material food, but spiritual nourishment, as, for example, obedience to the divine will, the inspired word of Holy Writ, etc.

[209] St. Matthew, who was writing especially for Jews, calls the theocratic capital by its glorious name of "Holy City," a title often used in the books of both the Old and New Testament (cf. Is. 48:2; 52:1; Dan. 3:28; Tob. 13:11; Apoc. 11:2, etc.), as also by Philo and Josephus.

gionaries to scourge Him and crucify Him. For Him all these
humiliations were part of the divine plan, to which He generously conformed.

It is impossible to indicate with certainty the exact place
which St. Matthew and St. Luke call "the pinnacle [210] of the
Temple," upon which Satan placed Christ. From the expression which they employ [211] it follows that there is here no
question of the sanctuary strictly so called, but of the Temple
in a broad sense, of the whole agglomeration of buildings that
composed it. Solomon's Porch and the Royal Porch have been
especially suggested in this connection. The former stood
up in the eastern part, the latter in the southern part of the
sacred edifice. As for the Royal Porch, Josephus says [212] that
from the top of it anyone would look down into so deep an
abyss as to make him dizzy. [213]

The devil, speaking again, said to Jesus: "If Thou be the
Son of God, cast Thyself down, for it is written: That He
hath given His angels charge over Thee, and in their hands
shall they bear Thee up, lest perhaps Thou dash Thy foot
against a stone." While remaining fundamentally the same,
the diabolic tactics now try to improve. The tempter, having
just experienced to his cost the power of an apt Biblical quotation, himself cites one to justify his odious proposal. He
takes it from the Psalter, [214] and it is certain that it expresses
with a tender beauty the watchfulness, which we might almost
call maternal, with which God constantly encompasses the

[210] We take this word from the Vulgate, which very correctly uses *pinnaculum*
to translate the corresponding Greek expression, τὸ πτερύγιον. This diminutive of
πτέρυξ, was often employed figuratively to designate the top of a building, particularly a wing-shaped pediment.

[211] τὸ ἱερόν, and not ὁ ναός.

[212] *Ant.*, XV, xi, 5. See Vol. I, p. 166.

[213] Eusebius of Caesarea, *Hist. Eccl.*, II, 29, and XI, 5, also relates, but without
further specification, that it was from the pinnacle of the Temple that St. James,
Bishop of Jerusalem, was later hurled by the Jews.

[214] Ps. 90: 11 f.

just, His faithful friends. At God's command, the angels will take them gently in their hands and snatch them from peril. With the more reason will He safeguard His Christ. Let Jesus, then, not hesitate to leap into space. Not only will He come to no harm, but, by such an unheard-of prodigy, He will amaze those who would be walking about the Temple courts and He would at once be acclaimed as the expected Liberator, the Messias coming directly down from heaven.

The Savior at once replied: "It is written again: Thou shalt not tempt the Lord thy God." It is true that God solemnly promised to rescue the just from the midst of their dangers; but He did not promise to come to their help when, without sufficient reason, they expose themselves to peril by reckless presumption, as Satan proposed to the Savior. So to act would be to tempt God, arrogantly to put Him to the test, to require that, upon one of our whims, He abandon the wise designs of His providence, in short, that He perform the oddest wonders in order to repair our shameful folly. This second reply of Christ also comes from Deuteronomy.[215] Moses used these words to reproach the Hebrews for their wrongful murmuring by which they had "tempted the Lord their God," when they were suffering thirst in the desert, imperiously demanding some great miracle.[216] Christ will not act thus, but will refrain from the criminal act proposed by the devil. The first Satanic suggestion He answered by affirming His perfect trust in God, who would not let Him die of hunger; the second He repels by declaring that He will not foolishly expose Himself to danger in consequence of a grievously blameworthy presumption. When His hour comes, He will without fear or hesitation go forth to meet death; but, for the present, He will manifest His heavenly mission only by winning hearts and convincing men's minds.

[215] Deut. 6:16, following the Septuagint.
[216] Cf. Ex. 17:2; Ps. 77:18 f.

Then, the Gospel narrative continues,[217] "the devil took Him up into a very high mountain and showed Him all the kingdoms of the world and the glory of them." Efforts to determine the mountain top from which Satan had the Savior behold so many wonders, have been in vain. Thabor and Nebo have been mentioned. But their height is not sufficient to justify the expression "very high" of St. Matthew's description. Furthermore, whatever mountain it may have been, it was not possible from its summit to behold "all the kingdoms of the world," even if we should considerably restrict the meaning of these last words. It is, therefore, probable that Satan had recourse to magical means, a sort of phantasmagoria and mirage, in order to bring before our Lord's eyes and imagination this gigantic and marvelous panorama: the beauties of nature and of art, cities and their magnificent buildings, armies and multitudes, material riches, in a word, all that constitutes our earth's outward glory. St. Luke's account favors this view, for he says that the wonderful sight lasted but a moment.[218]

Thinking to have amazed Christ by this grandiose sight, Satan continued speaking, to accomplish his seduction: "To Thee will I give all this power and the glory of them; for to me they are delivered, and to whom I will I give them. If Thou therefore wilt adore before me, all shall be Thine." As St. Jerome remarks,[219] the devil here makes use of bold, haughty language, but largely false, because it is not true

----

[217] Our readers know that St. Luke does not follow the same order as St. Matthew in the sequence of the last two temptations. He assigns the third place to the one we have just been considering, and the second place to the one which St. Matthew's account places third. Very generally preference is given—as it was in the opinion of St. Justin, in the second century (*Dial. cum Tryph.*, 103)—to the plan followed in the First Gospel, because it presents a more natural and logical gradation. Furthermore, how could the devil, after being ignominiously driven off by the words, "Begone, Satan," have returned to the attack?

[218] Ἐν στιγμῇ χρόνου. Vulg., *in momento temporis.*

[219] *Comment. in Matth., hoc loco.*

that he possesses such authority over the entire world and that he can bestow kingdoms as fiefs on whomsoever he chooses. Yet in this assertion the devil is not absolutely lying, since God permits him to exercise a certain power over the affairs of men, and men only too often yield to his fatal sway. In this sense it is that Christ Himself sometimes calls him "the prince of this world" [220] and that St. Paul even calls him "the god of this world." [221] There is a mixture of imposture and truth in the impudent proposal he here makes to Jesus. With what artfulness he brings out the value of the goods whose full and immediate enjoyment he offers! But this offer is far from being gratuitous. To his favors he attaches a monstrous and truly diabolical condition: Jesus must first prostrate Himself at his feet and thus show, in Oriental fashion, His absolute submission to the suzerain from whose hands He will receive His powers.

This time Satan has removed his mask. "Adore me!" such, in all its nakedness, is the horrible proposal he dares make to Christ. In ordinary souls, the sight of worldly goods at once arouses a desire to possess and enjoy them. The devil hoped to succeed the more easily in producing such a desire in Christ's heart since the Messias, as the devil knew, was destined to exercise a universal kingship. His error was gross. This he will comprehend when from the Savior's lips he hears the command, issued with all the force of contempt: "Begone, Satan!" [222] which drives him away in shame. The Savior, however, supplements His thought by another quotation from the Sacred Books: "It is written: The Lord thy God shalt thou adore, and Him only shalt thou serve." [223]

[220] John 12:31; 14:30.

[221] 2 Cor. 4:4. Cf. Eph. 2:2.

[222] The words "behind me," added by several manuscripts and some of the Greek Fathers, appear not to have belonged to the original text. The addition is borrowed from Matt. 16:23.

[223] As in the case of the preceding texts, this one is quoted with a certain freedom.

This text, which is likewise taken from Deuteronomy,[224] proclaims the fundamental law of all true religion. To adore God and serve Him, is the first and greatest of all commandments and sums up all the others.[225] In quoting it, Christ, as it were, took an oath of fidelity to the only living God, His heavenly Father, who alone had a right to His homage.

There was no better argument to silence His adversary. And so the devil, defeated along his whole front, was compelled to flee in disgrace. "All the temptation being ended," says St. Luke in expressive words.[226] In fact, as the moralists remark, the three special temptations to which the infernal spirit had recourse to bring Jesus to do evil, include the germ and abridgment of all others.[227] The same Evangelist, after mentioning the tempter's departure, adds that it was but "for a time." Satan did not altogether give up the strife. But he would await a more favorable opportunity before returning to the attack, and he counted on finding it some day. But it does not seem that he ever again personally engaged in a struggle with the Savior. At least he did attack Him and tempt Him by means of numerous tools: the Scribes and Pharisees, the Sadducees, the multitudes and their false Messianic ideal, the traitor Judas.[228] Even St. Peter one day became the tempter of his Master.[229] Jesus again experienced the trial of temptation, especially during the last days of His life. In His farewell address, alluding to Gethsemani and Calvary, He says to His Apostles: "The prince of this world cometh." [230] In the wilderness, Satan tempted Him by the

[224] Deut. 6: 13.
[225] Matt. 22: 36–38; Mark 12: 28–34.
[226] Luke 4: 13. That is, every kind of temptation.
[227] St. Gregory the Great, *Hom. in Matth.*, XVI; St. Thomas, *Summa Theol.*, 3a, qu. 41, a. 4.
[228] Cf. John 13: 27.
[229] Matt. 16: 23; Mark 8: 33.
[230] John 14: 30

lure of the gratification of the senses and by the attraction of glory; later he tempts Him by the dread of suffering and of death.

At the time of the first diabolic assault, the Savior had expressed His full trust in God, who, by a word, can provide for those who love Him the food needed to sustain life. The close of this episode shows that not in vain had He put hope in that powerful succor. In fact, so soon as Satan departed, "behold angels came and ministered to Him." We can easily suppose that their eager ministration consisted in miraculously bringing Him the food that He so greatly needed.[231]

Such were the principal circumstances of the temptation of our Lord Jesus Christ. This mysterious scene was, as our early doctors are wont to repeat, the counterpart of that which took place four thousand years earlier, in Paradise. The victory of Him who is justly called the second Adam, the head of redeemed mankind, compensated for the shameful and easy defeat of the first Adam. But, lest we deprive this episode of its true character and thereby lessen its significance, let us note that the trial undergone by Jesus in the wilderness consisted not merely of a threefold temptation of sense gratification, vainglory, and ambition, but was grave and decisive also in another way. Gospel commentators to-day all agree in recognizing that it was not as an ordinary man, but chiefly as the Messias that Jesus was tempted, at the very hour when He was about to present Himself as such to His countrymen. The images which the devil brought up before His eyes were cleverly chosen to seduce Him, had that been possible. Since it is an eminently important point in the history we are writing, we should not tire repeating that most of the Jews of that time, sadly distorting the holy and heavenly por-

---

231 The verb διακονεῖν (Vulg., ministrare) often has this special meaning in the New Testament. Cf. Matt. 8:15; 25:44; Mark 1:13, 31; Luke 4:39; 12:37; 17:8; Acts 6:2, etc.

trait which the prophets had sketched of the Messias, rendered it altogether earthly and unrecognizable. They were expecting a liberator who would strike in a theatrical manner, perform numerous miracles for no other purpose than to flatter his personal vanity or that of his race, manifesting himself as a mighty king whose ambition even the empire of the world could hardly satisfy.[232] It was this programme of a false Jewish Messianism that the devil, in his three consecutive assaults, proposed that Jesus should carry out. He wanted to make of Him, as has been said, a Messias "by the grace of Satan." Three times the Savior rejected and condemned this programme, the while attesting three great principles: (1) Even as the Messias, He did not consider Himself freed from the needs and trials to which other men are subjected, and He would not perform any miracle to evade them; (2) Nor to convince His countrymen of His Messianic rights, would He resort to useless prodigies or perform dazzling "signs," devoid of any moral purpose; (3) The kingdom He is going to found will have nothing political or human in it, but will be spiritual and religious. In a word, Jesus consents to perform the functions of Messias only in a manner conformable to God's will.

It is true that it will cost Him His life, for, by refusing to lend Himself to the rôle that Satan suggested, He will clash with the prejudices of His people and will gradually stir up a violent flood of hatred against Himself. Each time, therefore, that He repelled one of Satan's attacks, He ascended another step to the altar on which He was to be immolated. But at the end of His glorious career He could truthfully say that the prince of this world, the chief of devils, had not the least power over Him.[233]

---

[232] See Vol. I, p. 198.
[233] John 14 : 30. See Appendix III.

III. Further Eloquent Testimony of John the Baptist to Christ [234]

The Synoptics inform us with what fidelity John became the herald of the Messias in the presence of the Jewish multitudes, even before knowing Him and baptizing Him. The Fourth Gospel points out more direct and personal testimonies which the precursor rendered to Jesus about six weeks after His baptism. The account is an abridgment of four successive days of the Savior's life.[235]

It has been well said that John the Baptist stands like a sentry before the portals of the Kingdom of Heaven, as at the entry to a superb sanctuary, in order to open the gate to whosoever approaches with the requisite dispositions. But those before whom he renders the first testimony we have to explain here, did not come to him as humble penitents. The fact that they were official personages, sent by the Sanhedrin of Jerusalem,[236] to make a formal inquiry about him, enhances the force of his testimony. His ever growing fame, which attracted to the banks of the lower Jordan numerous multitudes, coming not only from all parts of Palestine, but also from the Jewish capital,[237] could not fail to stir the high assembly, which judged that it ought to obtain direct information.

By acting thus, the Sanhedrin nowise exceeded its rights, for one of its most essential duties had to do with the religious affairs of Judaism. The rabbinical writings of the time say explicitly [238] that the judgment to be passed on a prophet was a matter within its special jurisdiction. And John's prophecies concerned an article of faith, the coming of the Mes-

---

[234] John 1 : 19–34.
[235] John 1 : 19, 29, 35, 43.
[236] On this high assembly, see Vol. I, p. 140.
[237] Matt. 3 : 5; Mark 1 : 5.
[238] The tractate *Sanhedrin*, I, 5. Cf. Deut. 18 : 21 f.

sias, which at that time aroused the keenest interest throughout the nation. Furthermore, the rumor spread and daily assumed greater consistency, that the son of Zachary was himself the expected liberator. What was he in fact? Why this baptism, which he administered without first obtaining authorization? In itself it was quite legitimate for the constituted authorities to step in for the purpose of obtaining light on these disturbing questions. There is, consequently, no need of attributing a character of open hostility to their proceeding, even though several members of the Great Council may have voted for the inquiry while mindful of the severe words uttered by the precursor, in the presence of the people, against the Pharisees and Sadducees.[239]

If we could enter the soul of John the Baptist and observe the sentiments that filled it since the time he first had direct contact with Christ, we would see that his faith and zeal, and his desire to serve the Messias more energetically than ever, were remarkably quickened, while his deep humility and self-abnegation were still further developed. John's soul was in this wonderful state when the delegates came. They had been selected from the ranks of the priests and Levites. This was a very natural choice, since the points to be inquired into were specifically theological and consequently belonged to the priestly domain. In former times did not God say, by the mouth of the prophet Malachias, that "the lips of the priest shall keep knowledge, and they shall seek the law at his mouth, because he is the angel of the Lord"? [240] Under the present circumstances, then, the priests played the principal part; the Levites accompanied them as a guard of honor.

The well-ordered inquiry which John the Baptist underwent was conducted with a tone of authority. The dialogue was lively and rapid, for the precursor experienced no hesi-

---

[239] Matt. 3:7–12.
[240] Mal. 2:7. Cf. Osee 4:6.

tation in replying. "Who art thou?" he was first asked. As John at once comprehended, in the delegates' inner thought this question clearly meant: Art thou the Messias? And so he answered firmly: "I am not the Christ." [241] The Evangelist emphasizes the firmness, loyalty, and sincerity of this reply, introducing it by a formal expression, which is successively positive, negative, and again positive: "He confessed, and did not deny, and he confessed . . ." He, the Messias? This hypothesis he rejected promptly and thoroughly, as an intolerable blasphemy.

"What then?" the delegates asked. "Art thou Elias?" This second question should not surprise us. In fact, according to a prophecy of Malachias,[242] the prophet Elias, who was mysteriously taken up in a fiery chariot and reserved by the Lord for a future rôle, was to appear again on earth some day, in order to prepare the way for the Messias. The Book of Ecclesiasticus [243] also refers to this noble office of Elias and earnestly calls for his appearance. The same belief was held by the Jews in our Lord's time, as may be seen from many passages in the Gospels [244] and rabbinical writings.[245] Jesus Himself shared it, but with an important distinction: the prophet Elias will prepare for the Messias' second coming; it was reserved to John to prepare for the first coming.[246] Hence the angel Gabriel, when foretelling to Zachary

---

[241] The most authentic reading of the Greek text places the pronoun ἐγώ at the beginning of the sentence, to emphasize it still more. It has long been remarked that throughout this passage John the Baptist frequently repeats this same pronoun, to give greater force to his testimony. See verses 20, 23, 26, 27, 30, 31 (twice), 33, 34.

[242] Mal. 4 : 5 f. (3 : 23 f. in the Hebrew text).

[243] Ecclu. 48 : 1–11.

[244] Matt. 16 : 14 ; 17 : 10–13 ; John 1 : 21, etc.

[245] Cf. St. Justin, *Dial. cum Tryph.*, 8 ; J. Langen, *Das Judentum in Palästina zur Zeit Christi*, pp. 490 f.; Weber, *System der altsynagogalen palästinischen Theologie*, pp. 337–339; Bousset, *Die Religion des Judentums*, p. 220; Edersheim, *Life and Times of Jesus*, II, 703–706.

[246] Matt. 11 : 13 f. ; 17 : 10–13.

the birth of this privileged son, announced that he would be endowed with the spirit and power of Elias.[247] The precursor had no call to enter into these theological distinctions. To the question "Art thou Elias?" he simply replied: "I am not." As St. Gregory the Great says, he was, in reality, only a mystical and figurative Elias.

"Art thou the prophet?" the delegates then asked. The presence of the definite article ὁ in the Greek text [248] indicates that in putting this third question they had in mind a determinate person, known at least in a general way, who is mentioned twice again in the Fourth Gospel.[249] In the almost unanimous opinion of interpreters, this prophet is none other than the one whose distant advent Moses foretold under divine inspiration.[250] But, although a certain number of Jews distinguished him from the Messias, as the Sanhedrin's representatives do here,[251] and looked upon him as one of the Messias' precursors, other Israelites [252] and the early Christians [253] made of him and of Christ one and the same person. This latter interpretation is the true one. A simple emphatic "No" was John's reply.[254]

The delegates returned to the charge, indicating the reason why they felt they must still persist: "Who art thou, that we may give an answer to them that sent us? What sayest thou of thyself?" Their inquiry had thus far brought them only a negative result, and they could hardly depart without obtaining some positive information to put in their report.

---

[247] Luke 1 : 17.
[248] Ὁ προφήτης.
[249] John 6 : 14; 7 : 40.
[250] Deut. 18 : 15–18.
[251] Cf. John 7 : 40; also Matt. 16 : 14; Mark 6 : 15; 8 : 28; Luke 9 : 8, 19.
[252] John 1 : 45.
[253] Acts 3 : 22 f.; 7 : 37.
[254] The brevity and vigor of his answers are remarkable: "I am not the Christ"; "I am not"; "No."

The answer was no less prompt than were the previous replies. It consisted in Isaias' prophecy which the Synoptics quote in connection with the Baptist's first appearance on the historic scene,[255] a text which he now applies to himself: "I am the voice of one crying in the wilderness, make straight the way of the Lord." He is and wishes to be only a voice, an impersonal thing without a name. However, the sacred narratives have acquainted us with its power, eloquence, and wonderful success. But John thinks only of humbling himself before Christ.

At this point of his narrative the Evangelist pauses a moment to remark that the members of the deputation belonged to the sect of the Pharisees.[256] These great zealots of the faith and of the purity of worship put another and final question to John. Using his own avowals as their starting-point, they ask him: "Why then dost thou baptize, if thou be not Christ nor Elias nor the prophet?" The right of innovation in religious matters and of instituting a new ceremony would readily be acknowledged in the Messias and in the great personages who were to prepare for His coming. But since John is nothing, by what title does he baptize? This time he makes only an indirect reply; but how clear it is and how

---

[255] Is. 40:3. See page 21.

[256] Following Origen's view, some have interpreted this remark as if it indicated that at that moment another deputation, made up of Pharisees, had come looking for the precursor, to question him. But the very text of the narrative is opposed to such an interpretation, for its different parts (John 1:20-28) are bound together as portions of one inseparable whole. There is question of one and the same audience, one and the same delegation. Without sufficient grounds it has been said that the Sanhedrin would not have chosen its delegates from the party of the Pharisees. On the contrary, it is certain that, for a long time past, the latter had penetrated into the great Council, where their influence made itself felt as it did everywhere else. We know also from Flavius Josephus (*Ant.*, XVIII, i, 3) that they were particularly competent in whatever concerned religious ceremonies. Hence it was natural that the Evangelist should insert the retrospective detail just as he is about to speak of the baptism introduced by John. A certain number of priests and Levites were members of the Pharisaic sect.

well it justifies his whole conduct! With a few slight changes he therein inserts the first testimony that he rendered to Christ the Redeemer.[257] He humbly says: "I baptize in water; but there stands in the midst of you one whom you know not. . . . It is He that comes [258] after me; I am not worthy to loose the strap of His shoe."

These few words contain, after a fashion, John the Baptist's credentials. His questioners wanted to know by virtue of what privilege he was baptizing. First of all he answers that his baptism is merely an external rite—"I baptize in water"—by contrast with the baptism "in the Holy Ghost and in fire," which the Messias will confer. He adds that, with regard to Christ, the office that he fills is no doubt very lowly, but one which puts him in personal relations with Christ: it is as the precursor that he baptizes. Lastly, he now knows Christ, whom God deigned to manifest to him, while, as for them,[259] they do not yet know Him, although He is living near them, nay, in their very midst.

It is in this last feature that what we might call the new aspect, the point of this, the precursor's second testimony, consists. The Messias is "in the midst of you": what a stirring revelation! The Evangelist closes his account by indicating the locality where the incident took place: "These things were done in Bethania, beyond the Jordan, where John was baptizing." The words "beyond the Jordan," which are used to designate the province of Peraea, are employed to distinguish that Bethania from the other town of the same name in the vicinity of Jerusalem, where Lazarus, Martha, and Mary,

[257] In the Greek, ὁ ἐρχόμενος, in the participial form; one of the names of the Messias among the Jews. Cf. Matt. 11:3, etc. We have quoted John's answer conformably to what seems the most authentic reading of the text. After the words "Whom you know not," in the Vulgate and elsewhere we read: "The same is He that shall come after me, who is preferred before me; the latchet of whose shoe I am not worthy . . ."

[258] Matt. 3:11; Mark 1:7 f.; Luke 3:16.

[259] In the Greek there is a very emphatic ὑμεῖς, "you."

those close friends of our Lord, dwelt.[260] But where was this second Bethania?

Commentators and Palestinologists have offered several hypotheses, none of which is entirely satisfactory. The most recent, as also the most acceptable,[261] is that "Bethania was located about two miles above the present Jordan bridge, at Kirbet Tell-el-Medech on the left bank of the river, north of Wady Nimrin. A little below the bridge there is El-Ghoranyeh, the most frequented ford in the southern portion of the Jordan. At this ford three ancient routes meet, the most important ones of Judea, coming from Bethel, Jerusalem, and Bethlehem. Whereas the east bank of the Jordan, in all its southern portion, preserves no trace of any ancient town located near the river, Tell-el-Medech presents considerable ruins of an ancient site, dominated by the remains of a tower which must have served as a station for Roman soldiers." [262] This place possesses a special interest for us because, if it is authentic, it is perhaps there that Jesus was baptized.[263]

What feelings did the members of the Sanhedrin's deputation experience upon hearing these memorable words? Did

[260] John 11 : 1–18. We have no occasion here to enter into the discussion raised by the variant Βηθαβαρᾷ, which Origen injudiciously championed. He himself acknowledges that in his time the reading Βηθανία was the best vouched for. As, however, during a journey that he made in Palestine about the year 215, he failed to discover any place by the name of Bethania on the left bank of the Jordan, whereas he did find there a village called Bethabara, he adopted and had others adopt this reading, which is certainly erroneous and which the best critics condemn.

[261] We owe it to Father Féderlin, one of the White Fathers of St. Anne of Jerusalem.

[262] *La Palestine, Guide Historique et Pratique,* by professors of Notre Dame de France à Jerusalem, 2d ed., pp. 280 f. Among the other places with which attempts have been made to identify this Bethania, we cite the ruins now called Betane, on the wady Abu Muhaa, about an hour's walk southwest of Es-Salt, on the site of the ancient Botnin (Josue 13:26). See St. Jerome, *Onomasticon,* 103, 14.

[263] See, however, what is said above on the subject of the traditional site of our Lord's baptism. It is true that John the Baptist did not stay continually in the same place.

they ask for further explanations before leaving John the Baptist? The Evangelist's silence would seem to indicate they did not. Moreover, his purpose was simply to set forth the Baptist's testimony. Following his usual custom, he closes the incident without entering into other details and passes on to a still more remarkable episode.

The precursor had a threefold mission to perform: to preach the proximate coming of the Messias, to prepare the Jewish people for this coming, and to point out the Christ in the person of Jesus. The author of the Fourth Gospel shows us the Baptist in the exercise of this last office, the greatest of all, and cites his third testimony,[264] still clearer and more categorical than the two preceding ones.

A number of fervent disciples, mostly young men, had quickly gathered about the new prophet, as formerly disciples had done about Samuel, Elias, and Eliseus.[265] John selected them from the ranks of his best catechumens. To a certain extent imitating the austerity of his life,[266] they prepared themselves under his direction for the worthy reception of the Messias and His graces. Their master taught them a special prayer,[267] and they sanctified themselves at his side.

The day after the official visit of the Great Council's deputation, while John was surrounded by several of these disciples, he saw [268] Jesus, who was then returning from the wilderness after His temptation and who was passing at a little distance. Did Christ come hither to have another interview with His precursor? It does not seem likely. At any rate there is nothing in the sacred text to favor such a conjecture. But Jesus gives John an occasion to render a third testimony to Him, and the son of Zachary does not neglect the opportunity.

[264] John 1 : 29-34.
[265] Cf. 1 Kings 10 : 5-12; 3 Kings 18 : 4; 4 Kings 2 : 15; 6 : 1, etc.
[266] Matt. 9 : 14; Mark 2 : 18; Luke 5 : 33.
[267] Luke 11 : 1.
[268] In the Greek, the use of the present tense, βλέπει, dramatizes the fact.

Under the impulse of strong feeling, pointing to the Savior
—Raphael, in one of his masterpieces, represents the Baptist
in this attitude, glowing with holy joy—he utters these words,
which impressed themselves deeply in his disciples' memory:
"Behold the Lamb of God, behold Him who taketh away the
sin of the world. This is He of whom I said: After me there
cometh a man who is preferred before me; because He was
before me. And I knew Him not, but that He may be made
manifest in Israel, therefore am I come baptizing with water.
And John gave testimony, saying: I saw the Spirit coming
down as a dove from heaven, and He remained upon Him.
And I knew Him not; but He who sent me to baptize with
water, said to me: He upon whom thou shalt see the Spirit
descending and remaining upon Him, He it is that baptizeth
with the Holy Ghost. And I saw, and I gave testimony, that
this is the Son of God." [269]

"The Lamb of God who taketh away the sin of the world!"
This figurative language is gentle yet forceful. The humble
lamb of the fields held a considerable place in Jewish worship,
especially in the "everlasting" sacrifice offered every morning
and evening in the name of the whole people.[270] But the precursor is not here alluding to that sacrifice, repeated daily
since the time of Moses. The Paschal lamb also held a notable
place in the history of Israel, for, when it was immolated for
the first time in the land of Gessen, it had saved the firstborn
of the Hebrews from death.[271] The Old Testament certainly
contains no more touching symbol of the Messias, who became our victim. St. Paul and St. John[272] the Evangelist
quite rightly regard this lamb as a type of Christ.

Nevertheless, as all agree, when John the Baptist applied
this mystical name to Jesus, he had in mind especially one

[269] John 1: 29–34. See also John 10: 40–42.
[270] We have described it above. See Vol. I, pp. 244 ff.
[271] Ex. 12: 3–28.
[272] 1 Cor. 5: 7; John 19: 31, 36.

of the most beautiful and famous of Isaias' Messianic prophecies. In his fifty-third chapter, where he describes in advance the Passion of the "servant of Jehovah," that is, of Christ, more as an evangelist than as a prophet,[273] he compares the suffering Messias to a lamb "led to the slaughter" and opening not its mouth to complain.[274] There is no doubt but that the precursor, under a special inspiration of the Holy Ghost, was applying this prophecy to Jesus. "Looking upon Jesus as the Lamb of God, St. John already saw Him, as it were, covered with His own blood," [275] and thereby bearing, taking away,[276] and expiating the sins [277] of the whole world. It is not surprising, therefore, that the early Christians sang the praises of the Savior Jesus under this title in their canticles,[278] or that St. Peter calls Him "a Lamb unspotted and undefiled," [279] or that the beloved disciple twenty-nine times gives Him this name in his Apocalypse,[280] not to mention other passages in that same book where he depicts Him as immolated for our salvation.

After noting, by this fine metaphor, the greatness of the Messias' work, John the Baptist returns to His Person and dignity. What he previously asserted in general terms about the Messias, he repeats and applies directly to Jesus: "This is He of whom I said: After me there cometh a man who is preferred before me, because He was before me." Then he explains to his hearers the manner in which he learned that the Son of Mary was the Messias. That heavenly manifesta-

[273] St. Jerome, *Epist. ad Paulin.*, 53.

[274] Is. 53 : 7.

[275] Bossuet, *Élévations sur les Mystères*, 24th day, second elevation.

[276] Like the Hebrew *nacah,* the Greek verb αἴρω, which ordinarily means "carry," in this passage means : "to remove," to expiate by His personal sacrifice.

[277] The text uses the singular, "the sin," *i. e.,* all the crimes of mankind, here represented as an unclean and heavy mass.

[278] H. Leclerq, article "Agneau" in the *Dictionnaire d'Archéologie Chrétienne et de Liturgie,* published by J. Cabrol, Vol. I, cols. 877–904.

[279] 1 Pet. 1 : 19.

[280] Apoc. 5 : 6–14; 13 : 8; 15 : 3 f., etc.

tion, which the Synoptics relate with great detail, adds new strength to John's testimony. There is a splendid accent of faith, as also of triumph, in the final attestation: "I saw and I gave testimony, that this is the Son of God." [281] The precursor might have added that he had also heard the voice of God the Father, proclaiming Jesus His well-beloved Son; at least, the echo of that proclamation is to be heard in the profession of faith which we have just quoted.

A question is sometimes raised as to the sense in which John the Baptist here uses the title "Son of God." It is certain that he attributes to it its strictest and most literal meaning. We must bear in mind that this testimony of the Baptist is recorded by the author of the Fourth Gospel, who in his sublime prologue only a few verses before, relating the episode on the banks of the Jordan, lays stress on the divinity of our Lord Jesus Christ and on His glory, which is that "of the only begotten of the Father, full of grace and truth." The words "Son of God" could not have a different meaning less than a page later. Furthermore, the detail, "who is preferred before me because He was before me," here as in that prologue,[282] can mean only the eternal pre-existence of the Messias and consequently His divinity manifested to the precursor by a special revelation. From that we must judge the full extent and force of his later testimony.

IV. Our Lord Gathers a Few Disciples. He Performs His First Miracle [283]

These accounts have a delicious freshness about them. As we read them, we feel that the narrator was an eyewitness of

---

[281] The variant "the Elect of God," which we find in a few manuscripts and elsewhere, is insufficiently warranted.

[282] John I : 15, 30.

[283] John I : 35—2 : 11.

them.[284] Although he had reached extreme old age when he put these touching scenes in writing, yet their smallest details had remained present in his mind and heart. He sets them forth with feelings of love and gratitude, the warmth of which we sense through his lines. His charming narrative enables us to be present at the very first beginnings of the Church of Christ.

On the day following that on which he had spoken the significant words, "Behold the Lamb of God," the Baptist was standing with two of his disciples when, silently and majestically, Jesus again passed a short distance away. John, turning a penetrating look upon Him,[285] said, as he had the day before, but this time without any further comment: "Behold the Lamb of God!" This simple exclamation at once produced a remarkable effect. The two disciples understood that their master, by so emphatically drawing their attention to the divine Lamb, thereby invited them to join Jesus. The practical motto of that deeply humble and disinterested soul was now more than ever: "He [the Messias] must increase, but I must decrease." [286]

Drawn by an irresistible attraction, the two young men thereupon started to follow Jesus at a little distance, without venturing to overtake Him. The Savior, hearing steps behind Him, turned round, looked closely [287] at those following Him, and, with a gentleness which put them at their ease, asked them: "What seek you?" They replied: "Master"—the Evangelist uses this title here, although they addressed Him in their own tongue: "Rabbi"—"where dwellest Thou?" Thus did they indirectly express the earnest desire which they felt

[284] The verbs "see, behold, look upon" appear frequently in the first part, John 1 : 35–51.

[285] Ἐμβλέψας, says the Greek text; Vulg., *respiciens*.

[286] John 3 : 30.

[287] Literally: "having looked upon" (θεασάμενος).

of conversing with Him. "Come and you will see," [288] He simply said, not wishing to exercise any pressure on them. If they join Him, it must be spontaneously, freely. Then they accompanied Him to the place, doubtless not very distant, where He had fixed His temporary abode before returning to Galilee. The Evangelist remarks that "it was about the tenth hour" when they joined our Lord; that would be about four o'clock in the afternoon, according to our method of reckoning.[289] The beloved disciple has put a whole world of memories into this little detail. Was not that the most decisive hour of his whole life? "They came and saw," he continues, echoing the words of the Savior's kind invitation; and they remained with Him throughout the rest of the day. During this long visit, there began for those two privileged souls the magnificent "vision" of which St. John speaks in his prologue: "We saw His glory . . ." [290] How we would like to know in detail the words that were then exchanged! We can at least surmise their substance, since we know their result: Jesus proved to them that He was the Messias.

One of these disciples of the precursor was Andrew, the future Apostle. The name of the other is not given in the account. There is no doubt, however, but that he is identical with the Evangelist himself, whose custom it is to hide modestly behind a veil of anonymity. Many early authors acknowledged this identity,[291] which is almost universally recognized as a

---

[288] We adopt the reading ὄψεσθε, in the future tense, in place of ἴδετε, "see."

[289] According to the system then in use among the Jews, each day was composed of twelve hours, which were reckoned from six o'clock in the morning. Various commentators suppose, but, as it seems to us, without sufficient reason, that the Evangelist here abandons this system and conforms to that of the Greeks and Romans, which was identical with ours and according to which the hour mentioned in the text would be ten o'clock in the morning.

[290] John 1 : 14.

[291] V. g., St. Epiphanius, *Haer.*, LI, 14, 15, and Theodoret in his commentary, *hoc loco.*

legitimate inference. Andrew and John had each a brother, to whom they wished, on their return, to impart the good news. Andrew, more fortunate in his quest, was the first [292] to find his brother, Simon. As soon as he saw him, he called out, with a joy in which we can feel the faith and love of a worthy son of Abraham: "We have found the Messias!" But that Andrew's joy might be complete, it was necessary for his brother also to become a disciple of Christ. Andrew was, therefore, eager to lead him to Jesus. The Savior, turning upon the newcomer one of those penetrating looks that read the very depth of men's souls,[293] said to him: "Thou art Simon, son of John; [294] thou shalt be called Peter." In the Aramaic dialect, spoken by Jesus, the name Peter is called Kepha, which we find repeated in several New Testament passages [295] under the Greek form "Kephas." In promising this new name to Simon, our Lord made a play on words, after the manner of the Orient, to signify that Andrew's brother would one day become the unshakable foundation on which the Messias' Church would be built. But we should note that Christ at this time does not go beyond a promise: "Thou shalt be called Cephas." This surname becomes Simon's permanently only on the day when, enlightened by a special revelation, he publicly confesses that Jesus is both the Christ and the Son of the living God. [296] Everything leads us to suppose that John, the other disciple of the precursor, promptly found his brother James and brought him to Jesus.

The next day (the fourth from that on which the San-

---

[292] This fact is in consequence of the reading πρῶτος, "first," which has the best authority. Moreover, the sense remains almost the same with the variant πρῶτον, "at first" (Vulg., primum).

[293] The Greek has: ἐμβλέψας.

[294] The best reading of the original text is 'Ιωάννου or 'Ιωάνου, and not 'Ιωνᾶ. It is one and the same name under these three forms.

[295] Cf. I Cor. 1: 12; 3: 22; 15: 5; Gal. 2: 9, 14. Kepha is the equivalent of the Hebrew keph, "stone, rock."

[296] Matt. 16: 16.

hedrin's delegates came to the Baptist) Jesus, accompanied by his four new disciples, started out on His return to Galilee. Almost immediately He met Philip, who, like Peter and Andrew, was a native of Bethsaida, a village located on the western shore of Lake Genesareth.[297] To him He said: "Follow Me." Probably Philip also was one of John the Baptist's disciples, and from his two fellow-townsmen he must have heard about their meeting with the Savior. He, too, obeys the call without hesitation. In the case of the other four young men, it was they who presented themselves to Jesus; this time it is from our Lord that the first advances come.

Shortly afterwards Philip, upon meeting his friend Nathanael, who was from Cana of Galilee,[298] said to him: "We have found Him of whom Moses in the Law, and the prophets did write, Jesus the Son of Joseph of Nazareth." This is something more than Andrew's simple cry: "We have found the Messias"; it is almost a short demonstration of Jesus' Messianic character as evidenced by the Old Testament prophecies.[299] The friend of Andrew and Simon was indeed greatly in error when he spoke of Jesus as Joseph's son. But he could not help at that time sharing the popular view on this point. "Can any thing of good come from Nazareth?" is the disdainful reply of Nathanael, who evidently had not a very high regard for that humble village, hid, as it was, in the mountains and at that time lacking in any glory. Did he have some special reason for thus depreciating it? We do not know. But in our Lord's public life there are two episodes [300] which show us its inhabitants in a light not at all favorable. "Come and see," answered Philip, unwittingly making use of an expression like that with which Jesus encouraged Andrew and the

[297] Further on we shall try to determine the exact site.

[298] John 21 : 2.

[299] On Moses' prophecy, see Vol. I, p. 215. But it is possible that Philip had in mind all the Messianic prophecies of the Pentateuch.

[300] Matt. 13 : 58; Mark 6 : 5; Luke 4 : 20.

beloved disciple to follow Him. Philip's personal experience had shown him that to spend a few moments with Mary's Son was sufficient to be convinced of His divine mission.

When the Savior saw the two friends coming toward Him, He said aloud, referring to Nathanael: "Behold an Israelite indeed, in whom there is no guile." These words mean: Behold an Israelite who is such not by birth and in name only, like so many others, but who possesses all the qualities of a worthy member of the theocratic nation. "Whence knowest Thou me?" Nathanael asked in great surprise. Jesus, again showing His supernatural knowledge of all things, replied: "Before that Philip called thee, when thou wast under the fig tree, I saw thee." Commentators are agreed that the Savior in speaking thus implied something beyond the outward facts indicated by the words "when thou wast under the fig tree." He recalled to Nathanael's mind, in terms hidden from the others, but clear to him, a particular state of soul in which Nathanael then was and which he supposed that no one else was aware of. This unexpected revelation at once produced the conviction on which Philip counted. Nathanael's prejudice against Nazareth vanished in the face of the evidence, and he immediately made a full confession of faith: "Rabbi, Thou art the Son of God; Thou art the King of Israel."

Although weighty authors, both ancient [301] and modern, are of opinion that in this passage the title "Son of God" has simply the meaning of Messias, that view is rejected not only by St. Augustine and many Catholic interpreters, but also by several Protestant theologians.[302] In fact, Nathanael might well have had a presentiment of Christ's divinity, since he now looked upon Him as the "King of Israel," that is, as the Redeemer, whose superhuman character is presupposed by sev-

[301] Such as St. John Chrysostom and Theophylactus.
[302] See Godet, *Commentaire sur l'Évangile de S. Jean*, 2d ed., II, 187 f.; Zahn, *Das Evangelium des Johannes ausgelegt*, p. 139.

eral Old Testament texts.[303] Furthermore, the testimony of John the Baptist, whose disciple Nathanael also seems to have been, and the miraculous knowledge about him which Jesus just manifested, were proofs of great weight with him.

The Divine Master at once rewarded Nathanael's act of faith by a generous promise, saying: "Because I said unto thee: I saw thee under the fig tree, thou believest; greater things than these shalt thou see." These other prodigies, superior to the marvel which had just aroused Nathanael's admiration, prodigies that he would one day have the happiness of witnessing as an Apostle—for we shall soon find him in the Apostolic College under the name of Bartholomew—the Savior briefly describes in figurative language addressed to all the little band of disciples gathered about Him: "Amen, amen I say to you, you shall see the heaven opened, and the angels of God ascending and descending upon the Son of Man."

The words, *"Amen, amen dico,"* which appear in this double form only in the Fourth Gospel,[304] are a sort of oath, by which Jesus guarantees the certainty of His promise. As to the angels whose coming and going will form a continuous procession between heaven and earth, with Jesus as its center, they plainly recall Jacob's dream and its mysterious ladder along which the heavenly spirits kept ascending and descending.[305] In that instance their presence signified that the God of the patriarchs of Israel placed Isaac's son under the special protection of angels during his dangerous journey and his residence in distant Mesopotamia. In the passage we are considering, they represent the perpetual succession of divine favors of which Jesus was to be the object, the ceaseless display of miraculous powers which would proceed from His

[303] See Vol. I, pp. 209 ff.

[304] About twenty-five times, and always on the lips of Christ. This formula also occurs very often in the Synoptic Gospels, but with a single *Amen*. See the Concordances.

[305] Gen. 28: 12.

hands, the continual exchange of intimate communications which henceforth would take place, thanks to Him, between God and men.

Further on we shall have to explain the somewhat obscure title of "Son of Man," which Christ has just called Himself for the first time and which He will take very often in the four Gospels.[306] In itself it is an extraordinary name; it is especially so here, after John the Baptist and Nathanael have successively called Jesus "Son of God" and "King of Israel." For it is, in a way, a title of humility. It shows that, although our Lord is closely united to God by a divine sonship, and to the theocratic nation as being King of Israel, as Son of Man He belongs to the human race, the whole of which He came to save.

Let us return to the sacred narrative. After evincing Christ's supernatural knowledge, it now manifests His almighty power. The third day following that on which He set out after the calling of Philip and Nathanael, a marriage feast was celebrated at Cana of Galilee. This was a small town located, most probably,[307] on the site of the present village of Kefr Kenna, about four miles northwest of Nazareth on the road leading, then as now, from Nazareth to Tiberias and Capharnaum.[308] It was Nathanael's home town.[309] Anyone coming from Nazareth, before entering the village of Cana will see to his right an abundant spring, which must have supplied the water that was miraculously changed into wine. According to an early tradition, the house of the newly mar-

---

[306] According to a calculation which seems exact, about eighty times (thirty times in the First Gospel, thirteen in the Second, twenty-five in the Third, twelve in the Fourth). See Geden, *A Concordance to the Greek Testament*, 2d ed., pp. 966–968.

[307] Guérin, *Déscription de la Palestine: La Galilée*, I, 168–182.

[308] According to another, comparatively recent opinion, Cana of Galilee is identical with *Kana el Djelil*, or *Khirbet Kana*, eight miles north of Nazareth. See Robinson, *Palästina und die angrenzenden Länder*, III, 443–449.

[309] John 21 : 2.

ried couple stood on the spot now occupied by the Franciscan church. The country round about is fertile and fairly well cultivated. Thick hedges of prickly cactus surround and protect the fields. There are a few vineyards, producing an excellent reddish wine. The three days mentioned above were amply sufficient for Jesus and His disciples to cover the distance of about 56 miles from Bethania on the Jordan to Cana.

The author of the Fourth Gospel, as is his custom, passes over the secondary details and comes straight to the principal fact. After saying that our Lord's mother was present at the wedding feast—a fact which shows that she was related to the young couple or was a friend of theirs—he mentions the arrival of Jesus and His companions at Cana and the invitation which they at once received to take part in the festivities. Early commentators frequently refer to the Savior's gracious condescension in accepting the invitation and thus honoring a wedding banquet with His presence. Did He not put on our humanity in order to sanctify all the events of our life, our joys as well as our sorrows? [310]

An embarrassing incident came near disturbing the feast. The married couple were of modest circumstances,[311] and now there arrive six or seven unexpected guests. Among the Jews, wedding festivities ordinarily lasted several days—sometimes three days, sometimes as many as seven or even more [312]—and nothing in the account indicates that Jesus and His companions reached Cana in time for the first meal. Suddenly it was noticed that the supply of wine was exhausted.[313] Mary, in

---

[310] Cf. St. Epiphanius, *Haer.*, 57; St. Augustine, *Tractat. in Joan*, 19. In His discourses and especially in His parables, our Lord frequently alludes to marriage solemnities.

[311] The presence of several servants in the house was evidently for this special occasion.

[312] Gen. 29:27; Judges 14:10–18; Tobias 8:20 (according to the Septuagint). Cf. Selden, *Uxor Hebraica*, II, 11.

[313] The Greek text says explicitly: ὑστερήσαντος οἴνου. The Latin translation, *deficiente vino*, has the same meaning.

the kindness of her heart, thought of the promptest means to save the young couple from humiliation. Her Son was there; thanks to His intervention, all embarrassment could be immediately dispelled. She therefore said to Him in a low voice: "They have no wine." It would be a great mistake to see in these few words merely the simple communication of a fact. They certainly contain an urgent, even though indirect request to come to the aid of the young couple by some supernatural means. This discreet appeal reminds us of the analogous request of Lazarus' sisters, who sent word to Jesus, saying: "Lord, behold, he whom Thou lovest is sick." [314] In each case, a miracle was hoped for and expected. It is true, as the Evangelist tells us, that Jesus had not yet performed any miracles. But that reason would not stop Mary, who knew her Son's goodness of heart and infinite power. Seeing Him accompanied by disciples, she understood that He was about to begin His ministry as Messias and emerge from the voluntary obscurity in which He had lived until then.

Our Lord replied: "Woman, what is that to Me and to thee? My hour is not yet come." At first sight these words surprise us, for they seem cold, almost harsh, as if Jesus were rebuking His mother. Many Protestant commentators, even among the weightiest, claim to find therein a proof that, so far as it concerned the Kingdom of the Messias, Mary's suggestion was full of the false idea which Jesus so often had to repudiate.[315] The explanations by Catholic commentators have not always been happy, and those who criticize our filial devotion to the Blessed Virgin take advantage of the severe judg-

---

[314] John 11 : 3.

[315] Laidlaw, *The Miracles of Our Lord,* p. 41. Cf. Zahn, *Das Evangelium des Johannes,* pp. 150 f.; Godet, *Commentaire sur l'Évangile de S. Jean,* II, 205. This last speaks of "an encroachment by Mary in the domain exclusively reserved to Jesus," of an "indirect intervention in His office of Messias." Rationalist critics go still further and say that Jesus, "in the consciousness of His [wounded] dignity, replied to His mother as to an inferior, from the height of His greatness." H. J. Holtzmann, *Theologie des N. T.,* 2d ed., II, 470.

ment of several Fathers on Mary's conduct in this instance. Thus, St. John Chrysostom attributes her request to a sentiment of vainglory.[316]

Let us study the words of Christ to ascertain their true meaning. First of all, we may say that the apostrophe "Woman,"—as is generally recognized—when found in ancient languages, contains nothing but what is quite respectful. It was in common use among the Jews [317] as well as among the Greeks.[318] That Jesus did not consider it any way offensive to His mother is evident from the fact that He used it again on the cross, when He entrusted her to the care of St. John.[319]

The expression, "What is that to Me and to thee?" [320] which we find several times in the Bible, with slight variations,[321] and which is not unknown to the Greek and Latin classics, ordinarily implies a difference of opinion or lack of agreement on a given point, a veiled refusal: but its special significance depends largely on circumstances of the moment. Now, in the present case, the circumstances remove all harshness from it. A modern Rationalist suggests the following translation: "Allow Me to do it, mother"; [322] and a certain Anglican theologian considers that the expression "is perfectly consistent

316 *Hom. in Joan.*, XXI, 2. St. Thomas, *Summa Theol.*, 3a, qu. 27, a. 4, says on this subject: "*In verbis illis Chrysostomus excessit.*" See also St. Irenaeus, *Adv. Haer.*, III, 13. In Knabenbauer, *Comment. in Evang. sec. Joan.*, I, 118–122, and Bartmann, *Christus ein Gegner des Marienkultus?*, may be found the refutation of a certain number of false and artificial interpretations of Christ's reply to His mother.

317 *Matt.* 15:28, "O woman, great is thy faith"; Luke 13:12, "Woman, thou art delivered from thy infirmity"; John 4:21, etc.

318 They addressed even queens in this manner. Cf. Dio Cassius, *Hist.*, LI, 12, 5; Æschylus, *Agam.*, 1607, etc.

319 John 19:26. In Spain, the word *mujer*, "woman," is often used as an affectionate form of address.

320 In the Greek: τί ἐμοὶ καὶ σοί; κοινόν or πρᾶγμα being understood. In the Vulgate: "*Quid mihi et tibi est?*" rei or negotii being understood.

321 Josue 22:24; Judges 11:12; 2 Kings 16:10; 19:22; 3 Kings 17:18; 4 Kings 3:13; 2 Par. 35:21; Matt. 8:29; 27:19; Mark 1:24; Luke 8:28, etc.

322 E. Reuss, *La Théologie Johannique*, pp. 132 f.

with the most delicate courtesy." [323] The expression, "My hour is not yet come," further softens the words that precede and partly gives us the key to them. In the Fourth Gospel there is frequently [324] mention of Jesus' "hour," which stands especially for the time of His Passion. [325] In our present passage, however, this substantive is taken in another sense and indicates a precise moment, determined in advance by the divine plan. [326] As the question here is that of His first miracle, it was quite right that Jesus should wait to perform it until His Father's hour. The Savior means, then, that for the exercise of His Messianic office He is not dependent on His mother, however great His desire to gratify her, but solely upon God, whose will alone must serve as His rule. These words of our Lord are, therefore, analogous to those which He spoke while yet a boy, in the Temple at Jerusalem. [327] Even more than then, He must now freely consecrate Himself to His heavenly Father's business without let or hindrance from any influence even of those closest to Him. And so, without meaning to find the slightest fault with His mother, Jesus calls to her mind His utter independence whenever He must speak or act as the Messias.

Mary understood and did not insist; but, at the same time, so well did she comprehend that Her son's refusal was not absolute—did not the words "not yet" signify this?—and so little did she permit her confidence to be disturbed, that she told the servants: "Whatsoever He shall say to you, do ye."

In the vestibule or courtyard there were six enormous stone amphorae, each holding two or three "measures." [328] If, as is probable, the Evangelist had in mind the Attic "measure,"

[323] Farrar, *The Life of Christ*, 23d ed., I, 165.

[324] More than thirty times.

[325] Cf. John 7:30; 8:20; 12:23, 27; 13:1; 17:1.

[326] See John 7:6, a passage having a general resemblance to this one.

[327] Luke 2:49.

[328] A Greek word meaning "measure," which at that period designated the largest liquid measure.

which was equal to about ten gallons, each amphora would have contained 20 or 30 gallons, the six together holding 120 or 180 gallons. The Evangelist explains their presence by remarking that they were used for the ablutions and ceremonial purifications of the Jews. In fact, as we shall see later in St. Mark, "the Pharisees and all the Jews eat not without often washing their hands, holding the tradition of the ancients; and when they come from the market, unless they be washed, they eat not; and many other things there are that have been delivered to them to observe, the washings of cups and of pots and of brazen vessels and of beds." [329] Hence there was need for a plentiful supply of water in a Jewish household, the more so when a big dinner was being given.

Of a sudden, Jesus said to the waiters: "Fill the water-pots with water." His hour was now come; an inner voice had apprised Him of it, and He obeyed on the instant. Yet only a very short time had elapsed between His reply to His mother and this order to the waiters. But, to quote a very judicious remark, "a change in moral and spiritual conditions is not measured by length of time." Such majesty was there in our Savior's whole bearing that the waiters obeyed Him without the least hesitation, however extraordinary His direction may have seemed to them. And Mary's advice to them had not failed to produce its effect. The ablutions of the dinner guests had emptied the amphorae, at least for the most part. These jars were now filled "up to the brim": a detail added to note the extent of the miracle. A few moments later, Jesus said: "Draw out now and carry to the chief steward of the feast." When that one of the guests or of the waiters who filled the office of chief steward tasted the drink thus brought to him, the source of which he was unaware of, he declared that it was excellent wine. As he quite well knew that only one kind of wine had been placed at his disposal and that the supply

[329] Mark 7: 3 f.

was exhausted, he supposed the bridegroom had planned a pleasant surprise for his guests by unexpectedly serving this wine of better quality. Therefore the chief steward went up to him and in a familiar manner said: "Every man at first setteth forth good wine, and when men have well drunk,[330] then that which is worse. But thou hast kept the good wine until now." Thus, without realizing it, he did in his own way testify to the reality of the miracle, the rapid change of substance solely by the Miracle-worker's will. Some Rationalist interpreters are scandalized at what they term "a miracle of luxury"; we, on the contrary, admire the princely munificence of Christ's wedding gift.

We have already spoken of the Evangelist's habitual brevity. He is completely silent about the wonderment of the witnesses of this miracle, the thanks of the young couple, the evident investigation by the chief steward. He merely notes that it was the "beginning of miracles," that is, of the Savior's miracles, and mentions the happy result brought about by this striking prodigy: "His disciples believed in Him." In thus manifesting His creative power, Jesus attested the truth of His mission and the greatness of His nature, and furnished His disciples, whose faith was already intense, with an additional reason for believing in Him and for adhering more closely to Him.

[330] Literally: "when one has become drunk." But evidently it is unnecessary to take the expression literally in the present case.

CHAPTER III

Christ's Preliminary Ministry at Jerusalem, in Judea, and in Samaria [331]

I<small>T</small> was fitting that the first public manifestation of the Messias should take place at Jerusalem, the capital of the theocratic state, the center of Israel's religious and moral life, and that it should occur in the Temple, which was, so to speak, the royal palace of the true God. There it is that Jesus first reveals Himself, by a vigorous act of authority, by miracles, and by preaching. But his relative lack of success only too well forecasts the repeated thwarting that awaited Him at Jerusalem, and already we may see the shadow of the cross rising in the distance. After a brief stay in the Jewish metropolis, the Savior retires into Judea for several months, accompanied by His first disciples: this is a calm but hidden period, to which the Gospel accounts devote only a few lines. Upon leaving Judea and returning to Galilee to begin His real ministry, Jesus passes through Samaria, stopping there two days and winning a humble group to His cause: the modest prelude of great things.

I. Christ Celebrates the First Pasch of His Public Life At Jerusalem [332]

Immediately after the miracle at Cana, Jesus, in company with His mother, His "brethren," [333] and His first disciples,

---

[331] John 2: 13–4: 42.
[332] John 2: 13–3: 21.
[333] His cousins (Vol. I, p. 419).

betook Himself to Capharnaum, at that time an important city, located on the northwestern shore of Lake Tiberias, probably at the ruin-covered spot now called Tell Hum.[334] For some distance the road follows the high, verdant plateau on which the village of Cana stood. Before long, mountains rise up on the left. Farther on, facing the traveler is the Kurun Hattin—the "Horns of Hattin"—a very curious formation, like a spur. Then abruptly the view opens eastward, to the right, and there before one's eyes, like a gleaming mirror, is the beautiful lake which holds so great a place in our Lord's public life. The windings of the road as it descends in rapid turns bring into view now one, now another part of the lake. The mountains that hem in its eastern shore seem very close, although in reality they are five or six miles distant. The western shore, which is by far the most interesting, gradually comes into view. Here, from south to north, are Tiberias and its hot springs, the plain of Genesareth, and the sites of Magdala, Bethsaida, Capharnaum, and Corozain. We shall later give a fuller description of this region, then so singularly blessed, which was to become a second homeland for our Lord.

It took about seven or eight hours to walk from Cana to Capharnaum. Jesus does not seem to have stayed in the latter town at this time. It was not till a little later that He made it His permanent residence.[335] On this occasion He probably came there merely to join a caravan of pilgrims being formed to go for the Pasch to Jerusalem, where He purposed beginning His public ministry.

In previous years, when He visited the Temple, Jesus had been grieved at the sight of a whole series of deplorable abuses which had been introduced into the vast Court of the Gentiles

[334] Further on we will discuss the question of the site of Capharnaum. Tell Hum is about an hour's walk west of the point where the Jordan empties into the lake.

[335] Cf. Matt. 4: 13–17.

and the porches that surrounded it. But he did not undertake to remedy those abuses so long as His hidden life lasted and so long as He was outwardly leading the life of an ordinary Jew. Now that His Messianic career has opened, He will vindicate His Father's honor, so grievously outraged in the holiest place on earth through the guilty tolerance and even graver connivance of a priesthood without respect for God's house.

The numberless sacrifices that were offered during the religious festivals, especially during the Pasch and its octave,[336] required thousands of victims, not to speak of the flour, wine, oil, and salt which constituted the materials of the unbloody sacrifices. It was right and proper that some arrangement should be provided to facilitate their acquisition by pilgrims from distant places.[337] But what at first was a service of charity and religion, had degenerated into a regular trade. Merchants were allowed to install themselves even inside the sacred precincts, with their oxen, calves, sheep, lambs, goats, their cages of pigeons and doves, and other objects for use in the public worship, all of which they had for sale. The Court of the Gentiles thus became a veritable market place.[338] If we imagine the noise and endless discussions that took place between buyers and sellers, after the manner of the East, the cries of the animals, and all this curious transaction of business and these crowds so near the sanctuary, we will have some idea of that shocking profanation. But priests and Levites, at least some of them, derived so great a profit from this scandalous abuse that they were interested in maintaining it to the full.

In the same court, seated at their little tables, on which

[336] The lambs alone, the meat of which formed the principal element of the Passover feast, reached an enormous figure.

[337] Acts 2 : 7–11.

[338] For curious and painful details according to the Talmud, see Edersheim, *The Life of Jesus,* I, 368–372.

might be seen wooden bowls containing gold, silver, and copper coins of all sizes and values, were the money changers or bankers. They charged a commission of 5 or even 10 per cent for giving Jewish coins in exchange for Greek, Roman, or other monies which were not acceptable for the Temple treasury because of their pagan images and emblems. Many pilgrims, especially those coming from a great distance, took advantage of their journey to Jerusalem to pay the tax of a didrachma or half-shekel [339] which every Israelite of twenty years or more was bound to contribute annually for the public worship. That, too, gave rise to the most baneful haggling and to pitiless, usurious profits.

Jesus, though retaining complete self-control, was moved to indignation. He picked up a few cords which had been used for tying the animals, and from them made a scourge, with which, as He struck to right and left, He drove both beasts and merchants from the sacred precincts. Then He overturned the tables of the money changers, whose coins rolled in every direction. To those who sold doves, He said, as He pointed to their cages: "Take these things hence, and make not the house of My Father a house of traffic." These last words were addressed to all those who were thus profaning the Temple. By these words our Lord explained and justified the movement of holy anger with which He had acted. Has not a son the right and duty of avenging the honor of the paternal roof? Among the large crowd that witnessed this scene, no one offered the slightest resistance. That sudden and majestic appearance of wrathful holiness struck all present with terror. And further, the voice of their own conscience cried out that the profaners were in the wrong. This was one of those miracles of a moral order of which we shall have to speak later on.[340]

[339] Cf. Matt. 17: 23.
[340] See Fillion, *Les Miracles de N.-S. Jésus-Christ*, II, 311–334.

Their Master's energetic action recalled to the minds of the disciples accompanying Him a text of the Psalms, which they at once applied to it: "The zeal of Thy house hath eaten me up." [341] This ardent zeal, burning in Him like a sacred fire, was to cost Him His life, for it occasioned between Him and the Jewish religious authorities a conflict which gradually stirred up in them a violent hatred that would be satisfied by nothing short of His death. The religious chiefs—most likely some priests of the upper classes or perhaps the high Levitical officers charged with policing the Temple [342]—were unable to hide the acute displeasure they felt upon learning that Jesus had taken the liberty of exercising the rôle of reformer in their special domain, and of thus publicly condemning their culpable inaction or rather direct connivance. Being promptly informed or else attracted by the tumult which the scene of expulsion provoked, they sharply asked our Lord: "What sign dost Thou show us, seeing Thou dost these things?" They dared not criticize the act itself, so praiseworthy and well justified was it. But they hoped to place Jesus in an embarrassing position by calling upon Him to perform an immediate miracle, by way of credentials. Since He had received no authorization from them, He must needs, by some striking prodigy, show that He had a commission from God, the true Master of the Temple.

With calm dignity the Savior replied: "Destroy this temple, and in three days I will raise it up." Since it was a question of the sanctuary, it was from the sanctuary itself that He took the idea of the "sign" which they demanded of Him. But He intentionally made His words obscure and enigmatical. And so the officers were unable to grasp its genuine meaning. Interpreting it literally, as

---

[341] Ps. 68:10. Several other passages of this psalm are applied to our Lord in the New Testament. Cf. John 19:28; Acts 1:20; Rom. 11:9; 15:3.

[342] Acts 4:1; 5:24, 26; Josephus, *Bell. Jud.*, II, xvii, 2; VI, v, 3.

though Jesus had in mind the material edifice in which they stood, they answered in a tone of irony: "Six and forty years was this Temple in building; and wilt Thou raise it up in three days?" It would not have been possible to put in more conspicuous relief the extraordinary disproportion between the long years which thousands of workmen had taken to build the Temple, and the three days which Jesus said would suffice for rebuilding it if it were razed to the ground. From Josephus [343] we know that this vast structure, begun in the eighteenth year of Herod, consequently a considerable time before the Savior's birth, was even then far from being completed. It was not finished until A. D. 63 or 64, under the government of Agrippa II, shortly before its destruction by the Romans.[344] But, as the Evangelist adds, our Lord was referring to "the temple of His body." His sacred body was indeed the living sanctuary of the Divinity. Death destroyed it on Calvary; but on the third day it was raised up—"awakened," according to the literal meaning of the Greek text [345]—by the Resurrection.

This is the first example of the pedagogical method used by our Lord when He had before Him ill-disposed hearers, namely, to present the truth under a veil more or less hiding it. Furthermore, on another occasion He again refers His enemies to the "sign" of His Resurrection, to "the sign of Jonas the prophet," as He Himself calls it.[346] Is it not the most irrefutable proof of His Messianic character and divinity? And is it not notable that even at the first Pasch of His public life He prophesies what will be accomplished at the last one?

[343] *Ant.*, XV, xi, 1.

[344] A. D. 70. Josephus, *Ant.*, XX, ix, 7.

[345] The same verb ἐγείρω appears here and there in the New Testament writings to signify the resurrection of the dead. Cf. John 12: 1; Acts 3: 15; 4: 10; 13: 30; Rom. 4: 24. On the other hand, classical authors also use it with the meaning "to construct" a building.

[346] Cf. Matt. 12: 39 f.; 16: 1–4.

The religious officials were not the only ones to misunderstand the meaning of Christ's reply; the disciples themselves did not comprehend it, as the author of the Fourth Gospel candidly avows. It took them some years to believe that their Master would die a victim of His enemies. How then could they have had an idea of His Resurrection? But in the light of later events, especially when their risen Lord appeared to them, they recalled this saying, which had been impressed on their mind, and they rejoiced in its perfect fulfilment. As the Evangelist says, "they believed the Scripture," which had long before prophesied the Messias' Resurrection.[347] Others, too, remembered this same reply, when they introduced it in a distorted form before the tribunal of the Sanhedrin, as evidence that Jesus was guilty of blasphemy and should be condemned to death.[348]

We have one more word to say with regard to the expulsion of the sellers from the Temple. We read in the Synoptic Gospels [349] the account of a deed in the Savior's last days, that bears a great likeness to this one, which, according to St. John, occurred at the very outset of His public life. Might it not be one and the same incident, which the Evangelists, for reasons of convenience, assigned to different times? Or must the two episodes be regarded as historically distinct? In our own time, as in early days, interpreters have been divided between these two views. Nevertheless the great majority of Catholic commentators have always been in favor of the second opinion.[350] They base their conclusion on the following reasons, which seem to us convincing: "(1) It is difficult to suppose that if in reality there was only one event, the Evange-

[347] Cf. Ps. 15: 10; Is. 53: 10–12; Luke 24: 26 f., 44–46.
[348] Matt. 26: 60 f.; Mark 14: 58; 15: 29. Cf. Acts 6: 11–14.
[349] Matt. 21: 12 f.; Mark 11: 15–17; Luke 19: 45 f.
[350] This is likewise adopted by several Protestant theologians. See, for example, Godet, *Commentaire sur l'Évangile de S. Jean,* 2d ed., II, 244 f.; A. Plummer, *A Commentary on the Gospel according to St. Matthew,* p. 287; Wohlenberg, *Das Evangelium des Markus erklärt,* p. 300.

lists would have assigned such different and even contradictory dates for it. (2) In spite of a general resemblance and of certain points in common, each of the accounts has its own individual features and presents important small differences,[351] especially in the matter of the words spoken by Christ and the immediate consequences of that vigorous intervention. (3) The repetition of such an act contains nothing impossible, whether as regards the Jews, who, once the first emotion had subsided, would not be slow in resuming their deplorable practices under the tolerant eyes of the priestly caste, or as regards Christ Himself, who wished to mark the beginning and the end of His ministry by a manifestation of His religious zeal." [352] The incident fits in well at each of the points where it is narrated; and those who favor the identity are puzzled and divided as to the period of its actual occurrence.

With the account of the expulsion of the sellers the Evangelist connects a characteristic little picture, drawn with master hand, a picture that sums up the very short stay [353] which Jesus then made in Jerusalem. Although He refused the religious leaders the miraculous sign which they so arrogantly demanded, the Savior did perform numerous miracles, none of which, however, is related in detail. Of those persons who witnessed them, many "believed in His name" and acknowledged Him to be the Messias. But the Evangelist tells us that our Lord, whose wisdom was as great as His power, "did not trust Himself unto them,[354] for that He knew all men, and because He needed not that any should give testimony of man: for He knew what was in man." Thanks to His pene-

---

[351] The reader may easily note this by himself or by the aid of commentaries.

[352] Fillion, *L'Évangile selon S. Jean*, pp. 40 f.

[353] It seems not to have extended much beyond the Paschal octave.

[354] In the Greek text, the antithesis is more strongly emphasized by the use of one and the same verb: "They believed"; but "He did not believe."

trating look, often mentioned in the Fourth Gospel,[355] like
that with which God sees to the very depth of hearts and consciences,[356] our Lord knew the innermost dispositions of His
new followers and saw how weak and superficial was their
faith. He was not deceived as to the permanence of their attachment, which would promptly change to coolness, if His
conduct should be opposed to their Messianic preconceptions.
Hence, although He had such surpassing kindliness and although He was from the first hour so affable with those devoted disciples whom He met at the precursor's side, He kept
a reserve towards these unstable friends.

Yet there was one inhabitant of Jerusalem on whom Jesus
produced a deeper impression. He bore the Greek name of
Nicodemus, at that time rather frequent among the Jews.[357]
Although in Palestine, as later in the Greek world,[358] belief
in our Lord made its first conquests chiefly in the popular
classes, Nicodemus was reckoned among the great personages
of Judaism, for he was a member of the Sanhedrin.[359] He also
belonged to the Pharisee party, a fact which added still more
to his authority. In fine, the title of "a master in Israel," as
our Lord calls him, leads us to suppose he was a doctor of the
Law. Being better disposed than most of his colleagues, he
was impressed by our Lord's miracles and, while not yet regarding Him as the Messias, at least he saw in Him a man
of rare holiness, on whom God had bestowed particular blessings. Prompted by a desire to converse with Him, he visited
Jesus, but fearing by this step to compromise himself with
his colleagues, who had already taken a dislike to Jesus,

---

[355] John 1:49 f.; 4:19, 29; 6:62, 65; 11:4, 15; 13:11; 16:19; 21:17.
[356] Cf. 3 Kings 8:39; 1 Par. 28:9; Ecclu. 42:18–20; Jer. 17:9 f., etc.
[357] The Talmud mentions it in the slightly modified form of *Nakdimon*.
[358] 1 Cor. 1:26 f.
[359] It is thus we should here render the expression "a ruler of the Jews." Cf.
John 7:50.

through a feeling of quite human fear and prudence he chose
the night-time for meeting Him at the house where He was
residing during the feast.[360] Jesus, knowing what a fervent
disciple Nicodemus would one day become and by what acts
of courage that honest and upright soul would redeem his
present weakness,[361] received him with great kindness.

Inasmuch as we have here the first connected discourse
of the Divine Master in the Fourth Gospel, it will not be amiss
to make a few preliminary remarks upon the interview which
Christ deigned to grant this nocturnal caller. In spite of its
depth and its wealth of detail, it is only a very brief summary; in its recorded form, the conversation would have
lasted hardly a few minutes. As in all similar instances, the
Evangelist sets down the Savior's words only in what is essential and characteristic; but they lose nothing of their outward coloring.[362]

The general topic of the conversation is the necessity of a
rebirth, of a spiritual regeneration, in order to belong to the
Kingdom of God. From this great thought, Jesus passes to
other indispensable points of Christian faith and, lifting the
veil that hides the future, He pictures the Messias under the
figure of a victim generously offering Himself in sacrifice
for the salvation of the world. The whole scene is one of simplicity, dignity, and perfect calm. According to His custom,
Christ strives, but at first without great success, to raise the
mind of the one with whom He is conversing to a higher
plane. What an honor He confers on Nicodemus, revealing
such astonishing wonders to him and opening up such vistas
of truth!

[360] Perhaps in that which the beloved disciple seems to have owned at Jerusalem,
according to John 19:27.

[361] John 7:50-52; 19:39-42.

[362] Some have wondered how St. John knew the details of this interview. That
question is easily answered: perhaps from Jesus Himself, or later from Nicodemus; but it seems more natural to suppose that, along with the other disciples,
he was present at the scene which he describes so well.

Let us picture to ourselves the two speakers seated beside each other on a couch in a plainly furnished room, which was dimly lighted by a small earthenware lamp set on a lampstand. After the customary greetings, Nicodemus respectfully says to Jesus: "Rabbi,[363] we know that Thou art come a teacher from God; for no man can do these signs which Thou dost, unless God be with him." This beginning of the matter is significant. It acquaints us with the fact that other Jews of the upper classes had, like Nicodemus, felt the influence of Christ's miracles and preaching: hence the plural, "We know." Thus they acknowledged His right to teach in the religious domain, although He had received no official commission, God Himself having directly approved Him through the miraculous power with which He invested Him.

The Savior replied: "Amen, amen I say to thee, unless a man be born again,[364] he cannot see the Kingdom of God," that is, belong to it, be admitted to it. Commentators have noted that our Lord replies rather to Nicodemus' inner thought than to his spoken words. The thought was practically this: What must one do, what conditions must one fulfil in order to become worthy of the kingdom which the Messias is going to found presently? And Jesus tells him that, before aught else, it is necessary to be spiritually regenerated, to undergo, through divine intervention, an inner transformation of one's whole being.

Nicodemus asks for an explanation: "How can a man be born when he is old? Can he enter a second time into his mother's womb, and be born again?" Nicodemus remains in the purely natural realm, while Jesus wishes to draw him into

---

[363] Cf. John 1 : 49.

[364] The Greek adverb ἄνωθεν may here be taken in either of two distinct senses: "from on high" (the literal signification), consequently, from Heaven; or else, "again," as the Vulgate translates it, *denuo*. The thought remains fundamentally the same, whichever interpretation one accepts, for the rebirth of which Christ speaks can come only from Heaven, from God Himself.

the lofty realm of the supernatural.[365] Various Old Testament passages might have called to his mind that there exists a spiritual regeneration of mind and heart.[366] Did not the Jews give proselytes the name of "newborn babes"?[367] But he was blinded by his Pharisaic preconceptions. Or perhaps he was pleading the false so as to learn the true. Jesus answers: "Amen, amen I say to thee, unless a man be born again of water and the Holy Ghost, he cannot enter into the Kingdom of God."

We have here another practice of our Lord's pedagogical method. To a request for an explanation He replies by repeating almost the identical words, but at the same time accentuating them and giving them another turn so as to make them clearer. The new birth which He requires as a condition for entrance into the Kingdom of God consists in baptism, composed of two elements: one being material, water; the other spiritual and divine, the Holy Ghost. But this baptism is precisely what the precursor spoke of as an institution reserved to the Messias, in contrast to his simple baptism of water which was incapable of blotting out sins.[368] By means of a comparison taken from the law of resemblances, the Savior explains why regeneration through Christian baptism is necessary: "That which is born of the flesh, is flesh; and that which is born of the Spirit is spirit." The "flesh" is here human nature with its corrupt instincts; the "spirit" is spiritual nature with its heavenly instincts and loftier aspirations. But, as St. Paul says,[369] flesh and blood cannot enter into the Kingdom of God. Only the Holy Ghost is able to transform them

---

[365] St. Augustine: *"Spiritus ei loquitur, et carnem sapit."*

[366] Ps. 50: 9, 12; 85: 4 f.; Ezech. 11: 19 f.; 36: 26–28, etc.

[367] See Lightfoot, *Horae Hebr. et Talmud. in Evang.*, I, 984.

[368] The earliest Christian Doctors, such as St. Justin, *Apol.*, I, 61, St. Irenaeus, *Fragm.*, 35, St. Cyril of Jerusalem, *Cat.*, I, 4, recognized that Christ here intended to speak of Christian Baptism. See the Council of Trent, Sess. VII, can. 2, *De Baptismo*.

[369] 1 Cor. 15: 50.

and make them supernatural; and this transformation takes place by baptism.

Going still farther, the Divine Master makes use of another figure to prove the possibility, the reality, the immaterial character of the Christian rebirth: "The wind breatheth where it will; and thou hearest its voice, but thou knowest not whence it cometh and whither it goeth: so is everyone that is born of the Spirit." The wind is, indeed, a most capricious creature and, in more than one respect, is still a mystery for modern meteorology, in spite of the great progress made by this science. We perceive its presence by its sound and its effects. The new life which the Holy Ghost causes to enter into us through baptism is likewise very mysterious and most often manifests itself only by its results.

Nicodemus candidly acknowledges that he does not yet understand: "How can these things be done?" Not without a touch of irony, our Lord answers: "Art thou a master in Israel, and knowest not these things?" He, a doctor of the Law, charged with the instruction of others, should have known at least in their *ensemble* those details which, as we said, appear in several places of the Old Testament. Did he, then, like so many others, have his eyes covered when he read Holy Scripture? [370] Happily he has found the true "Master in Israel," who, with charming kindness, makes unspeakable revelations about His higher nature, about the office He was to fill here below, and about the results of His coming into our midst.

At this point the dialogue changes into an eloquent monologue, Nicodemus being reduced to silence and satisfied to be an attentive listener. Jesus' thought, as it were, takes a new flight, rising to the loftiest plane. We will quote in full that charming passage, in which everything is linked together like the parts of a chain:

[370] Cf. 2 Cor. 3:13.

"Amen, amen I say to thee, that we speak what we know and we testify what we have seen and you receive not our testimony. If I have spoken to you earthly things, and you believe not, how will you believe if I shall speak to you heavenly things? And no man hath ascended into heaven but he that descended from heaven, the Son of Man who is in heaven.

"And as Moses lifted up the serpent in the desert, so must the Son of Man be lifted up, that whosoever believeth in Him may not perish, but may have life everlasting.[371] For God so loved the world, as to give His only begotten Son, that whosoever believeth in Him may not perish, but may have life everlasting. For God sent not His Son into the world to judge the world, but that the world may be saved by Him.

"He that believeth in Him is not judged. But he that doth not believe, is already judged: because he believeth not in the name of the only begotten Son of God. And this is the judgment: because the light is come into the world, and men loved darkness rather than the light: for their works were evil. For every one that doth evil hateth the light, and cometh not to the light, that his works may not be reproved. But he that doth truth, cometh to the light that his works may be made manifest because they are done in God."

We cannot here present a detailed explanation of these words, although they are a mine of incomparable riches; that is the business of the commentators. It will suffice to point out briefly the general trend of the ideas and to dwell upon a few particular features. Three great thoughts are successively developed:[372] although Jesus brings to the world a new doctrine, superior to anything known before, He deserves to be believed on His own word, because He comes from Heaven; He will one day die on the cross for the redemption of man-

[371] It is without sufficient grounds that various commentators bring our Lord's words to a close at this point and consider the rest of the discourse as a series of reflections added by the Evangelist. See Fillion, *L'Évangile de S. Jean*, pp. 56 f.

[372] We have indicated them in the translation by the paragraphing.

kind; unfortunately, all men will not be saved, because not all will be willing to believe in the Son of God; but such as are lost will have themselves to blame for their own damnation.

The second of these developments possesses an appealing beauty. It shows us, long beforehand, the cross of Jesus set up like an infallible sign of salvation. The historical fact which our Lord regards as a symbol of His death on Calvary, occurred in the wilderness of Pharan during the fortieth and last year of the wanderings of the Hebrew people. The latter, influenced by their weariness, having hurled at Heaven one of those blasphemous cries which had already cost them so dear, God punished them by sending into their midst a multitude of fiery serpents whose bite produced death. The offending people soon repented and implored the divine mercy, which was not refused them. But their being saved was, by God's will, connected with an outward sign. Upon His command, "Moses made a brazen serpent, and set it up for a sign: which when they that were bitten looked upon, they were healed." [373] The brazen serpent was therefore a "sign of salvation," as it is called in the Book of Wisdom,[374] and it had the advantage of requiring and arousing faith, that virtue so precious in God's sight.

A look of faith and repentance turned upon the crucified Savior produces even more wonderful results: "That whosoever believeth in Him may not perish, but may have life everlasting." [375] Such is the noble and generous purpose of the Savior's death. As for the last reason, it is ineffable, since it consists in God's infinite love, who to save "the world,"—that

---

[373] Num. 21 : 4-9.

[374] Wis. 16 : 6.

[375] In two other passages of the Fourth Gospel (John 8: 28; 2: 32 f.) our Lord again mentions this mysterious "lifting up," by which, as St. John expressly says, He alludes to the manner of His death.

is, fallen, sinful man—[376] sacrificed even His only begotten Son, having Him die on a cross. Without exaggeration it may be said that this passage is one of the most beautiful and consoling in all of Holy Writ and that Christ's words, simple as they are, here possess an incomparable majesty.

The next lines are as terrible as those others are gentle. Despite the infinite value of the expiatory sacrifice offered to God by the Messias, not all men will be saved. On the other hand, Christ does not wish to exercise any office but that of Savior. That of a judge passing sentence is repugnant to His love and His heavenly Father's love. If many sinners are eternally damned, they can blame only themselves, and it will be their works and their own conscience that will pronounce their condemnation.

What was the practical effect of the conversation between Jesus and Nicodemus? The Evangelist does not say so explicitly, but we are probably right in supposing that the sincere and loyal soul of the "master in Israel" was deeply impressed and that when he left he took away with him in his heart the good seed which would gradually germinate, grow, and fructify so as to make of him a disciple of Christ and the friend of His cross. And so we shall one day hear him take up the Savior's defense before the Sanhedrin, which had issued an order for His arrest without a preliminary hearing. Nicodemus said to them: "Doth our law judge any man unless it first hear him and know what he doth?" [377] With a like fearlessness, along with Joseph of Arimathea, he will take a hand in Christ's burial and will pay the last respects to His sacred body with a pious prodigality expressive of his great devotedness.[378]

---

[376] Cf. John 1: 10; 6: 33, 52; 7: 7; 12: 31; 17: 14, 25; 15: 18 f., etc.

[377] John 7: 50 f.

[378] John 19: 39–41. On the historical character of the whole episode, see Appendix V.

II. Christ's Long Sojourn in Judea [379]

Taken all in all, Christ's preliminary ministry at Jerusalem bore but little fruit. One soul, that was later to become a great soul from the Christian viewpoint, had yielded to His influence, but in a way as yet incomplete. A number of followers gathered about the Savior; but their faith was wholly external, and He could hardly count on them. The positive results were indeed of modest proportions. On the other hand, at His very first Messianic manifestation, He had stirred up the religious chiefs of the nation against Him and His work. He saw the realization of the words which He but now addressed to Nicodemus: "You receive not our testimony." In the face of such a reception, He did not hesitate, but hastened to leave the unbelieving city. Yet the purpose He intended had been attained: He had inaugurated His rôle in the metropolis of the theocracy, in the very Temple; He had manifested Himself as the Messias by a vigorous act of authority, by His preaching, and by His miracles. His stay was not, then, altogether fruitless.

Although withdrawing from Jerusalem, He did not as yet wish to leave Judea. Therefore He retired to some rural district [380] which the Evangelist does not specify. His stay in Judea seems to have lasted about eight months.[381] Through-

---

[379] John 3: 22–36.

[380] In Greek, the words Ἰουδαίαν γῆν (Vulg., terram Judaeam) designate the country, as opposed to the city.

[381] This is very plausibly surmised from a remark of Christ to His disciples when He was about to leave Judea and return to Galilee (John 4: 35): "Do not you say: There are yet four months, and then the harvest cometh?" Since the harvest in Palestine occurs usually about the end of April, if we take these words literally, we may infer that our Lord uttered them about the end of December. As the Pasch was celebrated at the first new moon of April, there would be an interval of about eight months on which the Synoptics observe complete silence, while St. John merely says, in a few lines, that Jesus at that time joined in the ministry of His precursor. However this may be, the imperfect διέτριβεν (Vulg., demorabatur), "He abode," designates a prolonged sojourn.

out this period neither He nor the young men who had followed Him from Galilee to Cana, then to Capharnaum and
Jerusalem, remained inactive. He was announcing the near
coming of the Kingdom of God to the crowds that little by
little joined Him and soon gathered about Him in large numbers. The young Galileans, with His authorization and on
His responsibility, conferred baptism on those asking for
it. This detail presupposes that, without becoming established
in any one place, Jesus and His companions did not withdraw
far from the western bank of the southern part of the Jordan.

Ever since the first Christian centuries, commentators and
leading theologians have asked, without being able to agree,
whether the rite then administered by the Savior's disciples
was Christian baptism, the baptism "in the Holy Gohst," announced by the precursor. Many hold that it was; but the
contrary view has always found defenders [382] and, unless we
are mistaken, it is the preponderant opinion to-day. It rests
on excellent grounds. If the narrator had meant to designate
the Sacrament of Baptism, would he not in some way have indicated the fact, so as to prevent any regrettable confusion
in the minds of his readers, to whom he so often speaks of
John's baptism?

A still better reason is to be found in the following circumstance: further on,[383] after citing these somewhat obscure
words of our Lord, "He that believeth in Me . . . out of his
belly shall flow rivers of living water," the Evangelist adds by
way of explanation: "Now this He said of the Spirit which
they should receive, who believed in Him: for as yet the Spirit
was not given, because Jesus was not yet glorified." From
this remark it seems to follow that Christian Baptism, by
which the Holy Ghost is so abundantly communicated to souls,

[382] Among them, Tertullian, *De Bapt.*, II, St. John Chrysostom, and St. Leo.
[383] John 7 : 38 f.

was instituted only after the Savior's Resurrection. And, as a matter of fact, St. Matthew [384] places the institution of Christian baptism only a few days before the Ascension. The rite which our Lord's disciples were then administering scarcely differed from the precursor's baptism and, like it, symbolized the necessity of conversion in order to share in the Kingdom of the Messias. It is evidently for this reason that the Savior Himself refrained from baptizing. Had He done so, it might rightly have been supposed that He was conferring baptism "in the Holy Ghost." [385] Soon Jesus takes the general theme of His preaching from John the Baptist; [386] it is not surprising that He should also have taken his baptism, during the more or less extended period of His preliminary ministry.

Jesus and John, then, accompanied by their more intimate disciples, labored simultaneously, at some distance from each other and under almost identical conditions. At that time the Baptist was no longer at Bethania in Peraea, on the left bank of the Jordan,[387] but on the right bank, "in Ennon near Salim," where he had established himself, "because there was much water there," as was required for his baptism by immersion. Unfortunately it is not possible to determine with certainty the location of these two places, the names of which were and still are rather common in Palestine.[388] Following Eusebius and St. Jerome,[389] they have sometimes been located eight Roman miles south of Scythopolis or Bethsan; sometimes, with St. Epiphanius and the scholarly American Pal-

---

[384] Matt. 28: 19.

[385] On this question, see Suarez, *Opera Omnia,* (Vives ed.), XX, 326–333; Knabenbauer, *Comment. in Evang. sec. Joan.,* 2d ed., pp. 152 f.

[386] Matt. 4: 17; Mark 1: 15.

[387] John 1: 28.

[388] "Ennon" is derived from the Hebrew *'ain,* meaning "a spring."

[389] *Onomasticon,* under the words Ennon and Salim. See also St. Jerome, *Epist. ad Evang.,* 56.

estinologist Robinson,[390] a short distance east of Sichem or
Nablus; or again, in southern Judea, at the place formerly occupied by the villages which in the Vulgate bear the names of
Selim and Aen.[391] The first of these conjectures is the most
likely, although it involves (as also does the second) a very
real difficulty, that of placing the Baptist's temporary residence in a district that belonged to the Samaritans, so hostile
to the Jews.

The multitudes continued to flock to the precursor. But
the fame that was associated with Jesus' name at Jerusalem
spread throughout Judea and even beyond. Thus it came to
pass that ever increasing multitudes gathered about Him, so
that His renown soon threatened to eclipse that of John. The
evening twilight of the latter's day was beginning; the radiant dawn of Christ's day was rising. The Evangelist gives
us no details of His success, but news of it promptly reached
the precursor's disciples, who took umbrage at it. An almost
commonplace incident served to excite their jealousy still
further. One day a Jew [392] came to them—a notable personage, according to the opinion of some; [393] others consider he
was simply an ordinary Israelite—and began a lively discussion with them "concerning purification," evidently referring
to the baptism administered either by the precursor or by
our Lord's disciples. It is not difficult to surmise the origin
of the dispute. The unnamed Jew must have been a recent
follower won by Christ. Upon meeting some of John's disciples, in his neophyte's zeal he brought up the question of the
baptism conferred by Christ's disciples and by John, placing
the latter's in the second place.

[390] *Neue bibl. Forschungen in Palästina*, p. 400.
[391] Josue 15 : 32.
[392] 'Ιουδαίου in the singular, according to the best accredited reading; the Itala,
the Vulgate, etc., read 'Ιουδαίων, "Jews."
[393] These found their view, but with little probability, on the fact that,
in the Fourth Gospel, the word "Jews" habitually signifies the religious chiefs
of the people.

The blow had an immediate effect. The disciples of the Baptist were deeply hurt and went at once to their master. With a feeling of bitterness that may still be sensed in their words, they said to him: "Rabbi, He that was with thee beyond the Jordan,[394] to whom thou gavest testimony, behold He baptizeth, and all men come to Him." He baptizeth: this detail—strictly speaking, not true, because Christ Himself did not baptize—particularly stirred their indignation, for they regarded the baptism of penance as John's special prerogative. They were hardly less shocked upon considering that He who was thus usurping the Baptist's rights and rivaling him in his own domain, owed His reputation and success, as they thought, to the testimony which John had so generously rendered to Him. "All men come to Him": in speaking thus, they were considerably exaggerating. But such is indeed the language of jealousy, which cannot brook a rival's advantages: those of Jesus, however, were quite notable.

How poorly these narrow-minded disciples understood their master and his great soul! His reply, not unlike that which he gave to the Sanhedrin's delegates, was worthy of his humble character and unselfish loyalty. It is the more precious for us, since it contains the last and finest of his testimonies to the Messias. There are two parts to it. The first establishes a new parallel between Jesus and the precursor, setting Christ's superiority in high relief. The Baptist says: "A man cannot receive any thing unless it be given him from Heaven. You yourselves do bear me witness that I said, I am not Christ, but that I am sent before Him. He that hath the bride is the bridegroom. But the friend of the bridegroom, who standeth and heareth him, rejoiceth with joy because of the bridegroom's voice. This my joy therefore is fulfilled. He must increase, but I must decrease."

Thus, instead of putting himself in rivalry with Christ, the

[394] At Bethania in Peraea.

precursor places himself in all respects far beneath Him. Every success comes from God, he says. Christ's growing influence is therefore a heavenly attestation of His superiority. John then appeals to the still fresh recollection of his disciples, in whose presence he had more than once declared that he was only the Messias' herald and servant. The better again to point out Christ's preponderant office, he makes use of a charmingly expressive metaphor, taken from the wedding customs of his countrymen. In several Old Testament passages,[395] the covenant which the God of Israel had made with His people is compared to a marriage, the closest union that human creatures are able to contract between one another. Jesus made use of this same figure,[396] and the Apostles likewise employed it to represent the Divine Master as the mystical Spouse descended from Heaven to celebrate His nuptials with the Church.[397] Now, in the Jewish wedding ceremonies an important function was entrusted to him whom John the Baptist calls "the friend of the bridegroom." [398] He it was who regulated whatever concerned the preliminary questions of the marriage, such as the amount to be paid the girl's father by her future husband. Once the betrothals were concluded, he carried the messages of the betrothed back and forth, as custom did not allow them to visit each other before the marriage. Lastly he arranged the wedding feast and presided over it. However esteemed this office was, in itself it was but secondary and transient. The precursor aspired to no other and was joyfully happy to fill it. The conclusion of

---

[395] Is. 54: 6; 62: 5; Ezech. 16: 1–63; Osee 2: 18 f., etc.

[396] Matt. 9: 15; 25: 1–12; Mark 2: 19.

[397] 2 Cor. 11: 2; Eph. 5: 32; Apoc. 19: 7; 21: 2, 9.

[398] In Hebrew he was called *Shoshebheyna.* See Buxtorf, *Lexicon Talmudicum,* under this word; Lightfoot, *Horae Hebr. et Talm. in Evang.,* I, 998; Schoettgen, *Horae Hebr. et Talmud. in N. T.,* I, 335–340; Weber, *System der altsynagogalen palästinischen Theologie,* pp. 50 f. Among the Greeks, the "paranymph" performed similar functions; those of our "groomsman" are much less extensive.

his eloquent parallel throws light on his feelings of self-forgetfulness and deep humility. As a necessity proceeding from God's plan, "He must increase," says the Baptist, "but I must decrease." John understands that his career is approaching its end; he is content to disappear, giving place to Christ, whose coming he has prepared with all his power.

In the second part of his reply he rises to a still higher plane. It may be summed up as follows: Jesus' heavenly origin places Him far above all created beings; thence result the perfection and certitude of His teaching; He is the Son of God and as such possesses universal sovereignty; happy then are they who adhere to Him by faith, and woe to those who refuse to believe in Him.

"He [399] that is of the earth, of the earth he is, and of the earth he speaketh. He that cometh from heaven, is above all. And what He hath seen and heard, that He testifieth: and no man receiveth His testimony.[400] He that hath received His testimony, hath set to his seal [401] that God is true. For He whom God hath sent, speaketh the words of God: for God doth not give the Spirit by measure.[402] The Father loveth the Son, and He hath given all things into His hand. He that believeth in the Son, hath life everlasting; but he that believeth not the Son, shall not see life; but the wrath of God abideth on him."

[399] Here, as in the last lines of our Lord's discourse to Nicodemus, some commentators consider that we have remarks added by the Evangelist. Their arguments are not convincing. See Fillion, *L'Évangile de S. Jean*, p. 62.

[400] An evident hyperbole, as were also, in an opposite sense, the words of the precursor's disciples: "All men come to Him." Almost immediately the Baptist asserts that Christ's preaching was far from remaining barren.

[401] In the Greek: ἐσφράγισεν, "has placed his seal" (Vulg., *signavit*). This is a figure taken from the very ancient practice of imprinting one's seal on a document to authenticate and confirm it. Cf. John 6:27; Rom. 4:11; 15:28, etc.

[402] To His other representatives, whether prophets or apostles, God gave His gifts only by measure; He pours forth His Spirit on them only partially, and for a special purpose. Cf. 1 Cor. 12:7-11. With regard to Christ, "In Him it hath well pleased the Father that all fulness should dwell." (Col. 1:19.)

"The Father loveth the Son." These sublime words explain why God the Father put no bounds to His generosity towards this only Son, in whom He was so exceedingly well pleased. They are another echo of the revelation which the precursor received at the time of Christ's baptism: "This is My beloved Son."

The Pharisees, those austere and restless zealots, who were disquieted by the precursor's success and the renown of his baptizing, learned also that Christ's popularity was making rapid progress, to such an extent that His followers were becoming more numerous than those of John. They thereupon conceived a bitter jealousy, which they doubtless displayed by recriminations and threats. When news of this reached our Lord, He looked upon it as a providential sign, warning Him not to remain any longer in Judea, where the Pharisee party enjoyed powerful influence. Although His life was not in danger, He left that province and set out for Galilee. We shall again see Him several times resort to this same procedure under similar circumstances.[403] So long as His "hour" is not yet come, He avoids exasperating His enemies and thereby compromising His ministry. He withdraws from their neighborhood, of His own accord leaving ground that has become too dangerous, and betakes Himself to other districts more favorable to His activity. Thus He put into practice the advice which He later gave His Apostles for the period of their missions: "When they shall persecute you in this city, flee into another." [404] Further on, the Synoptics acquaint us with a second motive for this hurried departure: John the Baptist had just been imprisoned by Herod Antipas, and Jesus wished to transfer His ministry to Galilee.

[403] Cf. Mark 3:17; 7:24; John 7:1; 10:39 f.; 11:54, etc.
[404] Matt. 10:23.

III. Jesus in Samaria. His Conversation with the Samaritan Woman. John is Imprisoned by Herod.

We noted above that the Galilean caravans going to Jerusalem to celebrate the religious festivals or returning afterward to their own province, often made a considerable detour in order to avoid the affronts and even acts of violence that would be offered them by the Samaritans on those occasions.[405] Jesus Himself conformed to this custom at least once, at the time of His last journey to the Jewish capital.[406] But in the present case He wished to take the shorter route, directly north through Samaria, which formed, as it were, an enclave between Judea and Galilee. Probably on the second day of this journey, after a toilsome advance, much of which was by steep mountain roads, still accompanied by His faithful disciples, He reached the heart of the Samaritan country near a town called Sychar,[407] situated only a short distance from the field which the patriarch Jacob, centuries before, had bequeathed to his favorite son Joseph. "Now Jacob's well was there," says the Evangelist. "Jesus therefore being wearied with His journey, sat down simply [408] at the edge of the well. It was about the sixth hour," *i. e.,* about noon.

This lifelike and dramatic scene opens one of the most charming narratives in the Savior's life. All the delicacy and candor and ingenuousness of the Evangelist St. John are to be seen in this account. The story's setting, which St. John merely sketches and which has changed but slightly since then, was worthy of the episode about to take place there. The coun-

---

[405] Josephus, *Ant.,* X, v, 1 ; *Vita,* 52.

[406] Matt. 19 : 1 ; Mark 10 : 1.

[407] For the spelling of this name, we follow the best reading of the Greek text: Συχάρ, in place of Σιχάρ.

[408] This seems to be the most exact translation of the adverb οὕτως (Vulg., *sic*), "thus," constituting by itself a lifelike picture. The early Greek commentators, in fact, render it by ἁπλῶς, ὡς ἔτυχε, "simply, unstudied."

tryside where our Lord had just arrived has ever been one of
the most remarkable of all Palestine. Its details are never forgotten by anyone who stops there even for a few hours.

A traveler coming north from Jerusalem, after the usual
halt at Khan Lubban, reaches the plain of El Makhnah, which
is more extensive than all those enclosed by the mountains of
Ephraim. It is a vast wheat-field, divided by neither hedge nor
fence of any kind; its monotony is broken only by numerous
olive orchards planted here and there. After advancing almost in a straight line, the highway bends sharply to the left,
being forced to make a turn about a spur of Mount Gerizim,
which extends in a southeasterly direction. There, between
that mountain and Mount Ebal, which rises up just opposite,
begins the narrow smiling valley in the midst of which is located the city of Nablus, the ancient Sichem. The almost complete bareness of the two relatively gigantic mountains serves
the more conspicuously to display, especially in springtime,
the bright verdure of the little valley which is watered by
abundant springs. "Along flowing streams the traveler makes
his way under the shade of trees, delighted by the singing
of great numbers of birds." [409] The gardens and orchards
surrounding Nablus produce a vigorous growth. The principal fruit trees are the almond, fig, jujube, orange, citron, wal-
nut, and apricot.

But let us return to the Gospel story. Sometimes, following St. Jerome [410] and a few early pilgrims or travelers,[411]
writers have identified Sychar with the celebrated city of
Sichem which we have just mentioned and which has borne the
name of Nablus since its reconstruction by Vespasian.[412] But

---

[409] Van de Velde, *Reise durch Syrien*, I, 291. Cf. A. Stanley, *Sinai and Palestine,*
2d ed., pp. 233–235.

[410] *Quaest. in Gen.*, XLVIII, 22.

[411] Arculf in 700, Saewulf about 1102, Mandeville in 1372, etc.

[412] *Neapolis:* from two Greek words meaning "New City." It is the same name
as Naples.

to-day all are agreed in rejecting this identification and in
recognizing the Sychar of the Gospel in the humble village
now called Askar, which is to be seen at the foot of Mount
Ebal, ten or twelve minutes' walk from Jacob's well. The
historian Eusebius,[413] the Pilgrim of Bordeaux (in 333), and
other early authors clearly distinguish the two places from
each other. There is no sound reason for questioning this
ancient tradition. The Talmud also refers to a village located near Sichem and named Sukar or Sichar, with a well
by the same name, which could scarcely have been other than
Jacob's well.[414]

This well forms the central point of the episode we are
now considering. It is one of the best accredited monuments
of the geography of the Gospels and one of the precious relics
of Israelitic history as also of the history of Christ. Aside
from the Jewish, Christian, and Mohammedan tradition,
which has been invariable in this matter, there may also be
advanced in behalf of its authenticity, an indisputable physical argument. "In the Orient the wells and by-paths are very
reliable guiding-marks for historical or geographical research.
The springs, in fact, do not alter their positions and, in those
warm and arid countries, where water is always scarce, the
direction of roads is nearly always determined by the prospect of obtaining water for both men and beasts of burden at
the end of each stretch of a journey." [415] In this fact we may
see a further guaranty for Jacob's well.

It is found quite near the road going from Jerusalem to
Nablus and beyond, a little to the right and almost immediately after the sharp turn spoken of above, between one and
two miles from ancient Sichem. Unfortunately it has lost its
primitive features. In the third century it was covered over
with a sanctuary, which slowly fell into ruin and which the

413 In his *Onomasticon*, under the word "Sychar."

414 Neubauer, *Géographie du Talmud*, pp. 169 f.

415 Lortet, *La Syrie d'aujourd'hui*, p. 204.

Greek Orthodox Church has rebuilt; the well is therefore no longer in the open air as it was of old. "An ancient rectangular well-curb, about 3½ feet long and 2⅓ feet wide, pierced by a circular opening and marked with a groove which has been made by the rope used in drawing water, is placed at the opening made in the dome that covers the well." [416] The present depth of the well is 82 feet. Jacob dug it at great expense in the limestone. Its water is excellent. Magnificent plane-trees, said to be very ancient, shaded it at the time of the Pilgrim of Bordeaux. Between it and the village of Sychar may be seen the field which the patriarch bought from the people of the country and bequeathed to the most beloved of his sons. [417] In this field is pointed out Joseph's tomb, a humble half-ruined monument, but an object of great veneration in the locality. [418]

All these memories must have rushed to our Lord's mind while He was sitting on the edge of the well, waiting for His Apostles' return. It was at Sichem, quite near this spot, that Abraham erected the theocracy's first sanctuary, in the form of an altar consecrated to the God of the promise and the revelation. [419] Later on, in obedience to the order given by Moses before his death, [420] Josue built an altar on the top of Mount Ebal and immolated many victims there in honor of Jehovah. [421]

Did Jesus wait there quite alone? One would think so from the general expression used by the Evangelist: "His disciples were gone into the city to buy food." Yet it is possible, as has often been conjectured of late, that John remained at the beloved Master's side. This circumstance would partly explain

---

[416] L. Heidet, in Vigouroux' *Dictionnaire de la Bible*, Vol. III, col. 1080.

[417] Cf. Gen. 33: 18–20; 48: 21 f.

[418] Joseph, before dying, asked that his mortal remains should be carried to this place, and his wish was fulfilled after the departure from Egypt. Cf. Gen. 50: 24; Jer. 24: 32.

[419] Gen. 12: 6 f.

[420] Deut. 27: 4–7.

[421] Josue 8: 30.

the lifelike character and very circumstantial details of the account.

By the foot-path leading from Sychar to the well, there suddenly arrived a young woman, carrying an earthen jar on her head or shoulder, coming to replenish her supply of water, at the time of the principal meal of the day. She had a long rope which she let down over the well-curb, and soon filled her jar. Jesus said to her: "Give Me to drink." He was really thirsty after His long and wearisome journey. But His thirst was especially for this strayed soul, which He longed to lead back to better ways. "Give Me to drink." It was by these extremely simple words that one of the most sublime dialogues of sacred literature began. Following His custom, the Master associated a heavenly lesson with a commonplace incident. Above we saw Him in converse with one of Israel's sages, a member of the Jewish Sanhedrin. In this instance it is a woman from the ranks of the common people, a sinful woman, whom He instructs. What a difference, so far as concerns the two persons with whom He talks! And there is also a great difference in the subject matter treated of, in the truths He reveals. Yet He employs the same general method of teaching. In both cases the Savior takes advantage of the immediate circumstances. He skillfully passes from the natural to the supernatural. Words which at first were not understood, He merely repeats and develops in order thus to arouse attention and stir up faith. He tries to touch the heart after having convinced the mind. In this He gives us a divine model of the method to be used in converting souls.[422]

The woman, in astonishment, replied to Jesus: "How dost Thou, being a Jew, ask of me to drink, who am a Samaritan woman?" She had recognized our Lord's nationality by some detail of His dress or by His speech. The Samaritans pronounced certain vowels and guttural letters differently from

[422] Fillion, *L'Évangile de S. Jean*, pp. 71 f.

the Jews. As the Evangelist explains, the woman's surprise arose from the fact that Jews did not have relations, that is, friendly and cordial intercourse, with the inhabitants of Samaria.[423] That reciprocal antipathy reached such a point that a little later a Jew could not eat a Samaritan's bread or drink his wine without contracting a legal defilement. But evidently this extreme prohibition did not yet exist in the time of Christ, since His disciples were gone to Sychar to procure food.

The woman's question would have drawn our Lord onto barren ground. Therefore, instead of replying to it, He says: "If thou didst know the gift of God, and who He is that saith to thee: Give Me to drink, thou perhaps wouldst have asked of Him; and He would have given thee living water." By using this manner of speech, which is partly metaphorical, He wished to stir up in her mind an inkling of the dignity of Him who was speaking to her. The "gift of God" to which He alludes, seemingly consisted in the signal favor which Providence had accorded her in bringing about a conversation with the Messias Himself. In this text and elsewhere in Holy Writ,[424] "living water" is water flowing from springs, as opposed to the stagnant water of cisterns. It is the more precious in Palestine, as it is generally more rare. In this passage [425] it symbolizes the fulness of graces which the Holy Ghost pours into souls, the supernatural life which Christ brought to the world.

The woman, more and more astonished, replied: "Sir, Thou hast nothing wherein to draw, and the well is deep. From whence then hast Thou living water?" Fixedly she remains in the domain of things physical, unable as yet to rise higher.

---

[423] On the hostility that existed between the two peoples, and which still subsists among their descendants, see Vol. I, p. 103 f.; also Josephus, *Ant.*, XV, ii, 2; XX, vi, 1; *Bell. Jud.*, XII, 3; Schürer, *Geschichte des jüdischen Volkes zur Zeit Jesu Christi*, 3d ed., II, 22 f.

[424] Gen. 26:19; Lev. 14:5; Jer. 2:13; Zach. 14:8, etc.

[425] And also a little further on in the Fourth Gospel, John 8:37–39.

At least our Savior's remark produced a first effect upon her. She suspects that she has before her much more than an ordinary Jew, and she feels a certain respect towards Him. For that reason she addresses Christ now, and twice again later, by the honorable title of "Sir." But how could He procure "living water" for her? The water in Jacob's well possessed that quality. Yet, as the woman easily observed, Christ had at hand neither the rope nor the little leather bucket nor the little pitcher which travelers in Palestine [426] carried with them for use in drawing water according as they had need on their journey.

Then, in a tone of irony and disbelief, the woman proudly added: "Art Thou greater than our father Jacob, who gave us the well and drank thereof himself, and his children and his cattle?" Whatever might be the rank of him with whom she was talking, surely it could not be superior to that of the illustrious patriarch to whom the inhabitants of the district owed this well and who had been satisfied with its water. It was a point of national pride with the Samaritans, as Josephus relates,[427] to consider and proclaim Jacob as their ancestor, although most of them were of pagan origin.

Jesus again takes up and develops the allegory of living water. He says: "Whosoever drinketh of this water shall thirst again; but he that shall drink of the water that I will give him, shall not thirst forever. But the water that I will give him shall become in him a fountain of water, springing up into life everlasting." Our Lord, by these words, did not answer the woman's question any more directly than He had previously. But He replied to her inner thought, which was this: Of what water are you speaking? He disregards the secondary points, which would have uselessly changed or in-

---

[426] The Greeks gave this utensil the name of ἄντλημα (St. Augustine, *hauritorium*). The disciples, upon going off to the town, had not thought of leaving it with their Master.

[427] *Ant.*, XI, viii, 6.

terrupted the course of the dialogue, and He goes straight to the chief fact, pointing out the special, infinitely precious quality of the mystical water which He was mighty enough to procure. Ordinary water, even though taken from Jacob's well, quenches thirst only for a few hours: of this the Samaritan woman with her pitcher was a manifest proof. But the water that He will give, assuages thirst forever.[428] It possesses a marvelous privilege: within him who drinks it, it is changed into an abundant, inexhaustible spring which ceaselessly refreshes him and finally leads him to eternal life, where it immerses him, so to speak, in a boundless ocean. This is a rich figure of the never-failing graces which flood a believing soul united to Christ, when it has received the Holy Ghost.

Now convinced, but still under a misapprehension as to the nature of the water that Christ has just described in such eloquent terms, the woman said to him: "Sir, give me this water, that I may not thirst nor come hither to draw." No longer does she offer objections; but, by an exchange of their respective parts, she now addresses the Savior with the request by which He Himself had begun the conversation. Her imagination and desires are greatly aroused. She wishes to have a supply of this goodly water. But why did she come such a distance to Jacob's well, wheras quite near Sychar there flowed several abundant springs? Perchance because she preferred the water from Jacob's well above all the others; perhaps also on account of her ill-fame, which made her dread the jibes of her companions if she were to go with her pitcher to the same place and at the same hour as they.

Thus far our Lord had addressed Himself to the woman's mind. He now gave an unexpected turn to the conversation, appealing directly to her conscience. He said to her: "Go, call thy husband, and come hither." Did he really wish her to bring this man to Him, as has sometimes been supposed? Assuredly

[428] Cf. Apoc. 7: 16 i.

not. His real purpose was to awaken that sinful soul by a sudden blow. Blushing and embarrassed, the woman replied: "I have no husband." This answer was ambiguous, for it might simply mean: I am not married. It is quite possible that the Samaritan woman cleverly worded her answer thus in the hope of eluding any further questioning by Christ. But the Savior's prompt reply showed her that He read her sinful heart to its very depth: "Thou hast said well: I have no husband. For thou hast had five husbands, and he whom thou now hast is not thy husband. This thou hast said truly." It is generally believed that she had been legally married to all five in succession either because some had died or because some had been divorced; for in those lax times the practice of divorce allowed the bonds of matrimony to be easily severed.[429] On any supposition, this woman's lightness of morals was but too evident.

The blow was effective. In the presence of such plain allegations, the woman had no other alternative but simply to acknowledge her shame. She did so at once, for she was not without a certain frankness, as the course of her conversation already showed. Yet her avowal was still only indirect and implied: "Sir, I perceive that Thou art a prophet." Often, in fact, as she had been told, the prophets read the hidden things of the heart, and our Lord had just proved to her that He possessed such a power. His superhuman knowledge produced a deep impression on her and even inspired in her a beginning of faith.

Since He was a prophet, she at once proposed to Him the solving of a religious problem which her coreligionists had discussed for centuries past and to which she herself was not indifferent. She said to Him: "Our fathers adored on this mountain, and you [Jews] say that at Jerusalem is the place where men must adore." Many commentators see in these

[429] Matt. 19:3.

words merely a clever diversion to eliminate from the conversation a topic which may well have been especially unpleas-
ant for her. But, along with most interpreters, we prefer to
suppose that the Samaritan woman had a serious purpose in
putting this question to Jesus. While saying "on this mountain," she must have motioned with her hand in the direction of Gerizim, which rose directly above them. It held a
special place in the religion of those whom the woman calls
"our fathers," and who here stand for the ancient Samaritans.

About three hundred years before our era, on the top of
Mount Gerizim they had built a temple which was destroyed
in 128 by the High Priest John Hyrcanus I, the successor of
the Machabees.[430] Some ruins of it still exist. From that summit, situated in the center of Palestine, one may enjoy a splendid panorama in every direction. The view extends southward to the mountains of Ephraim; eastward to the heights
which rise like a wall, closing the horizon on the far side of
the Jordan; westward, as far as the plain of Sharon and the
Mediterranean; northward to the mountains of Sebaste or
Samaria, dominated afar by Hermon's snowy peak. Even
after the destruction of their temple, the Samaritans continued to regard Gerizim as the central place of their worship.

To-day their greatly reduced community,[431] living in the
city of Nablus, where they have a modest synagogue, call it the
holy mountain, turn toward it in prayer, connect all sorts
of legendary traditions with it, and every year go to its summit, there to immolate and eat the Paschal lamb. By way of
justifying this veneration, the Samaritans have at all times

---

[430] Josephus, *Ant.*, XIII, ix, 1. See Schürer, *Geschichte des jüdischen Volkes
zur Zeit Jesu Christi,* 3d ed., I, 264, 492, 651; II, 16, etc.; Felten, *Neutesta-
mentliche Zeitgeschichte,* 1910, I, 43–47.

[431] It barely amounts to about 170 members. See Baedeker, *Palästina,* 7th ed.,
1910, p. 204.

alleged the passage in Deuteronomy where Moses commands the Hebrews to erect an altar on Mount Gerizim in honor of the true God,[432] after they shall have crossed the Jordan. But, in reality, the authentic Hebrew text of this passage names Mount Ebal. It is in consequence of a deliberate fraud of copyists that we read the name of Gerizim in the celebrated manuscript of the Pentateuch which the Samaritans possess.[433]

Without wishing to enter into a discussion upon the point in dispute, Christ this time consented to follow the woman on the ground she had chosen, for it lent itself perfectly to the great revelations He desired to make. In a pathetic tone, He replied to her: "Woman, believe Me, that the hour cometh when you shall neither on this mountain nor in Jerusalem adore the Father. You adore that which you know not: we adore that which we know; for salvation is of the Jews. But the hour cometh and now is, when the true adorers shall adore the Father in spirit and in truth. For the Father also seeketh such to adore Him. God is a spirit; and they that adore Him, must adore Him in spirit and in truth."

What a prospect for the near future was opened up by these words of Christ, and to what a sublime height He raised the question! In the first part of His reply, He says that soon every religious particularity will cease, and everywhere will be seen a superior, perfect worship, which will overthrow all barriers introduced by time, place, nationality, or difference of tongue, thus abrogating the religion of the Jews as well as that of the Samaritans. This will be the literal fulfilment of Malachias' prophecy: "From the rising of the sun even to the going down, My name is great among the Gentiles, and in every place there is sacrifice and there is offered to My name

---

[432] Deut. 27 : 4.
[433] See Vigouroux' *Dictionnaire de la Bible*, Vol. V, cols. 1421–1424.

a clean oblation. For My name is great among the Gentiles, saith the Lord of hosts." [434] Barely forty years after the Savior's prophecy was uttered, the part concerning the Temple at Jerusalem was completely fulfilled. That celebrated sanctuary, in fact, suffered the same fate at the hands of the Romans which had befallen the temple on Gerizim: it became a heap of ruins. Although the Jewish religion far excelled all others, it was incomplete and imperfect. Therefore it, too, would have to give place to the new religion founded by Christ. This alone will create between God and man paternal relations on God's part, filial on ours. It was rather to the Master than to the "Father" that the Jews, as likewise the Samaritans, had rendered and were still rendering their homage.

After giving this general reply, Christ solves directly, according to the history of revelation, the problem presented by the Samaritan woman. Up to that time the Jews alone had practiced religion as willed by God. The Temple at Jerusalem was the sole legitimate sanctuary. By accepting only the Pentateuch and rejecting all the other parts of the Bible, the Samaritans had placed themselves outside the divine will. Their religion was schismatic, and Gerizim had not the least right to their superstitious veneration. "Salvation is of the Jews": were they not, in fact, the people chosen by God from all others, to safeguard the treasure of revelation? Was it not by them that the promise of redemption was transmitted? And was not the Messias to issue directly from their ranks, to save the whole world? St. Paul takes a certain pride in frequently mentioning this privilege of Israel.[435]

But the new state of things announced by Jesus has just begun. "The hour cometh, and now is." With what gentle firmness He must have uttered those prophetic words! With the little group of disciples who had joined Him, Christ had

[434] Mal. 1 : 11.
[435] Rom. 1 : 16; 2 : 10; 3 : 1; 9 : 4 f., etc.

already inaugurated the "true religion," the worship of "true
adorers," so happily characterized by the words "in spirit and
in truth." These qualities placed it above all other religions.
It was "in spirit," *i. e.,* interior, spiritual, consisting chiefly
in adoring with mind and heart; [436] and it was "in truth," no
longer in figure, as was the usual case in Jewish worship,
where the nation's homage to its God was expressed through
the intermediary of symbolic sacrifices, whereas the religion
of Christ possesses the reality in place of the shadow, and
immolates to the sovereign Lord the Victim *par excellence.*[437]
Such being the case, the new worship perfectly corresponds
to the nature of God, who "is spirit," and who is fully satisfied only by an adoration that is chiefly spiritual. Under the
Old Covenant there was an occasional glimpse of this higher
worship,[438] but its full realization was reserved to the New
Covenant.[439]

The woman to whom Christ deigned to make these revelations was evidently unable to grasp their full import. She did

[436] In the Greek πνεύματι, as opposed to ἐν σάρκι, "in the flesh." It is in the same
sense that St. Paul says: "God . . . whom I serve in my spirit." Rom. 1:9. Cf.
Eph. 6:18.

[437] Cf. Heb. 10:1.

[438] Ps. 39:7-9; 49:7-23; 50:18 f.; Is. 1:11-20; 29:13; Amos 5:20-26; Joel
2:13, etc.

[439] Even though admiring this passage as "one of the most important and most
beautiful in the New Testament" (Heitmuller, *Die Schriften des N. T.,* II, 233),
the Rationalist critics have sometimes curiously distorted its meaning, as if it
radically suppressed external worship and consequently churches, altars, sacraments, sacred ceremonial, and the priesthood. This conclusion is absolutely un-
justified. Jesus, who went regularly to Jerusalem to celebrate His people's religious
festivals in the Temple, did not for a moment entertain the thought of abolishing
external worship. Until the end of time, this sort of adoration will continue to be
a necessity, considering the conditions of our nature. Since we are composed
of body and soul, it is just that our whole being pay homage to the Lord. The
heavenly spirits alone may confine themselves to merely spiritual worship. Furthermore, man lives in society, and this fact requires that he offer public adoration
to God. In fine, Jesus instituted Sacraments and a priesthood, which no one is
authorized to suppress. The essential is that religion should not be a mere matter
of bodily acts and formulas, in which the spirit does not share. Appendix VI
points out other errors of Rationalism in connection with this episode.

at least understand that the great reform in question was connected with the coming of the Messias, for her coreligionists, like the Jews, were also looking for the advent of a redeemer whom they called Taheb ("he who reëstablishes").[440] They pictured him as an eminent prophet, according to these words of Moses: "The Lord said to me, . . . I will raise them up a prophet out of the midst of their brethren like to thee; and I will put My words in His mouth, and He shall speak to them all that I shall command Him." [441] This is why the Samaritan woman says to our Lord: "I know that the Messias cometh; therefore when He is come, He will tell us all things." With simple majesty, Jesus says to her: "I am He, who am speaking with thee." What a sublime revelation, with which He is pleased to honor this woman's nascent faith and good will! In His relations with His countrymen, for a long time He will avoid applying the title of Messias directly and openly to Himself, because of the use they would have been led to make of it in consequence of their extravagant hopes. The same inopportuneness did not exist amidst the Samaritans: Jesus therefore did not fear to present Himself to them as the Messias.

The conversation was at that point when the disciples returned, bringing the food for which they had gone to Sychar, or perhaps to Sichem. Their first impression, when they saw that their Master was talking with a woman, was one of surprise, because, thanks to the Scribes and Pharisees, in the Jewish world of that time the attitude regarding outward relations between men and women was extremely severe. One rabbi went so far as to prohibit even an ordinary salutation by a man to a woman.[442] So greatly was the disciples' respect for the Savior and so high an idea did they have of His conduct

---

[440] See Zahn, *Das Evangelium des Johannes*, 2d ed., p. 248. According to others, but less correctly, "he who returns," or "he who converts."

[441] Deut., 18, 17-18.

[442] *Kiddushin*, 70, 1. Cf. *Pirke Aboth*, I, 5, Fiebig ed., 1906, pp. 2 f.; *Erubin*,

that none of them, as the Evangelist remarks, made so bold as to question Him about it.

Upon their arrival, the woman silently withdrew, forgetting in her excitement to take her pitcher. She returned in all haste to Sychar and eagerly imparted her joy and faith to whomsoever she met, saying to them: "Come, and see a man who has told me all things whatsoever I have done." These words were very significant on her lips. Jesus had not told her everything she had done; but at least He had put His finger on the sore spot of her soul, and that psychological intuition was the beginning of her conversion. She said further: "Is not He the Christ?" She believed that He was. But she did not venture, in an outward and absolute manner, to pronounce on this weighty question. So impressive a piece of news at once produced its effect. Most of the inhabitants of the place straightway turned their steps toward Jacob's well, to see the mysterious stranger close at hand.

Meanwhile the Savior was engaged in another colloquy, this time with His disciples. "Rabbi, eat," they said, as they spread out their provisions before Him. But, just as He had shortly before forgotten His thirst, so now He forgot His hunger, His thoughts being raised aloft. He replied: "I have meat to eat which you know not." As previously the woman had failed to understand, so neither did the disciples comprehend the deeper meaning of these words, which they interpreted literally. They said one to another: "Hath any man brought Him to eat?" Jesus briefly explained His thought: "My meat is to do the will of Him that sent Me, that I may perfect His work." In His first reply He was not speaking of material food, but of a mystical nourishment, which was the filial and faithful accomplishment of the will of His heavenly Father. In our attempt to draw our Lord's moral portrait, we pointed

53, b; *Yoma,* 66, b. See also the collections of Lightfoot and of Wünsche, *in hoc loco.*

out with what love and promptness He always conformed to that holy will.[443]

He added these consoling remarks about the future of His work and the generous reward in store for His collaborators: "Do not you say, There are yet four months, and then the harvest cometh? Behold, I say to you, lift up your eyes and see the countries; for they are white already to harvest. And he that reapeth receiveth wages, and gathereth fruit unto life everlasting: that both he that soweth and he that reapeth may rejoice together. For in this is the saying true: That it is one man that soweth and it is another that reapeth."

As we saw above, the words, "Do not you say, There are yet four months . . . ," enable us to fix the approximate date of our Lord's passing through Samaria. It must have been the middle of January at the latest. Taking the disciples' remark as a starting-point and passing from the reality to the figure, Christ's thought at once rose to a higher plane. He said to them: It will not be long before the approaching harvest. As St. John Chrysostom and St. Augustine remark,[444] they had only to raise their eyes in order to perceive, in the direction of Sychar, a symbolic field in which the grain was already ripe. The inhabitants of the village were approaching, animated by the best dispositions, resembling a rich harvest. To gather it in, there was need only to take hold of the sickle.

Our Savior, contemplating in spirit the future ministry of His Apostles and their successors, continued His beautiful allegory and encouraged the disciples to become zealous harvesters, by describing the advantages they would derive from seconding Him in this task. Not in material granaries will Christ's laborers heap their sheaves, but in Heaven. It is

---

[443] On more than one occasion, on the busiest days of His ministry, our Lord was so active in the service of God and of souls that He did not have time to take His meals. Cf. Mark 3: 20, etc.

[444] In their commentaries, *in hoc loco*.

God Himself who will reward them. In this world "they that sow in tears," anxious lest the seed may not bear fruit, are not always sure to "reap in joy." [445] But when there is question of the field of souls, the sower and reaper rejoice together in Heaven, where they receive an eternal blessedness as their wage. On the other hand, the preachers of the gospel must not be puffed up at their success, which is often owing partly to the work of their predecessors, who prepared it for them without enjoying the firstfruits.

Jesus was at that point in His little discourse, when the inhabitants of Sychar reached Him. Several of them already looked upon Him as the Taheb, solely on the testimony of their townswoman, so greatly had they been impressed by His revelations to her. But they desired to see Him and know Him at closer range. So they begged Him to stay some time in their midst, in order to instruct them more fully. With His customary kindliness, He yielded to this so natural and legitimate request, and stayed two full days in their village. The number of those who believed in Him notably increased, although He seems not to have performed any miracle at Sychar. In speaking of Him, they said to her who had been the first occasion of their faith: "We now believe, not for thy saying; for we ourselves have heard Him and know that this is indeed the Savior of the world." A more exact name they could not have given Him. The ministry that He had gladly exercised in their midst, regardless of the fact that they were hated by the Jews, gave them to understand that He was bringing salvation not only to a privileged nation, but to all without exception. Their eagerness to be numbered among His disciples is remarkable and is their highest praise. It contrasts with the unbelief of the religious leaders of Israel, with the indifference of the people of Jerusalem and the super-

[445] Ps. 125 : 5. This is a proverbial saying which we also find in classical literature. Cf. Hesiod, *Theog.*, 599; Aristophanes, *Equit.*, 39.

ficial faith with which so many other Jews seemed to attach themselves to Jesus.[446]

It was about the time of our Lord's return to Galilee, although the exact date cannot be determined, that the precursor's imprisonment took place. The Synoptics set forth its occasion briefly.[447] John the Baptist was not satisfied with reminding the multitudes of their moral and religious obligations and with preparing them for the coming of the Messias. That intrepid man, who fearlessly reproached the ruling classes of Israel, also one day rebuked Herod Antipas "for all the evils which he had done";[448] especially did he loudly denounce a crying scandal which had burst upon the court of that weak and frivolous tetrarch. Already married to the daughter of Aretas IV, king of the Nabataean Arabs of Petra, whom St. Paul mentions in one of his Epistles,[449] and defying both human and divine laws, Herod dared publicly to wed Herodias, an ambitious, passionate, and violent princess, who was herself already married and who was also his niece and his sister-in-law. Her father was Antipas' brother Aristobulus, the son of Herod the Great by the Hasmonean princess Mariamne. Her husband, Herod Philip,[450] was also

[446] This is the only occasion when our Lord preached the glad tidings in Samaria. Soon afterwards He forbade His disciples to preach the gospel in that province (Matt. 10:5). But He removed His prohibition before ascending into Heaven (Acts 1:8), and the deacon Philip, then the Apostles themselves, subsequently made numerous conversions therein (Acts 8:4-25).

[447] Matt. 14:3-5; Mark 6:17-20; Luke 3:19 f. St. Mark's account is the most complete of the three. St. Luke merely gives a simple summary; but the point at which he places the incident is more in conformity with the chronological order. St. Matthew and St. Mark relate the Baptist's imprisonment only on the occasion of his martyrdom.

[448] Luke 3:19.

[449] 2 Cor. 11:32.

[450] We should not confuse this ruler with his other half-brother, the tetrarch of Iturea, who also bore the name Philip and whom St. Luke mentions in his synchronous date (3:1). Josephus (*Ant.*, XVII, i, 2, and elsewhere) calls him simply Herod, from his family name; St. Luke designates him by his personal name, Philip. There is, then, no contradiction between the two writers. It is, of course, surprising to see the same name given to two brothers; but that is by no

a son of King Herod by another Mariamne (the daughter of the High Priest Simon) and consequently half-brother of the tetrarch Antipas. They were married about 10 B. C. and of their union was born that Salome who played so lamentable a part in John the Baptist's martyrdom.

Herod Philip, who was politically disinherited by his father, but possessed an ample fortune, went to Rome, where he led the life of a private individual. This inferior status was not at all pleasing to his wife, the proud Herodias. And therefore, when her uncle Antipas, who had come to Rome on affairs of state, avowed his criminal passion for her, she easily allowed herself to be seduced, happy in the prospect of shining in the court at Tiberias. But, before following the tetrarch to Palestine, she required him to repudiate the daughter of Aretas. The latter, secretly informed, betook herself to her father, who shortly after avenged this affront by declaring war on Antipas and inflicting a crushing defeat on him.[451] Many of the Jews looked upon this disaster as a just punishment by which God took up the defense of grossly outraged morality. From the genealogical details given above, it follows that the union of Antipas and Herodias was a double incest and a double adultery. Each of them had already contracted a lawful marriage and their wedded partners were still living; and the Jewish law expressly forbade a matrimonial union between brother-in-law and sister-in-law as also between uncle and niece.[452] Furthermore, in view of their high station, their conduct was "a cynical and conspicuous violation of the conjugal law." [453]

means impossible, as we remarked in connection with the Blessed Virgin. Antipater and Antipas, two other sons of King Herod, had names almost identical. It was easy to distinguish the two Philips, who, moreover, were not born of the same mother.

[451] This war was caused partly by a question of boundaries. Cf. Josephus, *Ant.*, XVIII, v. 1.

[452] Lev. 18:10, 16; 20:21; Josephus, *Ant.*, XVIII, v. 4.

[453] A. Réville, *Jésus de Nazareth*, I, 452.

Voicing the public indignation which such indecency justly aroused, John several times [454] protested by his famous *Non licet* ("it is not lawful"), which he cast perhaps into the very face of the tetrarch, as Elias, his model, had sternly rebuked Achab and Jezabel.[455]

His courage in defending the cause of outraged morality was cruelly punished. Antipas "added this also above all" [456] and cast John into a dungeon of the fortress of Machaerus, built like an eagle's nest in one of the wildest spots of southern Peraea, east of the Dead Sea.

Josephus gives [457] a detailed description of that fortress, the ruins of which have been visited by several modern Palestinologists.[458] It was built by the Hasmonean prince Alexander Janeus,[459] then destroyed by Gabinius at the time of Pompey's wars,[460] and subsequently rebuilt and considerably enlarged by Herod the Great, who made of it, as it were, the defensive rampart of Palestine beyond the Jordan, to prevent incursions by Arab brigands. During the last war of the Jews against Rome, it stubbornly resisted the attacks of Lucilius Bassus; and, upon being forced to surrender, it was again destroyed. To-day nothing remains of it but a heap of ruins. It was made up of two distinct parts: a city protected by strong ramparts and towers, and a citadel perched on a much loftier rocky height. The citadel, "encompassed by deep valleys, was

---

[454] This is indicated by the use of the imperfect in the accounts of St. Matthew and St. Mark: ἔλεγεν (Vulg., *dicebat*), "he said." In St. Luke's, the participle ἐλεγχόμενος (Vulg., *cum corriperetur*) may be interpreted in the same way.

[455] 3 Kings 21: 17–24.

[456] Luke 3: 20.

[457] *Bell. Jud.*, VII, vi, 1–2.

[458] Seetzen, *Reisen durch Syria, Palästina . . .*, 1854–1859, II, 330–334; Tristram, *The Land of Moab*, 1873, pp. 253–265. See also G. A. Smith, *Historical Geography of Palestine*, pp. 569 f.; Chauvet and Isambert, *Syrie, Palestine*, p. 507; F. Parent, *Machœrous*, 1868; Duc de Luynes, *Voyage d'exploration à la Mer Morte . . . et sur la Rive Gauche du Jourdain*, 1894, Atlas, pl. 36–39; Abel, *Une Croisière autour de la Mer Morte*, 1910, pp. 32–40.

[459] On this ruler, see Vol. I, p. 127, note 382.

[460] Josephus, *Bell. Jud.*, I, viii, 5.

fortified by an enclosure 160 cubits (about 270 feet) high, within which the royal palace was located. Of this only the foundations remain, rising about five or six feet above ground. In the interior are a very deep well, a large vaulted cistern, and two subterranean cisterns." [461] From this point of observation nearly the whole length of the western shore of the Dead Sea may be seen, as also the Judean plateau as far as the neighborhood of Hebron, the cities of Bethlehem and Jerusalem, the wilderness of Juda, the oasis of Jericho, and the Jordan River, which appears like a silver thread. The altitude is 3772 feet above the Dead Sea, about 2400 feet above the Mediterranean. The ancient name of the fortress is easily recognized under the present Arab name, M'kaur.

Josephus,[462] speaking of the Baptist's arrest, seems to attribute it to a political motive. He says that Antipas feared that John would make use of his powerful influence to incite the Jews to revolt. But this information would be inexact and incomplete, had not the Evangelists shown us the real cause of the imprisonment. The harsh treatment accorded John the Baptist was far from assuaging Herodias' hatred and desire for revenge. This New Testament Jezabel, this Jewish Cleopatra, as she is sometimes called, wanted his immediate death, and she repeatedly asked it of the tetrarch,[463] who at first was on the point of yielding, but feared, doubtless not without good reason, thus to draw upon himself the wrath of his subjects, who were greatly devoted to the Baptist. However disreputable Antipas was, he could appreciate the servant of God, in whom he recognized "a just and holy man," and he conceived a sort of religious reverence for him. Knowing also that he no longer had any reason to fear John, he protected him for some little time from the bitter enmity and snares of

[461] Chauvet and Isambert, *loc. cit.*

[462] *Ant.,* XVIII, v, 2.

[463] The imperfects in the sacred text clearly show this sacrilegious insistance.

Herodias.[464] He even went much farther: when in residence at Machaerus, he visited the Baptist in his dungeon or had him brought into the palace, and gladly heard him and followed his wise counsels in many matters; for at intervals the truth exercised its power even over that corrupt soul. Thus at a later date, Felix, one of the Roman governors of Palestine after Pilate, visited St. Paul in his prison at Caesarea.[465]

[464] The Greek verb ἐνεῖχεν seems to be well translated by the Vulgate: *insidiabatur ei*. Others give it the meaning "to hate," or "to be angry with."

[465] Acts 24: 24-26.

SECOND PERIOD

From the Beginning of Our Lord's Preaching Until
the Second Pasch of His Public Life

CHAPTER I

Glorious Beginnings

I. The Savior Announces the Founding of the Kingdom of God [466]

ST. MATTHEW tells us that, "when Jesus had heard that John was delivered up [to the tetrarch Antipas], He retired [467] into Galilee." The precursor's imprisonment was, for Christ, a sort of signal by which God notified Him that the hour had come to begin His real ministry.[468] Up to that time, Jesus had kept Himself in the background; henceforth He takes the principal part, for the modest activity which He had displayed at Jerusalem, in Judea, and in Samaria, was hardly more than a work of preparation.

According to St. Luke's expression, it was "in the power of the [Holy] Spirit" [469] that the Savior took this momentous step, installing Himself in Galilee, there to establish the center of His preaching and, as it were, the cradle of His Church. No other province of Palestine could have lent itself better to the fulfilment of that design. Nowhere else would it have been possible for His ministry to be less hindered. Far removed from Jerusalem and Judea where the Pharisees were

---

[466] Matt. 4: 12–17; Mark 1: 14 f.; Luke 4: 14 f.; John 4: 43–45.

[467] In the Greek: ἀνεχώρησεν. The author of the First Gospel uses this verb several times to express the idea of a flight in the face of danger. In this instance, the danger came from the Pharisees, who were threatening to hinder Christ's activity.

[468] St. Jerome says on this subject (*Comment. in Matth.*, IV, 15): *"Joanne tradito, recte ipse [Jesus] incipit praedicare; desinente lege, consequenter oritur evangelium."*

[469] Literally: "by the power of the Spirit."

masters, Galilee kept Him safe for a time from the hostility which they already showed towards His Person and His work. The inhabitants of Galilee, with their candid and vivacious manner, were a fertile soil in which the good seed of the Messianic doctrine would quickly germinate and bear excellent fruit.

The Savior made a brilliant start, one full of promise and possessing "the character of springtime." It was a period of sunshine, filled with a divine animation on Christ's part, a joyful confidence on the part of the multitudes that gathered about Him and were led by Him. Scarcely had He entered Galilee, when His fame, which had preceded Him by several months, resounded throughout the province. This rapid enthusisam of the people was largely due to the impressive accounts of His miracles given by those Galileans who had witnessed them in Jerusalem at the time of the previous Pasch.[470] His preaching, which was soon heard in the synagogues on the Sabbaths and religious feastdays, did but add to His renown.[471] The rich substance of that preaching has been recorded by St. Mark in a beautiful rhythmic summary containing four members:

> "The time is accomplished,
>   And the Kingdom of God is at hand.
> Repent,[472]
>   And believe the gospel."

The Messias' whole programme is to be found in those few words. After indicating the fundamental idea of Christianity, that of the establishment of the Kingdom of God on earth, they point out in abridged form the preliminary and

---

[470] John 2: 23; 3: 2; 4: 45.

[471] In St. Matthew's account, the present participle δοξαζόμενος indicates an enduring fact.

[472] In the Greek: μετανοεῖτε (Vulg., paenitemini). We have already (page 31) given the meaning of this expression.

essential conditions of the redemption procured by the Messias: conversion or repentance, and faith. What depth there is in the first statement: "The time is accomplished!" The time here spoken of represents the long centuries during which God so directed the course of the world as to prepare for the coming of Christ. Those centuries have now passed, and the hour has come when the Savior is about to carry out the decrees that His love suggested to Him from all eternity to raise up fallen man. The old era is at an end; a new era begins with the preaching of Him about whom the whole history of the world gravitates. It is in this sense also that St. Paul later speaks of "the fulness of the time." [473]

John the Baptist, had likewise proclaimed the nearness of the Kingdom of God and the need of repentance.[474] But there was an important difference between the precursor's preaching and that of Jesus. As St. Mark notes,[475] Jesus added a new element to the Baptist's preaching. Not only does He say to His hearers, as John did: "Repent"; but He adds this essential admonition: "Believe the gospel." He preached, says the same Evangelist, "the gospel of God." [476] Therein, if we may so speak, was His specialty, His privilege, whereas John, although also proclaiming the "good tidings," [477] since he was announcing the Messias' coming, was especially the preacher of repentance. Taking a comparison from the liturgical chant, we might say that John the Baptist intoned the antiphon, but that Jesus, repeating it, modulated it on a warmer and more melodious tone.

But what was this "Kingdom of Heaven," this "Kingdom

---

[473] Gal. 4:4; Eph. 1:10.

[474] Matt. 3:2.

[475] Mark 1:15.

[476] Mark 1:14. This reading has the best authority, instead of "the gospel of the Kingdom of God." The gospel of God is that which has God for its author and source. St. Paul again and again also employs this phrase (Rom. 1:1; 15:16; 2 Cor. 11:7; 1 Thess. 2:8 f. Cf. 1 Pet. 4:17).

[477] *"Evangelizabat populo,"* says St. Luke, 3:18.

of God," the establishment of which Jesus after John the
Baptist, and the Apostles along with and after their Master,[478]
ceaselessly preached and furthered with all their power? We
must explain its nature because it forms an essential element
of our Savior's teaching.[479]

We have just mentioned the two names by which the Kingdom is referred to at almost every page of the Gospels. At the
outset we must make inquiry as to the meaning of these terms.
The first, "Kingdom of Heaven," [480] is used only in St. Matthew's Gospel.[481] St. Mark and St. Luke cite only the second,[482] which appears also three times in St. Matthew's Gospel,[483] and in St. John's,[484] then in various passages in the
Acts of the Apostles,[485] St. Paul's Epistles,[486] and the Apocalypse.[487] By these examples we see that the idea of the divine, heavenly Kingdom really constitutes the groundwork of
the Gospel revelation. Jesus made it the theme of His first
discourses and returned to it continually during His whole
public life. Only a few hours before His death, He again
spoke to His Apostles [488] about His Father's Kingdom.

By themselves the two expressions offer no difficulty. The

[478] Matt. 10:7; Luke 10:9.

[479] In our day it has been a subject of numerous studies, some of them very
extensive, for the critics have set up in this field, as we shall see, some of their
most destructive theories. Here we will merely cite a few of these works. Catholic
authors: B. Bartmann, *Das Himmelreich und sein König*, 1904; an article in the
Revue Biblique, 1899, pp. 346–360; P. Batiffol, *L'Enseignement de Jésus*, 1905,
pp. 139–188. Protestant authors: Lütgert, *Das Reich Gottes nach den synoptischen
Evangelien*, 1895; J. Orr, "Kingdom of God," in Hastings' *Dictionary of the
Bible*, II, 844–856. Rationalist authors: J. Weiss, *Die Predigt Jesu vom Reiche
Gottes*, 2d ed., 1900; Wendt, *Die Lehre Jesu*, 2d ed., 1901, pp. 209–212, 269–302.

[480] βασιλεία τῶν οὐρανῶν (Vulg., *regnum caelorum*).

[481] Thirty-four times, according to Geden, *A Concordance of the Greek Testament*, 2d ed., pp. 141 f.

[482] βασιλεία τοῦ θεοῦ. St. Mark, fourteen times; St. Luke, thirty-two times, according to the same concordance.

[483] Matt. 12:28; 21:31–43.

[484] John 3:3, 5; 18:36.

[485] Acts 1:3; 8:12; 14:21.

[486] Rom. 14:17; 1 Cor. 4:20; 6:9 f.; Col. 4:11, etc.

Kingdom of Heaven, as the Fathers often repeat, is a kingdom instituted by Heaven and leading to Heaven. Not only is it heavenly in its origin, but its purpose is likewise heavenly, as are its laws, its final consummation, and its King, who is the eternal King of ages. The Kingdom of God, in contrast with the kingdoms of earth, is one founded by that sovereign Master, a kingdom over which He alone exercises legitimate dominion. But it is proper to remark that the Greek word βασιλεία, based on the Hebrew "malkut," might better be translated here by "government" or "kingship" than by "kingdom." It is especially of the reign of God, of His royal government, that Jesus speaks, at least ordinarily. However, this is but a simple *nuance*. It is generally admitted that the two expressions, "Kingdom of Heaven" and "Kingdom of God," [489] are equivalent terms, since St. Matthew uses both without making any distinction between them. It seems—and such is the view of the best interpreters—that "Kingdom of Heaven" was the primitive form, the one used by our Lord most often, if not even exclusively, since it was at that time quite familiar to the Jews. St. Mark, St. Luke, and St. Paul, if this supposition be correct, slightly altered it in order to make it more easily understood by the Greco-Roman Christians.

The *regnum caelorum* is one of the great religious concepts. In the Old Covenant it was first stated in a simple way, then rapidly developed, then given a still more rapid, but nearly always regrettable, growth in the rabbinical writings; finally in the New Covenant it appears in all its fulness. A glance at the religious literature of Israel and then at the Gospels will make this threefold fact quite evident.

It is certain that the idea of God's absolute kingship forms

487 Apoc. 12 : 10.

488 Matt. 26 : 29; Mark 14 : 25.

489 We will continue to employ these two terms, familiar to our readers, without any distinction.

the very substance of the Old Testament in every phase of its history. It appears at the beginning of the world's existence. As soon as God created free beings, capable of knowing and serving Him, there existed in fact a kingdom of which He was the sole master. Therein everything was His and dependent on His providence. It was at first a very holy kingdom, so long as Adam and Eve remained submissive to the divine commands; but unfortunately sin entered in as a consequence of their fatal disobedience. The world would at once have been changed into a kingdom of Satan, had not the Creator in His immense pity taken prompt measures to save poor humanity, that *massa damnata,* as St. Augustine calls it. Thanks to these measures, the kingdom of Christ, in a broad sense, began with the very first Messianic prophecy.[490] But it had two long preparatory epochs, that of the patriarchs and that of the Judaic theocracy. During the patriarchal era, it existed in a latent condition, in the souls of those whom the Book of Genesis calls "The sons of God" [491] and who constituted the best portion of early humanity. It next clearly appeared, under the form of the theocracy,[492] when it pleased the Lord to choose the Hebrews as His people of predilection and when He concluded a solemn covenant with them on Sinai. He then became their King in a very special sense. He Himself dictated to Moses the legislation by which He willed to govern them. Throughout their history, He repeated His commands to them by the intermediary of the prophets. Their leaders, such as the judges and kings, were appointed "to sit upon the throne of the Kingdom of Jehovah," [493] in His name and as His representatives. The divine government was at the basis of everything, and the Lord had His place in the

---

[490] Gen. 3 : 14 f.

[491] Gen. 6 : 2.

[492] A happy expression, going back, it seems, to Flavius Josephus, *Contr. Apion.,* II, 16. It means : government of God.

[493] 1 Par. 28 : 5.

Temple at Jerusalem, while the priests and Levites formed
His immediate court.

Beginning with David, this idea became still more precise,
the Kingdom of God became more plainly the Kingdom of
the Messias, and its ideal was sketched by the prophetic
oracles. It was to be a spiritual kingdom, freed from all political and earthly elements, a kingdom as vast as the world,
because all kings of the earth and all nations would come to
it for enlightenment. Even during the humiliations of the
Exile, when everything seemed hopelessly lost, the prophets
proclaimed the future reëstablishment of that blessed reign.[494]
After the Exile, the notion of the Kingdom of Heaven—the
malkut shamaim, as it was called in Hebrew; the *malkuta
dichemayyam* according to its Aramaic name—became more
living than ever. The rabbis often make mention of this
idea; [495] the apocalyptical books call earnestly for its advent.[496] Every devout Jew, at his morning and evening prayers, recited and still recites a formula in which he "takes the
yoke of the kingdom upon him." [497] The Kingdom of Heaven
lived in all thoughts, it was referred to in every conversation;
it was a current idea. But we have already remarked how far
it had been gradually distorted. There were some holy souls,
however, who kept it in all its purity, though it was yet incomplete, even for them, until Jesus set it forth.

The Savior, therefore, could be understood when He
preached throughout Galilee "the gospel of the kingdom,"
since that good news had been announced long before and
since the precursor had but recently proclaimed it with burn-

---

[494] See especially Dan. 2 : 44 ; 7 : 13–18 ; Jer. 3 : 13–17 ; 30 : 16–23 ; Soph. 3 : 8–20 ;
Zach. 14 : 9.

[495] See Lightfoot, I, 212–214 ; Schoettgen, II, 1141–1143 ; Weber, *System der
altsynagogalem palästinischen Theologie,* pp. 58 f., 364 f ; Dalmann, *Die Worte
Jesu,* pp. 75–88 ; Bousset, *Religion des Judentums,* pp. 195–201.

[496] See the *Book of Henoch,* 46 : 3 ; 48 : 2 ; the Sybilline oracles, III, 698–726,
766–783 ; the *Psalms of Solomon,* 17 : 23–25, etc.

[497] *Pirke Aboth.*

ing zeal. But it was needful to correct the false views in the minds of the people, to perfect what was good, to lift to a higher plane what had not yet been fully revealed and, for this purpose, to return to the ideal of the prophets and even to go beyond it. This is why Jesus, utterly rejecting the shabby and commonplace notions of most of His countrymen, purging the idea of the Kingdom of God from the chimeras of Jewish eschatology, and especially protesting against the purely external and political aspect which Scribes and Pharisees gave to the Messianic hope, in such wise as to make it the monopoly of their nation, persistently stressed its spiritual nature and universal character.

Let it suffice to remind the reader of a few texts which, among a score of the same sort, emphasize this double condition. To Pilate's question: "Art Thou a king?" Jesus gave an affirmative answer, adding that His kingdom was not of this world,[498] *i. e.,* that it was chiefly interior, that it concerned minds and hearts rather than earthly territory. Hence the duties of the citizens of His kingdom are spiritual and consist of virtues and moral qualities, as may be seen from the Beatitudes, from the Sermon on the Mount, and from numerous other passages of the Gospels.[499] This is why that kingdom was first established in individual souls and not by outward conquests. Its catholicity is no less evident; the only ones forever excluded from it are Satan and his angels. The right to be the first to enter the kingdom was reserved for the Jews, as they were the theocratic people; but Jesus warns them, as John the Baptist did, that unless they fulfil the conditions required for membership in the kingdom, "the Kingdom of God shall be taken from you and shall be given to a nation yielding the fruits thereof," [500] and that nation will

[498] John 18: 36 f.
[499] Matt. 18: 4; 28: 20, etc. See also 1 Pet. 2: 1-10.
[500] Matt. 21: 43.

be made up of pagans and even of sinners, provided they resolve to alter their life.[501]

Furthermore, in the Savior's teaching the Kingdom of
Heaven is presented, from the viewpoint of its establishment,
sometimes as being present and already founded, sometimes
as a thing of the future. The expression is complex because
of its very richness. But it is easy to distinguish its various
aspects, which appear as so many different views of the kingdom described by Christ. Its real foundation dates from the
very moment when our Lord began to preach it. Whence
His words: "The Kingdom of God cometh not with observation; neither shall they say: Behold here or behold there. For
lo, the Kingdom of God is within you." [502] Whence again·
"From the days of John the Baptist until now, the Kingdom
of Heaven suffereth violence." [503] And again: "If I by the
Spirit of God cast out devils, then is the Kingdom of God
come upon you." [504] However, as the divine government was
destined to acquire an ever greater increase, Christ also describes it now and again as a future reality. This is so in the
case of several parables of the Kingdom of Heaven, which
set forth the more or less rapid progress of that growth.[505]
The Kingdom of God as established by Christ during His
mortal life is only in the first period of its existence. To this
phase, which will last until the end of the world, and in
which sin will continue to exist along with goodness,[506] there
will succeed another much more perfect one that will be the
period of consummation. It is now called "eschatological," [507]
because it will not begin till the end of time, when the glorified

501 Matt. 21 : 31.
502 Luke 17 : 20 f. Further proof that this kingdom is spiritual. But the phrase
may be translated: "is among you."
503 Matt. 11 : 12; Luke 11 : 20.
504 Matt. 12 : 28. See also Mark 10 : 15; Luke 18 . 17, etc.
505 Matt. 13 : 24–30, 31–33; Mark 4 : 26–29.
506 Matt. 13 : 47–50, etc.
507 From the two Greek words ἔσχατος and λόγος, "last things."

Christ will come a second time, for the purpose of the general judgment.[508] Then, after sin and death have been destroyed and all nature has been regenerated, Christ, as St. Paul teaches,[509] will give back His powers into the hands of His heavenly Father, and the Kingdom of God will shine in all its splendor and holiness, and its duration will be everlasting.

While awaiting that blessed eternity, the Kingdom of God, as many Gospel passages inform us, will appear on earth under the form of a special society, the first foundations of which were laid by the Savior during His mortal life and to which He gave a powerful organic structure. This society, whose members are joined together neither by bonds of race or blood nor by the bond of language nor by that of a common territory or material interests, is His Church. He laid its foundations upon a firm rock;[510] He gave it rulers in the person of Peter, of the other Apostles, and of their successors; He left it His Spirit and wise laws; He bestowed His graces and sacraments upon it; and He promised to assist it even to the end of time.[511] With Him and for Him it continues to strive until that day when it will become the Church triumphant and will live forever with Him. It belongs to Him, since He is its Founder and since He directs it from the height of Heaven. This is why the government of the mystical and yet very real kingdom, whose history we have just rapidly surveyed, is attributed to Him as well as to God the Father.[512]

Such are the chief aspects of the kingdom announced by John the Baptist and by Christ. "In fact, an analysis of 119 passages in the New Testament where the expression 'kingdom' occurs, shows that it means the *rule of God;* which

---

[508] Cf. Matt. 13:40–43; 19:28 f.; 22:29 f.; 24:29–35; Mark 13:24–37; Luke 21:25–33; John 5:28 f., etc.

[509] 1 Cor. 15:24–28.

[510] Matt. 16:17–19.

[511] Matt. 28:20.

[512] Matt. 13:41; 16:28; 20:21; Eph. 5:5; Col. 1:13; 2 Tim. 4:1, etc.

was *manifested in and through Christ;* is *apparent in the Church; gradually develops amidst hindrances; is triumphant at the second coming of Christ* ('the end') ; and finally *perfected in the world to come."* [513]

Twenty times a day we voice our longing for its coming in all its forms, as we recite the beautiful prayer bequeathed to us by our Lord, saying, *"Adveniat regnum tuum,* Thy kingdom come!" [514]

II. Christ's Messianic Consciousness. His Programme

By what title did Jesus present Himself to His fellow-Jews when He announced to them the coming of the Kingdom of Heaven? In the Catholic Church and in the case of orthodox Protestants, every child even but slightly instructed in the catechism, would answer without hesitation that the Savior, at the very first moment of His appearance on the scene of history, had a full and entire consciousness of being the Messias and that for this reason He was called JESUS CHRIST.[515] Fifty years ago it would scarcely have occurred to anyone to put such a question, although our Lord's Messianic character had been more than once denied.[516] But the errors that have recently grown up on this point [517] oblige us to examine it thoroughly.

When Jesus came to John to be baptized and when He

---

[513] Edersheim, *The Life and Times of Jesus,* I, 270.

[514] Matt. 6: 10; Luke 11 : 2.

[515] All our readers know that the word "Messias" is of Hebraic origin, *Mashiahh,* in Aramaic *meshihha,* from which is copied the Greek form Μεσσίας, whence come the Latin *Messias* and the English "Messias," meaning "Anointed." The Greeks translated it quite literally by Χριστός, from which we get the word "Christ." Among the ancient Hebrews, kings were consecrated by a religious anointing, as we learn from various passages of the Bible: Judges 9:8; 1 Kings 10:1; 16: 1, 13; 3 Kings 1: 39; 4 Kings 9: 1–10, etc. In the case of the Messias, there is no question of an unction, except a moral one.

[516] *V. g.,* by Reimarus, Strauss, Renan.

[517] We will point out the principal ones in Appendix VIII.

began His preaching, what did He think Himself to be? Were His ideas, as to the nature and conditions of the part He was preparing to fill, at that time clear and precise? Did He possess fully what it has been agreed to call "the Messianic consciousness"? [518] As serious critics, we will not have recourse to psychological hypotheses resting on sophisms and preconceived ideas, to elucidate this highly important point. Since it is a fact of history, it ought to be studied chiefly by the aid of historical documents and therefore, in the present case, by the aid of the Gospels, whose authenticity and truthfulness have been proved elsewhere. And their answer is not doubtful to anyone who peruses them attentively and impartially.

The chief and immediate purpose of the accounts of the Infancy is to show that Mary's Son was the Messias long promised to Israel. Jesus' genealogies, the words which the angel addressed to Zachary, then to the Virgin of Nazareth, the incidents of the shepherds of Bethlehem and the Magi, the mystery of the Presentation in the Temple, the four canticles: it is all a deliberate affirmation of the Child Jesus' Messianic dignity. There is one detail which, being especially significant, deserves to be singled out from all the others. It is the words addressed by Jesus to His mother and His foster-father when they found Him in the midst of the Jewish doctors: "Did you not know that I must be about My Father's business?" [519] These words contain a clear though indirect revelation of the Savior's Messianic consciousness.

After the long years of His hidden life, Jesus left Nazareth to begin His ministry. In this new sphere, in order to obtain His real thought as to His office, we must examine His words and acts, as also the conduct of His disciples and of the multitudes towards Him. That our proof may lose nothing of its

[518] *Das messianische Bewusstsein.*
[519] Luke 2:49.

force, it is important to distinguish, from our present special viewpoint, between two successive phases of our Lord's public life. The first extends from His baptism to St. Peter's confession and embraces about two years; the second extends from that confession to the Ascension. The Savior's Messianic consciousness underwent no variation during these two periods; but it showed itself very differently.

During the first phase, that is, during the greater part of His Galilean activity, it is certain that Jesus carefully avoided presenting Himself openly as the Messias. By attentively following the sacred narratives, we note that at that time He manifested a great reserve in the matter of His special mission. Thus at times He imposed silence upon the devils who were proclaiming His office,[520] and even upon the sick after curing them.[521] It is easy to see the reason for this prohibition. For the very sake of His cause, Jesus desired to avoid whatever might arouse among the Jewish multitudes, then so impressionable on the subject of the Messias, the political hopes and false ideas and dangerous enthusiasm which we have already pointed out and which we shall have occasion to mention again. We shall see these foolhardy ideas burst forth in a dangerous way at the first multiplication of the loaves,[522] and, unless Jesus had taken heed, it would have been the same after each of His principal miracles. This is why, at the start, He acted with so great discretion and prudence, revealing His Messianic character only on rare occasions, when He knew it would be safe to do so.

At the beginning of His active life, when He had no presentiment of peril, the Savior several times clearly referred to Himself as the Christ. His reply to John the Baptist when the latter at first declined to baptize Him: "Suffer it to be so

[520] Cf. Mark 1 : 25 and Luke 4 : 35; Mark 1 : 34 and Luke 4 : 41; Mark 3 : 10–12.
[521] Matt. 8 : 4; 9 : 30; 12 : 16; Mark 5 : 43; 7 : 36 f.; 8 : 26; Luke 8 : 36, etc.
[522] John 6 : 14 f.

now; for so it becometh us to fulfil all justice," [523] was an affirmation of His Messianic office. The words which He addressed to Nathanael a little later: "You shall see the heaven opened, and the angels of God ascending and descending upon the Son of Man," [524] leave no doubt as to the meaning He attached to His office. His revelation to the Samaritan woman [525] was still more explicit. The expulsion of the sellers from the Temple, [526] the tone of authority with which He preached the Kingdom of Heaven, His applying to Himself, in the synagogue at Nazareth, a prophecy which fits no one but the Messias, [527] the power which He attributed to Himself of forgiving sins, [528] the language He used in the matter of the mission confided to Him, [529] and on the subject of His personal relations with God, [530] the surprising rights which He claimed to exercise over the Sabbath [531] and over other precepts of the Mosaic Law, [532] the Sermon on the Mount taken as a whole, wherein He spoke as a real lawmaker, His claim to superiority over the Temple, [533] over Solomon, [534] and over the prophets, [535] His reply by word and deed to the envoys of John the Baptist, [536] His tender invitation to the afflicted, [537] the judicial authority with which He considered Himself vested, [538] His instructions to His disciples when He sent them

[523] Matt. 3 : 15.
[524] John 1 : 51.
[525] John 4 : 26.
[526] John 2 : 23–25.
[527] Luke 4 : 16–21.
[528] Matt. 9 : 2–6; Luke 5 : 20–25.
[529] Mark 1 : 38; Luke 4 : 43.
[530] Matt. 11 : 25–27; Luke 10 : 21–24, and several passages of the Fourth Gospel.
[531] Matt. 12 : 8, etc.
[532] Matt. 5 : 17, 22, 28, 31, 34, etc.
[533] Matt. 12 : 6.
[534] Matt. 12 : 42.
[535] Matt. 12 : 41.
[536] Matt. 11 : 2–6.
[537] Matt. 11 : 28 f.
[538] Matt. 7 : 22 f.; 10 : 14 f., etc.

to preach in His name,[539] His numberless miracles, the power which He bestowed on the Apostles to perform miracles,[540] His malediction of the unbelieving cities on the lake shore,[541] the manner in which He made Himself the center of the new religion,[542] the sacrifices He required of all His followers,[543] the firmness of His attitude towards His enemies: [544] all this reveals in Him, from the first days of His public life, the consciousness and certitude of possessing an office which, on the part of a Jew, could be none other than that of the Messias.

As we have already said, the devils acknowledged that dignity in Him and published it aloud. Satan, their chief, quickly suspected it and therefore came and tempted Jesus. John the Baptist also proclaimed it before and after the Savior's appearance. The first disciples had at least an inkling of it at the time of their first meeting with Jesus,[545] although it took them considerable time to recognize it fully and to accept its purely spiritual nature. During this same period of Jesus' ministry, the Jewish multitudes rendered Him a homage which was suited only to a superior being, to the expected Liberator. In fine, God Himself, immediately after Jesus' baptism, acknowledged Him not only as His Christ, but as His well-beloved Son.

We would have to cite the Gospel almost in its entirety if we wished to mention all the deeds and words that attest our Lord's Messianic consciousness.[546] And we should add that, although He was so humble and truthful, so loyal and holy,

---

[539] Matt. 10 : 5–42.
[540] Matt. 10 : 8, etc.
[541] Matt. 11 : 20–24.
[542] Matt. 10 : 38 f., etc.
[543] Matt. 16 : 24–28; Mark 8 : 34–38; Luke 9 : 23–27, etc.
[544] Matt. 12 : 25–45; 15 : 1–9; 16 : 1–4; Mark 3 : 23–30; 7 : 5–13, etc.
[545] John 1 : 41, 45, 49; Luke 5 : 8, etc.
[546] See Lepin, *Jésus Messie et Fils de Dieu*, 4th ed., pp. 77–216, where this proof is set forth with force and clearness.

He always accepted without protest the plainly Messianic homage that was paid to Him: wherein we see another proof that He was confident of His right to it. It is therefore incontestable that, with the above mentioned reservation which He kept for the first two years of His ministry, He took an attitude that befitted only the Messias: this is affirmed on every page of the Gospel.

During the succeeding period, the Messianic consciousness appeared with a much greater force and splendor. This period opens with St. Peter's confession.[547] When Jesus saw that His Apostles had overcome their grossest preconceptions about the Messias, He Himself stirred them to confess the faith. With this purpose in mind, He put the famous question to them: "Whom do men say that the Son of Man is?" Peter answered: "Thou art Christ, the Son of the living God." Not merely does the Savior openly accept the title of Messias, but He felicitates Simon Peter upon his providential intuition and rewards him, by appointing him His vicar on earth and the head of His future Church. From that moment He no longer refrained from manifesting Himself as the Messias before His disciples. Yet even then, to avoid the untimely enthusiasm of the populace, He admonished the disciples to remain very circumspect on the subject of His office, until after His death.[548] Furthermore, since He considered them still too imperfect to understand thoroughly the nature of His mission, He counterbalanced the revelation of His glory by often speaking to them of His humiliations and His death.[549] For some little time He continued to employ great caution with regard to the populace. Yet on some occasions He did not hesitate to show Himself directly as the Messias.[550] When His

[547] Matt. 16: 13–20; Mark 8: 27–30; Luke 9: 18–21.
[548] Matt. 16: 20; Mark 8: 30; Luke 9: 21.
[549] Matt. 16: 21; 17: 21 f.; 20: 18 f., etc.
[550] To the man who was blind from birth, John 9: 35–38; to the Jews in the Temple porch, John 10: 24–30.

"hour" approached, He lifted the veil, for it was quite needful that He make an official and public attempt to have His dignity recognized. Hence His triumphal entry into the Holy City a few days before His death—a triumph which, both on His part and that of the multitude, was a glorious Messianic manifestation. On Tuesday of Holy Week, in His discussions with various categories of His enemies, He made no secret of His office.[551] The description of His second coming and of the last judgment also very clearly places the Messianic crown upon His head.[552] His replies to the questions of Caiphas [553] and Pilate [554] are still more categorical.

In the face of so many proofs, it is undeniable that Jesus always believed that He was the Messias, that He exercised the functions of that office throughout His public life, and that if for a while He employed a certain reserve in His Messianic manifestations, that reserve formed part of a most prudent pedagogy, which perceived the difficulties of a too abrupt or too general revelation and overcame those difficulties mildly and ably.

Various titles which undoubtedly designated the Messias and which Jesus either gave Himself or allowed to be given to Him, in particular those of "Son of David," "Son of God," and "Son of Man," confirm the conclusion we have just drawn. Elsewhere we have explained the first of these titles; [555] at the proper point we will make a special study of the second. At present we will consider the third, which we have already heard three times on the Savior's lips,[556] and which was so well suited both to veil and to reveal His Messianic office.

[551] See particularly the parable of the unfaithful husbandmen, Matt. 21 : 33–46.
[552] Matt. chaps. 24–25; Mark chap. 14; Luke chap. 21.
[553] Matt. 26: 63 f.; Mark 14: 61 f.
[554] Matt. 27: 11; Mark 15: 2; Luke 23: 3; John 18: 37.
[555] Vol. I, pp. 310 ff.
[556] John 1 : 51; 3: 13 f.

The form of this expression is remarkable and quite Semitic. But its use in the Gospels is still more extraordinary. There it appears about eighty times—thirty times in the First Gospel, fourteen in the Second, twenty-five in the Third, and twelve in the Fourth—and always as a title which is applied to Jesus only by Himself, neither His disciples nor the multitudes ever attributing it to Him.[557] With a single exception,[558] it is met with nowhere in the New Testament writings outside the Gospels. In short, it is a quite personal appellation and one special to the Savior.

Like the expression "Kingdom of Heaven," the title "Son of Man" appears under different aspects, according to the occasions on which it is used. Our Lord employs it now as a title expressing lowliness and inferiority and now as a name indicating power and greatness. Thus this term shows us Jesus subject to every human necessity,[559] possessing not even a stone on which to rest His head,[560] as having come into this world to minister and not to be ministered unto,[561] betrayed by one of His followers,[562] destined to undergo every sort of ill-treatment. In fact, our Lord almost invariably took this name when preaching His Passion and death.[563] On the other hand, when thus calling Himself, the Savior often plainly intended to claim a lofty dignity, authority, and glory. At a very early date He announced to His disciples that they would see the angels of Heaven ascending and descending

[557] In one passage (John 12:34) we hear the Jews ask: "Who is this Son of Man?" But they do not directly apply this title to Jesus.

[558] Acts 7:55.

[559] Matt. 11:19; Luke 7:34.

[560] Matt. 8:20; Luke 9:58.

[561] Matt. 20:28; Mark 10:45.

[562] Matt. 26:24; Mark 14:21; Luke 22:22.

[563] Matt. 17:12 and Mark 9:11; Matt. 17:21 and Luke 9:44; Matt. 20:18, Mark 10:33, and Luke 18:31–33; Matt. 26:45 and Mark 14:41. After His Resurrection, however, Jesus twice uses the term "Messias" in place of the expression "'Son of Man" (Luke 24:26, 46).

upon the Son of Man.[564] In another place [565] He says that the Son of Man has the superhuman power to forgive sins. He is lord of the Sabbath.[566] He has come to redeem and save sinners.[567] He has the right to interpret and alter the Mosaic Law on important points.[568] He is the Divine Savior who, by His words, lays the foundation of the Kingdom of God.[569] He will be the supreme Judge at the end of time.[570] And, as He majestically affirms before Caiphas,[571] it is as Son of Man that He will so gloriously come a second time.[572]

This interesting title was no more invented by our Lord than was the expression "Kingdom of Heaven." The holy Fathers indicate its true origin [573] by connecting it, as do most commentators to-day, with a famous prophecy of Daniel: "I beheld therefore in the vision of the night, and lo, one like the son of man, came with the clouds of heaven, and he came even to the Ancient of days: and they presented him before Him. And He gave him power and glory and a kingdom: and all peoples, tribes, and tongues shall serve him. His power is an everlasting power that shall not be taken away: and his kingdom that shall not be destroyed." [574]

This prophecy certainly refers to the Messias. It was applied to Him by the Jewish apocalyptical literature of the first

[564] John 1:51.
[565] Matt. 9:6; Mark 2:10; Luke 5:24.
[566] Matt. 12:8 and the parallel passages.
[567] Luke 19:10.
[568] Mark 2:27 f.
[569] Matt. 13:27, 41.
[570] Matt. 25:31-33; Luke 21:36; John 5:27.
[571] Matt. 26:64; Mark 14:62; Luke 22:69.
[572] Matt. 24:4-27; Mark 8:38; 13:26; Luke 12:40; 17:24.
[573] Cf. St. Justin, *Dial. cum Tryph.*, 76, 100; Tertullian, *Adv. Marc.*, IV, 10; St. Epiphanius, *Haer.*, 57; Eusebius, *Hist. Eccl.*, I, 2, etc.
[574] Dan. 7:13 f. In this passage the Son of Man does not represent, as the critics affirm, the people of Israel idealized and glorified, but an individual being, whom God arms with great power to strive victoriously against the great empires of the world, which are figured by four monstrous animals in the preceding verses.

century before our era, particularly the Book of Henoch,[575] in which he figures as a superhuman personage, called also the Elect of God, to whom it is given to sit upon the divine throne and to exercise an all-powerful sway over the whole world.

The Messianic meaning of the title "Son of Man" is also required by a great number of the Gospel texts containing it—texts which, if otherwise interpreted, would lose their whole force. But it is certain that in our Lord's time this expression was not in current use among the Jews to designate the Messias. Only a few initiated individuals attributed this higher sense to it, of which the mass of the people did not possess the secret.[576] It was therefore a rather vague and even obscure name. And this is precisely the reason why Jesus, in conformity with the pedagogical method we have described, used it to half conceal, especially in the presence of the multitudes, the unique character of His Person and work. This title veiled Him and revealed Him, both at once. For the reasons indicated above, He could not at first directly and publicly present Himself as the Messias. And yet He needed to prepare His countrymen to recognize Him in that quality some day. In designating Himself by the extraordinary and mysterious appellation of Son of Man, He largely concealed His chief office. At the same time He thus aroused attention and curiosity; He provoked investigations and questions. To some few this title recalled Daniel's prophecy and led them gradually to see in Jesus the promised Messias, without His having need to disclose Himself openly. Hence the expression was very well suited to His purpose.[577]

When Jesus began to announce the coming of the King-

---

[575] See chaps. 37–71.

[576] See John 12:34, a text quoted above.

[577] It has been deeply studied from every angle and in a most interesting manner by Tillmann, *Der Menschensohn: Jesu Selbstbezeichnung für seine messianische Würde*, 1907.

dom of Heaven, at first with a certain reserve in Jerusalem, Judea, and Samaria, then more freely in Galilee, He had therefore a firm belief that He was the Messias. Such being the case, it may seem superfluous to ask whether He had a well-defined plan and what that plan was. But since these questions are much discussed to-day, it will not be useless to point out what the Catholic thought is on this point.

Assuredly Jesus did have a well-determined plan of action when He inaugurated His ministry, and that plan was infinitely wise and perfect, since it was elaborated in the divine counsels from all eternity. Its every detail was decided upon beforehand. The Christ, who was likewise the Incarnate Word, therefore knew, when He began the work, what there was for Him to do and in what way He would do it.

We may say that His plan consisted first in a great fundamental principle: to fulfil the will of God always and in all things. That was His constant, living rule. As He asserted in many different circumstances, the *oportet*—"it must be"— of that holy will never left His mind.[578] It was to obey God that He "came," that He was "sent" into the world.[579] For the details, He had only to abandon Himself to the direction of the Holy Ghost. But it often happened during the centuries previous to the Incarnation that the heavenly Father's will was expressed by the voice of prophets, so that the principal lines of Christ's life were already marked out. Hence that double formula which we so frequently read in the Gospels: "Such or such a thing was done that such and such a prophecy might be fulfilled.[580] And so it was fulfilled, that was fore-

---

[578] Matt. 16: 21; 26: 54; Mark 8: 31; Luke 2: 49; 4: 43; 9: 22; 17: 25; 22: 37; 24: 7, 44; John 3: 14; 20: 9. Cf. Acts 2: 23; 3: 18; 4: 28. These texts deserve to be meditated upon.

[579] Matt. 10: 40; 15: 24; 21: 37; Mark 9: 36; 12: 6; Luke 9: 48; 10: 16; 20: 13; John 5: 23, 24, 30, 36, 38; 6: 29, 38–40, etc.

[580] Matt. 1: 22; 2: 15, 23; 4: 14; 8: 17; 12: 17; 13: 35; 21: 4; 26: 56; Mark 14: 49; John 12: 38; 13: 18; 15: 25; 17: 12; 18: 9, 32; 19: 24, 36.

told . . ." [581] Thus, with His dying breath could Jesus say, with a feeling of love and triumph: *"Consummatum est,* It is consummated," [582] *i. e.,* "all prophecy has been fulfilled."

The plan was very simple as well as clear. The Evangelists disclose it at every turn. St. John especially is fond of showing us Jesus calmly advancing, with a thorough knowledge of the matter, with firm step, freely notwithstanding the divine *oportet,* toward the goal which had been thus set for Him, toward His "hour" which was to bring its integral fulfilment.

When we study the lives of great men, those most highly gifted from a moral point of view, those of surpassing intellect, even those who are most holy, we fear at times to see them fail in the presence of difficulties and dangers. But we never experience any such feeling in studying Jesus. From His first steps, we are confident that nothing will make Him weaken, that nothing will turn Him from His path. In His earthly existence, everything is linked together consistently. The events are connected according to a preëstablished order which no obstacle can disturb.

The Savior's aim and plan, the ideal which He constantly had before His eyes, was to found the Kingdom of Heaven and thereby procure the glory of God and the salvation of souls. No other plan could better befit the Messias. Jesus' words and His whole conduct bear witness that such was truly His unfaltering scheme. As He was conscious of being Christ the Redeemer, so too, when we respectfully study His mind, we see Him fully aware of His work and of the means at His disposal for bringing it to a successful issue. He foresaw everything, He knew everything that He should do, and He did it with all the perfection that we could expect from Him.

[581] Matt. 2:17; 26:54; 27:9; Luke 24:44.
[582] John 19:30. Cf. Luke 24:44.

III. Jesus Cures the Son of a Royal Officer. He Makes His Residence at Capharnaum. He Definitively Attaches Four Disciples To His Person.[583]

Let us again take up the thread of our narrative, which we were obliged to interrupt in order to explain certain general ideas of the highest importance.

The four Evangelists, each in his own way, sketch the beginnings of our Lord's active ministry in Galilee immediately after the Baptist's imprisonment. St. Matthew and St. Mark give us a summary of His preaching. St. Luke and St. John describe His success in brief form. Everything presages a brilliant career, of which we are now to become the happy witnesses for some time.

When Christ first returned from Judea to Galilee after His baptism and temptation, He performed at Cana the first of all His miracles.[584] On His second return He again stopped at that village and there performed another miracle, not less striking than the changing of water into wine. At that time there was at Capharnaum a personage of some rank, whose exact office it is hard to determine. The word by which it is designated in the Greek text [585] seems to indicate that he was an officer attached to the civil or military household of Herod Antipas. Sometimes he has been identified with Chusa, stew-

---

[583] John 4: 46–54; Matt. 4: 13–17, 18–22; Mark 1: 16–20; Luke 5: 1–11.

[584] John 2: 1–11.

[585] Βασιλικός, *i. e.,* "royal." This may mean: of royal lineage; or else, employed in the service of a king (here, of the tetrarch Herod Antipas, whom the people spoke of as king; cf. Matt. 14:9; Mark 6:25). St. John Chrysostom hesitates between these two meanings. But the form has no *raison d'être* in this place; we are, then, restricted to the classical usage, according to which the word βασιλικός signifies servants of various ranks, whether civil or military, who were attached to the person of a king or prince. Josephus uses it often, and always with reference to royal troops. St. Jerome, *Comment. in Is.,* 65: 1, proposes translating it by *palatinus,* servant of the palace. The Vulgate follows the reading of certain Greek manuscripts which have βασιλίσκος, *regulus;* literally, petty king, tribal chief, etc.

ard of that same ruler, whose wife Joanna was among the devout Galilean women who later accompanied Jesus on His mission journeys and generously ministered to His needs.[586] But this is a mere conjecture.

This officer had a son of tender years,[587] who was suffering from a violent attack of one of those malignant fevers which, in summer and even more so in autumn, even yet find many victims in that tropical region, which is marshy in places and abounds in mosquitoes. The disease had grown so bad that the boy's life was despaired of and his death was expected presently. When the news of Christ's return spread through the district, the afflicted father had the happy inspiration to implore His aid. Perhaps he was one of those Galileans who had with their own eyes beheld the miracles performed by our Lord in Jerusalem.[588] Moreover the fame of the first miracle performed at Cana had extended far and wide throughout that region.

From the lake shore the royal officer hurriedly made the long ascent leading to the lofty plateau on which Cana was located.[589] Then he hastened to find the Savior, whom he repeatedly [590] urged to go down with him to Capharnaum to cure the sick boy. He seems to have supposed that the Miracle-worker's presence was a necessary condition of the cure. The harsh reply which Christ makes would astonish us if we failed to remember that at times He liked to make trial of the faith of those who requested this sort of favor of Him.[591] He said:

[586] Luke 8 : 1-3.

[587] John 4 : 49, he is designated by the diminutive παιδίον, *puellus.* At the beginning of the account, we read ὁ υἱός, with the article, "the son," whence we may conclude that he was an only son.

[588] John 2 : 22 f.; 3 : 2; 4 : 45. Most of them had probably witnessed the miracles of healing.

[589] We mention above (page 90) the distance separating the two places. The difference in elevation is about 2600 feet. See our *Atlas Géographique de la Bible,* pl. XVIII, profile 2.

[590] The imperfect ἠρώτα (Vulg., *rogabat*) shows the insistent repetition.

[591] Matt. 15 : 23, 28; 17 : 16, etc.

"Unless you see signs and wonders, you believe not." These two nouns, "signs" and "wonders,"[592] here as in various other passages of the Old and New Testament,[593] are joined together to emphasize the idea. The latter rather accentuates the striking character of the miracles, while the former alludes to the higher truth which it is their purpose to teach. In speaking thus, Jesus was addressing not only the suppliant; this fact is evident from the use of the plural: "Unless you see . . . , you believe not." His blame fell upon the Jews in general, who throughout the course of their history had repeatedly demanded miracles of God or His representatives. Hence St. Paul's words: "The Jews require signs."[594] But we need not go back very far. Did we not see them, at the opening of our Lord's public life, attracted by His miracles in a purely human manner?[595] To see first, then to believe: that is what most of them wanted to do; to believe in Jesus' mission, not so much because of His personal testimony and His preaching, but rather by virtue of His miraculous powers. In many cases, however, this sort of faith was shallow and imperfect, and the Divine Master had His reasons for mistrusting it.[596] Without wishing to depreciate the proving force of His miracles, which were one of His credentials,[597] He preferred, as He one day clearly said,[598] those who believe without having seen, like the Samaritans of Sychar.

The officer, sustained by his paternal love, bravely stood the test. Instead of allowing himself to be vanquished by the Savior's harsh words, he humbly repeated his request, making it

---

[592] In the Greek: σημεῖα καὶ τέρατα.

[593] Deut. 28: 46; Neh. 9: 10; Is. 8: 18; Matt. 24: 24; Mark 13: 22; Acts 2: 19; Rom. 15: 19, etc.

[594] 1 Cor. 1: 22.

[595] John 2: 23–25; 3: 2–21; 4: 35.

[596] John 2: 23 f.

[597] John 5: 36; 10: 38; 14: 11 f.

[598] John 20: 29.

still more touching: "Lord, come down before that my son die." Jesus, whose refusal had been only apparent, answered: "Go thy way; thy son liveth." Since the boy was dying, for our Lord to speak thus was to announce his cure. But, by using this form of expression, our Lord subjected the suppliant's faith to another trial, since He declined to go down to Capharnaum with him and since He was merely curing the boy at a distance. Despite all this, the father believed and left Cana to return home. We may imagine the deep emotion and joy which reigned in that home when the sick child suddenly recovered his health.

As quickly as possible several servants were sent to meet the father and to tell him the happy news. They met him coming down the long descent that leads from Cana to Capharnaum. His first words were to ask at what hour the change for the better took place.[599] This verification was prompted by faith, not by doubt. The servants answered: "Yesterday, at the seventh hour—according to our method of reckoning time, it would have been at 1 o'clock in the afternoon [600]— the fever left him." In the present case, the cessation of the fever was equivalent to the boy's being safely removed from the danger of death. The father knew that such was the exact time at which Jesus had said to him: "Thy son liveth"; and

[599] The Greek in this place has a very elegant expression: κομψότερον ἔσχεν. It is the *belle habere* of the Latins.

[600] This little chronological detail has created a difficulty for a long time. It is asked how the royal officer, who must have been eager to return home in order to learn the result of Christ's promise, was still on the road the next day, although his meeting with our Lord took place at one o'clock in the afternoon. All sorts of reasons have been imagined to explain the delay in his departure. The need of giving some rest to his riding animal would have detained him at Cana a short while. After nightfall he could advance but slowly and might not have met his servants until after midnight. Still another solution is offered: the meeting of the master and his servants might have taken place after sunset, on the very evening of the miracle; since, among the Jews, the day began at the hour the sun disappeared below the horizon, one might say "yesterday" without a night having passed in the meanwhile.

he thus had, so to speak, a palpable proof of the miracle. And so his faith advanced another step toward perfection. He found the very best means of manifesting it and at the same time of testifying his gratitude to Him who had performed so great a miracle at a distance, simply by His will. Not only did he himself believe that Jesus was the Messias, but "his whole house," *i. e.,* his wife, his son, and his servants, shared in his faith. A few months earlier, the changing of the water into wine at Cana had already produced an increase of faith in a few well-disposed souls.[601]

Jesus was then at the village of Cana only in passing, for He was on the point of carrying out a project of considerable import. Although the humble village of Nazareth, hidden in the mountains and not easily accessible, was remarkably well suited for a life of retreat, it was not equally so for our Lord's purposes, once He had entered upon His ministry. He needed a more extended, more populous field of action, one more accessible and less cut off from the vital points of Galilee. Presently we shall see that very Nazareth, which had sheltered Him for so many years, treating Him most hatefully when He pays it a kindly visit; it will make itself unworthy to keep Him any longer in its midst. Even had He received the heartiest welcome, Jesus could hardly have continued to make Nazareth His habitual place of residence.

In the very first days of His Galilean ministry, therefore, He decided to make His residence in a place better suited to the new circumstances of His life. That place He found in the city of Capharnaum.[602] It was located on the northern shore of Lake Tiberias, on the road connecting Syria, or rather the whole East, with the Mediterranean and Egypt, in the richest, most populous, and most frequented part of all Palestine. It

---

[601] John 2: 11.

[602] In Greek, according to the best manuscripts and the best critics, Καφαρναούμ, *Capharnaum* in the Vulgate. The reading Καπερναούμ, "Capernaum," is incorrect.

possessed a custom-house,[603] a garrison,[604] and at least one synagogue.[605] By its very location it became the center of a flourishing commerce. From there the echo of the Savior's preaching and miracles would naturally reach afar, and Jesus would Himself radiate in all directions, across the whole of Galilee, accompanied by His faithful disciples. We can now understand why Jesus honored this city by making it His headquarters, to which He returned after each of His evangelizing journeys. For this reason also the Evangelists sometimes call it "His own city." [606]

Although so celebrated in the life of Christ, the city of Capharnaum is mentioned by none of the Old Testament writers. Possibly its founding had been comparatively recent. But it was not unknown to the Talmudists.[607] It had the great misfortune of not corresponding with the many graces which our Lord bestowed upon it. Hence He one day uttered against it a terrible malediction,[608] which was so literally fulfilled that to-day the exact site of the unbelieving city cannot be determined. The ablest Palestinologists are not agreed on this point; and so long as extensive excavations are not undertaken at the spots to which the discussion points, there is no reason to expect that the question will be finally settled.

If the reader consults a sufficiently detailed map of the region nearest the lake,[609] he will see on the northwest shore a name, Tell Hum, about three miles from the point where the Jordan empties into the lake. A little farther south, along the shore, will be found the name of Khan Miniyeh. It is between these two names that the geographers and commentators are divided. In favor of Tell Hum the following facts are

[603] Matt. 9:9; Mark 2:14; Luke 5:27.
[604] Matt. 8:5; Luke 7:2.
[605] Luke 7:5.
[606] Cf. Matt. 9:1.
[607] Neubauer, *Géographie du Talmud*, p. 221.
[608] Matt. 11:23 f.
[609] See our *Atlas Géographique de la Bible*, pl. XI.

alleged: (1) The general resemblance of the name: *Tell,* an Arabic word commonly used to designate a heap of ruins, having replaced the Hebrew *Caphar,* "village";[610] *Hum* is considered to be a contraction of *Nahum;* (2) The indication supplied by several ancient pilgrims, among others, Theodosius (A. D. 530); (3) Considerable ruins, especially those of a magnificent synagogue, which might well be that which the Roman centurion, a friend of the Jews, built at his own expense.[611] Khan Miniyeh seems not to contain any real ruins, although in summer, when the water of the lake is lower, near the shore may be seen some remains of constructions which are supposed to have been a port. In favor of Khan Miniyeh, the strongest argument is furnished by the historian Josephus; he mentions an abundant fountain in this district, and he calls it Kepharnome.[612] As a matter of fact, at the distance of a half-hour's walk north of Khan Miniyeh, there is a spring of this sort, which to-day is called Ain-et-Tabigha, which is none other than the Heptapogon, or "Seven Fountains," of the ancient writers. Nothing of a like character is to be found in the vicinity of Tell Hum. But Josephus does not say that this spring flows in the neighborhood of Capharnaum. On the other hand, Theodosius relates that, when coming from Tiberias and Magdala, he passed by the "Seven Fountains" before reaching Capharnaum: whence it follows that tradition at that time placed this latter city at Tell Hum and not at Khan Miniyeh.[613]

In this fact of Christ establishing His residence at Caphar-

[610] The equivalent of the Arabic *Kefr,* used so frequently.

[611] Luke 7 : 5.

[612] *Bell. Jud.,* III, x, 8. Cf. *Vita,* 72.

[613] Of late this question has been extensively studied, but without any certain solution being reached. Among those favoring Khan Miniyeh, as also among the defenders of Tell Hum, are to be found distinguished Palestinologists. At the present time, those who favor Tell Hum seem to be the more numerous. See the various Dictionaries of the Bible, under the word "Capharnaum," for the development of the arguments for and against each of these views.

naum, St. Matthew, faithful to his plan of showing our
Lord's fulfilment of the ancient prophecies, sees the realization of a celebrated prophecy of Isaias,[614] which he quotes
freely according to the Hebrew, at the same time abridging
it, for he repeats only the words which most directly apply to
the subject: "Land of Zabulon and land of Nephthalim, the
way of the sea beyond the Jordan, Galilee of the Gentiles. The
people that sat in darkness hath seen great light, and to them
that sat in the region of the shadow of death, light is sprung
up."

This prophecy is taken from the little "Book of Emmanuel," [615] which in most charming language describes the salvation which is one day to be obtained for the Israelites by the
divine Emmanuel, the son of a virgin, the Messias. The page
preceding the lines which St. Matthew quotes places before
our eyes a Palestine invaded and ravaged by terrible conquer-
ors, first the Assyrians, then the Chaldeans and Syrians, who
entered it from the north, putting everything to fire and sword
as they passed. To the unfortunate inhabitants of these northern districts, who were to suffer still more from barbarian
invasions, the prophet promises in the future a perfect rec-
ompense, and he directs their attention to the Messias-
Redeemer, who will fully console them when He establishes
His place of sojourn in their midst. He it is who in this passage, as in several other places of Holy Writ,[616] is designated
by the figure of a bright light which will disperse the gloom
of suffering, as the sun scatters the thickest mists. Five different districts are successively named: the land of Neph-
thali, which in this text is equivalent to the most northerly
portion of Galilee; the land of Zabulon, or the southern part
of that same province; the way of the sea, or the district

614 Is. 9: 1 f. (Hebrew text, 8: 23—9: 1).
615 This name is given to chapters 7-12 of Isaias.
616 Is. 42: 6; 49: 6; 60: 1-3; Luke 1: 78; John 1: 9; 8: 12, etc.

situated to the west of Lake Tiberias, in the direction of the Mediterranean; beyond the Jordan, or northern Peraea; Galilee of the Gentiles, that is, the Galilean region dependent on Tyre and Sidon.[617]

It did not, therefore, enter into our Savior's plan to remain habitually, like John the Baptist, in one place, there to await the multitudes in order to announce to them the coming of the Kingdom of Heaven. He Himself went forth to meet those whom He so ardently desired to save, and at the very start the most brilliant success attended Him. A majority of the Jewish rabbis, particularly the most learned and illustrious, used to gather about them a group of disciples, whose education they undertook and whom they thus prepared to continue their work.[618] In like manner Jesus, shortly after His baptism, gathered about Him a few young men, most of whom seem to have had John the Baptist as their first teacher.[619] He kept them with Him, at least for part of His preliminary ministry at Jerusalem, in Judea and Samaria.[620] But they do not all seem to have remained in His company. However this may be, their call had been simply transient, after the manner of a probation; and so the Evangelists do not mention them after Christ's return to Galilee. They had then resumed their ordinary occupations. But Christ is about to attach four of them definitively to His Person, and they form the nucleus of the Apostolic College which He instituted a little later.

Let us now consider the circumstances of that decisive call, which constitutes an important date in the Savior's public life. It was made up of two scenes, the first preserved by St.

[617] See our *Atlas Géographique de la Bible*, pl. X.
[618] Vol. I, pp. 182 f. Schürer, *Geschichte des jüdischen Volkes*, 3d ed., II, 423–426.
[619] John 1 : 29–51.
[620] John 2 : 1 f., 11, 12, 22; 3 : 22; 4 : 1, 27, 33.

Luke,[621] the second by St. Matthew and St. Mark.[622]

One day, as Jesus walked along the lake shore, He was surrounded by a large crowd eager to hear Him again. Two boats were moored at the shore, and the fishermen were cleaning their nets, as is the custom after each catch, in order to remove weeds, mud, and little stones that may be lodged in the meshes. One of these boats belonged to Simon, whom Jesus had already met on the banks of the Jordan and to whom He had promised the symbolic name of Peter.[623] The other belonged to Zebedee, whose two sons, James and John, were also destined to acquire fame. Being hindered by the growing crowd which was pressing around Him, Jesus went up into Simon's boat and asked him to take a few strokes with the oar so as to withdraw the boat slightly from the shore. Then, after being seated, He spoke to the multitude from this improvised pulpit, as it was gently rocked by the waves.[624] Early Christian writers remark that our Lord deliberately chose the boat of the future St. Peter; in fact, on more than one occasion of His public life and long before the glorious confession at Caesarea,[625] Jesus hinted that He intended to confer a high office upon that disciple. The "bark of Peter" has thus become a figure of the Church of Christ and it is represented as such on many ancient monuments.[626]

When Jesus had finished speaking to the people, He said to Simon: "Launch out into the deep and let down your nets for a draught." The first of these two requests was addressed to the owner of the boat; the second, to the entire crew, composed of several fishermen.[627] In a respectful tone, Simon an-

[621] Luke 5: 1-11.

[622] Matt. 4: 18-22; Mark 1: 16-20.

[623] John 1: 42.

[624] On still other occasions, and for the same reason, our Lord addressed the multitudes from a fisherman's boat. Cf. Mark 3: 9; 4: 1.

[625] Matt. 16: 16-19.

[626] See F. X. Kraus, *Real-Encyklopädie der christlichen Alterthümer*, II, 73 f.

[627] Luke 5: 9, we read: "He [Simon Peter] was wholly astonished, and all that were with him."

swered: "Master,[628] we have labored all the night and have taken nothing; but at Thy word I will let down the net." It is a fact of experience, pointed out in ancient times,[629] that the night is generally the most favorable time for fishing. Therefore Peter was persuaded that a further attempt in the middle of the day had little chance of success. Nevertheless, he considered Jesus' wish as a command, which he was ready to obey at once. Simon's words show that he was far from expecting a miracle, and that, had he heeded only his personal inclination, he would not have started fishing again at that time.

With the assistance of his comrades he cast the net. In all seas, at times one meets large shoals of fish, and such is particularly the case in Lake Tiberias. "The density of the shoals of fish in the Sea of Galilee can scarcely be conceived by those who have not witnessed them. Frequently these shoals cover an acre or more of the surface, and the fish, as they slowly move along in masses, are so crowded, with their back fins just appearing on the level of the water, that the appearance at a little distance is that of a violent shower of rain pattering on the surface." [630] Peter's net fell exactly into one of these shoals, which the Savior's almighty power had brought to the very spot or the presence of which had been revealed to Him by His divine knowledge—the latter being more likely. In a moment the net became so filled that, when it was lifted out of the water, it began to break and there was danger of it becoming completely ruined. Peter therefore and his companions made signs to the sons of Zebedee, who were in the other boat, not far away, to come as quickly as possible to their

---

[628] In the Greek: ἐπιστάτα (Vulg., *praeceptor*); St. Luke habitually uses this title in place of *Rabbi*. Cf. Luke 8: 24, 45; 9: 33, 49; 17: 13.

[629] Aristotle, *De Animal. Histor.*, XIX, 10, Pliny, *Hist. Nat.*, IX, 23. Cf. Tristram, *Natural History of the Bible*, 5th ed., p. 289.

[630] Tristram, *op. cit.*, p. 285. See also Lortet, *Poissons et Reptiles du Lac de Tibériade*, 1883, and *La Syrie d'aujourd'hui*, 1884, pp 504-511.

aid. The abundant catch filled both boats so that they ran the risk of being sunk.

However accustomed Simon and his companions were to fine catches in that lake, which was so well supplied with fish, they had no hesitation in regarding this extraordinary draught as a miracle. They perceived that it was owing neither to chance nor to their personal efforts, but solely to Jesus' supernatural intervention. Peter thereupon cast himself down at the Savior's knees, saying: "Depart from me, for I am a sinful man, O Lord." [631] He spoke thus under the influence of religious fear at sight of such a miracle, impressed by the eminent holiness which that prodigy showed to be in the Miracle-worker.

Jesus gently reassured him: "Fear not; from henceforth thou shalt catch living men." [632] These were profound words, by which He indicated the symbolic character of the miracle He had just performed. They were also an eloquent presage of the success which Peter would win in the exercise of the high office that was in store for him. The mystical net of the Prince of the Apostles would some day be filled with numberless souls, which it will be his happiness to win to the cause of Christ.[633]

Shortly after this scene, the lake shore witnessed another of the same sort, but still more decisive, for it ended with a formal call addressed by Jesus in turn to Peter, Andrew, and the two sons of Zebedee—a call which they promptly obeyed. St. Matthew and St. Mark [634] relate it in terms which are as simple as they are dramatic.

Jesus, walking along the shore,[635] doubtless still in the

---

[631] This time he calls Jesus κύριος, a much higher title than *Rabbi*.

[632] Such is the full meaning of the Greek word ζωγρῶν.

[633] See St. John Chrysostom, *Hom. in Matth.*, 14; St. Ambrose, *Expositio in Luc.*, 5:4; St. Augustine, *Quaest. Evangel.*, II, 2, etc.

[634] Matt. 4:18–2; Mark 1:16–20.

[635] Παραγῶν, says St. Mark: He "was passing by." St. Luke has περιπατῶν, "walking."

neighborhood of Capharnaum, saw Simon and his brother Andrew engaged in fishing with a cast-net. This sort of net, when adroitly thrown either from the shore or from a boat, falls in a circle on the surface of the water, rapidly sinks by means of the weights attached to it, and encloses whatever happens to be beneath it. Our Lord said to them: "Come after Me,[636] and I will make you to be fishers of men." It was by a like formula that Elias had invited his disciple Eliseus to join him.[637] In telling the two chosen ones that He would make them fishers of men, Jesus was making a play on words in true Oriental fashion. The duties that He will entrust to them, after gradually preparing them, will not be without analogy to the occupation they had previously followed. Moreover, such was the meaning of the promise recently made to Simon Peter. Thus it was that God formerly changed the young shepherd David into a shepherd of Israel.[638] Without hesitating an instant, Simon and Andrew left their nets and followed Jesus.

Going on a little farther, the Savior saw two other brothers, James and John, mending their nets. Them also He called, and they obeyed with the same promptness and generosity. As St. Mark says, "Leaving their father Zebedee in the ship with his hired men, they followed Him." Did the Evangelist, by mentioning their father, intend to emphasize their perfect detachment? It is possible; but the other two brothers also, in order to correspond to their vocation, had given up every-thing—as St. Peter reminds our Lord at a later date [639]—and their merit was no less great.

From the presence of hired men in Zebedee's boat it has been inferred that he was a well-to-do man. This conjecture

---

[636] In the Greek, with remarkable energy: Δεῦτε, ὀπίσω μου. Literally: "Here, behind Me."

[637] See the passage in 3 Kings 19:20.

[638] Ps. 77:70 f.

[639] Matt. 19:27; Mark 10:28; Luke 18:28.

is confirmed by the mention of Salome, the mother of James and John, among the holy women who were our Lord's friends.[640] Moreover, it is likely that Simon and Andrew, though not rich, were likewise in comfortable circumstances, since, according to St. Luke,[641] they were the "partners" of Zebedee and his sons and shared the results of their fishing.[642]

We cannot but admire the double conquest thus won by Christ. For this reason early Christian writers call Him a divine Fisherman.[643] These disciples will form among the twelve Apostles a specially marked group and will become the particularly intimate friends of Jesus. From the moment when He thus attached them to Himself, they had to give up their occupation of fishing, thenceforth incompatible with their new manner of life. But that rude trade was an excellent school to make of them worthy disciples of the Messias. They had been trained in patience and courageous labor. They brought to their Master a lively faith in His divine mission, since they had seen Him at work for some time, and brought loving, generous hearts and a good will ready for every trial.[644]

---

[640] Mark 15:40; cf. Matt. 20:20.

[641] Luke 5:7, 10; μετόχοι κοινωνοί.

[642] On the fishermen of Lake Tiberias, their income, and their organization, see Schwalm, *La Vie Privée du Peuple Juif à l'Époque de Jésus-Christ*, pp. 152-156. There was a considerable fish business, not only in the region of the lake itself, but also beyond, even as far as Jerusalem. The fishermen were, therefore, very numerous. Cf. Josephus, *Vita*, 12. Taricheae, to the south of the lake, possessed an important salting industry. Several towns on the shore bore significant names: *Bethsaida*, "fishing house"; *Migdol Nunia*, "Fish Tower," etc.

[643] On this symbol and on that of the fish (ἰχθύς), which have given birth to so many frescoes and sculptures in the catacombs and elsewhere, see Pitra, *Spicilegium Solesmense*, part III, pp. 419-425; Martigny, *Dictionnaire des Antiquités Chrétiennes*, 2d ed., pp. 622 f., 653-659; F. X. Kraus, *Real-Encyklopädie der christlichen Alterthümer*, I, 516-528.

[644] In the preceding pages, we have separated St. Luke's narrative from the accounts of St. Matthew and St. Mark, although several commentators, whose opinion we share up to this point, make one and the same incident of them. Between these accounts there are assuredly notable resemblances as to time, place, persons,

This is the proper place for us to give a brief description of the celebrated lake which has just been the scene of the miraculous draught of fishes and of another catch still more precious, one that will occupy so large a place in Christ's public life. Geographers, historians, and travelers have devoted to this lake many well merited pages, sometimes eloquent, sometimes simply learned.[645] It bore different names in sacred history. In ancient times it was called the "Sea of Cenereth."[646] Beginning with the period of the Machabees, it was named the Lake or Sea of "Genesar"[647] or "Genesareth."[648] St. John the Evangelist is the only one to use the appellation "Sea of Tiberias,"[649] to which the present Arabic name Bahr Tabariyeh corresponds. St. Matthew and St. Mark ordinarily say "Sea of Galilee."[650] Each of these names arose from some secondary circumstance. Cenereth was a city built on the western shore; Genesar or Genesareth, a fertile

and aim. Yet, more closely considered, they show serious divergences, which the reader can easily observe for himself. In the narratives of St. Matthew and St. Mark, the essential point consists in the calling of the four disciples; but this feature is precisely lacking in the Third Gospel. We may add that, according to the first two Synoptics, Jesus was alone on the shore, whereas St. Luke shows Him surrounded by a crowd, which He addressed after boarding Simon's boat. Further, in connection with this sermon, St. Luke relates the incident of the miraculous draught of fishes, on which the other two Evangelists are completely silent. He closes his account thus: "Having brought their ships to land, leaving all things, they followed Him"; this he does because, though wishing to pass over in silence the calling of the disciples itself, he purposes giving its result.

[645] See especially Josephus, *Bel. Jud.*, III, x, 7; A. Stanley, *Sinai and Palestine*, pp. 368–380; Chauvet and Isambert, *Syrie, Palestine*, 1887, pp. 454–456; Tristram, *The Land of Israel*, 3d ed, pp. 406–424; Lortet, *La Syrie d'Aujourd'hui*, pp. 501–525.

[646] Num. 34:11; Josue 13:27. The Septuagint transliterates this name by Χενερέθ, the Vulgate by *Cenereth*.

[647] I Mach. 11:67: Γεννησάρ in the Greek text (Vulg., *Gennesar*). Cf. Josephus, *Ant.*, XIII, v. 7; XVIII, ii 11; *Vita*, 65; *Bell. Jud.*, II, xx, 6; III, x, 7. Pliny, *Hist. Nat.*, V, 15, says "Gennesara"; the Targums have *Guinesar* or *Guinnesar*.

[648] Luke 5:1.

[649] John 6:1; 21:1.

[650] Matt. 4:1; Mark 1:16, etc. It is to be noted also that these two Evangelists designate the lake in the Hebraic manner by the general word θάλασσα, "sea." St. John does so, too. St. Luke alone uses the more correct expression λίμνη.

plain bordering the lake on its western side.[651] On that same shore, south of Genesar, is still located the important city of Tiberias.

In consequence of a volcanic depression which the Jordan valley underwent throughout nearly its whole extent, the basin of the lake is about 700 feet below the level of the Mediterranean. This volcanic origin is shown by the rocks and basaltic sediments which abound all over this region, by the hot springs near the lake shore,[652] and also by the craters which exist in considerable numbers in the Djaulan, on the plateau that rises up east of the lake. This latter seems even more deeply embanked when it is viewed from the height of the neighboring mountains.[653] Its length from north to south is thirteen miles; its greatest breadth, between Kersa on the east and Magdala on the west, is six miles; its area is sixty-five square miles. Because of the pureness of the air, its dimensions appear less than they really are. From the heights dominating Tell Hum and from the whole eastern side, its full extent can be viewed. Its shape is that of an irregular oval, narrower at the southern end, and has been compared to the shape of a harp. Hence, according to some authors, was derived the ancient name of Cenereth (or Kinnereth), since the Hebrews applied the name *kinnor* to a small harp often mentioned in the Psalms. The Jordan enters the lake at the north and flows out at the southern end. Its depth is not very great. Opposite Tiberias it is about 148 feet; near the southern end, it is not more than 70 or 80 feet. But at some exceptional points it is almost 800 feet deep.[654] Moreover, the surface level varies as much as six feet according to the season, for it rises in the rainy season

[651] We will later accompany our Lord thither.

[652] The principal one is that of Ammam, near Tiberias. See Lortet, *La Syrie d'Aujourd'hui*, pp. 513 f.

[653] Page 90.

[654] Lortet, *loc. cit.*

as also in spring, when the snow on Mount Hermon melts.[655]

The lake is magnificently encompassed by the mountains that close it in on the east and west. Their features are very unlike. Those to the east are more compact and form a gigantic wall, about 2000 feet high, supporting the Basan plateau and running indefinitely to the south. Their united and regular summit appears like a straight line against the sky. Here and there they are cut into by the beds of a few winter torrents. The mountains to the west are more varied and picturesque, rising one behind the other so as to present an interestingly irregular appearance. Even in the case of those that are very steep, at their foot they reach only to some little distance from the lake, thus leaving free a more or less considerable region along the shore; in early times a highway circled this lowland border. This setting offers the greater interest to us inasmuch as it has undergone but little modification since the time Jesus honored the neighborhood of this body of water with His presence. To the north the countryside is dominated by "the white dome of Hermon," which, "when lighted up by the rays of the setting sun, is wonderfully reflected in the blue ripples of the lake." [656] The water is ordinarily "of a beautiful blue, with a slightly opaque tint. Toward evening it reproduces the color of the sky, a brilliant sapphire blue. During the day, there may frequently be observed colored bands, either straight or curved, on the surface, due to currents or to light winds that ripple the water and make it sparkle in a special way." [657]

It is easy to understand that in the summer an intense and sometimes torrid heat is to be felt in this deep basin. On the other hand, the region knows no real winter and snow rarely falls there. On the average there is only sixty days' rain during the year, none at all in June, July, August, and Sep-

[655] Cf. Josue 3 : 15.
[656] Lortet, *op. cit.*, p. 502.
[657] *Ibid.*, p. 505.

tember. Here even more than in any other part of Palestine, life was spent in the open air. In the Gospel narrative we see whole multitudes who were nowise concerned at passing the night outdoors, although it was only springtime.[658]

This lake, immortalized by the Lord Jesus, unquestionably possesses real beauty, although it be not that of the great Swiss lakes or those of Savoy and northern Italy. We mentioned [659] the impression produced by a view of it when seen of a sudden by one coming from Nazareth and Cana. Whether the traveler is skirting its shores or sailing over its surface, he must admire its varied splendors. Some writers have said that the surroundings of the lake are lacking in the picturesque. In its present condition, this region surpasses all other districts of Palestine in natural charms. Its chief, we might almost say its sole defect, consists in its bareness, its vast solitude, its forlorn aspect. In other times the fertile soil of much of its shores and environs was vigorously and intelligently cultivated and produced the luxuriant vegetation of the tropics, yielding crops as rich as they were varied, following one another for the greater part of the year. Even to-day, the whole country, mountains included, is covered in the springtime with verdure and variegated flowers.[660] But in summer and autumn everything is burned and dried up, becoming as gray as ashes. Formerly cities, villages, country villas, and beautiful buildings rose up around the lake and formed a brilliant crown for it. Now the district is almost a desert. Only one city remains, still flourishing indeed, with

[658] Matt. 15:32; Mark 8:2 f., etc.

[659] Page 90.

[660] Lortet, *op. cit.*, p. 512, mentions this special feature, which we also found very striking: "The shore, particularly toward the Genesareth plain, is bordered with magnificent clumps of oleanders, which grow entirely in the water and form enormous bushes covered with a myriad of flowers. Nothing could be more smiling than this pink girdle, which is reflected in the blue transparent waters." On the same part of the shore may also be seen clumps of papyrus, several feet high.

here and there a few wretched villages, such as Medjdel, the ancient Magdala, to the northwest, and Semak to the south. Formerly there was life and movement, a thriving commerce on the highways, and on the lake hundreds of boats. To-day nearly everywhere is death. Formerly there was universal prosperity; to-day there is poverty and desolation. When we picture these earlier conditions to ourselves, we can understand the praise bestowed on the lake by Josephus, who speaks of it as a region of paradise, and by the rabbis, who speak of its charms as celebrated by God Himself: "Saith the Lord, I have created seven lakes in the land of Israel, but I have chosen only one of them for Myself: the Lake of Tiberias." [661] It is truly the "Jewel of Galilee." [662] Its beauty cannot be denied; but it is a special kind of beauty, a beauty at once calm, gentle, noble, and silent, which a Catholic pilgrim can enjoy with deep feeling, while looking for traces of Christ.

IV. One of Christ's Days at Capharnaum [663]

One of our Savior's days, at the beginning of His Galilean ministry, is described almost in full by St. Mark and St. Luke, only in part by St. Matthew. It was a laborious day, filled by prayer, preaching, and good works. Thanks to the four short and realistic accounts, we can form a clear idea of what our Lord's life was at that time.[664] It was a Sabbath. The morning was spent in the synagogue. After the religious service, Jesus went with His four disciples to Simon Peter's house, and remained there the whole afternoon. In the eve-

[661] *Midr. Tehillin,* 4.

[662] *La Palestine, Guide Historique et Pratique,* by professors of Notre-Dame de France à Jérusalem, 2d ed., p. 482.

[663] Matt. 8: 14–17; Mark 1: 21–39; Luke 4: 31–44.

[664] Dr. F. Delitzsch sets forth these accounts and develops them in a very interesting booklet, *Ein Tag in Kapernaum,* 1871.

ning after sunset, He cured the sick that were brought to Him
from all parts of the city. The next day we see Him, early in
the morning, at prayer on the lake shore, whence He sets out
on His first missionary tour.

None of the Synoptics indicates the exact spot where the
double scene occurred that ended in the call of the first disciples; but it must have been a short distance from Capharnaum, since St. Mark shows us Jesus entering that city immediately afterwards, with those whom He had just won.
The next day was a Sabbath. The Master and His disciples
therefore went to the synagogue for the morning services.[665]
We have already said something about these buildings and
the important place they occupied in the Judaism of that period.[666] In our Lord's time there was hardly any town in
Palestine inhabited by Jews which did not have its synagogue.
They were built as richly as the people's resources allowed
and, so far as possible, orientated in such a way that the people, when praying, would be facing toward Jerusalem. In the
rear there was a large cabinet, provided with a veil: this was
the *tabah,* the "ark" in which the Sacred Books were kept.
About the middle of the hall was a platform to accommodate
the "ruler" of the synagogue and the more distinguished
members of the congregation. On this same platform was the
reader's lectern. The rest of the furniture consisted of lamps,
poor-boxes, and cupboards for the sacred trumpets and other
liturgical objects. The men were on one side, the women on
the other, facing each other and separated by a partition.
Sometimes the women were placed in a special gallery. Meet-
ings were held several times a week, but especially on the Sabbath and on feastdays.

In recent years the remains of some synagogues have been
discovered in Northern Galilee, notably at Kefr Bireh, at

---

[665] We shall presently have occasion to describe the principal ceremonies.

[666] In Hebrew they were called *beth-hakkeneset,* "meeting house," almost equivalent to the Greek συναγωγή, from which we have the Latin *synagoga.*

Meinun, at Cades, at Itbid, and, as of special interest to us at this point, at Capharnaum.[667] The splendid ruins of this latter edifice show that the building measured seventy-eight feet in length and fifty-nine feet in width. "A broad doorway gave access to a large nave, surrounded by a gallery on three sides, east, north, and west. The bases of the sixteen columns that supported the roof are for the most part still *in situ*. The remains of the entablature and of the frieze, profusely adorned with sculptures, and the enormous quantity of yellowish stone that lies about on the ground" impress one deeply.[668] According to the view of several connoisseurs, it is not impossible that these remains are those of the synagogue which the Roman centurion of Capharnaum constructed at his own expense to show the high esteem in which he held the religion of the Jews.[669]

The synagogues were intended for religious instruction no less than for the exercise of worship, strictly so called. Hence our Lord frequently spoke in them. Some of His most important discourses were delivered in synagogues.[670] There, especially on the Sabbath, He was sure to find a fairly large audience, usually well disposed, because they were gathered to honor and invoke God. Although He was not a regularly titled doctor, He could freely preach in the synagogues, for the Jews allowed considerable liberty to their coreligionists in this matter. Every Israelite enjoying a good reputation and himself sufficiently instructed, could easily obtain from the *rosh hakkeneset,* or ruler of the synagogue, the requisite authorization. Transient strangers were nearly always invited

[667] See Schürer, *Geschichte des jüdischen Volkes,* 4th ed., II, 445 f.; Chauvet and Isambert, *Syrie, Palestine,* pp. 459, 467; V. Guérin, *Galilée,* I, 198–201, 227–231, 241 f.; II, 95, 100 f., 357 f., 429 f., 441, 447–449, etc.

[668] *La Palestine,* by professors of Notre-Dame de France à Jérusalem, 2d ed., p 493. The carving is in imitation of foliage. The building material is a beautiful limestone imitation of marble.

[669] Cf. Luke 7:4 f.

[670] Mark 6:1–6; Luke 4:16 f.; John 6:25–66.

to address a few words of edification to their brethren.[671] The Apostles, after the example of their Divine Master, profited extensively by this latitude in order to sow the good seed of the gospel.

Jesus, therefore, on that day spoke in the synagogue. The sacred writers say nothing as to the subject of His address. But they stress in most explicit terms the impression felt by the hearers. These latter were genuinely enthused.[672] As both St. Mark and St. Luke add, Jesus taught "as one having power, and," says St. Mark, by way of contrast, "not as the Scribes." In fact, there was a great difference between the two methods of teaching. On the one hand, we have the Divine Lawgiver, Himself interpreting His laws; the Incarnate Word, the uncreated Wisdom, going straight to men's souls to instruct them, to convince them, to console them, to encourage them in doing right. On the other hand, we have cold legists, the impersonal mouthpieces of a tradition often entirely human; they were not able men, and instead of giving life to the texts which they sought to explain, they stifled them under the weight of their stiff and punctilious commentary, most often introduced by the banal formula: "Rabbi so and so says . . ." For the past nineteen hundred years the Savior's doctrine has been spirit and life, in the Gospel writings which are handed down to us; the teaching of the Scribes and rabbis, which the Talmud reproduces in every shape, does not enlighten the mind and still less does it warm the heart. To read even a few consecutive pages of it is a tiresome undertaking.[673]

But now let us consider an unexpected incident which redoubled the admiration of the people gathered in the syna-

---

[671] Acts 13 : 15, etc.

[672] In the Greek ἐξεπλήσσαντο (Vulg., *stupebant*). Literally, they were as if struck with amazement, beside themselves.

[673] Presently we will treat more fully the beautiful subject of our Lord's eloquence.

gogue at Capharnaum. Among them was one of those "demoniacs" or persons "possessed by the devil," then so lamentably numerous in Palestine. As is indicated by the various names which these wretches are given in the Gospels,[674] and still more by the painful details which those same writings supply as to their horrible state, the demoniacs had become the prey and victims of devils that entered into them and exercised a usurped control over their minds and their members, subjecting them, absorbing them, so to speak, and to a certain extent changing them into themselves. Thus, although the will, that sacred and inviolable seat of the soul, continued to belong strictly to the possessed persons, yet the latter were habitually only docile instruments which the evil spirits manipulated at their pleasure. The demoniacs had lucid intervals, during which they regained possession of themselves. At such times we see them cast themselves at Jesus' feet, begging Him to deliver them; and then up they rise in fury, showering insults upon Him, as if there were within them two distinct personalities, one in subjection, despite themselves, to the harsh slavery of the devil, the other in the rôle of a cruel tyrant, commanding and arrogating to himself the right to torture both body and mind.

Sometimes it was not merely one devil, but several devils that seized upon the same person.[675] It also happened that Satanic possession was associated with physical diseases or infirmities. Such was the case of the young lunatic who was also an epileptic,[676] the possessed men of Gerasa, evidently

---

[674] In the Greek text, the most frequent of these terms is δαιμονιζόμενος; the Vulgate paraphrase, *daemonium habens*, does not translate its full force. In connection with the very event we are here considering, St. Luke (4:33) uses an extraordinary expression: "A man having the spirit of an unclean devil." St. Mark, 1:23, literally: "A man in [*i. e.*, in the power of] an unclean spirit."

[675] Cf. Mark 16:9, and Luke 8:2 (Mary Magdalen); Mark 5:9 and Luke 8:30 (the possessed men of Gerasa).

[676] Matt. 17:14-20; Mark 9:13-28; Luke 9:37-44.

afflicted with violent insanity,[677] the woman "bent over," who was suffering from partial paralysis.[678]

We need not be surprised if the demoniacs, who seem to have been quite rare among the Hebrews during the period of the Old Covenant, suddenly increased in extraordinary proportions in the Savior's time. "The realm of darkness marshalled all its forces to withstand its Conqueror, who had just entered the scene of history. But God had His plan, which was to make known, by His brilliant victory over the devils, the coming of the Kingdom of God in Christ and with Christ." [679] It is exactly what we shall observe at the first victory of this sort which Jesus is about to win over the devil. The loftiness of His personality will there appear to us in wonderful relief.

When the demoniacs were quiet, they were not forbidden to be present at the services in the synagogue. Hence we find one of them in the Capharnaum synagogue that Sabbath morning. Scarcely had the Savior finished His discourse, when this unfortunate wretch cried out: "Alas! [680] What have we to do with Thee, Jesus of Nazareth? Thou art come to destroy us.[681] I know who Thou art, the Holy One of God." These words of anguish and deep-seated antipathy express three undeniable truths: there is nothing in common between Jesus and the devils, as the latter openly avow; [682] He has come expressly to crush the head of the old serpent and to overthrow his empire; He is *par excellence* the Holy One, the Consecrated One, that is, the Messias.[683]

[677] Matt. 8:28–34; Mark 5:1–20; Luke 8:26–39.

[678] Luke 13:10–13.

[679] F Delitzsch, *System der bibl. Psychologie,* 2d ed., p. 305.

[680] The Greek word ἔα might here be the imperative of the verb ἐάω; in that case, it would be translated "Leave (us)." But it is rather an exclamation, the Hebrew *eahh,* "ah! alas!"

[681] The best critics of the text suppress the question mark here.

[682] Cf. 2 Cor. 6:14 f.

[683] Cf. John 6:69 (Vulg., 70), where Peter says to Christ, according to the most authentic reading: "Thou art the Christ, the Holy One of God."

These words are assuredly most remarkable. By the mouth
of the possessed man the devil speaks, now in the singular, "I
know . . . ," now in the plural, "to destroy us," according
as he expresses his individual thought or that of the whole
mass of infernal spirits. It is not surprising if thereafter
they all know our Lord's Messianic dignity. The voice of
God Himself at the time of Christ's baptism, then the repeated
testimony of John the Baptist, clearly revealed it to them.
And as St. James says, "the devils also believe and tremble." [684]

It is easy to understand that the Holy One of God could
not accept this testimony, even though forced and involuntary, of an "impure" [685] spirit, that is, one thoroughly evil,
one that thinks only of drawing men into sin. In a severe
tone,[686] Jesus issued two commands to him: "Speak no
more,[687] and go out of the man." The devil had to obey at
once; but he did not leave his victim without a last attempt
to harm him and without showing his hatred. He shook the
possessed man so violently as to hurl him to the ground in
the midst of the assembled people; then he left him with a
cry of rage.

An indescribable emotion, made up of two distinct elements, religious awe in the presence of the supernatural, and
admiration caused by the miracle, seized the entire gathering.
Soon the second of these feelings dominated, and the witnesses
of the prodigy remarked to one another: "What thing is this?

[684] James 2 : 19.

[685] This epithet (in the Greek ἀκάθαρτον, Vulg., *immundus*) is associated with
the name of devil, according to Geder's Greek Concordance, twice by St.
Matthew, eleven times by St. Mark, six times by St. Luke, twice in the Acts of
the Apostles. In every case it has the general signification we have indicated.

[686] The verb ἐπετίμησεν (Vulg., *comminatus est* in St. Mark, and *increpavit* in
St. Luke), occurring rather frequently in the Gospels, signifies a threat which one
has no right to resist.

[687] In the original text literally: "Be thou muzzled!" It is a vigorous metaphor.
Muzzles are put on vicious animals to prevent their biting.

It is a new doctrine accompanied with power.[688] With authority He commandeth the unclean spirits, and they obey Him."
After being first struck by the moral vigor of Christ's teaching, they were now impressed by the irresistible power He
exercised over the devils. A single word from Him was
enough to put to flight one of those beings so difficult to
overcome. As we said above, this was probably the first time
that Jesus performed a cure of this sort, and never had the
like been seen or heard. The fame of such a miracle, duly
observed and attested by the large number of those present,
rapidly spread through the length and breadth of Galilee.[689]

Upon leaving the synagogue, Jesus went directly to Simon
Peter's house, to spend the rest of the Sabbath in quiet there.
That modest abode was probably the house which served our
Lord as His occasional lodging whenever He was living at
Capharnaum.[690] The future Prince of the Apostles was married: this we learn indirectly from the present passage,
through mention of his mother-in-law, more directly from
St. Paul's testimony [691] and ecclesiastical tradition.[692] Simon Peter was a native of Bethsaida; [693] but it is possible
that he made Capharnaum his home at the time of his marriage.

When Jesus and His four disciples entered the house, Simon's mother-in-law was abed, "taken with a great fever,"
as St. Luke tells us; for him this medical detail was of special

[688] The commentators do not entirely agree on the punctuation and interpretation
of this passage. But their differences of opinion affect only simple shades of
meaning.

[689] Mark 1 : 21–28; Luke 4 : 31–37.

[690] In that case, it would be "the house" referred to in Mark 2 : 2; 9 : 32; 10 : 10.

[691] 1 Cor. 9 : 5.

[692] Clement of Alexandria, *Strom.*, III, vi, 52; vii, 19–63; Eusebius, *Hist. Eccl.*,
III, 30.

[693] John 1 : 44.

importance.[694] We know [695] that at certain periods of the
year fevers are rather frequent on the shores of Lake Tiberias. Perhaps the attack in question was as sudden as it was
severe. The disciples took the first step in drawing their
Master's attention to this sad event, and He, wishing to reward their generous devotedness, as also to give them a
special pledge of His affection, at once yielded to their earnest desire. Coming to the bed on which the sick woman lay,
He leaned over her, took hold of her hand, and gently raised
her, at the same time commanding [696] the fever to leave her.
The sickness vanished instantly and the cure was so complete that Peter's mother-in-law was herself able to prepare
the Sabbath evening meal and serve it to her guests. It was
like a miracle within a miracle, because when a severe fever
ends, either of itself or under the influence of medicines, it
usually leaves the patient in a state of great weakness, which
only gradually disappears.

This time the whole city was stirred. And so it happened
that, as soon as the sun had disappeared below the horizon,
thus putting an end to the Sabbath and its obligatory repose,
the inhabitants hurried to profit by the kind Miracle-worker's
presence to obtain other favors from Him. In a short time,
along the streets there was a procession of sick and demoniacs, who were being led or carried to Jesus. In the words
of St. Mark, who obtained this unforgettable detail from
St. Peter, "all the city was gathered together at the door" of
the house. The Savior's generosity was quite equal to this
enthusiastic confidence. "All that were sick He healed," remarks St. Matthew, and St. Luke adds that He performed
these wonderful cures simply by imposing His hands. With
a single word He drove out the devils, who despite themselves

[694] St. Matthew and St. Mark merely say that the sick woman was πυρέσσουσα
(Vulg., *febricitans*), "having a fever."
[695] Cf. Thomson, *The Land and the Book*, 1876, p. 238.
[696] Here we again meet with the verb ἐπετίμησεν.

abandoned the bodies of the possessed, crying out to the Savior: "Thou art the Son of God." But again He imposed silence upon them. Thus, not only on that day, but during all this first period of Christ's active ministry, there was a wonderful outpouring of His miraculous power. Independently of isolated cases of healing, the Synoptics again and again make mention of cures performed *en masse*.[697]

In connection with these numerous cures, St. Matthew cites a prophecy, saying: "That it might be fulfilled, which was spoken by the prophet Isaias, saying: He took our infirmities and bore our diseases." [698] The illustrious prophet, describing the sufferings which were one day to be undergone by the Servant of Jehovah, *i. e.,* the Messias, also pointed out their happy consequences for mankind, whose countless sins had aroused God's anger and provoked His vengeance. Christ offered Himself to His Father as a victim of propitiation and so carried and took away our crimes and the punishments of every kind, such as diseases, and physical and moral infirmities, which those sins had drawn down upon us. In curing the sick and driving out devils, Jesus was therefore exercising His providential office.

[697] Matt. 4:24 f.; 8:16; 12:15; Mark 3:10-12; Luke 6:18 f.
[698] Is. 53:4.

CHAPTER II

Jesus Goes About Galilee, Preaching the Gospel and
Performing Miracles

I. Occasion and Summary of Christ's First Pastoral Tour [699]

In spite of the weariness that He must have felt after a day of such strenuous activity, the zealous Pastor of souls was on His feet very early the next morning, even before that Sabbath night had quite passed; [700] without anyone being aware of it, he noiselessly left the house. "A remarkable feature of the lake is that it was so closely surrounded with desert solitudes. It was those 'desert places' thus close at hand on the table-lands, or in the ravines of the eastern and western ranges, which seem to be classed under the common name of 'the mountain,' that gave the opportunities of retirement for rest or prayer." [701] Jesus reached one of these retreats, and at once His soul was immersed in prayer. It was partly for the purpose of uniting Himself more completely with His Father by earnest prayer, [702] that He had left the house of His future Apostle. But He intended at the same time to escape the ovations of the people of Capharnaum, whose enthusiasm had been aroused by the miracles of the day before. As the sequence shows, He especially wished to execute with-

---

[699] Matt. 4 : 23; Mark 1 : 35–39; Luke 4 : 42–44.

[700] Well expressed by St. Mark by the use of an unusual phrase: πρωὶ ἔννυχα λίαν (Vulg., *diluculo valde*).

[701] Stanley, *Sinai and Palestine*, p. 282.

[702] On our Lord's prayers, see Vol. I, p. 464. Contrary to their usual practice, it is not St. Luke, but St. Mark who mentions this prayer on the shore of the lake.

out delay a great project that He had formed in His mind.

When His disciples noted His absence, they at once began to search [703] for Him under the direction of Simon Peter. Upon finding Him, they said to Him: "All seek for Thee." At daybreak the multitudes had gathered to see the mighty and merciful Miracle-worker. But the Son of God did not become incarnate to reserve His blessings for a privileged district. He therefore answered His disciples by reminding them that many other children of Israel had a right to His preaching and favors: "Let us go into the neighboring towns and cities,[704] that I may preach there also the Kingdom of God; for therefore am I sent." [705] This was in truth the first of the duties which His heavenly Father had entrusted to Him: to proclaim the near founding of the Kingdom of Heaven and to lay its foundations.

At least three different times we see Christ undertaking preaching tours through Galilee. The one here mentioned by the Synoptics was the beginning of that blessed series.[706] It must have been of considerable extent, as may be inferred from the expressions by which the three Evangelists sketch the main lines of this period of intense labor. St. Matthew tells us that "Jesus went about all Galilee, teaching in their synagogues and preaching the gospel of the Kingdom, and healing all manner of sickness and every infirmity among the people." In this brief but eloquent summary we find the customary elements of Christ's ministry: preaching, which was ordinarily done in the synagogues and the principal subject of which was the Kingdom of God; and the miraculous curing

---

[703] Κατεδίωξαν αὐτον is St. Mark's forceful expression (Vulg., *prosecutus est eum*). It was a veritable "search," in a friendly sense.

[704] St. Mark here uses another particular expression, κωμοπόλεις (literally, the "village-cities"), meaning all the localities, big and little.

[705] According to St. Mark, but in the same sense: "To this purpose am I come." Cf. John 3: 2; 8: 42; 13: 3; 16: 27 f., 30; 17: 8, etc.

[706] The beginnings of the other two are mentioned by St. Matthew 9: 35, and St. Luke 8: 1.

of the sick and of those possessed.[707] Thanks to this holy combination, Jesus acted as physician both of souls and of bodies. His numerous miracles attested the truth of His doctrine and disposed men's hearts to receive His teaching. The divine word, bountifully implanted in His hearers' minds, prevented the miracles from producing a merely superficial and transient effect.

All of Galilee was evangelized. According to a detail special to the Third Gospel,[708]—if the text be authentic—our Lord's first pastoral tour brought Him far beyond the limits of that province. This journey also extended to Judea, i. e., to the whole of Palestine, as this term is sometimes employed by St. Luke.[709] We have no indication regarding the itinerary followed by the divine Missionary and His disciples. From the words, "Let us go into the neighboring towns and cities," we may infer that the places nearest Capharnaum—Bethsaida, Corozain, Magdala, Dalmanutha—were the first to be evangelized. So considerable a labor evidently required weeks, perhaps months. The language used by the Evangelists, in particular the use of the imperfect tense and of the participle in connection with the imperfect,[710] points to a rather long period.

[707] St. Mark emphasizes the latter feature.

[708] Luke 4:44. Several of the most competent authorities in textual criticism adopt the reading: "in the synagogues of Judea" (instead of Galilee). It is true that other learned critics prefer to read: Γαλιλαίας.

[709] Cf. Luke 1:5; 7:17; 23:5; Acts 10:37, etc.

[710] St. Matthew: "Jesus went about all Galilee, teaching . . . preaching . . . and healing." St. Mark and St Luke: "He was preaching . . ." St. Mark (2:1), mentioning the end of the journey, says that it occurred "after some days." This is, of course, a vague expression, but may here very well indicate a considerable interval.

II. Healing of a Leper. Jesus is Rejected by His Fellow-townsmen of Nazareth.

After the setting which we have just described according to the accounts of the three Synoptics, we are surprised to observe that they do not directly mention more than a single event of that extensive preaching tour.[711] It was a case of extraordinary healing, one that attracted special attention. At the outskirts of a city, which the sacred writers do not name, a Jew afflicted with leprosy, forgetful of the prescription ordering lepers to remain at a certain distance from passers-by,[712] or else boldly disregarding it in the hope of obtaining a cure, approached Jesus suddenly—the three Evangelists mention the feeling of surprise caused by his abrupt appearance—fell upon his knees and then prostrated himself at full length on the ground before our Lord. The prayer that came from his lips, which were disfigured by the disease, was no less humble and touching than was his attitude: "Lord, if Thou wilt, Thou canst make me clean." "To make clean" was the technical expression which the Jews were accustomed to use ever since the time of Moses to designate the curing of leprosy. That hideous disease has always been one of the most desolating plagues of Egypt, its original country, of Palestine, Syria, and other Bible lands. It has also penetrated several parts of Europe.[713] In the thirteenth chapter of Leviticus it is described at considerable length. Travelers' accounts and medical reports make all its pitiful details well known.[714]

[711] Matt. 8: 2–4; Mark 1: 40–45; Luke 5: 12–16. St. Mark's account is very lifelike and complete; St. Matthew's is merely a short summary.

[712] Four cubits, according to a regulation established by the rabbis. The cubit was 20 inches.

[713] Especially Norway. There is also a small number of lepers in France, even in Paris.

[714] See particularly H. Lenoir, *Traité Pratique et Théorique de la Lèpre*, 1886; Dom Sauton, *La Lèprose*, 1901; H. Lesêtre, article "Lèpre," in Vigouroux' *Dictionnaire de la Bible*, Vol. IV, cols. 176 f.; Fillion, *Les Miracles de N.-S. Jésus-Christ*, II, 123–130.

(1) Its physical aspect. Starting from the skin, which it attacks first, the leprosy slowly penetrates to the inner parts of the body, affecting the flesh, muscles, tendons, the nervous system, and even the bones, which it gnaws, so to speak, and partly destroys. The various portions of the body are thus invaded, one after the other, with an accompaniment of atrocious physical and moral sufferings. The lips and the nose disappear; the face and the rest of the body are covered with fetid ulcers. Finger bones, sometimes an entire foot or hand, fall off. In many cases this condition lasts for several years, as the vital organs may be only gradually involved. Thus does the leper experience a living death. What is still more horrible about it is that the disease is generally incurable, as the ancient Hebrews long ago recognized [715] and as the best medical authorities still regard it. The rabbis, who recommended specifics for all other diseases, mentioned none for leprosy.

(2) Its social aspect. As this disease was then considered contagious,[716] the Hebrew lawmaker enacted strict measures to isolate so far as possible those afflicted with it. After a close examination had recognized the existence of the dread disease in them, they were declared legally impure and were forbidden to enter any city. In order that they might be known as lepers even at a distance, they had to wear torn clothes, keep their head uncovered, wear a veil over their chin, and warn passers-by of their presence by calling out: *Tame, tame* ("Impure, impure").[717] They were thus abandoned to themselves and became outcasts of society, generally reduced to the necessity of begging, like those who may even now be seen at the gates of Jerusalem. To make their existence

[715] Cf. 4 Kings 5:7.
[716] The question is to-day a matter of discussion in the medical world. The opinion that it is contagious is the more common and seems more probable.
[717] Lev. 13:45 f.; Num. 5:2; 4 Kings 7:3; 15:5.

somewhat more tolerable, they often joined together in little bands and thus pooled their misfortunes.[718]

(3) Its religious aspect. Among the Jews, lepers were not, strictly speaking, excommunicated. They were allowed to be present at religious services in the synagogues, but on most humiliating conditions: they were obliged to be the first to enter and the last to leave and had to occupy a place set apart.[719] But the idea which was universally held as to the causes of their disease did but increase their despair. It was considered as a fact beyond question that so horrible an affliction could be nothing but a punishment from God, incurred by great sins.[720] Hence came the Hebrew word for leprosy: *tsara'at,* a blow struck by God, a divine scourge.

St. Luke, being a physician, mentions a significant detail which emphasizes the sad state of the man who cast himself at the Savior's feet. He was "full of leprosy." His feet and hands, and especially his face, bore visible traces of his disease. But he had complete confidence in Christ's almighty power. "Thou canst make me clean," *i. e.,* cure me. But would the Miracle-worker do so? The leper, though not being certain of it, hoped so. His indirect petition sought to move the heart of the kind Master and incline His will to grant the favor.

St. Mark, who of all the Evangelists is most careful to note the Savior's feelings, informs us that the favor was granted at once. The Jewish rabbis, not satisfied with increasing the rigor of the rules decreed by Moses with regard to lepers, were far from showing to these unfortunates the pity which they deserved, by virtue of being human creatures and fellow-Jews. One of these rabbis boasts of hurling stones at lepers to drive them from his path. Certain others fled or hid themselves upon perceiving lepers at a distance. Still another for-

---

[718] 4 Kings 7:3; Luke 17:12.

[719] Edersheim, *The Life and Times of Jesus,* I, 494 f.

[720] This view claims to rest on certain Biblical facts. Cf. Num. 12:9-15; 4 Kings 15:5; 2 Par. 26:19-21.

bade them to wash their faces.[721] How different from our Lord's conduct! Upon seeing and hearing the afflicted man who was imploring Him, He was filled with a deep pity,[722] which He manifested by gesture and word. "Stretching forth His hand, He touched" the leper. The law forbade such contact; but, "when charity is joined with power, it can place itself above the law," [723] on such secondary points. At the same time the Savior spoke these gentle words, an echo of the suppliant's language: "I will. Be thou cleansed." As all three Evangelists note, "immediately" the leper was healed. It was a miracle of the first order, for not only the horrible disease disappeared, but also its traces, the ravages it had already produced on its victim's face and members.

The scene now suddenly changes. Jesus, again speaking, sternly [724] addressed two orders to the man He had just cured: "See thou tell no man; but go, show thyself to the priest and offer the gift which Moses commanded for a testimony unto them." Jesus had already used the former of these injunctions, in connection with the driving out of a devil. As He well knew, it was impossible to prevent the fame of His miracles from spreading afar, because they were ordinarily performed in the presence of many witnesses.[725] Moreover, He could not wish them to remain unknown, because they were intended to accredit Him as God's envoy and to give more weight to His preaching. How, then, could He thus absolutely prevent the outburst of gratitude on the part of those to whom

[721] Edersheim, op. cit., I, 495. The celebrated Rabbi Méir said he would not consent to eat an egg bought on a street where a leper lived.

[722] Σπλαγχνισθείς, we read in the Greek text. The author of the Epistle to the Hebrews three times mentions Christ's feelings of pity. Cf. Heb. 2:17; 4:15; 5:2. See also Phil. 1:8.

[723] Wohlenberg, Das Evangelium des Markus ausgelegt, p. 70.

[724] This results from St. Mark's use of the verb ἐμβριμησάμενος (Vulg., comminatus est), which, in the language of classical authors as well as of the sacred writers, ordinarily indicates severity of language or acts. Cf. Matt. 9:30 (a passage similar to this one); Mark 14:5, etc.

[725] Matt. 4:23 f.; 8:16; 9:6; 11:4; 12:15 f., 22–25; 14:1, 21, etc.

He had granted so great favors? But He strove, so far as depended on Him, to quiet the reports of His brilliant deeds, so as to avoid any profane or political agitation. Whatever happened, His end was partly attained by the very fact that He had imposed silence, because He thus proved that He did not seek the admiration of the multitude.

In the present case, He foresaw that the leper, with his enthusiastic temperament, would try to arouse public feeling and that, upon perceiving that he was entirely healed, he would consider himself freed from carrying out the legal prescription which still remained for him to fulfil. Hence the other and no less urgent command, by which Jesus reminded him that, before resuming his place in society, he was first of all bound to have his cure certified by the priest charged with such duty in the district, and secondly to go to Jerusalem, there to offer the sacrifice prescribed by Moses: namely, for the rich, a year old ewe and two lambs; for the poor, a lamb and two doves.[726]

"Jesus quite rightly did not wish that the exercise of His miraculous powers should seem to contravene the law in its important prescriptions. But in this matter the ordinance was really urgent, since it concerned the restoring to the cured leper of his social privileges, and since this right was exclusively reserved to the priests. Furthermore, this official examination and declaration would not be without advantage for the Savior Himself: it would constitute for the priests an undeniable testimony both of His respect for the Mosiac Law, which He would soon be accused of violating, and of His Messianic office, manifestly demonstrated by His miracles."[727]

The better to show the importance which He attached to His double command, Jesus "drove him away," according to

---

[726] See Lev. 14: 1–32, for the ceremonies of the purification of lepers.
[727] Fillion, *Les Miracles de N.-S. Jésus-Christ,* II, 132–134.

the forceful term employed by St. Mark.[728] Our Lord showed as much firmness towards the leper after curing him as He had shown kindliness before the miracle. But, so far as concerned the first of the two orders, it was utterly futile. In fact, the leper no sooner departed from the place where he had met the Savior, than he began to publish abroad the miracle of his cure. However natural this indiscretion may have been, its consequences were very bothersome to our Lord, who could scarcely enter into the cities openly and in daylight without arousing in spite of Himself popular manifestations which were blamed on Him and which even partly hindered His ministry. He was therefore constrained to abandon temporarily His plans of a very active apostolate in important places. But as He was also fond of a life of retreat, He now withdrew into the solitudes of the district, where He gladly spent the time in prayer. Moreover, He did but half conceal Himself, for the multitudes succeeded in finding Him, being eager, as St. Luke tells us, "to hear and to be healed by Him of their infirmities." He received them with infinite kindness.

We judge this the proper chronological place for the insertion of a sadly characteristic incident which St. Luke, in consequence of a slight transposition, relates quite at the beginning of the public ministry,[729] but which certainly took place only somewhat later, since there is question of numerous striking miracles performed by Christ at Capharnaum a short time before. About this time the Savior made a visit to Nazareth, the humble village "where He was brought up," as the Evangelist reminds us. There more than anywhere else He would have liked to bestow His divine favors. But it is pre-

---

[728] Ἐξέβαλεν (Vulg., *ejecit*). This detail in conjunction with ἐμβριμησάμενος completes the dramatic picture.

[729] Luke 4: 16–30. In Matt. 13: 53–58 and Mark 6: 1–6, we shall find an incident closely analogous to this one, but differing from it too much for us to regard them as identical.

cisely at Nazareth, "His country," that we note the first germs of that antagonism which could scarcely fail to break out in Galilee, as previously it had in Judea, against the Person and work of the Messias.

The Sabbath following His arrival, Jesus, according to His usual practice, attended the divine services in the synagogue. This was the synagogue where He had prayed so often during His life at Nazareth. According to an apparently early tradition, that building stood to the north of the present basilica of the Annunciation, as one ascends towards the center of the town, on the site now occupied by the church of the Greek Melchites.[730]

Let us follow the principal ceremonies of these synagogue services.[731] When the *rosh hakkeneset,* or head of the synagogue, and his official assistants took their places on the platform erected in front of the holy ark, the "delegate of the community"—his Hebrew title being *shelcahh zibbur*—began the recitation of the prayers. First were the two "blessings," one of them addressed to the Creator of all things, especially of light, who watches over His work, constantly maintaining and renewing it, the other addressed to the God of Israel, who showers graces on His people, having chosen them from all nations, and who gave them His law.[732] Then was recited the Shema,[733] famous among the Jews, made up of three passages from the Pentateuch,[734] calling attention to the unity of the true God and urging the people to take constant thought of Him. After another "blessing," which praises Jehovah as

[730] *La Palestine,* by professors of Notre-Dame de France à Jérusalem, 2d ed., pp. 454 f.

[731] See Edersheim, *The Life and Times of Jesus,* I, 438–448; Schürer, *Geschichte des jüdischen Volkes,* 3d ed., II, 450–463.

[732] The text of these "blessings" grew manifestly in the course of time; but the content remained substantially the same.

[733] This name comes from its first word, meaning: "Hear."

[734] Deut. 6:4–9; 11:13–21; Num. 15:35–41. All Israel was commanded to recite twice a day, morning and evening, this sort of profession of faith; Josephus clearly alludes to it, *Ant.,* IV, viii, 13.

King of Israel and its Savior, the officiant, standing before the ark, began, in the name of all present, the beautiful prayer known in Hebrew as *Shemoneh Esreh, i. e.,* "eighteen," be- cause it was originally composed of eighteen eulogies or praises addressed to the Lord.[735] But on the Sabbath he re- cited only the first three and last three eulogies. Outwardly the other persons present took no part in these various prayers beyond responding "Amen" at the points prescribed by the ritual. During the *Shemoneh Esreh,* everyone stood up, facing toward the ark, consequently toward Jerusalem.

These prayers were followed by two readings, both taken from the Bible: the first was from the Pentateuch, that is, the Law; the second, from the Prophetical Books.[736] The former bore simply the name of *haphtarah,* "act of dismissing," [737] because it ended the liturgical use of the Bible for the services of that day. The sacred text was read verse by verse in He- brew, when taken from the Pentateuch, and was immediately translated into Aramaic by the *meturgueman* or "translator." From the Prophetical Books ordinarily three successive verses were read and these were at once translated in like manner. All present remained standing during these readings. They sat down to listen to the preaching that followed.

The day when Jesus honored the synagogue at Nazareth with His presence, everything took place as we have just said, up to the point of the reading taken from the Prophets. At that moment He stepped forward to do the reading. Had

---

[735] In its present form, it contains nineteen. It may be found in all the Jewish Euchologies, because it is *par excellence* the Israelite "prayer," as, in fact, it is often called. The twelfth Eulogy was added, at Gamaliel II's request (toward the end of the first century of our era), against the *Minnim* or "apostates," *i. e.,* against the Jews who became Christians. Several Fathers mention the fact with great indignation. Cf. St. Epiphanius, *Haer.,* XXIX, 9; St. Jerome, *Comment. in Is.* 5: 18 f., etc. In the present text, in place of *Minnim* we read *malsimim,* "ca- lumniators." See Schürer, *op. cit.,* II, 463 f.; J. Derenbourg, *Histoire de la Pales- tine,* pp. 345 f.

[736] Cf. Acts 13: 15; 15: 21.

[737] An expression analogous to our *missa.*

He received a special invitation to do so from the presiding
officer, or did He volunteer, as custom allowed? This is difficult to say. However, St. Luke's text seems rather to favor the
second hypothesis. Jesus, then, mounted the steps of the platform and stood before the reader's stand. The *hazzan* or
sacristan at once handed Him the book, or rather the "roll"
(*meguillah*), which contained the Prophecies of Isaias. The
sacred volumes of the Jews did not consist of pages arranged
and bound together like our modern books, but of rectangular
sheets of parchment, sewed end to end and rolled about one
or two wooden cylinders.[738] Having unrolled [739] the parchment, Jesus "found," *i.e.*, according to the most natural meaning of this verb, had providentially before His eyes,[740] a gentle prophecy of Isaias, who, by means of striking examples,
depicts in a realistic manner the consoling and beneficent mission of the Messias, as also His love for the lowly and afflicted. This prophecy we read in St. Luke's account in these
words: "The Spirit of the Lord is upon me. Wherefore He
hath anointed me to preach the gospel to the poor, He hath
sent me to heal the contrite of heart, to preach deliverance to
the captives, and sight to the blind, to set at liberty them that
are bruised, to preach the acceptable year of the Lord and the
day of reward." [741]

The passage is quoted somewhat freely after the Septuagint
translation.[742] But it quite well renders the sense of the original text. In mentioning "the acceptable year of the Lord," the
prophet was alluding to the great jubilee year of the Hebrews,

[738] See Fillion, *Atlas Archéologique de la Bible*, 2d ed., pl. LXVII, fig. 8; pl.
LXVIII, figs. 1, 2, 4; pl. LXX, figs. 2 and 3.

[739] Ἀναπτύξας (Vulg., *revolvit*) : the expression is very exact.

[740] The passage read by our Lord is part of the *haphtarah* of the feast of
Expiation or Great Pardon. But this does not mean that this solemnity was being
celebrated at Nazareth on that day, because the cycle of assigned Bible readings
in the synagogues is more recent than the time of Christ.

[741] Is. 61 : 1 f.

[742] The principal divergences between that and the Hebrew original are pointed
out in our commentary on St. Luke's Gospel, p. 114.

which came every fifty years and which brought solace and consolation to great numbers of the afflicted, whom it freed from slavery or restored to the possession of their property.[743] It was therefore, in this sense, a particularly blessed year. This is why it is here put forth as a type of the Messianic epoch and its many blessings.

After Jesus had read this passage in distinct, dignified tones, He rolled up the parchment and handed it back to the *hazzan*. Then He sat down in the reader's chair, thus showing that He intended to speak upon the sacred text. The moment was a solemn one, and St. Luke has sketched it in a few brief words, showing us the eyes of all attentively fixed upon Jesus.[744] The people, already impressed, wondered what this young man was going to say regarding so remarkable a text; for His fame as a speaker and miracle-worker had been brought first from Jerusalem, then from Capharnaum, but until now He had appeared in the little village only under the aspect of a quiet, modest workman. With what eloquence, what accents of piety He must have commented on this magnificent theme and how we would wish to know His complete discourse! But the Evangelist gives us only the brief introduction: "To-day your ears have heard the fulfilment of these words." [745] This means: I am the Messias, the Redeemer and Consoler foretold by Isaias. The favorable period of the Lord had therefore opened, and each one might abundantly gather its blessings.

Although St. Luke does not report our Lord's instruction, he dramatically describes the effect it produced on those present. He says: "All gave testimony to Him; [746] and they won-

---

[743] See Lev. 25 : 8–55.

[744] The verb ἀτενίζω signifies a penetrating look, and the expression ἦσαν ἀτενίζοντες implies the prolongation of that look. For a little picture of a like kind, see Acts 6 : 15.

[745] It might be translated: "To-day is fulfilled this word which you have just heard."

[746] A testimony altogether favorable.

dered at the words of grace that proceeded from His mouth."
The expression, "words of grace," as in other passages of
Scripture,[747] means beautiful, gracious words, pleasant to hear
because of their substance as well as their form. Our Lord's
fellow-townsmen were able to appreciate them. First-class
documents—the Gospels, the Acts of the Apostles, the writings of Philo and Josephus—inform us that these people had
a taste for preaching and that among them were not a few
popular orators.[748] These latter, it is true, on more than one
occasion, when delivering their speeches, were less concerned
with the sanctification of their hearers than with the promotion of their own personal fame.

Unfortunately the people of Nazareth seem to have been
carried away rather by the outer charm of Christ's words
than by the thoughts expressed. Their own remarks tell us
what most impressed them as they were enraptured by the
speaker's words. When the Savior finished, they began to
exchange their impressions, saying one to another: "Is not
this the son of Joseph?" They could not understand how He
whom they regarded—so well had the virginal secret been
kept—as the son of a lowly carpenter and who had received
no special education, no scholarly training, could speak with
so much gracefulness and distinction. This detail betrays an
unpardonable light-mindedness.[749]

Did Christ, by virtue of His divine knowledge, read these
superficial comments in their hearts, or were they revealed
to Him by His hearing some of their conversation? However
that may be, He calmly replied to their curious reflections,
saying: "Doubtless, you will say to Me this similitude: Physician, heal Thyself. As great things as we have heard done

[747] Ps. 44: 3; Eccles. 10: 12; Ecclu. 21: 19; Col. 4: 6.

[748] Edersheim, *The Life and Times of Jesus*, I, 446.

[749] Such was St. Augustine before his conversion, letting himself be delighted
by the "suavity" of St. Ambrose's preaching, but remaining indifferent to its
substance, as he himself relates, *Expos. in Ezech.*, XXXIII, 32.

in Capharnaum, do also here in Thy own country." The sa-
tirical proverb which our Lord places on the lips of His towns-
men by way of objection, was then current in various forms
among the Greeks and Romans as well as among the Jews.[750]
It was applied to those who, while assuming to succor others,
did themselves need to have others come to their aid. Now, in
a certain sense, Jesus had just presented Himself as a physician able to cure all diseases. The thought is this: If Thou art
really the Savior of Israel, begin by improving Thy own condition; for all of us here know its obscurity and poverty. For
this purpose, do Thou here before our eyes perform miracles
like to those Thou didst perform at Capharnaum; we will then
be convinced.

After a short pause, Jesus continued: "Amen I say to you,
no prophet is accepted in his own country. In truth I say to
you, there were many widows in the days of Elias in Israel,
when heaven was shut up three years and six months, when
there was a great famine throughout all the earth. And to
none of them was Elias sent, but to Sarepta [751] of Sidon, to
a widow woman. And there were many lepers in Israel in the
time of Eliseus the prophet, and none of them was cleansed
but Naaman the Syrian."

Jesus answers the proverb which had been advanced by way
of objection to Him, by citing another proverb, admirably
suited to the circumstances.[752] He is not surprised at His
countrymen's feelings towards Him. "Familiarity breeds contempt." When anyone has lived in intimate association with a

---

[750] In the Fragments of Euripides (Fr. 247): "A physician for others, and he
himself covered with sores." Ovid, *De Re Amat.*, 216: "*Et fateor, medicus turpiter
aeger eram.*" Cf. Cicero, *Epist. ad Divers.*, IV, 5: "Physician, cure thy lameness,"
said the rabbis (*Tanchum*, IV, 2, and *Bereshit rabba*, 23). According to Wünsche,
Neue Beiträge, p. 426, the Jews still frequently say: *Rofe, velo lo*, "Physician, and
not for himself."

[751] To-day, *Surafend*, on the Mediterranean coast, 22 miles south of Sidon.

[752] St. Matthew, 13:57, and St. Mark, 6:4, also quote it, on the occasion of another visit of Jesus to Nazareth. See also John 4:44.

great person, even a great prophet, as Jeremias learned to his cost,[753] such a one is ordinarily less apt and prompt to recognize the great man's qualities. Then Jesus replied to the demand for miracles, which had been made by the people of Nazareth. No, He will perform none in their midst, and He justifies His refusal by examples taken from the history of two illustrious prophets of olden times, Elias[754] and Eliseus,[755] who, under circumstances similar to His, had performed none for their own countrymen. The Messias' blessings must be the reward of faith; they were not dependent on purely geographical circumstances.

Although Jesus did not apply these two examples directly to His fellow-townsmen, the allusion was altogether too evident not to be understood. Are we less worthy, said they to one another, than the pagan woman of Sarepta and Naaman the leper? The thought filled those violent and passionate Galileans with fury. Two or three voices shouted cries of death against Him who was in their eyes nothing more than a bold trouble-maker. The whole crowd rallied to this bloody plan, and brutal hands laid hold on Christ. They retained just enough self-control not to execute the horrible crime on the spot, an outrage which would have recalled the judicial murder of the deacon Stephen by an infuriated mob.[756] These exasperated fanatics dragged the Savior out of the synagogue, then out of the town. Upon reaching "the brow of the hill whereon their city was built," they prepared to hurl their victim down from that height. But Jesus, freeing Himself from their hands, passed through their midst, calmly and majestically, without anyone daring to seize Him again and stop

[753] Jer. 11 : 21 ; 12 : 6.
[754] 3 Kings 17 : 8–16.
[755] 4 Kings 5 : 2–14.
[756] Acts 7 : 57. The martyrdom of St. James the Less occurred at Jerusalem under similar conditions. Cf. Josephus, *Ant.*, XX, ix, 1. St. John, 8 : 59 and 10 : 31, cites two attempts by the Jews to stone our Lord. In acting thus, they thought to show a zeal for the Mosaic religion.

Him. *Ibat*, "He went His way": in this one word the Evangelist gives us a whole picture.

What happened? Are we to suppose, as many authors do, that Christ's dignified bearing, the nobility of His features and of His look, sufficed of themselves to fill these maddened people with fear? We think not; for, as various Rationalist commentators rightly acknowledge,[757] it is evident that St. Luke here intends to relate a genuine miracle. But some of our early exegetes went too far when they said that Jesus instantly struck with blindness or paralysis those who were on the point of killing Him. The account implies nothing of the sort. There was a miracle—what is called a moral miracle, which consisted in the victory won by Jesus' will over that of his enemies, reducing the latter to powerlessness. The driving of the sellers out of the Temple belongs to this category of miracles, and several other examples are mentioned by the Evangelists.[758]

According to a local tradition, the hill from which the Jews were going to hurl Christ, after dragging Him out of the synagogue, is at the end of the ravine which descends from Nazareth straight south towards the great plain of Esdraelon. It is the perpendicular cliff which overhangs this ravine on the east and which may be seen from a considerable distance by one coming from Djenin or Caiffa. [759] This cliff, which is called "Mount of the Precipitation," dominates the plain from a height of about 700 feet. Although it was well suited for the summary execution which the enemies of Christ intended, yet it has the serious inconvenience of being located more than two miles from Nazareth and of being difficult of access in many places. The Gospel text supposes rather that the precipice was quite close to the town, and the perpendicu-

---

[757] *V. g.*, H. J. Holtzmann, J. Weiss, Loisy.

[758] On this subject, see Fillion, *Les Miracles de N.-S. Jésus-Christ*, I, 35 f.; II, 311–334.

[759] *La Palestine*, by professors of N.-D. de France à Jérusalem, 2d ed., p. 457.

lar cliff, sixty-five feet high, to be seen near the church of the Maronites, at the northwestern end of Nazareth, may well have been the theater of the final scene, so well described by St. Luke.[760]

[760] Stanley, *Sinai and Palestine*, p. 367; Robinson, *Researches in Palestine*, II, 329 f. That, however, is only a hypothesis. Moreover, there is no lack of precipices at Nazareth and in its immediate neighborhood.

CHAPTER III

The Beginning of Christ's Conflict With the Pharisees

FROM the outset of His public life, Christ met with opposition, at first from the priestly caste,[761] then from the Pharisees.[762] Up to this point of the narrative, everything succeeded according to His wishes in Galilee. But there, too, the strife was about to begin between Him and the Pharisaic sect. We are now going to study the first skirmishes of that conflict, which ends only with the death of the Savior, apparently vanquished, but in reality victorious. The curing of a paralytic and the calling of St. Matthew furnish the opportunity eagerly sought by the Pharisees for openly declaring themselves His adversaries.

I. Curing of a Paralytic at Capharnaum [763]

After Christ's great preaching tour through Galilee, He returned to Capharnaum, "His own city," as St. Matthew calls it on this occasion. The report of His return at once spread abroad, and the house which served Him habitually as a residence (probably that of Simon Peter, as we said above [764]) was soon invaded by such a large crowd that the very entrance was blocked, so packed was it with people. The rooms of the ground floor were all filled, as also the little

761 John 2: 13–20.

762 John 4: 1–3.

763 Matt. 9: 1–8; Mark 2: 1–12; Luke 5: 17–26. St. Matthew's account is very brief; St. Mark and St. Luke supply concrete and picturesque details.

764 In St. Mark we read: ἐν οἴκῳ, without the article (εἰς οἶκον, according to another reading).

courtyard located in front of the house and separated from the street by a wall, and even the street itself, on which the courtyard gate opened. This large gathering recalls that of a certain Sabbath when Peter's house witnessed a procession of the sick and infirm, whom the Master restored to health. Since on that occasion He had left immediately afterwards and the people had been long deprived of His blessed presence, they feared lest He would do the same thing this time too. Therefore they hastened to come to Him.

The Savior's tireless zeal took advantage of this excellent opportunity to speak "the word," [765] *i. e.,* the word *par excellence,* the gospel, to all those eager listeners. St. Luke here inserts another characteristic detail: "And the power of the Lord [the power of God Himself] was to heal them." These words mean that at that period, perhaps at that very hour, numerous miracles were performed by Jesus, who possessed an almighty divine power to be used at His pleasure. This general expression prepares the reader for the great miracle about to follow. St. Luke also mentions a further significant detail. In the front rank of those crowding around Jesus, the Evangelist shows us, seated not far from the Master, "Pharisees and doctors of the law sitting by, that were come out of every town of Galilee and Judea," and even "from Jerusalem," their great center. Evidently they were present with hostile intent, for the purpose of watching Christ's conduct and teaching, because His fame, ever increasing throughout Palestine, had stirred up and revived their base jealousy.

The august speaker was suddenly interrupted by an extraordinary occurrence, which St. Mark and St. Luke relate in dramatic style. Four men carrying a paralytic, who was lying on a poor cot,[766] appeared before the doorway of the house.

---

[765] Τὸν λόγον, says St. Mark.

[766] Throughout the account, St. Mark uses the Greek word κράβαττος, from which the Latins formed *grabatus.* St. Matthew says κλίνη, "bed." In St. Luke κλίνη alternates with the diminutive κλινίδιον, "little bed." The *grabatus* was the

They saw at once that, encumbered by their burden, they would be unable to pass through the densely packed throng. At first they must have been sorely disappointed. But their earnest desire, or rather their strong purpose, to reach Jesus suggested a means of overcoming the difficulty. Still carrying the bed and the sick man, they mounted a ladder, or the outside stairs with which the houses in Palestine are usually provided,[767] to the flat roof.[768] In the Orient the roofs of dwellings are generally of very light construction, consisting of reeds or branches in place of laths, a coating of pounded clay, and at times also some tiles, as in the present case. Those carrying the sick man had only to remove a number of tiles and some of the clay and reeds, in order to form an opening large enough to let the sick man and his cot pass through. The task was simple, and whatever damage was done could be easily repaired. Through the gaping hole thus made, they let down their precious burden by means of ropes, into the midst of the gathering, to the very side of Christ.[769]

At this sight, what must have been the emotion of all present! Unbelief alone displeased the Savior. A suppliant's faith never left Him unmoved, and that manifested on this occasion was so intense, so touching, that we might almost call it heroic. There was the undaunted faith of the men carrying the cot. There was also the faith of the sick man, who consented to the procedure and patiently endured the rude jolts which it must have caused him. Neither they nor the paralytic

bed of the poor and was composed of a simple network of cords stretched on a wooden or iron frame and supporting a mattress. See A. Rich, *Dictionary of Roman and Greek Antiquities,* p. 319.

[767] Cf. Mark 13 : 15; Fillion, *Atlas Archéologique de la Bible,* 2d ed., pl. XII, figs. 3, 10.

[768] Cicero, *In M. Anton. Orat. Philipp.,* II, 18, 45, mentions an undertaking of the same sort.

[769] Cf. Tristram, *Eastern Customs,* pp. 34 f. Delitzsch, *Ein Tag in Kapernaum,* pp. 40–46, and Edersheim, *Life and Times of Jesus.* I, 501–504, offer different and interesting explanations, which, however, fail to take fully into account all the details of the Gospel narratives.

wanted to lose an opportunity which might never return. The firm confidence the three Evangelists mention by one and same expression: "Jesus, seeing their faith." Without even giving the paralytic time to make his request, which every detail of the scene clearly evinced, Jesus said to him with utmost kindness: "Be of good heart, son,[770] thy sins are forgiven thee."

Why this formula of absolution at the time when an immediate miracle of healing was expected? Our Lord, when later consulted by His Apostles,[771] denied the assertion of the rabbis of that time that every physical or moral affliction is a punishment for sin, and that no one could be freed of a sickness until God pardoned the faults which occasioned it.[772] But the Divine Master was then stating a general principle, while in the present case there is question of a particular fact. There certainly are cases where a guilty life is directly punished by bodily infirmity, and it is a fact of experience that paralysis in particular has more than once been the sad result of immorality.[773] In forgiving the sins of the sick man just brought to Him under such extraordinary circumstances, Jesus made known that they had been the real cause of his disease. He thus reassured him, for this unfortunate sufferer was aware of his moral miseries and he must have feared that because of them he would not be able to obtain his cure, even through an intermediary so powerful as Jesus. For that reason the Savior first of all attacked the inner evil and thus suppressed the cause before removing the effect. In this way

---

[770] In place of this comforting and reassuring appellation, St. Luke makes use of a general term: ἄνθρωπε, "man."

[771] John 9 : 1–3.

[772] The tractate *Nedarim*, 41, a. See Wünsche, *Neue Beiträge*, pp. 120 f.

[773] Cf. John 5 : 14. On this disease, see Fillion, *Les Miracles de N.-S. Jésus-Christ*, II, 142–144. St. Matthew and St. Mark designate the paralytic of Capharnaum by the popular term, παραλυτικός. St. Luke, following his usual custom, uses a medical term, παραλελυμένος. Cf. Hobbart, *The Medical Language of St. Luke*, p. 6; Harnack, *Lukas der Arzt*, pp. 127, 129.

He bestowed a double favor, purifying the soul before healing the body.

The words of Christ formed the heart of the incident. They immediately created the conflict to which we referred above. Upon hearing these words, the Scribes and Pharisees, who were present at the scene as veritable spies, were scandalized and at once assumed a hostile attitude towards Jesus. "Why doth this man [774] speak thus?" they say to one another; "He blasphemeth. Who can forgive sins, but God only?" Of a truth, in the Bible [775] the remission of sins is always looked upon as a divine prerogative, and no formula of absolution exists in Judaism, which does not recognize in any man, howsoever great or holy, the power of purifying sinful souls. But had not Jesus sufficiently proved that He was above human conditions? He was not encroaching upon the rights of God; this fact He at once proceeded to prove. "Knowing [776] in His spirit" (*i. e.,* in a wholly supernatural manner, without the aid of the senses) the malevolent judgment which the Scribes and Pharisees had formed about Him, He said to them, before they could express their impressions to one another: "Why do you think evil in your hearts? Which is easier to say to the sick of the palsy: Thy sins are forgiven thee; or to say: Arise, take up thy bed, and walk?"

The alternative was proposed in the simplest fashion. It left the unjust accusers no means of escape. In themselves, the two things are equally easy, if the only question is that of pronouncing the words. They are extremely difficult, if they are to be carried out; and in this case, the forgiveness of sins would present a special difficulty. It would be a simple matter for an impostor to attribute to himself in words the power

---

[774] The pronoun οὗτος (Vulg., *hic*), quoted by the three Evangelists, is full of contempt.

[775] Ex. 34:7; Is. 43:25; 44:22, etc.

[776] The participle ἐπιγνούς, used by St. Mark and St. Luke, indicates a full knowledge.

of forgiving sins: but who would venture, without feeling himself invested with a higher power, to declare that with a word he could heal bodily diseases, in particular a case of paralysis? [777] The argument was decisive, irrefutable. The Pharisees were reduced to humiliating silence. Jesus, after vainly waiting for them to reply, said: "That you may know that the Son of Man hath power on earth to forgive sins (He saith to the sick of the palsy), I say to thee: Arise, take up thy bed, and go into thy house." [778] A miracle so plainly and solemnly announced, if really accomplished, at once amounts to a proof. The words of the "Son of Man" were not uttered in vain, for, in obedience to Christ's threefold command, the paralytic suddenly rose up, took his bed on his shoulders, and went home, glorifying God. The wretched cot that had been the sign of his infirmity thus became the proof of his cure.

In the presence of the supernatural contemplated so close at hand, the witnesses of the miracle were at first filled with religious awe. But then rising to a feeling of a higher order, they voiced their wonderment, which they showed, like the paralytic, by glorifying God, who, as St. Matthew adds, "gave such power to men" in the person of His Christ. "We have seen wonderful things to-day," they said. As for the Scribes and Pharisees, the Evangelists do not trouble themselves about them. But we can easily imagine the feelings of hatred which their defeat stirred in their breasts. They will not forget, they will not forgive. The strife is on, and they will cease their attacks only on the day of seeming victory.

---

[777] As St. Jerome remarks, *Comment. in Matth.*, 4: 5, "*inter dicere et facere, multa distantia est; utrum sint paralytico peccata dimissa, solus noverat, qui faciebat.*"

[778] It is remarkable that these words of our Lord have been recorded in identical language by the three Synoptics, including the extraordinary parenthesis which interrupts them for a moment.

II. The Calling of Levi the Publican

After the great miracle in which He so well combined logic and action, Jesus left the house where the prodigy had taken place. He went forth from the city and turned toward the shore of the lake. There He was joined by a considerable multitude, to whom, according to His practice, He broke the bread of the word. After finishing His discourse, He continued walking along the shore.

The city of Capharnaum, by the very fact of its location on one of the busiest trade routes of the world, was the depositary and transportation center of an enormous quantity of merchandise carried from the Orient to the West, and vice versa. But nothing passed free. At this place, as at Jericho, there was an important custom house, maintained by a large number of publicans or taxgatherers. One of these officials was then sitting in his office, which perhaps was nothing more than a table placed under the shelter of a few boards. From there he was watching over the coming and going on the highway and in the harbor. St. Mark and St. Luke call him Levi.[779] But he is better known by the name of Matthew, as he is called in the First Gospel.[780] Levi was his Jewish name; Matthew or Mattai (*i. e.,* "gift of God"), probably the Christian name given him by Christ. Or perchance, like many other Jews, he had two names.

Jesus said to him: "Follow Me," thus inviting him to become His disciple in a strict sense. It was by these same words that Peter and Andrew, James and John, had heard the Sav-

---

[779] St. Mark adds that he was the son of Alpheus, but of an Alpheus whom we must not confuse with the father of St. James the Less (Matt. 10: 3; Mark 3: 18; Luke 6: 15; Acts 1: 13).

[780] Matt. 9: 9. The identity of Levi and St. Matthew was denied in very early times by the Gnostic Heracleon and by Origen, and frequently since then, but always without sound reasons.

ior's call, while they were in the midst of their ordinary duties. Exactly the same result was produced: "Leaving all things, he rose up and followed Him." Here again the sacrifice was immediate and complete, with this difference that the fishermen could, if occasion required, take up their occupation again, whereas it would be practically impossible for a publican to return to his post after thus abandoning it. But this call by Christ and this generous sacrifice by Levi had evidently been prepared for. It was not the first time that the Master and the new disciple had met in that city of Capharnaum, where our Lord returned from time to time. Even had the publican's conversion been the work of a moment, this psychological phenomenon would be in perfect agreement with the astounding power of attraction which Jesus exercised over minds and hearts.[781]

What may well amaze us more is to see that Christ feared not to choose and destine to the ranks of His intimate disciples and soon after to the ranks of His Apostles, a man who belonged to a corporation so justly held in disrepute,[782] the members of which were looked upon as public sinners. But Jesus had the holy daring, whenever He judged it useful for His work, to brave the prejudices of His fellow-Jews. In this instance we shall even hear Him justify His conduct.[783]

Shortly after this brief scene on the lake shore, Levi gave a banquet at his house in honor of his new Master. To this dinner he invited his former colleagues and a number of his friends in order to bid them farewell. For the Pharisees of Capharnaum this was a welcome opportunity to show their animosity toward Jesus. In fact, in their eyes, to eat at the

---

[781] See St. Jerome, *Comment. in Matth.*, 9:9.

[782] See Vol. I, p. 154.

[783] Matt. 5:46 f.; 11:19; 18:17; 21:31 f.; Luke 3:12; 7:29, 34; 15:1 f.; 18:9-14; 19:7, etc. A hundred and fifty years later, Celsus grossly insulted Christianity, with reference to the calling of Levi the publican. Cf. Origen, *Contra Celsum*, I, 62.

same table with publicans and other public sinners [784] constituted a veritable scandal, the more so as, according to Eastern
custom, participation in the same meal does of itself establish
close relations.[785] Nevertheless they did not venture to reveal
their sentiments directly to Christ, for they had already
learned to dread His crushing repartees. Therefore they
sought out His disciples and asked them: "Why doth your
Master eat and drink with publicans and sinners?"

The Savior, overhearing the insidious question, Himself
undertook to answer it: "They that are in health need not
a physician, but they that are ill. Go then and learn what this
meaneth: I will have mercy and not sacrifice. For I am come
not to call the just, but sinners."

This little apology is composed of three parts: a popular
maxim, a text from the Old Testament, and a reason *ex con-
venientia.* The proverb, which is to be found with interesting
variations in classical literatures, points to a fact of daily
experience. Says Pausanias in the same strain: "Physicians
are not accustomed to remain at the side of those who are
in health, but at the side of the sick." [786] If those at table
with Jesus were sinners, was that not the proper place for
Him, inasmuch as He is the Physician of souls? [787] The

---

[784] The three Evangelists distinguish two categories of guests on this occasion.
St. Matthew and St. Mark: "publicans and sinners"; St. Luke: "publicans and
others." The word "sinners" must here be understood from the Pharisaic point of
view. Cf. Matt. 11 : 19, and Luke 15 : 1, where these two expressions are likewise
associated. But it may also mean sinners properly so called, or at least men who
were easy-going with regard to many burdensome precepts.

[785] It was for this reason that strict observers of the Mosaic Law, even after
conversion to Christianity, were extremely sensitive on this subject. Cf. Acts 11 : 3;
Gal. 2 : 12. The rabbis forbade their disciples to take meals in company with the
"people of the soil," *i. e.,* the uninstructed common people (*Berakhoth,* 43, 2); all
the more so with men of questionable conduct.

[786] Plutarch, *Apophtegm. Lacon.,* 230. Cf. Dio Cassius, *Or.,* VIII, 8; Jülicher,
Gleichnisreden Jesu, II, 176 f.

[787] St. Augustine, *Serm.* 87: "*Jacet toto orbe terrarum, ab oriente usque ad
occidentem, grandis aegrotus; ad sanandum grandem aegrotum descendit omnipo-
tens medicus.*" Cf. St. Justin, *Apol.,* I, 15.

words, "I will have mercy and not sacrifice," are quoted from a prophecy of Osee.[788] In a paradoxical form it expresses the thought that Jesus much better corresponded with God's designs by acting mercifully toward sinners than by showing Himself harsh and pitiless with them, after the manner of the Scribes and Pharisees. The bloody sacrifices were necessary, since the law required them; but the God of Israel much preferred the practice of mercy towards one's neighbor, even if the latter were sinful. Lastly, did not the office of Messias consist in converting and saving sinners? Jesus develops this idea at a later date, when He explains the parable of the lost sheep.[789]

At that time there were at Capharnaum some disciples of John the Baptist, who, in imitation of the austerity of his life, practiced frequent fasting and made use of long prayer formulas at regular hours. The Pharisees also, and pious Israelites in general, fasted often, as we learn from the Gospels[790] and the Talmud.[791] They ordinarily did so on Mondays and Thursdays because, according to tradition, it was on those days that Moses ascended Sinai (a Thursday) and came down therefrom (Monday). Although the Mosaic legislation imposed on the Hebrews only a single fastday every year, for the feast of the Great Pardon (Yom Kippur) or Expiation,[792] this practice of penance and mourning was but too natural not to recommend itself as a good work to souls with faith. And so we find mention made of it again and again in

[788] Osee 6:6. The expression introducing the text, "Go and learn," is often used by the rabbis.

[789] Matt. 18:10-14; Luke 15:1-7.

[790] Matt. 6:16 f.; Luke 2:37; 18:12.

[791] See Schürer, Geschichte des jüdischen Volkes, 4th ed., II, 489-491; III, 104 f., 116 f.

[792] In September or October. Cf. Lev. 16:29-31; 23:27-32; Num. 29:7; Acts 27:9. Later on, others were introduced in memory of several painful happenings that occurred at the time of the destruction of Jerusalem by the Chaldeans. See Nowack, Lehrbuch der hebr. Archäologie, II, 201 f.

the Old Testament writings.[793] Jesus had no thought of abolishing the custom. The early Church preserved it and even imposed it on all Christians.[794]

As St. Mark tells us, the day of Levi's banquet coincided with one of the fastdays of the precursor's disciples and the Pharisees. The contrast was but the more striking, and the moment was well chosen to draw attention to it. The disciples of John,[795] coming up to the Savior, asked Him: "Why do we and the Pharisees fast often, but Thy disciples do not fast?" Was this question prompted by ill-will, in the hope of embarrassing our Lord? Probably it was, because the Baptist's disciples were already animated by feelings of jealousy toward Him.[796] This hypothesis seems to be confirmed by the presence of the Pharisees.

Thus questioned because He was considered responsible for His disciples' conduct, Jesus, in words both familiar and striking, gives all the explanation that could be desired. First He replies: "Can you make the children of the bridegroom fast, whilst the bridegroom is with them? But the days will come when the bridegroom shall be taken away from them, then shall they fast in those days."

This first part of His reply at once elucidates the whole question. The forceful and charming figure, which He takes from the marriage ceremonies of the Jews, was the more appropriate since only recently the Baptist himself had used it in the presence of several of his own disciples, comparing the Messias to a mystical spouse coming down from Heaven to celebrate His nuptials with the Church.[797] The friends of the bridegroom are, of course, the young men whom Jesus had at-

---

[793] 1 Kings 31:13; 2 Kings 12:16; Dan. 10:2; Joel 1:14; 2:12, 15, etc.

[794] Acts 13:2 f.; Tertullian, *De Jejunio*, II; *Constitut. Apost.*, V, 18.

[795] According to St. Mark's account, they seem to have presented themselves in company with some Pharisees.

[796] John 3:26.

[797] John 3:29–31.

tached to His Person, for it will be their principal duty to bring pure and holy souls to Him, souls that will be gathered to form His Church, His heavenly spouse.[798] That was precisely the time of the nuptials, consequently a time of festivity and joy. Fasting, on the contrary, is a manifestation of sadness and grief. Who, without violating the fitness of things, would think of condemning to fasting the people of the marriage feast while the nuptial solemnities lasted? Hence it follows that it would be unreasonable to impose fasting, supererogatory fasting, upon Christ's disciples so long as He, the Divine Spouse, was celebrating in their company the festivities of His marriage. But, continues the Divine Master, the days of His presence in their midst are numbered. It will not be long before He will be violently taken away,[799] and "then" —Jesus emphasized this adverb—they will be able to fast without any impropriety. This new allusion to Christ's Passion and death is striking, especially associated as it here is with the joyous comparison of the marriage. But even at the period of His most brilliant successes, Jesus constantly had before His eyes what He called His "hour."

The argument was the more peremptory as the Savior nowise found fault with the fasting of the Pharisees and of the Baptist's disciples. Only one thing He asked, liberty for His own followers in a matter which was, moreover, quite secondary. He then proceeded to corroborate His thesis by other considerations, presented in the form of little parables. They have the force of veritable principles. Continuing He said: "No man seweth a piece of raw cloth [800] to an old garment; otherwise the new piecing taketh away from the old, and

---

[798] 2 Cor. 11 : 2.

[799] The idea of violence is clearly affirmed by the Greek verb ἀπαρθῇ (Vulg., auferetur, ablatus fuerit).

[800] The adjective ἄγναφος (Vulg., rudis) literally refers to cloth that has not passed through a fuller's hands and is consequently stiff. When it shrinks, especially in being washed, it will produce the accident referred to.

there is made a greater rent.[801] And no man putteth new wine
into old bottles; otherwise the new wine will burst the bottles,
and both the wine will be spilled and the bottles will be lost.
But new wine must be put into new bottles; and both are preserved. And no man drinking old, hath presently a mind to
new; for he saith: The old is better."

What simplicity, and at the same time what force of language! Jesus gladly takes His comparisons from the lowliest
usages of domestic life, for the purpose of expressing lofty
truths. This time He justifies His disciples' conduct by an argument drawn from the very nature of the institution to which
they will thenceforth belong. What intelligent housewife
would put into practice the costly and ridiculous sort of mending so well described? What man, mindful of his interests,
would put new, still fermenting wine into old skin bottles [802]
which have shrunken by use and would be unable to withstand
the pressure generated by fermentation? Literally as well as
figuratively, worn-out cloth and new, unprepared cloth, old
skin bottles and new wine, cannot well go together. They are
heterogeneous things, which it would be a mistake to join
in close association.

A new spirit demands new forms. The religious spirit particularly is loath to be hindered in its force of expansion,
which is especially great. If it would be disastrous for the
old Judaism to try to rejuvenate itself by patching here and
there with pieces of new cloth, cut from the religion of Jesus, it

[801] We read in St. Luke, with a variant that still more emphasizes the thought:
"No man putteth a piece from a new garment upon an old garment; otherwise he
both rendeth the new, and the piece taken from the new agreeth not with the old."
In the case thus presented, not to mention the inelegance of such a patch, there
would be a double loss, a double foolishness, since one would spoil not only a
corner of a piece of new cloth, but a new garment, by cutting out a piece for the
repair of the old garment.

[802] In the Biblical East, as receptacles for water, wine, oil, and other liquids,
the people have always used leather bottles, of various sizes, which are frequently
represented on ancient monuments. See Fillion, *Atlas Archéologique de la Bible*,
pl. XX, figs. 10, 13, 14, 15, 17.

would likewise have been so for the latter to seek confine itself, if only for a time, in the superannuated forms of Mosa-
ism. Therefore let the Pharisees and the precursor's disciples
give themselves to many fasts, if that suits them. The disciples of Christ have something better to do, and their Master
will not ingraft His Church upon the half decayed trunk of
the Judaism of the Scribes, which could not possibly be rejuvenated. The worn-out garments and the old bottles well represent the theocracy of the Old Covenant and especially that
collection of traditions and stern practices which they wished
to impose on our Lord and His disciples. Likewise new cloth
and new wine are a very expressive figure of the new, generous spirit which the gospel was to bring to the world. A mixture of the two religions, of the two spirits, was impossible,
and would have produced the most lamentable consequences.
This fact is to be seen after the Savior's death, when the Juda-
izers caused a dangerous schism in the primitive Church under the pretext of patching the religion of Sinai with pieces
taken from Christianity.

The third comparison, "No man drinking old [wine], hath
presently a mind to new," [803] fundamentally expresses the
same truth. Just as a man finds it harder to tolerate the sharp-
ness of new wine if he is accustomed to drinking old wine,
which is mellower and more agreeable to the palate,[804] so he
who from childhood is accustomed to the ancient customs or
to a religious system of a particular kind, with difficulty habit-
uates himself to a new sort of life, and with greater difficulty
to a new religion. The old wine here symbolizes Judaism, the
new wine is a figure of Christianity. Might one not say that in
this instance Jesus gently excuses His adversaries' conduct, allowing them time to become accustomed to the new wine of the
gospel? At any rate, what an admirable method of teaching
His is!

[803] St. Luke is the only one to mention this.
[804] Ecclu. 9 : 15.

THIRD PERIOD

From the Second to the Third Pasch of Our Lord's Public Life

CHAPTER I

From the Second Pasch to the Choosing of the Apostles

I. Jesus Enters into Conflict with the Jewish Authorities at Jerusalem, on the Occasion of a Miracle Performed on the Sabbath [805]

NOTWITHSTANDING its exceptional importance, this event is passed over in silence by the Synoptics, since the Savior's ministry in Jerusalem and Judea was outside their scope. But, as it forms an essential part of Christ's manifestation before the religious leaders of Judaism, it receives all proper emphasis in the Fourth Gospel. The current of opposition which we saw beginning in Galilee, existed long before in the Jewish capital, and St. John refers to it more than once.[806] It was about to develop there suddenly and to assume a formidable appearance. Jerusalem becomes a center of unbelief in the Messias and of hateful resistance to Him, with the element hostile to Him enjoying considerable power. Faith and love, it is true, also grow without pause during this whole period and console the heart of Christ, who profits by every opportunity to reveal Himself to His compatriots. The account contains not the least allusion to Christ's disciples. We may well suppose that He came to Jerusalem without them, or that they were not with Him during the scenes taking place at Bethesda and in the porticoes of the Temple.

At the beginning of his narrative the Evangelist mentions

[805] John 5: 1-47.
[806] John 1: 11; 2: 14-25; 3: 18 f., 26; 4: 1-3, 44.

the circumstances of time and place. He says: "After these things was a festival day of the Jews,[807] and Jesus went up to Jerusalem." What was this festival? It is impossible to say with certainty, for St. John's expression leaves its identity undecided, and the succeeding part of the account contains no indication which helps to make the hint more precise. And so, ever since the earliest times, commentators have failed to agree on this point. They have identified it with every one of the great Jewish religious feasts: some with the Pasch, following Tatian, St. Irenaeus, and Eusebius of Caesarea; others with Pentecost, as did St. John Chrysostom and St. Cyril of Alexandria; still others with the feast of Purin or "Lots," instituted in memory of the great peril from which the Jews escaped in Persia, thanks to Queen Esther; [808] others again with the feast of Tabernacles. It is difficult to make a well founded decision. Everything considered, particularly the testimony of St. Irenaeus, who through St. Polycarp was so closely connected with St. John, we incline to the view that the feast here referred to was the Pasch, consequently the second Pasch of our Lord's public life.[809] This hypothesis would have St. John mentioning two Paschal festivals right after each other, since at the beginning of the next chapter he speaks of another in explicit terms.[810] Thus he would have passed over in silence a whole year of Christ's life. This, of course, presents a difficulty, not however an impossibility, because the author of the Fourth Gospel purposed omitting the Galilean ministry. It is well to note also that a little further on we see the Savior in Galilee surrounded by a large and enthusiastic multitude. This fact presupposes that a considerable

[807] According to another reading, which has equally good authority, we read with the article: "the festival day of the Jews."

[808] Esther 9: 17–20. It was celebrated in the month of March.

[809] For a discussion of these various opinions, see Fillion, L'Évangile de S. Jean, Introd. Critiq. et Commentaires, pp. 91–93; Knabenbauer, Comment. in Evang. sec. Joannem, pp. 186 f.

[810] John 6: 4.

time had passed since the beginning of His public life.[811]

St. John, continuing his account, briefly describes the place that was the scene of one of the Savior's great miracles: "There is at Jerusalem, near the Sheep Gate, a pond which in Hebrew is named Bethesda, "having five porches." [812] "Bethesda," or more exactly *Beithhesda,* "House of Charity," was, in the Aramaic idiom, a most appropriate name for a building whose purpose was to solace human afflictions.[813] The Sheep Gate, near which the pond was located, is spoken of several times in the Book of Nehemias.[814] Probably it was so called because through it were brought into the city and the Temple courts the large number of sheep that had been fattened on the eastern plains and were to serve either as food or for the sacrifices. The gate was situated northeast of the ramparts, almost on the site of the present St. Stephen's Gate.[815] According to information furnished by St. Cyril of Jerusalem,[816] the five porches built above the pond formed a quadrilateral, with one transverse porch connecting two of the sides.[817] This basin, which was destined to become celebrated in our Lord's history, has been long but mistakenly identified with the vast reservoir called Birket Israin,[818] which is now dry. Excavations, begun in 1871 about fifty yards northeast of the Church of St. Anne, brought to light its remains, and this location so well agrees with the data of a tradition going

[811] As we said above, this chronological problem is important for determining the length of our Lord's public life and the date of His death.

[812] There are some variants at this point in the Greek manuscripts. We have followed the reading which seems to us to have the best authority.

[813] In the Vulgate, the edifice bears the name of *Bethsaida.* Moreover, the form of the name varies in the Greek text. See Edersheim, *The Life and Times of Jesus,* I, 462; Zahn, *Das Evangelium des Johannes,* pp. 274 f.

[814] Neh. 3: 1-31; 12: 38. Cf. Fillion and Nicole, *Atlas Géographique de la Bible,* pl. XIV.

[815] Called in Arabic, *Bab Sitti Mariam.* Fillion and Nicole, *op. cit.,* pl. XIV.

[816] *Homil. in Paralyt.,* II.

[817] *La Palestine,* by professors of Notre-Dame de France à Jérusalem, 2d ed., p. 182

[818] See Chauvet and Isambert, *Syrie, Palestine,* pp. 290 f.

back to the first third of the fourth century, that there is a
growing tendency among Biblical scholars to accept it as the
genuine site.[819]

After these topographical details, the Evangelist completes
his general description by speaking of "a great multitude of
sick, of blind, of lame, of withered," [820] lying on the ground or
on cots. Then he adds that they were "waiting for the moving
of the water. And an angel of the Lord descended at certain
times into the pond; and the water was moved. And he that
went down first into the pond after the moving of the water,
was made whole of whatsoever infirmity he lay under."

As we wrote in another place,[821] these last lines [822] "have
for a long time past been a matter of endless discussion among
exegetes, from the standpoint of textual criticism and also
from that of the interpretation of the facts. The lines are
lacking in several early Greek manuscripts and in one of the
most important Syriac versions. Further, they appear with
numerous variants in the manuscripts containing them. For
these two reasons, learned critics, including some Catholic
commentators, regard them as a marginal gloss inserted in the
text. On the other hand, most of the Greek manuscripts and
ancient versions contain the words, and the general sense of
the passage seems to require their presence. In fact, a few
verses later [823] the paralytic, in reply to Jesus, mentions the
moving of the water in the pond as a condition of its healing
power. But this remark becomes scarcely intelligible if we
eliminate the disputed lines, since they furnish the key. We,
therefore, along with many authors belonging to all schools

---

[819] See Vigouroux' *Dictionnaire de la Bible,* Vol. I, cols. 1730–1732; Hastings'
Dictionary of Christ, I, 194 f.; *La Palestine,* by professors of Notre-Dame de
France à Jérusalem, 2d ed., pp. 182 f.

[820] The Greek word ξηροί, literally, "withered," is used of those whose members
are atrophied.

[821] Fillion, *Les Miracles de N.-S. Jésus-Christ,* II, 162 ff.

[822] John 5 : 3ᵇ–4.

[823] John 5 : 7.

of exegesis,[824] incline to consider the text authentic. If its authenticity be accepted, it is evident that the Evangelist by using these words intended to designate a periodical miracle, performed at certain times through the intermediary of an angel who, while remaining invisible, came and stirred the water and communicated to it the power of healing the one who should first succeed in entering it after that "moving." This was the interpretation of the Fathers and early doctors, as it is likewise the one adopted by most modern exegetes.

Nevertheless numerous commentators, even orthodox Christian scholars, though admitting the integral authenticity of the text, are of opinion that the whole passage involves nothing more than a purely natural phenomenon. One of them says: "The piscina of Bethesda was simply a basin of mineral waters where . . . the infirm waited, looking for the propitious moment when the subterranean caloric, suddenly breaking loose, caused considerable agitation on the surface of the water and stirred up the metallic salts that gave efficacy to the bath." [825] In this event the moving of the water would be intermittent and the curative effect would be present especially during the first moments after the disturbance. In the view of these same commentators, the Jews, unacquainted with the natural cause, attributed the healing property of the water to the intervention of an angel, and St. John merely reports the popular belief. But to this explanation one may reply: What mineral or gas-charged water is capable of curing not only paralytics and lame people, but even the blind? For these last are mentioned in the same breath with the other infirm people who waited for the moving of the water. Moreover, the Evangelist gives no intimation of a distinction

---

[824] Several Rationalist commentators, v. g., Reuss and Heitmüller, defend the authenticity of these lines. It is, of course, for the more or less avowed ulterior purpose of arousing lack of confidence in an author guilty of crediting such "superstitions."

[825] Le Camus, The Life of Christ, English trans., I, 335.

between his personal belief and that of the people. The terms in which he sets forth the facts—on the supposition that his whole account is authentic—describe a general belief. It therefore seems to us difficult not to admit in this passage a miracle which occurred periodically, probably at irregular intervals.[826]

The following lines, dramatically describing a scene observed at the hot springs of Ibrahim near Tiberias, enable us to imagine the sad picture which was presented to our Savior's compassionate gaze at the pool of Bethesda. "The hall in which the spring is located is surrounded by several porticoes, where we see a large number of people crowded together, lying on cots or rolled up in blankets, with pitiful expressions of wretchedness and suffering. . . . The white marble pool is circular in form and is covered by a cupola supported by columns; the inner side of the basin is surrounded by steps on which one may sit." [827]

Among the sick who gathered about the pool of Bethesda to profit by the properties of its waters, was a paralytic [828] who deserved special interest because his disease was of thirty-eight years' standing. From his own words we know that he was not reduced to a state of total immobility. He also tells how little hope he had of recovering his health, even at this place which witnessed so many cures. Yet we shall see him freed from his infirmity, but in a quite unforeseen way. Our Lord's infinite compassion drew Him to this assemblage of afflictions. He approached the man and asked him: "Wilt thou be made whole?" To put such a question to a helpless

---

[826] For a fuller discussion of the two points mentioned, see Fillion, L'Évangile de S. Jean, pp. 96–98; Knabenbauer, Comment. in Evang. S. Joannis, pp. 188–190; T. Zahn, Das Evangelium des Johannes, pp. 274–280.

[827] F. Bovet, Voyage en Terre Sainte, 3d ed., p. 378.

[828] One of the ἄρρωστοι mentioned above. His illness is not specified by the Evangelist. But, from the account as a whole it follows that he was afflicted with partial paralysis.

wretch, afflicted with an inveterate [829] disease, who was there precisely to obtain his cure, would seem strange if proffered by anyone else. But it had an excellent purpose: to arouse the infirm man's faith and hope and draw his attention to an unthought-of means of recovering his health. In fact, the all-powerful Wonder-worker, but the use of these words, was implicitly promising to restore the sick man's health. The paralytic's reply bears an imprint of deep sadness: "Sir, I have no man, when the water is troubled, to put me into the pond. For whilst I am coming, another goeth down before me." No one, in such a plight; no friend, not a single kindly soul directly interested in him, to render this indispensable service! Therefore was it in vain that he had often tried to approach the pool, dragging himself painfully along, at the favorable moment; someone was always there ahead of him.

In a mild tone of authority, Jesus then said: "Arise, take up thy bed and walk." These words, almost identical with those which He addressed to another paralytic not long before,[830] produced an immediate effect. The sick man was at once cured, took his cot on his shoulders, and went off. An undeniable miracle had been performed. But, as the Evangelist continues, "it was the Sabbath that day." This remark forms the heart of the whole episode. The religious leaders of the Jews, upon seeing this man carrying his couch along the street, were deeply scandalized and said to him: "It is the Sabbath; it is not lawful for thee to take up thy bed." A weighty tradition did, indeed, forbid the carrying of burdens on the Sabbath.[831]

[829] Our Lord, as the Evangelist (John 5:6) says, was aware of this detail by His supernatural knowledge.

[830] Following St. John Chrysostom, some commentators have thought it possible to identify this episode with the curing of the paralytic of Capharnaum. Most Rationalist critics eagerly adopt this view. But it is certainly erroneous. In fact, apart from Christ's words, "Arise, take up thy bed . . . ," which are almost the same in the two accounts, the whole incident is different: the time, place, occasion, the principal and accesory circumstances show that we have before us two entirely distinct episodes.

[831] Cf. Neh. 13:19.

But there were legitimate exceptions to that rule. The rabbis themselves recognized this fact, since they laid down the following principle: "If a prophet say to thee, 'Transgress the words of the Law,' obey him, except in what concerns idolatry." [832] The paralytic was unwittingly conforming to this rule, for he replied: "He that made me whole, He said to me: Take up thy bed and walk." He meant to imply: He had the right to give me this command, for in miraculously restoring my health, He proved that He possessed a superior authority, and of course I obeyed Him.

The Jews then asked him: "What is that man [an expression of contempt] who said to thee: Take up thy bed and walk?" Evidently it was for the purpose of preferring a formal charge against Jesus that they wanted this information. But the paralytic did not know his benefactor's name, because immediately after the miracle Jesus left the pond and disappeared in the crowd. It was not a flight, to escape a danger that did not yet exist, but an act of prudence, to prevent a tumultuous gathering and acclamations which at that time might have proved harmful to His ministry.

A little later, probably on the same day, in one of the Temple courts, Jesus met the paralytic, who had been led thither by a feeling of pious thanksgiving. Jesus said to him: "Behold thou art made whole; sin no more, lest some worse thing happen to thee." From this remark we may reasonably infer that so inveterate an infirmity, as in the similar case that we studied a few pages above, was a punishment for grievous moral faults. Jesus had cured the disease; but it might return, even in a more terrible form, if the recipient of so great a favor should again fall into sin.

Doubly happy at having obtained forgiveness as well as his cure, the paralytic went and told the Jewish authorities that it was Jesus who had miraculously restored his health. In taking

[832] *Sanhedr.* f. 90, 1.

this step, he certainly did not intend, as is sometimes supposed, maliciously to denounce his benefactor. Yet he did not
wish to defy the religious leaders. In his candor he supposed
that he was bringing esteem and honor to the powerful and
merciful Wonder-worker. It is not likely that he knew the
ill-will of our Lord's enemies, who "persecuted" Him "because He did these things on the Sabbath." From this fact
we may rightly surmise that the Jews went in search of Jesus
and heaped reproach and threats upon Him. These men, of
a narrow, evil spirit, stupidly identifying their human
traditions about the Sabbath with the genuine import of the
divine precept, did not even deign to note the brilliant miracle which Jesus had just performed. It was a minor circumstance that claimed their attention and aroused their anger.
At a later day Christ refers to this characteristic fact.[833]

For the time being, He first answered them with profound
words of majesty: "My Father worketh until now; and I
work." He thus went straight to the heart of the matter. He
claimed for Himself the dignity and prerogatives of Son of
God, thanks to which He was King and Lord of the Sabbath.
There is not and cannot be absolute repose for God. This is a
manifest truth, which the Jewish theosophist Philo expresses
thus: "Never does He cease acting; as it is the property of
fire to burn and of snow to cool, so it belongs to God to act." [834]
It is, of course, written that the Creator rested on the seventh
day, after finishing His vast work, and by this mysterious
rest He Himself supplied the reason for the establishment of
the Sabbath for His people.[835] But it is also evident that the
divine repose has nothing in common with inaction. It is not
a complete ceasing from all activity, even less is it the stopping of His fatherly favors. His perpetual action is neces-

[833] Cf. John 7 : 22 f.
[834] *Legat. all.*, I, 3.
[835] Gen. 2 : 1–3 ; Ex. 20 : 11 ; 31 : 16 f.

sary for the conservation of His creatures and for the government of the world. Such was also the view of some rabbis. "R. Pinchas made this remark: Although it is said that God rested from all His work, that refers only to the creation of the world, not however to His conduct towards the wicked and the just." [836] Like His heavenly Father, Jesus is constantly active, without His activity being limited to certain days or being obliged to cease on account of the Sabbath rest. By speaking thus, He shows Himself truly filial. His Father works; how could He remain inactive? In the final analysis, therefore, the charge made against Him falls indirectly upon God.

His enemies grasped the full import of this short reply. It was clear that on His lips the emphatic words, "My Father," did not have the broad sense in which every pious Jew might call God his Father, but that they designated God as "His own Father" in the strictest meaning of the words.[837] This is why the Jewish leaders, after hearing them, cherished even more hateful feelings against Jesus and went so far as to plot His death, as the Evangelist tells us. For a blasphemer openly to attribute the divine nature to himself, would, indeed, have been a far graver crime than a simple violation of the Sabbath.

The Savior then justified Himself in a charming discourse, delivered with a certain divine calmness,[838] the first of the discourses which are recorded in St. John's Gospel. Therein, repeating and developing His majestic assertion, He proves that He is truly the Son of God and the Messias. It is a sublime, vigorous, and closely reasoned page. The filial sentiment that we have just mentioned constantly shows itself. Sad im-

[836] He is engaged in punishing the former and blessing the latter. *Bereshith rabba*, 11. See also Clement of Alexandria, *Stromata*, VI, 141 f.; Eusebius, *Praeparat. evang.*, XIII, xii, 11.

[837] John 5: 18; πατέρα ἴδιον, *"Patrem proprium."*

[838] "It is like a stream whose waters, clear as a mirror, flow tranquilly along," writes the Rationalist Ewald (*Die Johann. Schriften übersetzt und erklärt*, I, 207), who usually has a fine appreciation of the literary beauties of the Bible.

pressions also appear in it, especially toward the end, when
Jesus denounces the unbelief of the Jews. It does not fall
within our purpose to explain it in detail.[839] But we will quote
it in full and note the chief turns of our Savior's thought.

We have here a frankly apologetic thesis, made up of two
almost equal parts. In the first,[840] Jesus openly lays claim to
a divine nature and the rights which it confers on Him. In the
second part,[841] He points out the various testimonies that have
been given in His favor; they are undeniable testimonies, but
His adversaries have refused to accept them.

He first develops the protest He has just made against the
attacks of the Jewish leaders, dwelling on the relations that
exist between His activity and that of God, His Father.

"Amen, amen I say unto you, the Son cannot do any thing of
Himself, but what He seeth the Father doing; for what things soever He doth, these the Son also doth in like manner. For the Father
loveth the Son and showeth Him all things which Himself doth:
and greater works than these will He show Him, that you may
wonder."

Three times in this discourse we hear the phrase: "Amen,
amen I say unto you," a sort of oath by which Jesus, as it
were, places under the seal of divine truthfulness the important declaration He here makes. In the first place He says that
a close community, or rather a complete identity of acts, exists
between His Father and Himself. When He adds that the Son
can do nothing of Himself, He nowise lessens His own freedom, spontaneity, or omnipotence, since He too possesses the
divine nature in all its fulness. But He cannot act otherwise

[839] See Fillion, *L'Évangile de S. Jean,* pp. 103–115; Knabenbauer, *Comment. in
Evang. S. Johannis,* pp. 196–211; Schanz, *Comment. über das Evangelium des heil.
Johannes,* pp. 240–259; Zahn, *Das Evangelium des Johannes,* pp. 288–312; Godet,
Commentaire sur l'Évangile de S. Jean, I, 440–444, etc.
[840] John 5: 19–30.
[841] John 5: 31–47.

than the Father, since they both have but one and the same will. The Father has a tender love for this only begotten Son, whose lovable qualities are infinite. But to those whom we love, we reveal our secrets; this is another reason for the perfect likeness between the Father's activity and that of the Son. It is touching to see Jesus, in order to give us some idea of His relations with God, basing a comparison upon the affection of human fathers, who communicate their inner thoughts and plans to their children, and who initiate their sons into the first elements of their trade or art. He had just referred to His miracles, especially to the curing of the paralytic, and He announced that He would perform still more wonderful works. The continuation of the discourse tells us of what they would consist.

"As the Father raiseth up the dead and giveth life, so the Son also giveth life to whom He will. For neither doth the Father judge any man, but hath given all judgment to the Son. That all men may honor the Son as they honor the Father. He who honoreth not the Son, honoreth not the Father, who hath sent Him."

The power of raising the dead, the right to judge all men— these are the two great works in question. Jesus entered into this subject in some detail, giving a spiritual and moral meaning both to the resurrection of the dead and to the judgment.

"Amen, amen I say unto you, that the hour cometh, and now is, when the dead shall hear the voice of the Son of God, and they that hear shall live. For as the Father hath life in Himself, so He hath given to the Son also to have life in Himself. And He hath given Him power to do judgment because He is the Son of Man."

As Jesus clearly predicts again a few days before His Passion,[842] there will be at the end of time a universal resurrec-

---

[842] Matt. 25: 31–46. Cf. I Cor. 15: 54–56.

tion in the strictest sense, followed by the general judgment, after which the good will be eternally rewarded, while the wicked will undergo everlasting punishment.

"Wonder not at this. For the hour cometh wherein all that are in the graves shall hear the voice of the Son of God. And they that have done good things, shall come forth unto the resurrection of life; but they that have done evil, unto the resurrection of judgment."

Jesus concludes the first part of His discourse with the thought that served as His starting-point:

"I cannot of Myself do any thing. As I hear, so I judge. And My judgment is just, because I seek not My own will, but the will of Him that sent Me."

It might have been objected that the superhuman rights and powers which Jesus claimed had no other reality that His own personal assertion. He anticipates and refutes this objection in the second part of His apology. From the consideration of His sublime office He passes quite naturally to three testimonies that proved its reality in an indisputable way. He cites three witnesses: His heavenly Father, His own miracles, and Holy Scripture. It is noteworthy that after thus far speaking in the third person—except in His opening assertion: "And I work"—He uses the first person during the rest of the discourse.

"If I bear witness of Myself, My witness is not true. There is another that beareth witness of Me. And I know that the witness which He witnesseth of Me is true. You sent to John, and he gave testimony to the truth. But I receive not testimony from man; but I say these things that you may be saved. He was a burning and a shining light; and you were willing for a time to rejoice in his light."

Somewhat later we shall hear our Lord saying: "Although I give testimony of Myself, My testimony is true." [843] And He will be perfectly right, so beyond suspicion did His holiness and divine origin place His truthfulness. But at this point He makes a concession. For the time being He consents to apply to Himself the very legitimate juridical rule that no one's testimony in his own behalf is to be considered as impartial evidence.[844] Various commentators have thought this "other" who rendered a truthful testimony to Jesus to be John the Baptist, who is referred to immediately afterwards. But they fail to note that Jesus mentions him only to set him aside almost at once, saying that He does not accept the testimony of man. In the present passage, therefore, the allusion is to God's testimony, which at first is simply mentioned and later is more fully developed.

Christ's praise of the precursor is as glowing as it is well deserved. Nevertheless John the Baptist was but a lamp, a torch, whose modest brightness could not be compared with the brilliant radiance of the Messias: *"Non erat ille lux."* The Savior alone *"erat lux vera quae illuminat omnem hominem venientem in hunc mundum."* [845] After praising the Baptist, Jesus utters a stinging rebuke to the Jewish religious leaders, whose national pride had for a while taken delight in the vain satisfaction of seeing suddenly arise in Israel this prophet who was evidently sent by God.

Our Lord next presents the testimony of the heavenly Father, who manifested Himself in three ways: by the numerous miracles which Jesus had performed; by the direct attestation of the divine voice itself, probably that which accompanied the Savior's baptism; lastly, by the Sacred Scriptures.

---

[843] John 8: 14.

[844] As the rabbis (*Ketuboth*, 23 b), also said, "No credence is placed in witnesses [who testify] in their own case." Cf. Cicero, *Pro Roscio*, XXXVI, 103, etc.

[845] John 1: 8 f.

"But I have a greater testimony than that of John: for the works which the Father hath given Me to perfect; the works themselves, which I do, give testimony of Me, that the Father hath sent Me. And the Father Himself who hath sent Me hath given testimony of Me; neither have you heard His voice at any time nor seen His shape. And you have not His word abiding in you; for whom He hath sent, Him you believe not. Search the Scriptures, for you think in them to have life everlasting; and the same are they that give testimony of Me. And you will not come to Me that you may have life."

Twice again in this passage Jesus severely rebukes the Jews. They would not let themselves be convinced by His "works," *i. e.,* His conduct as a whole, and especially His miracles, or by the various manifestations through which God sought to enlighten them, addressing Himself to their hearing, to their sight, and to their hearts. There is particular force to what our Lord says here about the testimony rendered to Him by the Scriptures. The Scribes and rabbis of the time were painstaking students of the Bible and even "searched" it assiduously.[846] But in this study they followed the shallow method which characterized them in all matters. Hence they derived therefrom almost no profit either for themselves or for others. Through their own fault, they had over their eyes the thick veil spoken of by St. Paul,[847] and consequently refused to see the portrait of the Messias in the Old Testament, where some feature or other is depicted on almost every page. Their Scripture reading was ordinarily labor lost.[848]

In concluding, Jesus takes the offensive still more vigor-

---

[846] Josephus also praises their zeal in this matter. Cf. *Ant.,* XVII, ii, 4; *Bell. Jud.,* II, viii, 14.

[847] 2 Cor. 3: 14–16.

[848] Cf. Rom. 2: 17–20.

ously, pointing out the causes of His enemies' unbelief and its deplorable consequences:

"I receive not glory from men. But I know you, that you have not the love of God in you. I am come in the name of My Father, and you receive Me not. If another shall come in his own name, him you will receive. How can you believe, who receive glory one from another: and the glory which is from God alone, you do not seek? Think not that I will accuse you to the Father. There is one that accuseth you, Moses, in whom you trust. For if you did believe Moses, you would perhaps believe Me also; for he wrote of Me. But if you do not believe his writings, how will you believe My words?"

What holy vigor these words contain, and what a touch of sadness, at sight of such resistance to grace and at the contemplation of the punishment that will overtake it! How could Jesus more plainly exhibit to His hearers the folly of their blindness? They wish to possess the true life, yet they turn from Him who brings it to them. They rightly consider Moses the chief personage of Israel's history, yet they reject the Messias, who is so often spoken of in his writings.[849] They fail to understand that Moses will be the first to condemn them. Before long the Savior's prediction will be fulfilled: namely, that these blind and senseless men, who are unwilling to receive Him, will eagerly welcome false Christs, who will serve as instruments of divine vengeance.[850]

What were the immediate results of this eminently apologetic and Christological discourse, which opens up such extensive views of the nature and work of the Incarnate Word? St. John closes the narrative at this point without telling us.

---

[849] It was not without a feeling of noble pride that Christ must have uttered those expressive words: "He wrote of Me." On the principal Messianic prophecies of the Pentateuch, see Vol. I, pp. 212–215. At this place, Jesus seems to be alluding to a passage in Deuteronomy, 18: 15–19.

[850] Cf. Matt. 24: 5, 24.

It would seem that the Jews were deeply impressed, since they found nothing by way of reply, and since they let our Lord depart peacefully, without daring to lay violent hands upon Him.

II. The Conflict Breaks Out also in Galilee, on the Occasion of Two Other So-called Violations of the Sabbath by Our Lord

The incident just described is related only by St. John. The Synoptics record two others, which took place about the same period, incidents which plainly exhibit the bitterness of the strife in which the Scribes and Pharisees, our Lord's relentless enemies, were then engaged against Him. These adversaries seek on all sides for opportunities to harm Him and they even stir up such occasions. But each time He promptly takes up the gage and triumphantly answers their hateful accusations. As we read in the Synoptics, and also in the Fourth Gospel, it is our Lord's apparent violation of the Sabbath that provokes the violent outburst of the conflict, this time in Galilee, where until then it had scarcely existed, except in a latent condition. Having returned to Galilee after the feast which He had gone to Jerusalem to celebrate, Jesus, followed by His disciples, was walking one day along a foot-path through a wheat field.[851] The place is not mentioned by name, but it was probably on the western shore of Lake Genesareth. As the grain was ripe, the time must have been the middle of spring, not far from the Pasch, because on the second day of that feast, the 16th Nisan, there were offered to God in the Temple the first sheaves of the barley crop,[852]

---

[851] Matt. 12: 1–8; Mark 2: 23–28; Luke 6: 1–5. St. Matthew places this episode at a very late period in the Savior's life; the other two Evangelists seem to conform to the real order of events.

[852] See Vol. I, p. 381, where we describe this interesting ceremony.

which ripened a little earlier than other grain. It was a Sabbath.

St. Luke designates the special place of this Sabbath in the liturgical year, but the expression he uses is so obscure that its exact meaning has never been ascertained with finality. Hypotheses, however, are not lacking [853] to explain the words "second first," [854] which are to be found nowhere else either in sacred or profane literature. The most likely opinion [855] is that the Evangelist means the first Sabbath following the second day of the Paschal octave. The Mosaic Law did, in fact, direct [856] that, starting with that day, seven Sabbaths were to be reckoned to Pentecost. In order to distinguish them, because of their special importance, from all the other Sabbaths of the year, it is supposed that there was prefixed to their serial number the word "second," i. e., second day of the Pasch, thus indicating their starting-point. However this may be, it seems that the event related took place a short time after the curing of the paralytic at Bethesda. If the festival day which brought Jesus to Jerusalem was the Pasch, the Savior had at that time been exercising His ministry for a year, and two more years were yet to elapse before his death.

For those who accompanied the Divine Master and shared His life of poverty, there was not always assurance of daily

---

[853] See Zahn, *Das Evangelium des Lucas,* pp. 269–272; Fillion, *L'Évangile de S. Luc,* pp. 133 f.

[854] Ἐν σαββάτῳ δευτεροπρώτῳ. Lately the authenticity of this expression has been denied, on the pretext that it is omitted in some manuscripts of high authority. Cf. Westcott and Hort, *The New Testament in the Original Greek,* II, 48. But its presence in the great mass of Greek manuscripts and in most of the early versions seems to prove that it is not the result of an interpolation. Its very obscurity is rather favorable to its authenticity. It is easy to understand that some copyists would have suppressed it because they found it unintelligible; but there was no reason for any of them falsely to insert it into the text. See Zahn, *loc. cit.* The learned critic Tischendorf several times changed his mind on the subject: after suppressing it in several editions of his Greek New Testament, he finally replaced the phrase in the eighth edition.

[855] Its author is Scaliger, *De Emendat. Temp.,* Book VI.

[856] Lev. 23 : 15–22.

bread. Thus it happened on this "second first" Sabbath that
His disciples, who were walking behind Him, were reduced
to the necessity of satisfying their hunger by plucking some
ears of wheat, which they rubbed in their hands to loosen
the grain. This act in itself was nowise blameworthy, for the
Jewish law expressly authorized anyone crossing through a
vineyard or a grain field to gather a few bunches of grapes or
a few ears of grain in order to satisfy thirst or hunger, on
condition that what was thus taken be eaten on the spot.[857]
This charitable tolerance subsists even yet in Palestine.[858]
Nevertheless, although such an act was free from any in-
delicacy, it might give rise to another sort of accusation. The
Pharisees of the place followed our Lord even into the open
country in order to spy on Him, perhaps to see whether in His
walk He would exceed the distance of 2000 cubits,[859] farther
than which the rabbis did not allow anyone to go on the Sabbath. These spies were not slow in discovering in the disciples' conduct a ground for accusation. They came to the
Savior, whom they naturally held responsible, and said to Him
in a tone of severity: "See![860] Thy disciples do what is not
lawful on the Sabbath day."

Elsewhere[861] we have given a large number of details
about the excessively rigid manner in which the Scribes of
our Lord's time required the Sabbath rest to be observed by
their fellow-Jews. Upon the authentic text of the law (Exodus 31: 12–17), which does not go beyond generalities, they
had superimposed a whole system of petty and often ridicu-

---

[857] Deut. 23: 24 f.

[858] Cf. Robinson, *Researches in Palestine*, I, 493–499.

[859] The Jewish cubit was the equivalent of about 20 inches.

[860] This is St. Mark's very expressive text: "Ἴδε. St. Matthew has ἰδού, "behold."
According to St. Luke, the Pharisees address the disciples directly, saying: "Why
do you that which is not lawful . . . ?" The two forms are easily reconciled; the
question may have been put to Jesus and to His disciples at the same time.

[861] See Fillion, *L'Évangile de S. Matthieu*, p. 236, and *L'Étude de la Bible*,
1922, p. 334; A. Wünsche, *Beiträge zur Erläuterung der Evangelien aus dem
Talmud*, pp. 148–152.

lous casuistry which, under the semblance of protecting the Sabbath, changed it into a veritable burden. It was the teaching of their extreme Sabbatism that to pluck two ears of wheat was to engage in the labor of harvesting, which was explicitly forbidden.[862] To rub these ears between one's hands so as to loosen the grain, was equivalent to threshing: another grievous wrong, said these narrow-minded critics. The Savior's disciples were therefore culpable, doubly so, and the Master who tolerated such a scandal on their part shared in their guilt.[863]

With an energy and appropriateness that promptly silenced the accusers, Jesus took up His disciples' defense and protested against an exaggerated interpretation which degraded the spirit of the commandment. His little address on that occasion advanced four arguments: the first two are taken from the history of revelation; the third is a text from the Prophets; the fourth is supplied by sound and sane reason. The following version is formed by combining the three Gospel accounts:

"Have you not read what David did when he was hungry, and they that were with him: how he entered into the house of God [864] and did eat the loaves of proposition, which it was not lawful for him to eat, nor for them that were with him, but for the priests only? Or have ye not read in the law that on the Sabbath days the priests in the Temple break the Sab-

[862] Ex. 34: 21.

[863] The Pharisaic spirit still exists in Israel with regard to the Sabbath. Orthodox Jews observe the Sabbath rest as rigorously as did their fathers. Among them are some who would not wind their watch nor open a letter on the Sabbath, who call a Christian to light their fire which they have prepared the day before, who consider it a grievous fault to write a single line. See E. Coypel, Le Judaïsme, Esquisse des Mœurs Juives, pp. 170–177.

[864] This refers to the Tabernacle, then at Nob, a city north of Jerusalem, in the tribe of Benjamin, not far from Anathoth. Cf. 1 Kings 21: 1–6; Neh. 11: 32; Is. 10: 32. St. Mark's mention of Abiathar, instead of his father Achimelech, who was then the real High Priest, gives rise to no serious difficulty. See Fillion, L'Évangile de S. Marc, p. 50.

bath and are without blame? But I tell you that there is here a greater than the Temple. And if you knew what this meaneth: I will have mercy, and not sacrifice, you would never have condemned the innocent. The Sabbath was made for man, not man for the Sabbath. Therefore the Son of man is Lord of the Sabbath also."

The example taken from the life of David [865] had particular force because that ruler was greatly venerated by all the Jews, who rightly looked upon him as a man after God's own heart. This example proves that at times, in a man's life, there is a conflict between various distinct obligations and that, in such case, the positive law yields to the natural law. Thus, among the Hebrews, it was forbidden for anyone except the priests to eat the twelve loaves which were renewed each Sabbath and which were called "loaves of proposition" because they were laid upon a golden table in the sanctuary of the tabernacle, to represent before God the twelve tribes of Israel.[866] Yet the High Priest of that earlier time did not hesitate to give some of them to David to satisfy his hunger. Should not the Pharisees, who prided themselves on a thorough knowledge of the Scriptures, have remembered this deed and have drawn therefrom an application to the present case? There is a genuine reproach in the words: "Have you not read?" which our Lord uses to introduce this example, and again after it. It has been noted that He makes use of this expression whenever He refers to the Scripture in the presence of educated hearers,[867] whereas, whenever He is addressing the common people or a mixed audience, He says, "Have you not heard?" [868]

The second example adduced by our Lord to justify His

[865] Cf. 1 Kings 21 : 1–6.
[866] Lev. 24 : 5–9; Fillion, *Atlas Archéologique de la Bible*, pl. CIV, figs. 3, 6, 8, 9.
[867] Cf. Matt. 12 : 3, 5; 19 : 4; 21 : 16, 42; Mark 2 : 25; 12 : 10, 26; Luke 6 : 3; 10 : 26.
[868] Matt. 5 : 21, 27, 33, 38, 43.

disciples' conduct was still more pertinent, since it directly concerned the Sabbath and its obligatory rest. If one were to weigh the facts in a purely material way, one would have to say that the priests and Levites constantly violated the Sabbath, because on that day they performed more than the ordinary amount of labor, since the prescribed sacrifices were more numerous. Hence the number of those needed for the service of the Temple was doubled on that day. Yet who would have thought of accusing them? Everyone adopted the Talmudic saying: "A servile labor performed for the public worship ceases to be servile." [869] There could, then, be exceptions to the general rule, as to all other laws. But the act imputed to the disciples as a transgression was not even a labor. How majestically Jesus adds, by way of conclusion to this second argument: "I tell you that there is here a greater than the Temple." It is to Himself, as Messias, that He refers by these words. In that capacity He had the right to interpret the law and, if need be, to dispense His disciples, just as God authorized the labor of the priests on the Sabbath.

On a previous occasion our Lord had met the Pharisees' unjust criticism by the divine words, "I will have mercy, and not sacrifice," taken from the prophet Osee.[870] In the present case this text emphasizes the degenerate casuistry and unspeakable hard-heartedness of those who condemned the innocent without even condescending to examine whether their acts were not wholly excusable.

Christ ends His eloquent defense with a most cogent argument from reason. "The Sabbath was made for man, and not man for the Sabbath." So evident and undeniable is this principle that at a later date several rabbis also proclaimed it, in this wise: "The Sabbath has been given into your hands;

[869] *Shabbath*, 19, 1.
[870] Matt. 9: 13.

you have not been given into the hands of the Sabbath." [871]
The meaning of the Savior's words is that the Sabbath rest
was instituted by God as a blessing for the Israelites, not as
an oppressive burden. The Scribes and Pharisees judged
otherwise, for they made man a slave of the Sabbath.

In conclusion our Lord lays claim, under the title of Son
of Man, of ideal man and Messias, to supreme authority over
the Sabbath. He is its "Lord," its Master. The Sabbath is
therefore under His direct control. To Him it belongs to decide, without contradiction, what is lawful and what is forbidden to be done on that day, in accordance with the spirit
of the law. We should note that Jesus has no more thought
of abolishing the Sabbath than of then abolishing the sacrifices and other similar institutions of Judaism. He does nothing more than explain the commandment and free it from
the false interpretations that had been heaped upon it by men
without authority or intelligence. The whole argument was
so sound and conclusive that no one attempted to refute it.
It was one of our Lord's first victories at that time.

He won another such victory a short time afterwards, likewise on a Sabbath, when He was directly attacked by His
enemies.[872] He had entered the synagogue in some town,
which the sacred writers do not name, with the intention, as
St. Luke says, of announcing the glad tidings to those present, at the close of the religious services. We are not told
whether He was able to carry out this intention. The Evangelists pass on to the special incident that raised His enemies'
hatred to the highest pitch. In the synagogue there was a
man whose hand—the right hand, says St. Luke with the exactness of a physician—was "withered." This expression
means that the hand was atrophied, stiff and motionless in
consequence of a local paralysis which had arrested the cir-

---

[871] See Wünsche, *Beiträge,* p. 149.
[872] Matt. 12:9–14; Mark 3:1–6; Luke 6:6–11.

culation in that member. This disease is regarded as incurable after it has lasted for a considerable time; and even if human skill and science does sometimes succeed in curing it, this is never a sudden effect. In his commentary on St. Matthew's account of this event, St. Jerome quotes several lines from the apocryphal Gospel of the Nazarenians, wherein it is said that the afflicted man was formerly a mason, and that he would have been reduced to begging if Jesus had not come to his aid. This detail may possibly be historical.

Seated in the places of honor which they were so ready and apt in assigning to themselves,[873] were several Pharisees, whose attention was fixed upon our Lord, with evil intent. They knew that the obligatory Sabbath rest did not stop His wonderful cures,[874] and they hoped He would heal the unfortunate sick man before their very eyes. They could then lodge a charge against Him with the religious authority. The severity of the Scribes was exercised in this direction no less than in all others. They did not allow a sick person to be cared for on the Sabbath unless his life were really in danger.[875] In all other cases they showed themselves inexorable and even classed as breaker of the Sabbath anyone who on that day offered a few words of comfort to the sick. Woe to anybody who broke an arm or a leg or who sprained a muscle on the Sabbath! He had to wait until after sunset to receive first aid; he was not even permitted to pour a little cool water on his painful wounds.

As Jesus was too slow to suit His impatient enemies in performing the miracle which would give them a pretext for accusing Him, they took the initiative and put this insidious question to Him: "Is it lawful to heal on the Sabbath days?"

[873] Matt. 23:6; Mark 12:39; Luke 20:46.
[874] Cf. Mark 1:21–26; Luke 4:33–35.
[875] Cf. A. Wünsche, *Beiträge zur Erläuterung der Evangelien aus dem Talmud*, pp. 150–152.

But He read their inmost thoughts. Instead of falling into the trap which they set for Him, He frustrated their wile with divine wisdom. Turning abruptly to the sick man, He said to him in a commanding tone: "Arise and stand forth in the midst." In this instance our Lord gave all possible publicity to His act, the better to protest against the Scribes' false principles regarding the Sabbath. Thus commanded, the sick man stepped into the midst of the assembly. The Savior then answered the Pharisees' question by asking another, a method that was not uncommon with Him. He said to them: "I ask you, if it be lawful on the Sabbath days to do good, or to do evil, to save life, or to destroy?" Although His question seems to differ but slightly from theirs, His words present the case of conscience under a new aspect. In place of "to heal," Jesus says "to do good"; then He sets forth a double alternative, the second supplementing the first and applying it to the actual case. He thereby transformed the import of the act and declared that, far from committing a fault by curing a sick man on the Sabbath, one would be guilty of sin in not curing him. The dilemma proposed by the Pharisees was: to do or not to do. The one put by our Lord was: to do good or not to do good—not to do so being almost equivalent to doing evil.

To the question thus put, the answer was plain, so plain that the Savior's adversaries refrained from stating it, because to do so would have been to condemn themselves. Jesus, again speaking, said to them in a tone of severity: "What man shall there be among you, that hath one sheep; and if the same fall into a pit on the Sabbath day, will he not take hold on it and lift it up? How much better is a man than a sheep?" In fact, the owner of an animal that had fallen into a ditch or into one of those cisterns often hidden by foliage in the fields of the Orient, was permitted by the Pharisaic school to do, even on the Sabbath, whatever might be necessary to draw out the beast.[876] This example, taken from common sense and from ordinary usage, succeeded in confounding the questioners, who sanctioned what at times would be a considerable labor in order to avoid a material loss, and yet who would not consent to Jesus healing an infirm man by means of a simple word.

Amid the general silence, the Savior said: "Therefore it is lawful to do a good deed on the Sabbath days." Then turning on His foes a look in which might be seen, says St. Mark, a mixture of anger and sadness—of anger because of their malice and bad faith, of sadness because of the hardness [877] of their hearts—He said to the infirm man: "Stretch forth thy hand." That hand, which had been lifeless perhaps for a long time, was easily stretched forth. It had been miraculously cured and made as healthy "as the other," says St. Matthew.

Furious [878] at having been thus worsted and humiliated in the presence of the whole assembly, the Pharisees were scarcely out of the synagogue before they took counsel with the Herodians, criminally plotting together how they might scheme to bring about Jesus' death. Here, as at Jerusalem, His death was decided upon; but the manner of carrying out that decision was beset with difficulties up to the very last. As we explained in the preceding volume,[879] the Herodians were Jews devoted to the dynasty of Herod; consequently they were to some extent Liberals in politics as also in religion.

---

[876] *Shabbath,* 128, b. Macrobius, *Sat.,* I, 16, alludes to this concession: *"Si bos in specum decidisset, eumque paterfamilias adhibitis operis liberasset, non est visus ferias polluisse."*

[877] In the Greek, according to most of the manuscripts, πωρώσει, "hardening." The Itala and the Vulgate follow the reading πηρώσει, *caecitate,* "blindness." We also find the reading νεκρώσει, the "death" (some Latin manuscripts: *super mortua illorum corda*). It is the same sense, with slight shades of difference.

[878] This word is none too strong. St. Luke shows us the Pharisees "filled with madness." Often great anger is a momentary fit of furious madness.

[879] Vol. I, p. 192.

At first glance it is therefore surprising to see the Pharisees joining forces with them, for their tendencies were quite the opposite. But history furnishes many examples of such alliances between people belonging to different parties, for the purpose of more readily obtaining a greatly desired result. Further on [880] we shall see that Herod Antipas was at heart not favorably inclined to our Lord; the assistance of his partisans, especially in Galilee, might indeed be of use to the Pharisees in carrying out their execrable scheme.[881]

III. Jesus Retires to the Shores of Lake Tiberias, Where Friendly Crowds Gather About Him [882]

This homicidal plot did not escape the Savior's knowledge; but it failed to disturb His peace of soul. Nevertheless, conformable to His principle of not exasperating His enemies so long as His "hour," the hour of His sacrifice, had not yet come, He retired [883] with His disciples to one of the solitudes in the neighborhood of Lake Tiberias. The Evangelists inform us that He was at once surrounded by devoted crowds which formed a sort of royal escort for Him, and that He responded to their affection by numerous favors. This is a consoling page of our Lord's life and an interesting summary of His ministry at that period.

St. Matthew and St. Mark draw up a significant list of the regions from which these multitudes came in groups to gather about the good Master. They came especially from the Jewish provinces: first of all from Galilee, where Jesus was then actively engaged; and from Peraea, east of the Jordan, and

---

[880] Luke 13:31 f.; 23:8–12. Cf. Matt. 14:1 f.; Mark 6:14–16; Luke 9:7–9.

[881] Later on we find the Pharisees and Herodians in league against our Lord. Cf. Matt. 22:16; Mark 12:13.

[882] Matt. 12:15–21 (and also 4:24 f.); Mark 3:7–12; Luke 6:17–19.

[883] Here as in certain other passages (Matt. 2:12, 14, 22; 4:12; 14:13, etc.), the Greek verb ἀναχωρεῖν (Vulgate., *recedere, secedere*) has the special meaning of "withdrawing" to escape from danger.

also from Judea. Of the four parts that formed Palestine
strictly so called, Samaria is the only one not mentioned as
sending any contingent. They came from Jerusalem, too,
where, despite the indifference of some and the unfriendli-
ness of others, Jesus had a number of followers from the beginning. But the Jewish districts were not the only ones to
take part in that enthusiastic pilgrimage. The neighboring
regions, although pagan, were also represented in the crowds
that gathered about our Lord. The sacred writers mention
the following: Idumea, south of Judea; Decapolis, east of
Galilee; the cities of Tyre and Sidon, northwest of that same
province; and Syria, northeast.[884] Their coming was facilitated by the existence of highways connecting all these districts with Capharnaum and Lake Tiberias. What a power
of attraction Jesus must have had, since, without the least
effort to seek popularity, He thus drew to Him such numerous and varied multitudes! It was a truly superb and thrilling
sight.

A few details, noted by the Evangelists, show how kind and
gracious Jesus was and how greatly these people loved Him.
We are happy to read, in St. Luke's account, that the crowds
came to the Savior "to hear Him" as well as "to be healed of
their diseases." His teaching was no less famous than were
His miracles. Those who came to be cured of their bodily
ills delivered a veritable assault upon the Master with the
indelicate familiarity of the Orient. But He showed unlimited
kindness to them all and healed them. "They pressed upon
Him," [885] the more confident of obtaining their cure if they
could succeed in touching His sacred Person. We know that
wonderful cures had taken place at mere contact with Him.[886]
Scenes of this sort happened so frequently that Jesus had to

---

884 See Fillion and Nicole, *Atlas Géographique de la Bible*, pl. X.
885 'Επιπίπτειν, St. Mark says with dramatic force.
886 Mark 1:41. Cf. 5:27; 6:56; 8:22, etc.

ask His disciples to hold constantly at His disposal a little boat, moored close to the shore and ready at all times to receive Him. To this boat they betook themselves whenever He was too hard pressed by the crowd or when He wished to obtain a moment's rest. In case of need, if His enemies should become more threatening, this ship could speedily carry Him to the other side of the lake. Demoniacs also came to Him and, falling at His feet, cried aloud: "Thou art the Son of God." This homage Jesus had already rejected,[887] and against it He again protested energetically. And it was not only those possessed upon whom He imposed silence; for reasons explained above,[888] He also constantly admonished all whom He cured at that time of any physical or moral ill, to observe this same silence. So far as depended on Him, He did not wish that the people's flocking to Him and their confidence in Him should aggravate the situation, already so painful, which the Pharisaic party had created for Him. For the time being, it would suffice for Him to be His own herald.

In this humble conduct of the Savior, St. Matthew, in accordance with his practice of mentioning the points in our Lord's life which were foretold by the prophets, sees the fulfilment of a beautiful prediction of Isaias,[889] which the Targum also applied to the Messias. It appears thus in the First Gospel: [890] "Behold My servant whom I have chosen, My beloved in whom My soul hath been well pleased. I will put My spirit upon him, and he shall shew judgment to the Gentiles. He shall not contend nor cry out, neither shall any man hear his voice in the streets. The bruised reed he shall not break; and smoking flax he shall not extinguish; till he send

[887] Mark 1 : 25 ; Luke 4 : 35.

[888] Page 194.

[889] Is. 42 : 1–4.

[890] It is quoted freely, in a way independent either of the Hebrew text or of the . Septuagint translation. For a detailed explanation of it see St. Jerome, *Epist. ad Algasiam,* as also commentaries on Isaias' prophecy and on St. Matthew's Gospel.

forth judgment unto victory. And in his name the Gentiles shall hope."

The second part of the Book of Isaias, to which these lines belong, is consecrated almost entirely to the "Servant of Jehovah" (*i. e.,* the Messias) and His work of redemption. Evidently all the elements of the portrait here traced by the prophet belong perfectly to Jesus, such as the four Gospels picture Him. On the banks of the Jordan, God proclaimed Him to be His Elect, His Christ, at the same time that He poured forth His Spirit upon Him in profusion. Jesus' attitude towards those to whom He was bringing salvation is described in negative details, which reveal Him as being full of a charming mildness, a merciful kindness, and an incomparable modesty. What a difference between Him and popular orators who think only of their own fame! So truly is He the Savior *par excellence* that He strives to revive life wherever even a spark of it remains. And He is the authentic Savior not only of the Jews: it is to all nations, to pagans as well as to the children of Israel, that He brings the good tidings of redemption and gives hope of true blessedness. His final triumph is beyond the shadow of a doubt in the prophet's mind.

CHAPTER II

From the Calling of the Apostles to the Anointing of Jesus by the Sinful Woman

I. Founding of the Apostolic College [891]

THIS is an event of extraordinary importance, to be counted among the culminating points of the Savior's life, for it must be considered as a decisive step undertaken with a view to the foundation of the Christian Church. The sacred writers have shown us Jesus winning rapid successes in Galilee. The good seed has been sown abundantly, and a rich harvest is already in preparation. The Messias has therefore need of zealous workers who can help Him in gathering it. But it is particularly in view of the future that He now chooses special helpers. In the divine plan a short duration had been assigned to His personal ministry. Hence it was needful that, after His return to Heaven, His nascent work should be continued without delay and developed by men to whom He communicates His spirit. He laid the foundation of this great act some little time before by attaching to Himself, at first in a transient way,[892] then more definitely,[893] several tried disciples, who had been living with Him and serving the apprenticeship of their future labors. But that step was not enough; the Savior now supplements it.

To grasp its significance more exactly, we should make a distinction between the various groups of the Savior's followers which are mentioned by the Evangelists. They all are

---

[891] Modern critics deny the historical character of this institution. See Appendix IX, 1.

[892] John 1 : 35–51.

[893] Matt. 4 : 18–22; 9 : 9 f., and the parallel passages of St. Mark and St. Luke.

called "disciples," because they look upon Jesus as their Master and Teacher. That name, "disciple," is given them in different degrees. There was the great mass of Christ's followers, His disciples in the broadest sense of the term. It is in this sense that the Acts of the Apostles [894] speaks of "the multitude of the disciples" who were dwelling in Jerusalem. This same name is given to another category of believers, much less numerous but more closely connected with our Lord, with whom they had very intimate relations. Such, before their call to the apostolate, were Peter and Andrew, James and John, Philip, Nathanael, and Matthew; such, later, were also the seventy-two disciples,[895] the one hundred and twenty disciples gathered in the upper room after Christ's Ascension,[896] the five hundred disciples to whom our Lord appeared in Galilee after His Resurrection.[897] Lastly, the Apostles, even after being called to the apostolate, are frequently still called disciples by the sacred writers. It was their first title and for a long while continued to be the one most frequently used. All these disciples formed about Jesus, to the very close of His earthly life, three concentric circles, surrounding Him with their sincere homage.

It is in simple yet grave and solemn terms that St. Mark and St. Luke [898] describe the delightful scene of the calling of the Apostles. St. Mark says: "Going up into a mountain, He called unto Him whom He would Himself, and they came to Him. And He made that twelve should be with Him and that He might send them to preach. And He gave them power to heal sicknesses and to cast out devils." St. Luke narrates the event thus: "It came to pass in those days [899] that He went

[894] Acts 6: 2.
[895] Luke 10: 1-24.
[896] Acts 1: 15.
[897] 1 Cor. 15: 6.
[898] Mark 3: 13 f.; Luke 6: 12 f.
[899] Shortly after the curing of the man with the withered hand. Cf. Luke 6: 6-11.

out into a mountain to pray, and He passed the whole night in the prayer of God. And when day was come, He called unto Him His disciples; and He chose twelve of them, whom also He named Apostles." It is on a much later occasion, when their Divine Master entrusted to them the mission of carrying the glad tidings through all Galilee,[900] that St. Matthew refers to the Apostles and the fact of their being called. But the way in which he then speaks of them presupposes that for some time they had existed as a distinct body. The place which St. Mark and St. Luke assign to their calling is in conformity with the chronological order. It was just before delivering the Sermon on the Mount that the Savior chose them.

It would gratify our piety to know exactly what mountain was the scene of these two events. None of the Synoptics mentions it by name, although in designating it they all employ an expression which seems to imply that it was then well known: for them it is "the mountain." [901] From the three accounts taken together it appears likely that it was not far from the western shore of Lake Genesareth. In the varied and picturesque block of mountains overhanging this shore almost opposite Tiberias, there is a curiously shaped ridge, 1134 feet above the level of the Mediterranean. The Arabs call it Karn or Kurun Hattin, "Horns of Hattin." [902] This might have been the Mount of the Beatitudes. "The southern side of this crest is 150 or 200 feet above the highway, whereas the northern side rises about 800 feet above the valley formed by the Wady El Tammam." From this height the panorama is remarkable. "Below may be seen the tranquil

[900] Matt. 10 : 1-4.

[901] Τὸ ὄρος, with the article, although there was no previous mention of it.

[902] *Hattin* is a Moslem village, sadly famous on acount of the frightful disaster which, July 4, 1187, there befell the army of the Crusaders, under the command of Guy de Lusignan, king of Jerusalem.

waters of the lake, on whose surface the hills opposite cast sharp reflections. Beyond, the mountains of Djaulan come down to the very shore and shut off the view in that direction. On the right, to the south . . . is a low lying plain, the Ard-el-Ahma; further away is Thabor, its summit, framed in by other mountains, resembling a camel's hump. On the left, toward the north, rises Great Hermon with its snow-capped top." [903] The summit of this hill consists of a plateau about 300 feet long, terminating at each end in a rounded projection which, when viewed from a certain angle, has the appearance of a horn: hence its present name. Some travelers have regarded its appearance as that of a saddle with its two pommels. The thirteenth century is the earliest that we find traces of the tradition that regards the Kurun Hattin as the historic scene of the choosing of the Apostles and the Sermon on the Mount; possibly its curious shape, rather striking even at a considerable distance, favored this choice. While this may be only a hypothesis, it is not at all unlikely, because the locality is solitary, as our Lord wished, and yet easily reached. The latter circumstance would explain the presence of the large crowd that came there to meet Him.[904]

Let us return to the details of the choosing of the Apostles, as recorded by St. Mark and St. Luke. Jesus wished to give this act all due solemnity. He ascended the mountain one evening, in company with a large number of disciples, and together they passed the night there. But while the disciples slept, Jesus engaged in fervent prayer.[905] He took counsel with

[903] A. Legendre, in Vigouroux' *Dictionnaire de la Bible,* Vol. I, cols. 1530 f. Cf. Fillion and Nicole, *Atlas Géographique de la Bible,* pl. X.

[904] Matt. 4: 25; Luke 6: 17. See A. Legendre, *op. cit.,* cols. 1529–1531; Robinson, *Palestine,* I, 482–486; V. Guérin, *Description de la Palestine: La Galilée,* I, 195–198; Stanley, *Sinai and Palestine,* 2d ed., p. 369. St. Jerome declares that he knew nothing for certain on the subject of the Mount of the Beatitudes. He says that several of his contemporaries identified it with Thabor or one of the neighboring mountains.

[905] St. Luke's language is particularly expressive: ἦν διανυκτερεύων ἐν τῇ προσευχῇ τοῦ θεοῦ (Vulg., "*erat pernoctans in oratione Dei*").

His heavenly Father and recommended to Him the choice He was about to make; He prayed the Father to bestow His graces on those to whom so lofty and delicate an office was to be entrusted. With all proper respect, we may suppose this prayer was one of the most earnest supplications of the God-Man made during His public life.

When morning came, the Savior called together the disciples whom He had led to the mountain. Then, in the presence of this notable gathering, which represents for us the beginnings of the Christian Church, He announced one by one the names of the chosen Twelve. The latter, stepping forth from the group of disciples, took their places at His side, proud and happy at this unexpected promotion. St. Mark adds a significant detail to this picture: "He called unto Him whom He would Himself," that is, those whom He deemed the best fitted for the office He was to entrust to them, those whom He had named to His Father during His long prayer. It was truly a spontaneous choice, an act of His free will. He reminds His Apostles of this fact later, when He says: "You have not chosen Me; but I have chosen you." [906] To His Divine Father He will say what amounts to the same thing: "Thine they were, and to Me Thou gavest them." [907] The rule that we shall see Him follow in the choice of His disciples of second rank guided Him *a fortiori* in the choosing of the Twelve. He did not accept indifferently those who offered themselves to Him and wished to attach themselves regularly to His Person, but only those whom He Himself called and chose. [908] It was fitting that the Messias-King should thus select His future ministers.

"Whom also He named Apostles." Apostle is a characteristic name; it means "one sent," a messenger, an envoy. [909] Yet

[906] John 15: 16.
[907] John 17: 6.
[908] Cf. Matt. 4: 19, 21; 8: 18–22; Mark 5: 18–20; Luke 10: 1–16.
[909] In Greek, ἀπόστολος, from the root ἀποστέλλω, "I send"; the Latin *apostolus*,

it is used only ten times in the Gospels,[910] which ordinarily call the Apostles "disciples," in a very special sense. But after the Savior's Ascension this name came into much more frequent use, as may be seen from the Acts of the Apostles[911] and from St. Paul's Epistles. From the sacred text it is evident that Jesus personally bestowed this glorious name upon them, doubtless at the very time of their being chosen.

"He made that twelve should be with Him." The three Synoptics here mention and emphasize this number, the importance of which we can understand, since it came to be frequently employed to designate the members of the Apostolic College.[912] Evidently the number was symbolic, and it is commonly admitted that Jesus, in designating twelve Apostles, neither more nor less, purposed in a visible way to connect the New Covenant with the Old, choosing that number in memory of the twelve great patriarchs who had been the founders of the twelve tribes that originally composed the people of God. He later refers to this fact when He tells the Twelve that they will judge the tribes of Israel.[913] It was because of the mystical character of this number that St. Peter, after our Lord's Ascension, considered that Judas' place in the Apostolic circle "must" be filled without delay.[914]

After supplying these details about the choosing of the Apostles, the Synoptics give their names in three lists which,

whence our word "apostle," is copied from the Greek. John 13: 16, Christ in an indirect way interprets it Himself.

[910] Once by St. Matthew, 10: 2; twice by St. Mark, 3: 14 and 6: 30; six times by St. Luke, 6: 13; 9: 10; 11: 49; 17: 5; 22: 14; 24: 10; once by St. John, 13: 16.

[911] Twenty-nine times.

[912] It is used, with or without the article in the Greek text, four times by St. Matthew, nine times by St. Mark, six times by St. Luke, four times by St. John. It is found also in Acts 6: 2; 1 Cor. 15: 5, and in the writings of the Apostolic Fathers.

[913] Matt. 19: 28; Luke 22: 30. Cf. Apoc. 21: 12.

[914] Acts 1: 22: δεῖ (Vulg., *oportet*).

in conjunction with a similar enumeration in the Acts of the Apostles,[915] are of great interest.

ST. MATTHEW	ST. MARK	ST. LUKE	THE ACTS
Simon	Simon	Simon	Peter
Andrew	James	Andrew	John
James	John	James	James
John	Andrew	John	Andrew
Philip	Philip	Philip	Philip
Bartholomew	Bartholomew	Bartholomew	Thomas
Thomas	Matthew	Matthew	Bartholomew
Matthew	Thomas	Thomas	Matthew
James of Al-pheus	James of Al-pheus	James of Al-pheus	James of Al-pheus
Thadeus	Thaddeus	Simon Zelotes	Simon Zelotes
Simon the Ca-nanean	Simon the Ca-nanean	Jude of James	Jude of James [916]
Judas Iscariot	Judas Iscariot	Judas Iscariot	

Comparing these four lists, we remark that they are all easily divisible into three groups of four names each, each group always containing the same names. Peter, Andrew, James the Greater, and his brother John form the first group. Philip, Bartholomew, Thomas, and Matthew constitute the second. James the Less, Simon the Cananean (or Zelotes), Jude (or Thaddeus), and Judas Iscariot compose the third. In all the lists it is the same Apostle who is named at the head of each group: Simon Peter in the first group, Philip in the second, James the Less in the third. But the other Apostles

[915] Matt. 10: 2–4; Mark 3: 16–19; Luke 6: 14–16; Acts 1: 13. The Fourth Gospel contains no list of this sort. But on different occasions St. John names most of the Apostles individually: Peter, Andrew, John, and perhaps also his brother, Philip, Nathanael (Bartholomew), Thomas, Jude, and Judas.

[916] The traitor's name naturally disappears from the list after his shameful death.

do not regularly occupy the same place in their respective groups. In the lists of the Second and Third Gospel, the Apostles are also joined in pairs by the conjunction "and," perhaps according to the combinations established by our Lord Himself, when He sent the Twelve to preach for the first time.[917] The names seem to follow each other according to a certain order of precedence, the most celebrated Apostles being mentioned first, the others following. St. Peter heads all the lists; and Judas is named last, with an epithet of infamy: "Judas Iscariot, who was the traitor," "Judas Iscariot, who also betrayed Him." It is noteworthy that among the Twelve were two or three pairs of brothers: Peter and Andrew, James the Greater and John, very probably also James the Less and Jude.

Long ago the question was raised whether some of Christ's relations had not been elevated to the dignity of the Apostolate. The matter has been and still is much in dispute. Without entering deeply into this complex problem, we will point out the chief reasons in favor of an affirmative answer. (1) In his Epistle to the Galatians,[918] St. Paul, speaking of the visit which he made to St. Peter shortly after his conversion, says that with St. Peter at Jerusalem, "other of the Apostles I saw none, saving James the brother of the Lord." This evidently refers to James, the son of Alpheus, called James the Less, because the other James, the elder son of Zebedee, had been martyred several years before.[919] A little further on in the same Epistle,[920] St. Paul refers to this same James, along with Cephas and John, as a foundation pillar of the Church: this is virtually equivalent to reckoning him among the members of the Apostolic College. The Jewish historian Jose-

---

[917] St. Mark, 6:7, says explicitly that He sent them "two and two."
[918] Gal. 1:19.
[919] Acts 12:1 f.
[920] Gal. 2:9.

phus [921] also calls James the Less the brother of Jesus.[922]
(2) At the beginning of his Catholic Epistle, St. Jude calls
himself the brother of James; hence it would follow that he
too was one of the Savior's relations. Moreover, the list of
the "brothers" (*i. e.,* cousins) of Jesus, as recorded by St.
Matthew and St. Mark,[923] contains the names of James (Jacob) and of Judas (or Jude). True, these names, which recall
two illustrious patriarchs, were very common among the Jews
and might well be found in families not at all related to
Christ. It is also a fact that, according to other Gospel texts,[924]
the Savior's "brethren" did not believe in His mission at the
time when He formed the College of the Apostles. But this
assertion, true in a general sense, did not refer to all the
"brethren" of Jesus, so that He might have numbered some
of them among the Twelve.[925] Because of these difficulties and
because of the fact that the Acts of the Apostles [926] and St.
Paul [927] seem to make a distinction between the Apostles and
the "brethren" of our Lord, many commentators hesitate or
frankly refuse to admit the identity. However, we consider it
more probable.

As we read over these lists of the Apostles, we observe with
regret, as expressed by St. John Chrysostom,[928] how little we
know of the lives of these chosen ones of Christ beyond what
is contained in the New Testament. We would be exceeding
the scope of our plan if we were to give even a condensed summary of the authentic facts which ancient writers have re-

[921] *Ant.,* XX, ix, 1.
[922] By correlating Matt. 27 : 56, Mark 15 : 40, and John 19 : 25, we are led to the
same conclusion, which has been adopted by numerous commentators.
[923] Matt. 13 : 55; Mark 6 : 3.
[924] John 7 : 5. Cf. Mark 3 : 21.
[925] On this historical problem, which was much disputed in the early Christian
ages, see the various Dictionaries of the Bible, and Corluy, *Les Frères de Notre-
Seigneur,* 1878, pp. 23–27.
[926] Acts 1 : 14.
[927] 1 Cor. 9 : 5.
[928] *Comment. in Epist. ad Philem.*

corded about them. We must, therefore, confine ourselves to a mention of the most salient items.[929]

We will defer speaking of the primacy of St. Peter, a real primacy of honor and of jurisdiction, until we come to the conferring of it upon him by the Divine Master in a plain and decisive manner. But it is well to remark at once that, after having been intimated at the time of Christ's first relations with His future vicar,[930] it is here clearly insinuated by the place which is uniformly accorded to Simon at the head of all four lists and even more so by the remarkable expression that introduces his name in St. Matthew's list: *"Primus, Simon."* [931] This epithet is certainly not a mere ordinal number, but the statement of a real preëminence, since the numbering is not carried beyond him. Simon Peter's character, with its contrasts, is conspicuous in many incidents of the Savior's life. At once determined and wavering, bold and timid, impulsive and generous, the Prince of the Apostles was a Galilean to the marrow of his bones. His ardor no less than his high dignity often impelled him to take the initiative in speaking and acting. More than once he is the spokesman of the Apostolic body. His love for his Master knows no bounds; yet, after rashly attempting to defend Him with the sword, he denies Him. But he valiantly repairs his fault throughout the rest of his life.[932]

His brother Andrew, like him a disciple of the precursor, had the distinction of being the first to go to Jesus with John, the future beloved Apostle.[933] If his renown pales beside that of St. Peter, neither by his labors nor by his death does he

---

[929] Those of our readers who have a taste for this sort of inquiry can satisfy it by consulting the Bible Dictionaries and Encyclopedias, and especially the Bollandists' *Acta Sanctorum.* See also Fillion, *L'Évangile de S. Matthieu,* pp. 191–196.

[930] John 1 : 42.

[931] Πρῶτος Σίμων.

[932] See Canon Fouard, *St. Peter and the First Years of Christianity,* English trans.; Fillion, *Saint Pierre,* 1906 (in the collection *Les Saints*).

[933] John 1 : 35–40.

belie the meaning of his Greek name, which suggests virility, vigor. It is almost surprising that he did not belong to the little group, composed of Peter, James the Greater, and John, which St. Chrysostom calls the group of "the intimate among intimates." St. Mark here informs us that Jesus, doubtless a little later, gave to the two sons of Zebedee and Salome the surname of "Boanerges," [934] i. e., "Sons of Thunder." This characteristically Oriental appellation was a delicate allusion either to the eager temperament and active zeal of the two brothers,[935] or to their powerful eloquence.[936] To the name of James is ordinarily added the epithet of "the Greater," to distinguish him from James of Alpheus, called by way of contrast "the Little," [937] or "the Less." He it was who was the first among the Apostles to have the glory of shedding his blood for Christ.[938] John, his younger brother, "the disciple whom Jesus loved" and to whom He confided His mother before expiring on the cross, the organizer of the Church of Ephesus after St. Paul, was the one of the Twelve who lived the longest, for he did not die until the end of the first century of our era. In him we venerate, not only the Apostle and beloved friend of the Savior, but also the Fourth Evangelist and the author of three Catholic Epistles and of the Apocalypse.[939]

Since the Middle Ages it has been rather commonly held that Bartholomew is none other than Nathanael, that "good Israelite" who was brought to Jesus by his friend Philip, at the very outset of the public life and who, though skeptical at

[934] The probable etymology of this Aramaic term is *boane,* "son," and *reguesh,* "thunder." See Fillion, *L'Évangile de S. Marc,* pp. 56 f.

[935] Some traces of it are to be found in the Gospels. Cf. Mark 9 : 38 ; 10 : 37 ; Luke 9 : 54. See also 1 John 2 : 22 ; 3 : 8 ; 3 John 7–11.

[936] Origen mentions the "mystical thunder," νοητὴ βροντή, which reverberates in St. John's writings.

[937] Mark 15 : 40.

[938] Acts 12 : 2.

[939] His life has been written often. See especially Mgr. Baunard, *L'Apôtre Saint Jean,* 1869 ; Fouard, *Saint Jean et la Fin de l'Âge Apostolique,* 4th ed., 1906 ; Fillion, *Saint Jean l'Évangeliste, sa Vie et ses Écrits,* 1907.

first, was promptly won by the Divine Master.[940] This identification rests on several grounds. Among the five persons mentioned at the close of the first chapter of St. John, four became Apostles, and there is no apparent reason why Nathanael should have been the only one left out. In this same passage Jesus informs him that He has destined him for a higher rôle, which could hardly be anything but that of an Apostle. Bartholomew is connected with Philip in the four lists of Apostles as Nathanael is in the episode to which we have just referred. On the last page of the Fourth Gospel,[941] Nathanael again is a member of a group of Apostles, seemingly because he was himself one of the Twelve. Moreover, Bartholomew, in Aramaic *Bar-Tolmai,* "son of Tolmai," is a patronymic and presupposes a personal name, which in the present case would have been Nathanael.

According to a very early tradition, and in spite of Heracleon and Origen, Levi and Matthew are one and the same person. In him we recognize the author of the First Gospel, the Gospel of the Messias. St. John [942] more than once gives the Greek translation of the name "Thomas"—in Hebrew, *Teom;* in Aramaic, *Toma*—which means "Didymus," *i. e.,* twin. This Apostle's character in some respects resembled that of Peter: he was ardent and generous,[943] but he also had moments of weakness.[944]

In the case of some of the Apostles, the same name was duplicated, and it was therefore necessary to distinguish them by surnames. Hence we see the names of James the Greater and James the Less or the Little. In the four lists the latter is called "James of Alpheus," *i. e.,* the son of Alpheus. It is the view of a large number of interpreters that Alpheus

[940] John 1 : 45–51.
[941] John 21 : 2.
[942] John 11 : 16; 20 : 24; 21 : 2.
[943] John 11 : 16.
[944] John 20 : 24–29.

is, in the half-concealed Hebraic form of the name,[945] the same as Cleophas, mentioned by St. Luke and St. John [946] in connection with Christ's Passion and Resurrection. The opinion has been almost universal in the Latin Church that the Apostle "Judas of James," as St. Luke calls him, was the brother of St. James the Less and a near relation of our Lord. To this view it is objected that in the preceding line the words "James of Alpheus" certainly mean the son of Alpheus and that it is hardly permissible, after so short an interval, to translate a similar expression differently. The objection has weight; but the tradition has weight too, and classical literature offers examples of combinations like this, in which the second name does not always indicate paternity, but sometimes the relation of brother. St. Jude has this peculiarity, that he is designated by three different names in the lists.[947] In fact, he is also called Thaddeus [948] and Lebbeus,[949] two diminutives expressing tenderness.[950]

Simon the Cananean, or more exactly, following St. Luke, Simon the Zealot,[951] had belonged, as this epithet signifies, to the party of Galilean zealots, which was already in existence in Palestine at the time of our Lord, but generally in a moderate form, very different from the form it assumed at the time of the war with the Romans. To-day we would translate it "Nationalist."

[945] Halpai. In Greek, 'Αλφαῖος (Vulg., *Alphaeus*).

[946] Luke 24: 18; John 19: 25.

[947] This is why early writers, with St. Jerome, sometimes said of him that he was the Apostle "with the three names."

[948] In St. Matthew's and St. Mark's lists.

[949] In several manuscripts of the First Gospel.

[950] The former, *Taddai*, seems to be derived from the noun *tad*, "breast," and might be translated "beloved." The latter, *Lebbai*, comes from *leb*, "heart." Both, therefore, have almost the same meaning.

[951] The Greek name Καναναῖος, from which the Latin *Cananaeus* and the English "Cananean" are copied, is the reproduction of the Aramaic *Kan'ana*, which means zealot. It does not at all refer to the country of Chanaan nor to the town of Cana. The reading Καναντης, found in a certain number of Greek manuscripts, is faulty.

The epithet "Iscariot," independently of the infamous
words, "who betrayed Jesus," serves to make a distinction between the two Apostles who bore the name of Judas; it is
almost unanimously considered as the equivalent of the Hebrew *ish Keriot,* "man of Kerioth," *i. e.,* living in the place
that formerly bore this name. It is a geographical designation, which was likewise applied to the traitor's father.[952]
The town in question was not the Kerioth of the country of
Moab,[953] east of the Dead Sea, but that of northern Judea.[954]
Judas seems to have been the only one of the Twelve who was
not a Galilean.

The presence of a traitor in the ranks of the Apostles raises
a problem that is both psychological and theological, one that
we cannot pass over in silence. How are we to explain the fact
that Jesus chose this wretch and placed him among the
Twelve? And how are we to explain that an Apostle fell so
low as to betray such a Master? Therein is surely a deep,
sorrowful mystery which, for the past hundred years especially among Rationalists, has at times received the strangest
interpretations,[955] as though Judas had purposed rendering
a service to our Lord by delivering Him into the hands of
His enemies. Sometimes, also, there has been exaggeration
in the opposite direction, by taking from Judas every human
feeling and considering him as hostile to Jesus from the very
first. The question must not be decided *a priori,* with preconceived notions in either sense, but by the aid of the documents, *i. e.,* our four Gospels.[956]

---

[952] John 6:72, in the Greek text: "Judas [son] of Simon Iscariot." The Vulgate,
by mistake, has: *Judam Simonis Iscariotem.*

[953] Jer. 48:24, 41. Hebrew, *Keriot;* Vulgate, *Carioth.*

[954] Josue 15:2. Hebrew, *Keriot Hesron;* Vulgate, *Carioth Hesron.*

[955] See Appendix IX, 2.

[956] For a thorough solving of this problem, it would be well to consider, one
after the other, all the Gospel texts in which the traitor is mentioned, namely:
(1) the lists of Apostles: Matt. 10:2-4; Mark 3:16-19; Luke 6:14-16; (2) the
passages referring to Judas during our Lord's public life: Matt. 26:8 f.; Mark

The traitor's character is, indeed, complex. At the time when the Savior honored him by choosing him as an Apostle, it cannot be doubted that he possessed all the qualities required for worthily filling that office. He certainly had defects, prejudices. But none of the Twelve was entirely free from defects and, in that holy association with Jesus, he might easily have overcome them. But he allowed ambition, jealousy, and especially avarice (that passion which makes one excessively brutal and selfish) to take possession of his heart. These vices gradually led him to commit the most horrible crime in the annals of history. About a year before Christ's death, when Judas observed the defection of many disciples and when he comprehended that the bright hopes which he had based on his title of Apostle were ruined, inasmuch as Jesus would not lend Himself to the proud expectations of the Jewish national Messianism, his apostasy was a settled thing in the depth of his soul.[957]

Yet Jesus had loved him as He did the other Apostles and had even given him a particular mark of confidence by making him the treasurer of the little community.[958] Again and again did our Lord clearly warn him, though always with the utmost delicacy, of the moral danger he was running, showing him, in veiled words that would not arouse the suspicions of his fellow-Apostles, that He was not unaware of his dark schemes.[959] It was all in vain. Judas' heart kept growing more hardened up to the very moment when he made his horrible proposal to the members of the Sanhedrin: "What will you give me, and I will deliver Him unto you?" Even then Jesus

14:4 f.; Luke 22:3; John 6:64–72; 12:4–6; 13:11; (3) the accounts of the betrayal: Matt. 26:14–16; Mark 14:10 f.; Luke 22:3–6; John 13:2; Matt. 26:21–25; Mark 14:18–21; Luke 22:21 f.; John 13:21–30; Matt. 26:47–50; Mark 14:43–45; Luke 22:47 f.; John 18:2 f.; (4) the accounts of the traitor's death: Matt. 27:3–5; Acts 1:16–20.

957 John 6:67–72.
958 John 12:6; 13:29.
959 John 6:71 f.; 13:21–30.

still tried to lead him into better dispositions and to awaken his conscience,[960] but without success. Finally, He had to abandon the traitor to himself and let him perpetrate his crime. To save him, it would have been necessary to violate the conditions to which God attached man's individual redemption. That Jesus was morally unable to do.

After all, the problem of Judas' fall is but part of another more general problem: the reconciling of divine foreknowledge with human free will, in other words, the problem of predestination. "Judas was among the Apostles by the same title as the serpent in the earthly paradise, Cain in the home of the first human family, Sham in the ark, evil always and everywhere with goodness. He was in the Apostolic College to serve as an instrument in the carrying out of the providential decrees regarding the Messias. And this instrument acted in the full exercise of his free will, nay more, even though he was the recipient of choice graces, by the aid of which he could have rescued himself from his ignominious rôle. . . . But the traitor abused it all. Whose, then, is the blame?" [961]

After mentioning the choosing of the Twelve, St. Mark briefly indicates the twofold purpose which Jesus intended by that solemn act: He wished to have the Apostles with Him and to send them to preach. This was but the immediate purpose, because, with regard to His Apostles, our Lord had much more far-reaching aims, which He reveals to them in due time. Meanwhile it is enough that He have them always at His side, gradually to train and instruct them, and also at times to entrust them with the ministry of preaching, as a sort of apprenticeship. St. Mark further says that Jesus bestowed upon the Twelve the power to heal diseases and to drive out devils. It may be, however, that this detail is in-

---

[960] Matt. 26: 20–25; John 13: 27.
[961] Fillion, *L'Évangile de S. Matthieu,* pp. 195 f. See Appendix IX, 2.

serted at this point by anticipation, because we see the Apostles exercising this wonderful gift only when they go forth to preach for the first time.[962]

Let us now take a general glance at the list which we have been considering in detail. St. Paul wrote to the recently converted Christians of Corinth: "See your vocation, brethren, that there are not many wise according to the flesh, not many mighty, not many noble. But the foolish things of the world hath God chosen, that He may confound the wise; and the weak things of the world hath God chosen, that He may confound the strong. And the base things of the world and the things that are contemptible, hath God chosen, and things that are not, that He might bring to nought things that are: that no flesh should glory in His sight." [963] This remark also applies to the providential choosing of the Twelve. Upon considering the four lists containing their names, we observe that none of the Apostles belonged to the influential classes of contemporary Judaism. In vain do we look among the Apostles, at the time of their being called, for a member of the priestly caste, a Scribe, a Pharisee, the possessor of a large fortune, a genius, a capable organizer. The fact is that Jesus had no need of human means to found His Church. Once it is firmly established, with the concourse of these plain, weak men, taken from the ranks of the common people, accustomed to hard labor, men who earned their bread by the sweat of their brow, it can in all truth be said: "The finger of God is there." Men imbued with Pharisaic prejudices, filled with the vainglorious sentiments of their personal strength, would not be fitted to help in the work of the Messias. With supreme contempt, the Sanhedrin will treat the Apostles as "illiterate and ignorant men," [964] and Celsus will ridicule them because

---

[962] Mark 6: 12 f.; Luke 9: 6.
[963] I Cor. I: 26–29.
[964] Acts 4: 13; ἀγράμματοι καὶ ἰδιῶται (Vulg., *sine litteris et idiotae*).

of their lack of worldly knowledge.[965] Although they did not attend the Scribes' classes—this is what is meant when they are called "illiterate"—the Apostles were men of good sense and sound judgment, capable of mental development, as their acts and writings prove. Let us not expect of them a worldly influence and knowledge which in reality they did not possess. Jesus and His Divine Spirit will be able to instruct them and make them apt in learning and preaching Christian truths. Several of them will fill that office with admirable loftiness of vision. Will there not be among them one of the greatest theologians that ever lived?

So far as we can judge, the Twelve were in the strength of young manhood when Jesus called them. At that time they were probably between twenty and thirty years old, the age of full vigor. This was an excellent condition, since they would have to endure wearisome labor and privations. It is supposed that St. John was the youngest of them. Many, perhaps most of them, were married, as was Simon Peter.[966] St. Jerome's beautiful saying about the beloved disciple is well-known: "John, who was virginal when he first believed in Christ, remained always so, and this is why he was more beloved of the Savior, and why he leaned on the breast of Jesus." [967] The Apostles' individual characters, as they are occasionally manifested in the Gospels, were most varied, complementing one another, so that the community of the Twelve formed an interesting "microcosm."

Those whom Jesus thus attached to Himself for the purpose of making them His witnesses and heralds, were, of course, of Jewish origin, since the Christian Church was to

---

[965] Origen, *Contra Celsum*, I, 62; III, 29; VI, 7; VIII, 47; *De Princip.*, II, vi, 1. Cf. St. Justin, *Apol.*, I, 39; Clement of Alexandria, *Stromata*, I, ix, 45.

[966] Matt. 8:14; 1 Cor. 9:5 f.

[967] *Contr. Jovinian.*, I, 26. Cf. *Epist. ad Princip.*, CXXVII, 2; Fillion, *Saint Jean l'Évangeliste*, pp. 31–35.

be the direct successor of the Synagogue and since the Messianic salvation was first offered to the Jews. They were devout men, full of faith and piety, fearing God and obedient to His laws, men of great uprightness and integrity, loyal, humble, prudent, and active. Abandoning as they did, at a single word from the Divine Master, whatever they held most dear, they showed how greatly they possessed the spirit of detachment.[968] We scarcely need to add that they were united to Christ by bonds of an affection that was both deep and respectful. This they proved by sharing His life of poverty and mortification for several years and, all except the traitor, by laboring for Him after His Resurrection with unwavering fidelity. All things considered, they were individually and collectively endowed with fine qualities that grew day by day. Thus we may say, without disrespectful presumption, that their selection did honor to the Savior's human wisdom and sagacity.

It is unnecessary to exaggerate, as was often done in the early centuries,[969] in order to realize, from many a detail in the Gospels, that the Apostles, even after passing considerable time in the Savior's school, were still imperfect from a moral standpoint. We see that they were slow to grasp certain of Christ's teachings;[970] in particular that they were unable to convince themselves of the necessity of His Passion and death;[971] that they were jealous of one another,[972] ambi-

---

[968] Peter and Andrew, James and John were perhaps in comfortable circumstances, and the others also; St. Matthew still more so, without however there being any justification for the epithet πλούσιος, "rich," which Clement of Alexandria associates with his name (*Quis Dives Salv.*, 13).

[969] On this subject, see the interesting quotations taken from the Christian literature of the first centuries, in W. Bauer, *Leben Jesu*, pp. 430, 432–434. The Epistle of Barnabas, V, 9, makes of the Apostles, at the time of their being called, scandalous sinners (ὄντας ὑπὲρ πᾶσαν ἁμαρτίαν ἀνομωτέρους). Origen also, *Hom. in Joan.*, I, 13, judges them very severely. See also his *Comment. in Matth.*, XII, 40 f.

[970] Matt. 16: 5–12; Mark 8: 14–20, etc.

[971] Matt. 16: 20–23; Luke 9: 44 f., etc.

[972] Mark 9: 32–35.

tious,[973] vindictive,[974] narrow-minded and exclusive,[975] weak-willed to such an extent that the chief of them denied His Master to a servant,[976] that all abandoned Him in the hour of danger,[977] and that one of them shamefully betrayed Him. Notwithstanding all these imperfections, they truly formed an "élite," to use Tertullian's expression,[978] and were fitted to receive a training as a result of which that crude gold, after passing through the hands of the great goldsmith, became a most pure metal, free from all dross.

We must now describe that training, at least in its broad outlines. It will show us Jesus under a new aspect, that of the wisest, most patient, and most devoted of teachers.[979] From the moment when He gathered the Twelve around Him, He devoted Himself with untiring zeal to the task which He had generously assumed. So excellent was His method and so assiduous His labor that He gradually accomplished His purpose.

As St. Mark tells us, it was Christ's wish to have His Apostles, once He had chosen them, constantly with Him. This decision was not without good reason. Habitual association with Him would be the best and chief element of their training, for never has the earth possessed a personality even remotely comparable to our Blessed Lord. His outward distinction, His bearing, His speech, and most particularly His moral perfection placed Him infinitely above all other men. With this model ever before their eyes, the Apostles were constantly learning to know Him and esteem Him better, to

[973] Matt. 20: 20–28; Luke 22: 24–30.
[974] Luke 9: 51–56.
[975] Mark 9: 37–40.
[976] Matt. 26: 69–75.
[977] Matt. 26: 56.
[978] *De Praescript. Haeret.,* 20.
[979] Details on this subject will be found in H. Latham, *Pastor Pastorum, or the Schooling of the Twelve by Our Lord,* and A. Bruce, *The Training of the Twelve,* 3d ed., 1883.

imbibe His spirit, and to imitate Him. His virtue was so simple and natural! Into it there entered no austerities like those of John the Baptist, no peculiarities like those of the Pharisees. In him everything breathed humility, detachment, modesty, poverty, trust in God, perfect holiness, the sincerest spirit of religion. In His school His intimate disciples learned true, solid piety instead of rigid formalism. His sympathy for every kind of suffering, His mercy toward sinners, His love for His heavenly Father, all formed an ideal that could not fail to impress them. The sight of their Master's miracles also had a share in their training. Those repeated wonders, which produced so deep an impression on the multitudes, as we have already seen in the Gospel narrative, doubly affected the Apostles, who saw their Divine Master performing these prodigies of all sorts day after day. In those miracles they found an invincible argument in favor of His Messianic character. Their faith became purer as they observed that the Savior's miracles were of an utterly different sort from those which their fellow-Jews were then expecting from the Messias. Moreover, many of these miracles were performed directly for the sake of the Apostles—for example, the first and second miraculous draughts of fishes,[980] the stilling of the tempest,[981] the walking on the water,[982] the stater in the fish's mouth,[983] the cursing of the fig tree [984]— and must have exerted a special influence upon their minds. For at least two years they were thus close observers of the deeds of the great Miracle-worker.

One cannot help but be moved when picturing to oneself what the life of the Apostles must have been in the intimate companionship of the most perfect of teachers. Although they

[980] Luke 5 : 1-7 ; John 21 : 1-11.
[981] Matt. 8 : 23-27.
[982] Matt. 14 : 25-32.
[983] Matt. 17 : 23-26.
[984] Matt. 21 : 18 f. ; Mark 11 : 12-14.

shared His labors, fatigues, and privations, what indescribable joys were theirs in His holy presence! One day He congratulated them on this unique privilege: "Amen, I say to you, many prophets and just men have desired to see the things that you see and have not seen them, and to hear the things that you hear and have not heard them." [985] One is still more impressed upon thinking of what must have been, for a delicate and exquisite nature like that of the Incarnate Word, a life in common with those men, who were naturally somewhat crude. He was henceforth deprived of His freedom, His peaceful solitude. Furthermore, did He not have to provide for their temporal needs, since He had required them to give up what was formerly their means of livelihood?

Jesus' words constituted another effective element in the Apostles' training, and unquestionably exercised a powerful influence upon them. They derived immense profit from His general preaching. Whatever this incomparable teacher imparted to the people about the Kingdom of Heaven, the nature of God, His own Person, Christian perfection, fraternal charity, and the future Church, enlightened their minds and elevated their hearts. But every day the Savior's teaching also came to them in a special form, the direct aim of which was their Apostolic training. The Gospels contain a comparatively large number of these special instructions, these precise lessons which were addressed solely to them. The Divine Master thereby imparted His spirit to them, inculcated them with His wishes, and enlightened them upon their present and future office. There were lessons about how they should conduct themselves as preachers of the gospel,[986] lessons of humility,[987] lessons of tolerance,[988] of good example,[989] of love

[985] Matt. 13:17.
[986] Matt. 10:1-42.
[987] Matt. 20:25-28; Mark 10:42-45.
[988] Mark 9:37-40; Luke 9:49 f.
[989] Matt. 18:6-9; Mark 9:41-49.

for their neighbor.[990] What a wealth of instruction was contained in the discourse about the end of the world,[991] and in the farewell address delivered in the Cenacle and on the way to Gethsemani![992] When we study these pages of the Gospel later on, we shall understand how well suited they were to the moral conditions of the Twelve, and how effective for producing in the Apostles the transformation which Jesus desired.

We should note that, in these familiar conversations of Christ with His Apostles, no trace is to be seen of any esoteric teaching, nothing that may not be "preached from the house-tops," when the proper hour comes. This unique educator was wonderfully skilful in adapting His instructions and counsels to the circumstances of the occasion. Only gradually and in due season did He reveal to the disciples certain truths harder to understand. That was one of His pedagogical principles. "I have many things to say to you; but you cannot bear them now."[993] Whenever His teaching presented some obscurity, He gave the Apostles all desirable explanation.[994] At times what pains He took to make them understand, despite their obtuseness, certain essential teachings, notably the necessity of His Passion and death! Sometimes He complained of their dullness of mind. It is charming to see with what frankness the Evangelists record these complaints, so little to the credit of the Apostles. Another trait of the excellence of the Savior's pedagogy is to be found in the fact that, in the matter of moral perfection, He required of His disciples only what they could easily perform at the time. He waited until they had grown strong before calling upon them to make harder sacrifices.[995]

---

[990] Matt. 18: 15–35.

[991] Matt. chaps. 23–25.

[992] John chaps. 13–16.

[993] John 16: 12–25.

[994] Mark 4: 34: Τοῖς ἰδίοις μαθηταῖς ἐπέλυεν πάντα. Cf. Matt. 13: 10–17, 36–43; 16: 10–13; 18: 21–35, etc.

[995] Matt. 9: 14–17, etc.

The most successful means which our Lord employed in training His Apostles was certainly the fatherly love with which He encompassed them. How could they have withstood such tenderness or have refused so loving a Master whatever He asked? His guidance was ever that of a most devoted friend. Together with Him they formed a united family, in which He was the profoundly respected head.[996] He addressed them by tender, loving names, calling them His friends,[997] His brethren,[998] His little children.[999] With a mother's solicitude He was watchful that they should want for nothing, and He even thought to procure a few days' rest for them after their hard labors.[1] His kindness to them was unlimited. The remark with which St. John introduces the scene of the washing of the Apostles' feet, demonstrates this most eloquently: "Having loved His own who were in the world, He loved them unto the end";[2] or, according to a translation that is perhaps more exact, "He loved them even to excess." And in His solemn prayer to His heavenly Father upon setting forth from the Cenacle,[3] looking back over the years during which He had kept the Twelve at His side, He could truthfully say that He had fulfilled toward them all the obligations of a most deep attachment. His influence was always mild and penetrated their souls like a sweet fragrance. It is noteworthy that He never did the least violence to His Apostles' moral temperament, in a way to stifle their individual character, but sought to suppress only their defects, leaving to each his own personal nature, adorned and perfected.

His affection always remained firm and vigorous, without, however, changing to harshness. For the sake of those whom

[996] Matt. 10:24 f.; 23:8, 10; 24:42 f.; John 13:13 f.
[997] Luke 12:4; John 15:14 f.
[998] Matt. 25:40; 28:10; John 20:17.
[999] John 13:33; 21:5.
[1] Mark 6:30 f.
[2] John 13:1.
[3] John 17:6, 8, 12.

He was preparing for so lofty an office, He let no occasion
pass to correct their imperfections. His rebukes were sometimes justly stern,[4] but at other times they were marked by
the most winning gentleness. Such were His words to St.
Peter when He said: "Simon, sleepest thou? Couldst thou
not watch one hour?" [5] Such also was the Master's look that
penetrated the very depth of Peter's heart after his denial.[6]
The Apostles were always at ease with Him, for He allowed
them a familiarity which, however, did not for a moment cease
to be imbued with the deepest respect.

The loyal candor, as also the gentleness of His method of
training, has ever been admired. Says Guizot: "You might
read and reread the history of all the religious or political
revolutions that have ever taken place in the world; but nowhere would you find, between the leader and his companions,
between the founder and his workers, this divine character
of perfect and strict sincerity that is to be seen in the acts
and language of Jesus Christ towards His Apostles. He had
chosen them, and He loved them; to them He confided His
work, but He made use of no leniency or reticence, no falter-
ing encouragement, no exaggeration either of promise or
hope, in dealing with them. He told them nothing but the
pure truth; and in the name of truth He gave them His commandments and handed on His mission to them." [7] The Savior's method of teaching His Apostles, therefore, bore the
happiest fruit.

II. The Sermon on the Mount [8]

St. Luke connects this remarkable portion of the Savior's
teaching directly with the choosing of the Apostles, and every-

[4] Matt. 16: 22 f.; Mark 8: 32 f.
[5] Mark 14: 37.
[6] Luke 22: 61.
[7] Guizot, *Méditations*, pp. 269 f.
[8] Matt. 5: 1–7: 27; Luke 6: 20–49.

thing leads us to believe that is its right place. The chronological place which the First Gospel assigns to it is not strictly
correct. St. Matthew anticipates the facts by inserting it at
the beginning of Christ's public life, by way of a worthy opening of His preaching, of which it is an eloquent abridgment.
For a discourse of this sort to be fruitful, Jesus must have
already begun His ministry some time before and must have
acquired numerous disciples, whom the three Evangelists
show us then gathered about Him. According to the natural
order of events, we are thus transported to within a short
time of the feast which we have called the first Pasch of our
Lord's ministry. It was in the midst of the "happy year," although, as a famous passage in the sermon itself shows, the
first indications of the opposition of the ruling classes had already appeared.

The founding of the Apostolic College and the Sermon on
the Mount are connected events, both of them having a notable significance in Christ's life. Quite rightly they are regarded as the first steps taken by Him for the founding of
His Church. By the choosing of the Apostles, He acquired
assistants whom He would prepare as official successors. By
delivering His great Sermon, He promulgated what has been
well called the Charter of the Kingdom of Heaven.

"Seeing the multitudes, He went up into a mountain and
. . . He taught them." [9] By these words St. Matthew introduces the wonderful discourse which, because of the place
where the words were first heard, is called the Sermon on
the Mount.

We have already described the region which, at least in its
ensemble, served as the scene of this discourse. It was one
of the natural terraces of the hilly country on the northwest
shore of Lake Tiberias, not far from Capharnaum. Jesus
came to this solitary region the previous evening and passed

[9] Matt. 5 : 1 f.

the night in prayer, before forming the College of the Twelve. The crowds that were continually drawn to Him by His miracles and words and by the charm of His Person, rejoined Him there in the morning and furnished the occasion for delivering this masterful sermon. Like His subject, His pulpit was also one of grandeur, in contrast with the little boat from which not long before He had preached to the people gathered on the shore.[10] Since the Sermon on the Mount is, in a sense, to the Christian Church what the legislation of Sinai was to the theocracy of the Old Testament, it was equivalent to a solemn promulgation of the New Law. But what a difference in the outward circumstances in which the two divine codes were given to the world! "In the one case there was the arid desert, a forbidding, gigantic rocky mountain, crowned with lightning flashes, an awesome region; in the other case, there was a grass-covered plateau from which one looks down upon a region which in former times was reckoned among the most charming in the world. At Sinai God's word reverberated like awful thunderclaps; here the divine word is full of mildness. There the people were commanded to keep aloof; here with cordial familiarity they approach the Lawgiver, who is the Savior of mankind. There the law was promulgated; here, the gospel." [11]

Those who had the blessed privilege of being the first to hear this memorable sermon formed three distinct categories, as the sacred writers clearly state. In the foremost rank were the Apostles whom Jesus had just chosen. In the second rank, forming a compact group around the Divine Speaker, were the numerous disciples whom He led thither the day before. Behind these were gathered the multitudes that had come from every quarter of Palestine to see our Lord and to hear His words. From St. Matthew's and St. Luke's narratives we

[10] Mark 3:9; Luke 5:1-3.
[11] Fillion, L'Évangile de S. Matthieu, p. 100.

can see that it was especially the two former classes that Jesus addressed. And this clearly follows from the very substance of the discourse, since in part it describes the qualities of perfect Christians, to whom alone were suited, for example, the Beatitudes, the words "You are the salt of the earth. . . . You are the light of the world," and many other details.[12] But it is no less certain that, according to Christ's intention, numerous other details applied likewise to the great mass of His audience, since it was composed mostly of friendly groups. St. Matthew pictures these crowds at the close of the Sermon as lost in admiration.[13] St. Luke says: "When He [Jesus] had finished all His words in the hearing of the people." [14]

St. Mark does not include the Sermon on the Mount in his Gospel. Deeds entered into his plan much more than discourses. Furthermore, the sermon we are about to study has a Jewish coloring which would not have greatly interested the Roman readers of the Second Gospel. Both St. Matthew and St. Luke have preserved it, but with considerable variants, both of content and form. It occupies three whole chapters, one hundred and seven verses, in the First Gospel and only twenty-nine verses in the Third. St. Matthew [15] tells us that the sermon was delivered on a mountain, but St. Luke [16] says that Jesus, after choosing the twelve Apostles, came down from the mountain and stopped in a plain, where He preached to the disciples and the multitude. From these divergences it has sometimes been concluded, in early times as well as in our own day,[17] that we have here the reports of two different

---

[12] Matt. 5 : 1 f.: "His disciples came unto Him and . . . He taught them, saying . . ." Luke 6 : 20: "And He, lifting up His eyes on His disciples, said . . ."

[13] Matt. 7 : 28.

[14] Luke 7 : 1.

[15] Matt. 5 : 1.

[16] Luke 6 : 17.

[17] *V. g.*, St. Augustine and St. Gregory the Great in the early centuries; in recent times, Dr. Keim.

discourses, the longer one delivered on the mountain in the presence of the Apostles and disciples, the shorter one in the plain, somewhat later, before the multitude that had rejoined our Lord.

All things being considered, we prefer the view of most commentators [18] that the two accounts, in spite of their very marked differences, refer to one and the same sermon. All the divergences are easily explained, and the resemblances are such that it is hardly possible not to maintain the identity. The external circumstances are alike: we have the same audience, made up of the disciples and the multitude; the location is the same, for the plain mentioned by St. Luke deserves that name only by reference to the height from which Jesus had just come down; it was a level spot in the hilly country. The theme is likewise identical: in both cases it is real justice, Christian holiness. This subject, although much abridged in the Third Gospel, is treated in the same manner in each account. At the beginning are the Beatitudes; then come rules of conduct, often expressed in identical words; at the close is a warning in the form of a characteristic parable. Moreover, the sermon, as we read it in St. Luke, is contained in its entirety in St. Matthew's account. Here, as in other instances, the author of the Third Gospel, following the document at his disposal, suppresses certain details that he judged useless for his Greek readers; notably the lengthy comparison which our Lord makes between Jewish holiness and Christian perfection,[19] as also the description of Pharisaic hypocrisy.[20] He also omits other passages which appear elsewhere in his narrative, since Jesus on different occasions repeated certain of His particularly significant precepts.[21] It is possible, too, that

[18] In early times, St. John Chrysostom and St. Jerome.
[19] Matt. 5: 17–48.
[20] Matt. 6: 1–18.
[21] "*Vitae totius praecepta, quae non potuerunt nimium saepi repeti.*" Grotius, *In Luc.*, 6: 17.

St. Matthew, as he frequently does, has detached from their chronological place certain sayings of the Divine Master— especially some of those that St. Luke sets forth elsewhere [22] —in order to join them with other similar sayings. This, however, is only a hypothesis. The Sermon on the Mount, as we find it in the First Gospel, must be very close to the form it had when it left the heart and lips of the Savior. We should not be surprised at its length, because Jesus did not hesitate to develop His thought when He was teaching the multitudes.[23] As it comes down to us, it could have been delivered in less than a half hour.

Christian interpreters all agree in praising its perfect unity. Its dominant idea, set forth under different aspects, is that of the Kingdom of Heaven, in its essence and principles, and in the conditions required of those who wish to belong to it, in a word, in the holiness that ought to shine forth in each of its members. This beautiful subject of Christian morality, contrasted with the moral teaching of the Old Testament and more notably with that of the Judaism of our Lord's time, is clearly defined and amply developed. Herein we have a proclamation of the Messias, who, as founder and lawgiver of the New Covenant, declares to His subjects what He requires and expects of them if they wish to serve Him faithfully, not in words, but in deeds. Until then, Jesus had announced to His countrymen the coming of the Kingdom of God and urged them to enter therein. But He had not yet described in detail the moral qualities they must possess to become worthy of it. On the present occasion He does so. It was needful for His disciples, as also for the multitudes, to be acquainted with His thought and His will on this subject. He employs, not the form of exhortation, but rather that of exposition, sketching the constitution of the Kingdom of

---

[22] *V. g.*, Matt. 5 : 25, 32 ; 6 : 7–13 ; 7 : 6, 7–11, 22 f.
[23] Cf. Mark 4 : 1 f., 33 ; 6 : 34 f., etc.

Heaven and enumerating its principal laws. What He proposes as their goal is the most beautiful and lofty of ideals.

In the general order of ideas and in their connection with one another a plan is evident, although we should not look for an arrangement as closely reasoned as that to which we people of the Occident are accustomed.[24] The Beatitudes form, as it were, the exordium, wherein Jesus sets forth the essential conditions on which citizenship in His Kingdom depends.[25] Then, in the body of the sermon,[26] He indicates what are the chief obligations of His subjects and points out some of their rights. In an eloquent epilogue,[27] He urges His hearers to put into practice the rules of conduct which He has just outlined.

Before quoting the text of the sermon, the two Evangelists draw attention to its importance by a few dramatic details. St. Luke tells us that it was preceded by an extraordinary display of our Lord's miraculous power: "They that were troubled with unclean spirits were cured. And all the multitude sought to touch Him, for virtue went out from Him and healed all." [28] Then St. Matthew notes [29] that the Savior, when about to begin speaking, sat down. This He usually did when preaching at considerable length.[30] A solemnity is evident from a detail given by St. Luke: "lifting up His eyes on His disciples" [31] a look full of hope and joy and tenderness —and from St. Matthew's words: "Opening His mouth, He taught them." [32]

---

[24] In our rapid exposition we will follow St. Matthew's presentation, since it most closely approaches the authentic expression of the discourse.

[25] Matt. 5: 3–16; Luke 6: 20–26.

[26] Matt. 5: 17–7: 23; Luke 6: 27–46.

[27] Matt. 7: 24–27; Luke 6: 47–49.

[28] Luke 6: 18 f. Cf. Matt. 4: 24 f., and Mark 3: 7–12, passages referring to the same event.

[29] Matt. 5: 1.

[30] Matt. 13: 2; 26: 55; Mark 13: 3; Luke 4: 20.

[31] Luke 6: 20.

[32] Matt. 5: 2. We find this same detail in several other places in the Bible (Job

If, as has been said, the Sermon on the Mount may be compared to a magnificent palace, the Beatitudes are its fitting vestibule.[33] Their name of "Beatitudes" comes from the Latin adjective *Beati* ("Blessed") with which each of them begins.[34] They appeal to a universal craving of the human heart, always and everywhere so eager for happiness, and they promise the satisfaction of that longing. But here there is evidently question of a pure and lofty satisfaction, which can be enjoyed, first on earth, then eternally in Heaven, by all who faithfully obey the law imposed by Christ.

The number of the Beatitudes is not the same in the two accounts. Ordinarily we speak of eight, according to St. Matthew's enumeration;[35] Bossuet calls them "the octave of Beatitudes."[36] St. Luke[37] mentions only four, to which he adds four maledictions exactly corresponding to them, but which are lacking in the First Gospel. He omits those concerning the meek, the merciful, the pure of heart, and the peacemakers. Possibly in the first instance there were eight maledictions, as there were eight Beatitudes, since it was natural that Jesus, after felicitating those who would be fully imbued with the Christian spirit, should foretell the evil fortune of those who would refuse to acquire it.

If we consider the Beatitudes according to their external form, we see that they are in rhythm, in cadence after the man-

3:1; Acts 8:35; 10:34) and also in classical authors (Aristophanes, *Ar.*, XVII, 9; Virgil, *Æneid*, II, 246).

[33] Fairbairn, *Studies in the Life of Christ,* p. 139.

[34] The Greek μακάριος has the same meaning. It is equivalent to the Hebrew *'ashere,* often used in a similar manner in the Psalms and elsewhere. Cf. Ps. 1:1; 2:13; 31:1 f.; 32:12; 40:1; 64:4, etc.

[35] Matt. 5:1–12. Various recent authors reduce this number to seven, others raise it to nine or even ten. But as Dr. Zahn well says, *Das Evangelium des Matthäus,* p. 176, "there are neither seven nor nine nor ten Beatitudes; there are eight, as during all the centuries it has been customary to reckon them." St. Ambrose, *De Offic.,* I, 6, already spoke of this number in his day.

[36] *Méditations sur l'Évangile,* 1st day.

[37] Luke 6:20–26.

ner of Hebrew poetry. Each of them is composed of two hemi-
stichs. In the first Jesus mentions a Christian virtue and calls
those "blessed" who possess it; in the second He states the
reason for His felicitations, a reason which in every case is
some special privilege that His faithful disciples will enjoy
in the Messianic Kingdom. The second hemistich is closely
connected with the first, inasmuch as the promised reward is
appropriately adapted to the nature of the virtue recommended. Yet this reward is constantly the same, although
given different names. In each case it is the same ideal happiness. This is represented "in the first Beatitude as the Kingdom; in the second, as a promised land; in the third, as true
and perfect consolation; in the fourth, as the satisfaction of
all our desires; in the fifth, as utmost mercy, which removes
all evils and bestows all good things; in the sixth, by its proper
name, as the sight of God; in the seventh, as the perfection
of our adoption; in the eighth, again, as the Kingdom of
Heaven." [38] Since the Kingdom of Heaven has two stages,
one present, the other future, so we should distinguish two
degrees in the fulfilment of the promises here made by the
Savior. They will be partly fulfilled on earth, before being
completely realized in Heaven.

"Blessed are the poor in spirit: for theirs is the Kingdom of
Heaven. Blessed are the meek: for they shall possess the land. Blessed
are they that mourn: for they shall be comforted. Blessed are they
that hunger and thirst after justice: for they shall have their fill.
Blessed are the merciful: for they shall obtain mercy. Blessed are
the clean of heart: for they shall see God. Blessed are the peacemakers: for they shall be called the children of God. Blessed are they
that suffer persecution for justice' sake: for theirs is the Kingdom
of Heaven. Blessed are ye when they shall revile you and persecute
you and speak all that is evil against you untruly for My sake. Be
glad and rejoice, for your reward is very great in heaven. For so
they persecuted the prophets that were before you."

[38] Bossuet, *loc. cii.*

In this "wonderful beginning" [39] of the Sermon, each line is an exalted moral teaching. The language is partly that of the Old Testament, which Jesus often takes as a basis for His preaching. But nowhere can there be found a group of more comforting and encouraging thoughts. And, as St. Ambrose remarks,[40] what paradoxes they are, at least in appearance! Those whom Christ proclaims blessed are the very ones that the world considers wretched. But the world is not a good judge when it comes to appreciate real happiness and the conditions of happiness. Yet the Savior's audience must have experienced a great surprise when they heard these sublime but astonishing words. Some may have doubted; but most of His hearers admired these sayings and little by little learned to value their truth. Most fittingly they came from the lips of Him who was bringing true blessedness to the earth. The type of virtue which they propose is that of perfection. A Christian practicing them would attain a high degree of holiness, for he would be like to Jesus Himself, the divine exemplar, who possessed to an infinite degree the lofty virtues which He here recommends so charmingly. These are eminent qualities, solid and generous virtues that are not acquired in a day, but by dint of many struggles and repeated sacrifices.[41]

By the "poor in spirit" are meant not persons of humble station nor those aware of their moral wretchedness, but those, whether rich or poor, who are guided by the spirit of

[39] J. Weiss, *Schriften des N. T.*, I, 239.

[40] *Exposit. in Luc.*, 6: 19.

[41] St. John Chrysostom, *Hom. in Matth.*, V, 2, remarks, as a noteworthy circumstance, that "Christ does not use the commandment formula to enumerate the conditions of entrance into the Kingdom of Heaven, but expresses His will by means of mild, gracious words which draw hearts spontaneously. He does not say: Be poor in spirit, be merciful and pure of heart, if you wish to share in My Kingdom; He does not threaten like Moses; He prefers to command while seeming to praise and felicitate. He surrounds His prescriptions with promises. Yet this series of Beatitudes demands the exercise of the loftiest virtues. It begins with tears and closes with blood; the weak are summoned to the most virile heroism. Thus do Christ's words here possess an astonishing courage." (Fillion, *L'Évangile de S. Matthieu*, p. 102.)

poverty.[42] There are rich people who are not attached to worldly possessions, and there are poor people who tolerate their state of poverty with great impatience. The meekness praised by Christ is not to be confused with weak compliance; it is not a weakness, but rather a power. The land which Jesus promises as an inheritance [43] to those who acquire meekness, represents the Messianic Kingdom, considered both in its earthly and in its heavenly, eternal phase. "Those who mourn" are, in general, the afflicted, those who suffer, but on condition that they endure their physical or moral sufferings patiently. It is not in vain that many Old Testament passages bestow on the Messias the name of "Consoler." [44] No one knew better how to dry the tears of sufferers. The "justice" after which we should "hunger and thirst," if we are one day to merit being filled, is nothing other than Christian holiness.[45] The merciful, as Bousset says,[46] are those who show themselves "tender for the misfortune of others." God will treat them with fatherly mercy, especially on judgment day. The meaning of the sixth Beatitude is unduly restricted if it is applied only to chastity, to virginity strictly so called, because the purity of heart which it requires signifies the flight of sin, innocence in its various aspects. A superb reward is promised to those possessing this virtue: not only God's friendship, as the Old Law announced,[47] but the very sight of God, i. e., supreme and everlasting bliss.[48] The Kingdom of Heaven is a kingdom of peace, its Founder is the Prince of Peace.[49] According to the full force of the Greek text,[50] the

[42] "Blessed are the poor," we read simply and clearly in St. Luke's account.

[43] Such is the exact sense of the original text.

[44] In Hebrew, *Menahem.* See W. Bousset, *Die Religion des Judentums,* 2d ed., p. 261.

[45] The Psalmist (Ps. 16: 15) thought with delight of this blessed satisfaction.

[46] *Loc. cit.*

[47] Prov. 22: 11.

[48] 1 John 3: 2.

[49] Is. 9: 6.

[50] Οἱ εἰρηνοποιοί,

seventh Beatitude concerns those who, by word and deed, become promoters of peace: these will be called the children of God, who is pleased by a holy union of hearts.

The eighth and last Beatitude is developed at greater length than are the others. It foretells the generally hostile attitude that the Jewish and pagan world would take towards the Savior's disciples, and for these latter it marks out how they should conduct themselves in the presence of their persecutors. Insults, calumnies, all sorts of violence they are to suffer patiently, courageous to the point of heroism. It will be an honor for them to be treated like their Master, and it is but just that they should imitate the patience and courage which He exhibited amidst cruel torments.[51] And the infinite happiness which they are to enjoy in Heaven will be an ample and everlasting reward for all their sufferings. How forcible are the words, "Be glad and rejoice," [52] in which the paradox reaches its climax! [53]

Such are the conditions on which one may become a worthy citizen of the Kingdom of Heaven. Whoever fulfils these conditions, to whatever race or period he belongs, will deserve to become a subject of the Messias, because His Kingdom is without bounds, His Church will be catholic. To all who are willing to practice this ideal of Christian perfection, especially to the Apostles and those of His disciples who with them are to exercise the duties of superior officers in the Messianic Kingdom, Jesus then sets forth, in expressive and figurative language, the holy and useful influence which they will be called upon to exercise in the midst of an unfriendly or indifferent world.

---

[51] Cf. John 15: 18–21; Heb. 12: 2–5; 1 Pet. 2: 21–25.

[52] The verb σκιρτήσατε, used by St. Luke, means literally "to jump with joy."

[53] The maledictions which we read in the Third Gospel after the Beatitudes, are these: "Woe to you that are rich; for you have your consolation. Woe to you that are filled; for you shall hunger. Woe to you that now laugh; for you shall mourn and weep. Woe to you when men shall bless you; for according to these things did their fathers to the false prophets."

"You are the salt of the earth. But if the salt lose its savor, wherewith shall it be salted? It is good for nothing any more but to be cast out, and to be trodden on by men. You are the light of the world. A city seated on a mountain cannot be hid. Neither do men light a candle and put it under a bushel, but upon a candlestick, that it may shine to all that are in the house. So let your light shine before men, that they may see your good works and glorify your Father who is in Heaven." [54]

The metaphors of the salt and the light are readily understood. Salt lends an agreeable and wholesome savor to food. It is also an antiseptic. It is particularly from this last viewpoint that Christians can be the salt of the earth, because they are a preservative against the corruption of the world. But they must be watchful not to lose so precious a property. When salt loses its savor, as often happened in ancient Palestine, which was provided with the coarse and impure salt of the Dead Sea, it is good for nothing but to be thrown away among the filth and refuse that encumber the streets of Oriental cities.[55] By their holy life and blameless conduct and, in the case of Apostles and their helpers, by their preaching, Christians are also the light of the world, which is plunged in intellectual darkness as well as in moral corruption. They will seek only to please God; but they can no more hide the brightness of their virtues than a lamp on a stand can fail to radiate its light,[56] or than a city built on a mountain can fail to be seen. This was the case with the city of Safed, perched on one of the southernmost spurs of Lebanon. It may well be that Jesus had in mind this very city, which was facing Him as He spoke.

[54] Matt. 5: 13–16.

[55] Thomson, *The Land and the Book*, p. 381: "I saw large quantities of it literally thrown into the road, to be trodden under foot of men and beasts."

[56] Our readers are acquainted with the appearance of the little clay lamps that have been found by thousands in Palestine and elsewhere; the ancients used them indoors. To enable these lamps to cast their modest light to a greater distance, it was customary to place them on a more or less elevated stand.

288 THE PUBLIC LIFE OF OUR LORD

There is a noble grandeur in the office thus entrusted to the Apostles and to all true disciples of the Savior. They will be the conserving and enlightening force of mankind. It might be said that the Sermon on the Mount is contained in abridged form in this majestic exordium. But it contains many other wonderful things. Christ had just established on earth a new city of God. Yet He does not wish to suggest that everything is absolutely new in that city. It is new; but its foundations are old, for they are the Mosaic Law, developed and brought to perfection. Jesus does not think of overthrowing the legislation of Sinai; His purpose is to transfigure it. To clarify this point, He makes a lengthy comparison between the old law and the new code introduced by Him. And first He announces a few general principles of the highest importance.

"Do not think that I am come to destroy the law or the prophets. I am not come to destroy, but to fulfil. For amen I say unto you, till heaven and earth pass, one jot or one tittle [57] shall not pass of the law, till all be fulfilled. He therefore that shall break one of these least commandments, and shall so teach men, shall be called the least in the Kingdom of Heaven. But he that shall do and teach, he shall be called great in the Kingdom of Heaven." [58]

This energetic protest shows forth Jesus' thought about the Law of Moses and His respect for it. We are at once struck by the calm dignity with which He introduces Himself personally on the scene,[59] as the religious reformer *par excellence,* as the Messias. He knows that He speaks with supreme authority. The personal pronoun appears again and again in this part of the sermon.

[57] The *iota,* equivalent to our letter "i," is the smallest letter of the Greek alphabet. Christ must have said in Aramaic: Not one *yod;* but in that language *yod* is the smallest consonant of the alphabet. The "tittle" consisted, as the Greek text says, in a little "horn," which the Jews wrote above certain of their letters to prevent their being confused with other letters closely resembling them.

[58] Matt. 5 : 17–19.

[59] He had already done so, but only in passing, in the eighth Beatitude: "Blessed are ye when they shall revile you and persecute you . . . *for My sake."*

Until then, "the law and the prophets," *i. e.,* the whole Old Testament, considered in its two principal parts,[60] had served as a rule for numerous generations of Jews. Is Christ going to abrogate them? [61] Certainly not; on the contrary, it is His firm purpose to "fulfil" [62] them, that is, according to the view of most commentators,[63] to perfect them by raising them to the ideal willed by God. Since the law of Sinai was the authentic expression of God's will, to destroy it utterly could not enter the Messias' mind. But it was His duty to make it still finer, more perfect, more sanctifying. The language which He here employs is undeniably true, if we consider it in its *ensemble* and if we give it its correct meaning. As expressed by an early Greek interpreter,[64] Jesus' action regarding the Jewish Law is like that of a painter who, by going over a charcoal sketch with colored paints, does not destroy the sketch, but perfects and embellishes it, giving it its true aspect.

In the prescriptions of the Old Law, Jesus fulfilled what was there only in figure; He replaced the shadow by the substance, rejuvenated what had become aged. In His hands the Mosaic legislation underwent an evolution that was necessitated by the loftier spirit of Christianity: but this new spirit cannot be said to have destroyed it, unless in the sense in which we speak of the destruction of a seed by the full growth

---

[60] This technical expression recurs frequently in various New Testament writings. Cf. Matt. 7:12; 11:13; 22:40; Luke 16:16, 29, 31; 24:27; Acts 13:15; 24:14; 28:23; Rom. 3:21. It is to be found often also in the Talmud.

[61] In the Greek: καταλῦσαι (Vulg., *solvere*). With regard to a law, it means "to abrogate, to annul."

[62] Πληρῶσαι (Vulg., *adimplere*). It would be a singular weakening of our Lord's thought if we merely made Him say that He came to obey the law.

[63] The Fathers are explicit on this point. St. Irenaeus, *Adv. Haer.*, IV, 13: "*Extendit* [*legem*] *et implevit.*" Tertullian, *De Paenit.*, 3: "*Adjectionem legi superstruit.*" St. Jerome, *in hoc loco*: "*Rudia et imperfecta complevit.*" St. Augustine, *In Matth., hoc loco*: "*Addit*"; *In Joan.*, V: "*Perficit.*" St. John Chrysostom, *Hom. in Joan.*, 5:19: Διόρθωσις νομοθεσίας, etc. Strauss, Keim, and several other Rationalist critics are in favor of this interpretation, which is, moreover, the only acceptable one.

[64] Theophylactus, died about 1107.

of the plant, of a flower by the fruit. It had to be so, since the old bottles of Judaism could not hold the new wine of the Gospel.[65] Jesus desired to explain Himself on this point, doubtless to refute His adversaries' accusations. Did they not say that He wished to destroy the Temple,[66] that He violated the Sabbath rest,[67] that He rejected the traditions of the ancients, which they considered no less binding than the Law itself?[68] Not merely does He repeat His assertion under oath (*"Amen dico vobis"*) and promise to the Mosaic Law a perpetual duration[69] under the Christian régime, but He explicitly forbids His disciples to abrogate it in its essential parts. He even threatens punishment on those who, without good reason, break the least of its commandments, while He promises a special reward to those who obey it faithfully.

By itself this language is very clear. Yet it will be profitable to explain it more thoroughly because of the double attitude that Jesus seems to have taken toward the Mosaic Law. When studying His acts and words in this connection, one is readily convinced of His respect and perfect obedience. He was born under the law, as St. Paul says,[70] and He remained subject to it throughout His life. It would be vain to attempt to show that He personally violated a single really legal prescription. He was circumcised eight days after His birth. While still a child, He went on pilgrimage to Jerusalem for the solemn feasts. He frequented the Temple, which He con-

---

[65] See pages 217 f.

[66] John 2 : 19 ; Matt. 26 : 60 f.

[67] Matt. 12 : 2–14 ; John 5 : 10–18, etc.

[68] Mark 7 : 3, etc.

[69] The saying, "till heaven and earth pass," means: till the end of time. It is quite Hebraic. Cf. Ps. 71 : 5, 7 ; 88 : 38 ; Jer. 33 : 20 f. See also Mark 13 : 31 ; Luke 16 : 17. Again and again the rabbis attribute an everlasting duration to the Mosaic Law. "Every thing will have an end," they say (*Bereshith Rabba*), "heaven and earth will have their end ; one only thing will have no end : it is the Law." Philo, *Vita Mos.*, II, 14 f., and Josephus, *Ant.*, III, viii, 10, and *Contra Apion.*, II, 38, use words to the same effect.

[70] Gal. 4 : 4.

sidered His Father's house, and He protected it from blameworthy irreverence. On the Sabbath He was regularly present at the religious exercises in the synagogue. Upon curing
a leper, He sent him to the priests to have his cure attested
and to offer the sacrifices prescribed by the law. In the matter
of legal interpretation, He wished the official authority of the
Scribes to be respected. More than once we hear Him praise
the Decalogue as an abridged statement of the divine will.
In short, His thought and His outward attitude towards the
Jewish law were always those of a pious and dutiful Israelite.
Those Judaizing Christians, the Ebionites, declared Him justified before God, because of His exemplary fulfilment of the
law.[71] And the Talmud puts on His lips these words, which
are evidently taken from the passage in St. Matthew which
we explained: "I have not come to take away anything whatsoever from the law of Moses, but to add to the Law of
Moses." [72]

On the other hand, it cannot be denied that His words
sometimes show a considerable independence of Mosaic institutions. Though He did not directly abrogate any legal
statute, leaving this task to His Apostles, who later on did so
little by little as circumstances required, some of His instructions prepared the way for that abrogation. We note it, for
example, with reference to sacrifices,[73] fasting,[74] the Sabbath,[75] divorce,[76] the law of talion,[77] and ablutions.[78] With
full consideration of all the facts, we may assert that Jesus
did not attack and did not destroy the law. In some instances
(as in the matter of ablutions) He liberated the law by de-

[71] St. Hippolytus, *Philosoph.*, VII, 36.

[72] *Shabbath*, 26, a–b. Cf. Laible, *Jesus Christus im Talmud*, pp. 62–64.

[73] John 4 : 21, 24. Cf. Mark 12 : 33, where our Lord places the love of God far
above sacrifices.

[74] Matt. 9 : 14 f.

[75] Matt. 12 : 5–8.

[76] Matt. 5 : 31 f.

[77] Matt. 5 : 38–42.

[78] Mark 7 : 1–23.

taching it from the human traditions with which the Scribes
had encumbered it; in other cases (*e. g.*, with regard to the
Sabbath) He explained it, showing that under certain circumstances it ceases to be obligatory; or again, He replaced the
figure by the ideal, the carnal sacrifices by the august V. tim
of our altars. In every instance He elevated and transformed
the law, delicately suppressing its transient elements and making it eternal.

Although He declared that He came to fulfil the law, it is
worthy of note that He never said or even insinuated that the
Old Covenant would retain its primitive form, that the legislation of Sinai would endure to the end of time as a ritualistic, social, and constitutional code. To do so would have been
contrary to the fulfilment of the divine plan, so clearly described by the prophets of old. Did not Moses himself announce that God would some day give Israel a prophet like
to him,[79] who would supplement and perfect his works as lawgiver? But the perfecting of it required that it be modified.
Hence "for Jesus the [Jewish] law possesses both a temporary and an eternal character. Therefore He gives to the
immutable what belongs to it, and to the transient what belongs to it." [80]

It is thus the earliest Fathers explained the Savior's conduct with respect to the Mosaic legislation. He fulfilled its
precepts, says St. Justin.[81] But many of those precepts, having as their chief purpose to prepare for the coming of Christ,
ceased to be binding after His coming. The others, by their
very nature, have a perpetual duration.[82]

After setting forth the great principles, Jesus proceeds to

[79] Deut. 18 : 15.

[80] Ehrhardt, *Der Grundcharakter der Ethik Jesu im Verhältnis zu den messian-
ischen Hoffnungen seines Volkes,* p. 66.

[81] *Dial. cum Tryph.,* 27, 43, 46, 67, etc. So, too, Tertullian, *De Paenit.,* 3; St.
Irenaeus, *passim;* Origen, *Contra Celsum,* II, 5 f. Cf. W. Bauer, *Leben Jesu,*
pp. 352–359.

[82] On the interesting question of Christ's relations with the Jewish Law, see

apply them in the succeeding part of His sermon. Passing from generalities, He enters upon practical details. He surveys, one after another, six precepts of the Old Law and explains them in accordance with the spirit of the New Law, showing in what way the latter perfects the former by spiritualizing it and raising it to a moral level which the Mosaic legislation had been incapable of attaining.

"For I tell you, that unless your justice [83] abound more than that of the Scribes and Pharisees, you shall not enter into the Kingdom of Heaven.

"You have heard that it was said to them of old: Thou shalt not kill. And whosoever shall kill shall be in danger of the judgment. But I say to you, that whosoever is angry with his brother, shall be in danger of the judgment. And whosoever shall say to his brother, Raca, shall be in danger of the council. And whosoever shall say, Thou fool, shall be in danger of hell fire.[84] If therefore thou offer thy gift at the altar and there thou remember that thy brother hath any thing against thee, leave there thy offering before the altar,[85] and go first to be reconciled to thy brother; and then coming thou shalt offer thy gift. Be at agreement with thy adversary betimes, whilst thou art in the way with him, lest perhaps the adversary deliver thee to the judge, and the judge deliver thee to the officer, and

Benz, *Die Stellung Jesu zum alttestamentlichen Gesetz*, 1914; W. Bousset, *Die Predigt Jesu in ihrem Gegensatz zum Judentum*, 1892.

[83] That is, your moral conduct, your holiness.

[84] The word *Gehenna*, which comes to us from the Greek (γεέννα) through the intermediary of the Latin (Vulg., *gehenna*), is of Hebraic origin (*gue Hinnom*) and originally designated the "valley of Hinnom" or "valley of the sons of Hinnom" which is mentioned in several places in the Old Testament. Cf. 4 Kings 23:10; Jer. 7:31 f., etc. It was a ravine located south of Jerusalem (the present Wady er Rebabi) and in which formerly children had been sacrificed to the god Moloch. The devout King Josias purposely profaned that sinister place, to show the horror it inspired in faithful Jews. Thereafter all sorts of refuse and offal were thrown there and it remained a place of disgust and execration (4 Kings chap. 23). Finally, its name served to designate hell, in the popular speech which our Lord Himself uses in this passage.

[85] The altar of holocausts, in the innermost court of the Temple at Jerusalem. See Vol. I, p. 167.

thou be cast into prison. Amen I say to thee, thou shalt not go out from thence till thou repay the last farthing." [86]

In the previous volume [87] we studied the "justice" of the Scribes and Pharisees at some length and without difficulty were convinced of its imperfections. Such a holiness did not suffice even from the standpoint of the Old Testament, the spirit of which it falsified. Moreover, it was altogether superficial. For the New Covenant to compromise with it was impossible. The first example by which Jesus sets forth the ideal of virtue which He desired all His followers to attain is taken from the fifth commandment of the Decalogue [88] and concerns homicide. The text of the Old Law, the Scribes' interpretation of it, and the Christian ideal are successively passed in review, as in the succeeding examples. The "ancients" to whom the Savior refers represent all the Jewish generations of the previous centuries. The code of Sinai directly forbade only murder, *i. e.,* the most grievous external wrong that can be inflicted on one's neighbor; Christ condemns even a simple interior movement of anger and *a fortiori* words of insult.[89] The two living rules of conduct, one taken from the religious, the other from the civil life of the epoch, show the need for the practice of fraternal charity, whether to please God or to avoid inflicting great suffering on others.

The second and third examples are as follows:

"You have heard that it was said to them of old: Thou shalt not commit adultery. But I say to you, that whosoever shall look on a woman to lust after her, hath already committed adultery with her

[86] Matt. 5 : 21–26.

[87] Vol. I, pp. 180, 188.

[88] Ex. 20 : 13; Deut. 5 : 17.

[89] There is a gradation in the three cases of culpability mentioned by our Lord: anger, an insult expressed in words (*Raca* an Aramaic word which has the meaning of "empty," stupid), a further insult ("senseless," in the moral order, impious). There is likewise a gradation in the punishment, which will be pronounced first by the court of first resort, then by the Sanhedrin, and lastly by God Himself.

in his heart. And if thy right eye scandalize thee, pluck it out and cast it from thee. For it is expedient for thee that one of thy members should perish, rather than that thy whole body be cast into hell. And if thy right hand scandalize thee, cut it off, and cast it from thee. For it is expedient for thee that one of thy members should perish, rather than that thy whole body go into hell. And it hath been said, Whosoever shall put away his wife, let him give her a bill of divorce. But I say to you, that whosoever shall put away his wife, excepting for the cause of fornication, maketh her to commit adultery; and he that shall marry her that is put away, committeth adultery." [90]

These words concern the sanctity of marriage, both for husband and for wife, a sanctity which the old code but imperfectly protected. The old prohibition refers chiefly to outward acts: "Thou shalt not commit adultery." [91] Jesus goes farther and forbids voluntary lustful glances. The better to make it understood how important it is to keep oneself chaste at any price, in the internal as well as the external forum, He uses two metaphors which declare relentless war upon whatever might lead to sins of impurity. "We are obliged to give up illicit associations, not only the most agreeable, but also the most necessary, rather than imperil our salvation." [92] This is what is signified by that right eye or right hand which must be ruthlessly plucked out or cut off.

The law authorizing divorce,[93] which came to be strangely abused in the course of time,[94] had brought great harm to

[90] Matt. 5 : 27–32.

[91] Ex. 20 : 14; Deut. 5 : 18. Nevertheless, the tenth commandment of the Decalogue (Ex. 20 : 17; Deut. 10 : 21), also condemns, in a general way, evil desires. Cf. Job, 31 : 1.

[92] Bossuet.

[93] Deut. 24 : 1–4.

[94] The passage of the Pentateuch (Deut. 24 : 1) authorizing divorce says: "If a man take a wife and have her, and she find not favor in his eyes, because he has discovered in her *something repulsive* (in the Hebrew: *ervat dabar*), he shall write for her a bill of divorce . . . and send her out of his house." The words we have italicized, rather vague by themselves, received from Hillel and his school

conjugal fidelity. But it was only a temporary concession which Moses made to the Hebrews "by reason of the hardness of their hearts," as the Divine Master says later.[95] In proclaiming forever the indissolubility of marriage, He restored it to its primitive unity, willed by the Creator in the beginning.[96]

The fourth example is as follows:

"Again you have heard that it was said to them of old, Thou shalt not forswear thyself: but thou shalt perform thy oaths to the Lord. But I say to you not to swear at all, neither by heaven, for it is the throne of God, nor by the earth, for it is His footstool, nor by Jerusalem, for it is the city of the great King. Neither shalt thou swear by thy head, because thou canst not make one hair white or black. But let your speech be yea, yea: no, no; and that which is over and above these is of evil." [97]

This antithesis is about oaths, which the Jews were guilty of employing with too little consideration. Even the pagans were shocked at this practice, and their writers mention the readiness with which the Jews living throughout the Roman provinces unscrupulously violated their oaths.[98] They had no hesitation in resorting to mental reservations and in using forms of oaths which they claimed did not bind in conscience.

a scandalous interpretation which threw wide open the door to passion. A man was considered authorized, on the most frivolous pretexts, to send away even a faithful wife. The poor preparation or omission of some dish at table, the sight of a more beautiful woman, the rabbis dared even to say, were sufficient reasons for divorce. Do not the Pharisees ask our Lord: "Is it lawful for a man to put away his wife for every cause?" (Matt. 19:3). Such abuses evidently could not be tolerated under the law of holiness. The parenthesis, "except it be for fornication," which we find only in the First Gospel, gives rise to a difficulty that is more apparent than real. In no case does Christ allow divorce, as He clearly says later (Matt. 19:6, 9; Mark 10:9–12; Luke 16:18. Cf. 1 Cor. 7:10 f.). All that He authorizes in case of adultery, is the separation of the husband and wife; but He absolutely forbids their contracting a new marriage. See Fillion, *L'Évangile de S. Matthieu*, pp. 369–374.

[95] Matt. 19:8; Mark 10:5.
[96] Gen. 2:18–24.
[97] Matt. 5:33–37.
[98] See, among others, Martial, *Sat.*, XI, 94.

The Talmud also treated the matter and asked whether the words "Yes" and "No" were not by themselves a sufficient guaranty of veracity among honorable men.[99] With greater reason ought this be so under the Gospel.[100] Yet it is evident that Jesus does not absolutely forbid the taking of oaths, because there are circumstances in which their usefulness is undeniable. This is notably so in courts of justice. The Savior Himself took an oath before Caiphas.[101]

The fifth example is that of retaliation, the law of the talion.

"You have heard that it hath been said, An eye for an eye, and a tooth for a tooth. But I say to you not to resist evil; but if one strike thee on thy right cheek, turn to him also the other. And if a man will contend with thee in judgment and take away thy coat, let go thy cloak [102] also unto him. And whosoever will force thee [103] one mile, go with him other two. Give to him that asketh of thee, and from him that would borrow of thee turn not away." [104]

The *lex talionis* existed in most ancient codes. The recently discovered Code of Hammurapi expressly speaks of it,[105] as did the Roman code also.[106] But our acquaintance with it is chiefly through the Mosaic legislation, which enters into details on the subject.[107] Before religion and civilization

---

[99] Wünsche, *Neue Beiträge*, p. 57. Cf. Ecclus. 23: 9–11.

[100] "*Evangelica veritas non recipit juramenta,*" says St. Jerome (*hoc loco*). The Mosaic law does not explicitly mention oaths; it merely condemns perjury (Ex. 20:7; Lev. 19:12) and requires the complete fulfilment of vows (Num. 30:3; cf. Matt. 23:16–22).

[101] Matt. 26:63.

[102] The Greek χιτών here designates the under-tunic; ἱμάτιον represents the outer garment, the ample piece of cloth that usually serves Orientals as a cloak during the day and as a blanket at night.

[103] The verb ἀγγαρεύω, Latinized under the form *angariare*, is of Persian origin and corresponds to the expression "to requisition." Cf. Herodotus, VIII, 98; Xenophon, *Cyrop.*, VIII, 6, 17.

[104] Matt. 5:38–42.

[105] Cf. Scheil, *La Loi de Hammourabi*, 1904.

[106] *Tabula* 8.

[107] Ex. 21:23–25; Deut. 19:18–21 etc.

moderated the harshness of human customs, the law of the talion offered real advantages, since it established the quite legitimate principle that there should be a parity between a brutal, unjust offense and the reparation. Ordinarily the talion was commuted to a money payment, the amount being determined by the judges. But it had the serious drawback of encouraging the spirit of revenge and retaliation. Against this danger various passages in the Old Testament warn all those who wish to remain faithful to God.[108] And Jesus entirely excludes it from the Gospel charter, since the law of His Kingdom is distinctly a law of love. While not wishing to condemn the protective measures which society or private individuals are obliged to adopt against assassins, robbers, and other criminals, He points out, in four rules of conduct, but without at all purposing to impose their literal observance on His disciples, what should be the disposition of all true Christians in the face of outrage. St. Paul sums these rules up in this sentence: *"Noli vinci a malo, sed vince in bono malum."* [109]

The sixth example concerns the love of our enemies:

"You have heard that it hath been said, Thou shalt love thy neighbor and hate thy enemy. But I say to you, Love your enemies; do good to them that hate you; and pray for them that persecute and calumniate you; that you may be the children of your Father who is in heaven, who maketh His sun to rise upon the good and bad, and raineth upon the just and the unjust. For if you love them that love you, what reward shall you have? Do not even the publicans this? And if you salute your brethren only, what do you more? Do not also the heathens this? Be you therefore perfect, as also your heavenly Father is perfect." [110]

Love of one's neighbor was not forgotten in the Mosaic leg-

108 Lev. 19:18; Deut. 32:35; Ecclu. 28:1-7.
109 Rom. 12:21.
110 Matt. 5:43-48. Here again, for the moment, we find St. Luke, 6:27-35.

islation,[111] and in many other places in the Old Testament it is recommended in beautiful terms.[112] Unfortunately most Jews gave the word "neighbor" an extremely restricted meaning, refusing to apply it to the pagans, whom they considered *in toto* as enemies. Under the Christian law, all men are brothers and ought to be loved as brothers. Not only are enemies not outside the pale of charity, but Jesus grants them, in a way, a privileged place, by insisting on the duty of generous forgiveness, without being concerned with the difficulty presented by the performance of this precept. Never before had such language been heard. The example of God showering His blessings on the wicked as well as on the good, is a cogent reason which Jesus suggests to His disciples to urge them to love their enemies.

The golden rule, "Be you therefore perfect, as also your heavenly Father is perfect," [113] forms a fitting conclusion to this first part of the discourse. It is a noble but formidable ideal [114] of Christian holiness, so different from the "justice" of the Scribes and Pharisees. We can now better understand in what way Jesus perfected the Jewish law, and what a distance separated His interpretation from that of the lawyers of Israel. The latter were attached to the letter, to external acts; He penetrated to the deepest feelings, which He wished to be free from all alloy. The Scribes and Pharisees were often satisfied with apparent holiness; Jesus requires a deep, solid virtue. The six times repeated "I say to you" reveals the Master who has a right to require obedience.

We have now come to the principal part of the sermon, in which Jesus develops some of the great obligations incum-

[111] The first part of the passage quoted by our Lord is taken from Leviticus 19:18. The words "[thou shalt] hate thy enemy" are not in that text; but they were indeed in the spirit of the Scribes.

[112] Cf. Ps. 7:4 f.; 34:12–14; Prov. 17:5; 24:29, etc.

[113] Matt. 5:48.

[114] "Never did the founder of a religion propose to his disciples an ideal so unattainable." H. Monnier, *La Mission Historique de Jésus*, p. 139.

bent on the citizens of His Kingdom. In the first part of the sermon, in contrast to the Scribes' false interpretation of the Decalogue, He set forth the true sense of the spiritualized law; here, as opposed to the false and boastful virtue of the Pharisees, He proclaims the purity of intention with which He wishes His disciples to perform the threefold duty of almsgiving, prayer, and fasting.

These three works of faith, by which Jewish piety was manifested in the course of the ages,[115] and which were in full vigor at the beginning of our era,[116] were also to serve as perpetual nourishment for Christian piety. But what the Pharisees spoiled by their ostentation and hypocrisy, Christ's disciples are to do with discretion and simplicity, so as to lose none of the merit of their acts. This is well expressed by the principle which opens this new series of recommendations: "Take heed that you do not your justice before men, to be seen by them;[117] otherwise you shall not have a reward of your Father who is in heaven."

Jesus applied this principle from the three points of view just mentioned. As to almsgiving, He says:

"Therefore when thou dost an almsdeed, sound not a trumpet before thee, as the hypocrites do in the synagogues and in the streets, that they may be honored by men. Amen I say to you, they have received their reward. But when thou dost alms, let not thy left hand know what thy right hand doth. That thy alms may be in secret, and thy Father who seeth in secret will repay thee."[118]

We scarcely need to take literally the admonition, "Sound not a trumpet." This is rather a vivid picture of the vanity

---

[115] Cf. Tobias 4:7-11; 12:8-10; 14:9-12; Ecclus. 3:14, 33; 4:3 f.; 5:10; 16:14 etc.

[116] See E. Schürer, *Geschichte des jüdischen Volkes*, 4th ed., II, 252, 440 f., 452-454, 528, etc.; W. Bousset, *Religion des Judentums*, pp. 119, 457.

[117] Matt. 6:1. Seneca also says, *Epist.*, XIX, 4: "*Qui virtutem suam publicari vult, non virtuti laborat, sed gloriae.*"

[118] Matt. 6:2-4.

that animated the Pharisees whenever they gave alms. They did in fact seek the publicity of the synagogues and street-corners and other places where they would have the best chance of attracting attention.[119] In contrast to this sorry practice, Jesus depicts Christian almsdeeds, modest, quiet, seeking to be hidden.[120] God sees the generous deed: this is all it asks, knowing that, in the words of a fine popular proverb, "Who gives to the poor, lends to God."

The same sort of conduct is urged in the matter of prayer.

"And when ye pray, you shall not be as the hypocrites, that love to stand [121] and pray in the synagogues and corners of the streets, that they may be seen by men. Amen I say to you, they have received their reward. But thou when thou shalt pray, enter into thy chamber, and having shut the door, pray to thy Father in secret; and thy Father who seeth in secret will repay thee. And when you are praying, speak not much as the heathens. For they think that in their much speaking they may be heard. Be not you therefore·like to them, for your Father knoweth what is needful for you, before you ask Him. Thus therefore shall you pray: Our Father who art in Heaven, hallowed be Thy name. Thy Kingdom come. Thy will be done on earth as it is in Heaven. Give us this day our supersubstantial bread. And forgive us our debts, as we also forgive our debtors. And lead us not into temptation. But deliver us from evil. Amen. For if you will forgive men their offences, your heavenly Father will forgive you also your offences. But if you will not forgive men, neither will your Father forgive you your offences." [122]

For prayer, our Lord recommends to His disciples the same delicate reserve as for almsdeeds, directing them to pray with

---

[119] Matt. 23:5: "All their works they do for to be seen of men."

[120] The saying "Let not thy left hand . . ." is proverbial to express the secrecy with which an act is done.

[121] This was frequently the posture of the Jews when praying. Cf. 1 Kings 1:26; 3 Kings 8:22; Mark 11:25; Luke 18:11 etc. They prayed also kneeling or prostrate. See Fillion, *Atlas Archéologique de la Bible,* pl. XCV, fig. 3; pl. XCVI, figs. 5, 6, 7.

[122] Matt. 6:5-15.

their door closed, their chamber being transformed into a secret oratory. But He does not in the least criticize public prayer, formulated in the name of society. In this place He speaks only of individual prayer, which takes place between God and the soul, without outward formality, like that which He Himself was wont to offer in retired places. Nor does He say that lengthy prayers are in themselves to be condemned. What he does condemn, as is indicated by the characteristic expression used in the Greek text of St. Matthew,[123] is the vain and superstitious repetition of formulas by which, so to speak, one seeks to force God to grant the favors requested. Such practices were good for the pagans;[124] they would be unbecoming on the part of Christians.[125] St. Augustine points out the true meaning of Jesus' words, when he says: *"Aliud est sermo multus, aliud diuturnus affectus. Absit ab oratione multa locutio, sed non desit multa precatio."* [126] As usual, our Lord adds to the precept a concrete model, the better to show His disciples how in a few words one can offer a fervent prayer to God. It is a perfect abridgment of what is best for God's glory and for our own good. Like the Beatitudes, the "Our Father" appears in the Third Gospel [127] in a condensed form. But both versions of it may well have been original, since it is quite possible that the Savior repeated this prayer on different occasions, with slight changes. It has its exquisite art, "its rhetoric." In the manner of some of the Psalms, it begins with a sort of *captatio benevolentiae,* con-

---

[123] Βαττολογεῖν. The etymology is not certain. Consult the Greek lexicons.

[124] The Third Book of Kings, 18:26, cites the example of the priests of Baal. Even to-day the Mohammedans and Tibetans still resort to this ridiculous "redundance." This is what Roman writers jestingly called, *fatigare deos, deorum aures contundere.*

[125] Certain Jewish prayers were not free from this prolixity, which many rabbis openly approved. "Whoever repeats prayers over and over is heard," they said (Wünsche, *op. cit.,* p. 82). Repetitions abound in the *Shemone esre* and in the *Kaddish,* which has been mentioned above.

[126] *Epist.* CXXX.

[127] Luke 11:1-4. It is quoted on another occasion.

sisting of the words "Our Father who art in heaven," and intended to move the heart of God. After this filial invocation comes the body of the prayer, divided into two parts, the first of which concerns the glory of God, the second our temporal and spiritual needs.

The prayer begins with the words "Our Father," not "My Father," because we belong to one single family and should be solicitous for the welfare of all the members.[128] In honor of the great God whom we invoke, we utter three distinct wishes, worded in a beautiful symmetry. The first is addressed to the loving and beloved Father, whose name we desire to see hallowed, that is, to be everywhere acknowledged and treated as holy, to be blessed and reverenced as it deserves. The second is addressed to the glorious, eternal, almighty Sovereign, whose Kingdom we wish to see established in all places, thus joining our humble efforts to those of the Messias Himself. The third is addressed to the absolute Master of Heaven and earth, whose all-holy and all-just will should be, as far as it depends upon us, fulfilled as joyously and perfectly on earth as it is by the angels and saints in Heaven.

A Christian at prayer, after occupying himself with God's interests and honor, has a right to think of his own personal concerns and to implore the heavenly Father in their behalf. This is done in the second part of the Lord's Prayer, in four requests. To his Creator, who does not leave even the young ravens without food, he speaks of his material needs, represented by the daily bread,[129] which in most countries is man's

[128] St. Augustine (loc. cit.): "Oratio fraterna est. Non dicit [Jesus], Pater meus sed Pater noster, omnes videlicet una oratione complectens."

[129] The Greek epithet ἐπιούσιος, corresponding to this adjective, appears in extant literature only in this place of the First Gospel and in the parallel passage of St. Luke. Its exact meaning has not yet been definitely established, because it has greatly varied since the earliest times. The Syriac Version translates it by "necessary"; the Syriac Cureton by "continual"; the Vulgate by *supersubstantialem* in St. Matthew, by *quotidianum* in St. Luke. According to others, the entire ex-

staple food.[130] The next petitions concern our numerous spiritual wants. Aware of being in continual need of divine pardon, we implore the Father of mercies to grant it to us and,
to be the more sure of obtaining it, we declare that we fully
and generously forgive those who have offended us. To this
request, which concerns the past, we add two others,[131] regarding the dangers to which we are exposed by countless
temptations and regarding the malice of the devil,[132] whose
power contrasts with our weakness.

Such is the Lord's Prayer, admired even by those who
rarely recite it. No other formula of supplication can be compared with it. The Word made flesh, who by His double nature knows as none other what is fitting towards God and
what is needful for man, drew this prayer from His heart as
much as from His mind. Its gentleness and fervor came from
that soul which never breathed aught but His Father's glory
and man's blessedness. Its sublimity is as great as its simplicity. We never tire repeating it.

With regard to fasting, as in the matter of almsgiving and
prayer, Jesus reproves the boastful and hypocritical attitude
of the Pharisees, who paraded their mortifications, putting
on sad looks at such times and even coming into public with
a shaggy beard and disordered hair and unwashed face,[133]
in the hope of attracting praise. Christ's disciples, on the contrary, will hide their fasting, which they will undertake only
to please God and to win supernatural merits. The words

pression is equivalent to "our bread of to-morrow" (according to the Gospel of
the Hebrews) or "of the future" (St. Athanasius: τὸν μέλλοντα; St. Cyril of
Alexandria: τὸν ἥξοντα). Consult the commentaries and lexicons.

[130] In the early centuries, some (St. Irenaeus among them) considered this
"supersubstantial bread" to mean the Holy Eucharist; but in this passage that
meaning could at best be only secondary.

[131] They really constitute only one, according to St. John Chrysostom.

[132] The Greek πονηροῦ, like the Latin malo, is ambiguous. These words may be
either neuter (badness, evil) or masculine (the evil one par excellence, i. e., Satan).
The latter interpretation is the better and the more commonly accepted.

[133] Buxtorf, Synagoga Judaica, XXVII.

"Anoint thy head and wash thy face" are evidently a hyperbole, intended to accentuate the thought.

"And when you fast, be not as the hypocrites, sad. For they disfigure their faces, that they may appear unto men to fast. Amen I say to you, they have received their reward. But thou, when thou fastest, anoint thy head, and wash thy face; that thou appear not to men to fast, but to thy Father who is in secret; and thy Father who seeth in secret, will repay thee." [134]

From duties of piety the Savior passes to those which arise from the possession of this world's goods.[135] The Messias-King wishes His subjects' hearts to be undividedly His. Two things there are which can rob Him of those hearts, totally or partially: immoderate love of riches and exaggerated anxiety for temporal necessities. Hence there are two rules of conduct, which our Lord sets forth and explains in what is reckoned as one of the most beautiful and consoling pages of the Gospel.

The first rule is this: True riches consist not in the goods of this world, which are frail and perishable, and the possession of which is therefore precarious, but in heavenly treasures, which are safe from all danger of loss.

"Lay not up to yourselves treasures on earth, where the rust and moth consume and where thieves break through and steal. But lay up to yourselves treasures in Heaven, where neither the rust nor moth doth consume, and where thieves do not break through nor steal. For where thy treasure is, there is thy heart also. The light of thy body is thy eye. If thy eye be single, thy whole body shall be lightsome. But if thy eye be evil, thy whole body shall be darksome. If then the light that is in thee be darkness, the darkness itself

---

[134] Matt. 6: 16-18.

[135] Matt. 6: 19-34. Cf. Luke 12: 33 f.; 11: 34-36; 16: 13; 12: 22-31. We cite these passages from St. Luke according to the order of the parallelism with those of St. Matthew.

how great shall it be? No man can serve two masters. For either he will hate the one and love the other; or he will sustain the one and despise the other. You cannot serve God and mammon." [136]

The words, "Where thy treasure is, there is thy heart also," constitute a psychological truth the force of which is experienced in every human life. Christian hearts are to long only for the treasures of Heaven, which alone are worthy of them, alone are lasting. What Jesus says about the eye being single, that is, healthy and well formed, refers to the same thought, expressed figuratively. If our heart is pure and simple, as it will be if we do not allow ourselves to be seduced by a craving for worldly goods, our whole moral life will remain holy and lightsome. Love for riches will produce the contrary effect. The adage, "No man can serve two masters," which is to be found among most races, and the Savior's application of it in this passage, supplement and strengthen the idea. The disciple of the Messias must choose between these two opposite paths: to serve God or to serve Mammon.[137] Should there be a moment's hesitation? Should he turn to the service of Mammon, that despot whose rule is so tyrannical?

The second rule is this: The disciple of Christ should cast from his mind all excessively human solicitude in the matter of his material needs.

"Therefore I say to you, be not solicitous for your life, what you shall eat, nor for your body, what you shall put on. Is not the life more than the meat, and the body more than the raiment? Behold the birds of the air, for they neither sow nor do they reap nor gather into barns; and your heavenly Father feedeth them. Are not you of much more value than they? And which of you by taking thought

[136] Matt. 6: 19–24.

[137] "Mammon" (*mammona*), is an Aramaic word meaning wealth. St. Augustine informs us that it likewise belonged to the idiom of the Carthaginians, which was also a Semitic language.

can add to his stature [138] one cubit? [139] And for raiment why are you solicitous? Consider the lilies of the field, how they grow; they labor not, neither do they spin. But I say to you, that not even Solomon in all his glory was arrayed as one of these. And if the grass of the field, which is to-day, and to-morrow is cast into the oven, God doth so clothe, how much more you, O ye of little faith? Be not solicitous therefore, saying, What shall we eat; or what shall we drink, or wherewith shall we be clothed? For after all these things do the heathens seek. For your Father knoweth that you have need of all these things. Seek ye therefore first the Kingdom of God and His justice, and all these things shall be added unto you. Be not therefore solicitous for to-morrow; for the morrow will be solicitous for itself. Sufficient for the day is the evil thereof." [140]

This passage is wonderful both in content and form; the language which our Lord uses is truly exquisite. "Be not solicitous," [141] is the dominant note of this whole series of admonitions. They do not at all exclude a prudent and moderate foresight or the labor necessary for meeting the various needs of life, because man has been condemned to eat his bread by the sweat of his brow. Jesus is here protesting only against fretful preoccupations, absorbing anxieties, and lack of confidence in God. He mentions five reasons why a Christian ought to remain calm about his temporal necessities. The Creator, who gave us life, will not fail to provide us with all

---

[138] In agreement with most commentators, and contrary to the Vulgate, which here translates the Greek word $\dot{\eta}\lambda\iota\kappa\iota\alpha$ by *statura*, we believe this substantive in this place does not designate the length of the human body, but the length of life. In fact, the word does have these two meanings in the New Testament; but the second meaning is evidently the one that is more suitable here, because to add twenty inches to a man's height would be something enormous, whereas the Savior has in view only a small dimension.

[139] The cubit was the chief linear measure among the Jews. It is thought that it was equal to about twenty inches. It was so called because it equaled the length of the forearm of a man of ordinary size, measured from the elbow to the tip of the middle finger.

[140] Matt. 6: 25-34.

[141] $M\dot{\eta}\ \mu\epsilon\rho\iota\mu\nu\hat{\alpha}\tau\epsilon$ (Vulg., *ne soliciti sitis*).

that is absolutely necessary to preserve that life; the infinitely good God, who takes fatherly care of the humblest creatures, even of the sparrow, will relieve the needs of man, His privileged creature. Anxious solicitude serves no good purpose. Even the most brilliant genius is in reality powerless to prolong his life for a single minute against the divine will; the delicate attentions which even beings without reason, such as ephemeral flowers,[142] receive from the Creator, bear witness to man that his temporal needs will not be forgotten. To lack confidence in the care of Providence would be a pagan sentiment, unworthy of members of the Kingdom of Heaven. The conclusion is that Christians ought to seek spiritual goods before all else, assured that God will compensate them by amply providing for their temporal needs. Furthermore, since each day brings man his share of cares, of what use is it to worry about them in advance? To do so would be to suffer doubly and uselessly.

After these important declarations, the sermon passes to instructions of various kinds,[143] the first of which concern reciprocal duties of Christians. Jesus says that no one has a right to constitute himself a severe judge of his neighbor's faults and to pronounce sentence of condemnation. Yet it is sometimes necessary to judge so as not lightly to give holy things over to others. In this passage the Savior's language assumes a lively and remarkably vigorous form:

"Judge not, that you may not be judged. For with what judgment you judge, you shall be judged; and with what measure you mete, it shall be measured to you again. And why seest thou the mote that is in thy brother's eye, and seest not the beam that is in

[142] It is not absolutely certain that the flower mentioned here by our Lord is the lily, although there are several varieties of this flower in Palestine. The little picture which contrasts the charming adornment of the lily of the field with the splendor of Solomon's raiment is exquisite.

[143] Matt. 7 : 1–23.

thy own eye? Or how sayest thou to thy brother: Let me cast the mote out of thy eye; and behold a beam is in thy own eye? Thou hypocrite, cast out first the beam out of thy own eye, and then shalt thou see to cast out the mote out of thy brother's eye. Give not that which is holy to dogs; neither cast ye your pearls before swine, lest perhaps they trample them under their feet and, turning upon you, they tear you." [144]

"With what judgment you judge, you shall be judged." This is the very legitimate divine law of retaliation, which is in striking contrast to the fifth petition of the Lord's prayer: "Forgive us . . . as we forgive . . ." The little parable of the beam and the mote in the eye, appearing also in the Talmud and in Arabic literature, emphasizes the defect in question and makes the blame more severe.[145] Holy things and pearls, which should not be thrown to unclean animals, here stand for the gospel doctrine in general, the mysteries of faith, the sacraments, particularly the Eucharist.[146]

Jesus now returns to the subject of prayer, to consider it from another point of view and to point out the irresistible power of Christian supplication. He has imposed many difficult obligations upon His disciples. For their encouragement He promises them that divine grace, if they ask for it perseveringly, will powerfully help them to remain faithful. Whereas earthly kings often reject their subjects' petitions, even the most deserving, the requests of Christians will always be favorably received by God. By repetitions and eloquent figures, the Savior stresses the need of persevering in prayer if one wishes assuredly to be heard, on condition, however, of asking from God only "good things."

---

[144] Matt. 7: 1–6; Luke 6: 37–42.

[145] For the same thought, see Cicero, *De Offic.*, I, 41; *Tuscul.*, III, 3; Horace, *Sat.*, I, 3, 73–75; Seneca, *De Vita Beata*, 27. "To judge thy neighbor, wait until thou art in his place," said Hillel, *Pirke Aboth*, II, 5.

[146] See the *Didache*, IX, 5; Tertullian, *De Paenit.*, LIV, etc.

"Ask, and it shall be given you; seek, and you shall find; knock, and it shall be opened to you. For every one that asketh, receiveth; and he that seeketh, findeth; and to him that knocketh, it shall be opened. Or what man is there among you, of whom if his son shall ask bread, will he reach him a stone? Or if he shall ask him a fish, will he reach him a serpent? If you then being evil, know how to give good gifts to your children, how much more will your Father who is in Heaven, give good things to them that ask Him?" [147]

Christ then announces a truly "golden rule," as it has been well called, a rule summarizing all He had said thus far: "All things therefore whatsoever you would that men should do to you, do you also to them. For this is the law and the prophets." [148]

The universal practice of this royal law of charity would contribute very largely to the restoration of the earthly paradise. It is an entirely natural law, which we find stated not only in several places in the Old Testament, as our Lord declares,[149] but likewise in many pagan authors.[150] It may also be found in the Talmud, which records this saying of Hillel: "Do not to thy neighbor what thou thyself dost detest." In this form the counsel is purely negative and recommends nothing more than to refrain from all injustice, whereas "our Lord's precept is essentially positive and calls for unlimited activity. In contrast with the passive attitude of justice, He sets forth the free initiative of love." [151]

A generous Christian will not succeed in obeying these different commands of Christ without pain and struggle. Along

[147] Matt. 7:7–11.

[148] Matt. 7:12.

[149] Tobias 4:16: "See thou never do to another what thou wouldst hate to have done to thee by another"; Ecclus. 31:18: "Judge of the disposition of thy neighbor by thyself."

[150] *V. g.*, Isocrates, *Orat.*, I: "What angers you when others afflict you therewith, see that you do not to others"; Diog. Laert., V, i, 21: "How should we treat others? . . . As we would have them treat us," etc.

[151] H. Monnier, *La Mission Historique de Jésus*, p. 137.

his path will arise many sorts of obstacles, some of them springing from the very essence of the new religion, which requires constantly repeated sacrifices; other hindrances will come from perverse guides who endeavor to seduce the souls of men striving for perfection; still others will arise from dangerous illusions about the practice of holiness. Hence there are three successive exhortations.

The difficulties inherent in the Christian life are metaphorically set forth as follows:

"Enter ye in at the narrow gate; for wide is the gate, and broad is the way that leadeth to destruction, and many there are who go in thereat. How narrow is the gate, and strait is the way that leadeth to life; and few there are that find it!" [152]

These two gates and these two paths clearly symbolize the easy life which is so pleasing to human nature and which provides worldly men with an unrestrained license for all their desires, and, on the other hand, they symbolize the trouble and mortification and suffering which must be undergone to follow Jesus. But what a contrast in the journey's end! The narrow, steep road of perfection leads to eternal happiness; the broad road, to everlasting perdition. Unfortunately a large number of men blindly and foolishly risk the latter.

The false guides, whom the Savior here calls "false prophets," also cause the Messias' disciples to run great dangers.

"Beware of false prophets, who come to you in the clothing of sheep, but inwardly they are ravening wolves. By their fruits you shall know them. Do men gather grapes of thorns, or figs of thistles? Even so every good tree bringeth forth good fruit, and the evil tree bringeth forth evil fruit. A good tree cannot bring forth evil fruit, neither can an evil tree bring forth good fruit. Every tree that bring-

[152] Matt. 7 : 13 f.

eth not forth good fruit, shall be cut down, and shall be cast into the fire. Wherefore by their fruits you shall know them." [153]

To be safe from the pernicious influence of these false guides, a good Christian needs only to observe closely their words and deeds and their whole conduct. Before long they disclose their true inner nature. In developing His thought on this subject, our Lord uses figures taken from the plant kingdom. [154]

A sincere disciple of the Divine Master will not be satisfied with a merely external profession of Christian faith, because such a profession, even though accompanied by the gift of miracles, will alone not lead him to Heaven. To theoretic faith he must add works, consisting in the exact fulfilment of God's will on all points. As was said long ago, "it is not the name, it is the life that makes a Christian."

"Not every one that saith to Me, Lord, Lord, shall enter into the Kingdom of Heaven; but he that doth the will of My Father who is in Heaven, he shall enter into the Kingdom of Heaven. Many will say to Me in that day: Lord, Lord, have not we prophesied in Thy name, and cast out devils in Thy name, and done many miracles in Thy name? And then will I profess unto them, I never knew you; depart from Me, you that work iniquity." [155]

Jesus suddenly transports His hearers to the scene of the last judgment, which has something tragical about it. The words, "I never knew you; depart from Me," will terribly dispel the illusion of those who think themselves assured of their salvation and even of a place of honor in the assembly of the elect, but who will hear themselves called workers of iniquity. [156]

[153] Matt. 7 : 15–20.
[154] Cf. Luke 6 : 43–46; James 3 : 12. See also Epictetus, II, xx, 18.
[155] Matt. 7 : 21–23.
[156] Our readers know that the gift of prophecy and that of miracles do not

The Sermon on the Mount comes to a close with a peroration, which brings to the hearers' attention the priceless advantages of obedience and the awful consequences of disobedience, and urges them to put into practice the instructions they have just heard.

"Every one therefore that heareth these My words and doth them, shall be likened to a wise man that built his house upon a rock. And the rain fell and the floods came and the winds blew, and they beat upon that house, and it fell not, for it was founded on a rock. And every one that heareth these My words and doth them not, shall be like a foolish man that built his house upon the sand. And the rain fell and the floods came and the winds blew, and they beat upon that house, and it fell, and great was the fall thereof." [157]

In this passage we have two little contrasted parables dramatically described. The short clauses, abruptly following one another, joined by the conjunction "and" recurring again and again, eloquently depict the sudden origin and impetuous character of those short storms, especially frequent in Palestine, which cause so much damage. In the second case, to the tumult of rain, wind, and overflowing torrents is added the crumbling of the house. This is a sad figure of virtue which lacks solidity and is shaken and overwhelmed by the storm of temptation or passion.

St. Matthew [158] briefly acquaints us with the impression which the sermon produced on the hearers. All were charmed and beside themselves with admiration.[159] This does not sur-

necessarily presuppose sanctifying grace in those who have received these gifts. Witness Balaam, the traitor Judas, and others. Cf. 1 Cor. 13: 1-3. The grace *gratis data* (gratuitously given), as the theologians express it, consisting in miraculous powers granted at times to sinners, is one thing; another is the grace *gratum faciens* (which renders the soul pleasing to God). See St. Thomas, *Summa Theolog.*, 1a 2ae, qu. 3.

[157] Matt. 7: 24-27; Luke 6: 47-49.
[158] Matt. 7: 28 f.
[159] In the Greek: ἐξεπλήσσοντο.

prise us, because Jesus "was teaching [160] them as one having power, and not as the Scribes and Pharisees." Everything contributed to enhance the Preacher's authority: in His Person, a majesty of features and bearing, a confident tone of voice, a persuasive mildness of look; in His teaching, the truth, the simplicity, the loftiness, and even the difficulty of His precepts. His audience felt, in His accent, that it was not only a holy personage or a prophet, but a wise and mighty lawgiver that spoke. From every standpoint, what a difference between Him and the Scribes, those spiritless interpreters of the Law, who failed to rise above meticulous and commonplace explanations, which no powerful breath elevated to the serene heights where religious truth appears more beautiful and consoling. [161]

III. General View of Christ's Preaching [162]

Let us attempt, less briefly than the Evangelists, to describe the character of this new preaching. But we will here concern ourselves mostly with its external form. The study of the rich and transcendent content we postpone to a later chapter.

The Savior's words occupy a considerable space in the Gospel accounts, of which they form about a quarter. They appear at every turn, chiefly in two forms: connected discourses and isolated sayings. The former are divided into three categories, as they are recorded by the Synoptics, by

[160] This expression generalizes the thought and here characterizes our Lord's entire eloquence.

[161] For a detailed explanation of the Sermon on the Mount, see St. Augustine, *De Sermone Domini in Monte;* Hugo Weiss, *Die Bergpredigt Christi,* 1892; G. Heinrici, *Die Bergpredigt quellenkritisch . . . untersucht,* 1900; E. Lyttleton, *Studies in the Sermon on the Mount,* 1905; C. W. Votaw, in Hastings' *Dictionary of the Bible,* V. 1–20. Consult also the commentaries, among others: P. Schanz, *Das Evangelium des Matthäus,* pp. 156–246; Knabenbauer, *Comment. in Evang. S. Matthaei,* I, 180–317; Fillion, *L'Évangile de S. Matthieu,* pp. 77–150; T. Zahn, *Das Evangelium des Matthäus ausgelegt,* pp. 173–329. On the assertions of Rationalists and Jews in the matter of this sermon, see Appendix X.

[162] See Appendix XI.

St. John, or in the form of parables. Under each of these aspects, their authenticity is free from all shadow of doubt. The arguments proving that our four Gospels are authentic and genuine apply equally well to the spoken words as to the other details. True, they were first uttered in Aramaic, the language which our Lord habitually spoke and of which the Greek dress in which we possess them is only a translation that necessarily loses something of the primitive coloring. But this translation is so exact and it comes down to us through such faithful hands that it has almost the value of the original text. It is true that Christ's words were not at once consigned to writing and that in passing from mouth to mouth they must have undergone some modification, as we see by the variants which appear in the different accounts. Nevertheless, as several Rationalist critics unhesitatingly acknowledge,[163] so sure and retentive is the memory of Orientals generally,[164] so striking and easily remembered were our Lord's words, and so carefully did the first Christians preserve them, after the manner of a sacred treasure, that we have the most solid guaranties of their authenticity. They have scarcely lost the savor and freshness which they had when Jesus pronounced them.[165]

We have already said what is to be thought of the special character of the Savior's discourses, as we read them in the Fourth Gospel, and in due course we will give special attention to the parables. What we wish to say at this point about the

[163] Cf. J. Weiss, *Die Schriften des N. T.,* I, 48 f.; O. Frommel, *Die Poesie des Evangeliums Jesu,* p. 35; Dalman, *Die Worte Jesu,* pp. 34 f., etc.

[164] Talmudic literature was preserved in this way for several centuries by oral tradition, before being consigned to writing.

[165] In fact, "in consequence of one of those mysterious phenomena that seem to be a sort of miracle in the intellectual realm, we possess a considerable treasure of Christ's words, with such clearness, with such plasticity of expression, with such a depth of content . . . that it is impossible for us not to consider Christ as their author and to attribute them to some great unknown personage." (O. Frommel, *loc. cit.*)

form of Christ's doctrine applies to both those parts of His preaching as well as to His other discourses and His isolated sentences. These last are rather numerous, and there is hardly a page of the Gospels that does not include some.[166] Many of them are so sparkling with beauty and force and truth that they became proverbial among all the peoples of Europe.[167] They have been compared to arrows penetrating deeply into men's minds for their enlightenment and into their hearts for their moral betterment. Considered all together, they evince Christ's superior mind, the moral power of His Personality, and His superhuman holiness. They have had a prominent share in the formation of the Christian spirit and in the civilization of the world. The sayings of great thinkers or heroes have sometimes been collected. But what collection of sayings can hold a place beside those of our Lord?

Orientals, particularly the Jews, always relished this manner of teaching, these figurative expressions which become engraved in the mind. The books of the Old Testament abound in such sentences and axioms. Some of those books—Proverbs, Ecclesiastes, Ecclesiasticus, and Wisdom—are made up

---

[166] Crooker exaggerates when he counts about two hundred of them (*The Supremacy of Jesus*, p. 98).

[167] There is a very large number from which to choose: "There shall be weeping and gnashing of teeth" (Matt. 8:12); "He hath not where to lay his head" (Matt. 8:20); "Let the dead bury their dead" (Matt. 8:22); "They that are in health need not a physician, but they that are ill" (Matt. 9:12); "Thy faith hath made thee whole" (Matt. 9:22); "Wise as serpents and simple as doves" (Matt. 10:16); "The disciple is not above the master" (Matt. 10:24); "Preach ye upon the housetops" (Matt. 10:27); "A cup of cold water" (Matt. 10:42); "Out of the abundance of the heart the mouth speaketh" (Matt. 12:34); "Many are called, but few are chosen" (Matt. 22:14); "Render to Cæsar the things that are Cæsar's; and to God, the things that are God's (Matt. 22:21); "These things you ought to have done, and not to leave those undone" (Matt. 23:23); "The spirit indeed is willing, but the flesh weak" (Matt. 26:41); "Physician, heal thyself" (Luke 4:23); "No prophet is accepted in his own country" (Luke 4:24); "But one thing is necessary" (Luke 10:42); "I have sinned against heaven and before thee" (Luke 15:18), etc., etc. Numerous passages from the Sermon on the Mount have become popular proverbs. Cf. Matt. 5:15; 6:3, 21, 24, 34; 7:3, 6, 7, 15, 18, 19, etc.

almost entirely of them. In the style of the ancient writers of
His race, Jesus often uttered such proverbial sentences in the
form characteristic of Hebrew poetry. Therein we find what
is called the "parallelism of the members," consisting in the
repetition of the principal thought by means of varied expressions, which in some cases develop and strengthen the thought,
at other times set up an antithesis in contrast to it.[168] The
following examples will serve as illustrations:

> "So shall the last be first,
>   and the first last." [169]
> "He is not the God of the dead,
>   but of the living." [170]
> "Whosoever will save his life, shall lose it;
>   and whosoever shall lose his life for My sake and
>   the gospel, shall save it." [171]
> "Give not that which is holy to dogs;
>   neither cast ye your pearls before swine." [172]

At times, instead of a distich, we find three or four members or sentences grouped together:

> "We have piped to you,
>   and you have not danced.
>   We have mourned,
>   and you have not wept." [173]
> "Ask, and it shall be given you;
>   seek, and you shall find;
>   knock, and it shall be opened to you." [174]
> "Be not solicitous for your life, what you shall eat,

[168] See Fillion, *La Sainte Bible Commentée*, III, 482–486.
[169] Matt. 20:16.
[170] Matt. 22:32.
[171] Mark 8:35.
[172] Matt. 7:6.
[173] Luke 7:32.
[174] Matt. 7:7.

nor for your body, what you shall put on.
Is not the life more than the meat,
        and the body more than the raiment ?" [175]

It sometimes happens that the members are arranged in symmetrical stanzas, as in this "hymn of finished beauty," [176] this lyric so full of feeling:

"I confess to Thee, O Father, Lord of heaven and earth,
        because Thou hast hid these things from the wise and prudent,
        and hast revealed them to little ones.
Yea, Father; for so hath it seemed good in thy sight.

All things are delivered to Me by My Father.
        And no one knoweth the Son, but the Father;
        neither doth any one know the Father, but the Son,
        and he to whom it shall please the Son to reveal Him.

Come to Me, all you that labour and are burdened,
        and I will refresh you.
Take up My yoke upon you and learn of Me,
        because I am meek and humble of heart.
And you shall find rest to your souls;
        for My yoke is sweet and My burden light." [177]

But this rhythm and this poetic parallelism are by no means to be found in all our Lord's sayings.

As Clement of Alexandria wrote, "to save mankind Christ uses every accent and infinitely varies His manner of speech. Now He warns and threatens, now He expresses wrath, and now He shows His pity in tears." [178] We might add that at times He instructs, or again He moralizes, or converses in a familiar way, or He rises to the very highest sublimity of language. He offers us every kind of preaching: formal ser-

[175] Matt. 6:25.
[176] Frommel, *Poesie des Evangeliums*, p. 43.
[177] Matt. 11:25-30.
[178] See what we said in Vol. I, pp. 438 ff. about the feelings and emotions of the Savior.

mon, catechism, homily, informal dialogue, polemical discourse, simple repartee. His speech has a graver tone in the
synagogues, but becomes simpler with His disciples and the
multitudes. He even has, if we may be permitted the expression, His table-talk, which is not the least interesting part of
His teaching. Under all circumstances He is a master: when
He consoles, when He rebukes, when He encourages, when
He tests someone's faith, when He repudiates a rôle that
does not befit Him. He raises questions, He replies to objections that are proposed to Him, He exposes men's inmost
thoughts. And His speech ever remains sober and dignified,
even when taking on a popular tone. In no instance does it
exhibit the slightest lack of good taste; never is it marred by
those puerilities or repulsive details which so often mark the
writings of the rabbis.

Jesus' habitual method in preaching or in simple conversation is "intuitive" rather than "discursive." He does not reason things out, like Plato; He does not comment, like a Scribe.
He knows fully and absolutely, He contemplates by direct
sight. He reports what He sees and hears.[179] But this
does not prevent His words from conforming to the ordinary laws of reasoning. His thoughts follow one another
in logical order. His argumentation leaves nothing to be desired.[180] He appeals directly to the mind, the soul, the heart,
sometimes to His hearers' personal experience.[181] He clearly
enunciates principles and cogently deduces conclusions. And
withal there shines a remarkable talent for raising minds
above things of sense and the commonplaces of life, trans-
porting them to the spheres of heavenly truth and the Kingdom of God. Never is there a superfluous word on His lips.
It is certain that His words owe part of their power to their

[179] Kilpatrick in Hastings' *Dictionary of Christ*, I, 287.
[180] See, by way of example, Matt. 23:29–31; Mark 11:30; 12:36.
[181] Cf. Matt. 7:9–12; Luke 12:42–48; 13:15 f.; 15:4–7, 8–10; 17:7–10, etc.

rigorous conciseness and condensation. Everywhere they are marked by clearness and balance.

Jesus makes vigorous use of irony, hyperbole, and paradox, as we remarked when considering the Sermon on the Mount. "Blessed are the poor. Woe to the rich. If thy right eye scandalize thee, pluck it out. If any man come to Me, and hate not his father and mother, . . . he cannot be My disciple. He that is not with Me, is against Me. Whosoever shall lose his life, . . . shall save it. I came not to send peace, but the sword. It is easier for a camel to pass through the eye of a needle, than for a rich man to enter into the Kingdom of Heaven. When thou makest a dinner or a supper, call not thy friends nor thy brethren nor thy kinsmen nor thy neighbors. . . . But call the poor, the maimed, the lame, and the blind." This purposely exaggerated manner of expressing His thought had as its aim to render His thought more salient and to make it penetrate His hearers' memory more deeply. Sentences of this sort must be interpreted according to their spirit, and not solely according to the letter, because Jesus wishes to impose upon His disciples only "that which is just." [182] These licenses are met with not only in poetry, but also in ordinary speech, to which they communicate energy and life.

The Evangelists quote numerous questions addressed by our Lord under most diverse circumstances, to His Apostles and disciples, His friends and His enemies, to the crowds gathered about Him. Every intelligent teacher has recourse to this method which Socrates made famous. [183] The questions, when ably put, stir the hearers to reflect and give the teacher an opportunity to explain his doctrine more thoroughly. It is, therefore, not surprising that Jesus again and again made use

[182] Luke 12: 57.
[183] The rabbis also commonly made use of this method.

of this method. He asks a question to elicit a bit of information by way of preparation for one of His miracles,[184] or to
introduce a parable; [185] or again to half conceal a rebuke,[186] or
to draw out from His hearers themselves the sometimes tragic
conclusion of His preaching.[187] Often, in reply to a question addressed to Him, He asked another, which obliged the
questioner to reflect further and solve his problem himself.[188]
Jesus acted thus especially when He was asked an insidious
question.[189]

Another notable characteristic of the Savior's speech is
that ordinarily it is very concrete, rarely abstract, save for a
few passages in the Fourth Gospel; in these latter cases Jesus
was addressing mostly educated hearers who could understand
Him without difficulty. When He spoke to the common people, He gave His instructions the form most pleasing to them.
He used many figures and comparisons, as a capable teacher
who knows the influence they exert over the imagination.[190]
There are but few pages of the Gospels that do not contain one
or more of these well-chosen metaphors. Thus Jesus compared
the future Prince of the Apostles to a foundation stone; the
Pharisees, to blind leaders of the blind; Herod Antipas, to
a fox. He advised His disciples to have the wisdom of the
serpent and the simplicity of the dove; He sent them into the

---

[184] Mark 6:38: "How many loaves have you?" Luke 8:30: "What is thy
name?" John 11:34: "Where have you laid him?" etc.

[185] Mark 4:30: "To what shall we liken the Kingdom of God?" etc.

[186] Matt. 8:26: "Why are you fearful, O ye of little faith?" Matt. 20:22: "Can
you drink the chalice that I shall drink?" Mark 9:32: "What did you treat of in
the way?" etc.

[187] Matt. 21:40: "When therefore the lord of the vineyard shall come, what
will he do to those husbandmen?"

[188] Cf. Mark 2:18 f.; John 6:5, etc.

[189] Cf. Matt. 12:10 f.; 15:1–3; 21:23–25; Mark 2:6–9, 24 f.; Luke 7:39–42;
John 6:62–64, etc.

[190] Cf. Frommel, *Poesie des Evangeliums*, pp. 56–58; Jülicher, *Gleichnisreden
Jesu*, I, 50–52; H. Weinel, *Die Bildersprache Jesu, passim*.

world as lambs among wolves. He one day saw Satan falling from heaven like lightning. His parables and allegories are merely spun-out metaphors.

What wonderful local coloring is to be observed in the choice of all these figures and comparisons! Jesus takes them freely from every feature of the Palestine of that time. When we were considering the subject of His intellectual growth, we mentioned the deep impressions which nature and the social, political, and religious life made on His mind.[191] All these were a rich treasure-house, from which, during His ministry, He continually brought forth "things old and new" for the purpose of greater emphasis in His preaching. The agricultural activities and climatic conditions of the country, its flora and fauna, its outward configuration, commerce and industry, houses and their furniture, publicans and soldiers, the thousand details of daily life and social usages, the political institutions, religious beliefs and practices, all supplied Him with arguments and examples, with illustrations for His doctrinal and moral teaching. Thus the varied aspects of Palestine and its history in our Lord's time are continually reflected in the Gospel narratives.[192]

Our Lord's preaching, considered in its outward form,

---

[191] See Vol. I, pp. 403 ff.

[192] Cf. Frommel, *op. cit.*, pp. 71 f. This subject is so interesting that we will cite a few additional examples. The rain which is usually brought by the east wind, the fig tree blossoming and announcing the approach of the fine season, the reed bending with the wind, new wine fermenting and threatening to burst old skin bottles, the carefree joyousness of the birds, the passing beauty of the flowers, the stupidity of the sheep straying away, the tenderness of a hen for her little ones, the wolf's cruelty, the bird of prey swooping down upon a carcass, litttle children playing in the market place, marriage and funeral ceremonies, physicians and patients, the rich and poor, priests and Pharisees, the relations between friends and enemies, the various members forming a household (parents, children, servants of different rank), robbers and brigands, angels, saints, and devils, God and the Messias: all these details and many others form a collection no less instructive than delightful. Christ thus places before our eyes the whole life of His country and time, and depicts the finest part of it to raise hearts to God.

wins our admiration, no matter from what angle we view it.
It is always simple and clear, even when it becomes sublime
and rises to the height of Heaven. Never is it affected or
professorial, but always fresh and original, bright and picturesque. We cannot hope fittingly to describe its lifelike realism,
its exquisite poetry, its irresistible logic, its strength and
gentleness, its brilliance and eloquence, its gracefulness and
appropriateness, its depth, its permeating sweetness. Is it
not a remarkable fact that it preserves all its qualities even
when translated into foreign languages? In every literary
masterpiece, both form and content should be perfect. They
are so in the Savior's words, which will continue to exercise
their gentle and salutary influence to the end of time, winning great and small by their heavenly charm. Therein we
hear the Son of Man speaking to men. His brethren, to show
them the way of holiness and to teach them where they will
find true happiness. If we might be permitted to apply such
terms to Jesus, we would say that, in the matter of language,
He is a poet, an esthete of the highest rank, as He is also,
from the standpoint of ideas, the greatest of thinkers and
doctors. But we may offer a more worthy praise of His preaching by simply saying that, in its outward expression as well
as in its content, it possesses an incomparable perfection,
worthy of the Messias and Son of God. As rarely happens,
the Savior succeeded in becoming popular,[193] while opposing
current practices and combating the passions and prejudices
of His compatriots. In very truth, "never did man speak like
this Man." [194]

[193] The Evangelists several times mention the popularity which came to Jesus
from the charm of His words. Cf. Matt. 7:28; 13:54; Mark 1:22; 6:2; Luke
4:22; 19:48, etc.
[194] John 7:46.

IV. Curing of the Centurion's Servant and Raising to
Life of the Son of the Widow of Naim

The two Evangelists who relate the cure of the centurion's
servant [195] connect it closely with the Sermon on the Mount. St.
Matthew mentions only one incident, in the interval, namely,
the curing of a leper. St. Luke, with his customary exactness,
indicates a still closer connection between the two events. He
says: "When He had finished all His words in the hearing of
the people, He entered into Capharnaum"; and it was shortly
afterwards that the miracle seems to have taken place.

At Capharnaum there was a detachment of soldiers who
guarded the port and the commercial highway. With them
resided a centurion, in the service of the tetrarch Herod Antipas; the latter had reorganized his military forces after the
Roman system. His little army was made up almost entirely of
foreign mercenaries. [196] A centurion, as the word indicates, [197]
was in command of a company of a hundred men, that is, one-
sixth of a cohort, which in turn formed the tenth part of a
legion, this last being composed of about six thousand men.
There were, consequently, sixty centurions in a legion. [198]

The centurion who is the hero of this episode was certainly
a pagan, as is evident from the Savior's remark: "I have not
found so great faith in Israel." At the very most he might
be reckoned among the proselytes; but even this supposition
is without sound reasons. Like the other officers of this same
rank who are mentioned in the New Testament, [199] he had

[195] Matt. 8: 5–13; Luke 7: 1–10. See Appendix XIII.

[196] Cf. Josephus, *Ant.*, XVII, viii, 3.

[197] In the Greek ἑκατόνταρχος, or ἑκατνταρχης, "who has command over a
hundred men." The Syriac text of the Sinaiticus is wrong: χιλιαρχος, "head of a
thousand," corresponding to the *"tribunus"* of St. Hilary.

[198] See Vigouroux' *Dictionnaire de la Bible*, Vol. I, cols. 994–997; Daremberg
and Saglio, *Dictionnaire des Antiquités Grecques et Romaines*, under the word
"Centurion."

[199] Matt. 27: 54; Acts 22: 26; 23: 23 f.; 24: 23; 27: 43.

a noble, generous soul, and likable traits of character. He had an opportunity to observe Judaism at close range and, as in the case of many other pagans, was attracted by the beauty of its doctrines and the loftiness of its moral teaching. Evidently he had heard of Jesus,[200] of His holiness and kindness, of His miracles, particularly of His curing the daughter of the royal officer at Capharnaum,[201] which made such a stir. It is even highly probable that He had seen Jesus on the streets of the city and had been present at some one or other of His sermons. He had conceived a high regard for the Savior, without, however, having had personal relations with Him.

In this centurion's service was a slave,[202] "who was dear to him," according to St. Luke's remark.[203] A fact of this sort was extremely rare among the Greeks and Romans, who ordinarily treated their slaves with utmost contempt and often with harsh cruelty.[204] So exceptionally was the contrary true [205] that Cicero [206] excuses himself for having shown fondness for one of these unfortunate creatures. The Evangelist's remark explains the centurion's extraordinary interest in his servant and the active measures he undertook in his behalf upon seeing him suddenly suffer a stroke of paralysis, which caused him horrible suffering and put his life in immediate danger.[207] Ordinary measures were plainly insufficient. But

[200] Luke 7:3.
[201] John 4:46–53.
[202] The two accounts alternately designate him by the words δοῦλος, "slave," and παῖς, which sometimes means "son" and sometimes "servant." The former of these terms is here the more exact.
[203] The Greek adjective ἔντιμος means: "held in honor," *pretiosus*, as the Vulgate translates it; hence "dear."
[204] Aristotle, *Polit.*, I, 3; Plato, *De Leg.*, VI; *Republ.*, VIII.
[205] See Seneca, *Epist.*, XLVII, and *De Clement.*, I, 18.
[206] *De Offic.*, I, 19.
[207] St. Matthew: παραλυτικός, δεινῶς βασανιζόμενος (Vulg., *paralyticus, et male torquetur*). St. Luke: κακῶς ἔχων, ἤμελλεν τελευτᾶν (Vulg., *male habens, erat moriturus*). The two Evangelists mutually supplement each other. The verb βέβληται (Vulg., *jacet*), added by St. Matthew, seems to indicate a sudden attack of the ailment.

Jesus was at hand, and the centurion, in his desolation, did not doubt but that He could promptly and miraculously cure the sick slave.

We must here point out a notable divergence as to the order of events in the two narratives. According to St. Matthew, the centurion himself came to the Savior and made his request directly. From St. Luke's account we would suppose that he did not come in person, but sent to Jesus in succession two deputations, charged with presenting his request to the Master. Yet there is no real contradiction between the two accounts. The author of the First Gospel, who considerably abridges, goes straight to the chief event, suppressing all secondary details. On the principle that, "what one does through the agency of another, he is regarded as doing himself," St. Matthew attributes to the centurion the steps taken by his envoys and the words spoken by them in his name. This literary procedure is quite proper, and not infrequently is employed by secular historians. We will follow St. Luke's narrative, which is more exact and complete.

The centurion, in his humility, did not think himself worthy to present his petition personally to Jesus. He therefore deputed some notables [208] of the city to convey this request: "Lord, my servant lieth at home sick of the palsy, and is grievously tormented." The envoys, mindful of the favors which the pagan officer had generously bestowed upon the city, forgot their Jewish prejudice and, after making the request, warmly pleaded his cause, saying: "He is worthy that Thou shouldst do this for him. For he loveth our nation; and he hath built us a synagogue." His good will was shown in deeds. The most important one, and very significant on the part of a pagan, was the building of a synagogue in Caphar-

---

[208] St. Luke calls them πρεσβύτεροι (*Vulg., seniores*), "the ancients," *i. e.,* according to the Jewish meaning of this word, the chief personages of the city; but not necessarily, as various interpreters would have it, the principal men of the Synagogue. These are habitually designated by their official title.

THE CENTURION'S SERVANT 327

naum at his own expense. This was the richest and finest in
the city if it is the one whose extensive ruins, discovered at
Tell Hum, we referred to above.[209] Some time before, Emperor Augustus had issued a laudatory edict about the synagogues,[210] and this centurion may have drawn a practical
conclusion from it.

Jesus received the notables' request with the greatest kindness, saying: "I will come and heal him." [211] He at once started
with them toward the centurion's house. The centurion, having been informed of the Savior's approach, changed his first
decision and hastily sent other messengers to meet him. This
delegation was made up of several of his friends and was
instructed to say to Jesus: "Lord, trouble not Thyself,[212] for
I am not worthy that Thou shouldst enter under my roof.
For which cause neither did I think myself worthy to come to
Thee. But say only a word,[213] and my servant shall be healed."
The Church has honored these remarkable words of faith and
humility by inserting them in the liturgical prayers which the
priest recites at the moment of communion. The centurion,
through his friends, explains the motive for the sudden change
in the form of his request. He gives a military reason, based
on the experiences of his own daily life: "For I also am a
man subject to authority, having under me soldiers; and I say
to one: Go, and he goeth; and to another: Come, and he cometh; and to my servant: Do this, and he doth it." He knew

[209] The Greek text, with the article, says: *"the* synagogue," *i.e.,* the well-
known building, the special synagogue.

[210] Josephus, *Ant.,* XVI, 6.

[211] Many contemporary interpreters (Wellhausen, Zahn, etc.), with no sufficient
reason, give an interrogative turn to our Lord's reply: "Shall I go and heal him?"
They have Him speak as if He had hesitated to enter the house of a pagan and
thereby contract a legal defilement. Cf. John 18:28; Acts 10:28; 11:3, etc. But
Christ scarcely permitted Himself to be disturbed by pre-occupations of that sort
when there was question of rendering a service to His neighbor.

[212] In the Greek: μὴ σκύλλου (Vulg., *noli vexari*), a vigorous expression.

[213] Εἰπέ λόγῳ (Vulg., *dic. verbo*); literally: "Say by a word" (the dative of
instrument).

the prompt effect of orders given; and he also knew what it is to obey. If he, a subordinate officer, was able to effect such results by his mere word, and if the word of his superior officers obtained from him, even at a distance, whatever was commanded, with all the more reason would an order from Jesus, the mighty Miracle-worker, succeed in accomplishing whatever He might will. He had only to command the disease to go, and however grievous it might be, it would instantly disappear.

The two sacred writers remark that the Savior, upon hearing these words, could not repress a feeling of admiration.[214] It has been fittingly said that it is a rule of divine perfection to marvel at nothing, because, in a strict sense, wonderment supposes surprise and, to some extent, an ignorance which is incompatible with the Savior's infinite knowledge. But Christ was man as well as God, and it was His human soul that experienced this astonishment and admiration. As we have already shown,[215] He was subject to all the feelings of our nature which were not evidences of weakness and corruption.

The centurion deserved public praise, and Jesus at once bestowed it upon him. Turning to the crowd about Him, He said: "Amen I say to you, I have not found so great faith, not even in Israel." [216] These words, "not even in Israel," said much, for our Lord, by His preaching and miracles, and by the holiness of His life, had done everything to arouse in His fellow-Jews faith in His superhuman nature; although He had won a large number of faithful disciples, yet at this period of His ministry there were few among them, whose faith was as perfect as that of the centurion.[217]

[214] See also Mark 6:6.

[215] Vol. I, pp. 435–442.

[216] In St. Matthew, with a slight shade of difference: "With no one have I found so great faith in Israel."

[217] Let us remark, further, that here our Lord's words have a general character and that they do not necessarily prove that the centurion's faith surpassed, as has

Looking into the future and considering the centurion as a type of those countless pagans who would one day believe in Him, Jesus continued: "And I say to you that many shall come from the east and the west and shall sit down with Abraham and Isaac and Jacob in the Kingdom of Heaven. But the children of the Kingdom shall be cast out into the exterior darkness. There shall be weeping and gnashing of teeth." This prophecy of the Savior was a joyous one for the Gentiles, but tragic for the Jews. It throws light on the future of His Church. At first we are surprised not to find it at this point in the Gospel of St. Luke, who is so glad to introduce everything that is favorable to the pagans. But he keeps it for mention later on,[218] since Jesus repeated it on another occasion. The language of this prophecy has a thoroughly Hebraic coloring. The "children of the Kingdom" are the Jews, who, by virtue of the divine promises, were its born heirs and had a right to be the first to enter therein. What a punishment for them to be excluded *en masse*,[219] while the converted pagans will gather there from all parts of the earth! But the aged Simeon, many years before, had announced that Christ would be an occasion of ruin for many Israelites;[220] and the ancient prophets[221] had foretold the large place that would be accorded in the Church to the Gentile world.[222] As in Isaias and in various New Testament passages,[223] the happiness which the elect will enjoy in the Kingdom of Heaven is represented by the figure of an evening banquet in a brightly

sometimes been said (even by such masters as St. Ambrose, St. Augustine, St. Thomas Aquinas), that of the Apostles themselves.

[218] Luke 13: 28.

[219] A violent exclusion, according to the reading ἐκβληθήσονται, which is the most authentic reading and the one followed by the Vulgate (*ejicientur*). Elsewhere we read: "they will go out."

[220] Luke 2: 34.

[221] Is. 2: 2-4; 45: 6; 49: 12; 59: 19; Jer. 3: 18; Mich. 4: 1-7; Mal. 1: 11, etc.

[222] Christ Himself more than once repeats that promise. Cf. Matt. 21: 42; 22: 9; 24: 14; 25: 32; 28: 19; John 10: 16; 12: 20, etc.

[223] Is. 25: 6; Matt. 26· 29; Luke 14: 15; 22: 30; Apoc. 3: 20; 19: 9, etc.

lighted hall,[224] while darkness reigns outside. Those who, through their own fault, will have no share in this feast, which is presided over by Israel's three most illustrious patriarchs, will therefore be cast out into the "exterior darkness." Their grief and despair are briefly and tragically described by the expression: "There shall be weeping and gnashing of teeth."

Close upon the praise of the centurion's faith, came his consoling reward, the healing of the sick servant, performed from a distance by a powerful act of the will. The officer's friends had the happiness to see this result themselves when they returned to report the Savior's words.

From this prodigy we pass to an incomparably greater miracle, the raising of the widow's son to life. It is related only by St. Luke.[225] This new incident takes us to a village of southern Galilee, called Naim,[226] which is mentioned nowhere else in the Bible. The name, which in Hebrew means "the Beautiful," "the Charming," was justified by its location. It stood on the northern slope of Little Hermon (now called Djebel ed Duhy, or ed Dahy), southwest of Nazareth and not far from Sunem, about an hour's journey west of Endor. From its lofty site it looked down upon the extensive fertile plain of Esdraelon; opposite, to the north, was Thabor and the wooded hills of Lower Galilee, surmounted by the snowy peak of Great Hermon. This fine perspective has hardly changed since then. But Naim itself is now only a wretched hamlet of a few huts scattered amid the remains of the past.[227]

This miracle took place shortly after the curing of the

---

[224] This metaphor appears frequently also in rabbinic literature. See Volz, *Jüdische Eschatologie,* p. 331; the *Book of Henoch,* 62:14; the *Apocalypse* of Baruch, 29:4; the Talmudic tractate *Aboth,* III, 20, etc.

[225] Luke 7:11-17.

[226] Ναίν or Ναείν, according to the Greek text. The present Arabic name is "Nein."

[227] See V. Guérin, *La Galilée,* I, 115 f.; Vigouroux' *Dictionnaire de la Bible,* Vol. IV, cols. 1469-1471; Sanday, *Sacred Sites of the Gospels,* pp. 24, 101.

paralytic servant. According to a variant of the original text,[228] it was the very next day. By leaving Capharnaum in the morning, Jesus would have had time to reach Naim, about twenty-four miles away, by evening, the hour when funerals often take place in the East. He was accompanied, not only by His Apostles, but by a large throng that never tired seeing and hearing Him. The presence of the multitude was quite providential, since it increased the number of witnesses of the new miracle.

The Savior had climbed the slope leading to Naim and, with His escort, was on the point of entering the city gate, such as most Palestinian towns had, when another procession, a sad one, came through in the opposite direction.[229] In accordance with Jewish custom, the cemetery was located outside the city and at some distance from the dwellings. Thither was being borne the corpse of a young man who had died in the flower of youth, an only son, leaving a widowed mother without support or hope or joy. Out of sympathy for so distressful a grief, which is regarded in the Bible [230] and elsewhere as a figure of overwhelming misfortune—"*Orba cum flet unicum mater*" [231]—most of the townspeople took part in the funeral procession.

Ten minutes' walk east from Naim, at the spot where the cemetery probably was located, may still be seen several tombs cut out of the rock. They are at the side of the road up which Jesus came before reaching the entrance to the city. The rabbis, whose regulations provided for all contingencies, had established special rules for a case like the present, when two such processions should meet. Even as a natural feeling of

---

[228] It is difficult to decide between the two readings ἐν τῷ ἑξῆς (*scil.*, χρόνῳ), "afterwards," and ἐν τῇ ἑξῆς (*scil.*, ἡμέρα), "the next day," which are equally accredited. The Vulgate adopts the former, which it translates by *deinceps*.

[229] The words καὶ ἰδού, "and behold," emphasize the suddenness of the meeting.

[230] Prov. 4: 3; Jer. 6: 26; Amos 8: 10; Zach. 12: 10, etc.

[231] Catullus, XXXIX, 5.

respect and humaneness would dictate, the living were to allow the funeral procession to pass and were then to join it and accompany it to the cemetery. But Jesus did a thousand times better than this. At sight of that desolated mother, His heart was moved with deep pity.[232] As she passed Him, just in front of the bier and following the hired mourners,[233] He gently said to her: "Weep not." For Him to speak thus, He must have been sure of the result that He intended; otherwise this word of encouragement would have been, as it often is on men's lips, merely an empty phrase. But Jesus never consoles in vain. He is the source of all true joy, and He can put an end to the greatest afflictions.[234]

On the low, open bier was laid, in the manner of the East, the body of the deceased, wrapped in a shroud, with the head uncovered. Jesus came to the bier and touched it. The bearers, usually chosen from the friends and neighbors of the deceased, were struck by the majesty that shone from Jesus' face. Rightly understanding His act and interpreting it as a command, they stopped at once. Then, amidst the silence and attention of all, the Divine Master, turning to the dead youth, whose face was livid and whose hands were clasped on his breast, pronounced these simple words, but in a tone of irresistible authority: "Young man,[235] I say to thee arise." He spoke to him as though he were merely asleep. His death was, in truth, only a sort of transitory sleep; for at once his soul returned to his body; he sat up and began to speak,[236]

---

[232] Ἐσπλαγχνίσθη (Vulg., *misericordia motus est*). On this expression, see Vol. I, p. 466, note 692.

[233] On Jewish funeral ceremonies of that time, see Edersheim, *Sketches of Jewish Social Life in the Days of Christ,* pp. 168–181.

[234] Cf. Apoc. 21 : 4.

[235] Some manuscripts and St. Ephrem, *Carm. Nisib.,* XXXIX, 179 f., repeat twice the apostrophe "Young man."

[236] It has been very justly remarked that the author of a legendary account would not have failed to quote the words uttered by the young man brought to

thus showing a complete return to life. We marvel at the ease with which the Savior performed such a miracle. As Massillon says, "He raises the dead as if He were performing the commonest act. He speaks as a master to those sleeping the eternal sleep, and we are aware that He is the God of the dead as of the living, never calmer than when performing the greatest deeds." [237] Another eminent writer says that there is something ineffably gentle [238] in the closing detail: "And He gave him to his mother." The expression was strictly exact, since death had snatched that only son from the grief-stricken widow. Jesus restored her precious treasure to her.

A tremendous sensation was produced by this miracle. Those close at hand were at first seized with a sort of fright, seeing this corpse come back to life before their very eyes. But presently nobler feelings arose within them, and they said, one to another, "A great prophet is risen up among us, and God hath visited His people." For many centuries the theocratic nation had not been honored or rejoiced by the presence of any prophet, and God had visited it in terrible ways to punish its faults. But Jesus was at least equal to a prophet sent from Heaven, since He raised the dead, as formerly Elias and Eliseus had done.[239] God, who endowed Jesus with such a power, thus showed that He had not abandoned His people. St. Luke concludes his account by saying that from Naim and the neighborhood the report of the miracle soon spread over all Judea,[240] and even to the adjoining regions.

---

life. As conscientious historians, the Evangelists omit details of this sort, which, moreover, are of no importance in themselves.

[237] *Discours sur la Divinité de Jésus-Christ.*

[238] Card. Wiseman, *Mélanges Réligieux, Scientifiques, et Littéraires,* 1858, p. 129.

[239] 3 Kings 17: 17–24; 4 Kings 4: 11–27.

[240] In the view of some interpreters, in this passage the name of Judea designates all Palestine. Cf. Luke 4: 44 (according to the Greek text); 23: 5.

V. General Survey of Christ's Miracles

Again and again the Evangelists present Jesus as an all-powerful miracle-worker, at whose word nature changes her most stable laws, all manner of disease and also the devils and even death take to flight. As the portion of the Gospel narrative which we have thus far been studying contains accounts of several such miracles, it seems fitting for us to take a general view of His miracles as we have already done regarding His preaching. We shall see that from this point of view also Christ is absolutely unique in the history of the world.[241]

The Evangelists employ several characteristic expressions to designate Christ's miracles. They call them "wonders," [242] or brilliant, marvelous deeds, "powers," [243] that is, acts manifesting the superior power of him who performs them, "signs" [244] of a divine mission, "works" [245] *par excellence*. In the mind of the sacred writers these terms do not correspond to distinct categories of miracles, but merely point to the varied aspects under which they may be considered.

The ancient prophets announced that the Messias would perform numerous wonders. Isaias especially, when describing the blessings of the Christ, said: "Then shall the eyes of the blind be opened, and the ears of the deaf shall be unstopped. Then shall the lame man leap as a hart, and the tongue of the dumb shall be free." [246] Jesus carried out that part of the divine plan as perfectly as He did all the rest. From the time that He presented Himself as the the special envoy of Heaven,

---

[241] For fuller details on this weighty question, see our study: *Les Miracles de N.-S. Jésus-Christ.*

[242] In the Greek, τέρατα (Vulg., *prodigia* or *portenta*) ; sometimes θαυμάσια (Vulg., *mirabilia*), marvelous deeds, or παράδοξα (Vulg., *mirabilia*), extraordinary, astounding deeds.

[243] Δυνάμεις (Vulg., *virtutes*).

[244] Σημεῖα (Vulg., *signa*).

[245] Ἔργα (Vulg., *opera*).

[246] Is. 35: 5 f.; cf. Matt. 11: 5.

as the Savior of Israel and of the world, He had to furnish proofs by which He would be fully accredited. Of these, one of the best was His miracles. If we were to eliminate them from His life, the faith of the early Christians would become an almost insoluble enigma. It is well to add that Jesus, being the Incarnate Word, was a perpetual miracle, "Wonderful," as Isaias names Him,[247] and that, in accord with the divine and human fitness of things, He must needs perform numerous wonders.

He superabundantly fulfilled this condition of His nature and office. At various places in the Gospels there are certain phrases which presuppose that, independently of the miracles related by the sacred writers, our Lord, during the brief period of His public life, performed almost countless other miracles. As St. Matthew says, "Jesus went about all Galilee . . . preaching the gospel of the Kingdom and healing all manner of sickness and every infirmity among the people. And His fame went throughout all Syria; and they presented to Him all sick people that were taken with divers diseases and torments, and such as were possessed by devils, and lunatics and those that had the palsy, and He cured them." [248] St. John [249] refers to the Savior's performing many miracles at Jerusalem at the beginning of His ministry; and the Synoptics make mention of a remarkable display of His miraculous power at Capharnaum.[250] At the time of our Lord's brief sojourn in the plain of Genesareth, as St. Mark informs us, "they began to carry about in beds those that were sick, where they heard He was. And whithersoever He entered, into towns or into villages or cities, they laid the sick in the streets, and besought Him that they might touch but the hem of His

247 Is. 9:6. In Hebrew, *Pele* (Vulg., *admirabilis*). Cf. St. Augustine, *Tractat. in Evangel.*, XVII, 1.

248 Matt. 4:23 f. Cf. Mark 1:39; Luke 4:44.

249 John 2:22 f.

250 Matt. 8:16 f.; Mark 1:32-34; Luke 4:40, etc.

garment: and as many as touched Him were made whole." [251]
From St. Matthew we learn that, at the time of the second
multiplication of loaves, "there came to Him great multitudes,
having with them the dumb, the blind, the lame, the maimed,
and many others; and they cast them down at His feet, and
He healed them; so that the multitudes marveled seeing the
dumb speak, the lame walk, the blind see. And they glorified
the God of Israel." [252] "When the Christ cometh, shall He do
more miracles than these which this man doth?" is the remark exchanged in Jerusalem itself between men who had
been impressed by the great number of miracles which our
Lord performed.[253] From these repeated statements we may
conclude, without exaggeration, that hundreds and thousands
of miracles must have proceeded from the Savior's heart and
hands. St. Thomas Aquinas [254] says they were like "an ineffable ocean of prodigies," not to mention the Savior's supernatural prophecies, of which we shall speak later on.[255]

Although we cannot calculate the total number of miracles
performed by Jesus Christ, the number of those for which
we have detailed accounts is comparatively limited. There
are not more than forty, according to the highest figure; some
authors place the total at thirty-three.[256] The Gospel that reports the largest number, mentions no more than twenty. On
this point, as in the matter of the Savior's teaching and His

[251] Mark 6 : 55 f. Cf. Matt. 14 : 35 f.

[252] Matt. 15 : 30 f. Cf. Mark 7 : 37.

[253] John 7 : 31. See also John 11 : 47; 12 : 37; 20 : 30; Matt. 19 : 2; 21 : 14; Luke 7 : 21; 8 : 2; 23 : 8, etc.

[254] *Summa Theolog.*, 3a, qu. 43, a. 4.

[255] "It is doubtful whether we have a correct notion of the immense number of Christ's miracles. Those related [in the Gospels] form only a small portion of those which He performed." (A. Maclaren, *In Matth.*, IV, 23–25.)

[256] This difference in calculating them comes from the fact that certain events in Christ's life, regarded as miraculous by some, are considered by others as not exceeding the limits of the natural order. In this number are the driving of the sellers out of the Temple, the falling to the ground of the servants of the San-hedrin at Gethsemani, etc.

deeds taken as a whole, it was impossible to narrate every-thing. The first biographers of Christ have likewise recorded only extracts, chosen examples of His miracles. It would gratify our piety to be more fully informed. But the report of a hundred additional miracles would have taught us noth-ing more regarding the essential features of Christ's life. Not only would a complete account of all His miracles have been difficult, as St. John says,[257] but it would have been use-less, since the examples that have come down to us, selected with exquisite judgment by the sacred writers,[258] amply suf-fice to acquaint us with our Lord as a miracle-worker and to prove the divinity of His mission.

We have seen that Jesus performed His first miracle at Cana, at the outset of His public life. The prodigies which the apocryphal gospels attribute to His childhood and youth [259] are, therefore, certainly not genuine, quite aside from their improbable and amazing and often coarse and shocking de-tails, which of themselves prove their falsity. From the time of the inauguration of His ministry, the Savior's miracles continually accompanied His preaching. Yet they seem to have been more numerous during the "happy year," and thereafter to have decreased because of the lessening of the faith of the masses. They ended only with the second miracu-lous draught of fishes after His Resurrection.

As we wrote in another work,[260] it is interesting to study the special character of our Lord's miracles in each of the Gospels. St. Matthew recounts them with the noble simplicity that distinguishes his whole work. It is well known that his

---

[257] John 21 : 25.

[258] On the rules which, independently of divine inspiration, guided their choice, see Fillion, *Les Miracles de N.-S.*, I, 23-25. In the same work (I, 25-30) will be found a complete list of the miracles recorded in the Gospels, with an indication of the part special to each Evangelist.

[259] *Ibid.*, pp. 158-163. Cf. Graffin and Nau, *Patrologia Orientalis*, Vol. XII, fasc. 4 and 5.

[260] Fillion, *op. cit.*, pp. 30-32.

method is frequently to group his materials according to a logical arrangement; this is just what he does with a number of Christ's miracles. In the ninth and tenth chapters of his Gospel, he gathers ten of them, one-half of all that he relates, so as to place before his readers in one group numerous and varied examples of the Divine Master's almighty power. The short Gospel of St. Mark is sometimes called "the Gospel of the Miracles." In fact, he flies, so to speak, from miracle to miracle; and in his lifelike pages our Lord's miracles appear to us in the brightest light. In the Savior's miracles as recounted by St. Luke, we find the gentle kindness and incomparable lovableness which characterize the Son of Man as depicted in the Third Gospel. In the Evangelist himself we find an artist with a wonderful power of description, a physician who specifies pathological details,[261] and a disciple of Paul, stressing the universal nature of the salvation brought to men by Jesus Christ. St. John recounts in detail only a small number of miracles.[262] But it is easy to see the importance he attaches to these "works" of his beloved Master.[263] He skilfully chose them from the greatest that our Lord performed.[264] And we find that with them Jesus Himself nearly always connects important discourses, which or-

---

[261] See Fillion, L'Évangile de S. Luc, Introd. Critique et Commentaires, pp. 2 f., 9–11, 13–16, etc.; A. Harnack, Lukas der Arzt, der Verfasser des dritten Evangeliums, 1906.

[262] Only eight or ten, depending on the character to be attributed to the driving out of the sellers, John 2: 13–21, and the falling down of the soldiers who came to arrest Jesus, John 18: 4–6.

[263] "As to those which he does report, he describes them with such exactness and accompanies them with such minute details and such conclusive proofs that not only do they most keenly interest us, but they also clearly show us his aim." (Cardinal Wiseman, l. c., p. 94.) See particularly the curing of the paralytic, John 5: 1–18; that of the man born blind, John 9: 1–38; and the resurrection of Lazarus, John 11: 1–44.

[264] Strauss himself makes this remark, Leben Jesu, I, 74. The paralytic had been suffering from his infirmity for thirty-eight years; the blind man had been afflicted from birth. Lazarus had been dead four days, etc.

dinarily concern His own Person and His divine office.[265]
Whereas the Synoptics often call attention to the impression
which our Lord's miracles produced on the friendly multitudes,[266] St. John repeatedly notes the effect upon the Savior's
enemies.[267]

Studying the miracles separately, we observe that they are
of a wide variety. Attempts to classify them have resulted in
different sorts of grouping.[268] The following seems to us the
most logical and natural: there were miracles performed in
the realm of nature (e. g., the changing of water into wine
at the wedding-feast of Cana, the calming of the tempest on
the lake, the walking on the water, etc.), supernatural cures,
the driving out of devils, victory over hostile forces (notably,
the expulsion of the sellers from the Temple, the way Jesus
thwarted the murderous attempt of the inhabitants of Nazareth), the raising of the dead. The Gospels give most notice
to cures of different diseases and infirmities: fever, leprosy,
dropsy, paralysis, hemorrhage, blindness, deafness, congenital
dumbness, and many other infirmities.

The historical reality and credibility of all these miracles,
to whatsoever category they belong, are guaranteed by the
soundest arguments, based on textual criticism, the character
of the Evangelists, and the miracles considered in themselves.

(1) The Gospel texts relating our Lord's miracles present,
as well as any part of His biography all the requisite conditions of authenticity, integrity, and veracity. In this threefold
respect, they nowise differ from the other portions of the
narrative. To attack or reject them solely because of the
supernatural element contained in them would be evidently
unjust, as the part devoted to this element, though not neg-
ligible, is by no means exaggerated and nowhere exceeds the

[265] John 9 : 3 ; 11 : 15, 42, etc.
[266] Cf. Matt. 9 : 33 ; 12 : 22 ; Mark 1 : 27 f., 45 ; Strauss, *Leben Jesu*, II, 708.
[267] Jülicher, *Einleitung in das N. T.*, 5th ed., p. 377.
[268] Fillion, *Les Miracles de N.-S. Jésus-Christ*, I, 34-36.

bounds of likelihood. It is of the highest importance to note the fact that it is impossible to eliminate the miracles from the Savior's history without mutilating it in the most arbitrary fashion and without at times making it unintelligible. Christ's miracles are so interwoven with His teaching and other acts of His life, that they cannot be removed without tearing the whole fabric to pieces.[269]

(2) The Evangelists are not less trustworthy in their accounts of our Lord's miracles than in the other portions of their narratives. Therein they display the same honesty and simplicity. They are satisfied with a purely objective and ordinarily brief exposition in which not the least sign leads us to suspect that they are embellishing or exaggerating, or that they are inventing. We should not forget that two of them, St. Matthew and St. John, were eyewitnesses of their Master's miracles, and that the other two, St. Mark and St. Luke, knew those same facts through the most reliable testimony. Should they be suspected of undue credulousness, the words of Jesus would protest in their behalf, since, on the occasion of several of His miracles,[270] He blamed the Apostles for their astonishing unbelief. It is also worthy of note that, when two or more of them recount the same miraculous event, they do so in an independent manner, with slight differences that are a guaranty of their truthfulness.

(3) The Savior's miracles were easy to verify. "They were performed in public places, in the presence of large crowds representative of all conditions of life, and even before bitter enemies,"[271] to whose interest it was to protest if they had remarked anything suspicious, but who, in spite of themselves,

---

[269] Lacordaire, Œuvres, IV, 45 f.; Fairbairn, Studies in the Life of Christ, p. 159; F. Nolloth, The Person of Our Lord, pp. 196-198; A. Bruce, The Miraculous Element in the Gospels, p. 116, etc. "The miracles cannot be eliminated from the Gospel narratives without destroying the latter to their very foundation," says Harnack, Lehrbuch der Dogmengeschichte, 3d ed., I, 64.

[270] Matt. 16: 8-10; Mark 9: 31.

[271] Lacordaire, op. cit., p. 48.

were obliged to bow before the evidence of the facts. "What do we?" they said to one another in their chagrin; "for this man doth many miracles." [272] This avowal of theirs is of the greatest value to us. And there is another decisive proof, namely, the attitude of Jesus Himself regarding His miracles. On several occasions He spoke about His marvelous "works" in such a way as to indicate that, in performing them, He was conscious of being a miracle-worker without the least doubt about His supernatural powers. He drives out devils by the Spirit of God;[273] He refers to the two multiplications of loaves as to genuine miracles; [274] He affirms that His miracles are manifest testimony in His favor.[275]

It is, therefore, easy to believe in the reality of the Gospel miracles. They withstand every attack.[276] They have been the basis of the faith of nineteen centuries in Jesus Christ and His Church. "What men, what geniuses have believed in them with simple sturdy faith, after the manner of the Apostles and their successors! Polycarp, Justin, Irenaeus, Origen, Clement of Alexandria,[277] Leo, Gregory the Great, Lactantius, Hilary, Jerome, Augustine, Basil, Gregory Nazianzen and John Chrysostom; later on, St. Anselm and Albert the Great, St. Thomas Aquinas and St. Bonaventure, Dante and Milton,

---

[272] John 11:47. Cf. Matt. 27:42; Mark 15:31 f. St. John (9:7-38) sets forth at length an official inquiry, conducted successively by the people and by the Sanhedrin, into the matter of the curing of the man born blind. No doubt our Lord's other miracles had often been the subject of similar investigations.

[273] Matt. 12:28; Luke 11:20.

[274] Matt. 16:8-10; Mark 8:17-20.

[275] John 5:20; 10:37 f., etc.

[276] Those of the latest Rationalists we will consider by themselves, in Appendix XIII.

[277] The following are some of the passages in which the earliest ecclesiastical writers treat of the miracles of Christ. St. Justin, *Apol.*, I, 22, 48, and *Dial. cum Tryph.*, 65; St. Irenaeus, *Adv. Haer.*, III, xi, 5; Melito of Sardis, *Fragm.*, XVI; Origen, *Contra Celsum*, II, 48; III, 28, 33; Tertullian, *Apol.*, 21; *De Carne Christi*, 4, etc.; St. Cyprian, *De Cath. Eccl. Unit.*, 3, etc.; Eusebius, *Demonstr. Evang.*, IX; Lactantius, *Divin. Institut.*, IV, 14. See W. Bauer, *Leben Jesu*, pp. 364-370.

Bossuet and Fénelon, Newton and Pascal. Savants and thinkers and saints and philosophers and theologians . . . did not
believe in Christ's miracles without weighing the reasons for
accepting them.[278] We who believe in the Gospel miracles are
in the excellent company of great numbers of noble men." [279]

Certain characteristics of the Savior's miracles deserve
special attention. We note that He performed none of them
in His own personal interest. "He suffered hunger at the
close of His forty days' fast, although, as the devil suggested,
it would have been easy for Him to change the stones of the
wilderness into bread; but He refrained from resorting to
that ready means. He was thirsty at Jacob's well and had no
means of drawing water; but He did not produce a miraculous flow of water to relieve His thirst. By casting Himself
from the pinnacle of the Temple He might have converted the
inhabitants of Jerusalem and obtained glory for Himself;
but this proposal of the evil spirit He rejected with horror.
He would have won many of His enemies to His cause, had
He consented, at their request, to perform some extraordinary
marvels; but He steadfastly refused to satisfy them.[280] He
allowed His executioners to lay hands on Him, to spit upon
Him, to strike Him; yet He had only to express a simple wish
to His heavenly Father,[281] and legions of angels would have
come to defend Him." [282]

On the contrary, save for rare exceptions,[283] the Gospel
miracles were glowing manifestations of Christ's merciful
goodness and compassionate love, for He never wearied in
alleviating the physical and moral sufferings of fallen man.[284]

---

278 Luther and Calvin themselves, with all their first followers, frankly admitted their reality.

279 Fillion, *Les Miracles de N.-S. Jésus-Christ,* I, 179 f.

280 Matt. 16: 1–4; Luke 23: 8 f.

281 Matt. 26: 53 f.

282 Fillion, *op. cit.,* pp. 138 f.

283 *V. g.,* the expulsion of the sellers, and the cursing of the barren fig tree.

284 This feature has impressed the Jewish writer J. Salvador, notwithstanding

His infinite kindness, expressing itself in wonderfully salutary acts, appears clearly in the sacred narratives, which mention it as the determining motive in several of His miracles. "He coming forth saw a great multitude and had compassion on them and healed their sick." [285] A few days later, He twice multiplied loaves [286] to provide nourishment for the crowds that had followed Him to a desert place and would otherwise have suffered from hunger.[287]

Although Jesus unceasingly performed miracles of every sort, He was never prodigal. "To the Evangelists the most miraculous thing in Christ was His determination not to be miraculous." [288] Christ always performs His miracles with a precise end in view: each of them corresponds to a need in the physical or moral order. So soon as the need is met, He at once becomes economical. With five loaves and two fishes He satisfied the hunger of several thousand men; but He directed His Apostles to gather up the fragments that remained, lest they be lost.

We marvel at the majestic serenity and divine calmness with which Jesus accomplished the most wonderful works. Under no circumstances, even when commanding the tempestuous lake or the devils or incurable diseases or even death, does He show the least hesitation or the slightest effort. The means He employed were astonishingly simple. Generally a word, a gesture, a mere touch was sufficient. "I will, be thou made clean"; [289] "Arise, take up thy bed, and walk"; [290]

his antichristian prejudices. Speaking of our Lord's miracles, he says that "love of neighbor and interest in the suffering classes shine in His miracles," and he finds therein an essential distinction between them and other religions. *Jésus-Christ et sa Doctrine*, 2d ed., I, 402.

[285] Matt. 14: 14.
[286] Matt. 15: 32.
[287] See also Matt. 20: 34; Mark 1: 41; Luke 7: 13, etc.
[288] Fairbairn, *Christ in Modern Theology*, p. 354.
[289] Matt. 8: 3.
[290] John 5: 8; cf. Matt. 9: 6.

"He said to the sea: Peace, be still"; [291] "Lazarus, come forth." [292] In some instances He cured at a distance.[293] With a single exception,[294] evidently willed by the Savior, the result was instantaneous, entire, and final. Thus, Simon Peter's mother-in-law was so completely cured that she was able at once to perform her household duties; the paralytics of Capharnaum and Bethesda went home carrying their beds on their shoulders; the daughter of Jairus, as soon as she was awakened from the sleep of death, was able to take food.

Ordinarily Jesus waited to perform His miracles until there was an appeal to His power or His goodness.[295] However, sometimes He Himself generously took the initiative, as in the case of the two miraculous draughts of fishes, the two multiplications of loaves, the resurrection of the widow's son and that of Lazarus, the curing of various sick persons. His loving heart could not withstand the sight of certain kinds of suffering.

From whatever angle we consider them, Christ's miracles constitute a unique fact in the history of mankind. As He Himself said, they were "works that no other man hath done." [296] This appreciation, which was also that of the Jewish multitudes,[297] is ratified by the judgment of all Christian ages. Never has the world witnessed such divine, transcendent deeds as the miracles of our Lord Jesus Christ. And they are in perfect harmony with all the other details of His life. As St. Augustine says, all these miracles "have their own

[291] Mark 4 : 39.

[292] John 11 : 43.

[293] Matt. 8 : 7 f.; 15 : 28; John 4 : 46-53.

[294] Mark 8 : 23.

[295] It was so in the case of Mary at Cana, John 2 : 3; of the royal officer of Capharnaum, John 4 : 46-50; of Jairus, Matt. 9 : 18; of the Syrophenician woman, Mark 7 : 25-28; of the father of the young lunatic, Mark 9 : 16-23; of the Apostles and the crowds on many occasions, Matt. 8 : 25; 14 : 28; Luke 4 : 38, etc.

[296] John 15 : 24.

[297] Matt. 9 : 33, on the occasion of one of our Lord's miracles, they cried out: "Never was the like seen in Israel."

language for those who know how to understand them"; [298] and this language is clear and eloquent, most convincing for anyone who listens to it attentively and without bias.

What do the miracles teach us about the Savior and His mission? What was their ultimate purpose in His mind and that of God, His Father? He has enlightened us on this subject in memorable words that emphasize the testimony which His miracles render to Him. In His discussion with the Jewish authorities after the curing of the paralytic of Bethesda, He said: "The works [*i. e.,* the miracles] which the Father hath given Me to perfect, the works themselves which I do, give testimony of Me, that the Father hath sent Me." [299] Later on when the Baptist, from his prison at Machaerus, sent two of his disciples to obtain from Jesus an official, categorical answer to the question, "Art Thou He that art to come?" that is, the Messias,—our Lord performed several miracles in sight of the messengers, and said to them: "Go and relate to John what you have heard and seen. The blind see, the lame walk, the lepers are cleansed, the deaf hear, the dead rise again, the poor have the gospel preached to them." [300] This testimony was all the plainer for having been taken from Isaias' prophecies relative to the Messias.[301]

Another day, when refuting the blasphemy of the Scribes and Pharisees, who accused Him of driving out devils by the help of Satan, Jesus drew this peremptory conclusion: "If I by the Spirit of God cast out devils, then is the Kingdom of God come upon you." [302] Hence the Messias, the founder of the Kingdom of God, must have made His appearance and was, in fact, Jesus Himself. In other passages [303] the Divine

---

[298] *Tractat. in Joan.,* XXIV, 2.
[299] John 5 : 36; cf. 10 : 24 f.
[300] Matt. 11 : 4 f.; Luke 7 : 18–22.
[301] Is. 35 : 4 f.; 61 : 1 f.
[302] Matt. 12 : 28. Cf. Luke 11 : 20.
[303] Matt. 16 : 5–12; Mark 8 : 11–21.

Master chides His Apostles for not believing enough in Him, notwithstanding the miracles they had witnessed. At one of the most momentous hours of His life, on the way to Geth-semani, the Savior said to His disciples: "If I had not come and spoken to them [the Jews who refused to believe in Him], they would not have sin; but now they have no excuse for their sin. . . . If I had not done among them the works that no other man hath done, they would not have sin; but now they have both seen and hated Me and My Father." [304] Christ's miracles, by conclusively proving that God had con-ferred full powers on Him, condemned the unbelief of the Jews.

It is, therefore, quite within the truth to affirm that the language of the Savior's miracles is precise and eloquent. Those miracles prove most cogently that Jesus is God's envoy *par excellence,* the Messias of Israel, and the Savior of man-kind. This was comprehended by those who in large numbers "believed in His name, seeing His signs which He did"; [305] by those who said to one another when the widow's son was raised to life: "A great prophet is risen up among us, and God hath visited His people"; [306] and by those who, after the curing of a certain possessed man, said: "Is not this the Son of David?" [307] Nicodemus, too, understood it, as appears from his words, "Rabbi, we know that Thou art come a teacher from God; for no man can do these things which Thou dost, unless God be with him." [308] If the faith of the first disciples and of the Apostles was so prompt and lively, this was because it was partly based on the Savior's miracles.[309] Hence St. John the Evangelist writes: "Whereas He had done so many

[304] John 15 : 22–24. See also 11 : 15, 41 f.
[305] John 2 : 23. Cf. Matt. 4 : 24; 14 : 33; 27 : 40–42; Mark 1 : 28; 2 : 12; John 7 : 31; 11 : 45, 48, etc.
[306] Luke 7 : 16.
[307] Matt. 12 : 23.
[308] John 3 : 2.
[309] Cf. Luke 8 : 25; John 2 : 11, etc.

miracles before them [the Jews], they believed not in Him." [310] This unbelief seemed to St. John something almost impossible, nay, monstrous in a way. Near the end of his Gospel he remarks: "Many other signs also did Jesus in the sight of His disciples, which are not written in this book. But these are written that you may believe that Jesus is the Christ, the Son of God; and that believing, you may have life in His name." [311]

"The conclusion is inevitable. In the minds of those who witnessed Christ's miracles, as in His own mind, that series of astounding prodigies contained the decisive, unanswerable proof of His close union with God, of His special mission, of His Messianic office. They were His credentials and the infallible attestation of His supreme dignity." [312] To what extent did they furnish a proof of His divinity? This is a question that we shall consider in a later chapter. [313]

VI. The Baptist's Embassy to Jesus. The Anointing by the Sinful Woman

The former of these episodes is justly reckoned among the most remarkable events in our Lord's life. St. Matthew

---

[310] John 12: 37.

[311] John 20: 30 f.

[312] Fillion, *Les Miracles de N.-S. Jésus-Christ*, I, 17.

[313] In Volume I of our work, *Les Miracles de N.-S. Jésus-Christ*, pp. vii–xi, we have drawn up a considerable list of recent works in which the question of our Lord's miracles is treated more or less profoundly by friends or foes. We will cite here only a small number of them. 1. Catholic authors: Chable, *Die Wunder Jesu in ihrem Zusammenhang betrachtet,* 1897; Corluy, S.J., art., "Miracles des évangiles," in J. B. Jaugey's *Dictionnaire Apologétique de la Foi,* 2d ed., 1892, cols. 1194–1229; Fonck, S.J., *Die Wunder des Herrn im Evangelium exegetisch und praktisch erklärt,* 2d ed., 1907; Hugueny, *Catholique et Critique,* Vol. I, nos. 109–124; H. Wallon, *De l'Autorité de l'Évangile,* 3d ed., 1913. 2. Protestant authors, relatively conservative: A. Bruce, *The Miraculous Element in the Gospels,* 5th ed., 1902; Fairbairn, *Studies in the Life of Christ,* 13th ed., pp. 149–164, 197–298; J. Laidlaw, *The Miracles of Our Lord, Expository and Homiletic,* 4th ed.,

and St. Luke,[314] especially the latter, describe the principal circumstances with great exactness. True, the two Evangelists do not assign the event to the same juncture in the Savior's life. This is owing to the fact that the author of the First Gospel is here influenced by the logical order, while St. Luke conforms more to the chronological.

We left the precursor in the fortress of Machaerus, where he had been unjustly imprisoned by Herod Antipas, partly for political reasons, but mostly as a victim of Herodias' hatred and vengeance. The Baptist's disciples, who were allowed to visit him, brought him word of Jesus' many miracles and of the growing success of His preaching. In this passage, St. Matthew calls the Savior's miracles "the works of Christ," [315] meaning works of such a sort as to testify that their author was certainly the Messias. The Baptist then chose two of his disciples and sent them to Jesus to ask Him in the precursor's name: "Art Thou He that is to come, or look we for another?" The expression, "He that is to come," or more exactly, "He that comes," [316] was frequently used at that time [317] to designate the Messias, who was so ardently longed for and whose coming was so eagerly awaited.

But how could it happen that John the Baptist, after the revelation he had received from the Holy Ghost,[318] after the

1900; Selby, Milligan, etc., *The Miracles of Jesus,* 1907; Trench, *Notes on the Miracles,* 9th ed., 1870; F. Westcott, *Characteristics of the Gospel Miracles,* 1913. For Rationalist authors, see Appendix XIII.

[314] Matt. 11:2–19; Luke 7:18–35. St. Mark did not insert it in his account.— For the Rationalist view, see Appendix XIV.

[315] Τὰ ἔργα τοῦ χριστοῦ, with two articles. St. Luke's language is more general: "John's disciples told him of all these things"; *i. e.,* by relating the series of deeds, the resurrection of the widow's son, the curing of the centurion's servant, the Sermon on the Mount, the choosing of the Apostles and all the preceding events. But these were also truly Messianic works.

[316] The Greek ὁ ἐρχόμενος is the equivalent of the Hebrew expression *habba;* literally, "the one coming."

[317] Cf. Matt. 3:11; Mark 11:9; Luke 13:35; 19:38; Heb. 10:37, etc. The Talmud uses it more than a hundred times.

[318] John 1:33.

scene he had beheld on the bank of the Jordan,[319] after his own repeated, official public testimony,[320] now asked Jesus whether He was really the Messias? Did his sufferings and the isolation and inactivity of his imprisonment gradually stir up some doubt in his mind? This hypothesis was sometimes held in the early centuries and unfortunately has still a large number of defenders even among orthodox Protestants and, of course, among Liberal theologians.[321] But such an interpretation of John's conduct is utterly inadmissible, as Jesus Himself presently declares. There was nothing firmer and more unshakable than the Baptist's great soul. How could he have so quickly forgotten the Holy Ghost's coming and appearing in the form of a dove over Jesus' head? And did he not still hear the echo of the divine voice proclaiming the lofty dignity of Mary's Son? "John had had such convincing evidence that Jesus was the Messiah, that he could hardly doubt now."[322]

The exegetical problem arising from the Baptist's action was long ago solved by most of the Fathers[323] and Catholic commentators and by many Protestant theologians. It was not for himself that John put this question to Jesus; he already knew the answer. He acted thus for the sake of his disciples, a number of whom were still incredulous with regard to our Lord, unfriendly or hostile to Him, and jealous of His authority, which they regarded as rivaling that of their master.[324] John had every reason to hope that, if they were placed in direct communication with Christ, they would

---

[319] Matt. 3: 13–17.

[320] John 1: 29–32, 35 f.; 3: 22–36.

[321] See Appendix XIV.

[322] Plummer, *An Exegetical Commentary on the Gospel according to St. Matthew*, p. 160.

[323] *V. g.*, Origen, St. Hilary, St. John Chrysostom, St. Jerome, St. Augustine, St. Gregory the Great. See Knabenbauer, *Comment. in Evangel. sec. Matth.*, I, 431–435.

[324] Cf. John 3: 25 f.

become favorably inclined to the Savior and would be led to recognize that He was the Messias.

John's messengers could not have reached the Savior more opportunely and providentially, because they found Him in the full exercise of His miraculous power. It was one of those particularly blessed moments when numerous wonders proceeded from His hands.[325] Before the eyes of the two disciples He cured many sick and possessed persons and restored sight to some that were blind.[326] This was His first reply: the clear and unmistakable answer of facts, the public exercise of manifestly supernatural powers. To that He added a no less decisive verbal reply: "Go and relate to John what you have heard and seen.[327] The blind see, the lame walk, the lepers are cleansed, the deaf hear, the dead rise again, the poor have the gospel preached to them. And blessed is he that shall not be scandalized in Me." As the question was asked in John's name, naturally Jesus addressed His reply to him, although it was first received by the two messengers and other disciples of the Baptist. It was the more suited to convince them since it was taken almost literally from an ideal picture which, centuries before, Isaias had sketched of the Messias' blessed activity. In a famous passage the great prophet, mingling reality with figure, said: "Then [in the days of the Christ] shall the eyes of the blind be opened and the ears of the deaf shall be unstopped. Then shall the lame man leap as a hart, and the tongue of the dumb shall be free." [328] In another passage,[329] which Jesus applied to Himself when

[325] Cf. Matt. 4:24 f.; 8:16, 26; 12:15; Mark 3:10–12; Luke 4:40; 5:17; 6:18 f., etc.

[326] St. Luke, the physician-evangelist, enumerates the miracles under four distinct heads: the curing of lingering illnesses, that of acute suffering, the driving out of devils, the restoring of sight to the blind.

[327] According to the Greek text: "What you hear and see."

[328] Is. 35:5 f.

[329] Is. 61:1.

speaking in the synagogue at Nazareth,[330] the prophet represents Christ as the protector of the afflicted and the bearer of
the glad tidings to the unfortunate. This last trait was a
special characteristic of the Messias, particularly at the time
of Jesus, when the doctors of the Law, the Pharisees and the
Jewish religious chiefs despised the common people and neglected them, whereas the Son of Man, faithful to His vocation, went forth to meet every form of suffering and became
eminently the preacher to the lowly and the poor. Jesus, after
enabling John's messengers to witness several miracles, recalled these prophecies to their minds, saying to them in substance: Verify for yourselves what Isaias prophesied about
the work of the Messias; I fulfil its every word; therefore I
am the Christ in person. We have already heard His words,
"The works themselves which I do, give testimony of Me,
that the Father hath sent Me";[331] and He added that this
testimony was superior to that of the Baptist. Some have
complained that in the present case our Lord did not answer
John's question directly; His reply has even been called
"evasive."[332] For anyone considering the circumstances of
the occasion and studying this reply without preconceptions,
it is the most striking legitimation that Jesus could have furnished of His Messianic office. We should, of course, take
the various details of this reply literally, not figuratively, or
"in a moral sense,"[333] as if they referred only to spiritual
cures. The texts are most precise.

As the reader must have remarked, Christ's message to
the precursor closes with an important announcement in the

[330] See page 198.

[331] John 5 : 36.

[332] H. J. Holtzmann, *Die Synoptiker*, 3d ed., p. 66. According to A. Réville,
Jésus de Nazareth, II, 115, they denote "a certain embarrassment."

[333] Reuss, *Synopse Évangélique*, p. 295. "This interpretation forces itself upon
us," says Réville. How, in that case, would the Baptist's messengers have *seen*
these purely moral cures?

delicate form of a Beatitude: "Blessed is he that shall not be scandalized in Me." Could the Messias become the cause of fall or scandal? Yes. More than thirty years previously. Simeon had foretold it; [334] and long before the Presentation in the Temple, Isaias had also prophesied it: "He shall be a sanctification to you. But for a stone of stumbling, and for a rock of offence to the two houses of Israel, for a snare and a ruin to the inhabitants of Jerusalem. And very many of them shall stumble and fall, and shall be broken in pieces, and shall be snared and taken." [335] These lines of Isaias explain the meaning of those words, "he that shall not be scandalized in Me." Etymologically, "scandal" means a snare, a trap. To be scandalized with regard to Jesus—as the conduct of John's disciples but too well showed—meant to find in His words and acts a false reason for not regarding Him as the Messias. Happy are those loyal souls whom no prejudice of this sort can bring to doubt Him or withdraw from Him! Let us hope that the Baptist's messengers comprehended the peril to which they exposed themselves and that they returned to their master better disposed toward Jesus and satisfied with His answer!

After their departure, Jesus made an address to those gathered about Him. It gives us an example of the simple and lofty character of His eloquence. Rhetorical questions, metaphors, and similitudes alternate with ordinary speech and reasoning, impressing certain important truths more deeply in His hearers' minds. This short discourse [336] opens with a glowing encomium of John the Baptist. [337] The scene just recounted took place in the presence of a large throng,[338] who were unaware of the secret reasons for the question put to

[334] Luke 2 : 34 f.
[335] Is. 8 : 14.
[336] Matt. 11 : 7-19; Luke 7 : 24-35.
[337] Matt. 11 : 7-15; Luke 7 : 24-30.
[338] The two Evangelists speak of "multitudes," in the plural.

Jesus in the Baptist's name. There was reason to fear that many of them would remain under a regrettable impression with respect to the precursor, whom they might be tempted to regard as a fickle person with a vacillating faith in the Messias. Even Christ's authority might be questioned if John's testimony to Him should become a matter of dispute. The Messias' public praise of the precursor would destroy all suspicion. The Baptist's whole history is summed up in those words of praise, which are as delightful in their lifelike form as in the noble, lofty thoughts they express.[339]

"What went you out into the desert to see? a reed shaken with the wind? But what went you out to see? a man clothed in soft garments? Behold they that are clothed in soft garments, are in the houses of kings. But what went you out to see? a prophet? yea, I tell you, and more than a prophet. For this is he of whom it is written:[340] Behold I send my angel before thy face, who shall prepare thy way before thee. Amen I say to you, there hath not risen among them that are born of women a greater than John the Baptist: yet he that is the lesser in the Kingdom of Heaven is greater than he. And from the days of John the Baptist until now, the Kingdom of Heaven suffereth violence, and the violent bear it away. For all the prophets and the Law prophesied until John. And if you will receive it, he is Elias that is to come. He that hath ears to hear, let him hear."

The beginning of this eulogy is negative. Jesus starts by stating what His precursor is not. Directly blaming His hearers, the Savior asks them six questions in rapid succession. These He answers for them. He reminds them of the holy enthusiasm which had led them out into the desert, and He

---

[339] As St. Jerome (*hoc loco*) well remarks, they prove that the assertion made by Jesus in the form of a Beatitude does not refer to the precursor, but to his disciples. "*Si superior sententia contra Joannem prolata fuerit . . . , quomodo nunc Joannes tantis laudibus praedicatur?*" The Savior would not thus contradict Himself within the space of a couple of sentences.

[340] Mal. 3: 1.

asks them what they went there to see.[341] He who had drawn
them thither had nothing in common with the reeds that grew
in abundance on the banks of the Jordan and that are shaken
in every direction by "the least breeze that ripples the surface
of the water." John, a reed, he who was as firm and inflexible
as a bronze column, who withstood the Pharisees, the Sadducees, and the mighty tetrarch; he, the sturdy oak that persecution was unable to uproot? Nor was he one of those effeminate men, dressed in soft, rich garments, living in the palaces
of kings; this fact was clearly proclaimed by his rude tunic of
camel's hair and his coarse leathern cincture.

What was he, then? the Divine Speaker asks for the third
time, passing to the positive side of the eulogy. A prophet?
Yes, and even more than a prophet, for to him and him alone
had been reserved the incomparable honor of preparing the
way of the Messias, of being His precursor, as Malachias, the
last of the Old Testament prophets, had foretold in a prophecy
to which the Jews of the time unhesitatingly attributed a Messianic character. In quoting this prophecy, Jesus slightly modified it. In the original text we read: "Behold I send My angel,
and he shall prepare the way before My face. And presently
the Lord, whom you seek, and the angel of the testament,
whom you desire, shall come to His temple. Behold He cometh,
saith the Lord of hosts." In this passage, God momentarily
identifies Himself with the Messias and announces that His
coming will be prepared by a herald expressly chosen to fill
that office; in the words of the text, as quoted by our Lord,
He addresses His Christ and promises Him a precursor. In
both cases the meaning is the same.

The eulogy then rises to still loftier heights; for Jesus
adds under oath ("Amen, I say to you") that John the Bap-

---

[341] In the first question the idea of seeing is expressed by the verb θεάσασθαι,
which means "to contemplate." In the following questions, the Evangelists use
ἰδεῖν, which indicates sight, pure and simple.

tist was higher in dignity than all other men [342] who had lived before him. Ancient times had seen holy and illustrious men: the patriarchs, Moses, Samuel, David, Elias, Eliseus, Isaias, Jeremias and a great many others. But Zachary's son was greater than any of them, since he was the precursor of the Messias. Yet without detracting anything from his praise, Jesus limits it somewhat by saying that, however great John's distinction may be, "he that is the lesser in the Kingdom of Heaven is greater than he." At first glance these words seem obscure, but the key is to be found in the words, "the Kingdom of Heaven." That kingdom is precisely the Kingdom of the Messias, which Jesus Christ had come to found. But it has two distinct phases: that of its establishment, extending from the Messias' appearance to the end of time, and that of its consummation in heaven. It is the former phase that Jesus has here in mind and, without taking anything from John's dignity, He affirms that the lowliest of the members of His Kingdom (of His Church) is, in a sense, higher than John. "The precursor is the greatest among men; but Christians, by the very fact that they are Christians, belong to a transfigured, divinized race. John the Baptist was the intimate friend of the Messias-King; but it was not granted him to cross the threshhold of the Kingdom, whereas the least of Christians has received that favor. John the Baptist is the groomsman; but the Church to which Christians belong is the very spouse of Christ. Christianity has placed us on a plane much loftier than that of Judaism, and the members of the New Testament excel the members of the Old Testament as much as the New Covenant excels the Old." [343] The comparison does not, therefore, bear upon the precursor's moral excellence, but upon his relations with the Messianic Kingdom, into which it was not granted him to enter.

[342] The expression "those that are born of women" is here a solemn periphrase, signifying the whole human race. Cf. Job 14: 1; 15: 14; 25: 4.

[343] Fillion, *L'Évangile de S. Matthieu*, p. 222.

However, continues the Savior, this kingdom it was John's glory to announce and prepare, and his preaching, joined to his holiness, was so successful that from the beginning of his ministry [344] up to the hour of Christ's eulogy many had striven to enter therein and to become citizens of that kingdom. The Messianic Kingdom is here [345] represented as a fortress violently assaulted by those who wish to seize it.[346] It is an assault of love by those seeking to enter, not an assault of hatred by men seeking its destruction. At this period of Christ's life, notwithstanding His very just complaint regarding the coldness with which He and His precursor were received by their fellow-Jews, large numbers eagerly advanced to the conquest of the Kingdom of Heaven. Jesus credits this success partly to the preaching of John the Baptist.

In this whole passage the Savior's thought is rich and condensed, and calls for some explanation. Continuing the Baptist's praise, He reminds His hearers that "all the prophets and the Law prophesied until John." In the religion of Israel, as it had existed up to that time, everything had a prophetic character, as Jesus says here and as St. Paul eloquently affirms later.[347] In addition to the prophecies strictly so called, there were types and figures. The Law itself was an *ensemble* of prophecies. But the precursor inaugurated a new era, that

[344] This is the meaning of the words "from the days of John the Baptist."

[345] The part of the discourse contained in Matt. 11:12-15, is omitted at this point by St. Luke; but he cites it on a later occasion, Luke 16:16, in an abridged form.

[346] With most interpreters, we give the Greek verb βιάζεται a passive meaning, which it certainly has in the parallel passage of St. Luke. The second half of the expression, "the violent bear it away," requires this translation. But there can be no question here, as some exegetes seek to make out, of a violence issuing from hatred and striving to oppress and destroy the kingdom, although such hatred appeared in the hostility of the Pharisees and hierarchs. In this passage our Lord is alluding only to the violence aroused by love. Those who take βιάζεται as being in the middle voice translate it *"sese vi obtrudit."* According to them, the Savior meant that the Kingdom of Heaven introduced itself vigorously, after a fashion forcing the entrance of minds and wills.

[347] See especially 1 Cor. 10:11.

of fulfilment. Before him men were looking forward to the realization of the divine oracles. But now, since the coming of the Messias is an accomplished fact, the passive waiting, which was allowable in previous times, is no longer justified; each one's duty is to strive earnestly to obtain a place in the Kingdom of Christ. Jesus gently exacts these efforts by saying: "If you will receive it," that is, if you wish to understand. But it is evident that it must be wished, since that is the price of salvation. The Savior closes His panegyric of the Baptist by connecting him with Elias, as the angel Gabriel did [348] when informing Zachary of the coming birth of John: "He is Elias that is to come." In the previous volume [349] we pointed out how and why Jesus could say that John the Baptist was another Elias. This first part of Christ's discourse closes with a short admonition, "He that hath ears to hear, let him hear," which our Lord uses on various occasions to draw His hearers' attention to important truths.[350]

Jesus then briefly describes the results of the Baptist's preaching upon the Jewish nation as a whole and the very different results produced upon its religious leaders. "All the people hearing, and the publicans, justified God, being baptized with John's baptism. But the Pharisees and the lawyers frustrated [351] the counsel of God against themselves, being not baptized by him."

St. Luke is the only one to record this consoling and sorrowful reflection,[352] which confirms and sums up the details the four Evangelists give of the Baptist's ministry. The Pharisees, those counterfeit saints of Judaism, and the Scribes, the

---

[348] Luke 1 : 16 f.

[349] See Vol. I, p. 252, and also Ecclus. 48 : 10; Matt. 17 : 10–13; Mark 9 : 10–12;

[350] Cf. Matt. 13 : 9, 43; Mark 4 : 9; Luke 8 : 8.

[351] Such is the meaning of the Greek: $\dot{\eta}\theta\acute{\epsilon}\tau\eta\sigma\alpha\nu$. The Vulgate translation (spreverunt, "they despised") is less exact.

[352] It is sometimes attributed to the Evangelist as a personal reflection of his own. But, along with most interpreters, we see no reason for not regarding it as the continuation of Christ's discourse.

scholars of the nation, and the Sadducees were especially the religious leaders, the ruling classes of the Jews. They had received John with coldness and censure and, by refusing to believe in his mission or to receive his baptism of penance, they had thwarted God's merciful designs so far as concerned themselves. In contrast with these upper classes, the rank and file of the nation, and even the publicans [353] and other public sinners, in large numbers received the precursor's message and baptism in a spirit of faith and thus contributed to the realization of the divine plan.

Jesus rebukes those who show themselves defiant and unbelieving. In figures taken from daily life, He depicts those men's appreciation of Himself and His precursor: [354]

"Whereunto then shall I liken the men of this generation? and to what are they like? They are like to children sitting in the market-place, and speaking one to another, and saying: We have piped to you, and you have not danced; we have mourned, and you have not wept. For John the Baptist came neither eating bread nor drinking wine; [355] and you say: He hath a devil. The Son of Man is come eating and drinking, and you say: Behold a man that is a glutton and a drinker of wine, a friend of publicans and sinners. And wisdom is justified by all her children."

The little parable at the beginning of this passage is certainly charming. "Whereunto shall I liken . . . ?" [356] Jesus seemed to be seeking for something with which to compare the sinful and ungrateful conduct that He wishes to describe. There came to His mind a scene of children at play. He had often watched their games; perhaps in His boyhood He had

[353] Luke 3 : 12.

[354] Matt. 11 : 16–19; Luke 7 : 31–35.

[355] According to St. Matthew's account: "neither eating nor drinking."

[356] This expression seems to have been much in use at that time to introduce a figurative discourse. Cf. Matt. 11 : 16; Mark 4 : 30; Luke 13 : 18 etc. It is to be found frequently also in the rabbinic writings.

taken part in them. He here pictures two groups of children in the market-place, that old and ever new playground of children. With the instinct of imitation so characteristic of children, one of these groups mimics a wedding scene, then a funeral scene, and the children composing the group wanted the other group to take up the joyous or mournful tone of their singing at once. As they failed to do so, the children who sought to impose their wishes on them shouted their discontent and reproaches. But these children had no right to force their whims on the others; rather ought they to have yielded to their comrades' wishes.[357]

The language which our Lord here puts on the children's lips is quite in agreement with the customs of the time. Among the Jews and most races of antiquity, the flute was regarded as indispensable both for funeral ceremonies [358] and for joyous functions, especially wedding festivities.[359] The Talmud mentions "the flute for a dead man" and "the flute for a bride." [360] In St. Matthew's account, the Greek verb that we translate "You have not mourned" [361] means rather, "You have not struck your breast," referring to another ancient practice in vogue in the East at funerals and on the occasion of national or private mourning.[362]

Jesus applies the parable to His fellow-Jews who criticised His conduct and that of the Baptist and remained unsubmissive to their preaching. These ill-disposed men are represented in the parable by the first group of children,[363] for they wished

[357] Bishop Le Camus' interesting little work, *Les Enfants de Nazareth,* 1900, with the charming scenes that it describes and the numerous pictures that make it still more lifelike, is a dramatic commentary on this passage of the Gospels.

[358] Jer. 48: 36; Matt. 9: 23; Josephus, *Bell. Jud.,* III, ix, 5; Elien, *Var. Hist.,* XII, 43.

[359] 3 Kings 1: 40; Is. 5: 12; 30: 29; Ecclus. 11: 21; 1 Mach. 3: 45.

[360] *Baba Mezia,* VI, 1. Cf. *Kethuboth,* IV, 4.

[361] Οὐκ ἐκόψασθε (Vulg., *non planxistis*); St. Luke says οὐκ ἐκλαύσατε.

[362] Zach. 12: 10–14; Matt. 24: 30; Luke 8: 52; 23: 27, etc.

[363] And not by the second group, as a rather large number of commentators seem to think. The text itself is quite clear on this point: "This generation . . .

to force their wills upon the Savior and John, whose conduct they took the liberty of insolently criticising. They were shocked at the austerity of John's life, which at first they had admired, and they dared to speak of him as possessed by a devil.[364] In vain they played joyous airs to him; he would not join in them. Soon they showed indignation because Jesus accepted invitations to great dinners and because He appeared not to practice a more mortified life than that of most Jews. They outrageously accused Him of being fond of wine and good cheer. He had not mourned with them. They were therefore displeased with both divine messengers and were scandalized in their regard.

But Heaven's graces and illuminations that fell upon Palestine were far from being in vain. It was with a tone of thankfulness that Jesus ended His address by saying that the absolute "wisdom," that of God, which had employed the most varied means to save the Jews,[365] had been "justified," that is, clearly approved, proclaimed just and perfect, by all "her children"—a Hebraism meaning those Jews who, by receiving Jesus and John as envoys of God, had shown that they were truly wise.[366]

St. Matthew adds to the discourse, as we have just read it, Christ's direful curse against three cities located on the shores of Lake Genesareth—Corozain, Bethsaida, and Capharnaum. Then follows Christ's praise of His heavenly Father for having deigned to make His revelations to the lowly and little ones. Lastly, we have the gentle invitation, "Come to Me, all

is like to children . . . who crying to their companions say: We have piped to you . . ." The "companions" can be none other than Jesus and John the Baptist, according to this construction of the sentence. The Gospel history, moreover, fully justifies this interpretation.

[364] Before long the Jews address this same sacrilegious insult to Christ Himself. Cf. Matt. 10: 24 f.; John 7: 20; 8: 48; 10: 20.

[365] Eph. 3: 10; Heb. 1: 1.

[366] In St. Matthew's text, 11: 19, some Greek manuscripts have the variant ἔργων, "works," instead of τέκνων, "children."

you that labor and are burdened." [367] It is likely that these three sayings belong to a later date, toward the end of the Savior's public life. At least that is where they are placed by St. Luke,[368] who ordinarily follows the chronological order. We therefore postpone consideration of them until we come to that period.

The anointing of Christ by the sinful woman is one of the incidents special to the Third Gospel.[369] It fits well into the plan of St. Luke, who takes advantage of every opportunity to show Christ's infinite mercy for repentant sinners and thereby the universality of the salvation which He brought to the world. St. Gregory the Great, who devotes one of his finest homilies to this episode,[370] says, at the beginning of his commentary on it, that in the presence of such a touching scene it would be easier for him to weep than to write. This passage is, in fact, "a charming description, which has a place of honor in the collection of pictures sketched by St. Luke's pen; it relates a wonderful cure, which well deserves to be described by him whom St. Paul calls his most dear physician. The account abounds in psychological truths and, for this reason was sure to attract the attention of the most psychological of the Evangelists." [371]

The sacred writer does not state the exact date of the incident, which he merely connects with the preceding events by a particle.[372] Yet there is every reason to believe that it is inserted in its proper chronological order. The place where it occurred is only vaguely indicated as being "in the city." [373] This may mean the city where Jesus was at the time. Com-

---

[367] Matt. 11 : 20–30.

[368] Luke 10 : 13–15, 21 f.

[369] Luke 7 : 36–50.

[370] *Hom. in Evang.*, XXV.

[371] Fillion, *L'Évangile de S. Luc*, p. 160. This incident inspired Père Lacordaire with some beautiful reflections; *Sainte Marie Madeleine,* chap. 3.

[372] Δέ in the Greek text (Vulg., *autem*).

[373] 'Εν τῇ πόλει, with the article.

mentators mention Naim, where the Divine Master's presence is indicated a few verses previously, Jerusalem, and Bethania: this last city is named because the sinful woman is sometimes identified with Mary, the sister of Lazarus. But St. Luke's expression may refer to Capharnaum, at that period "the city" of the Savior and His usual center.

Jesus, having been asked with pressing insistence, as the sacred text implies,[374] by a Pharisee named Simon to dine with him, accepted the invitation. Although our Lord was far from seeking invitations of this sort, yet He did not absolutely decline them. This fact provoked His enemies to taunt Him with insult and reproach. In this instance, as at all times, He was confident that He was accomplishing His lofty mission and doing the will of His heavenly Father. The different scenes of this sort which we read of in the Gospels, especially in that of St. Luke, [375] picture our Lord as most edifying in what might be called His table-talk.

The narrative shows Simon's reception of our Lord as being less than cordial. But there is no reason to suppose that the invitation was prompted by sinister motives. Jesus does blame His host for the coldness of His reception; He does not complain that He had been treated as an enemy by Simon. This Pharisee, like so many other persons, wished a closer view of the remarkable man who was being talked of everywhere and who was drawing multitudes to Him. It is even possible that Simon was attracted by His holiness and preaching and miracles, and that he desired to study Him more intimately. Such reasons would be sufficient to explain the invitation.

We shall understand the scene better if we recall the manner of sitting at table in the homes of the well-to-do, as indi-

[374] Ἤρώτα (Vulg., *rogabat*), in the imperfect, expressing repeated, continued action.

[375] Matt. 26:6–13; Mark 14:3–9; Luke 10:38–43; 11:37–52; 14:1–16; 19:1–27; John 2:1–11, etc.

cated in various passages of the Gospel and described by ancient authors and historians. "The posture of reclining . . .
was one between lying and sitting, the legs and the lower parts
of the body being stretched out at full length on a sofa, whilst
the upper part was slightly raised and supported upon the left
elbow, which rested on a pillow, the right arm and hand being
left free to reach out and take the food." [376] The position of
the diners was such that their heads were close to the rather
low table, which was in the center of the semi-circle formed
by the couches. Everyone thus reclined with his feet stretched
away from the table and toward the space where the waiters
went back and forth.

Abruptly [377] a woman entered the dining-room. She was
well known in the city as a woman of ill repute. The sacred
writer delicately refrains from mentioning her name; he
merely says that she was "a sinner." In spite of some interpreters' efforts [378] to lessen her guilt, it is hardly possible to
misunderstand the force of that expression, when applied to
a woman. While, perhaps, she was not a common prostitute,
there is no doubt but that for some time past she had led an
improper life. Simon also intimates as much, although he, too,
is reserved in the words he uses. And Jesus speaks plainly of
the converted woman's "many sins." St. Augustine says:
"Accessit ad Dominum immunda, ut rediret munda." [379]

[376] A. Rich, *Dictionary of Roman and Greek Antiquities*, p. 6. For fuller details,
see Daremberg and Saglio, *Dictionnaire des Antiquités Grecques et Romaines;*
Norwack, *Lehrbuch der hebräischen Archäologie*, I, 181 f.; Fillion, *Atlas Archéologique de la Bible*, 2d ed., pl. XXI, figs. 14, 15; pl. XXII, figs. 4, 6; pl. XXIII,
figs. 1, 3, 4, 6.

[377] The words καὶ ἰδού (Vulg., *et ecce*), "and behold," draw the reader's attention to the unexpected character of the event.

[378] In particular Dr. Keil, who is habitually more judicious: "The word 'sinner'
merely tells us that this woman's conduct was not in harmony with the moral
order, as then existing." *Commentar über die Evangelien des Markus und Lukas,*
p. 297. According to this view, she would have been merely worldly-minded. The
weighty Maldonatus very justly protested against this opinion, which was unknown to the early commentators.

[379] *Sermo* 94.

How are we to explain that a woman of this type was allowed to penetrate to the interior of a respectable home, even into the dining-room? The rigid customs of the West make such freedom appear strange to us. But it is quite in accord with the more informal practice of the Biblical East.[380] Moreover, it is true that this intrusion took place under the impulse of holy daring and courageous resolve. The sinful woman was determined to approach Jesus to obtain forgiveness from Him. Little did it matter to her that, to reach Him quickly, she was exposed to annoyance, insult, or even violence. As we may easily surmise, she had recently [381] come under the influence of the Savior's preaching, but without meeting Him personally. Understanding the ignominy of her manner of life and influenced by divine grace, she had promised God to lead a new life in reparation for her former misdeeds. Her first desire was publicly to testify her gratitude to Him who had wrought her conversion and to receive from His pure hands a blessing which would help her keep the good resolution she had taken. Therefore she entered the Pharisee's house quickly, as if she feared to let the hour of God pass without profiting by it.

The Gospel account is so precise that we are able, as it were, to witness the smallest details of the episode. The woman readily perceived where Jesus was at the table. Having placed herself behind Him, she intended first to pour upon His sacred feet a liquid perfume which she had brought in an alabaster vase. His feet were bare, since according to custom, He had removed His sandals at the door of the house. But the woman, overcome by her strong feelings of repentance, thanksgiving, and respectful affection, could not hold back her tears, which

---

[380] Cf. F. Robinson, *The Evangelists and the Mishna*, pp. 214 f.; Tristram, *Eastern Customs in Bible Lands*, p. 36.

[381] This appears clearly from the account. One is therefore not justified in accepting the view of some modern exegetes who refer her conversion to a more or less distant past.

fell upon Christ's feet. This detail made her act of devotion the more ingenuous. Unfastening her hair, she used it as a towel to wipe away the traces of her tears from the Savior's feet, which she then covered with pious kisses,[382] and upon which she poured perfume from an alabaster vase. Not a single word did she utter. But there was unspoken eloquence in every detail of her conduct, which so vividly showed the sincerity of her feelings. Her overflowing gratitude, her bitter regrets, and her generous devotedness found expression in the most natural and exquisite manner.

St. Luke makes no remark as to the astonishment of all those present. He merely describes the impressions of the host. The latter failed to comprehend this scene which made the angels rejoice. He was deeply shocked and, true Pharisee that he was, reasoned within himself thus: "This man,[383] if He were a prophet, would know surely who and what manner [384] of woman this is that toucheth Him, that she is a sinner." Simon was aware that the multitudes called Jesus a prophet.[385] From several events in the Old Testament,[386] he also knew that, although the prophets, even those most illumined from on high, are not able to read everything that is hidden in the depths of human hearts, God sometimes reveals these secrets to them. Therefore Simon thought that if Jesus were endowed with the gift of prophecy, He would have known at once the character of the woman whose homage He

---

[382] The compound verb κατεφίλει is very expressive. Cf. Matt. 26:49; Mark 14:45; Luke 15:20; Acts 20:37. Kissing anyone's feet was a mark of very great respect. Cf. Xenophon, *Cyrop.*, VII, 5, 36; Aristophanes, *Vesp.*, 608, etc. This homage was sometimes paid to the rabbis. It should also be noted that the last three verbs describing the sinful woman's marks of respect are in the imperfect: "she was wiping, she was kissing, she was anointing," expressing the repetition and continuation of the acts.

[383] The pronoun οὗτος (Vulg., *hic*), which begins the sentence, is very emphatic and is here not without a certain contempt.

[384] Τίς καὶ ποταπή (Vulg., *quae et qualis*) : a very expressive wording.

[385] Cf. Luke 7:16 f., etc.

[386] Cf. 3 Kings 14:6; 4 Kings 1:3; 5:26; Is. 10:3 etc.

so calmly received and would have driven her away instead of
tolerating her impure touch. The words, "that touchest Him,"
are very indicative here. A rabbi was once asked by his disciples: "How far off should one remain from a harlot?" He replied: "Four cubits," that is, about seven feet. But what a
difference between Jesus and the rabbis!

This feeling of misgiving, though hidden within Simon's
mind, did not elude the supernatural knowledge possessed by
Christ, who, as St. Augustine remarks, "heard the Pharisee's
thoughts." [387] The Savior then proved that, although He
patiently allowed the woman to show Him reverence, He was
not ignorant of her sad history and that He was consequently
a true prophet. But His remonstrance is gentle and kindly.
"Simon," He began, "I have somewhat to say to thee." "Master, say it," the Pharisee politely replied, giving Jesus the
title of "Rabbi," which corresponds to "Master." Jesus continued, at first half concealing His thought under the form
of an interesting case of conscience: "A certain creditor [388]
had two debtors, the one owed five hundred pence, and the
other fifty. And whereas they had not wherewith to pay, he
forgave them both. Which therefore of the two loveth [389] him
most?"

These last words amount to saying: Which of the two debtors ought to show his gratitude more warmly and heartily?
The answer was obvious. Simon said: "I suppose that he to
whom he forgave most." An insolvent debtor, whose debt of
about eighty dollars [390] is remitted, would be curiously ungrateful if he did not show his creditor more thankfulness
than one who was forgiven a debt only one-tenth as great.

---

[387] *Loc. cit.*

[388] In the Greek: δανειστής (Vulg., *foenerator*), a money-lender.

[389] In the Greek text this verb is in the future tense (ἀγαπήσει). Several manuscripts and the Vulgate have the present tense (*diligit*).

[390] Supposing the *denarius* to be worth about 17 cents.

But why the words, "I suppose"?[391] Might we not say that Simon gives his opinion reluctantly, as though he feared to commit himself or as though he were not interested in the proposed case? Many exegetes thus interpret the expression.

Jesus replied: "Thou hast judged rightly."[392] Then turning to the woman, who was still at His feet, our Lord, as though He had but then remarked her presence, continued, addressing the Pharisee: "Dost thou see this woman? I entered into thy house, thou gavest Me no water for My feet; but she with tears hath washed My feet, and with her hairs hath wiped them. Thou gavest Me no kiss; but she, since I came in,[393] hath not ceased to kiss My feet. My head with oil thou didst not anoint; but she with ointment hath anointed My feet. Wherefore I say to thee: Many sins are forgiven her, because she hath loved much. But to whom less is forgiven, he loveth less."

In this contrast[394] between Simon's behavior towards Him and that of the converted woman, our Lord refers to three of the principal ceremonies of Oriental hospitality on the occasion of a great dinner. Upon the arrival of the guests, one of the house-servants or sometimes the host himself washed and dried their feet,[395] which were protected from the dust and mud of the roads only by sandals. The host then welcomed his guests with a kiss.[396] In Bible lands this is still the ordinary manner of salutation, even between men. During the meal, a few drops of oil, usually scented, were poured on the heads

---

[391] Ὑπολαμβάνω (Vulg., *aestimo*).

[392] Ὀρθῶς ἔκρινας. It has been remarked that Socrates, in his famous Dialogues, again and again uses the expression πάνυ ὀρθῶς, "quite right," when he has caught the person to whom he is talking in the net of his reasoning.

[393] Such is the reading of the original text. *Intravit* of the Vulgate is a faulty correction, intended to palliate what at first seems to be an exaggeration. But the woman might quite well have entered shortly after our Lord.

[394] The rhythm of the language and the frequent repetition of the pronouns μου and μοι (Vulg., *meis, meos, meum, mihi*) surprisingly strengthen the thought.

[395] Gen. 18:4; Judges 19:21; 1 Kings 25:41; John 13:5; 1 Tim. 5:10.

[396] Gen. 33:4; Ex. 18:7; 2 Kings 15:5; 19:39; 20:9; Matt. 26:48 f., etc.

of the guests.[397] But Simon thought he might dispense with these various ceremonies in the case of Jesus, thus showing that his feeling towards his guest was not simply one of respect. There was a cold reserve in his attitude. In reality, it was the sinful woman who performed toward Jesus the honors of the proud Pharisee's house. The Divine Master may have intended to imply a criticism of the Pharisee's conduct when He said: "To whom less is forgiven, he loveth less." [398] There is, then, a rightful correlation between love and forgiveness. Great love, great pardon; little love, little pardon. The woman showed her immense love and contrition. Hence her grievous sins were entirely forgiven her.

Jesus did not wish her to depart before she had received the consoling assurance of her pardon. Addressing her for the first time, He said gently: "Thy sins are forgiven thee." This was a genuine absolution. At these words, as on a former occasion,[399] those present were scandalized and thought within themselves:[400] "Who is this [401] that forgiveth sins also?" At the basis of this reflection was an implied accusation of blasphemy. Undisturbed by their unspoken protest, the Savior again addressed the woman, saying to her: "Thy faith hath made thee safe; go in peace." A lively faith, joined to deep contrition and great love, had produced this marvelous regeneration.[402]

[397] Ps. 22 : 5; Eccles. 9 : 8; Amos 6 : 6.

[398] It has often been remarked that Christ here gives an unexpected turn to the thought. If He had finished His sentence as He began it, He would have said: "To him who loves less, less is forgiven." This transposition of the axiom nowise alters the idea which it expresses.

[399] Matt. 9 : 2 f. and parallel passages.

[400] Ἐν ἑαυτοῖς (Vulg., intra se). They do not at once communicate this rash judgment to one another; Christ did not give them time to do so.

[401] Again the contemptuous οὗτος.

[402] We have no occasion here to enter upon the discussion, once very heated and not yet entirely extinguished, which the close of this episode aroused between Protestant theologians or exegetes and Catholic theologians or commentators. The former, in conformity with Luther's famous principle and because of the words "Thy faith hath made thee safe," maintain that the faults of the sinful

Our piety longs to know exactly who was the woman who has given all Christian ages so beautiful an example of conversion. But St. Luke's natural feeling of delicacy let her name fall into oblivion, if indeed he knew it. From early times there have been conjectures and investigation on this subject. But the question almost at once assumed larger proportions and has become so complicated that it is no longer possible to solve it with certainty. Three women, who have a rather prominent place in the Gospel, are involved in this problem: the sinful woman of the episode we have just considered, Mary Magdalen, and Mary the sister of Lazarus and Martha. According to the view of St. Gregory the Great,[403] they were one and the same person. Owing to the weight of that great scholar's authority, his opinion was generally adopted by the Latin Church from the seventh century to the sixteenth. St. Ambrose, however, hesitated to commit himself to it.[404] St. Jerome[405] made a distinction between the sinful woman and Mary of Bethania, whereas St. Augustine considered them the same person.[406] At an early date the Greek Church decided against the identity[407] and has remained firmly of the same view, celebrating on different dates the feasts of the sinful woman, of Mary Magdalen, and of the other Mary. In the sixteenth and seventeenth centuries a reaction took place in the West, especially in France, in favor of a distinction be-

---

woman were pardoned solely on account of her faith; the latter, in accordance with the *ensemble* of the account and the Savior's words, hold that the forgiveness was obtained by *fides caritate formata,* by the union of faith and charity. On this point, see Knabenbauer, *Comment. in Evang. sec. Luc.,* pp. 268 f.; Schanz, *Commentar über das Evangel. des heil. Lucas,* pp. 248–250; Maldonatus, *in hunc locum.*

[403] *Hom. in Evang.* XXXIII. See also *Hom.* VIII.

[404] *Expositio in Luc.,* VI, speaking of the sinful woman and of Mary, Martha's sister, he says: "*Potest non eamdem esse.*" But he adds that it may also have been the same person, at first *peccatrix,* then *perfectior.*

[405] *Comment. in Matth.,* 26: 2.

[406] *Tractat. in Joan.,* 49; *De Consensu Evangelist.,* II, 154.

[407] See Origen, *In Matth.,* 35; St. John Chrysostom, *Homil. in Joan.,* 62.

tween the three saints. Participating in this movement were not only enthusiasts like Launoy and Dupin, but weighty scholars of the stamp of Estius, Tillemont, Calmet, Mabillon, and Bossuet. "It is more in conformity with the letter of the Gospel to distinguish three persons," said the Bishop of Meaux,[408] after a careful examination of the Gospel texts that speak of them. Nevertheless, the difficulties presented by these texts are not absolutely insoluble. But between the sinful woman, Mary Magdalen, and Mary the sister of Lazarus, as we see them in the Gospels, there exists a very real likeness of soul and character. They all were in like manner devoted to Jesus, generous and active in showing their holy attachment. This fact, of itself, would not prove their identity, but at least it helps to lessen the difficulties encountered in the solution of the problem.[409]

---

[408] In his dissertation "On the Three Magdalens," *Œuvres*, Versailles ed., XLIII, 3–10.

[409] For a more complete treatment, see Tillemont, *Mémoires*, Vol. II; the Bollandists, *Acta Sanctorum*, for July 22; Wouters, *Delucidationes Selectae S. Scripturae, De Concord. Evangel.*, c. XV, quaest. 1; Faillon, *Monuments inédits sur l'Apostolat de Sainte Marie-Madeleine en Provence*, 148; Lacordaire, *Sainte Marie-Madeleine*; Vigouroux' *Dictionnaire de la Bible*, Vol. IV, cols. 814–817.

CHAPTER III

Jesus Goes About Galilee a Second Time, Preaching the Gospel

WE beg the reader to keep in mind that it is impossible to determine in a thoroughly satisfactory manner the chronological order of events related by the Evangelists and to accompany our Lord step by step in His missionary activity. The sacred writers have not seen fit to confine themselves to that order and, while ordinarily grouping the events as a whole according to their true sequence, they do not always assign the same place to the details. A biographer of Christ, before deciding upon what is to be judged the most authentic arrangement, must compare the accounts, study the often vague terms by which the sacred authors introduce them, and consult the commentators who have closely examined the texts and have striven to ascertain the order of events. Even extensive labor of this sort frequently leaves one undecided. As we have done thus far, we will continue to arrange the events in the most probable order and the one most generally accepted. What is of the highest importance in a Life of the Savior, is His divine, charming portrait, His words, works, and example, combined and presented, if not in a strictly chronological order, at least so as not to deprive them of their beauty and truth.

In the period we are now entering, the Lord Jesus gives a greater scope to His general ministry, especially to His preaching. We shall have the happiness of observing His brilliant successes. But our joy will be clouded by the antagonism of the Pharisaic party, a hostility that develops in the same proportions as the attachment of the common people. This strife, which first appeared at the time of the curing of the paralytic at Capharnaum,[410] increased on different occasions. The Sermon on the Mount clearly presupposes its existence; and again, at the close of His panegyric of the precursor, Jesus dwelt still more on this fact. He had to expect this opposition: "His own received Him not." [411] But presently we shall see it reach an unexpected intensity, when it dares to look upon Christ as a demoniac and in league with Satan.

I. The August Preacher and His Following

St. Luke,[412] after recounting the episode of the sinful woman, introduces this new period of preaching as follows: "And it came to pass afterwards that He traveled through the cities and towns, preaching and evangelizing the Kingdom of God." We have already seen in the three Synoptics an indication of this same kind,[413] announcing and summing up the Savior's first apostolic journey through Galilee. In the present passage the words are perhaps even more expressive, especially in the Greek text; they show us the Divine Missioner journeying from city to city, from village to village,[414] everywhere breaking the bread of the gospel message, not disdaining to stop in the most insignificant towns. Two different terms are used to designate His preaching. The first is more general and formal: [415] He was "preaching." The second points out the special theme that He habitually treated of: He was "evangelizing," announcing the good tidings,[416] establishing the Kingdom of God and of the Messias. All Galilee,

---

[410] Matt. 9 : 1–8 and parallel passages.
[411] John 1 : 11.
[412] Luke 8 : 1.
[413] Matt. 4 : 23; Mark 1 : 38 f.; Luke 4 : 43 f.
[414] Διώδευεν κατὰ πόλιν καὶ κώμην.
[415] Κηρύσσων (Vulg., praedicans).
[416] Εὐαγγελιζόμενος (Vulg., evangelizans).

therefore, was again privileged to hear the Savior's eloquent voice, inviting His hearers to practice penance, preaching the gospel of pardon and grace, elevating their hearts, and winning numerous followers. As usual, His preaching was seconded by miracles, their manifestly divine character rendering faith easier and stronger. According to the Evangelist's brief description, our Lord must have devoted several weeks, perhaps some months, to this journey.

The former journey He began with only four disciples, whom He had associated with Him a short time before. This time He sets out accompanied by two friendly groups. The twelve Apostles, but recently chosen, formed, of course, the chief part of the procession. But St. Luke mentions also in the Savior's entourage "certain women who had been healed [evidently by Him] of evil spirits and infirmities." He had bestowed great favors upon them, restoring bodily health to some and freeing others from the devils that possessed them. He permitted them to testify their thankfulness by the services they were able to render Him during His journeys.

The Evangelist records the names of three of them. "Mary who is called Magdalen" is the most famous. According to the best authenticated opinion, her surname, intended to distinguish her from the many other Marys, is derived from the name of her birthplace, the town of Magdala,[417] "The Tower" (*i. e.,* watchtower), the only locality on the shores of the Sea of Galilee besides Tiberias which exists to-day. The ancient town, located near the middle of the western shore of the lake, on the plain of Genesareth, about halfway between Capharnaum (to the north) and Tiberias (to the south), was noted for its beauty and the wealth that came to it from its dyeworks and its manufacture of fine wool;[418] the present el Medjdel

[417] Whence the primitive form of the name: Μαγδαληνή in Greek, *Magdalene* in Latin.

[418] Neubauer, *La Géographic du Talmud,* p. 216; Edersheim, *Life and Times of Jesus the Messiah,* I, 571.

is nothing more than a wretched hamlet, containing a score of miserable mud huts, which shelter the only inhabitants of this formerly so populous and fertile district. St. Luke, after mentioning the name of Mary Magdalen, adds: "out of whom seven devils were gone forth." Sometimes, under the impression that this Mary is the sinful woman whose conversion St. Luke has just described, these words have been given a symbolic interpretation, as if they meant a life given up to every sort of vice. But the context itself shows that the reference is to a real diabolic possession, since the sacred writer, in the preceding line, says that many of the devoted women accompanying Jesus had been freed by Him from evil spirits. There is no reason for suddenly changing the meaning of the expression. After the general fact, the Evangelist cites a particular and very extraordinary fact, namely, that Mary Magdalen had been in the power of seven devils at the same time.[419]

St. Luke then mentions Joanna and Susanna. The latter, whose Hebrew name, *Shoshannah,* means "lily," does not appear elsewhere in the Gospel history. We will find Joanna among the holy women who remained faithful to the Divine Master up to and even after His death.[420] The Evangelist says that she was the wife of a certain Chusa, who was the steward [421] of the tetrarch Herod Antipas. It has sometimes been conjectured that she was a widow at this time; but there is no reason to suppose so.

The group of pious women following our Lord did not

[419] There will soon be question of other multiple possessions and there will be the case of the demoniacs of Gerasa. St. Mark, 16:9, characterizes Magdalen by the same detail. We should bear in mind that diabolical possession was neither habitually nor necessarily the punishment of a guilty life. It is also to be noted that St. Luke here introduces Mary Magdalen as an entirely new personage; he does not establish the least connection between her and the sinful woman. As we said above, he seems to wish positively to suppress the latter's name.

[420] Luke 24:10.

[421] The Greek word ἐπίτροπος (Vulg., *procurator*), by which his office is designated, is variously interpreted: treasurer, majordomo, steward, etc.

consist only of these three. Several others [422] also had the honor of belonging to this group. We can add to St. Luke's list by inserting Mary, the mother of James the Less and of Joseph, Salome, the mother of the sons of Zebedee, whom the two other Synoptics [423] speak of by name, as among those "who also when He was in Galilee followed Him and ministered to Him." These are the very terms used here by St. Luke. But he says that, besides their motherly or sisterly care for Jesus and the Apostles, these women provided them with material and financial assistance which providentially facilitated the Savior's exercise of His office. They were mostly wealthy women. It was owing to their constant generosity that the common purse of Jesus and His Apostles, which St. John mentions,[424] was rarely empty and that, in addition to the daily maintenance of thirteen young men, it enabled the Apostolic band to give alms to the poor.[425] The needs of these young men were very modest, as their life was of the simplest; but they had to be provided with food and clothing so long as Christ's preaching journeys lasted.

After the Last Supper our Lord asked the Apostles: "When I sent you without purse and scrip and shoes, did you want anything?" They answered: "Nothing." [426] Their not suffering for lack of material necessities was to some extent owing to Oriental hospitality; but to a much greater extent, probably, to the aid furnished by those devoted women whose generous services are mentioned by St. Luke. Although the nature and origin of Christ's financial resources during His public life are a matter of secondary importance, yet the subject is not without interest. He quit the exercise of His trade that He might devote Himself wholly to the founding of His

---

[422] Ἕτεραι πολλαί (Vulg., aliae multae).
[423] Matt. 27:56, 61, and Mark 15:40 f., 47.
[424] John 12:6; 13:29.
[425] John 13:29.
[426] Luke 22:35 f.

Church; His Apostles also, to lend their humble assistance to His great work, had abandoned their ordinary occupations. But the grateful love of those women who had been recipients of the Master's great spiritual favors provided for their material needs.

In like manner Jewish women were permitted to supply the rabbis with whatever was necessary for their maintenance; and frequently they showed their piety in this manner.[427] The Talmud did its best to encourage this useful practice, the purpose of which was so praiseworthy. In one place the Talmud says: "Whoever receives under his roof a disciple or a learned man, giving him food and drink and bestowing goods upon him, does the same thing as if he offered a daily sacrifice." [428] But nowhere do we find that women followed the Jewish rabbis in their journeys. Only Jesus could introduce an innovation in so delicate a matter. It was hardly more than a year since His disciples had been astonished at seeing Him converse with a woman in public.[429] With His divine hand He opens out the narrow circle in which the Orient had jealously confined its women. Thanks to Him, the vast field of good works was accessible to their activities. This field they have admirably cultivated in the Christian Church, making it yield a varied and abundant harvest. After Christ's Ascension, when the Apostles began to evangelize the world, as He had commanded them, they followed His example and were often accompanied by some pious woman, who was usually a relative.[430]

Let us pause to view the humble caravan. Jesus was in the midst of the Twelve, who grouped themselves around Him with a tender reverence. Some of them walked ahead of Him, others beside Him, the rest behind Him, but all as near Him

[427] Cf. St. Jerome, *In Matth.*, 27 : 58.
[428] *Neveh Shalom*, f. 156.
[429] John 4 : 27.
[430] 1 Cor. 9 : 5.

as possible, that they might lose none of His divine instruction. Generally it is He who speaks. But He readily allows His disciples to question Him in friendly familiarity, and He even provokes their questions. At a short distance there followed several veiled women, those spoken of by St. Luke. They carried baskets of provisions and talked together in a low voice. They were few in number, because it was useless for them all to come at the same time. Therefore they came in relays, to offer their services to Jesus and the Apostles.

Our Lord was, of course, the one to whom their looks and thoughts were directed. He was of medium height; His face was serious, but resplendent with a heavenly beauty.[431] Because of the sun's heat and in accord with Eastern custom, He was not bareheaded. Contrary to the usual representations of artists, His head was covered with a sudar (the keffyeh of the Arabs), that is, a sort of scarf fastened beneath the chin and resting loosely on the neck and shoulders.[432] His principal garment was a long tunic covering the whole body, but caught up in a girdle for greater convenience in walking. Over this tunic of somber color, He wore a tallith or blue mantle, the ample folds of which permitted an occasional glimpse of the tunic. His feet were bare, except for the sandals which He wore.[433]

II. Jesus Refutes an Infamous Calumny of the Scribes and Pharisees

The Gospel narrative does not allow us to remain long under the agreeable impression of the scene just described, which represents the Church in its infancy. The very imper-

---

[431] See Vol. I, pp. 432 f.

[432] To go out of doors with the head uncovered was regarded as improper, says the Talmud (tractate *Kiddushin,* 39 a).

[433] For this sketch, we have profited by the similar picture given by the elder Delitzsch in the charming little work entitled *Sehet, welch ein Mensch,* 1872, pp. 3–5.

fect dispositions of some of the Savior's relatives and the Pharisees' fanatical hatred presently give rise to a series of sorrowful incidents. But we are still in the period of Christ's great success. The Jewish multitudes, more and more attached to Him, continue to flock to Him wherever His zeal leads Him; in fact they leave Him not a moment's rest.

The first of these painful events is related only by St. Mark,[434] and in such concise terms that it is difficult to determine the meaning of all the details.[435]

One day Jesus returned to Capharnaum with His Apostles,[436] intending to set out again in another direction. An enormous crowd filled the house where He was staying and, in their eagerness to hear Him and to profit by His power and goodness, remained so long that neither the Savior nor the Twelve had a chance to take food.[437] On a previous occasion the throng of visitors had placed Jesus and His disciples in a similar though less painful situation,[438] and the same thing would happen again more than once [439] during this period of the Savior's public life; for He heeded only His zeal and at such times gladly fulfilled His own words: "My meat is to do the will of Him that sent Me, that I may perfect His work." [440]

Upon learning what was taking place, some people, whom the Evangelists speak of in a very general way as "His

[434] Mark 3 : 20 f.

[435] Victor of Antioch (second century), the earliest commentator on St. Mark's Gospel, complained of this semi-obscurity.

[436] The name of the place is not given. It is supposed to be Capharnaum because of the detail at the beginning: "He comes [ἔρχεται in the singular, according to best reading; the Vulgate has the plural, veniunt, as have several Greek manuscripts] to the house." It is supposed that this house was none other than that of Simon Peter, several times mentioned as Christ's place of abode when He was at Capharnaum. Cf. Mark 2 : 2, etc.

[437] Literally: "to eat bread." This Hebraism comes from the fact that, in the East as with us, bread is the basic food. Cf. Gen. 3 : 19; 31 : 54; 43 : 25; Ex. 2 : 20; Jer. 41 : 1, etc.

[438] Mark 2 : 1 f.

[439] Mark 8 : 20.

[440] John 4 : 34.

own," [441] and who may have been either relatives or simply disciples, suddenly appeared with the avowed intention of seizing Him and carrying Him off by force.[442] As justification for such an act of violence they dared to say: "He is become mad." [443] How is this scene to be explained? Maldonatus is right in saying [444] that a feeling of piety, which is laudable within bounds, but which in this case was not as intelligent as it should have been, instead of facilitating the interpretation, on the contrary has really increased the difficulty. Some early commentators place the insult, "He is become mad," on the lips of the Scribes and Pharisees, whom they substitute for "His own" in the text. Others give the words, "They said," an impersonal meaning, "It was said," an expression not altogether foreign to St. Mark.[445] Modern exegesis declines to sanction such arbitrary and profitless methods and prefers to retain the natural meaning of the text, endeavoring to explain the somewhat ambiguous phrase, "His own." This expression may designate either Christ's relatives or His disciples in a broad sense. Various Catholic, Protestant, and even Rationalist [446] exegetes accept the latter hypothesis. It would give rise to a less odious situation and seems to be favored by the account itself, which, with reference to the violent intruders, says that "they went out" of their houses and hastened to Jesus for the purpose of seizing Him. But

---

[441] Οἱ παρ' αὐτοῦ (Vulg., sui). This expression is both classical and Biblical. Prov. 31:21, the Septuagint uses it to translate the Hebrew expression "his house" (i. e., the family and the servants). It has the same meaning in Dan. 13:33. In the First Book of Machabees (cf. 9:44; 12:27; 13:53; 15:15; 16:16), it is several times used in a broad sense to designate someone's followers or members of his party. See also Josephus, Ant., I, x, 5. The Syriac Version of the Syr. Sin. has: 'his brothers.'

[442] Κρατῆσαι (Vulg., tenere).

[443] Ἐξέστη. Literally, "He is outside of Himself." The Vulgate translation, in furorem versus est, goes a little beyond the signification of the Greek, which does not necessarily indicate violent insanity.

[444] In his commentary on this passage of St. Mark.

[445] Mark 3:2.

[446] Among these last, v. g., Dr. Keim.

if the incident occurred at Capharnaum, there is no evidence that relatives of our Lord were there. As for His near relatives, it is supposed they were still in Nazareth and would not have had time to come from such a distance.

However, with most early and contemporary interpreters, we can apply the words "His own" to the Savior's relatives, without going contrary to the Evangelist's thought, if we draw a sharp line between these base insulters and our Savior's blessed Mother together with those of His "brethren" who come before long to pay Him an affectionate visit.[447] And we learn from St. John, who explicitly mentions it [448] in connection with a later event, that many of Christ's near relatives did not believe in Him, did not acknowledge His Messianic office, or at least understood it in a different way than He. However regrettable we may consider this attempt, so briefly described by St. Mark, and the insulting statement that sought to justify it, we should not be too much surprised at them. Furthermore, there is no proof that these men came with unfriendly dispositions, in spite of their rude language. They are generally credited with good intentions towards Jesus. They were disquieted by the agitation about Him, especially when they thought of the many enemies He had stirred up, whose displeasure might be visited upon all His relatives. All this puzzled them. Possibly they had planned this extravagant deed so as to rescue Jesus from the dangers that threatened Him.[449]

Shortly afterwards, as we read in St. Matthew and St. Luke,[450] a blind and dumb man, possessed by a devil, was brought to our Lord. Jesus drove out the devil, and the afflicted man at once recovered his sight and speech. In this

[447] Matt. 12: 47–50; Mark 3: 32–35; Luke 8: 20 f.
[448] John 7: 5.
[449] On the conclusion which certain extreme Rationalists have drawn from this incident and from other events of the Savior's life, see Appendix XVI.
[450] Matt. 12: 22 f.; Luke 11: 14.

case the blindness and dumbness were the result of diabolical possession, and not of any organic defect. As St. Jerome
remarks, these miracles were performed at once. This deliverance was witnessed by many persons, who could easily
confirm it. "All the multitudes were amazed," [451] says St.
Matthew, and he quotes their enthusiastic words: "Is not
this the Son of God," that is, the Messias in person? But they
hesitated as to how they should answer the question, not venturing to decide in this delicate matter, because Jesus, in spite
of His holiness, His miracles, and the loftiness of His teaching, did not correspond to His countrymen's false ideal of
the redeemer.

There were present a number of Scribes and Pharisees,
some of them having come from Jerusalem for the very purpose of spying on Jesus and criticizing Him. If a single Scribe
or Pharisee had raised his voice and cried out: "Yes, in very
truth, this is the Christ of the Lord," this seed of faith would
have quickly grown and would have overcome the prejudices
and low ideas. Unfortunately those bitter, unscrupulous enemies were blinded by hate and, instead of drawing from the
threefold miracle a conclusion favorable to Him who performed it, made so bold as to utter against Him a senseless
accusation, which was also an infamous calumny. They said:
"He hath Beelzebub, and by the prince of devils He casteth
out devils." [452] It is to be noted that they were careful not to
deny the miracle, as they might easily have done if their ad-

[451] 'Εξίσαντο: the same verb as that which was used above to express the odious
opinion of our Lord's disciples or neighbors. In this passage the Vulgate translates
it very exactly by *stupebant*. It describes very different states of mind, from simple
admiration (St. Luke has ἐθαύμασαν) to insanity, including exaltation and illu-
minism. St. Mark and St. Luke several times use it in a sense like that which we
find here in St. Matthew.

[452] The blasphemy is cited, with slight differences, by the three Synoptics. We
have here translated the text given by St. Mark, 3:22, which is divided into two
distinct but connected assertions. In St. Matthew we read: "This man casteth not
out devils but by Beelzebub the prince of the devils"; and in St. Luke: "He casteth
out devils by Beelzebub the prince of devils."

versary had been merely an impostor. But they gave it an interpretation which, if accepted, was calculated to destroy the Savior's growing prestige very quickly. As the facts clearly proved, He possessed real power over the devils. But, say these perverse men, He holds that power not from God, but from the chief of devils. The more outrageous the accusation, the more chance it had to produce upon the credulous multitudes the moral effect which the calumniators hoped for.[453]

We need not enter upon a discussion of the name Beelzebub; its pronunciation, origin, and exact meaning are uncertain.[454] Let it suffice to say that it was a contemptuous nickname by which the Jews of our Lord's time ironically designated Satan. Nowhere outside the Gospels is it applied to the devil. If we accept the spelling "Beelzebub"—adopted by the Vulgate, the Syriac Version, and some Greek manuscripts— this name represents the prince of devils as the "god of flies," an idol adored by the ancient Philistines of Accaron.[455] If, in agreement with most Greek manuscripts, we read Beelzebul, the meaning is: "Master of filth, of dung"; or, less probably, "Master of the (infernal) habitation." In any event, it was an opprobrious name, applied to Satan as chief of the bad angels.[456]

The Divine Master, whose patience was as great as His mercy, sometimes took no notice of the insults which His enemies cast at Him. But this time the accusation was too monstrous not to be answered on the spot. If the people should

---

[453] Fillion, *Les Miracles de N.-S. Jésus-Christ,* II, 279.

[454] See the Dictionaries of the Bible and the large Gospel commentaries.

[455] 4 Kings 1:2 f., 6. In Hebrew, *ba'al* means: "master," then by extension, "god," *zebub* is the word for a fly. Βαὰλ μαῖα θεός is the Septuagint translation. Cf. Josephus, *Ant.,* IX, ii, 1. The "god of flies" was invoked as a protector against that disgusting plague of Oriental countries.

[456] Without erecting demonology into a system, the Jews admitted the existence of a certain hierarchical order among evil spirits. See F. Weber, *System des*

come to believe that it was well founded, it might imperil the whole Messianic work. He whom God so mightily and patently accredited as the Messias, transformed into an agent and emissary of Satan! He, receiving His miraculous powers from the prince of the infernal regions! He could not possibly consent to remain silent under the blow of such a perfidious insult. He therefore refuted this calumny in a form of argumentative pleading, which has always been praised for its vigor, wisdom, and clearness. "All the qualities we have already admired in His discourses and answers, we find gathered here: mildness and humility, which no personal affront, not even the most contemptible insult, can weaken; a calm, serene temperament which does not return insult for insult; the just severity of a judge, in harmony with love that persuades and instructs; fulness of wisdom that makes known the secrets of hearts and declares the truth with penetrating power; the majesty of His person, affirming itself in all things." [457]

The three Synoptics record this apology: [458] abridged in St. Mark and St. Luke; more fully set forth in St. Matthew, whose account we will quote. It may be divided into two parts. Jesus first stands on the defensive and refutes His adversaries' odious hypothesis by invincible arguments which He takes from reason and experience. Then, assuming a vigorous offensive, He discloses the guilt of His calumniators and consequently the eternal punishment to which they expose themselves. The Scribes and Pharisees had not dared to make their insulting remark to our Lord's face, as they did later on at Jerusalem.[459] They slyly spread it through the crowd. But

altsynagogalen palästinischen Theologie, p. 243; Bousset, Religion des Judentums, pp. 327 f.

[457] H. Stier, Reden des Herrn Jesu.
[458] Matt. 12: 25–37; Mark 3: 23–30; Luke 11: 17–28.
[459] John 8: 48–52.

Jesus had knowledge of it in a supernatural manner.[460] Being ever open and fearless, He called them to Him,[461] so as to combat them face to face in the presence of the whole multitude.

The first part of His reply is set forth almost entirely, as St. Mark notes, in the form of "parables," that is, in figurative language.

"Every kingdom divided against itself shall be made desolate; and every city or house divided against itself shall not stand. And if Satan cast out Satan, he is divided against himself. How then shall his kingdom stand? And if I by Beelzebub cast out devils, by whom do your children cast them out? Therefore they shall be your judges. But if I by the Spirit of God cast out devils, then is the Kingdom of God come upon you. Or how can any one enter into the house of the strong, and rifle his goods, unless he first bind the strong? and then he will rifle his house. He that is not with Me, is against Me; and he that gathereth not with Me, scattereth." [462]

At the beginning we find what logicians call an *argumentum ex absurdo*. "How can Satan cast out Satan?" Jesus asks, according to the Second Gospel. The prince of devils in open warfare against himself, is a contradiction in terms, an absurdity. It is a law of history, as appears from daily experience and from well-known examples, that an empire, a family, a moral organism, can last only if all its parts remain closely united. If there is a schism or intestinal strife, destruction comes rapidly.[463] But Satan himself and his realm are no exception to this law. The expression, "to cast out devils by Beelzebub," is therefore a meaningless word-play, a sophism that cannot bear inspection.

[460] Matt. 12 : 25; Luke 11 : 17.
[461] Mark 3 : 23.
[462] Matt. 12 : 25–30.
[463] Cicero's saying (*Laelius*, VII, 23) is well known: "*Quae enim domus tam stabilis, quae tam firma civitas est, quae non odiis et excidiis funditus possit everti?*"

Jesus then made His equally unanswerable *argumentum ad hominem,* basing His reasoning on the example of the Jewish exorcists, that He might reduce the Scribes' accusation to nothingness. The "children" (*i. e.,* disciples) of the Pharisees [464] used to try to drive the devil out of the bodies of the possessed, and their efforts were sometimes successful, as is proved by the Savior's allusion.[465] Did their masters, the Pharisees, think of considering them the confederates of Satan? On the contrary, they admired them and congratulated them on their victories. Why, then, did the Pharisees show this partiality, why this injustice toward Jesus?

Jesus deduces two manifest consequences from these two arguments. Since He does not hold His powers from Satan, it is God Himself who has conferred them upon Him.[466] And since the kingdom of Satan is visibly beginning to crumble and is moving on to its destruction, it follows that the Kingdom of God, the Messianic Kingdom, has become a living reality in the midst of Israel.

Jesus next offers a third proof, in the form of a dramatic little parable. The devil is represented as a robust warrior, armed from head to foot,[467] on guard at the door of his house. To disarm him, completely overcome him, bind him, seize his fortified house and its amassed riches, it is necessary to be stronger than he. This "stronger" one who ousts Satan and

[464] This expression is analogous to that of "children of the prophets," which we often meet with in the historical books of the Old Testament.

[465] This fact is also attested by the historian Josephus, *Ant., VIII,* ii, 5; *Bell. jud.,* VII, vi, 3, and by several Fathers (*e. g.,* St. Irenaeus, *Adv. Haer.,* II, 7, and Origen, *Contra Celsum,* I and IV). See also Acts 19:13. The Talmud mentions the formulas, some of them magical and superstitious, by the aid of which these labored exorcisms took place (*Shabbat,* XIV, 3; *Sanhedrin,* X, 1; *Abhodah Zarah,* f. 12, 2).

[466] He drove out the devils "by the Spirit of God," we read in the First Gospel; "by the finger of God," says St. Luke. This latter expression was, according to Ex. 8:19, that used by the sorcerers of Egypt to explain the miracles performed by Moses.

[467] St. Luke, καθωπλισμένος (the Vulgate has simply: *armatus*).

seizes his booty, is Jesus Himself. How, then, can anyone maintain that He is indebted to Satan for His power, that He is the servant of Satan?

Jesus continues, saying: "He that is not with Me, is against Me; and he that gathereth not with Me, scattereth." These words contain a warning. There were among our Lord's hearers, as also elsewhere in Galilee and throughout Palestine, many wavering persons, who, although impressed by the Savior's preaching and miracles and holiness, were, unhappily, also swayed by the hostility which the nation's religious leaders showed toward Him, and consequently were undecided which side to join. Jesus warns them against this perilous indifference, inasmuch as neutrality in His regard was impossible, nay, even culpable. When principles are at stake—never had they been more so—indifference becomes opposition. In the relentless war that would be waged between the Messias and the diabolical powers, there was no choice but this: to be *for* Christ or *against* Him; to gather the harvest with Christ, or with Satan to scatter it to the wind.

Having refuted His enemies, Jesus takes the offensive, pointing out the extent of their crime and the punishment that awaited them if they persisted in their sinful conduct. The following lines are among the most terrible uttered by Christ: "Therefore I say to you: [468] Every sin and blasphemy shall be forgiven men, but the blasphemy of the Spirit shall not be forgiven. And whosoever shall speak a word against the Son of Man, it shall be forgiven him; but he that shall speak against the Holy Ghost, it shall not be forgiven him, neither in this world nor in the world to come." [469]

Might we not think we were listening to the voice of a

[468] This transition expression has here a very solemn quality. "Therefore": because, in spite of the evidence to the contrary, you dare to accuse Me of performing My miracles by favor of Satan's assistance.

[469] Matt. 12:31 f.; Mark 3:28–30. This passage is omitted by St. Luke.

judge pronouncing sentence? But, if we meditate upon the
terms of this sentence, they will not surprise us. Jesus wished
to strike hard, in the attempt to lead back to better dispositions those culpable men who stood before Him or at least to
prevent their example from becoming contagious. For this
reason He repeated His sentence of condemnation. The first
declaration is more general, the second somewhat more developed. In both cases it is expressed in lapidary style, with
every word significant. The general proposition declares that,
with a single exception, God in His infinite mercy is disposed
to grant a generous pardon to all sinners who humbly approach the tribunal of the sovereign Judge, sincerely contrite
for their sins and resolved to sin no more. God had formerly
made this consoling promise through His prophets;[470] in
the life of Christ, it has a new force and value. But, says the
Savior, there is one sin which by its very nature is unfor-
givable, "the blasphemy against the Holy Ghost."[471] And
when repeating His thought, Jesus makes it more precise.
This time, in place of mentioning sin in general, He speaks of
a particularly grievous form of sinful words: to speak ill of
the Son of Man.[472] Yet even in this case forgiveness is promised, on the usual conditions of contrition and purpose of
amendment. Jesus here intentionally calls Himself the Son
of Man, the name which often stands for the Messias on the
more lowly side of His nature,[473] His appearance in human
form. Men seeing Him so poor, outwardly so like the other
sons of Adam, and so lacking in the brilliant qualities which
were falsely attributed to the liberator of Israel, might to

[470] See especially Is. 1: 16–18, a very expressive passage.
[471] St. Mark: "He that shall blaspheme against the Holy Ghost." According to
St. Matthew: "The blasphemy of the Spirit." It is the same formula, abridged.
[472] Here St. Mark's account is less exact. In place of the Son of Man, he introduces "the sons of men": "All sins shall be forgiven unto the sons of men"; this
notably weakens the thought.
[473] Page 155.

some extent be led into error by preconceptions and ignorance.[474] For this reason, those who failed to recognize Him
and those who insulted and blasphemed Him will be able to
obtain forgiveness. But, says the Savior, the same is not true
in the case of blasphemy against the Holy Ghost, because this
sin, by its very nature, is such that God cannot pardon those
who become guilty of it. "It shall not be forgiven him, neither
in this world nor in the world to come." [475] It is "an everlasting sin," [476] that will be punished eternally. But why is
blasphemy against the Holy Ghost unpardonable? Evidently
because of its particular gravity. Its unforgivableness is not
on the side of God—at least, not directly—since His power
and mercy are infinite. It exists only on the side of the sinner,
whose state of soul is such that his pardon is morally impossible. The scene we have just been describing furnishes the
explanation needed for understanding this awful curse. Jesus
had just performed a miracle, in which God's action was
clearly manifested. The Scribes and Pharisees, voluntarily
closing their eyes to the light, deliberately and most hatefully
travestied the facts and attributed the miracle to the prince
of devils. It is following this accusation that our Lord says
that blasphemy against the Holy Ghost will not be forgiven.
Evidently His insulters had committed, or were on the point
of committing, the unpardonable sin. It therefore consists in
sinful obduracy in evil, in extraordinary bad faith, which
identifies the evident work of God with the work of Satan,
in open and deliberate strife against Heaven itself. In such
case we can understand that there is no possibility of forgiveness. Jesus spoke thus, "because they said: He hath an

[474] St. Peter, Acts 3: 17, and St. Paul, 1 Tim. 1: 13, clearly make this supposition, following therein our Lord Himself, Luke 23: 34.
[475] An expression often used by the rabbis. Cf. Dalman, *Die Worte Jesu*, pp.
121–125.
[476] Mark 3: 29.

unclean spirit." These are the significant words that conclude St. Mark's account.[477]

Jesus continues:

"Either make the tree good and the fruit good; or make the tree evil and its fruit evil. For by the fruit the tree is known. O generation of vipers, how can you speak good things, whereas you are evil? For out of the abundance of the heart the mouth speaketh. A good man out of a good treasure bringeth forth good things; and an evil man out of an evil treasure bringeth forth evil things. But I say unto you, that every idle word that men shall speak, they shall render an account for it in the day of judgment. For by thy words thou shalt be justified, and by thy words thou shalt be condemned." [478]

Our Lord again draws attention to the inconsequence of His enemies' conduct. Constrained by the evidence of the facts, they admitted that Jesus really delivered the possessed man from the power of the devil. He was a good tree, producing good fruit. But, according to the Pharisees' declaration, He was an evil tree producing evil fruit, since they called Him the associate of Beelzebub. Were they not thus guilty of another flagrant contradiction, an impossible absurdity? At this point the Divine Master loses patience, and, as the Baptist did before,[479] flays these "evil men," calling them a "generation of vipers." Indeed, insult and calumny were but natural on the part of these men, since "out of the abundance of the heart the mouth speaketh," and since in them was naught but iniquity. We may, then, surmise how

---

[477] On the unpardonable sin, see St. Jerome, *Epist.* 42, *ad Marcel.;* Suarez, *Com. in 3 Part. S. Thomae,* qu. 86, disput. 8; Knabenbauer, *Comment. in Evang. S. Matth.,* I, 503–508.

[478] Matt. 12:33–37.

[479] Matt. 3:7.

severely they will be condemned by the just Judge, who does not let an "idle" [480] word go unpunished.

Jesus had just finished His apology when, from the midst of the crowd, was heard a woman's voice,[481] crying out: "Blessed is the womb that bore Thee, and the paps that gave Thee suck." This was the same as saying: Blessed is Thy mother. This woman had been much impressed by the vigor and ability of Jesus' pleading, and in her naïve simplicity, she could not refrain from voicing her admiration. She was probably a mother herself and comprehended the holy pride that must have been experienced by her who gave birth to a son whose works and words were so marvelous. Her exclamation was, then, quite natural. It recalls Mary's early prophecy, "All generations shall call me blessed." [482] The rabbis represent the Jewish people as crying out, at sight of their redeemer's advent, these joyous words of felicitation: "Blessed is the hour when the Messias was created. Blessed is the womb from which He came forth." [483]

This beatitude of the woman in the crowd did not rise above the domain of nature. But Jesus added to it a beatitude in the realm of the supernatural. "Yea rather,[484] blessed are they who hear the word of God and keep it," that is, who put it into practice. Jesus was nowise contesting the truth of the praise to the honor of her whom He had made the most blessed of mothers and who had always faithfully kept the divine word. Our Lord, as was His practice, profited by this opportunity to raise His hearers' thoughts to a loftier sphere. Hence He affirms that it is more profitable to be united to

---

[480] St. Jerome thus defines it: *"Verbum quod sine utilitate loquentis dicitur et audientis,"* (*i. h. l.*).

[481] Luke 11:27: "Lifting up her voice."

[482] Luke 1:48.

[483] Passage quoted by Edersheim, *The Life and Times of Jesus the Messiah,* II, 201.

[484] Here the adverb μενοῦν (Vulg., *quin immo*), while confirming the assertion that precedes, modifies it in the sense of making it better or stronger.

God's commandments by obedience than by merely outward
relations, however close and noble these may be. Both beatitudes apply to Mary, as the holy Fathers often remark.[485]

There were some Scribes and Pharisees present who did
not take part in the calumny refuted by our Lord.[486] They
now said to Him, with a mixture of respect and boldness:
"Master [Rabbi], we wish to see a sign from heaven, performed by Thee." These men were representative of a
numerous party. For them the previous miracles of Christ,
particularly the one which gave rise to their colleagues'
blasphemy, were not enough to prove the divine origin of His
office and His Messianic character. To convince them, He
must, at their request, perform a "sign," an extraordinary
and decisive miracle that would take place, not on the earth,
but in the air, for example, an eclipse, or a storm out of a
clear sky.[487] Would they have believed, even if their request
had been granted? This may well be doubted, since "there
is no limit to the exigent demands of skeptics in matters of
the supernatural." [488] They arrogate to themselves the right
to criticize even the most indubitable miracles. As St. Luke
says, this request was made for the purpose of "tempting"
our Lord. But He treated those tempters as they deserved,
silencing them by another short and remarkably firm discourse.[489] He begins His reply by saying: "An evil and
adulterous generation seeketh a sign; and a sign shall not be
given it, but the sign of Jonas the prophet. For as Jonas was

[485] In particular St. Augustine, *Tractat. in Joan.*, X, 3: *"Hoc in ea magnificavit
Dominus, quia fecit voluntatem Patris, non quia caro genuit carnem; inde felix
quia verbum Dei custodit."* And also, *De Virgin.*, 3: *"Beatior Maria percipiendo
fidem Christi, quam concipiendo carnem Christi."*

[486] This clearly results from St. Luke's account: ἕτεροι, "others."

[487] Less probably, according to some interpreters, a prodigy so brilliant and
striking that one would be forced to regard it as a divine work.

[488] Girodon, *Commentaire Critique et Moral sur l'Évangile selon S. Luc*, 1903,
p. 337.

[489] Matt. 12 : 39–45; Luke 11 : 29–36, 24–28.

in the whale's belly three days and three nights, so shall the Son of Man be in the heart of the earth three days and three nights." [490]

In severe terms Jesus peremptorily refused to produce the sign. And His refusal is stated, not only for those who requested a sign, but for all those other Jews who shared their culpable dispositions.[491] They will not be given the sign which they presume to demand. In His infinite goodness, however, aside from His daily miracles that continue to the close of His life, He will grant them the exceptional prodigy, the miracle of miracles, which He calls the "sign of Jonas." Of late it is sometimes said that our Lord, by this comparison of Jonas with Himself, was referring only to their preaching. But Jesus' words, as we read them in St. Matthew, are opposed to such an interpretation; before they speak of Jesus' preaching and that of Jonas, they most clearly mention another point of comparison: namely, the prophet's sojourn in the whale's belly,[492] and Christ's sojourn "in the heart of the earth." [493]

The expression "three days and three nights" should be explained, at least so far as it concerns our Lord, according to the broad sense in which the ancient Jews used these words. In expressions of this sort, they reckoned a day already begun, as a full day of twenty-four hours. Thus the last hours of Good Friday, all Holy Saturday, and the first hours of Easter Sunday are considered equivalent to three days and three nights.

[490] Matt. 12:39 f.

[491] The epithet "adulterous" has here the sense of unfaithful, the Jewish people as a whole being compared to a wife who forgets her most sacred promises, as in many Old Testament passages: Is. 1:21; 50:1; Jer. 2:2; 3:6–15; Ezech. 16:8–14; 23:27; Osee 1:2—2:15; 7:13–16, etc.

[492] The term κῆτος (Vulg., cetus) is general, corresponding to the words "great fish" in the Book of Jonas, 2:1.

[493] In the canticle which he composed after his deliverance, Jonas represents himself as lost "in the heart of the sea" (Jonas 2:4). Christ evidently is alluding

The entire Old Testament history contains no more striking example of miraculous preservation from death than that
of Jonas. Thus God, in performing that unique miracle, intended to make it the type of a much more marvelous resurrection, that of our Lord Jesus Christ Himself. The Savior,
at the very beginning of His public life, was urged by the
Jewish religious leaders to justify His daring act of authority
in the Temple, by performing a "sign" in their presence. But
He referred them to the great miracle of His Resurrection.[494]
On that occasion His reply was more obscure than in the
present instance.

In His condemnation of the "evil generation" which He
was unable to bring to a belief in Him, Jesus cites two other
famous events in the history of Israel, the better to point
out the culpability of a large number of His fellow-Jews.
"The men of Ninive shall rise in judgment with this generation, and shall condemn it; because they did penance at the
preaching of Jonas. And behold a greater than Jonas here.
The queen of the south shall rise in judgment with this generation, and shall condemn it; because she came from the ends
of the earth to hear the wisdom of Solomon, and behold a
greater than Solomon here." [495]

The first of these two examples is also taken from the Book
of Jonas.[496] It describes the conversion of the Ninivites, proud
pagans though they were, who did penance at the bidding of
a stranger, a foreigner. The "queen of the south" is the Queen
of Saba, whose realm, which is supposed to have been part of
modern Yemen, was situated southeast of Palestine. She
came from a great distance ("from the far limits of the
earth," as the Oriental hyperbole expresses it) to see Solo-

to this detail when He speaks of His own sojourn "in the heart of the earth,"
i. e., in the tomb.
[494] John 2: 18 f.
[495] Matt. 12: 41 f.
[496] Jonas 3: 1–10.

mon and consult him; and she went back, astonished at what she had seen and heard.[497] These contrasts recall certain details in our Lord's discourse in the synagogue at Nazareth [498] and also the anathemas which He later pronounced against three unbelieving cities located on the shore of Lake Tiberias.[499] There is extraordinary force in the personal comparison which He twice makes. This is especially true of the words, "Behold a greater than Jonas here," "Behold a greater than Solomon here," uttered in a tone of authority and conviction which must have impressed many of His hearers.

St. Luke inserts after these words a few lines [500] that we have already seen in the Sermon on the Mount.[501] They are equivalent to telling those who demanded that Jesus gratify their whim by performing a miracle: You have received numerous evident proofs of My divine mission and, to recognize their value, you have but to open the eyes of your understanding; but, through your indifference or passionate hatred, you freely let yourselves be blinded.

"No man lighteth a candle and putteth it in a hidden place nor under a bushel, but upon a candlestick, that they that come in, may see the light. The light of thy body is thy eye. If thy eye be single,[502] thy whole body will be lightsome; but if it be evil, thy body also will be darksome. Take heed therefore, that the light which is in thee, be not darkness. If then thy whole body be lightsome, having no part of darkness, the whole shall be lightsome; and as a bright lamp, shall enlighten thee."

This passage sets forth three familiar truths. Our eyes are the lamps that furnish light to our body and its move-

---

[497] 3 Kings 10: 1–13.
[498] Luke 4: 25–27.
[499] Matt. 11: 20–24; Luke 10: 13–15.
[500] Luke 11: 33–36.
[501] Matt. 5: 15; 6: 22 f.
[502] *I. e.*, healthy, well constituted.

ments. If they are in good condition, our physical being is
full of light; if they are sickly, we walk in darkness. Since
they are a necessary organ, we ought to watch over them most
carefully. But it is still more important that we care for our
intellectual and moral vision, lest it become obscure and unable to comprehend the most manifest truths.

Jesus concludes this second discourse by referring indirectly to the calumny which He refuted in His preceding address. His adversaries had shamefully accused Him of being possessed by Beelzebub. He hurls back the accusation by
showing, in veiled words, that the real demoniac was that
wicked generation on whom exorcisms were tried in vain. It
remained insensible to all the offers of salvation that came
to it from Heaven. To punish it for so grievous a fault, God
will allow it to fall more and more into Satan's power. This
thought is presented in the form of an allegory, remarkable
for its psychological penetration.

"When an unclean spirit is gone out of a man, he walketh through
dry places,[503] seeking rest, and findeth none. Then he saith: I will
return into my house from whence I came out. And coming he findeth
it empty, swept, and garnished. Then he goeth, and taketh with him
seven other spirits more wicked than himself, and they enter in and
dwell there; and the last state of that man is made worse than the
first. So shall it be also to this wicked generation." [504]

The application of these words is evident. The ancient de-
mon of idolatry had brought the punishments of divine wrath
upon the ancestors of the Jews whom Jesus was addressing.
But this evil was expelled through the sufferings of the Babylonian Captivity, from which the Jewish nation emerged very
much purified. Upon returning to Palestine, the Jews for a

---

[503] That is, across deserts and ruins of cities, places where the Scripture rather
often locates the habitation of evil spirits (Is. 13: 21 f.; Tobias 8: 3, etc.).
[504] Matt. 12: 43–45; Luke 11: 24–26.

while became morally better than at any other period of their
history. Unfortunately this improved condition did not long
endure. The devil, angered at having been driven from his
old abode, returned to the charge under a different form,
stronger and more wicked than before. Aided by Sadducean
errors and Pharisaic hypocrisy, he succeeded in recovering
his former dwelling-place and in exercising therein an influence seven times more pernicious than before. The effects
of that influence were to be seen at the time of Christ and help
to explain why He was not acknowledged by all as the Messias. But these effects were still more evident after His Ascension, until the hour of the nation's complete ruin, its supreme punishment.[505]

While Jesus was thus speaking [506] to the multitude, part
of whom were seated about Him, His mother and cousins
(whom the Evangelists continue to call "His brethren") arrived, desiring to see Him and speak with Him.[507] But
it was impossible for them to reach Him, so compact was
the crowd that filled the house and gathered outside. The
news of their arrival passed from mouth to mouth and in
this way reached one of those near the Savior. This man,
thinking he ought to inform Jesus, said to Him: "Behold
Thy mother and Thy brethren [508] stand without, seeking
Thee."

To prevent any confusion, it is necessary to repeat that
this visit had nothing in common with the curious undertaking a short time before by some of our Lord's relatives or
disciples. St. Mark, who is the only one to relate the two in-

---

[505] See St. John Chrysostom, *Hom. in Matth.*, 43.

[506] The use of this expression by St. Matthew presupposes that this new episode
followed immediately after Christ's discourse to the Pharisees. St. Mark and St.
Luke do not set any date for it.

[507] This episode is related by the three Synoptics: Matt. 12:46–50; Mark
3:31–35; Luke 8:19–21.

[508] The words καὶ αἱ ἀδελφαί σου, "and thy sisters," which appear in some
manuscripts, are probably apocryphal.

cidents, clearly distinguishes them from each other.[509] Christ's
mother took no part in the first incident. What was her special
reason for coming to her Son at this time? The sacred writers are silent on this point. But we may suppose that the
Pharisees' growing hostility toward the Savior had something to do with this journey of His blessed Mother. It may
be that, upon learning that Jesus was in danger, she hastened to Him with motherly love and courage, as she later
comes to the foot of the cross on Calvary. At any rate, since
she accompanied the "brethren" of our Lord, we may be
sure that the visit was for a good purpose.

To the one who informed Him of their arrival, Jesus replied: "Who is My mother, and who are My brethren?"
Then, as He turned His eyes lovingly upon those assembled
about Him and held forth His hand as though to take possession of them, He continued: "Behold My mother and My
brethren. For whosoever shall do the will of My Father that
is in Heaven, he is My brother and sister and mother." Our
Lord chose this delicate and forcible way of telling His disciples, who were there in large numbers, what is the extent
of His affection and devotedness and how closely He is united
to those who zealously strive to obey God's will in all things.
For Him such obedience, even unto death, was a perpetual
and supreme aim. This bond established a relationship between them and Him comparable to that between members
of a family. He shows infinite condescension; for, as St. Paul
says, "He is not ashamed to call them brethren." [510]

But do these tender words of our Lord with regard to the
disciples imply a reproach to His relatives, especially His
mother? It was so supposed by some writers in the early centuries of our era. And this view is repeated and exaggerated

[509] Mark 3: 20 f., 31–35.
[510] Heb. 2: 11. See St. John Chrysostom, *Hom. in Matth.*, 44. Some commentators wrongly apply these words of our Lord only to the twelve Apostles.
They referred to all His disciples, present and future.

to-day by men who seem to have inherited feelings toward Mary that are akin to those which the Pharisees entertained toward the Savior.[511] If, however, this saying of our Lord be examined without bias, it will be found to contain nothing offensive or derogatory to Mary, and that it deprives her of none of her privileges as the Savior's mother. Moreover, our Lord's words were not addressed directly to her. This saying reminds us of His profound words in the Temple when the Blessed Virgin and St. Joseph found Him there in the midst of the doctors,[512] and of His words at the marriage feast at Cana at the time of His first miracle.[513] Here again He considers His family relations, not from the natural point of view, but from that of His duty as Messias. This duty outranks any other. To perform it with complete freedom, to consecrate Himself entirely to His office, it was necessary for Him to live disengaged from His relatives and other attachments which, however holy in themselves, might distract Him in the exercise of His vocation. The attitude which He here takes toward His relatives is that which He soon urges upon His Apostles [514] and, to a certain extent, upon all Christians.[515] But this attitude is not to be understood as something absolute, since Jesus kept a tender filial regard for His mother to the very end,[516] and He vigorously defends the rights of parents against undutiful sons.[517] On this occasion, as earlier in the Temple, He displays no coldness toward His mother, but He shows preference for His heavenly Father.[518] Mary is not one who would complain of this.

[511] See Appendix XVII.
[512] Luke 2 : 49.
[513] John 2 : 4.
[514] Mark 10 : 29 and parallel passages.
[515] Matt. 10 : 37.
[516] John 19 : 26 f.
[517] Matt. 15 : 3–5.
[518] *"Ostendit paternis se ministeriis amplius quam maternis affectibus debere."* St. Ambrose, *i. h. l.*

When Jesus dismissed the crowd, did He then receive His visitors? The Evangelists do not pause over information of this sort. But it is altogether likely that the Blessed Virgin then had an affectionate meeting with her Son.

CHAPTER IV

The Parables of the Kingdom of Heaven

I. Our Lord's Preaching in the Form of Parables

WE must define and describe this interesting method of teaching. Our Lord several times employed it in His public life previous to the point we have now reached,[519] and henceforth He uses it very frequently, for a special reason which He Himself points out.

The word "parable" comes to us from the Greek, through the Latin.[520] Etymologically it means the juxtaposition of two things, then the resulting comparison.[521] It represents in general a literary form in which there is placed beside the truth an image which makes it more living and more easily grasped.

We need not concern ourselves with the many and often brilliant parables of the Greek classics, with which those of the Gospel have no connection.[522] The Gospel parables are of an altogether Semitic kind, many examples of which are contained in the writings of the Old Testament and which the Hebrews called *machal*, "similitude," usually translated in the Septuagint by the word "parable." Just as the *machal* covers a wide field and appears in varied forms—simple

---

[519] Cf. Matt. 5: 13–16, the salt of the earth and the light of the world; 6: 26, 28, the birds of the air and the lilies of the field; 7: 13 f., the two gates and the two ways; 7: 24–27, the wise builder and the foolish builder; 9: 16 f., the patched garments and the bottles; 11: 16 f., the capricious children, etc.

[520] Παραβολή, *parabola*.

[521] It is composed of the adverb παρά, "beside," and the verb βάλλω, "I cast." Literally: "I place beside." Cicero translates it by *collatio*, "comparison"; Tertullian, by *similitudo*, "likeness."

[522] See Lagrange in the *Revue Biblique*, 1909, pp. 198–214.

proverb,[523] enigmatic sentence,[524] metaphorical narrative,[525] prophetic discourse,[526] etc.—so, too, the Gospel parable assumes various aspects. St. Luke, for example, gives the name of parable to the proverb, "Physician, heal thyself"; [527] St. Matthew and St. Mark call a mere comparison a parable.[528]

Nevertheless, when the Synoptics mention the Savior's parables,[529] they generally do so in the sense that became popular at an early date, meaning those charming little fictitious accounts—not intrinsically improbable—the elements of which are taken from nature or daily life. They set forth in somewhat dramatic form religious or moral truths which thus are made clearer and enter more deeply into men's minds and hearts. However varied these figures may be, the essential part is a comparison, sometimes very much developed, at other times simply indicated. The parable is, therefore, "a composite made up of body and soul. The body is the account itself in its obvious and natural sense. . . . The soul is a series of ideas parallel to the former, unfolded in the same order, but on a higher plane, so that one must be warned and must be attentive to grasp them." [530] The parable bears some analogy to the fable. But it differs therefrom in two respects. The animate or inanimate beings introduced are not allowed to exceed the laws of their nature: a wolf or a lamb, for example, is not represented as talking. And the parable, by

[523] 1 Kings 10:12: "Is Saul also among the prophets?" 24:14: "From the wicked shall wickedness come forth."

[524] Prov. 1:6 etc.

[525] Ex. 12:22.

[526] Num. 22:7, 18; 24:3 etc. See Gesenius, *Thesaurus Linguae Hebr. et Chald. Vet. Testam.*, II, 828.

[527] Luke 4:23.

[528] Matt. 15:15; Mark 7:17.

[529] The word παραβολή is used 56 times in the New Testament: 48 times in the Synoptic Gospels (17 times by St. Matthew, 13 by St. Mark, 18 by St. Luke), not at all by St. John, who employs the analogous expression παροιμία (John 10:6; 16:25, 29).

[530] Lesêtre, in Vigouroux' *Dictionnaire de la Bible*, Vol. IV, col. 2107.

its moral or religious trend, is much higher than the fable, which scarcely rises above the level of the natural world. The parable differs also from the allegory, which is more lengthy and complex and which directly personifies ideas, as we see in the two examples to be found in the Fourth Gospel: the allegories of the Good Shepherd and of the vine.[531]

With reference to what are called the parables of the Kingdom of Heaven, which we are going to study in this chapter, St. Matthew says: "All these things Jesus spoke in parables to the multitudes; and without parables He did not speak to them." [532] Although the second part of this statement is obviously hyperbolic, yet it proves that the number of our Lord's parables, beginning at this point of His ministry, must have been considerable. The Evangelists record about thirty [533] and, as in the case of Christ's miracles, they have made a most happy choice.

The Savior, of course, used parables day after day, according to the circumstances of the moment; but there is a real order among them, enabling us to classify them. They form three series, distinct from each other by their general theme as well as by the periods of Christ's ministry to which they belong. In the first series we find the eight parables of the Kingdom of Heaven grouped by themselves. A little later we find a larger series of a new type, conformable to the new purpose which their Divine Author intended. This latter series includes the parables of the good Samaritan, the unmerciful

---

[531] John 10: 1–16; 15: 1–11.

[532] Matt. 13: 34. St. Mark, 4: 33, makes a similar remark, couched in almost the same words.

[533] As to the number of parables in the Gospel, the disagreement among commentators would be hard to understand were it not for the fact that the reason for such difference of opinion arises from the difference of judgment as to the literary classification of the passages involved. Some authors speak of 71 and even 79 parables; but they include simple metaphorical expressions, such as the invitation to bear the Savior's yoke (Matt. 11: 29 f.), the reference to a millstone about the neck of one who gives scandal (Luke 17: 2), etc. Usually only the "story parables" are reckoned.

servant, the friend at midnight, the rich fool, the barren
fig tree, the great supper, the lost sheep, the lost drachma, the
prodigal son, the unjust steward, Dives and Lazarus, the
unjust judge, the Pharisee and the publican, the laborers in the
vineyard.[534] The third series includes six parables: those of
the pounds (*minae*), the two sons, the wicked husbandmen,
the marriage of the king's son, the ten virgins, the talents.
They concern the Kingdom of God, as do the parables of the
first series, but from a special point of view. Most of the
parables of the first and third series are recorded by St.
Matthew, who is the Evangelist of the Kingdom of Heaven.
Those of the second group almost all belong to St. Luke's
Gospel. St. Mark inserts only a small number of parables in
his narrative because he is more concerned with the Savior's
deeds than with His preaching. The Gospel according to St.
John does not contain a single parable; but it contains the two
allegories mentioned above.

It would be a mistake to regard our Lord as the origina-
tor of this form of teaching. Long before Him, wise men
such as Solomon and prophets such as Nathan and Isaias
had composed parables.[535] Throughout the Gospels it is evident that this literary form was well known at that time. In
fact, the rabbis made constant use of it. Some of them—for
example, Hillel, Shammai, Gamaliel, and Meir—won a well
deserved reputation in this matter. These rabbinical parables
have been much studied of late and interesting collections
of them [536] have been published, which enable us to compare

[534] To this group we might refer the little parable of the two debtors (Luke
7:40–42), which belongs to it, if not in time, at least by reason of its form
and thought.

[535] Cf. Eccles. 9:14–16; 2 Kings 22:1–7; Is. 28:23–29, etc.

[536] Cf. P. Fiebig, *Altjüdische Gleichnisse und die Gleichnisse Jesu,* 1904; *Die
Gleichnisse Jesu im Lichte der rabbinischen Gleichnisse des neutestamentlichen
Zeitalters,* 1912. See also Lightfoot, *Horae Hebr. et Talmud. in Evangelia,* I,
133; A. Wünsche, *Neue Beiträge zur Erläuterung der Evangelien aus Talmud
und Midrasch,* p. 160; Edersheim, *Life and Times of Jesus the Messiah,* I, 180–185.

them with Christ's parables. In both cases there are certain resemblances: for instance, in the manner of presenting the little imaginary accounts and even in the introductory formulas.[537] Many of the rabbinical parables are beautiful; but neither as a whole nor in detail can they stand comparison with those of our Lord. They are generally lacking in charm, picturesqueness, and naturalness. Their moral conclusions are not always lofty; often their application is clumsily made.

The following is the opinion of an enthusiastic Rationalist about the Gospel parables: "Centuries have passed and the parables remain. Interesting, vivid, easily impressing themselves in the memory . . . they offer substantial nourishment to the reflecting mind of great thinkers and the understanding of plain people. Therein Jesus appears as an incomparable artist. The beauty of these parables has the classical merit of obtaining a powerful effect by means of extreme simplicity."[538] The highest praise and admiration are due these little poems—for they are such in a literary sense—these perfect and inimitable models, these charming pictures in which the dominant idea is made to stand out by means of most varied details and colors. There is never a word too little, not a word too much. What could be more exquisite and dramatic than the parable of the prodigal son? What more tender than that of the lost sheep? What more tragic than that of the ten virgins? But we shall meet them all as we go along and shall observe their individual perfection.

Our Lord's astonishing power of observation is revealed better in the parables than anywhere else. However incomparable their outer form, the lessons which they teach and the moral truths which they enunciate are even more impressive. In St. Bernard's words, "their outer covering is most

---

[537] We find the rabbinic parables introduced by such expressions as these: "I will tell thee a parable," "What is this like?" "A parable: what is this like?"
[538] A. Réville, *Jésus de Nazareth*, II, 119.

pleasing; but, upon breaking the almond, we find something much more delectable within." Who but the Incarnate Word could so well understand and describe the close relations between the external world and the spiritual world? It is also to be noted that, although the parables were intended primarily for the Jews of Palestine, they contain nothing very specifically Jewish or Oriental. Hence they are suited to all races and countries, and have been relished and admired by all.

The Savior's parables contain inexhaustible treasures of doctrine. As an eminent theologian of the last century said,[539] they offer us a great variety of apparently independent lessons and, when considered separately, they give only partial results; whereas, if we bring them together and compare them, they throw no small light on the entire theory of religion and of the Church. This same scholar says further that, embraced in our Lord's parabolic teaching may be found all the doctrines and precepts that were to belong to the Church which He founded. The parables are an abundant mine for exploitation by theologians. At every new meditation of the parables, they are found to contain riches not before noted. They possess a simplicity suited to the minds of the untutored, and a profundity for the greatest thinkers. We may apply to them the words that St. Gregory the Great uses with reference to the

---

[539] Cardinal Wiseman, *op. cit.,* p. 28. On the parables the following works may also be consulted: Catholic authors: Fonck, S.J., *Die Parabeln des Herrn im Evangelium,* 1903 (3d ed., 1910) ; D. Buzy, *Introduction aux Paraboles Évangéliques,* 1912 (an excellent work) ; Z. Sainz, S.J., *Las Parabolas del Evangelio y el Reino de Jesucristo que es la Iglesia,* 1915. Protestant authors: R. Trench, *Notes on the Parables of Our Lord,* 11th ed., 1870; S. Goebel, *Die Parabeln Jesu methodisch ausgelegt,* 2 vols., 1879; A. Bruce, *The Parabolic Teaching of Christ,* 1882; Bugge, *Die Hauptparabeln Jesu,* 1903. Rationalist authors: Jülicher, *Die Gleichnisreden Jesu,* 2 vols., 1899; H. Weinel, *Die Bildersprache Jesu in ihrer Bedeutung für die Erforschung seines inneren Lebens,* 1906, and *Die Gleichnisse Jesu,* 5th ed., 1916. A number of serious errors by the Rationalist critics in the matter of the parables is pointed out in Appendix XVIII.

whole Bible: they are like a stream wherein a lamb may wade
and in which an elephant may easily swim.

As they express a great variety of dogmatic and moral
truths, so the images are taken from the most varied objects.
"That He might shed light upon what is lofty and divine,
upon the nature, the gradual establishment, and the laws of
the Kingdom of God, and that He might render heavenly
things accessible to His hearers, enslaved to things material,
Jesus gently led them from the known to the unknown . . . ,
from the commonplace to the eternal. With royal magnanim-
ity, He brought into His service the entire world, even with
its imperfection, that He might overcome the world. And
He fought it with its own weapons. He neglected none of the
means that words could supply, to make the grace of God
penetrate the hearts of His hearers." [540] Jesus took the outer
elements of His parables from every realm: the world of
plants and the world of animals, every domain of contemporary Jewish life (agricultural, economic, social, political,
religious), and even the divine world. We see God Himself
appear with His angels, priests and Levites, Jews and Samaritans, a Pharisee and a publican, rich and poor, an unjust
judge and an oppressed widow, playful children and a prodigal son, a generous landowner and a dishonest steward,
vine-dressers, farmers, fishermen and bankers, humble house-
wives and sons of kings. And these numerous details are
grouped with marvelous skill, with the result that each parable truly expresses the lessons that Jesus purposed. In short,
by their charm and variety, their originality, and the lessons
they contain, the Gospel parables reflect the greatness of their
Author, in whom they reveal, if we may use these terms in
speaking of Him, a deep thinker, an author of the highest
order, a genius. These masterpieces have a unique place in
the world's literature. Yet it would be a mistake to think

[540] Jülicher, *op. cit.,* I, 118.

they were composed with great labor and time, then improved and finished off. They came spontaneously from the Savior's mind and imagination, as living examples intended to complement and corroborate His teaching.

II. The First Group of Parables

We interrupted our narrative at a point when our Lord had just won a brilliant victory over His enemies. After that contest He left the house where it took place and sought rest at the lake shore.[541] There He sat down. The intimate circle of His disciples gathered around Him. But again His rest did not last long, because the multitude that had recently crowded about Him in the house soon rejoined Him, and continued to increase through the addition of new contingents that came from the neighboring towns.[542] Jesus knew that the multitude was eager to see and hear Him. Finding it inconvenient to address them as they crowded so closely about Him, He acted as on the day of the miraculous draught of fishes.[543] A small boat was there, perhaps the one that was held in reserve for occasions like this.[544] Thither He betook Himself, sat on the deck, and began speaking to the multitude that stood on the shore. He thus had all His hearers in front of Him. We owe this delightful picture to St. Matthew and St. Mark.

These Evangelists, after thus sketching the scene, say: "He taught them many things in parables."[545] It was there-

---

[541] St. Matthew explicitly says, 13:1, that these events occurred the same day.

[542] The three Synoptics insist on this detail. St. Matthew: ὄχλοι πολλοί, "great multitudes"; St. Mark, according to the best reading: ὄχλος πλεῖστος, "a very great multitude"; St. Luke: ὄχλου πολλοῦ, "a great multitude."

[543] Luke 5:3.

[544] Cf. Mark 3:9. If the hypothesis is correct, the preceding scene and that which is about to follow took place at Capharnaum.

[545] Matt. 13:3; Mark 4:2.

fore a whole sermon that Jesus then delivered under this form. According to the most probable view, this is where we should place the eight parables of the Kingdom of Heaven, composing the first of the three groups mentioned above and apparently all delivered on the same day. This fact seems to follow from the close connection between them in the matter of the subject treated. They form an unbroken chain, all the parts linked together, mutually explaining and supplementing each other. This undeniable unity leads us to suppose they were delivered at the same time.[546] Further, from end to end of his account, St. Matthew shows that he purposed following a strictly chronological order. This appears from the care with which he joins all the sections together by means of connective formulas.[547]

Jesus, following after the precursor, had, in the first hours of His public life, announced the near coming of the Kingdom of Heaven, that is, the Messianic Kingdom. From that time He continually spoke of it and preached it in every form of speech, so as to prepare men's minds and hearts to become worthy of it. In the Sermon on the Mount He had recently promulgated its laws. On the present occasion He resorts to a new manner of exposition to describe its nature and development and its successive stages, as also the means of securely possessing it. The parables of the Kingdom are in everyone's memory. But we will quote them in full and will then draw the reader's attention to their chief features.

The first is the parable of the sower. It serves to introduce the whole series.[548] Jesus said: "Hear ye." [549]

---

[546] The difficulty comes from the fact that St. Luke, who cites only three of them—the sower, the mustard seed, and the leaven—places the last two at a later period. Cf. Luke 8: 4-15; 13: 18-21. But it is quite possible that our Lord repeated them.

[547] Cf. Matt. 13: 1, 3, 10, 14, 31, 33, 34, 36, 53.

[548] Matt. 13: 3-9; Mark 4: 3-9; Luke 8: 5-8.

[549] An urgent call for attention, which St. Luke is the only one to point out here. Christ repeats it several times in this first group of parables.

"Behold the sower went forth to sow. And whilst he soweth some fell by the way side, and the birds of the air came and ate them up. And other some fell upon stony ground, where they had not much earth; and they sprung up immediately, because they had no deepness of earth. And when the sun was up they were scorched; and because they had not root, they withered away. And others fell among thorns; and the thorns grew up and choked them. And others fell upon good ground, and they brought forth fruit, some an hundredfold, some sixtyfold, and some thirtyfold. He that hath ears to hear, let him hear."

The description, though so simple, is sketched with a master hand. We have quoted it according to St. Matthew's Gospel. A great resemblance is to be observed between all three versions of this parable. But we recommend those who have the time and inclination, to compare the accounts and note the variations. It is an interesting study. This parable proposes the following problem: Since the seed is the same, whence comes the difference in the results? The answer is given. The difference comes from the diversity of conditions of the soil on which the grain fell from the sower's hand. The sower did his best. It is in spite of him that part of the seed fell on unpromising soil, was trodden under foot by passers-by, was devoured by thieving birds, sprang up only to be dried up presently by the heat of the sun or stifled somewhat later by the thistles, nettles, briars, and other thorny plants. Yet his labor will be rewarded at harvest time, for its yield will be thirtyfold, sixtyfold, nay, even a hundredfold. These figures show the great fertility of the soil, but they are not surprising for certain districts of Palestine, particularly Galilee, the Hauran plateau, and the shores of Lake Genesareth. Did not Isaac harvest "a hundredfold" in the neighborhood of Gerasa, in the Philistine country? [550] But

[550] Gen. 26:2. Speaking of Palestine as regards its agriculture, Tactitus (*Hist.*, V, 6), characterizes it thus: *"Uber solum, exuberant fruges."* Modern travelers

it is merely in passing that Jesus mentions this happy result of most of the sowing. He dwells upon three unfavorable conditions that the seed encountered. And the same will be the chief point in the application of the parable.

Travelers have again and again remarked how perfect is the local coloring of the scene which our Lord depicts in this parable. One of them writes: "A slight recess in the hillside close upon the plain disclosed at once, in detail, and with a conjunction which I remember nowhere else in Palestine, every feature of the great parable. There was the undulating cornfield descending to the water's edge. There was the trodden pathway running through the midst of it, with no fence or hedge to prevent the seed from falling here or there on either side of it or upon it; itself hard with the constant tramp of horse and mule and human feet. There was the 'good' rich soil, which distinguishes the whole of that plain and its neighborhood from the bare hills, elsewhere descending into the lake, and which, where there is no interruption, produces one vast mass of corn. There was the rocky ground of the hillside protruding here and there as elsewhere through the grassy slopes. There were the larger bushes of thorn, springing up in the very midst of the waving wheat." [551]

Good seed, even when sown in excellent ground, is exposed to other dangers than those just described. This is the lesson taught by the parable of the cockle, the second in the series, which is found only in the First Gospel.[552] It is therefore closely connected with the first parable.

"The Kingdom of Heaven is likened to a man that soweth good seed in his field. But while men were asleep, his enemy came and

and geographers say the same thing. Cf. Raumer, *Palästina*, p. 92; G. H. Smith, *Historical Geography of Palestine*, pp. 83, 439–441, 612; Chauvet and Isambert, *Syrie, Palestine*, p. 9. See also Vol. I, pp. 95 ff., of this work.

[551] A. Stanley, *Sinai and Palestine*, chap. 12.

[552] Matt. 13:24–30.

oversowed cockle among the wheat and went his way. And when the blade was sprung up, and had brought forth fruit, then appeared also the cockle. And the servants of the goodman of the house coming said to him: Sir, didst thou not sow good seed in thy field? Whence then hath it cockle? And he said to them: An enemy hath done this. And the servants said to him: Wilt thou that we go and gather it up? And he said: No, lest perhaps gathering up the cockle, you root up the wheat also together with it. Suffer both to grow until the harvest, and in the time of the harvest I will say to the reapers: Gather up first the cockle, and bind it into bundles to burn, but the wheat gather ye into my barn."

This little picture is even more dramatic than the preceding one. The mischievous practice which is the basis of this parable is by no means purely imaginary. Genuine instances of it have been detected both in the Orient and elsewhere.[553] The plant thus oversown by a foe in the wheat field is the cockle, the *lolium temulentum* of the botanists. It is often seen in Palestine, as also in our Western countries. It produces grain very similar to that of wheat, but smaller and generally darker: if the flour made from it is mixed with bread flour in notable quantity, it produces vertigo and convulsions.[554] During the early period of its growth it scarcely differs from wheat and can hardly be recognized even by the most practiced eye.[555] Hence the owner of the field would not allow his servants to root it up too soon. But when the head of grain issues from the sheath, a child can readily dis-

---

[553] Robert, *Oriental Illustrations,* p. 541.

[554] Hence the epithet *infelix,* which Virgil applies to it in his Georgics. Its Greek name ζιζάνια, of which the Latin *zizania* is a transliteration, is probably of Semitic origen. See Buxtorf, *Lexicon Talmudicum,* under the word "Zonim"; Lagarde, *Semitica,* I, 63; Lewy, *Aramäische Pflanzennamen,* p. 133.

[555] St. Jerome remarked this fact: *"Inter triticum et zizania, quod nos appellamus lolium, quamdiu herba est et nondum culmus ad spicam, grandis similitudo est, et in discernendo aut nulla aut perdifficilis distantia." Expos. in Matth. i. h. l.* We, too, have observed the same thing, when we sowed wheat and tare on the same piece of land.

tinguish the two plants. The separation can thus easily be made at harvest time. It is a common practice among Palestinian farmers, to weed out the cockle and other noxious growths a little while before the harvest.

The third parable, which we find only in the Second Gospel,[556] is likewise based on facts of agricultural life. As its first words indicate, it also is directly concerned with the Kingdom of God and of the Messias.

"So is the Kingdom of God, as if a man should cast seed in the earth, and should sleep, and rise, night and day, and the seed should spring and grow up whilst he knoweth not. For the earth of itself bringeth forth fruit, first the blade, then the ear, afterwards the full corn in the ear. And when the fruit is brought forth, immediately he putteth in the sickle, because the harvest is come."

The growth of plants is no less mysterious than wonderful. It hardly depends upon man's will. When the sower has carefully prepared his field and has placed the seed in the soil, he returns home and devotes his time to his usual occupations, leaving the rest to the forces of nature, the spontaneous action of the soil, and the government of Providence. He has done all that he can. He must patiently wait for the germination, then the growth, then the ripening to follow their course, until the happy hour when the harvesting of the crop will again require his intervention. Meanwhile he does not remain indifferent to the success of his sowing. On the contrary, it is a matter of much concern to him and is often in his mind. But, aside from a general foresight, which is not very far-reaching, he has no control over what is taking place in his field. The chief idea here is the spontaneity with which the earth fructifies the seed. "Of itself it bringeth forth" [557]— this is the essential detail. We will endeavor to explain it after

[556] Mark 4: 26–29.
[557] Αὐτομάτη (Vulg., *ultro*).

we have noted the interpretation which Christ gives His disciples of the first two parables.

In the following parable, given by all three Synoptics,[558] there is again, for the fourth time, question of sowing seed, but this time the point of view is quite different. Like the parable of the cockle, this one is not elaborately developed. Jesus merely sketches the principal outlines, which are perfectly clear. In St. Mark's version, it is introduced by two questions intended to arouse the attention of the hearers.

"To what shall we liken the Kingdom of God? or to what parable shall we compare it? The Kingdom of Heaven is like to a grain of mustard seed, which a man took and sowed in his field. Which is the least indeed of all seeds; but when it is grown up, it is greater than all herbs, and becometh a tree, so that the birds of the air come, and dwell in the branches thereof."

The plant that figures in this little account is the one from which mustard is prepared. Botanists call it *sinapis nigra*. It has always been grown in the gardens of Palestine on account of its pharmaceutical properties, and this is why our Lord places it among the vegetables.[559] But it grows wild throughout the East and is often found in the West. The seed consists of very small black round kernels, four to six of them being enclosed in a pod. It is by hyperbole that Jesus speaks of it as the smallest of seeds. Its small size was proverbial among the Jews. "Small as a mustard seed," was a common saying.[560] In Bible lands the *sinapis nigra* reached a height of six or seven feet,[561] and its principal stalk subdivides into numerous sturdy branches, whence, by hyperbole, it is called a tree in this text.[562] Birds are fond of its seeds;

[558] Matt. 13 : 31 f. ; Mark 4 : 30-32 ; Luke 13 : 18 f.
[559] Luke 13 : 19.
[560] Cf. Matt. 17 : 19 ; Luke 17 : 6.
[561] Thomson, *The Land and the Book*, pp. 414-416 ; Tristram, *Natural History of the Bible*, p. 472.
[562] This detail, taken literally by some exegetes, has led them to suppose that

and they come to it in large numbers and perch on its branches, where they can more conveniently peck at the seeds. All these details, so true to nature, are introduced for the purpose of drawing attention to the interesting fact that a very small seed, due to the mysterious power with which it is endowed, brings forth a plant of considerable size.

It was remarked long ago that, in the group of the eight parables of the Kingdom of Heaven, six are connected in pairs by their subject and meaning. The preceding parable is thus connected with the parable of the leaven, which is cited by St. Matthew and St. Luke.[563]

"Whereunto shall I esteem the Kingdom of God to be like? It is like to leaven, which a woman took and hid in three measures of meal, till the whole was leavened."

Our Lord takes us from the garden to the interior of the house, where we see the housewife making bread for the family. In another work [564] we pointed out that in the ancient world this task is ordinarily performed by women. In the present case we know that the family is a large one, since the leaven is kneaded with forty quarts of flour.[565] Sara had prepared this same quantity of bread when Abraham received the visit of his three mysterious guests.[566] As in the parable of the mustard seed, though under a different aspect, the Savior here describes the rapid and powerful result that can be effected by an apparently very small cause. St. Paul says: "Know you not that a little leaven corrupteth the whole

our Lord had in mind the tree called *Salvadora persica*, which is frequently to be seen in Egypt and of which a few specimens are to be found near the Dead Sea. But the words "greater than all herbs" are against this opinion.

[563] Matt. 13:33; Luke 13:20 f.

[564] *L'Évangile de S. Matthieu*, p. 273. Cf. Lev. 26:26.

[565] The Greek word σάτον (Vulg., *satum*) comes from the Aramaic *sa'ta'*, which corresponds to the Hebrew *se'ah*, meaning a measure equal to about fourteen quarts. See Josephus, *Ant.*, IX, ii, 5, and St. Jerome, *Expos. in Matth.*, i. h. l.

[566] Gen. 18:6.

lump?" [567] In the previous parable, the power of expansion is considered in its outward effects. Here it acts within, entering into and transforming whatever it can reach. Later on we shall see that the mustard seed and the leaven express parallel ideas regarding the Kingdom of Heaven, and that there is an important shade of difference in the ideas.

St. Matthew and St. Mark [568] at this point insert a remark which separates the first five parables of the Kingdom of Heaven from the three that we have yet to consider. The first part of the remark, as we read it in St. Matthew's Gospel, is this: "All these things Jesus spoke in parables to the multitudes; and without parables He did not speak to them." The last detail, which is repeated verbatim by St. Mark, must not be pressed to excess and must not be applied to all the rest of our Lord's public life, for again and again we shall find Him using the ordinary and direct form of teaching when He addresses the multitudes. But it shows beyond question that at this period He really modified the form of His preaching, usually presenting it in parables. We shall soon learn the reasons for this fact. St. Mark, after saying: "With many such parables He spoke to them the word," adds: "according as they were able to hear," which most naturally and probably means that He kept His preaching within the grasp of His hearers, adapting it to their mental capacity.

St. Mark acquaints us with another interesting fact. These many parables were often hard to understand. But the Savior "apart, explained all things to His disciples." And presently we shall hear some of His interpretations from His own lips. Many ancient philosophers and leaders of sects held certain esoteric and hidden doctrines, which they made known only to the initiated, but kept secret from all others. Not so Christ. He revealed Himself openly. When Caiphas asks

[567] 1 Cor. 5 : 6.
[568] Matt. 13 : 34 f.; Mark 4 : 33 f.

Him about His teaching, He can answer in all truth:
"I have spoken openly to the world. I have always taught in
the synagogue and in the Temple, whither all the Jews resort;
and in secret I have spoken nothing." [569] Whoever wished to
be enlightened on such or such a parable or on any other
point, had only to imitate the disciples and ask the Master, for
He was always willing to answer. And whenever there was
question of truths regarding practical morality, Jesus always
expressed Himself with the greatest simplicity and clearness.
St. Mark's words refer especially to the Kingdom of Heaven
and to its "mysteries"; Jesus had sound reasons for maintaining a prudent reserve about them at that time.

St. Matthew also adds to his general remark about the
Savior's parables. In accordance with his usual manner, he
emphasizes the relation that existed between this new sort
of preaching and the Old Testament prophecies. He says:
"Without parables He did not speak to them, that it might be
fulfilled which was spoken by the prophet, saying: I will open
my mouth in parables, I will utter things hidden from the
foundation of the world." This passage, taken from Psalm
77,[570] is quoted faithfully, although somewhat freely. The
author of the psalm is Asaph,[571] a famous Levite. The Old
Testament calls him "the seer," [572] which is equivalent to "prophet." He recounts the marvelous deeds which God had performed for the sake of the Hebrew people, from the time of
their exodus from Egypt until after their settling in the promised land. Whereas Asaph made known only the mysteries of

---

[569] John 18: 20.

[570] It is Psalm 78 in the Hebrew text, where we read: "I will open my mouth
[to express myself] in *machal;* I will publish the mysteries [*hhidot*] of ancient
times."

[571] On the curious reading διὰ 'Ἡσάιου τοῦ προφήτου, "by the prophet Isaias,"
which slipped into some manuscripts, and which St. Jerome, *Tractat. in Ps.*, 77,
mentions for the purpose of rejecting it, see T. Zahn, *Das Evangelium des Matthäus ausgelegt,* p. 477.

[572] 2 Par. 29: 30.

Israel's history, Jesus disclosed those which were included in the history of the whole human race, from the very time of creation. Thus, while imitating the literary form employed by the poet who had been His mystical representative, He fulfilled a prophecy which referred finally, though indirectly, to His sacred Person. That was one of the secret reasons why Jesus adopted this method of teaching.

Jesus now makes known to His more intimate circle a much deeper reason for His conduct. This we read in all three Synoptics.[573] When Jesus had dismissed the crowds and returned to the house where He was then staying, the Apostles and the other disciples who had followed Him [574] asked Him this question: "Why speakest Thou to them in parables?" [575] Their astonishment presupposes that on that day there had been something out of the ordinary in their Master's preaching. Contrary to His custom, He had used a large number of parables. This figurative style of speaking had dimmed the clearness of His teaching. It is true that, although a parable, accompanied by its authentic commentary, facilitates the understanding of an idea, yet a series of parables in immediate succession and without explanation is apt to produce obscurity.

The Savior, considering the question a reasonable one, replied with His usual condescension: "Because to you it is given to know the mysteries of the Kingdom of Heaven; but to them it is not given. For he that hath, to him shall be given, and he shall abound; but he that hath not, from him shall be taken away that also which he hath. Therefore do I speak to them in parables; because seeing they see not, and hearing they hear not, neither do they understand. And the prophecy

[573] Matt. 13: 10–17; Mark 4: 10–12; Luke 8: 9 f. St. Matthew's narrative is by far the most complete; St. Luke's is much abridged.

[574] In the Greek text St. Mark makes use of an extraordinary expression: οἱ περὶ αὐτὸν σὺν τοῖς δώδεκα, "those [who were] about Him with the Twelve."

[575] Matt. 13: 10.

of Isaias is fulfilled in them, who saith: By hearing you shall hear, and shall not understand; and seeing you shall see, and shall not perceive. For the heart of this people is grown gross, and with their ears they have been dull of hearing, and their eyes they have shut, lest at any time they should see with their eyes, and hear with their ears, and understand with their heart, and be converted, and I should heal them. But blessed are your eyes, because they see, and your ears, because they hear. For, amen I say to you, many prophets and just men have desired to see the things that you see, and have not seen them, and to hear the things that you hear and have not heard them." [576]

Jesus first makes a distinction between those who believed in Him—Apostles, disciples who followed Him more or less frequently, disciples in a broader sense—and those "that are without." This last expression He used, as we read in St. Mark's account,[577] to designate all those who obstinately kept themselves outside the friendly circle which formed the nascent Church. To the former, God granted the immense privilege of having clearly manifested to them the mysteries of the Kingdom of Heaven. That kingdom is itself a deep mystery and, besides, it has its state secrets, which no one can learn or understand without a particular revelation. Many truths regarding the nature of the Messianic Kingdom and the conditions of its foundation had been proclaimed by the prophets and recorded in the writings of the Old Testament, but in terms that were often obscure. To His disciples Jesus gradually disclosed all these things; to the others, at least for the time being, He announced those truths enclosed in parables. On the one hand, therefore, this form of teaching had a pedagogical character; on the other hand, it was what we might call disciplinary.

[576] Matt. 13: 11–17.
[577] Toís ἔξω (Vulg., *illis qui foris sunt*). St. Paul designates the pagans by this

Hence the parables have, in a way, two quite different aspects: one luminous, the other obscure. In this respect they are like the cloud and the pillar of fire that gave light to the Hebrews and hid them from the eyes of the Egyptians. Literary critics and philosophers alike are unanimous in acknowledging the existence of this double effect. It is undeniable that, as Quintillian remarks,[578] the parable sheds light on the thought and helps the understanding of it. And it is no less true, as Macrobius says,[579] that it obscures the thought, "protecting its secret by means of the figures." Tertullian says [580] that the parables "cast a shadow upon the light of the Gospel"; and in another place he says that "God comes to the aid of faith, assisting it by means of figures and parables." [581] The parable, by its attractive and vivid nature, by its varied colors, and by the beings that it introduces, excites attention, arouses curiosity, and awakens the understanding, which at once begins to search for the meaning. It becomes deeply imprinted in the memory, provoking investigation and inquiry.[582] It played the part of stimulator, especially among the Jews, who, like all Orientals, preferred concrete to abstract language, the popular and dramatized expression of an idea to its philosophical and methodical expression.[583] But the other side of the question is equally true. "If the matter is very elevated, the parable, approaching the subject only indirectly, is not of such a nature as to shed full light upon it." [584]

---

same phrase. Cf. 1 Cor. 5:12 f.; Col. 4:5; 1 Tim. 3:7. The rabbis applied it to non-Jews. See Lightfoot, *Horae Hebr. et Talmud.*, p. 4.

[578] *Institut.*, VIII, 3–72.

[579] *Somnium Scip.*, I, 2.

[580] *De Resurrect. Carnis*, 32.

[581] *De Anima*, 18.

[582] Seneca, *Epist. ad Lucil.*, LIX, 6.

[583] St. Jerome wrote, *Exposit. in Matth.* XIII: *"Familiare est Syris et maxime Palaestinis, ad omnem sermonem suum parabolas jungere, ut quod per simplex praeceptum teneri ab auditoribus non potest, per similitudinem exemplaque teneatur."*

[584] Lagrange, *Revue Biblique*, 1909, p. 367.

"Jesus' parables are not sufficiently clear with regard to their object, which naturally is mysterious." [585]

The obscurity of this literary form is attested in the Old Testament and also in Talmudic literature. The poets and prophets of Israel more than once add to the word *machal* another noun,[586] which likewise designates a literary production that requires an explanation in order to be understood. In the Talmud [587] we read: "God spoke face to face with Moses; to Balaam He spoke only in parables" (that is, in obscure terms).[588] The very features which make the parables pleasing and partly luminous, contribute to veil and complicate the thought which it is their purpose to express. Of this we have a proof in the disciples' failure to understand. In all literatures, the more concise and elegant language of poetry is usually less clear than that of simple prose.

Let us now pass to the second part of our Lord's reply. It indicates the reason why His preaching, when thereafter it is addressed to the crowds, would, at least for a while, frequently have to take the form of parables. He will act thus by virtue of a divine decree, based on the moral difference that separated His hearers into two distinct classes. To well-disposed souls it will bring light, if not immediately, at least after they have reflected or, if need be, consulted so as to reach an exact interpretation. But, on the contrary, it will put a bandage over the eyes of those who are indifferent or hostile, and it will thus possess a penal character in their case.

---

[585] *Ibid.*, 1910, p. 18.

[586] In Hebrew *hhidah,* which the Septuagint translates quite exactly by πρόβλημα, αἴνιγμα, "problem, enigma." Cf. Prov. 1:6; Ex. 17:2 etc. See also Ecclu. 39:3; 47:15, 17.

[587] *Midrash, Bemidbar,* 14.

[588] An allusion to Ex. 33:11 and Num. 23:7, 18. In this last passage, the revelations which God made to Balaam are designated by the word *machal.* John 16:25-29, the expression "speak in proverbs" (ἐν παροιμίαις) is likewise used as opposed to "speak plainly," openly (παρρησίᾳ).

Again will be fulfilled Isaias' terrible prophecy,[589] which he uttered in God's name against his sinful compatriots. In both cases, the obstinate unbelief of some and the wilful indifference of others and their great ingratitude will be punished by the withdrawal of the graces which they had abused. Of what use would it be to continue giving "that which is holy," the "pearls" of the gospel, to unworthy men? [590] Rather was it an act of kindness not to bestow these gifts upon them. In this way their punishment was accompanied by mercy, since it prevented a new sin on their part, the guilt of again knowingly rejecting God's grace, and since it offered them another opportunity to seek, question, understand, and be converted. It is evident that Jesus, even while punishing them, did not purpose to blind absolutely the men whom He had come to save.[591]

After this condemnation, which Jesus must have uttered reluctantly, He speaks of the choice and privileged graces conferred upon His blessed disciples. Their eyes see, their ears hear, their minds understand, while thousands of their fellow-Jews remain blind and deaf. In fact, they are more highly favored than were so many prophets and saints of the Old Covenant—so many kings, too, as the Third Gospel says—who had longed for the coming of the Messias and eagerly desired to behold Him, but who had been deprived of that happiness.[592]

We have just explained at some length Jesus' answer to His disciples' question. At the same time they asked Him another question,[593] as to the meaning of the parable of the

---

[589] Is. 6:9 f. This prophecy is here quoted rather literally, according to the Greek of the Septuagint. St. Matthew is the only one to quote it in full.

[590] Cf. Matt. 7:6.

[591] See Appendix XVII.

[592] Cf. Heb. 11:13, 39 f.

[593] Mark 4:10; Luke 7:9.

sower, which they frankly acknowledged that they did not understand. Jesus seemed to be surprised. He said to them: "Are you ignorant of this parable? And how shall you know all parables?" To some extent it contained the key to the others. These words of our Lord throw light on the state of mind of His best disciples at this period of His ministry. They were imperfect, slow to grasp His teaching. But at any rate they were desirous of being informed and they took the best means to arrive at a full understanding. The figurative language of the parables produced in them the very result desired by the Savior: it aroused their curiosity and their eagerness to know. With such a Master it was easy for them to have explained what they had not understood. Jesus then interpreted the parable as follows:

"Hear you therefore the parable of the sower. When anyone heareth the word of the kingdom, and understandeth it not, there cometh the wicked one and catcheth away that which was sown in his heart: this is he that received the seed by the wayside. And he that received the seed upon stony ground, is he that heareth the word, and immediately receiveth it with joy. Yet hath he not root in himself, but is only for a time; and when there ariseth tribulation and persecution because of the word, he is presently scandalized. And he that received the seed among thorns is he that heareth the word, and the care of this world and the deceitfulness of riches choketh up the word, and he becometh fruitless. But he that received the seed upon good ground, is he that heareth the word, and understandeth, and beareth fruit, and yieldeth the one an hundredfold, and another sixty, and another thirty." [594]

Jesus does not say that He is the Sower; but this fact is evidently implied in the account. As He had distinguished four kinds of ground and four different fates of the good seed, so He distinguishes four kinds of souls, three of which

[594] We have quoted according to St. Mark, 4: 13-20. The text in St. Matthew, 13: 18-23, and that in St. Luke, 8: 11-15, differ from it merely in simple shades of expression.

do not profit by the preaching of the gospel. If that preaching does not always bear fruit, the fault is to be found in the imperfect or evil dispositions of many hearers. Our Lord shows Himself to be a profound psychologist as, in a few words, He sketches these portraits of hardened hearts, of shallow hearts, of dissipated hearts, none of them profiting by the divine word, and of well-disposed hearts which produce abundant fruit.

As we read in the Second and Third Gospels,[595] Jesus added a few pregnant words which showed the disciples how necessary it is to hear the word of God with attention and zeal. St. Matthew omits these lines here because he had occasion to quote them at other points in His Gospel.[596] They express important general truths. It is therefore not surprising that our Lord repeated them. "Doth a candle come in to be put under a bushel, or under a bed? and not to be set on a candlestick? For there is nothing hid, which shall not be made manifest; neither was it made secret, but that it may come abroad. If any man have ears to hear, let him hear. And He said to them: Take heed what you hear. In what measure you mete, it shall be measured to you again, and more shall be given to you. For he that hath, to him shall be given; and he that hath not, that also which he hath shall be taken away from him."

These words, which are in the style of proverbs, contain no obscurity. The mysteries of the Kingdom of Heaven are not intended to be kept hidden. Jesus communicates them to His disciples that they may preach them in due time from the housetops. It is not sensible to set a lighted lamp under a bushel. Therefore Christ's future missionaries should listen attentively to the divine word, that they may become filled with it and generously spread it abroad. The greater their zeal, the

---

[595] Mark 4: 21–25; Luke 8: 16–18.

[596] In the Sermon on the Mount, Matt. 5: 15; 7: 2, and in the pastoral instruction addressed to the Twelve, Matt. 10: 26.

greater will be their reward in Heaven. The proverbial saying, "He that hath, to him shall be given," [597] expresses a law
of the moral as well as of the physical world. Equivalent sayings are to be found in the proverbs of many peoples.[598] In
fact, no one acquires anything save by means of what he has
and in proportion thereto. The Savior's disciples saw their
religious knowledge constantly increasing, whereas the mass
of the people, having become indifferent or unbelieving, day
by day were losing what they had at first acquired by listening
to Jesus.

The disciples were pleased at having their question answered. They then make a third request: "Master, expound
to us the parable of the cockle of the field." That parable presented a serious difficulty. Why does that pernicious plant,
the cockle, exist in the Kingdom of Heaven, the great abode
of all good things? Again the kind Master at once heeds the
prayer of His devoted friends and gives them a clear, concise commentary on the third parable.[599]

"He that soweth the good seed, is the Son of Man. And the field
is the world. And the good seed are the children of the Kingdom.
And the cockle are the children of the wicked one. And the enemy that
sowed them is the devil. But the harvest is the end of the world. And
the reapers are the angels. Even as cockle therefore is gathered up
and burnt with fire, so shall it be at the end of the world. The Son
of Man shall send His angels, and they shall gather out of His Kingdom all scandals, and them that work iniquity. And shall cast them
into the furnace of fire; there shall be weeping and gnashing of teeth.
Then shall the just shine as the sun, in the Kingdom of their Father."

This entire passage is a striking antithesis: The Son of
Man and the devil working beside each other in this world,
the one to save men, the other to destroy them; "the children

---

[597] St. Matthew inserts it a little earlier, 13:12.
[598] *"Dantur opes nulli nunc nisi divitibus."* (Martial, V, 81.)
[599] Only St. Matthew has preserved it, 13:37-43.

[*i. e.,* the subjects] of the Kingdom" and "the children of the wicked one," [600] the devil; the present time when, even in the Church of Christ, evil coexists with good, and the consummation of the ages; the elect and the damned; the everlasting glory of the former, symbolized by the resplendent brightness with which "the Father" will surround them, and the eternal suffering of the latter in the flames of hell. "He that hath ears to hear, let him hear"—such are the final words of this dramatic and tragic description.

To reward His disciples' good dispositions, Jesus continued the conversation, telling them three other parables of the Kingdom of Heaven. They are found only in the First Gospel, where the account leads us to suppose that the Divine Master had then no other hearers. The sixth and seventh parables, those of the hidden treasure and of the pearl of great price, are closely connected, as were the third and fourth, to express the same thought with only slight differences.

"The Kingdom of Heaven is like unto a treasure hidden in a field. Which a man having found, hid it, and for joy thereof goeth, and selleth all that he hath, and buyeth that field. Again the Kingdom of Heaven is like to a merchant seeking good pearls. Who when he had found one pearl of great price, went his way, and sold all that he had, and bought it." [601]

Orientals, inclined to be suspicious, have always been accustomed to bury articles of great value whenever those articles were considered to be in danger, for they thought there was no better means of security.[602] It is sometimes asked whether the man who found the treasure and who, to be sure of its possession, bought the field without letting the owner know of his discovery, acted in a manner conformable to justice. But in this parable as in that of the dishonest steward,

---

600. This is the import of the Greek text: οἱ υἱοὶ τοῦ πονηροῦ.
601 Matt. 13:44–46.
602 Cf. Job 3:21; Prov. 2:4; Jer. 41:8 etc.

Jesus does not pass judgment on the morality of the acts. He simply proposes an example and urges that it be imitated in that respect in which it contains something good to help in acquiring the Kingdom of Heaven. Moreover, the Jewish law of that time did not regard the acquisition of a field under such circumstances as unjust.[603] The ancients attached immense value to beautiful pearls, considering them, as Pliny the Elder informs us,[604] the most estimable of all gems. Hence the joy of the merchant who succeeded in finding one of very great price and who did not think he was giving too much when he sacrificed all he had in order to possess it. Like the treasure in the field, this single gem would constitute a fortune much greater than the goods sold in exchange for it. These two little parables have as their basis the fact that men are ready to give the most valuable things they have, that they may acquire something which seems to them still more precious. Since the Kingdom of Heaven is an incomparable treasure, a pearl of great price, we should make personal efforts to discover it and should eagerly sacrifice whatever we have in order to gain possession of it.

The eighth and last parable [605] is somewhat more developed and accompanied by a brief commentary. It parallels that of the cockle; fundamentally it teaches the same lesson.

"Again the Kingdom of Heaven is like to a net cast into the sea, and gathering together all kind of fishes. Which, when it was filled, they drew out, and sitting by the shore, they chose out the good into vessels, but the bad they cast forth. So shall it be at the end of the world. The angels shall go out and shall separate the wicked from among the just. And shall cast them into the furnace of fire; there shall be weeping and gnashing of teeth."

---

[603] See Edersheim, *Life and Times of Jesus the Messiah*, I, 595; Fillion, *L'Évangile de S. Matthieu, Introd. Critiq. et Comment.*, p. 278.

[604] *Hist. Nat.*, IX, 34.

[605] Matt. 13 : 47–50.

Thus, even in the Kingdom of God, even in the Church of the Messias, as in the wheat field where an enemy sowed cockle, as in the net [606] which gathers in its meshes bad fish as well as good, evil exists at the side of virtue; and it will be so to the end of time. Then only will take place, and for ever, the separation of the two opposite elements. If we read again Christ's interpretation of the parable of the cockle, we are struck by the similarity of details in the two parables. We also note the antagonism that will continue till the last hour between the devil and the Son of Man for the destruction or the salvation of mankind, and we observe the majesty with which Christ announces His decisive victory. But in the present parable our Lord dwells more on the future separation of the good from the wicked, and on the final transformation of the Kingdom of Heaven.

Having finished His explanations, Jesus asked His disciples: "Have ye understood all these things?" [607] "Yes, Master," they answer with some pride. They had not comprehended everything in detail; but, thanks to the Savior's interpretations, they had grasped the general sense of many of the parables of the Kingdom, and they divined the meaning of the others. Jesus then said, by way of encouragement: "Therefore every scribe instructed in the Kingdom of Heaven is like to a man that is a householder, who bringeth forth out of his treasure new things and old." These words contain another important lesson for them all. Since they are destined for the noble office of teachers in the Church of the Messias, they should imitate the example of a wise and prudent father, who opportunely procures all sorts of provisions and knows how to make proper use of them ac-

---

[606] There is question here of a seine (σαγήνη, sagena), a long net drawn through the water, the two ends of which are then brought together so as to enclose all the fish that are along its route. See Fillion, *Atlas Archéologique de la Bible,* 2d ed., pl. XLI, figs. 1, 6, and Lucian, *Piscat.,* p. 51.

[607] Matt. 13: 51.

cording to the needs of his children or his guests, serving things old and new so as to satisfy everyone. Hence the disciples should strive to acquire a wide knowledge that they may become fitted to announce the gospel with greater fruit.

Let us now cast a retrospective glance over this first series of parables, and let us try to obtain a better view of their harmonious connection by means of a few notions that apply to them as a whole. Each of them relates to the Messianic Kingdom. But this relation does not take place in the same manner in each case; for these parables show us the Church of Christ under different aspects, one after the other, so that each time we receive a new lesson. "It is a most happy diversity in a perfect unity. The parables enable us to witness the growth and development of the Kingdom of God on earth, from its foundation by our Lord Jesus Christ to its glorious transfiguration in Heaven. . . . It has sometimes been considered that each parable corresponds, in an exclusive way, to a precise epoch of Church history: for example, the parable of the sower to Apostolic times; that of the cockle, to the period of the early heresies; that of the mustard seed, to the Constantinian epoch, and so forth. But this view is not correct. The parables of the Kingdom thus far considered prophesy, not so much particular details of her history, but rather the general future of the Church, the universal laws that are to direct her in the course of ages, not during definite, isolated periods. Thus the parable of the sower sets forth the reasons for the success, and especially the lack of success, which it will encounter in the world. The parable of the cockle describes the obstacles that await the Kingdom of Heaven when it has been established in some place and labors to attain its complete development; this parable also makes known the real author of that hostile opposition and foretells the final triumph of the gospel. The parable of the seed which was sowed and then left to its own powers represents the divine Kingdom, which grows slowly at first, without any human action, and then passes through its successive evolutions and makes magnificent progress. The next two parables express the growth of the Messianic Kingdom on earth, according to the double mode of its manifestation: there is the extrinsic energy, figured by the mustard seed, which becomes a great tree capable of sheltering all the birds of the air, that is, all the nations of the earth; there is also the intrinsic force, figured by the leaven, by which the whole world is fermented. . . . The parables of the hidden treasure and of the pearl of great price declare what are men's duties with regard to the Kingdom founded by Christ, and their obligation to abandon everything in order to belong to it, after they have searched for it and discovered it. Lastly, the parable of the net shows us how good and evil, after long existing beside each other in the Church of Christ, will be eternally separated by God at the end of time, and how each person will be treated according to his merits. There is a logical connection between the eight parables, so that they mutually explain and supplement one another." [608]

The Savior, in explaining some of His parables, marked out rules that are very useful to the exegete for explaining all the others. It is important to separate, by a sufficiently deep study, the principal idea which each parable directly purposes to emphasize. In seeking to decide what this idea is, we are aided by the historical situation that served as the occasion for the parable, by such or such a remark with which Jesus or the Evangelists introduced it. [609] In the first and third series, the words, "The Kingdom of Heaven is like . . . ," largely contain the dominant idea. Once this is

---

[608] Fillion, *L'Évangile de S. Matthieu*, p. 281.

[609] Cf. Matt. 18: 21–35; Luke 10: 29–37; 14: 15–24; 15: 1–32, etc. Sometimes it is the conclusion that reveals the parent idea. Cf. Matt. 7: 9–11; Luke 11: 11–13, etc.

known, we can group about it, as their center, the various
details that develop it, at the same time having a care to distinguish essential details from those which are simply literary.
No account need be taken of these latter, which add nothing
to the meaning of the parable, but merely constitute its frame-
work. By wishing to explain everything and by departing
from the literal sense, a commentator often falls into forced
and exaggerated applications, as Tertullian and St. John
Chrysostom complained.[610] It is better to follow the example
of the Divine Master, who, in the interpretation of the parables of the sower and of the cockle, attaches value to details
that apparently are only secondary (for example, the birds,
the thorns, the burning heat), in applying them to the spiritual life; and He passes over other incidents of the same class
(the sleep of the landowner in whose field the cockle was
sown, the servants' offer of their services, the wheat gathered
into sheaves). In this domain, the limits of which cannot be
exactly laid down, the interpreter's prudence and discernment
play an important and delicate part.[611]

III. A Series of Great Miracles. Another Lack of Success at Nazareth

Within a period of less than twenty-four hours (so it
would seem) Jesus performs six miracles. They greatly add
to His reputation and arouse the enthusiasm of the multitudes more than ever. In the first miracle He subdues one of
the most terrifying forces of nature; in the second He wins
a victory over the devils; in the third, fifth, and sixth, He
restores health to certain sick people; in the fourth, He restores life to one who was dead.[612]

[610] Tertullian, *De Pudic.*, IX; St. John Chrysostom, *Hom. in Matth.*, LXIV, 3.
[611] Buzy gives some excellent guiding principles on this point, in the *Revue Biblique*, 1916, pp. 406–422.
[612] Appendix XIX replies to some objections of the Rationalists.

All three Synoptics relate the episode of the calming of the tempest.[613] St. Matthew sketches the incident briefly; St. Mark gives a dramatic and more ample description of it; St. Luke's account falls between these two. All three narratives are, to an unusual degree, in harmony with the circumstances of time and place.

As St. Mark expressly says, the event occurred in the evening of the memorable and laborious day when Jesus refuted the calumny of the Pharisees and propounded the parables of the Kingdom of Heaven. Being desirous of withdrawing from the plaudits of the populace, He left to His Apostles the task of gently dismissing the crowd. When the Apostles rejoined Him in the little boat from which He had addressed the people and which He seems not to have left,[614] He said to them: "Let us pass over to the other side" of the lake. As He was then on the western side, He was indicating the eastern shore, a less populous and quieter district, where His followers were then less numerous. He departed "even as He was," says St. Mark, that is, without making any special preparations. Other boats, probably carrying disciples who were loath to be separated from the Divine Master, set out shortly afterwards. As they are not mentioned in the rest of the account, this little flotilla must have been scattered by the tempest. Jesus, tired by the overwhelming labors of the day, lay down in the bottom of the boat, at the stern near the deck, His head resting on a rough cushion. St. Mark, who records these details, evidently obtained them from St. Peter. The Savior soon fell into a deep sleep. This is the only passage in the Gospel where there is mention of Jesus sleeping. This detail shows the reality of His human nature and the share it had in the weaknesses of our nature.

When Christ and the Apostles set out, the lake was calm.

613 Matt. 8: 18, 23–27; Mark 4: 35–40; Luke 8: 22–25.
614 Cf. Mark 4: 1 f., 35 f.

There was no sign of a coming storm. But inland lakes, surrounded by high mountains, are subject to sudden gales which stir up frightful tempests. This fact is especially true of Lake Tiberias because of the depth of the basin in which it lies.[615] The neighboring gorges serve as passageways through which the wind hurls itself with dreadful violence. Travelers and Palestinologists have often referred to this characteristic of the Sea of Galilee, which is ordinarily very calm. "It is always necessary to take the greatest precautions when you sail on this treacherous lake, where the wind often attains extraordinary violence. Twice we experienced the deepest anxiety when our boat was shaken by furious waves. . . . The least false maneuver would have capsized the boat. In fact, we kept shipping so much water that two men hardly sufficed to bail it out with metal pails. Huge black clouds piled up on the horizon. The wind, coming down from the mountain, blew a tempest, and the surface of the lake was covered with whitecaps." [616] It is a similar description which the Evangelists give of the storm which broke loose upon that same lake and raged over its surface. St. Matthew designates it by a word that is generally used to represent the violent disturbance caused by an earthquake.[617] St. Mark and St. Luke call it by its correct name: it was a whirlwind.[618] Enormous waves rose up, shook the little boat, poured into it, and threatened to smash it or sink it. Humanly speaking, the danger was extreme, as St. Luke says in explicit terms. Yet Jesus "was asleep." What a contrast is expressed by these simple words of St. Matthew! But the Savior was soon awakened

---

[615] We should bear in mind that it is situated about 680 feet below the level of the Mediterranean.

[616] Lortet, *La Syrie d'Aujourd'hui*, p. 502. See also Robinson, *Palästina und die angrenzenden Länder*, III, 571; K. Ritter, *Erdkunde*, XV, 308; Tristram, *Land of Israel*, p. 43; G. A. Smith, *Historical Geography of Palestine*, p. 441.

[617] Σεισμός.

[618] Λαῖλαψ.

by the cries of distress which the Apostles began to utter, thinking their last hour had come. "Master," they called to Him, "save us, we perish. . . . Master, doth it not concern Thee that we perish? . . . Master, Master, we perish." It is not unlikely that these three expressions, mentioned by one or other of the Synoptics,[619] were uttered at the same time. They voice the same request. The abrupt character of the phrases indicates anguish in the face of a dreadful peril.

Jesus at once stood up, threatened [620] the wind, which was the direct cause of the storm, then said to the sea in a stern voice: "Peace, be still." He rebuked the wind and the sea as though they were rational but rebellious beings and commanded them to be peaceful. In obedience to that command, the wind ceased at once and the angry waves became calm. This last detail was by itself a miracle, because, after a tempest, the surface of the ocean or of lakes does not become completely calm for hours. There is a delightful beauty in this identical remark of the three Evangelists: *"Et facta est tranquillitas magna."*

But the Savior gently rebukes the Twelve, saying: "Why are you fearful, O ye of little faith? Have you not faith yet?" They had faith up to a certain point, and had just shown it by calling upon their Master for succor in their peril. But it was far from perfect in spite of so many proofs which Jesus had given them of His power, since they were not at once convinced that His presence was enough to guarantee their safety, and since it was impossible that He should perish in the waves, as His work on earth was far from being completed.

Following this great miracle, a different sort of fright

---

[619] The first by St. Matthew, the second by St. Mark, the third by St. Luke.

[620] In the Greek, ἐπετίμησεν, which the Vulgate translates by three different expressions: *imperavit* (Matth.), *comminatus est* (Mark), *increpavit* (Luke). In other passages the Evangelists make use of this same verb to designate Christ's commands to a fever (Luke 4:39), to the devils (Mark 9:24), etc.

seized them for a moment, the awe which everyone feels in the presence of the supernatural. They said to one another: "Who [621] is this (think you), that He commandeth both the winds and the sea, and they obey Him?" No one knew better than did these fishermen that the wind and the sea are untamed, impetuous creatures which only the divine power can rule. Hence, although the Apostles had, with their own eyes, beheld so many great miracles of the Savior, this which they just witnessed stirred within them a new degree of admiration, because of its more grandiose character. Never had the annals of Israel seen its like.[622]

And yet, on that very day, the disciples were to be present at other miracles scarcely less impressive. The first one is a victory which their Master wins over the devils.[623] Jesus disembarked on the eastern shore, "which is over against Galilee," says St. Luke, in a district which is hard to determine. All three Evangelists mention the name of a region. But such a complication of variants on this point has crept into the three texts, that the determination of the primitive reading is beset with difficulties. The Greek manuscripts and the versions speak of the Gadarenians, the Gerasenians, and the Gergesenians,[624] so that we have to choose between the districts of the cities of Gadara, Gerasa, and Gergesa. We can eliminate Gerasa (the Sherach of to-day), which is located

---

[621] Ποταπός. St. Matthew: *Qualis et quantus.*

[622] For the Rationalist interpretations, see Appendix XIX. Our readers are acquainted with the beautiful spiritual applications of this episode to the Christian Church, like a bark tossed on the waves and seeming to be in danger; but it will not sink because its divine Founder is always with it to protect it. Tertullian (*De Baptismo,* 12), developed this allegory. See also St. Hippolytus, *Antichr.,* 59.

[623] Matt. 8:28–34; Mark 5:1–20; Luke 8:26–39. Again this time St. Matthew gives only a short sketch, whereas St. Mark's account is brilliant and quite detailed.

[624] Γαδαρηνῶν, Γερασηνῶν, and Γεργεσηνῶν. For the discussion of this point of textual criticism, see the large commentaries, notably T. Zahn, *Das Evangelium des Matthäus ausgelegt,* 2d ed., p. 360, and also Westcott and Hort, *The New Testament in the Original Greek,* 2d ed., Vol. II, p. 11 of the Appendix.

about forty miles southeast of Lake Tiberias. Gadara (to-day Mkes) to the south, although much nearer, was three hours' journey (seven miles) from the lake shore, whereas the account supposes a place whose territory was in the immediate vicinity of the lake. There remains Gergesa, which is now generally identified with the ruins called Kersa or Kursi (discovered in 1860), not far from the eastern shore, opposite Magdala, near the place where the Semak River flows into the lake. Nearby are some natural grottoes in the rocks which may formerly have been used as tombs. This is the only place along the shore where there is a hill rising from the water's edge and corresponding to the one which figures in the final scene of the episode.[625]

Jesus and His companions had taken but a few steps on shore, when two demoniacs [626] rushed toward them from a distance, coming out from the tombs, which were their place of abode. Having reached our Lord, they prostrated themselves at His feet in involuntary homage, and cried out: "What have we to do with Thee, Jesus, the Son of the most high God? Art Thou come hither to torment us before the time?" These are almost the identical words that were used by the possessed men of Capharnaum in addressing the Savior.[627] The words, "before the time," mean before the end

[625] See Thomson, *The Land and the Book,* pp. 375–378; Wilson, *Recovery of Jerusalem,* p. 369; Buhl, *Geographie des alten Palästina,* p. 243; Eusebius, in his *Onomasticon,* mentions a κωμή (*viculus* in St. Jerome's translation) named Gergesa and in his time still existing in those parts. Procopius of Gaza (about 500) also points out this locality, but as being in ruins.

[626] There is another little problem to be solved, the question as to the number of possessed persons in the Gergesa episode. St. Matthew introduces two; St. Mark and St. Luke speak only of one. St. John Chrysostom and St. Augustine offer a quite reasonable solution. There were in reality two demoniacs; but St. Mark and St. Luke point out only the fiercer and better known of them (*"personae alicujus clarioris seu famosioris,"* St. Augustine, *De Cons. Evang.,* II, 56), the one who plays the principal part in the account.

[627] Mark 1: 24; Luke 4: 34. Here the devils add to the name of God the epithet ὑψίστου, *altissimi,* frequently occurring in the Old Testament under the Hebraic form *Eliyon.*

of the world and the time of the general judgment; for until
then the devils, by God's permission, enjoy over nature, and
especially over man, a real power, which enables them to
gratify, at least in part, their hatred against the Kingdom
of Heaven by striving to injure it as much as possible. To
torment them before the time would therefore be to send them
"into the abyss," as St. Luke expresses it, that is, into the
depths of hell. This is why their adjuration is so urgent. Like
fugitive slaves that have been captured, they tremble upon
approaching their Master, certain that a severe punishment
awaits them.

St. Mark and St. Luke give us a vivid and terrible picture
of one of these demoniacs, who had been in the power of the
evil spirits for a long time. He wore no clothes and lived in
a perpetual paroxysm of madness. To prevent his inflicting
injuries on others, his hands and feet had often been bound
with iron; but, like Samson,[628] he had broken the chains and
fetters. No one had been able to tame him. He was wont to
run madly over the mountain, uttering cries like wild beasts
and wounding himself with stones, as if he wished to kill
himself. The other demoniac was scarcely less dreadful; for
St. Matthew speaks of both of them as being "exceeding
fierce," so that they frightened the whole country round. No
one dared pass along the roads which they were accustomed
to use. "Amid all the boasted civilization of antiquity, there
existed no hospitals, no penitentiaries, no asylums; and unfortunates of this class, being too dangerous and desperate
for human intercourse, could only be driven forth from
among their fellowmen, and restrained from mischief by
measures at once inadequate and cruel." [629]

The two possessed men of Gergesa earnestly begged Christ
not to disturb them. He ordered them to leave their un-

[628] Judges 16:8 f.
[629] Farrar, *Life of Christ*, I, 334.

fortunate victims in peace. Before finally driving them out, He asked that demoniac whose mad state we described, "What is thy name?" The purpose of this question was to show the full extent of the miracle which He was about to perform. The devil answered: "My name is Legion, for we are many." He haughtily took this name in an effort to defy the Savior. The Roman legion was but too well known in Palestine ever since Judea had become an integral part of the Empire. It usually contained five or six thousand soldiers. Evidently we need not here take this figure literally. But it does indicate that the man by whose mouth the devil was speaking, had been transformed into a Satanic camp where numerous spirits were garrisoned.

Notwithstanding the proud boastfulness of their reply, this diabolic assemblage felt their powerlessness; for, as St. Mark adds, they made a second request of Jesus, beseeching Him not to drive them out of the district. As men do, so too the fallen angels experience fears and desires. Those who thus implored Jesus' mercy were much pleased with this half-pagan country, where they could more freely exercise their harmful power. But our Lord made no reply. Then they presented their third request: "If Thou cast us out hence, send us into the herd of swine." A large herd of those animals was grazing on the mountain-side not far away. "Go," said Jesus. At once the devils, quitting the bodies of the possessed men, cast themselves into the bodies of the swine. Those irrational beasts, thereupon becoming mad, ran wildly along the steep side of the mountain and soon tumbled into the lake, which closed over its prey. These swine were two thousand in number. It has often been remarked that animals living in herds are sometimes seized by an attack of uncontrollable panic, from which serious consequences follow. Evidently the devils were not expecting this disaster, which thus caused their loss. In yielding to their wishes, Jesus caught them in their own trap, and the region was rid of their presence.

It is sometimes questioned, from the theological stand-point, whether Jesus had a right to impose so great a loss upon the owners of the swine. This query has been answered in various ways. If the herd belonged to Jews, they were justly punished, since they were engaging in a pursuit for-bidden them by the Mosaic Law. If the owners were pagans, they were at fault, because, by raising swine, they were in-sulting or tempting their Jewish neighbors. These are merely theological conjectures. But we need not concern ourselves with the morality of the Savior's act. "There are cases when power, by the very fact that it exists, guarantees the right," [630] and in this case "the service rendered was well worth such a price." [631] Otherwise, why might we not accuse Divine Provi-dence of sending to the earth either too much dry weather or too much rain? Moreover, Jesus did not command the devils to enter into the herd of swine; He simply allowed them to do so, as St. Augustine remarks: *"Expulsa et in porcos permissa dæmonia."* And the Gospel accounts make no allusion to any complaint by the inhabitants.

The news of the miracle was soon spread by the swine-herds to the neighboring town and the hamlets or farms which they passed through on their way. The people hastened from all sides to get more complete details and to obtain a close view of the Miracle-worker who had succeeded in freeing the country from such a plague. The sight presented to the public curiosity was one never to be forgotten. That one of the de-moniacs who had been the more alarming and troublesome, was sitting down near his liberator, like a disciple at the feet of his master, quiet, clothed, and in full possession of his mental faculties. Our Lord's disciples and the other witnesses of the miracle recounted what had taken place more fully and

---

[630] Godet, *Commentaire sur l'Évangile de S. Luc,* 2d ed., I, 485.
[631] A. Réville, *Jésus de Nazareth,* II, 488.

exactly than the swineherds had done. After the people's curiosity was satisfied, another feeling took possession of them, an ill-considered mercantile dread. They began to request Jesus to leave their district as soon as possible. We may easily surmise that they feared His presence might occasion them other material losses. This is the only instance in which we see the Savior's miracles produce a result of this kind.

Jesus, who did not purpose remaining in the midst of a population so ill-disposed toward Him, acceded to their pitiful request. Just as He was embarking to return to the western side of the lake, there occurred a little incident that was in conspicuous contrast with the conduct of the Gergesens. The demoniac who had been the more violently tormented by the devils begged of Christ the privilege of going with Him and of remaining with Him as one of His disciples. He wished never more to be separated from his Benefactor. But Jesus judged it best not to grant his request. However, He consoled him by entrusting to him a very estimable mission, which at once appealed to his zeal. He said to him: "Go into thy house to thy friends and tell them how great things the Lord hath done for thee and hath had mercy on thee." Happy at being thus able to serve the Savior's cause, the man departed and published his wonderful deliverance throughout Decapolis.[632] Upon hearing him, "all men wondered," [633] and no doubt this zealous missionary won many adherents for the Messias.[634]

Jesus left this region, where perchance He had intended to take some repose. He recrossed the lake, so as to return to Capharnaum. His return was impatiently awaited there; for the crowds which had regretfully seen Him depart were keep-

[632] On this province, see Vol. I, pp. 111 f.
[633] Mark 5 : 20.
[634] On the Rationalist interpretations of this prodigy, see Appendix XIX.

ing watch along the shore, to welcome Him as soon as He should reappear. "They were all waiting for Him," says St. Luke, thus noting another contrast with the request of the people of Gergesa. The Savior had scarcely stepped ashore, when He was surrounded by a large crowd. But the people respectfully drew back to open a passage for one of their religious leaders, a man named Jairus, who was the chief of one of the synagogues in the city.[635] His features bore traces of deep anguish. Jairus approached the Savior and humbly prostrated himself at His feet saying: "Lord, my daughter is at the point of death; come, lay Thy hand upon her, that she may be safe and may live." The dying girl was an only daughter, twelve years old.[636]

The kind Master could not resist such prayers. Accompanied by His Apostles, He started off toward Jairus' house, guided by the afflicted father. The crowd followed, in the hope of witnessing a great miracle of healing. The old streets of Oriental cities are narrow and crooked; a large crowd, therefore, moves along through them with difficulty, and in this case everyone tried to be close to Jesus; so that the throng pressed upon Him from all sides.

Someone has said that "grace so superabounds in this Prince of life that, while He is hastening to perform a work of power, He produces another." It is, so to speak, one miracle encased in another. The double event is related by the Synoptics, with the slight differences that we noted in connection with the two preceding miracles. St. Matthew limits himself to a brief sketch of the facts; St. Mark recounts them

---

[635] On the functions of a *rosh hakkeneseth*, or ruler of a synagogue, see Vol. I, p. 171.

[636] Hence, in St. Mark's account, the diminutive θυγάτριον, *filiola*, which was doubtless used by the father. According to St. Matthew, whose account is much abridged, Jairus said to our Lord: "My daughter is even now dead." In fact, she was dead when the Savior entered the house.

with all their details, which he obtained from St. Peter, who was a direct witness of them; St. Luke relates them with an artistic touch.[637]

The Savior and His entourage were advancing with difficulty, when the woman known in Christian history as the "hemorrhissa" [638] profited by this situation to steal, as it were, her cure without the Savior's knowledge, as she thought. She was indeed deserving of pity. For twelve years [639] she had been suffering from a flow of blood and had been thus reduced to a pitiful condition. She had consulted numerous physicians. Yet, instead of receiving the least help from them, she had suffered much at their hands and had spent her entire fortune for medicines and fees. St. Mark dwells upon these various details,[640] which make our Lord's immediate and complete success the more conspicuous. When we were describing the social conditions of Palestine in Christ's time,[641] we stated what the practice of medicine then amounted to. When we read in the rabbinical writings the recipes for curing precisely the ailment of which there is question in this incident,[642] we can well understand the pitiful despair of this woman. In fact, the Jewish physicians, as also most Greek, Roman, and other physicians, had scarcely any competency except in treating external ailments; internal diseases, which are the most frequent and the most serious, were nearly always a profound mystery to them. Hence we find them the

[637] Matt. 9: 18–26; Mark 5: 21–43; Luke 8: 40–56.

[638] It is based on the technical Greek word αἱμορροῦσα, used in the translation of the First Gospel. The other two authors have recourse to a periphrase to express the same idea: οὖσα ἐν ῥύσει αἵματος (Vulg., *quae erat in fluxu,* or *in profluvio, sanguinis*).

[639] Coinciding with the age of the girl who is to be providentially associated with her in Christ's miraculous action.

[640] St. Luke also; but he somewhat spares the physicians, his colleagues.

[641] Vol. I, p. 156.

[642] See our commentary on St. Mark's Gospel, p. 83, and our *Miracles de N.-S. Jésus-Christ,* II, 183.

object of bitter taunts in the writings of ancient [643] as well as modern authors.

Whence did this woman come? The Evangelists do not say. From St. Mark's account we might infer that her home was not in the vicinity of Capharnaum; for he uses the expression, "when she had heard of Jesus," and does not speak of her as of one who had witnessed His miracles. Further on we shall point out the traditional developments based on this statement. This woman knew by hearsay the Savior's almighty power which no physical ill withstood; she knew His merciful goodness that rejected no one, and she came to Him with boundless confidence, as to the only physician capable of restoring her health and strength. The very nature of her infirmity prevented her from openly seeking her cure at the hands of Jesus. But in her desolate soul, now filled with a holy confidence, she contrived a little scheme to obtain the much desired miracle secretly. She said within herself: "If I shall touch only the hem of His garment, I shall be healed." It is probable that by the "hem" [644] she meant the ornament (regarded as possessing a sacred character [645]), called *zizzith* in Hebrew. They were woolen tassels, each being made of three white threads and one blue thread, and were fastened to the four corners of the ample cloth that served as a cloak. This garment was worn in such a way that two corners reached over the shoulders and hung down behind. Therefore the tassels attached to those corners could easily be touched without attracting the attention of the person wearing the cloak.[646] The "hemorrhissa," with a mixture of daring and timidity, came behind Jesus as closely as possible and succeeded in touching one of these fringes. Her faith did not deceive her;

[643] Cf. Pliny, *Hist. Nat.*, XXIX, 5.
[644] We owe this interesting detail to St. Luke.
[645] Cf. Num. 15 : 37–40; Deut. 22 : 12.
[646] Fillion, *Atlas Archéologique de la Bible,* pl. CIX, figs. 2, 3, 9, 10.

for the well-being and strength which she at once felt within her revealed her complete cure to her. What joy must have been hers, after so many years of suffering!

But Jesus did not wish this miracle to pass unnoticed. On the contrary, He desired that it should serve to strengthen the faith of all who were there. He was, of course, not unaware of the cure which had taken place at the touch of His cloak. Whereas the woman "felt in her body" the favor that had been granted her, Jesus "knew in Himself," by divine perception, by His supernatural knowledge, "the virtue that had proceeded from Him." [647] Turning around quickly, He asked: "Who hath touched My garments?" This, too, He knew quite well; but He spoke thus to provoke the woman's avowal. As all those nearest Him denied having touched Him, Peter and the other disciples ingenuously showed what, as they thought, was singular in their Master's question. "The multitude throng and press Thee," they said, "and dost Thou say: Who touched Me?" They wrongly supposed that He was complaining of being jostled and shoved roughly. Without replying to them, Jesus continued to turn searching glances about Him,[648] looking for her who had touched Him. Then the woman, seeing that she was found out, cast herself, trembling and abashed, at the Savior's feet, and in the presence of all she avowed the reasons that had prompted her act and how she had been instantly cured. The Savior's purpose was attained. It remained for Him merely to confirm her cure. Still turned toward her, He said: "Daughter, thy faith hath made thee whole. Go in peace, and be thou whole of thy disease." These words show that in His eyes the woman's conduct was not tainted with any superstition, but was in all respects prompted by a sincere faith.

[647] Mark 5 : 29 f.

[648] St. Mark, περιεβλέπετο, Vulg., *circumspiciebat*. As we said above (I, 428), St. Mark is fond of noting Christ's glances and looks.

The apocryphal Gospel of Nicodemus [649] mentions the heroine of this episode under the name of Veronica and tells of her
appearing before Pilate's tribunal to testify in behalf of
Jesus at the time of His Passion. But this information does
not rest on any genuine foundation. According to an early
tradition, vouched for by Eusebius of Caesarea,[650] the "hemorrhissa," who was a pagan,—a native of Paneas, or Caesarea
Philippi, in northern Galilee—erected in her native city, in
front of her house, a bronze monument representing herself
kneeling before Jesus and suppliantly stretching her hands
toward Him, showing the Savior standing, and wearing a
cloak with fringes, with a hand extended toward the woman.
Eusebius says that he saw this monument, erected by the
"hemorrhissa" in memory of her miraculous cure. It was destroyed by Julian the Apostate, according to the statement of
the historian Sozomen.[651]

Whatever we are to think of the disputed authenticity
of this information, we know that the happy woman had
just finished her confession, when there came someone to the
chief of the synagogue, saying: "Thy daughter is dead. Why
dost thou trouble the Master any further?" This was indeed
a hard trial for Jairus. The miracle at which he was but now
present, had increased his lively faith; but of a sudden his
hopes are dashed. Jesus, who had overheard the sad news, and
who knew the distress which it caused in the soul of the
afflicted father, said to Jairus with the greatest kindness:
"Fear not; believe only and she shall be safe." Thereupon they
continued walking toward the house. When they arrived
there, a thoroughly Oriental tumult, in remarkable contrast
with the quiet with which we of the West surround our dead,
filled the house. The hired weepers were giving vent to their

[649] Chap. 7. Cf. Thilo, *Codex Apocryphus N. T.*, I, 501; Brunet, *Les Évangiles Apocryphes*, 2d ed., p. 240.

[650] *H. E.*, VII, 18.

[651] *Ibid.*, V. 11.

affected and noisy manifestations, shouting, crying, singing the praises of the deceased,[652] and wildly gesticulating as though to tear their hair. The flutists were playing their shrill and mournful airs; for these musicians were to be found at Jewish funerals, as well as at those of Rome. Since the child's death had been expected, weepers and flutists were warned to be in readiness, and they came at once upon word of the sad event. And with them relatives and neighbors, who filled the house.

Jesus, upon entering, sought to quiet all these people, saying: "Why make you this ado and weep? The damsel is not dead, but sleepeth." Evidently, by this figurative language, our Lord simply meant that, in the present case, death would not be of long duration and that, so prompt would be the return of life,[653] it would be like a short sleep. But these people, who had beheld the dead child and touched her, interpreted His words literally; they openly mocked Him who spoke thus without even having seen the child. With His calm authority, Jesus bade them leave the house. No one dared to refuse. He then entered the room where the lifeless body of the child was lying, allowing no one to go in with Him except the father and mother, and His three most intimate Apostles, Simon Peter, James the Greater, and John, that they might be witnesses of the great miracle. He came to the bed and, taking the cold hand of the dead child, said to her, in the Aramaic dialect which He ordinarily spoke: *"Talitha cumi,"* [654] that is, "Damsel, arise." He restored life to

---

[652] St. Mark, κλαίοντας καί ἀλαλάζοντας πολλά (Vulg., *flentes et ejulantes multum*).

[653] On this subject see Appendix XIII. On ancient Jewish tombs at Rome we frequently read the inscription: Ἐν εἰρήνη ἡ κοίμησις αὐτοῦ (or αὐτῆς in the feminine), "May his sleep be in peace." Cf. Schürer, *Gemeindeverfass. der Juden in Rom,* pp. 33–35.

[654] More correctly perhaps, according to some excellent Greek manuscripts: *Talitha cum.* St. Mark inserts other Aramaic expressions in his account. Cf. 7: 34; 14: 36.

her as easily as He might awaken a sleeping person. Immediately she arose and began to walk. We may imagine the parents' surprise, joy, and thankfulness.[655]

The Savior ordered that the girl be given something to eat. Thus He made it evident that He had not only restored her to life, but also to perfect health. Before leaving the house, He bade the father and mother to remain silent about this miracle. This injunction was, of course, only momentary, because it was not possible that the event should be kept secret, since a dense crowd was in the street, awaiting the result of the Savior's visit. But Jesus wished at least to have time to withdraw quietly and to avoid an enthusiastic ovation. The fame of the miracle spread through the whole country, and the Miracle-worker's glory was further increased.

As He was on His way home from Jairus' house, two blind men followed Him,[656] crying out: "Have mercy on us, O Son of David." To make Him favorable to their prayer, they gave Him the most popular title of the Messias.[657] It was an explicit act of faith, which merited and received its reward. But at first Jesus continued on His way without answering them, probably to try them and also to avoid a scene of public enthusiasm.

The Gospels contain rather frequent mention of blind men. This is not surprising, since blindness has ever been and still is one of the principal afflictions of the Biblical East. The fine dust that is in the air and gets into the eyes, the glaring sunlight, the whiteness of the ground, the coolness of the nights which are often spent outdoors, all these circumstances cause

[655] The Evangelists, who, as we have seen, scarcely pause over details of this sort, merely point out the first of these feelings, which was very keen: ἐξέστησαν ἐκστάσει μεγάλῃ, says St. Mark (Vulg., *obstupuerunt stupore magno*).

[656] St. Matthew is the only one to relate this other miracle, 9:27-31.

[657] See Vol. I, pp. 310 ff. We will meet with this title again and again. Cf. Matt. 12:23; 15:22; 20:31; 21:9, 15; 22:42-45, etc.

the eyes to become inflamed. In many cases, the lack of care and cleanliness leads to total blindness.

When Jesus reached His house, the two blind men, who had followed Him gropingly, approached Him and repeated their petition. The Savior asked them: "Do you believe that I can do this unto you?" He liked to stir up faith. "Yea, Lord," they replied, with an earnestness that showed their confidence in His miraculous powers. Then Jesus touched those sightless eyes, as though to open them to the light, and said: "According to your faith, be it done unto you." Instantly they recovered their sight. Before sending them away, Jesus bade them not to make the miracle known. But, like many others, they were unable to obey His command fully; scarcely had they gone out of the house, when they began to publish abroad in that whole region the blessing which they had received from Him whom they regarded as the Messias.

When they had gone, some kind neighbors brought to the Savior a dumb person possessed by a devil. As in a former case,[658] the dumbness was not caused by any organic defect, but by diabolic possession. And so, as soon as the devil was driven out by Christ's all-powerful exorcism, the dumb man recovered his speech. The crowd, which had again gathered, was in admiration at this miracle, and all gave voice to their enthusiasm, saying: "Never was the like seen in Israel." Their wonderment was provoked not merely by this last miracle.[659] It referred to all the prodigies that Jesus had performed at Capharnaum that day. But the jealous Pharisees utter their odious blasphemy: "By the prince of devils He casteth out devils." Unable to deny the reality of the miracle, they endeavor at least to lessen its worth and to destroy the effect of it by this perfidious insinuation. Having learned to their cost, they perhaps did not venture to make their accusa-

[658] Matt. 12: 22 f.; Luke 11: 14.
[659] It is mentioned only by St. Matthew, 9: 32-34.

tion in His presence, or it may be that He did not deign to answer them.

It was about this time that the Savior paid a visit to His fellow-townsmen of Nazareth, as described by St. Matthew and St. Mark.[660] The purpose of this visit may have been to escape from the public demonstrations which His recent miracles had aroused in Capharnaum. Considered as a whole, it is so like the visit mentioned by St. Luke,[661] which we placed shortly after the beginning of Christ's public ministry,[662] that several commentators identify the two events.[663] According to their view, St. Luke, in the case of this passage, purposely changed the order of events so as to show, at the outset of the public life, what obstacles Jesus would have to overcome in order to bring the Jews to a belief in His mission. The question is a delicate one; for every solution that has been proposed has reasons *pro* and *con*.[664] Yet it seems to us more conformable to the Gospel narrative to admit two separate visits. Between these two visits there was time enough for the passion of the people of Nazareth to subside, and it was natural that our Lord would give them a chance to repair their fault. Moreover, although it is undeniable that great resemblances exist between the accounts, yet several important details in St. Luke's narrative bear such a special stamp that they can hardly be explained save by supposing two visits.

Leaving the lake shore, Jesus, this time accompanied by His disciples,[665] traveled the eighteen miles which separated Capharnaum from the little town which both Evangelists call "His own country," because that was where He had been

---

[660] Matt. 13: 54–58; Mark 6: 1–6.

[661] Luke 4: 16–30.

[662] See pages 195–204.

[663] Catholic exegetes as well as others have always been divided on this question. St. Augustine and Maldonatus (to mention only two of the most illustrious scholars) favor a single visit.

[664] See Fillion, *L'Évangile de S. Matthieu*, pp. 280–283.

[665] There is no question of them in St. Luke's narrative.

brought up [666] and where He passed all of His hidden life. On the Sabbath following His arrival, He spoke in the synagogue and deeply impressed His hearers, as on a previous occasion, by the force and beauty of His preaching.[667] But most of them [668] let themselves be influenced by their narrow prejudices. St. Mark, who quotes their remarks more fully, describes them as holding a sort of deliberation together. They ask one another: "How came this man by all these things? And what wisdom is this that is given to Him, and such mighty works as are wrought by His hands?" They plainly recognize in Jesus a learned doctor and a mighty wonder-worker. His wisdom, which had just again shone in their presence, and His miracles, the fame of which had reached them, were too incontestable to be denied. But they knew not, or rather they did not wish to understand the why and the how. "Strange stupidity," says St. Jerome; "as if it was a difficult matter to point out whence the incarnate Wisdom came by His wisdom, whence the uncreated Providence came by His miraculous power." [669]

But the people of Nazareth were not large-minded enough to reconcile these superior gifts with His apparently lowly human origin and with His modest education, outwardly like theirs. "Is not this the carpenter," [670] they said, "the Son of Mary, the brother of James and Joseph and Jude and Simon? Are not also His sisters here with us?" Instead of being proud of Him, they reduced Him to their own image; instead of concluding, as all the circumstances should have per-

---

[666] Cf. Luke 4: 16.

[667] Ἐξεπλήσσοντο, (Vulg., *obstupescebant*) ; they were, so to speak, beside themselves.

[668] Οἱ πολλοί, St. Mark says explicitly; the *multi* of the Vulgate does not render the full force of this phrase.

[669] *Exposit. in Matth., i. h. l.*

[670] Such is the reading in St. Mark: ὁ τέκτων. In St. Matthew we read ὁ τοῦ τέκτονος υἱός, "the carpenter's son." On this trade, which had been St. Joseph's occupation before being that of Christ, see Vol. I, pp. 415 ff.

suaded them to do, that Jesus received His superhuman wisdom and exceptional power directly from Heaven, they clung to the negative result to which the crassest sophism had led them. As both Evangelists remark, "they were scandalized in regard of Him." At least we are grateful to the people of Nazareth for the authentic information they here supply regarding the Savior's relatives. But they were victims of their own unbelief; for it prevented Jesus from performing any brilliant and striking cures in their midst. Of course, for Him the obstacle was only a moral and relative one. But it would have been an anomaly for Him to exercise His supernatural power for the sake of these unworthy people, since He ordinarily required faith on the part of those who implored His mercy.[671] He merely cured a few sick people by laying His hands upon them. No doubt, in them He found some spark of faith. He wondered, says St. Mark, at such unbelief. He departed, therefore, but not without first repeating to His fellow-townsmen the proverb which was quoted to them at the time of His former visit and which was again realized with regard to Him: "A prophet is not without honor but in his own country and in his own house and among his own kindred."

[671] Cf. Matt. 8: 2, 13; 9: 2, 22, 28 f. etc. It is in this sense that we must interpret St. Mark's words: "He could not do any miracles there, only . . ." St. Matthew says simply: "He wrought not many miracles there . . ."

CHAPTER V

*From the Savior's Third Preaching Journey to the Third
Pasch of His Public Life*

1. Christ's Instructions to the Apostles for Their Present and Future Mission

ACCORDING to St. Mark's clear indication, it was at this period that Jesus began His third preaching tour through Galilee. St. Matthew summarizes it in almost the same words as those he employed in connection with the first mission: "Jesus went about all the cities and towns, teaching in their synagogues and preaching the gospel of the Kingdom and healing every disease and every infirmity." [672] But this time the Divine Master is not alone; He has the Apostles join Him in His evangelizing task. St. Matthew, in a few eloquent words, states the reason that led Jesus to undertake this new series of fatiguing sermons: [673] "Seeing the multitudes, He had compassion on them,[674] because they were distressed and lying like sheep that have no shepherd." In this passage we have one of those brief but characteristic descriptions which enable us to see the Savior's soul to its very depth. And at the same time we are given a desolate picture of the moral wretchedness in which the Jewish people were then languishing. In several passages of Holy Writ, Israel is represented as a

[672] Matt. 9: 35. Cf. 4: 23. St. Mark's summary (6: 6) is still more concise: "He went through the villages round about, teaching."

[673] Matt. 9: 36-38.

[674] Ἐσπλαγχνίσθη. On the use of this very expressive verb, see Vol. I, p. 466, note 692.

flock of sheep.[675] But it is a fact of experience, referred to by ancient writers, that the sheep is an essentially domestic animal, unable to live far away from man or deprived of his care. The words: "like sheep that have no shepherd" are sadly significant. The Jewish nation had its official spiritual guides, the priests and doctors of the law. Although they did not openly mistreat the nation, as at other epochs of Jewish history,[676] they abandoned it to itself, loaded it down with practices that often made religion odious, and scandalized it by their bad example. As Jesus tells them,[677] they were selfish and blind guides. At this sight, the delicate, loving heart of the Good Shepherd was filled with grief.

Instead of being disheartened in the face of such a state of affairs, He has recourse to a powerful means to save these neglected, abandoned sheep. Turning toward His Apostles, He says to them: "The harvest indeed is great, but the laborers are few. Pray ye therefore the Lord of the harvest, that He send forth laborers into His harvest." Jesus was fond of this joyous and hopeful figure of the harvest. Some time previous He employed it at Jacob's well,[678] to designate the vast field of Palestine, where in spirit He beheld the already whitening wheat that would soon be in need of harvesters. This wheat had ripened, and the hour was at hand to reap it and fill the barns with it. Hence the invitation which Jesus addressed to the Twelve: Pray the Master of the harvest, God, to send workers into His field as quickly as possible.

Whilst awaiting the coming of more numerous harvesters, the Savior, without further delay, sends His Apostles to gather with Him and for Him the precious and bounteous harvest. It was, in fact, for this very work that He had

[675] Cf. Ps. 22: 1–5; 79: 2; 99: 3; Is. 40: 11; Ezech. 24: 5 etc.
[676] Cf. 3 Kings 22: 17; Is. 53: 6; Jer. 50: 6; Ezech. 35: 5.
[677] Matt. 15: 14; 23: 16, 24.
[678] John 4: 35–38.

chosen and already partly trained them. The moment was a solemn one. The Synoptics indicate this by an expression that recalls the one they used when Jesus established the Apostolic College: [679] "He called the Twelve." [680] Having gathered them about Him, He provided them with spiritual powers analogous to His own, which were to serve them as credentials and confirm their preaching. The three Evangelists dwell on the fact, even before quoting the words by which the Savior communicated this privilege to them. "He gave them power over unclean spirits, to cast them out, and to heal all manner of diseases and all manner of infirmities." [681] He reserved for a later date the still loftier powers which would enable them to administer the Sacraments and bring divine grace directly to men's souls.

Before sending forth His Apostles through the cities and villages of Palestine to undergo what we might call the apprenticeship of their future office, Jesus indicated a few practical rules that, in addition to His example, should guide them in this important ministry which was so new for them. His address, occupying only a few verses in St. Mark's and St. Luke's account, fills a whole chapter in the First Gospel.[682] Even in the content of those few verses which the three Synoptics have in common, St. Matthew is much more complete, as he usually is in reporting the Savior's discourses: The following is the first part of our Lord's instruction to His Apostles, according to St. Matthew:

"Go ye not into the way of the Gentiles, and into the city of the Samaritans enter ye not. But go ye rather to the lost sheep of the house of Israel. And going, preach, saying: The Kingdom of Heaven is at hand. Heal the sick, raise the dead, cleanse the lepers, cast out

[679] Mark 3: 13; Luke 6: 13.
[680] Matt. 10: 1; Mark 6: 7; Luke 9: 1.
[681] Matt. 10: 1; Mark 6: 7; Luke 9: 1 f.
[682] Matt 10: 5–42; Mark 6: 8–11; Luke 9: 3–5.

devils; freely have you received, freely give. Do not possess gold, nor silver, nor money in your purses, nor scrip for your journey, nor two coats, nor shoes, nor a staff; for the workman is worthy of his meat. And into whatsoever city or town you shall enter, inquire who in it is worthy, and there abide till you go thence. And when you come into the house, salute it, saying: Peace be to this house. And if that house be worthy, your peace shall come upon it; but if it be not worthy, your peace shall return to you. And whosoever shall not receive you, nor hear your words; going forth out of that house or city shake off the dust from your feet. Amen I say to you, it shall be more tolerable for the land of Sodom and Gomorrha in the day of judgment, than for that city."

St. Gregory Nazianzen sums up these prescriptions in a few lines. The Apostles, as missionaries of Christ, should be "so virtuous, so constant and humble, in a word, so heavenly, that the gospel teaching may be propagated by their manner of life no less than by their words." [683]

Let us enter into a few details. First of all, Jesus fixes the limits within which the Apostles will exercise their ministry, beyond which they are not to go until further orders. For the time being, they will not carry the gospel to the pagan territories of the neighborhood, for example, Decapolis and the half-pagan province of Samaria; they will preach only to the Jews, to those "lost sheep" for whom Christ's heart had a tender pity. The principle that guided His preaching all during His public life [684] will serve as a rule for that of His envoys. Like Him, they will take into account the right reserved to the Jews, to be the first to receive the gospel. But this was only a temporary restriction, which Jesus removed when He was about to ascend into heaven, [685] by opening a worldwide field for their activity. Meanwhile, the Jewish na-

[683] *Exposit. in Evang.*, 6.
[684] Matt. 15:24: "I was not sent but to the sheep that are lost of the house of Israel." (Cf. Rom. 15:8.)
[685] Acts 1:8.

tion is to form the basis of the Christian race, the primitive trunk on which, to use St. Paul's metaphor, the Gentiles will be divinely grafted.[686]

The Savior then set forth the nature of the ministry He was confiding to the Twelve: "Going, preach." This will be their chief function. As they go from city to city they will preach incessantly, as He had been doing for several months. But what is to be the subject of their preaching? It will be that of John the Baptist,[687] that of Jesus Himself: [688] the coming of the Kingdom of Heaven, the Messianic Kingdom. They are not yet commissioned to announce the glad tidings in all their fulness; it will be enough at first that they open the hearts of their fellow-Jews to the graces and the salvation brought by the Messias.

Then came the conferring of the miraculous powers which the Evangelists mention at the beginning of their description of this episode. Jesus proclaims them in rhythmic language, containing six parallel statements, arranged in pairs.

> "Heal the sick;   cast out devils.
> Cleanse the lepers;   raise the dead.
> Freely have you received freely give."

The second of these supernatural gifts is so extraordinary that several manuscripts and some ancient versions surreptitiously suppress it. But it is the view of excellent critics [689] that the authenticity of these words is beyond doubt, for it is guaranteed by witnesses on whom we may fully rely. The instruction regarding the gratuitousness of the Apostolic ministry is well founded: by what right should anyone derive a pecuniary profit from a supernatural power received gratu-

---

[686] Rom. 11 : 16.
[687] Matt. 3 : 2 etc.
[688] Matt. 4 : 17.
[689] Among others, Westcott and Hort, B. Weiss, Nestle, H. von Soden, T. Zahn.

itously from Heaven? Simon Magus was the first to commit
the odious crime which has been stigmatised by the name of
simony.[690] All true missionaries, on the contrary, have, like
St. Paul,[691] gloried in suffering, in laboring with their hands,
so as not to be a burden to those whom they were evangelizing, although they had a right to live by the altar.[692]

When anybody is about to undertake a journey that is to
last some little time, he makes preparations, providing himself
with money, clothing, and food. Jesus entered into these practical details so as to show His Apostles what He expected of
them. The preparations, in accord with His orders, would not
require much time or expense, since His thought amounts
to this: Go, provided as you now are; you will need nothing
more, for Providence will take care of you. This is why the
Savior does not let them take with them either money in
their girdle,[693] or food in a napsack hanging from their shoulder, or an extra tunic, in a word anything superfluous. The
sandals and the tunic which they wear will suffice. They are
not to be solicitous for anything material; they are to be
satisfied with a staff, that faithful companion of travelers on
foot, at all times and in all countries.[694] Those to whom they
preach the gospel will, in return, furnish them with what they
need to live decently, without their having any preoccupations
to distract them from their weighty mission. God, whose workers they are, will treat them as a householder does those who
labor for him. "The laborer is worthy of his hire." Jesus did

[690] Acts 8: 18–24.

[691] Acts 20: 33–35; 1 Cor. 9: 12, 15, 18; 2 Cor. 11: 9–12; Phil. 4: 15; 1 Thess.
2: 9; 2 Thess. 3: 8.

[692] 1 Cor. 9: 13 f.

[693] The primary purpose of the belt or cincture was to gather up about the
waist the loose garments of the ancients. It was also so contrived as to hold a
sum of money, sometimes a considerable amount of it. Cf. Aulus Gellius, *Noct.
Att.*, XV, 12, 4; Suetonius, *Vitell.*, 16.

[694] Cf. Gen. 32: 10; Ex. 12: 11 etc. On the shades of difference to be found in
the three narratives, see the commentaries.

not deceive His Apostles when He made them this promise. In the cenacle, the night before He died, when He looked back upon this period of His life, He asked them whether they had wanted for anything while they went preaching through the land. Without hesitation, they answered: "Nothing." [695] But these prescriptions were transitory. Although they were easily carried out in Palestine, owing to the hospitable customs of the country, it would be morally impossible to follow them abroad, in pagan lands, especially in localities where there was no Jewish colony.

The rules as to where and how long they are to remain in the places where they preach, are very plain. The Apostles are not to ask hospitality from the first person they meet; they must gather reliable information before deciding this question. Without a careful choice, they would run the risk of compromising their personal reputation and also the cause of the Kingdom of Heaven. They will not prefer the home of the richest or most influential inhabitant, but that which they find out is the most worthy. Once installed in a house, they are to abide there until their departure from that town. To leave that house and go to another would be a mark of fickleness or lack of mortification, little in accord with the Apostolic character. Upon those who generously receive them, their presence will draw down rich blessings, which Jesus sums up by the word "peace."

As their time is precious and limited, if, on arriving in a city or village, they perceive that, in consequence of prejudice, indifference, or unbelief, their message is not well received, they must not seek to prolong their stay, for the gospel is not imposed by force. They shall leave for some other place, yet not without forcefully protesting by word and act against the affront offered the "good tidings." Upon quitting the inhospitable district, they shall strike their sandals together, as

[695] Luke 22 : 35 f.

the Jews generally did when leaving a pagan territory,[696] thus showing they wished to have nothing in common with the inhabitants. This will be an appeal to the latter's conscience and will also be for a testimony against them on the day of judgment.[697] Their refusal to receive the gospel would be so grievous a fault that Jesus predicted a punishment for them, before the great tribunal at the end of time, more terrible than that of Sodom and Gomorrha, the two cities whose very names symbolized the greatest crimes and misfortunes.[698]

In the accounts of St. Mark and St. Luke, the instructions given by our Lord to His Apostolic missionaries end at this point. In St. Matthew's Gospel they form only the first part, about one-third, of the Savior's discourse. Upon reading the rest of it, anyone will see that the perspective suddenly enlarges and that Jesus transports His disciples to a much vaster field of action and a more distant time. In place of the almost universally favorable reception which He just promised them, He tells them of persecutions they will have to undergo, not only in Palestine, at the hands of their countrymen, but also from pagans, whose territory He has just forbidden them to enter for the time being.

This remark is immediately followed by another. A whole passage, which we shall cite presently, is to be found in the other two Synoptics, but much further on, as an integral part of Christ's discourse on the Mount of Olives, a few days before His death. Therein He prophetically describes the future of His Apostles and His Church.[699] We shall have occasion to mention, in the course of the discourse, another analogous

[696] Vol. I, p. 158.

[697] Sts. Paul and Barnabas, when repulsed by the Jews of Antioch of Pisidia, carried out our Lord's advice literally. (Cf. Acts 13: 50 f.)

[698] Is. 1:9; Ezech. 16:46–50; Amos 4:11; Matt. 11:23 f.; Luke 17:29; Rom. 9:29; 2 Pet. 2:6, etc.

[699] Cf. Matt. 10:17–22; Mark 13:9–13; Luke 21:12–17.

but less striking detail. Ought we not conclude that St. Matthew, as at other points in his Gospel, has transferred some of the Divine Master's words from their chronological place and grouped them logically with others treating of the same subject? It is no more impossible in this instance than in the case of the Sermon on the Mount. But it can hardly be admitted that the Evangelist himself put together the rest of the discourse, with predictions and instructions given by Christ to His Apostles at different times and places. Perhaps this second part of the discourse was delivered at a later date. But it bears no sign of an artificial grouping, because there is a truly logical order between the thoughts that compose it. Further, although it was our Lord's direct and immediate purpose at that time to give the Twelve certain practical admonitions for the preparatory mission which He was about to confide to them, it would not be at all surprising that He should then broaden the horizon and, lifting the veil of the future before them, describe, in a miniature picture, what they must expect to encounter in the future exercise of their apostolate.

Let us now quote this other series of the Savior's pastoral instructions. "Behold I send you as sheep in the midst of wolves. Be ye therefore wise as serpents and simple as doves. But beware of men. For they will deliver you up in councils, and they will scourge you in their synagogues. And you shall be brought before governors and before kings for My sake, for a testimony to them and to the Gentiles. But when they shall deliver you up, take no thought how or what to speak: for it shall be given you in that hour what to speak. For it is not you that speak, but the Spirit of your Father that speaketh in you. The brother also shall deliver up the brother to death, and the father the son, and the children shall rise up against their parents, and shall put them to death. And you shall be hated by all men for My name's sake; but he that shall persevere unto the end, he shall be saved. And when they shall persecute you in this city, flee into another. Amen I say to you, you shall not finish all the cities of Israel, till the Son of Man come." [700]

These words are so clear as to call for little explanation. But how the horizon suddenly becomes darkened, as the field of action assigned to the first preachers of the gospel enlarges, so as to be limited only by the boundaries of the earth! Persecution enters the foreground and becomes the dominant note. Christ's missionaries are like sheep transported into the midst of wolves. All sorts of outrages await them from the implacable hatred of enemies. The Jews, their own coreligionists, will be the first to attack them, even dragging them before their lower courts and the Sanhedrin.[701] The pagans will also mercilessly pursue them and hale them like criminals before proconsuls and even to the bar of their kings.[702] Hence our Lord gives them a twofold warning: "Be ye therefore wise as serpents and simple as doves," [703] and "Beware of men."

These threatening predictions, however, are accompanied by consoling promises. It is Jesus Himself who thus sends His Apostles into the midst of perils. *"Ecce ego mitto vos . . ."* It is "for Him" and "for His name" that they must suffer humiliations, hatred, torture, and even death. He will not forget nor forsake them. When given over to the vengeance of judges by their relatives and friends, they will be

---

[700] Matt. 10: 16–23.

[701] These various tribunals are designated in the Greek text by the words εἰς συνέδρια. The synagogues are mentioned because their rulers and officers had the right, under certain circumstances, to exercise judicial power and to sentence culprits to a mitigated flogging. Cf. Luke 12: 11; 21: 12; Acts 22: 19; 26: 11; 2 Cor. 11: 24. See also Acts 22: 30—23: 11.

[702] Thus it was that St. Paul appeared before Felix, then before Festus, and even before Nero. Cf. Acts 24: 1–27; 2 Tim. 4: 16–18.

[703] Both profane and sacred antiquity always regarded the serpent as a type of wisdom and cunning, and the dove as a model of candor and simplicity. For this view, so far as the Bible is concerned, see especially Gen. 3: 1 and Osee 7: 11.

protected by Him. When they stand before the courts of justice, the Holy Ghost will suggest to them decisive arguments for their defense, and the best manner of presenting those arguments. The Acts of the Apostles and the Acts of the Martyrs contain many examples of this divine assistance, which communicated irresistible eloquence to men from the ranks of the common people, to young virgins, as well as to the Apostles and the early bishops. Moreover, Jesus needs His missionaries, because their life is precious for His cause and that of His Church. Perseverance in the faith and valiant constancy amidst the greatest dangers do not oblige a preacher of the gospel to expose himself uselessly. The Savior's wish is that, when persecution becomes too violent wherever His Apostles may be, they seek the shelter of another city. This flight will be a noble act of prudence, and the gospel will lose nothing thereby, since its spread will thus be the more rapid.

Our Lord concluded by saying: "Amen I say to you, you shall not finish all the cities of Israel, till the Son of Man come." These words present some difficulty, for commentators are not at one on the subject of the special advent which Jesus had in mind here. According to the most likely and natural opinion, there is no question of a personal coming, for no such event is found which can easily be harmonized with this prophecy. Rather we have here a reference to the manifestation which Christ will make of His power, when, through the intermediary of the Romans, He will punish the Jewish people and Jerusalem, guilty of obstinate rejection of the salvation which was so generously offered. When that time comes, the Apostles, at least those still living, will have had ample time to evangelize all the cities of Palestine.

In the third part of the Savior's discourse we again hear the two dominant notes that resounded in the second part. The idea of persecution is here closely associated with the reasons for encouragement and confidence.

"The disciple is not above the master, nor the servant above his lord. It is enough for the disciple that he be as his master and the servant as his lord. If they have called the goodman of the house Beelzebub, how much more them of his household? Therefore fear them not. For nothing is covered that shall not be revealed; nor hid, that shall not be known. That which I tell you in the dark, speak ye in the light; and that which you hear in the ear, preach ye upon the housetops. And fear ye not them that kill the body, and are not able to kill the soul; but rather fear him that can destroy both soul and body in hell. Are not two sparrows sold for a farthing? And not one of them shall fall on the ground without your Father. But the very hairs of your head are all numbered. Fear not therefore; better are you than many sparrows. Everyone therefore that shall confess Me before men, I will also confess him before My Father who is in heaven. But he that shall deny Me before men, I will also deny him before My Father who is in heaven.

"Do not think that I came to send peace upon earth. I came not to send peace, but the sword. For I came to set a man at variance against his father, and the daughter against her mother, and the daughter-in-law against her mother-in-law. And a man's enemies shall be they of his own household. He that loveth father or mother more than Me, is not worthy of Me; and he that loveth son or daughter more than Me, is not worthy of Me. And he that taketh not up his cross, and followeth Me, is not worthy of Me. He that findeth his life, shall lose it, and he that shall lose his life for Me, shall find it. He that receiveth you, receiveth Me; and he that receiveth Me, receiveth Him that sent Me. He that receiveth a prophet in the name of a prophet, shall receive the reward of a prophet. And he that receiveth a just man in the name of a just man, shall receive the reward of a just man. And whosoever shall give to drink to one of these little ones a cup of cold water only in the name of a disciple, amen I say to you, he shall not lose his reward." [704]

[704] Matt. 10 : 24–42.

This final series of admonitions may be summed up in a few words, which connect them in groups: It is fitting that the disciple be not treated better than his master; Fear not; The profession of faith and apostasy; The sword and the cross; The reward promised to those who cordially receive the ambassadors of the Messias.[705] In the second group, the triple repetition of "Fear not" is impressive. Equally so are the reasons by which our Lord justifies the confidence that His Apostles should have in His Father and in Him. Fearlessly preach these good tidings, which are destined to acquire world-wide publicity; [706] it is only for a time that I order you not to publish certain points of My doctrine. Have no fear even of death; though your persecutors can take the life of your body, they have no power over the higher part of your being; in depriving you of something which is of secondary rank and essentially transitory, they will procure for you another possession, Heaven, which is of infinite value and cannot be taken from you. God alone is to be feared; yet there is nothing to be feared from Him, if you remain faithful to Him. Trust in the loving Providence of Him who has a care for even the least creatures, as the common sparrow which is sold in the market for so small a price; [707] His watchful care extends even to our hair, that insignificant part of our being. These details, as also those referring to apostasy and the profession of faith, are nearly all given elsewhere by St. Luke.[708] As most commentators, Catholic, Protestant, and Rationalist, admit, there is nothing astonishing in this; these proverbial

[705] For developments of this thought, see Fillion, *L'Évangile de S. Matthieu*, pp. 208–216.

[706] As our readers know, the roofs in Palestine are generally flat and can be used as places from which all sorts of proclamations may be published. To preach from the housetops, therefore, is to preach openly, publicly.

[707] "Two for one *as*." The *as* was a Roman bronze coin worth about one cent in American money.

[708] Matt. 10:27–33. Cf. Luke 12:2–9.

sayings expressed what Jesus repeated on different occasions.

We have the same remark to make touching several thoughts of the next group: The sword and the cross.[709] The sword, that terrible instrument which symbolizes warfare, hurled by the Messias into the midst of the family, into the midst of the entire world: what could be more abnormal, more unexpected—so it seems? Is it not with an olive branch, the pledge of happiness and security, that He should have presented Himself, He whom the prophets called the Prince of Peace,[710] He of whom the angels sang at the hour of His birth, "On earth peace"?[711] Although Jesus says that He has come to bring war, and not peace, this does not mean that His coming was for the world a direct cause of strife and discord; but the strife and discord would be the natural consequence of the establishment of His Kingdom. Christ Himself can offer the kiss of peace only after cutting off passions and vices with the sword. When His gospel enters a family, it necessarily brings about violent separations, which, on the part of the members who remain in unbelief, will lead even to hatred, as if the very bond of blood ties were suddenly severed. However, never will there be anyone who will defend and maintain those sacred ties more firmly than Jesus did; but the salvation brought by Him, faith in Him, and love for Him must prevail above all the rest. Whoever should think or act otherwise would not be worthy of Him. *"Non est me dignus,"* He repeats three times. He who spoke thus, with so great assurance and vigor, had a truly lofty idea of His own nature and His divine mission. And in the major part of this address, Christ presents Himself as the universal center of minds and hearts. We shall later on draw the conclusion that follows from the truly royal and unique position

[709] Matt. 10: 34–36; cf. Luke 12: 51–53; Matt. 10: 37 f.; cf. Luke 14: 26 f.; Matt. 10: 39; cf. Luke 17: 33.

[710] Is 9: 6.

[711] Luke 2: 14.

which He takes here and in other passages of the Gospels.

Beside the sword, mention is made of the cross. This is the first time in the Savior's history that we hear the sacred name of the cross. The Apostles must have trembled with fright when He said to them without circumlocution, as a quite natural thing, that they must bear their cross, that instrument of cruel and infamous execution. There was no one in Palestine who did not know, ever since the Romans had established themselves as masters in a considerable part of the country, what crucifixion was; in fact, it was only a short time before that several Jews, who had participated in the revolt of Judas and Simon, had undergone its tortures. And it was well known that a condemned man had to carry his cross to the place of execution. But Jesus had just said that the disciple is not above the master; and the Master would one day be laden with a cross before dying upon it. In this passage, however, the Savior is speaking especially of moral crucifixion, which puts to death our nature's evil tendencies, and the generous acceptance of sufferings and sacrifices imposed by the practice of Christianity.

To save his life by losing it; to lose it while seeming to save it,—here we have, in the Oriental style, a play on words that is based on the double meaning of the Greek noun designating the soul, but also meaning life.[712] The sense of this proverbial expression is that it is better to suffer death as a martyr for Christ, than to lose eternal life by apostasy. The Stoic philosophers sometimes urged one another to have no dread of evils that could reach only their bodies. In the works of Epictetus,[713] we read the following dialogue apropos of this subject:

Tyrant.—I am going to load you with chains.

[712] Ψυχή (Vulg., *anima*).
[713] *Disc.* I, I. See also Euripides, *Bacc.*, 492–499.

Philosopher.—Me in chains? You can chain my leg; but Zeus himself is unable to subdue my will.

Tyrant.—I will throw you into prison.

Philosopher.—You mean that you will throw my body there.

Tyrant.—I will cut off your head.

Philosopher.—When did I say that my head could not be cut off?

These words are not devoid of nobility and courage. But, at bottom, what self-sufficiency! what pride! and how different from the reasons that Jesus offers His disciples for persevering in the midst of torments! Those motives have convinced and sustained thousands of Christian martyrs amidst their tortures.

In the last lines of our Lord's discourse, the question is no longer one of persecutions and sufferings to be undergone in preaching or practicing the gospel, but only of the reward God has in store for all who receive the Apostles with faith and respect. The Savior briefly sketches a wonderful synthesis. Just as the closest union exists between Him and His heavenly Father "who sent Him," so also between Him and His own envoys. To receive them is, therefore, to receive Him; it is also to receive His Father. But, to obtain the promised reward, the reception must be supernatural, it must be made to the ambassadors of Christ. The cup of cold water, which is more precious in the Orient than elsewhere because there the weather is hotter and water is scarcer, must be offered in Jesus' name "to one of these little ones," as the Apostles were in the eyes of the world, although they were so great in the sight of God and to the eyes of faith.

Provided with these instructions and strengthened with their Master's encouragement, the Twelve left Him, and went through the towns of Galilee, perhaps also beyond that province, announcing that the Kingdom of God was near at hand, exhorting to penance, driving out devils, and healing the sick, thanks to the powers Jesus had conferred on them

They departed in pairs, St. Mark notes,[714] as our Lord had willed, in order that they might stimulate and encourage each other. St. Matthew, in the list of the Apostles which he gives immediately after the Savior's discourse,[715] names them in pairs: Peter and Andrew, James the Greater and John, Philip and Bartholomew, Thomas and Matthew, James the Less and Jude, Simon Zelotes and Judas. It is quite possible that this arrangement corresponds to the grouping which our Lord Himself made when He sent the Twelve forth to preach in the districts which He had indicated. After their departure the Divine Master resumed His preaching in Galilee, probably accompanied by some disciples. Thus the glad tidings were spread more widely than before.

II. The Martyrdom of John the Baptist

This renewal of preaching and miracles made the Savior's name more renowned than ever and carried it even into the palace of Herod Antipas. The city of Tiberias, where the tetrarch[716] of Galilee and Peraea frequently resided, was so near Capharnaum that we would be surprised at learning that Antipas heard of Jesus only at such a late date, unless we remembered that the life of pleasure which he led with his frivolous and dissipated court and the cares of a political policy, then much embarrassed, scarcely left this ambitious and effeminate monarch time to concern himself with religious matters, even when they were occurring not far from him. It is also true that he sometimes resided at the fortress of Machaerus in the most distant part of Peraea. It is probable, too, that he had already heard of our Lord; but his shallow mind

714 Mark 6:7.

715 Matt. 10:2-4.

716 St. Mark in this passage calls him king, in a broad, popular sense. In fact a tetrarch was a little king in his states. On Herod Antipas, see Vol. I, p. 136.

had not been impressed. As we learn from the three Synoptics,[717] in the present instance he had a special reason for listening attentively to what the ever growing rumor brought to his ears about Jesus of Nazareth. Some time earlier he had sacrilegiously murdered John the Baptist, and his imagination was haunted by the specter of his victim. The Evangelists, in a genuine psychological portrait, picture the monarch as agitated by perpetual remorse and terror at the remembrance of the precursor. As we noted above, conscience was not altogether dead in him, since he had sometimes followed the suggestions and advice of the Baptist, whom he visited in his prison. Such being the case, he must have been deeply impressed by what he heard concerning our Lord.

Opinion was very much divided on the subject, although the Jewish multitudes regarded Jesus as a mighty and holy personage. "This is John the Baptist; he is risen from the dead," said some; among the Jews of that time, the resurrection of the dead was a generally accepted doctrine, which the skeptical Sadducees were the only ones to reject.[718] Many of those who knew Jesus only by His latest fame saw no better way of explaining the power of His words and works than by considering Him to be John the Baptist risen from the dead, beginning a second ministry more brilliant than the first. "That Elias had appeared," was the opinion of others, who preferred to seek farther back in their people's annals and there to take, for comparison with Jesus, the great Seer of Thisbe, who was likewise a magnificent religious orator and a powerful miracle-worker. The Jews believed that this holy prophet would reappear some time before the coming of the Messias, to prepare His ways.[719] Still others

---

[717] Matt. 14:1 f.; Mark 4:14-16; Luke 9:7-9.

[718] Cf. Matt. 22:23; Mark 12:18; Luke 20:27; Acts 23:6-10; Weber, *System der altssynagogalen palästinischen Theologie,* pp. 371-373; Bousset, *Die Religion des Judentums,* pp. 174 f.

[719] Cf. Matt. 17:10-12; Mark 9:10-12.

there were who would not decide explicitly, but merely expressed a general opinion "that one of the old prophets was risen again," one of the great prophets, but distinct from Elias.

The tetrarch was disturbed by the first of these conjectures, which, as Origen says,[720] would have been favored by a notable resemblance of features between Jesus and John the Baptist. But he endeavored to eliminate that hypothesis by an apparently very simple bit of reasoning: "John I have beheaded"; therefore it could not be John. But, he asked himself, "who is this of whom I hear such things?" He became more and more perplexed. Swayed to some extent by superstition, in the end he adopted the very hypothesis which he most dreaded, and one day plainly declared to those about him: "It is John the Baptist. He is risen from the dead, and therefore mighty works show forth themselves in him." Although the Baptist had performed no miracle during his ministry,[721] it was natural to suppose that God, upon raising him from the dead, would have endowed him with supernatural powers which he did not enjoy before his death. Having come to this conclusion, Antipas sought to have a meeting with Jesus, that he might render his conclusion more certain. Since he knew the Baptist personally, merely to see our Lord would suffice to put his judgment of the matter beyond all doubt.[722]

St. Matthew and St. Mark, after mentioning the aveng-

---

[720] *In Joan.*, VI, 31.

[721] John 10:41.

[722] May we not find an allusion to these terrors in the following lines of the Roman poet Persius (*Satires*, V, 169–185)?

> "At cum
> *Herodis venere dies, unctaque fenestra*
> *Dispositae pinguem nebulam vomuere lucernae,*
> *Portantes violas, rubrumque amplexa catinum*
> *Cauda natat thynni, tumet alba fidelia vino:*
> *Labra moves tacitus, recutitaque sabbata palles.*
> *Tunc negri lemures, ovoque pericula rupto.*"

ing terrors which we have just described, retrospectively relate the tragic details of the Baptist's martyrdom.[723]

It was especially to pacify the hatred of the cruel and shameless Herodias that the tetrarch had cast John into prison. Personally, Antipas had no wish to go farther than this: it was enough that he had rendered John incapable of harming him with the people by his severe language. He even showed regard for his prisoner and confidence in him; at times, when staying at Machaerus, he conversed with John and listened to his views. But the hateful woman, who had a fatal influence over him, would be satisfied with nothing less than the death of him whom she regarded as her most dangerous foe. Thus far Antipas had repeatedly refused to grant Herodias' urgent requests. But she hoped to find, some day or other, a favorable occasion which would enable her to obtain a sentence of death against John. Before long the opportunity came; for meanwhile the tetrarch's birthday anniversary arrived. It was a very old custom among the ancients to celebrate their birthday with great festivity. In the Book of Genesis,[724] for example, we see the pharaoh of Egypt celebrating it with magnificence. In conformity with this custom, Herod Antipas gave a great birthday banquet (which the Romans called *natalitiae dapes*), to which he invited the chief personages of his States. St. Mark mentions three categories of guests: the officials of the tetrarch's household, the officers of his little army, and the chief men of Galilee. The Evangelists do not state where the feast was held; but from the context we know that it must have been celebrated in the fortress of Machaerus, within which Herod the Great had built a splendid palace.[725]

[723] Matt. 14: 3-12; Mark 6: 17-29. St. Luke earlier in his narrative (3: 19 f.) alludes to this event.

[724] Gen. 40: 20. Cf. Josephus, *Ant.,* XII, v, 7; Schürer, *Geschichte des jüdischen Volkes,* I, 439. The Greeks called the birthday festival τὰ γενεσία.

[725] Josephus, *Bell. Jud.,* VII, vi, 2; Schürer, *op. cit.,* I, 366.

During the dinner given by Antipas, in place of professional dancers, Salome,[726] the daughter of Herodias by her lawful marriage to Herod Philip,[727] performed one of those usually licentious pantomimes of which Oriental dancing is composed.[728] At that time she must have been a little less than twenty years old. Her performance was more than an indecency; it was a veritable degradation; the fact that it was she who danced, is mentioned as something extraordinary. To a common courtesan, they would doubtless have given only divided attention. But Salome so far succeeded in winning the favor of the tetrarch, who was overheated with wine, that he foolishly promised, under an oath, to give her whatsoever she would ask for; and added, "though it be the half of my kingdom." Assuerus had made a similar promise to Esther, but under more decent circumstances.[729] The expression was proverbial, signifying that the request would be granted, however extraordinary it might be.

The girl was proud of her success and wanted to derive all the profit she could from this extravagant promise. Leaving the banquet hall at once, she went to her mother and consulted her as to what she should ask. Neither of them was among the dinner guests; for them to have a place at the banquet table would have been contrary to the etiquette of those times.[730] Herodias did not hesitate a moment. So prompt was her decision that it has sometimes been supposed she herself suggested the idea of her daughter dancing at the banquet, in the hope that the sensual monarch would be entrapped and would grant the dancer whatever she might ask. However this may be, Herodias did not wish to lose an opportunity that

---

[726] This was her name, according to Josephus, *Ant.*, XVIII, v, 4.

[727] See page 130.

[728] St. Ambrose, *De Virgin.*, III, 6.

[729] Esther 5 : 3. See also 3 Kings 13 : 8.

[730] Cicero, *In Verrem*, I, 26: "*Negavit moris esse Graecorum ut in convivio accumberent mulieres.*"

might never return. Taking advantage, therefore, of the royal imprudence, which made her all-powerful for the moment, she counselled Salome to ask for the head of John the Baptist. The girl hastily [731] returned to the tetrarch with her answer; brazenly she said: "I will that forthwith thou give me in a dish the head of John the Baptist." What words! They show how worthy Salome was of such a mother and to what an extent she shared Herodias' aversion for the precursor. For both of them he was a personal enemy who must be got rid of at any price, because he might some day bring about their ruin and cause them to fall back into their humble and comparatively poor condition of former days. And the dancer wants her request to be granted forthwith. She demands of the tetrarch, by virtue of his promise, that he have brought to her at once on a platter, probably taken from the banquet table, the bleeding head of the man of God. The criminal demand was made still more horrible by these barbarous details. [732]

Antipas was not expecting such a demand; and so, upon hearing it, he was genuinely grieved and regretted his mad offer. He might have retracted his promise and given Salome some rich gift. But he considered himself bound by an oath carelessly made before those at table and, rather than break it, was willing to make himself guilty of a criminal atrocity. Like many other weak and evil men, he was more concerned about what might be said of him than about committing a crime, more hesitant about violating a point of etiquette than about violating one of the Ten Commandments. The terrible tragedy was immediately consummated. The tetrarch, calling one of his guards, [733] gave him the fatal order, which was

[731] St. Mark mentions this detail: εὐθὺς μετὰ σπουδῆς, "at once with haste."

[732] St. Gregory the Great, in his commentary on this passage, draws attention to the atrocious nature of the request and of its execution under such circumstances.

[733] A σπεκουλάτωρ says the Greek text of St. Mark. This word, which is plainly

promptly carried out. After a short absence, the soldier returned to the banquet hall, carrying upon a blood-smeared platter the head of the Baptist, and placed it in the hands of Salome, who at once brought it to Herodias. Of an execution which took place under similar circumstances, Livy wrote: "Cruel and atrocious crime, committed in the midst of food and drink." [734]

John did, at least, receive decent burial. When his disciples learned of his martyrdom, they went to Machaerus to claim his mortal remains. Antipas, notwithstanding the baseness he had shown, allowed them to take the corpse away. According to a tradition mentioned by St. Jerome, they buried their master at Sabastiyeh, the ancient Samaria, where later on a church was built in his honor, the remains of which may still be seen. Then they went to Jesus with the sad news. Let us hope that they forgot their former prejudice and became hearty disciples of Him whom John had ceaselessly pointed out to them as the Messias.

III. The First Multiplication of the Loaves

Jesus was again on the shore of Lake Tiberias, probably at Capharnaum, when His Apostles rejoined Him at the end of their preaching tour. They were doubly happy; they rejoiced because of being again with the kind Master whom they loved so much, and because of the success which had everywhere attended their efforts. They recounted to Him in detail the various incidents of which they had been the

copied from the Latin *speculator,* means primarily a scout, then an officer acting as aide-de-camp, then (as in this passage) a soldier of the royal or pretorian guard, whose office it was to execute those sentenced to death. The rabbis use it frequently, giving it a Hebraic form. The following lines from Seneca, *De Ira,* I, 16 (or 18), confirm the meaning which St. Mark gives to the word: *"Centurio supplicio praepositus condere gladium speculatorem jubet."* Cf. Suetonius, *Claud.,* 35; Schürer, *op. cit.,* I, 471.

[734] *Hist.,* XXXIX, 43. Cf. Diogenes Laertius, *Anaxarch.,* IX, x, 2.

heroes and witnesses.[735] He shared their satisfaction and congratulated them upon having so well carried out the mission which He had entrusted to them. Their success augured well for the future. But they were tired; having labored without sparing their strength, they were in need of a little rest. Where might they obtain it? Certainly not in Capharnaum or its immediate vicinity. "There were many coming and going," so many, in fact, that Jesus and His Apostles "had not so much as time to eat," [736] as had happened to them before.[737] No doubt, it was the nearness of the Pasch that drew so great a crowd of visitors to Jesus at this time. Pilgrims, coming in crowds from the different districts of northern Palestine, gathered at Capharnaum and from there set out in long caravans for Jerusalem. Most of them, knowing that Jesus was ordinarily in the country near the lake, were eager to see Him, attracted especially, as St. John says,[738] by the many miraculous cures which He performed. All about Him was a ceaseless going and coming. He wished to cut this short for a while, because He wanted to avoid an excess of fatigue, not for Himself, since He never considered His own personal comfort, but for His tired Apostles. With delicate consideration He said to them: "Come apart into a desert place, and rest a little." It is touching to see Him taking such fatherly care of their health.

He embarked with the Twelve for the solitudes northeast of the lake, not far from the place where the Jordan flows into it. St. Luke records the name of the city nearest this spot, upon which one of the Savior's greatest miracles conferred everlasting fame. It was Bethsaida Julias, a village which the tetrarch Philip (whom St. Luke names among the

[735] There is a certain emphasis in these words of St. Mark (6:30): "They related to Him all things that they had done and taught."
[736] Mark 6:31.
[737] Mark 3:20.
[738] John 6:2.

rulers of Palestine of that time [739]) had made into a city, enlarging and beautifying it. The location which the historian Josephus attributes to it in several passages of his writings [740] exactly corresponds to that which the Evangelist here indicates. Probably the ancient city stood on the site of the heap of ruins to which the Arabs have given the name of Tell,[741] north of the El Batika plain, which extends along the northeast part of the shore. This territory did not belong to Galilee, but to the province of Gaulanitis, the modern Djaulan. It is possible that, apart from the principal purpose indicated by St. Mark and St. Luke, Jesus intended thus to avoid for a while the vicinity of Herod. There was reason to fear that this ruler, at first simply curious to see Jesus, might take umbrage at His growing fame, become hostile to Him, and thwart His ministry. On the other side of the Jordan, "over the Sea of Galilee," as the Fourth Gospel says, Jesus would be safe from persecution by that ruler.

For the remaining part of the account, we find the four Evangelists closely united.[742] The fact is so rare in the narrative of the Savior's public life, that it deserves special mention. It is explained by the striking character of the miracle therein set forth and also, so far as concerns St. John, by the important discourse which Jesus delivered on the occasion of that miracle.

Our Lord and His Apostles did not long enjoy the quietude and rest which they sought in the neighborhood of Bethsaida Julias. Their departure had been observed, as also the direction taken by their little boat. A large multitude, made up of men, women, and children, started out at once to join them,

---

[739] Luke 3 : 1.

[740] *Ant.*, XVIII, ii, 1; *Bell. Jud.*, II, ix, 1, and XIII, x, 7; *Vita, 72.* See also Pliny, *Hist. Nat.*, V, 16, and St. Jerome, *Exposit. in Matth.* XVI, 31.

[741] See Fillion and Nicole, *Atlas de Géographie Biblique,* pl. XI.

[742] Matt. 14 : 13–21; Mark 6 : 30–44; Luke 9 : 10–17; John 6 : 1–13. St. John shares with St. Mark the honor of supplying the most exact and complete details.

following the road that skirts the lake. They hurried so as to arrive before our Lord and His Apostles would have time to proceed very far inland. The voyage by water was only half as far as by land. But the wind must have been unfavorable for sailing, or else Jesus, desirous of conversing leisurely with His Apostles, was perhaps in no hurry to disembark. At any rate, scarcely were the Master and His disciples installed on a hillside, overlooking the plain and the lake, when they saw the crowd approaching them. Jesus, abandoning all idea of rest, rose up and went forward to meet His visitors, whom He welcomed with His customary kindness. "He had compassion on them," says St. Mark,[743] repeating St. Matthew's remark, "They were distressed and lying like sheep that have no shepherd." [744] Without losing a moment, Jesus entered upon His two usual occupations in such cases: He spoke at some length about the Kingdom of God, and restored health to the infirm who were brought to Him.[745]

The hours passed swiftly in this way. As the day began to close, the Apostles came to their Master and drew His attention to the situation. "This is a desert place," they said, "and the hour is now past. Send away the multitude, that going into the towns, they may buy themselves victuals." The season was only a short time before the equinox, when the sun sets at six o'clock. In the Orient, dusk quickly gives way to night. What the Twelve suggested was a worthy act of human foresight, since many of these people must have set out without providing themselves with food, so eager was their haste to rejoin the Savior; the others had already consumed the food which they had brought. All were so happy near our Lord that they seem not to have been concerned about their evening meal or a shelter for the night.

[743] 'Εσπλάγχνισθη (Vulg., misertus est).

[744] Matt. 9: 36.

[745] St. Luke here makes use of two most expressive imperfects: "He spoke . . . and healed."

Jesus quietly replied to His Apostles: "Give you them to eat." Then, speaking to Philip, who came from this district, He said to him: "Where shall we buy bread, that these may eat?" "This He said," says St. John, "to try him; for He Himself knew what He would do." Since it was impossible in this place, devoid of resources, to provide food for such a multitude by natural means, He would have wished that His Apostles, so often witnesses of His miraculous power, should remind Him that nothing was impossible to Him. Therein consisted the trial to which He subjected their faith. But that faith, though real, was timid and slow. And so Philip knew not how to reply, except by a remark that amounted to nothing: "Two hundred *denarii* worth of bread is not sufficient, that every one may take a little." This amount in Roman money was equal to about thirty-six dollars, and it is hardly probable that the purse of the little Apostolic community contained a fortune of that size, which moreover would certainly have been insufficient to buy a piece of bread for each of the five thousand men that Jesus then had before Him, "besides women and children."

Nevertheless Andrew, Simon Peter's brother, had made a rapid investigation. He said: "There is a boy here that hath five barley loaves and two fishes." Then in all candor he adds: "But what are these among so many?" Barley bread is of a very inferior quality. Then, as it is to-day, it was the bread of the poor. The fishes were probably dried and salted, according to the usage of the country.[746] Jesus directed that this modest supply of provisions be brought to Him. And these dinner guests, sent Him by Providence, He ordered to be seated by hundreds and fifties, to facilitate the distribution of the food. Having at His disposal the basis of the meal that He was about to give them, He sees to it, like a host at the hour

---

[746] At the south of Lake Tiberias, at Taricheae, there was a considerable fish salting industry.

of a great dinner, that His guests are conveniently placed, in order to make the serving easier and to avoid the confusion that would ensue if this immense throng should all rush from every side to receive, each one his share of the food.

It was in the midst of Palestinian springtime, and the grass was abundant in this region.[747] The Apostles promptly obeyed the Savior's orders and made the crowd sit down. If we bear in mind that in the Biblical East the men, even more so than the women, have always preferred multicolored garments, we can imagine the picturesque appearance of this multitude, as they sat in well arranged groups.[748] When all the people had been properly placed, Jesus took in His hands, first the loaves, then the fishes, raised His eyes toward His heavenly Father, and pronounced the prayer which the Jews recited before their meals: "Blessed be Thou, Lord our God, who hast sanctified us by Thy precepts and who bringest forth bread from the earth." The five loaves were somewhat of the shape and size of round ship biscuit, about ten inches in diameter and half an inch thick. These and the fishes Jesus broke into several pieces which He then handed to His Apostles, who distributed them to the crowd. St. Mark and St. Luke, by their choice of words, partly reveal the manner of the miracle. Jesus "broke" the loaves and the fishes; it was a matter of a moment. But again and again He "gave" the pieces thus broken until everyone in the vast multitude had been served. The two kinds of food were continually multiplied in His divine hands, and perhaps also in the hands of the Apostles.

What simplicity of language to relate one of the greatest

---

[747] In 1914, a few days after Easter, with our own eyes we were able to verify this fact, which St. Matthew, St. Mark, and St. John all mention.

[748] St. Mark uses the picturesque expression: πρασιαί πρασιαί (imperfectly translated in the Vulgate by *per partes*), equivalent to the Latin *areolatim*, a term which is used to designate the flower beds and borders of a garden. As the men sat down they presented the appearance of a living parterre.

marvels since the beginning of the world! [749] When Christ
changed the water into wine at Cana, He acted upon the very
substance; in this instance He acts on the quantity, which He
increased many hundredfold, owing to His unlimited creative
power. The Evangelists remark that each person received "as
much" of the food "as they would," and that all "were filled";
this is saying a great deal when there is question of five thousand men, "besides women and children," who must have been
very hungry after so long a journey on foot and so long a
fast. As an ancient Greek commentator [750] says, "this miracle
was a work of superabundant power. . . . Moses gave
manna, but to each one only the needed amount. . . . Elias,
when he fed the widow, gave her no more than was necessary.
But Jesus, being God, gave superabundantly." Yet, as we
noted above,[751] in the Savior's miracles we find a combination
of economy and prodigality. Of this we have a striking example in the present case. When the meal was ended, Jesus said
to His Apostles: "Gather up the fragments that remain, lest
they be lost." All four Evangelists mention this detail. With
these fragments the disciples filled twelve baskets,[752] each
disciple filling his own basket. There remained, therefore,
more than twelve times the quantity that had served as material for the miracle.[753]

St. John alone refers to the unusually deep impression
which this prodigy produced upon those who witnessed it and
who shared in its fruits. They said: "This is of a truth the
prophet that is to come [754] into the world." They were con-

---

[749] From this point of view, these narratives have been admired by many a
Rationalist critic. Cf. J. Weiss, *Die Schriften des N. T.*, I, 120.

[750] Theophylactus († cir. 1107).

[751] Page 343.

[752] In Greek, κόφινοι (Vulg., *cophini*), a sort of basket often represented on
Egyptian monuments.

[753] For the Rationalist interpretations of this prodigy, see Appendix XX.

[754] The Greek text has a double article: ὁ προφήτης ὁ ἐρχόμενος. Literally: "The
prophet, the coming . . ."

vinced that Jesus was the eagerly awaited Messias. In a few
moments their enthusiasm, which unfortunately was too
carnal-minded, assumed enormous proportions. They purposed nothing less than to seize our Lord and proclaim Him
King of Israel, even in spite of Himself, so inflamed was
their exaltation. The utter incompatibility between Christ's
Messianic ideal and that of the Jewish multitudes (a fact
which several times caused our Lord to grieve) could not but
create a deeper gulf between Him and them.

We see here the beginning of a grave crisis, which caused a
large number of His disciples to leave Him. It was the brilliant, striking aspect of this miracle that pleased them. It
represented the kind of ceaseless wonders which these enthusiasts expected of their glorious Messias. They did not
understand that, by building such hopes on Him, they were
lowering Him to their own moral level and were making Him
a mere instrument of their national pride, which thought only
of deliverance from the Roman yoke, the conquest of the
world, and unalloyed temporal happiness. Up to this point in
our Lord's life there had not been so enthusiastic a manifestation of Messianic faith in the ranks of the Jewish people. But
the Savior's refusal to accept this unenlightened and superficial popular favor caused it promptly to decrease and very
largely to grow cold.

On this point the Apostles shared their countrymen's feelings and impressions. If they remained for a while in contact with the crowd, it was to be feared that they too might
rally to its curious projects and might become an additional
hindrance to their Master at this critical juncture. To remove
them from this dangerous temptation, He hastened to send
them away. He ordered them to embark and to depart at once,
without waiting for Him; He would rejoin them at the other
side of the lake, after He had dismissed the people. They not
only obeyed reluctantly, but even somewhat objected to doing

so; for St. Matthew and St. Mark explicitly say that He had to "oblige" them to go up into the boat.[755]

St. Mark mentions the meeting place designated by our Lord. The Apostles were to go "over the water to Bethsaida"; this was not Bethsaida Julias, near which Jesus then was, but "Bethsaida of Galilee," which St. John speaks of in another passage,[756] when he says it was the country of Simon Peter, Andrew, and Philip. These indications show us that it was on the shore of the lake opposite the scene of the miraculous multiplication of the loaves and that it belonged to Galilee. These data seem to settle the dispute regarding the existence of two Bethsaidas at that time. The one of which St. Mark is here speaking, to which Jesus directed the Apostles to proceed, was in Galilee; Bethsaida Julias belonged to the district of Gaulanitis. The former stood on the northwestern shore of the lake; the latter was a little distance from the northeastern shore. It is certainly indicated with great clearness that there were two distinct Bethsaidas. It is not altogether surprising to find two towns of the same name only six miles apart, because the word Bethsaida, in Aramaic, means "fish house," and was well suited to localities on the lake shore. In the present case the word Julias was sufficient to distinguish one of these cities from the other.[757]

Night had almost fallen, when the Apostles weighed anchor.[758] Jesus succeeded in escaping—St. John says that He "fled"—from the midst of the crowd and retired alone to a

---

[755] Ἠνάγκασεν, Vulg., compulit, coegit.

[756] John 12: 21. Cf. 1: 44.

[757] On this question, see Vigouroux, Dictionnaire de la Bible, Vol. I, cols. 1714–1717; Hastings' Dictionary of Christ and the Gospels, I, 198; Tristram, Topography of the Holy Land, pp. 259–261; Buhl, Geographie des alten Palästina, pp. 241–243; Van Kasteren, in the Revue Biblique, 1894, pp. 65–70, etc. The question is a much disputed one. Later on we will endeavor to locate the exact site of western Bethsaida.

[758] The episode that follows is related by St. Matthew, 14: 22 f.; St. Mark, 6: 45–52; and St. John, 6: 14–21.

neighboring hill. As at other decisive hours of His ministry, He entered deeply into prayer. These prayers of the Incarnate Word will ever remain a profound mystery for us. They are unique: they were the adorations, the outpourings, the thanksgivings, and the supplications of a soul hypostatically united with the Divinity. They form one of the chief acts of the priesthood of our sovereign Priest.[759] A grave crisis was beginning in the life of Jesus; it was therefore natural that He should turn again to His heavenly Father for counsel and encouragement.

The crowd, seeing that it was impossible to carry out its design, gradually dispersed, especially as night was approaching. Meanwhile the little ship bearing the Twelve was struggling with difficulty against the waves that were raised by a violent west wind. We have already spoken of the frequency and suddenness of phenomena of this sort on the Sea of Galilee.[760] They are thus described by an eminent author who lived for a long time in Palestine: "I spent a night on the mountains east of the lake, at the head of Wady Shukaiyif. The sun had scarcely set when the wind began to blow towards the lake, and it continued all night long with increasing violence, so that when we descended to the shore next morning the surface of the lake was like that of a boiling cauldron. The wind swept down every wady from the northeast and east with such fury that no efforts of the rowers could have brought a boat to land at any point along that coast. It was no matter of wonder to me, therefore, that the disciples toiled and rowed hard all that night over the sea toward Capernaum." [761] The Apostles were truly to be pitied. According to St. Mark's expression, these stalwart young men were "laboring in rowing" with all their might for several hours. "About the fourth watch of the night," that is, about three o'clock in

[759] On the questions of these prayers, see Vol. I, p. 464.
[760] Page 432.
[761] Thomson, *The Land and the Book*, p. 374.

the morning,[762] they had covered a distance of not more than twenty-five or thirty stadia,[763] whereas in good weather the lake at its widest part (about six miles) could be crossed in two or three hours. To reach Bethsaida, near Capharnaum, they would have had to row for several hours more; for they had scarcely covered half their voyage. St. Matthew, using the same expression as St. Mark, says that the boat "was tossed with the waves."

Of a sudden the Apostles perceived, emerging from the darkness, a human form that seemed to be walking on the water, appearing and disappearing in the midst of the tossing waves. They were already alarmed by the storm; but they were more frightened by their troubled imagination. They thought they had before them one of those harmful phantoms, implicitly believed in at that time by sailors, and in general by Jews, Egyptians, and Orientals.[764] At the sight they uttered a cry of fright. The apparition came nearer the boat and continued, for a few steps, in a direction parallel to it, as though intending to pass it. But suddenly the figure stopped, and a kindly voice, which the disciples joyfully recognized, called out to them from the midst of the tempest: "Be of good heart; it is I, fear ye not." These gentle words are quoted identically by the three Evangelists who narrate the incident. In thus walking, contrary to all laws of gravity, upon the angry waves, Jesus again showed His power over the most terrible elements of nature.

The scene which then took place is recounted only by St.

---

[762] In our Lord's time the Jews divided the night, after the Roman method, into four "watches," of three hours each. They began respectively at 6 P. M., 9 P. M., midnight, and 3 A. M.

[763] The Greek stadium was a linear measure, equal to about 600 feet. The distance indicated by St. John was therefore between 3 and 3½ miles.

[764] Cf. Weber, *System der altsynagogalen palästinischen Theologie,* pp. 242–250; Edersheim, *The Life and Times of Jesus the Messiah,* II, 759; Bousset, *Religion des Judentums,* 2d ed., pp. 387–394; Stauben, *Récits de la Vie Juive en Alsace,* p. 147.

Matthew.[765] Peter, ever prompt and eager, was the first to recover from his fright. "Lord," he said, "bid me to come to Thee upon the waters." He knew that a word from the Savior would suffice for the accomplishment of this other miracle. And his request was discreetly expressed. It is not his desire to be the hero of a prodigy, but the more quickly to rejoin his well-beloved Master.[766] Moreover, he purposes entirely to remove his doubts as to the apparition. "Come," Jesus replies. The Apostle is satisfied; he steps over the side of the boat and begins walking toward the Savior on the surface of the water. But the tempest still raged. When Peter saw himself in the midst of the wild waves, which threatened to engulf him and in which he soon felt himself sinking, he lost his *sang-froid*. In terror, he cried out: "Lord, save me!" He knew that his ability as a swimmer would avail but little in such a sea. "It is indeed Peter, with the features which the Gospels habitually reveal in him: spontaneous, full of faith, enthusiastic, generous, braving danger at first, but impressionable, changeable, and letting himself be alarmed and discouraged by the first obstacle." [767] Jesus hastened to his rescue, took him by the hand, and raised him up. Peter deserved to receive a lesson, and the Divine Teacher gave it to him with mingled gentleness and firmness, saying: "O thou of little faith, why didst thou doubt?" Peter's request is not blamed, for it evinced an excellent heart and great confidence in Jesus. His fault lay in not persevering in that disposition of unbounded trust. It was the imperfection of his faith that caused his humiliating failure.

As soon as the Master and the disciple were in the boat, the wind suddenly ceased, as in the episode of the calming of the tempest. This would seem to be a third miracle by the

[765] Matt. 14:28-31.
[766] Cf. John 21:7.
[767] Fillion, *Saint Pierre*, p. 182.

Ruler of nature. Although accustomed to so many marvels, the Apostles could not restrain their wonderment, which St. Mark sets forth in terms that can hardly be translated into our tongue.[768] We might paraphrase them in this wise: "They were wholly amazed within themselves, and at the very height of astonishment." Had they reflected, they could easily have reasoned from this miracle and from all those which they had witnessed, that nothing was impossible to their Master. In fact, St. Mark states that "their heart was blinded," and that "they understood not concerning the loaves." These words are a sad reflection on their state of mind at this period of our Lord's life. They still had much progress to make. Yet their understanding, which had received so great enlightenment, was not wholly blinded. This fact they proved at that very moment by falling down at Jesus' feet and saying to Him, with deepest respect: "Indeed Thou art the Son of God." They began to feel that He who possessed such power was endowed with a superhuman nature. We may suppose that, while not yet attributing to the title of "Son of God" the fulness of its strict value, they did give it, in the present instance, a meaning higher than that of Messias.

The storm having been calmed, the wind became favorable; and thus the ship bearing Jesus and the Twelve quickly reached the western shore.[769] The Savior disembarked at the beautiful plain of Genesar or Genesareth.[770] It is situated at the foot of the mountains, between Magdala and Khan Mini-yeh. Its shape is roughly that of a triangle with the apex to-

[768] In the Greek: καὶ λίαν ἐκ περισσοῦ ἐν ἑαυτοῖς ἐξίσταντο, Vulg., et plus magis intra se stupebant.

[769] There is no reason for supposing that this constituted a fourth miracle. We should not, therefore, stress too much the words with which St. John closes his account of Christ walking on the water: "And presently the ship was at the land to which they were going."

[770] The former of these two forms of the name seems to be the one that was most commonly used. It is the one used by the Talmud (Neubauer, Géographie du Talmud, p. 15), by Josephus, and likewise by several Greek and Latin manuscripts.

ward the west. On the south and north it is bounded by large folds of the Galilean mountains, on the east by the lake;[771] but its size is not large, about three miles in length along the shore, and even less in width. But its richness was unequalled in the country. Josephus [772] gives a glowing description of it. He says: "The country also that lies over against this lake hath the same name of Genesareth. Its nature is wonderful as well as its beauty. Its soil is so fruitful that all sorts of trees can grow upon it, and the inhabitants accordingly plant all sorts of trees there. For the temper of the air is so well mixed that it agrees well with those several sorts; particularly walnuts, which require the coldest air, flourish there in great plenty. There are palms trees also which grow best in hot air, fig trees also and olives grow near them, which require an air which is more temperate. One may call this place the ambition of nature, where it forces those plants that are naturally enemies to one another to agree together. It is a happy contention of the seasons, as if every one of them laid claim to this country. For it not only nourishes different sorts of autumnal fruit, beyond men's expectation, but preserves them a great while. It supplies men with the principal fruits, with grapes and figs continually, during ten months of the year, and the rest of the fruits as they become ripe together through the whole year." The plain of Genesar was therefore like an immense orchard (a "paradise" Josephus calls it) dotted with villages and villas. Every bit of soil was cultivated with great care.

But the splendor which the Jewish historian boasted of, disappeared centuries ago. The towns and country villas have fallen into ruin; no longer are there any cultivated fields or vineyards or fine trees. In place of a happy, prosperous population of extraordinary density, there are only a few

---

[771] See Fillion and Nicole, *Atlas Géographique de la Bible*, pl. XI.
[772] *Bell. Jud.*, III, x, 8.

poor inhabitants, living in miserable huts. Nevertheless the visitor still finds much to admire. The whiteness of the bay, all sparkling with shells, the rose-colored laurel bushes that flourish along the water courses, the cliffs that appear to guard the two extremities of the plain and gently unite with the foot of the mountains, all these present a sight far from commonplace. Moreover, the soil has lost almost none of its fertility and, as in ancient times, is ready to enrich those who will carefully till it.[773]

Jesus had visited these districts during His great preaching tours. Hence He was immediately recognized when He landed. He was remarkably well loved there, as we learn from the interesting details which St. Matthew and St. Mark [774] furnish about His brief stay at this time. In His honor the inhabitants held a demonstration which must have brought joy to His heart. Messengers of good will carried word to the whole district, and in a short time the Savior saw Himself surrounded by a friendly crowd. Since it was known that He would merely cross the plain without tarrying on the way, sick people were brought on beds in all haste, that He might cure them. In response to these advances, which were so full of faith, He was willing to pass through the villages and hamlets of that prosperous region, leaving everywhere the evidence of His all-powerful goodness. For greater convenience, the sick were gathered in the public squares. They begged the Savior to let them touch the sacred fringe of His cloak, the mere touch of which had restored health to the woman with a flow of blood only a short time before. He graciously allowed them to do this, and all who touched it were healed. Those few hours were a time of joy for Jesus, as also for that respectful and friendly population.

---

[773] See Stanley, *Sinai and Palestine*, pp. 374–382; Chauvet and Isambert, *Syrie, Palestine*, pp. 460–463.

[774] Matt. 14: 34–36; Mark 6: 53–56.

IV. The Promise of the Eucharist

From this point onward for some time we have only St. John as our guide.[775] And an excellent guide he is, since we shall have to do with one of the most important events in the life of his Divine Friend, an event which he witnessed with his own eyes.

In the course of that day which Jesus began in the plain of Genesareth, He returned to Capharnaum and was soon joined by a number of those whom He had miraculously fed in the desert and from whose enthusiasm He had escaped. After they had unsuccessfully waited and searched for Him, they crossed the lake in boats which had come for them to a point on the shore nearest the scene of the miracle. They knew that Jesus made Capharnaum His center and ordinary place of residence, and they hoped to find Him there, because, despite their disappointment of the previous day, they were eager to see and hear Him again.

The meeting occurred in the synagogue,[776] where there began between Him and them a conversation which quickly became a discourse of the greatest significance, full of sublime revelations. It contains things "unheard-of" even in the Savior's life, in which so many deeds and sayings deserve this epithet. The dominant idea is that of a mystical food which every true disciple of Jesus must receive if he is to share in the Messianic redemption. This heavenly food first represents faith in Christ as the Savior of the world;[777] then, with equal clearness, it designates the Sacrament of the Eucharist.[778] St. John does not relate the Last Supper, where this divine mystery was instituted; he judged that the three previous Evan-

---

[775] John 6 : 22–72.
[776] John 6 : 60.
[777] John 6 : 25–47.
[778] John 6 : 48–72.

gelists had recounted it with sufficient fulness. On the other hand, he here shows us, exactly one year before that institution, our blessed Lord announcing and promising the Eucharistic manna in terms as precise as those of the institution. It is a promise full of love, as will be the gift itself. However, it provokes a schism even in the ranks of the Savior's disciples, and a beginning of apostasy in the very midst of the college of the twelve Apostles.

The discourse contains four groups of thoughts,[779] marked by transitional phrases expressing the surprise and dissatisfaction that our Lord's words aroused in His hearers.[780] Passing from one of these groups to the other, the ideas which the Divine Master wished to set forth, majestically evolve and become more emphatic.

The first part is an informal conversation, made up of four little dialogues,[781] in each of which we find a question by those present and an answer by Jesus. This questioning by the crowd shows to what an extent they were captivated by the Savior's words: no sooner does He reply to one question, than He is asked another. "Rabbi [Master], when camest Thou hither?" they first ask; for they did not know under what circumstances He had returned to Capharnaum. Without directly replying to the question, which was prompted by affectionate curiosity, the Master, according to His custom, at once raises the conversation to a higher plane, saying: "Amen, amen I say to you, you seek Me, not because you have seen miracles, but because you did eat of the loaves and were filled. Labor not for the meat which perisheth, but for that which endureth unto life everlasting, which the Son of Man will give you. For Him hath God, the Father, sealed."

The first words of this reply contain a well merited rebuke.

779 John 6: 25-40, 41-52, 53-60, 61-72 (in the Greek text: 6: 25-40, 41-51, 52-59, 60-71).

780 John 6: 41, 53, 61 (in the Greek text: 6, 41, 52, 60).

781 John 6: 25-27, 28-29, 30-33, 34-40.

Our Lord's miracles were always and primarily "signs," as
He here reminds His listeners, by using the most characteristic name by which they were called. They were striking, eloquent signs, showing forth His divine mission, because they
were, as Jesus says, the "seal" of God Himself, affixed to the
credentials which presented His Son to the world as the Messias. But the multitudes, far from grasping the lofty meaning
of those signs, had merely seen in them brilliant deeds, as also
the self-centered gratification of their material interests.
Thus, on the previous day, instead of seeking "the sign in the
bread," they saw only "the bread in the sign." In contrast with
this vain quest which, in the case of many of His superficial
admirers, was addressed less toward His person than toward
His gifts, Jesus in the second half of His reply speaks of the
courageous labor He requires of whosoever wishes to be a
real disciple: it is a labor that He will reward, not, as in the
desert, by perishable food, that sustains life only for a little
while, but by an incorruptible food that gives everlasting life.
Here we have, at the beginning of the discourse, the magnificent idea which, gradually rising higher and higher, becomes
the idea of the Eucharistic bread.

The first of the little dialogues introduces the idea of the
heavenly bread; the second indicates how it must be obtained.
The audience entered into Jesus' thought. They understood
that they must exercise a personal activity to make themselves
worthy of so precious a food. But what is to be the nature of
their activity? They ask, therefore, "What shall we do, that
we may work the works of God?" that is, works pleasing to
God in a special way in each separate case. In this expression
we recognize the disciples of those Pharisees, those doctors of
the law, whose constant preoccupation was this: By what particularly meritorious act (fasting, almsgiving, sacrifice,
prayer) can I obtain such or such a favor from Heaven?
Their thought always turned toward outward things, at the

expense of the interior life. With these many works which they proposed to perform with zeal, Jesus, in His reply, contrasts one single work, not difficult in itself, yet of the greatest value: "This is the work of God, that you believe in Him whom He hath sent." Evidently one could not do an act more pleasing to God than to receive His ambassador, His authorized representative, with earnest faith.

Our Lord's hearers then ask Him: "What sign therefore dost Thou show, that we may see and may believe Thee? What dost Thou work? Our fathers did eat manna in the desert, as it is written: [782] He gave them bread from heaven to eat." At first sight, this language is astonishing; it might almost be considered insolent. Those men, who the day before saw in the miracle of the multiplication of the loaves a sufficient reason to treat Jesus as the Messias, now demand that He perform a still more conspicuous prodigy, like that of the manna. This fact by itself shows the superficial and altogether human character of the confidence which they had in Him at first. True, He had deliberately lost it by refusing to accept their homage in the form they wished. Besides, He had just offered them a food of supreme worth, and had thus aroused among them a desire to see another great miracle performed by Him in their presence. They cite the miracle of the manna as an example, because an old Jewish tradition said that, "as the first redeemer [Moses] made manna fall from heaven, so the second redeemer [the Messias] will also make manna fall from heaven." [783] If Christ wishes to be honored as the liberator of Israel, let Him, then, furnish undeniable evidence of His rights.

To this formal demand He makes a noble reply: "Amen, amen I say to you; Moses gave you not bread from heaven,

[782] Ps. 77:24. On the miracle of the manna, see Ex. 16:11-36; Num. 11:7-9; Wis. 16:20 f.

[783] *Midrash Koheleth*, fol. 73, c. Cf. A. Wünsche, *Neue Beiträge zur Erläuterung der Evangelien aus Talmud und Midrasch*, p. 521.

but My Father giveth you the true bread from heaven. For the bread of God is that which cometh down from heaven and giveth life to the world." They speak of manna, which was in reality a heavenly bread, produced by a perpetual miracle for many years. But it was a small matter when compared with the infinitely loftier food which Jesus was promising to those who would believe in Him. Only of this food could anybody say that it is "the true bread from heaven";[784] it alone fulfilled the idea of heavenly nourishment. And, strictly speaking, it was not Moses, but God who gave the manna; and it did not really descend from Heaven, whereas the mystical bread announced by our Lord came from Heaven in very truth and could give life, not only to a small nation, but to the entire world.

Influenced by this enticing description, but still clinging to the external side of the thought, the Savior's questioners said: "Lord, give us always this bread." Their request was like that of the Samaritan woman who asked for the living water that was so much better than the water of Jacob's well.[785] In the Savior's words they see a magnificent but mysterious promise, which they at once interpret in conformity with their carnal desires. Let Jesus give them this priceless bread, and they will decide to join Him as faithful disciples.

Jesus, narrowing His subject still further, then makes a sublime answer to that fickle multitude. "I am the bread of life; he that cometh to Me shall not hunger; and he that believeth in Me shall never thirst. But I said unto you, that you also have seen Me, and you believe not. All that the Father giveth to Me shall come to Me; and him that cometh to Me, I will not cast out. Because I came down from heaven, not to do My own will, but the will of Him that sent Me. Now

---

[784] In the Greek, with two articles which emphasize the thought: τὸν ἄρτον . . . τὸν ἀληθινόν, "the bread (come) from heaven, the true."

[785] John 4 : 15.

this is the will of the Father who sent Me: that of all that He hath given Me, I should lose nothing; but should raise it up again in the last day. And this is the will of My Father that sent Me: that everyone who seeth the Son, and believeth in Him, may have life everlasting, and I will raise him up in the last day."

What dignity and beauty and depth in these words! How well the Divine Teacher profits by any circumstance to elevate the minds and hearts of men! In the course of this dialogue, His thought continues to advance and to rise higher. After speaking in veiled terms of the wonderful bread that He was ready to give the world, He now clearly and openly declares that this bread of immortality, this ideal and only true bread, is Himself. Consequently it is His own Person He offers, as a generous, incomparable gift. "I am the bread of life." By identifications of a like kind, He later says that He is the light of the world, the gate of the sheep, the good Shepherd, the way, the truth, and the life, the true vine.[786] Each of these appellations draws attention to some quality of His nature. He calls Himself "the bread of life," that is, the bread whose very essence consists in procuring life in its full extent, in its most varied manifestations.[787]

But this spiritual bread must be eaten and assimilated spiritually. For it to produce its marvelous effects, one must needs go to Christ and adhere to Him by a firm, active, living faith. When these two conditions are fulfilled, the feast will be complete, the blessed dinner guest of Jesus will no more hunger or thirst. But those who were listening to the Master did not fulfil those conditions, as He told them in great sorrow. And yet they had seen Him close at hand, with all the prerogatives with which God had endued Him, with all the signs

[786] John 8:12; 10:7, 11; 14:6; 15:1.
[787] Compare the analogous expressions: the tree of life (Gen. 2:9; Prov. 3:18, etc.), the fountain of life (Apoc. 21:6, etc.), the words of life (John 6:69; 1 John 1:1).

by which the heavenly Father attested His mission. But they had been unable, or rather unwilling, to be convinced. In a sort of monologue,[788] Jesus tried to derive some consolation. After all, notwithstanding the unbelief of so large a number of men, His work will succeed. All whom His Father has destined for Him and given to Him, will come to Him; these He will not reject, but will receive warmly. How could He refuse to receive them, since He came down from Heaven, by His Incarnation, to do the will of God and since the purpose and end of that will is precisely the salvation of all those who come to His Christ? Jesus dwells upon this profound thought, repeating it several times and promising His disciples eternal life and resurrection at the end of time.

As soon as the Savior had finished the first part of His discourse, loud murmurs were heard all about him. The Jews, in the early period of their history, had often murmured against God.[789] Our Lord's last words quoted above particularly shocked His hearers; whereupon they exchanged words of dissatisfaction so rudely as to interrupt the speaker. Referring to an assertion that had especially scandalized them, they said to one another: "Is not this [790] Jesus, the Son of Joseph, whose father and mother we know? How then saith He, I came down from heaven?" The objection is almost the same as that offered by the people of Nazareth on two occasions.[791] It shows a remarkable narrowness of mind and a deep ignorance of God's ways. The Evangelist here calls them "the Jews," alluding to their hostility to Jesus; [792] they could not, of course, know the well-guarded secret of the Incarnation of the Son of God. But they should have re-

---

[788] John 6: 37–40.

[789] Cf. Num. 11: 1; 14: 1; 1 Cor. 10: 11, etc.

[790] Contemptuous pronoun, as on other occasions.

[791] Cf. Luke 4: 22; Matt. 13: 55 f. (Mark 6: 3).

[792] In the Fourth Gospel, the word "Jews" ordinarily designates certain categories of the theocratic nation, insofar as they were ill-disposed towards our Lord.

called that the Lord of Israel had often chosen His prophets, kings, and highest representatives from the lowliest ranks
of society.

We wish here to make a remark apropos of our Savior's
audience. The crowd that filled the synagogue in Capharnaum
was made up mostly of unlettered people, very ordinary from
the standpoint of their education and social status. However,
throughout the dialogue they understand the Savior's thought
quite well. They murmur, and later become exasperated; but
that is precisely because they grasp the full significance of
the terms used by Jesus and because they cannot reconcile His
words with the idea they had of Him. In this connection, they
are a help to our understanding of the meaning of this memorable discourse. Let us now consider the second part, which
is begun by the murmuring of a portion of the listeners.

Our Lord speaks with perfect calmness, not entering upon
any explanation with regard to the error about His birth;
He merely repeats His assertions with new emphasis. But
the thought advances a step, for Jesus informs His hearers
how they can come to Him and what hinders them from believing in Him. And presently He gives the metaphor of
the heavenly bread a meaning much loftier than it had up
to this point. He says: "Murmur not among yourselves. No
man can come to Me, except the Father, who hath sent Me,
draw him; and I will raise him up in the last day. It is written
in the prophets: And they shall all be taught of God. Everyone
that hath heard of the Father, and hath learned, cometh to
Me. Not that any man hath seen the Father; but He who is
of God, He hath seen the Father. Amen, amen I say unto
you: He that believeth in Me, hath everlasting life."

He thus delicately and clearly indicates what prevented so
many of the Jews from believing in Him: owing to their
own fault, they had not received the teaching by means of
which God purposed leading them to His Christ. No one has

excelled St. Augustine [793] in describing that divine attraction
of which our Lord speaks here, those gentle though powerful
solicitations of grace by which the Father urges souls to go
to His Son and give themselves to Him. But that attraction
does violence to no one's free will, and is but too often resisted.
The text quoted by Christ, "They shall all be taught
of God," is taken from the prophet Isaias,[794] who portrays
the blessings that God will bestow on His people at the time
of the Messias. For predestined souls, one of His choicest
favors will consist in their being instructed and drawn directly
by Him and, if they accept His teaching with faith, in their
being thus led to the Savior, who will obtain eternal life for
them.

The hearers might object that they had not seen the Father and had not received any direct message from Him.
Jesus forestalls the objection by affirming that He at least,
who had come "from God," [795] knew this Divine Father by
a perfect knowledge. Let them, therefore, be instructed by
the Son! This passage is one of those most clearly attesting
the Divinity of our Lord Jesus Christ.

Abruptly at this point the idea of the spiritual food with
which the Savior identified Himself from the very beginning
of the discourse, is again introduced under a still nobler and
more generous aspect. Jesus now speaks, not only of faith
in Him and His mission, but of the Eucharist, which He
promises to give to men, to obtain the true life and salvation
for them. "I am the bread of life. Your fathers did eat manna
in the desert, and are dead. This is the bread which cometh
down from heaven; that if any man eat of it, he may not die.
I am the living bread which came down from heaven. If any

---

[793] *Tract. in Joan.*, XXVI, 4.

[794] Is. 54 : 13. Cf. Jer. 31 : 34. The words "in the prophets" stand for that
part of the Hebrew Bible which bore the title of *Nebi'im*, "Prophets."

[795] In the Greek: ὁ ὢν παρὰ τοῦ θεοῦ, "who is close to God." Here the preposi-
tion παρά is equivalent to πρός in John 1 : 1.

man eat of this bread, he shall live forever; and the bread
that I will give, is My flesh, for the life of the world."

Through these short, abrupt sentences we hear the beating
of the Sacred Heart of the Good Shepherd, promising to
become the nourishment of His sheep. The style of the language, as well as the thought, shows His emotion. But is
this passage really about the Holy Eucharist? Beyond any
doubt; for we have many solid proofs of it. This is not the
place to set forth those proofs at length;[796] for our purpose
it will suffice to point out the chief ones. Some are derived from
the text itself, others from the context, and still others from
the traditional interpretation of this whole part of our Lord's
discourse.

The text leaves nothing to be desired. If studied according
to the ordinary rules of language, the expressions used by
Christ from this point onward cannot, like the preceding expressions, be applied to faith; they are suited only to the Eucharist. After again mentioning the bread of life, for the
purpose of connecting this portion of His discourse with the
first part, Jesus repeatedly employs new and quite characteristic expressions ("My flesh, My blood," and especially, "to
eat My flesh, to drink My blood") the meaning of which is not
at all doubtful. This new phraseology certainly introduces a
new subject. It is also in perfect accord with the words that
the Savior pronounced when instituting the Eucharist. There
also He gave His body, that is, His flesh as food and His blood
as drink to His Apostles.[797] The promise, then, conforms entirely to the institution itself, which completes and explains

[796] See the commentaries on St. John's Gospel, e. g., Corluy, Commentarius in
Evangelium S. Joannis, 2d ed., pp. 57–62; Knabenbauer, Commentarius in Evangelium secundum Joannem, pp. 230–245; Schanz, Commentar über das Evangelium
des hl. Johannes, I, 284–295; Fillion, L'Évangile de S. Jean, pp. 133–143. See
especially Cardinal Wiseman's scholarly work, The Real Presence; also the chief
theologians, and Patrizi, Commentatio de Christo Pane Vitae, 1851. Appendix
XXI replies to certain objections of Protestant and Rationalist critics.

[797] Cf. Matt. 26: 26–29; Mark 14: 22–25; Luke 22: 15-20.

it, so as to render any doubt impossible. And let us note an important difference established by Christ Himself between the bread of life and the eating and drinking of His flesh and blood. God the Father distributed the former by drawing to His Son disciples who adhered to Him by a living faith; as to the Eucharistic food, it is not to be distributed until a later period, and by Jesus in person.

Presently we shall see that the context, that is, the remainder of the discourse, together with the incident that was provoked in the audience, requires the same conclusion. The words and the intention there expressed are so clear and precise that they have very commonly received, at all periods in the history of exegesis, the meaning we have just indicated. The Apostolic Fathers considered them as allusions to the Holy Eucharist.[798] Scarcely a single one of the early doctors applies the whole discourse to faith in Jesus;[799] one of them, St. Augustine, retracted later.[800] The vast majority apply this second half of our Lord's discourse integrally to the Eucharist.[801] All the interpreters and theologians, whether of the Middle Ages or of modern times, rallied to this practically unanimous opinion of the Fathers, save for very rare exceptions.[802] In our day, Catholic theology and exegesis recognize no other view. And this interpretation is so strictly required by the study of the text that a large number of Protestants have abandoned the theories of Luther and Cal-

---

[798] Particularly St. Ignatius of Antioch, *Epist. ad Rom.*, VII, 3; *Epist. ad Philad.*, IV, 1, and XII, 2; *Epist ad. Eph.*, V, 2; *Epist. ad Smyrn.*, II, 1.

[799] Such are Origen, *Hom. in Levit.*, VII, sec. 5, and elsewhere; Eusebius of Caesarea, *De Theol. Eccl.*, II, 12; St. Augustine, *De Doctr. Christ.*, III, 16.

[800] *Tractat. in Joan.*, XXVI, 15; *De Civitate Dei*, XX, 25.

[801] This proof is developed in the following works: V. Schmitt, *Die Verheissung der Eucharistie bei den Vätern*, 1900; *Die Verheissung der Eucharistie bei Cyrill von Jerusalem und Joannes Chrysost.*, 1903; Adam, *Die Eucharistielehre des heil. Augustinus*, 1908. See also Corluy, *op. cit.*

[802] Bérengar in the Middle Ages; in modern times, Cajetan and Jansenius.

vin on this point and have acknowledged [803] that, although in the first part of the discourse Jesus was speaking of faith, the rest of the passage can apply only to the Eucharist, and that He was then promising its institution at a later date. Several Rationalists and recent critics [804] also adopt this view as being required by the natural sense of the language. They add, however, that it was the author of the Fourth Gospel who introduced this idea; but the avowal is of value.

Let us now return to the Savior's beautiful words, which we find so consoling. In replying to an objection by His audience, He had already contrasted the manna with the true bread from Heaven, to show the inferiority of the miraculous food of the Pharan desert. He here resumes the antithesis from another point of view. The ancestors of the Jewish people did eat manna and, thanks to it, they were able to exist in a barren country; but it could not procure perpetual existence for them. Only the Eucharistic bread, only the flesh of Christ, when it is worthily received, can give everlasting life, for it is a food that veritably descends from heaven and possesses in itself a principle of eternal life.

At this point Jesus was again interrupted by murmurs and loud shouts. A tumultuous discussion [805] had begun in the audience between the two parties that were formed apropos of the Savior's last words. One party, still impressed by the speaker's personality, and also by the miracle of the preceding day, accepted His promise, though not fully understanding it, and acknowledged Him to be the promised Messias. The other party loudly and indignantly protested, saying: "How can this man give us His flesh to eat?" They had,

[803] Notably F. Keil, *Commentar über das Evangelium des Johannes*, pp. 270–274; T. Zahn, *Das Evangelium des Johannes ausgelegt*, pp. 348–356.

[804] Cf. Strauss, *Das Leben Jesu*, 1835, I, 649–652; recently H. J. Holtzmann, *Das Johannesevangelium*, p. 110; W. Bauer, *Das Johannesevangelium*, p. 71.

[805] In the Greek, ἐμάχοντο, Vulg., *litigabant*.

therefore, grasped the general meaning and import of the Savior's words. But they made the great mistake of taking the words in their crudest and most material acceptation, as though the speaker meant to have His flesh cut up and the bleeding pieces given them as food.

What will Jesus do now? Will He offer a further explanation of His words? Will He furnish some details about the manner of His presence in the Eucharistic food? No, He merely repeats His promise, stressing the terms He has just used and the necessity, for all true believers, of eating His flesh and drinking His blood if they wish to share in eternal life and remain in close union with Him. "Amen, amen I say to you: Except you eat the flesh of the Son of Man and drink His blood, you shall not have life in you. He that eateth My flesh and drinketh My blood, hath everlasting life; and I will raise him up in the last day. For My flesh is meat indeed; and My blood is drink indeed. He that eateth My flesh and drinketh My blood, abideth in Me, and I in him. As the living Father hath sent Me, and I live by the Father; so he that eateth Me, the same also shall live by Me. This is the bread that came down from heaven. Not as your fathers did eat manna, and are dead. He that eateth this bread, shall live forever."

What clearness there is in these words, and what infinite goodness in this promise! Jesus enlarges on His thought. That the Eucharistic banquet may be complete, He adds a heavenly drink to the heavenly food. He will give His disciples His flesh to eat and His blood to drink. He does not simply invite them to His table; He orders them, and threatens with the loss of spiritual life all those who absent themselves. On the other hand, obedient souls who do not tire of being nourished with this sacred food, will enjoy immense advantages, which the beloved disciple expresses in beautiful language. In this world there will be the "communion": He abiding in us; we abiding in Him; we living in Him and by Him, as He lives in His Father and for His Father. It would be impossible to think of a more intimate union, one more divine, blessed, and strengthening. And after death there will be everlasting life, assuring this union of unending duration. After hearing these words of the Good Shepherd and meditating on them, who would not wish to be always nourished with His flesh and blood?

But very many of Christ's hearers did not feel this holy desire. The fourth and last part of the discourse shows this. A hostile portion of those present had already murmured and loudly disputed. Now the opposition comes from the ranks of the Savior's disciples properly so called, from those who accompanied Him with the Apostles in His preaching journeys. A large number of them, as the text explicitly says,[806] uttered violent and bitter protests: "This saying is hard,[807] and who can hear it?" They too interpreted the Savior's words as though referring to a Thyestean feast, in which the food was parts of the human body. They were so shocked as to wish to withdraw from the best of masters. This was a terrible crisis for their faith. What will Jesus do, seeing and understanding what was taking place in their minds? He explains Himself; not, however, by recanting, but by affirming that nothing is impossible to Him and that His promise, while remaining literally true, is not to be taken in a material, carnal sense. "Doth this scandalize you?" He says. "If then you shall see the Son of Man ascend up where He was before? It is the spirit that quickeneth: the flesh profiteth nothing. The words that I have spoken to you are spirit and life. But there are some of you that believe not."

By the words "ascend up where He was before," Christ

---

806 Πολλοί, Vulg., *multi*.
807 The Greek adjective σκληρός means hard morally, "intolerable," as Tertullian translates it.

plainly refers to His Ascension,[808] which will bring Him back to Heaven, clothed in His sacred humanity. If those of His disciples who were on the point of apostatizing witnessed in advance this glorious mystery, which attested infinite power, they would have no difficulty in believing that He could keep His Eucharistic promise in a simple, natural manner by changing the consecrated bread and wine into His flesh and blood. They would then put full trust in Him and would no longer be scandalized.

The words, "It is the spirit that quickeneth; the flesh profiteth nothing," are a general statement, meaning that, in the human organism, it is the spirit, the soul, that confers life. The flesh, if it remains alone, is dead, inert, and promptly decays. In quoting this proverb, Jesus makes the sense of His words more precise: He did not have in mind to distribute His flesh separated from His spirit, as had been crudely supposed. His words were spirit and life, and must be interpreted according to the spirit. The flesh that is to be eaten and the blood that is to be drunk will be the flesh and blood of the Son of Man ascended into Heaven, transfigured, living forever. They will not be carnal food, because they will be spiritualized and will be presented in a mystical even though real manner.

Then Jesus continues, in a tone of sadness: "But there are some of you that believe not." Apropos of these tragic words, the Evangelist makes a profound remark: "For Jesus knew from the beginning who they were that did not believe, and who he was that would betray Him." The Divine Master was not deceived about the disciples whom He had drawn to Him. From the very outset He foresaw the frailty of the faith and the apostasy of some of them, and that foreknowledge included particularly the treason of Judas. Not only was

[808] Not, as has at times been said, His Crucifixion.

our Lord not surprised by the present crisis, but He warned His followers that it would happen. Therefore He adds these words, which bring His discourse to a close: "Therefore did I say to you, that no man can come to Me, unless it be given him by My Father."

The schism occurred despite this final delicate appeal. Thereupon many disciples left Jesus permanently. They "went back," says the Evangelist, by way of branding this ungrateful abandonment. It was a grave, decisive moment. Notwithstanding the pain He felt at this separation, the Savior judged it well to test also the faith of His Apostles, who were then gathered around Him.[809] He therefore put this plain question to them: "Will you also go away?" The reply came at once, and it was Simon Peter who took upon himself to answer in the name of all. In the Fourth Gospel, as in the Synoptics, he is the spokesman of the Apostolic College. In the present instance, we see him with all his earnestness of character, with all his faith and his love for the Master. He said: "Lord, to whom shall we go? Thou hast the words of eternal life. And we have believed and have known that Thou art the Holy One of God." The Savior was satisfied, for this profession of faith, a worthy prelude to that which the same Apostle will make on a still more solemn occasion, was as explicit as it could be at that time. The Apostles will not leave Jesus, for in Him they found the most perfect ideal, the ablest teacher for their intellectual and religious needs, the Messias in person. The expression, "We have believed and have known," is remarkable. At first they were attached to their divine Friend by faith; and that faith led them to an ever growing acquaintance, thanks to the continual relations they had with Jesus. The significant title, "Holy One of

---

[809] No doubt, the crowd had dispersed and our Lord had left the synagogue with His disciples.

God," [810] had already been addressed to our Lord in the synagogue at Capharnaum.[811] It designated the Messias, as being eminently consecrated to God and endued by Him with great holiness.[812]

Jesus, still under the impression of the deep grief caused Him by the departure of so many ungrateful followers, says: "Have not I chosen you twelve? And one of you is a devil." Among His closest and most privileged disciples, among those who should have been faithful above all others, there was a germ of apostasy, even a germ of treason, which supposes a diabolical nature in the future traitor. St. John reveals the name of this devil: "He [Jesus] meant Judas Iscariot, the son of Simon: for this same was about to betray Him, whereas he was one of the Twelve." The traitor so well concealed his scheme that the other Apostles, except perhaps the beloved disciple, suspected nothing until the consummation of the treason.

---

[810] This is the best authorized reading. The corresponding words, "the Christ, the Son of God," which we find in several Greek manuscripts, the Vulgate, etc., seem to be taken from Matt. 16: 16.

[811] Mark 1: 24; Luke 4: 34.

[812] See Appendix XXII.

FOURTH PERIOD

From the Third Pasch to the Feast of Dedication

The numerous and varied events that have engaged our attention from the outset of Christ's personal ministry, extended over a period of about two years and a half.[813] We have now reached the third Pasch of His public life, the beginning of its last year. Its dominant note is that of the fierce opposition of His powerful enemies. We have already witnessed several serious conflicts, which created an impassable gulf between Him and them. In the religious domain they were always vanquished by His forceful argumentation, and they were jealous of the multitude's growing attachment to Him, an attachment that was caused by His holiness and miracles and doctrine. And already they had formed the criminal design of removing Him *per fas et nefas;* but they dared not yet adopt effective measures to accomplish their purpose. Now that the favor with which the populace surrounded our Lord has visibly diminished, His foes' hostility becomes more active. They will have less fear of attacking Him to His face, of threatening Him, and of combining for more assured success in destroying Him. As Jesus Himself foretells, their hatred will triumph.

The Savior does not change His principles of action, but He somewhat modifies His ordinary manner of conduct. Since He has less success before the people, He lives in comparative retirement and does not appear publicly as much as

[813] See pages 4-8.

before. The curiosity of a large number of His countrymen, who wanted more brilliant prodigies, is no longer so fully satisfied by His miracles, which now become less frequent. Sometimes protests are raised against His doctrines; and revelations, which presuppose an infinite love on His part, are even called "hard"; He will give His divine lessons in public less often than formerly. On the other hand, He will show redoubled zeal in devoting Himself to the essential task of training His Apostles and intimate disciples, so as to prepare them for the difficult and important office which they will have to fill after His Resurrection and Ascension.

CHAPTER I

The Savior's Journey into the Regions of Phenicia, Upper Galilee, and Decapolis

WE here enter upon a little series of episodes about which St. Luke is silent. St. Matthew and St. Mark, especially the latter, relate them with vivid details.

I. New Conflict with the Scribes and Pharisees [814]

These rigid, narrow-minded doctors had seen for themselves or had learned through others that some of Christ's disciples, before their meals, neglected the washing of hands, which was prescribed by the Jewish traditions. This was an opportunity, like a former one regarding fasting, to blame the Savior for the fault of His disciples, and thus to compromise Him. In fact, negligence of this sort was a very serious offense in the eyes of the Scribes.

In passing, let us again note the Evangelists' correct knowledge of Jewish things and customs, and the confidence we should therefore have in all they relate. The Talmudic writings confirm all the details here set down by St. Matthew and St. Mark. The latter's description is the more complete. He uses the technical expression, to eat "with common hands," and explains that it means, "with unwashed hands." We would say, "with profane hands." [815] The adjective "common" is

---

[814] Matt. 15: 1–20; Mark 7: 1–23.

[815] The adjective κοινός, "common," is here equivalent to the rabbinical expression hhol. It is used in this same sense in various passages of the Old and New Testament. See in the Greek text, 1 Mach. 1: 47, 62; Acts 10: 14, 28; 11: 18; Rom. 14: 14; Heb. 10: 29; Apoc. 21: 27.

opposed to "holy, pure" (in a moral sense). Abundant information is furnished on the point in question by the Talmud in the curious tractate entitled *Yadaim*, "The Hands," the four chapters of which consider all imaginable cases and also treat of unrelated matters.[816] You will find there, for example, the discussion of what makes hands legally impure, the quantity of water needed to purify them, the requisite qualities of that water, the first and second ablutions, the way they are to be performed. This purificatory ablution was called *netilath yadaim*, "the raising of the hands," because anyone purifying them according to the rules had to raise them so that the water poured on the finger tips would run down to the knuckles. There was really no question of washing the hands completely, but only of letting a little water flow upon them.[817] Our two Evangelists state under what circumstances this ceremony was obligatory. It was performed by anybody returning home after being exposed to the possibility of having contracted a legal impurity, even innocently and unwittingly. Such a defilement would be caused by mere contact, on the street or in the market-place or in another person's house, with any person or object which the law classified as impure; for example, by brushing against a leper's garment, or the garment of a pagan or of a man who had touched a corpse.

[816] Cf. H. Strack, *Einleitung in den Talmud*, 2d ed., 1874, p. 43. For the details, see the large collections of Lightfoot, Schoettgen, and Wetzstein, *In Matth.*, 15:2; A. Wunsche, *Neue Beiträge zur Erläuterung der Evangelien*, p. 180; Edersheim, *Life and Times of Jesus the Messiah*, II, 9–13; Lagrange, *L'Évangile selon S. Marc*, pp. 171–174.

[817] A detail in St. Mark's description offers a very real difficulty. In the Greek text it is said that the Jews "wash their hands πυγμῇ." According to several interpreters, this means, "with closed fist," *i. e.*, each hand in turn being vigorously rubbed by the other fist. The Vulgate translates this word by *crebro*, "often," as if it were a synonym of πυκνά (cf. Luke 5:33). According to ancient Greek commentators, Theophylact and Euthymius, the meaning is "up to the elbow." The expression has not yet been clarified. Moreover, for this liturgical washing, the rabbis seem to say that it sufficed if it reached the end of the fingers. Cf. *Kullin*, 106, 1, a.

Moreover, as St. Mark informs his Roman readers, the washing of hands was not the only washing prescribed in connection with meals. He says: "Many other things there are that have been delivered to them to observe, the washings of cups and of pots and of brazen vessels and of beds." [818] This detail also is true to facts. [819] For purposes of legal purification, all wooden, stone, or metal utensils employed at meals, were dipped into water, washed, and rubbed. As for an earthenware vessel, when it had contracted any ritualistic stain, it had to be broken. These "traditions of the ancients" were highly prized by the Jews of our Lord's time; [820] the Talmud is full of them. Even to-day a large number of these prescriptions are rigorously followed by many of their descendants, [821] who are still impregnated with the Pharisaic spirit. Tradition has always played a considerable and legitimate part in the history of revealed religion. But such exact observance of it in matters of secondary importance was not really honoring it. Yet the Pharisees were as strict about these petty details as about the higher commandments of the Law. What senseless things their doctors have said with regard to the purification of the hands! "If anyone eats bread [*i. e.,* eats a meal] without washing his hands, it is as though he went to a harlot"; "whoever despises the [religious] washing of hands will be extirpated from this world"; "there are devils especially charged to injure those who do not wash their hands before meals." [822] A certain rabbi, named Eleazar, who presumed to neglect these ablutions, was excommunicated by

[818] That is, the couch on which one stretched out when dining.

[819] Cf. Schürer, *Geschichte des jüdischen Volkes,* 3d ed., II, 478–483; the Talmudic tractates *Kelim and Abodah zarah.*

[820] Gal. 1:14; Josephus, *Ant.,* XIII, x, 6.

[821] See C. Coypel, *Le Judaisme, Esquisse des Mœurs Juives,* 1887, pp. 54–63. "The Jews of Palestine, with whom we happened to eat when traveling, only with great reluctance loaned their dishes to strangers, so as not to be obliged to break them, if they were earthenware." Lagrange, *L'Évangile selon S. Marc,* p. 174.

[822] Cf. Schürer, *op. cit.*

the Sanhedrin; after his death, a large stone was placed on his coffin to show that he had deserved death by stoning.[823]

We can easily understand what severe judgment was passed on the liberty which several of the Savior's disciples took with those regulations, looked upon as sacrosanct. And, of course, their Master was held to be responsible for their conduct. But the Pharisees dared not accuse Him directly; they asked Him this insidious question: "Why do Thy disciples transgress the tradition of the ancients? For they wash not their hands when they eat bread."

Our Lord's reply was crushing. Without making a direct apology for His disciples, without concerning Himself with the immediate question about the traditional ablutions, He at once raises the problem to a higher plane, so as to solve it with finality. His concise and forcible argument urges two reasons. Replying to His adversaries by a counter-attack and meeting their accusation with a much more serious complaint, He shows them that they were wont to transform and grievously injure the weightiest commandments of the Decalogue, on the pretext of observing their traditions. He then condemns their sacrilegious hypocrisy with a text from Holy Writ: "Why do you also transgress the commandment of God for your tradition? For God said: Honor thy father and mother; and: He that shall curse father or mother, let him die the death. But you say: Whosoever shall say to father or mother: Corban (which is a gift), whatsoever proceedeth from me, shall profit thee. And he shall not honor [824] his father or his mother. And you have made void the commandment of God for your tradition. And many other such like things you do. Hypocrites, well hath Isaias prophesied of you, saying: This people honoreth Me with their lips; but their

---

[823] *Bab. Berashoth*, 46, 2.

[824] The word "honor" is here used in the special sense which St. Paul gives it, I Tim. 5:3, 17, to designate financial succor.

heart is far from Me. And in vain do they worship Me, teaching doctrines and commandments of men." [825]

We have here, from first word to last, an *argumentum ad hominem* which deals a heavy blow to the accusers. They well deserved the reproach of violating God's commandments for the sake of their purely human tradition. The justice of that reproach is shown by a consideration of the Jewish casuistry of the time and by the disastrous moral consequences that resulted from substituting the Pharisaic regulations for the law of God. Jesus takes the fourth commandment of the Decalogue by way of example. By two sacred texts, one positive,[826] the other negative,[827] He reminds His questioners that the divine Lawgiver attached special importance to this precept. By virtue of this commandment, which so well agrees with the dictates of nature, parents have a right not only to their children's love and respect under ordinary conditions of life, but, in the case of poverty, also to their effective assistance. Yet the Scribes established and authorized blameworthy reservations which made it possible and permissible for an unnatural son to escape from this latter duty. He had merely to say: "Whatever I possess is corban," that is, an "offering" made to God; at once he was considered as no longer having anything of his own and was forbidden to succor his father and mother. The Talmud contains fine admonitions with respect to filial devotion; but on this point it confirms the Savior's accusation. The case had been explicitly foreseen by the rabbis, who solved it in the manner indicated by our Lord. "The man is bound by the corban," they heartlessly reply.[828] Unscrupulous debtors had recourse to the very same

---

[825] St. Mark cites these two arguments in inverse order. It is hard to say what was the order followed by our Lord. It seems more natural that He first directly attacked the Pharisees, as St. Matthew indicates.

[826] Ex. 20: 12. Cf. Deut. 5: 16.

[827] Ex. 21: 17. Cf. Lev. 20: 9.

[828] Tractate *Nedarim*, 5, 9; 9, 1 etc.

procedure to injure the rights of their creditors and to rid themselves of their debts.[829] To tolerate such abuses and, still worse, openly to encourage them, was to reduce to empty words the weightiest precepts and obligations; it was to replace the divine commandments by prescriptions of a very inferior order and sometimes immoral prescriptions, invented by men.

To this iniquitous conduct of the doctors of the law and the Pharisees, Jesus with just indignation applied the words by which the prophet Isaias [830] branded the false piety and purely outward and insincere worship of many of his fellow-Jews. God has nothing but aversion for this formalism and hypocrisy. What He requires is a worship that comes from the heart.

After quoting this text, the Savior abruptly terminates the interview. Without directly replying to their question, He had refuted and confounded these insincere men. The large crowd that was gathered around our Lord when the Pharisees approached Him, had respectfully made room for their doctors and had withdrawn a little distance away. Jesus now called them to Him, for He purposed enlightening them on the point which had been the subject of discussion. Why did the Jewish lawyers attach that exaggerated importance to the washing of hands before meals? It was because of a fear that a person might have been contaminated by contact with some legally impure object or person. It was believed that, in case of real contamination, the latter would be communicated to the food that one might eat, and one's whole being would thereby be defiled. But the Savior replies that such defilement does not exist; no food can of itself contaminate the moral being. To express this thought, He employs

---

[829] Cf. Origen, *Hom. in Matth.*, XII, 9.

[830] Is. 29: 13. The passage is quoted somewhat freely and approaches the Septuagint translation more closely than the Hebrew.

paradoxical expressions, which He uses so effectively as to arouse attention and reflection: "Hear ye and understand. Not that which goeth into the mouth defileth a man; but what cometh out of the mouth, this defileth a man. If any man have ears to hear, let him hear."

These words go to the heart of the question; they enunciate a fundamental rule, separating the spirit from the letter, the moral law from a wretched and often sinful formalism. This rule, composed of a negative and a positive assertion, is for the moment somewhat obscure. But the Master presently interprets it. After dismissing the crowd, He enters into a house with His Apostles.[831] Immediately they say to Him:[832] "Dost Thou know that the Pharisees, when they heard this word, were scandalized?" This scandal was inevitable, because, in the few enigmatic words which Jesus addressed to the people, His enemies at once suspected, especially after the interview which had occasioned them, a threat regarding the laws about pure and impure food. Jesus answered the Apostles, saying: "Every plant which My heavenly Father hath not planted shall be rooted up. Let them alone: they are blind and leaders of the blind. And if the blind lead the blind, both fall into the pit."

The Pharisees were, therefore, injurious plants, like the cockle of the parable, or thorns and brambles which, unless care be taken, soon overrun the most fertile soil; and God will ruthlessly tear them up.[833] According to a metaphor often used by ancient writers,[834] the Pharisees are also compared,

[831] Probably St. Peter's house, if the scene took place at Capharnaum. But the Evangelists do not furnish us any geographical information on this point.

[832] St. Matthew is the only one to relate this incident (15: 12–14).

[833] St. Ignatius of Antioch plainly alludes to this passage when he writes, *Epist. ad Trall.*, IX: "Flee from the evil plants [the heretics]; the fruit which they bear brings death; whoever eats thereof will perish, because it is not of the Father's planting."

[834] We find this figure in the writings of Horace, Cicero, and Plutarch. Cf. Jülicher, *Gleichnisreden Jesu*, II, 51. Philo also uses it, *De Fortitud.*, 2 St. Luke,

from the moral standpoint, to blind men. The Jewish people might well complain, directed as they were by such guides, who were leading them to the abyss.

Simon Peter then asked our Lord: "Expound to us this parable." Under the generic name of parable, he was referring, according to one of the meanings of that term,[835] to the somewhat obscure remark which Jesus had made to the crowd a few moments before. The Savior answered: "Are you also yet without understanding? Do you not understand, that whatsoever entereth into the mouth, goeth into the belly,[836] and is cast out into the privy? But the things which proceed out of the mouth, come forth from the heart, and those things defile a man. For from the heart come forth evil thoughts, murders, adulteries, fornications, thefts, false testimonies, blasphemies. These are the things that defile a man. But to eat with unwashed hands doth not defile a man." [837]

The reply begins with a rebuke to the Apostles, because the Savior was grieved at their slowness in understanding His words, after about two years spent with Him. Nevertheless, with His usual kindness, He gives them the requested solution. Rarely do we find His language so realistic: but it elucidates the question perfectly. The traditions elaborated by the Scribes, regarding food and ablutions, made the serious mistake of confusing two different spheres: the sphere of the physical life and that of the moral life. Nutrition is a physiological phenomenon, with which religion is not directly concerned. How can material food defile a man spiritually, since it is foreign to his moral being, and reaches only his outer organism? Therefore, what difference does it make to

too, quotes this saying of our Lord, but on another occasion (Luke 6:39). See also the Talmudic tractate *Baba Kama*, 52, a.

[835] See page 401.

[836] St. Mark adds: "it entereth not into his heart."

[837] Matt. 15:15-20; Mark 7:17-23.

the soul whether a man does or does not wash his hands before meals? That is only a matter of hygiene and cleanliness.
But the morality of his acts comes from within a man—
from his heart, according to the Jewish psychology. Hence
the heart is the laboratory where everything is prepared that
is good or evil in a man, considered as a moral being. Jesus
ends his explanation by enumerating some of the vices and
evil acts that proceed from a corrupt heart. The list in St.
Mark's Gospel is more complete than that recorded by St.
Matthew, quoted above. St. Mark says: "From within out
of the heart of men proceed evil thoughts, adulteries, fornications, murders, thefts, covetousness, wickedness, deceit, lasciviousness, an evil eye, blasphemy, pride, foolishness." [838]

Our Lord did not, by these words, intend to abolish at once
the Levitical prescriptions regarding pure and impure food,
which, since the time of Moses, had occupied a considerable
place in the life of the chosen race. But the principle was laid
down and before long exercised an influence; shortly after
the admission of Gentiles into the Christian Church, it led
the Apostles to abrogate the Mosaic food laws, at first partially, then totally.[839]

II. The Healing of the Daughter of the Syrophenician
Woman and the Curing of Many Other Sick Persons

Shortly after the incident just narrated, Jesus made the
longest of His journeys recorded in the Gospels. The two
Evangelists who briefly indicate its general direction [840] seem
to present it as a prudent retreat, intended to divert for the
time being the attention of Christ's enemies, who had become

[838] A Hebraicism, meaning envy.
[839] Cf. Acts 10: 14 ff.; 15: 1–35.
[840] Matt. 15: 21, 29; Mark 7: 24, 31.

more offended and irritated than ever. The tour must have taken several weeks.

Leaving the lake shore with His Apostles, from whom He never again separated, He journeyed northwest and, after crossing all of Upper Galilee, arrived near the district of Tyre and Sidon.[841] Since the time of Pompey (64 B. C.), all Phenicia was a Roman province joined to Syria. Its two former capitals, once so powerful, had fallen from their greatness; but they still enjoyed a measure of fame. At the present day, Tyre or Sur, as the Arabs call it, is a town of only about 6,000 population, and no longer has any commerce. Sidon or Saida, located twenty-two miles farther north, has a population of 12,000 and is surrounded by rich gardens and orchards. In our Lord's time this whole country was pagan. Josephus [842] describes it as being very hostile to the Jews. Did Jesus really penetrate into the Phenician territory? Various interpreters doubt that He did; in support of this view, they claim that the two expressions used by the Evangelists are vague and general.[843] Yet both terms designate, not the boundaries of a district, but the district itself.[844] Furthermore, why should our Lord not have entered a pagan country, since He had no intention of exercising His ministry there, to do which would have been contrary to His designs? He retired into Phenicia only momentarily, as the prophet Elias had done.[845] It was His express desire, as St. Mark notes, "that no man should know it"; but news of His presence soon spread abroad. From the very beginning of His public life, His fame had spread to these regions, which furnished a contingent to the crowds which then came to Him from all parts of Pales-

---

[841] Fillion and Nicole, *Atlas Géographique de la Bible*, pl. X.

[842] *Contra Apion.*, I, 13.

[843] St. Matthew: εἰς τὰ μέρη, Vulg., *in partes;* St. Mark: εἰς τὰ ὅρια, Vulg., *in fines.*

[844] Cf. E. Preuschen, *Griechisch-deutsches Handwörterbuch zu den Schriften des N. T.*, 1910, pp. 707 and 820.

[845] 3 Kings 17: 8–10.

tine.[846] In His person there was a certain distinction and majesty which at once attracted attention. The little caravan could hardly succeed in concealing itself for long.

Before He set foot on Phenician territory, but when He was very near its frontier, the cessation of His incognito led to a touching incident.[847] Its heroine is celebrated under the popular appellation of "a woman of Canaan," by which St. Matthew designates her, while St. Mark more correctly calls her "a Syrophenician born." [848] The two titles together tell us what she was: she belonged by birth to the Canaanitish race, which occupied Palestine at the time the Hebrews took possession of it; but geographically she belonged to Phenicia, and in a political and administrative sense to the Roman province of Syria. St. Mark adds that she was a "Hellene," with respect to language and religion, therefore a pagan.[849] This woman, having learned of Jesus' arrival, suddenly and boldly [850] entered the house where He then was, which was in Galilean territory, not far from the frontier. Approaching the Savior with signs of deepest respect, she prostrated herself at His feet, saying: "Have mercy on me, O Lord, Thou Son of David; for my daughter is grievously troubled by a devil." Cases of diabolic possession existed at that time among the pagans as among the Jews,[851] and often manifested themselves by violent, painful convulsions.

The title "Son of David" (i. e., Messias) is at first astonishing on the lips of a pagan; but the suppliant evidently had

---

[846] Mark 3:8; Luke 6:17.

[847] Matt. 15:21-28; Mark 7:24-30.

[848] Συροφοινίκισσα, Vulg., Syrophoenissa, by way of distinction from the Phenicians of Libya (Strabo, XVII, 19) or Libyan Phenicians.

[849] The Vulgate well indicates the meaning of this word, translating it by Gentilis.

[850] The two Evangelists emphasize the unexpected character of the event, each by his favorite adverb—St. Matthew: ἰδού, ecce, "behold"; St. Mark: εὐθύς, "immediately."

[851] Cf. Sophocles, Ajax, 244; Eusebius, Praeparat. Evangelica, IV, xxiii, 4.

heard it applied to Jesus. She partly comprehended its significance, and she hoped, by using it, to make the powerful
Miracle-worker, whose prodigies had reached her ears, more
favorably inclined to her. At first, instead of granting the
petition of this afflicted mother, Jesus subjects her to a harsh
trial. He whose compassion frequently anticipated the en-
treaties of the unfortunate, and who always answered their
prayers with infinite goodness, did not even deign to reply
to this woman by a single word. This was because He was
aware of her extraordinary strength and wished to give her
an opportunity to show all her faith. He Himself makes known
another reason for the painful delay which He imposed on
her. Notwithstanding His silence, the woman continued humbly to set forth her request.[852] So touching was the scene
that the Apostles themselves were moved, although they were
accustomed to behold physical and moral suffering. From St.
Matthew's account it would seem that the rest of the episode
took place on the highway, since Jesus had meanwhile set
out from the house. Taking up the poor mother's cause, the
Twelve besought their Master to have pity on her and answer
her prayer, which she kept repeating aloud; this might become annoying for Jesus and His companions and might attract a crowd. The Savior merely answers coldly and sternly:
"I was not sent but to the sheep that are lost of the house of
Israel." [853] It is true that, although the work of redemption
undertaken by Christ was as vast as the world, His direct,
personal intervention, according to the divine plan, was to be
limited to the Jewish people, as He already had declared more
than once. The pagans were outside of that plan.

In the face of such a situation, of refusal so clearly and
forcibly expressed, anyone but a mother would have been

---

[852] The imperfect used by St. Mark, ἠρώτα (Vulg., rogabat), "she besought,"
indicates a repeated petition.

[853] On this expression, see Matt. 9 : 36.

disheartened. But the woman of Canaan had no intention either of being discouraged or of going away. On the contrary, she came closer to Jesus and, with her whole soul, she said, "Help me!" This time He consented to speak to her; but it was only to humiliate her still more. He said to her: "Suffer first the children to be filled; for it is not good to take the bread of the children and cast it to the dogs." This is not merely a refusal, but a harsh and contemptuous refusal. The children of whom He speaks are evidently the Jews; the dogs are none other than the pagans, of whose number was the suppliant woman. Nevertheless, the commentators observe that Jesus employs a diminutive form [854] designating, not the ownerless and half-wild animals that roam the streets of Oriental cities, feeding on filthy garbage, but the domestic "whelps," cared for in the house and sharing in the children's play. And when the Savior said, "Suffer *first* the children to be filled," He was no doubt affirming the prior right which the Jews had to the blessings of the Messias; but at the same time He implied that this right was not exclusive and that the Gentiles' turn would come later. These two circumstances relieve Jesus' words of a little of their harshness. Yet they remained crushing for the woman, whose daughter needed immediate help. With a courage equal to her faith and humility, in what might have caused her to lose hope, she found a telling argument to obtain the favor so earnestly desired. "Yea, Lord," she replies, "for the whelps also eat under the table of the crumbs of the children." Entering into the Savior's thoughts, she thus reminded Him that, without the least prejudice to the interests of the Jews, He could answer the prayer of a pagan and let a crumb of His favors fall upon her.

Not long before Jesus had marveled at the faith of the

---

[854] The two Greek texts have: τοῖς κυναρίοις. The Vulgate takes account of this diminutive only in quoting the Canaanitish woman's reply (*catelli*).

centurion, who likewise belonged to the Gentile world. How could He help but acknowledge Himself vanquished by the words of the Canaanitish woman, who so ably and respectfully turned against Him the argument which He used to humble and overwhelm her? [855] "O woman," said He, "great is thy faith; be it done to thee as thou wilt." On the instant, the devil was compelled to abandon his victim. The mother, upon returning home, found her daughter quietly lying on her bed, enjoying a repose which was in contrast with the terrible crises that occurred before she was freed from the devil.

Jesus seems to have made only a brief stay on Phenician soil. St. Mark says: "Going out of the coasts of Tyre, He came by Sidon to the Sea of Galilee, through the midst of the coasts of Decapolis." Anyone acquainted with the geography of Palestine will recognize that these few words sum up a rather extensive journey through the northern regions of the Jewish country. From the district of Tyre, our Lord turned northward, probably by the road which follows the Mediterranean shore line and crosses the Leontes (now the Litany) River before reaching Sarepta. He could have arrived at Sidon the same day, for the two ancient cities were not more than twenty-two miles apart. From Sidon, or the adjacent district, to reach the midst of Decapolis, which was located almost entirely on the left bank of the Jordan,[856] east and southeast of Lake Tiberias, Jesus had to recross the Leontes, but much farther up stream, then the massif of the southern Lebanon and the deep gorge formed by Celosyria ("hollow Syria"). There was a highway connecting Damascus and the Mediterranean coast.[857] After the Savior

---

[855] "*Christum suis verbis irretit, comprehendit et capit. Rationem contra se factam in ipsum leniter retorquet.*" Cornelius à Lapide, *Comment. in Matth.*, XV, 27. St. John Chrysostom has a beautiful treatment of the whole episode in his *Homil. in Matth.*, 52.

[856] Vol. I, p. 111.

[857] Cf. Merrill, *Galilee*, p. 58; G. A. Smith, *Historical Geography of Palestine*, p. 426; Hastings' *Dictionary of the Bible*, V, 370.

thus reached the headwaters of the Jordan, He turned south
by way of Cæsarea Philippi and Bethsaida Julias. The reader,
by consulting a map of Palestine, will see that our Lord's
route formed a semicircle. Those districts were rich in natural
beauty. Their comparative isolation enabled Jesus and the
Apostles to enjoy the rest and quiet which they had sought
in vain a short time before.

But it was not long before the usual throngs gathered about
them. So soon as it was learned that the Savior had returned
to those regions which He habitually frequented, large multitudes hastened to Him, accompanied by sick and infirm people who came to implore His help. St. Matthew mentions
"the dumb, the blind, the lame, the maimed, and many others."
The people's eagerness was the greater because for some time
they had been deprived of Christ's presence. In order to come
to Him, the crowds climbed a hill on which He had stopped.
They found Him sitting there. The Evangelist tells us that
the first thing they did was to "cast down at His feet" their
sick, thus abandoning them to His merciful goodness. Their
confidence was not disappointed, for Jesus cured all that were
brought to Him. The witnesses of these many prodigies marveled, "seeing the dumb speak, the lame walk, the blind see,
and they glorified the God of Israel," who had given such
power to His envoy and who through Him bestowed such
blessings upon His people.

We have been following St. Matthew's account,[858] which
furnishes merely the general details. St. Mark, with his
customary precision, describes one of these miraculous cures
in particular.[859] The manner in which our Lord performed
it was different from that of any cure we have thus far considered. Among the sick brought to Him by their relatives or
friends, was a man suffering from deafness and partial dumb-

[858] Matt. 15 : 29-31.
[859] Mark 7 : 31-37.

ness.[860] The Savior was besought to lay His hands upon him, as He sometimes did in curing the sick.[861] Instead of immediately restoring the man's speech and hearing, the Savior took him by the hand and led Him aside from the crowd. At no time did He perform His miracles with ostentation; but He now more than ever avoided performing them before the eyes of the easily excitable populace. Instead of effecting the cure merely by an act of the will or by a word or gesture, He placed His fingers in the deaf-mute's ears—probably the index finger of His right hand in the man's left ear, the index finger of His left hand in the right ear—and wet the man's tongue with a drop of His own saliva. So far as we can interpret those acts, they were symbolic gestures by which our Lord in some way prepared the diseased organs to resume their normal functions. Thus He opened those closed ears and loosed that halting tongue. By signs He made the infirm man understand that the cure would be His personal work, thereby arousing his faith and confidence. Jesus then raised His eyes to Heaven, as though for intimate converse with His Father. He sighed, thinking of the countless evils that overwhelmed fallen mankind, and pronounced this single word, in the idiom of the country: *"Ephpheta"* ("Be thou opened"), which St. Mark records as it was pronounced.[862]

At once the man's ears were opened and he heard perfectly; the fetters that held his tongue were broken and he spoke distinctly. As an early commentator of the Second Gospel remarks: "The Creator of nature had supplied what nature

---

[860] The adjective μογιλάλος means, literally, a man "who speaks little"; that is, in the present case, a man who, in consequence of a defect in his organs of speech, can express himself only with difficulty.

[861] Matt. 9: 18; Mark 5: 23; 6: 5, etc.

[862] The best reading of the Greek text is ἐφφαθά, which more exactly corresponds to the Aramaic *ephtah*, an abbreviated form of *etpetah*, imperative "*itpaal*" or "*etpaal*." The reading ἐφφεθά is also found; it is the one followed by the Vulgate. On this word, see Dalmann, *Grammatik des jüdisch-palästinischen Aramäisch,* 2d ed., 1905, p. 278, and A. Meyer, *Jesu Muttersprache,* p. 52.

lacked." [863] Jesus, who performed this miracle as it were clandestinely, ordered the man to remain silent about it; but this admonition was to no avail. As the Evangelist remarks, [864] the more explicit our Lord's prohibition was, the less it was observed, and the more were His wonderful blessings noised abroad; moreover, it was impossible for them to remain entirely hidden. We have already pointed out the chief reason for this injunction, which also was in conformity with Christ's perfect modesty. Those who learned of this double cure were greatly impressed by it, [865] and loudly praised Him who performed it. "He hath done all things well," they said; "He hath made both the deaf to hear, and the dumb to speak." This pious exclamation contains one of the most charming of all our Lord's praises. It recalls a detail of the description which Isaias gives of the epoch of the Messias: "Then shall the eyes of the blind be opened, and the ears of the deaf shall be unstopped . . . and the tongue of the dumb shall be free." [866]

III. Second Multiplication of Loaves; the Leaven of the Pharisees and Sadducees

It was at this period and probably in the territory of Decapolis during this sojourn of our Lord there, [867] that the second multiplication of loaves [868] occurred. The incident, as a whole and in its main details, took place in the same manner as on the occasion of the similar miracle a few months before. The large multitude that, as we have just seen, brought

---

[863] Victor of Antioch.

[864] In a very expressive and redundant phrase: $\mu\hat{a}\lambda\lambda o\nu\ \pi\epsilon\rho\iota\sigma\sigma\acute{o}\tau\epsilon\rho o\nu$, Vulg., *tanto magis plus*.

[865] St. Mark recounts this fact very forcefully: $\dot{\upsilon}\pi\epsilon\rho\pi\epsilon\rho\iota\sigma\sigma\hat{\omega}s\ \dot{\epsilon}\xi\epsilon\pi\lambda\acute{\eta}\sigma\sigma o\nu\tau o$.

[866] Is. 35: 5 f.

[867] Mark 7: 31. On the historical reality of the two miracles, see Appendix XXIII.

[868] Matt. 15: 32–39; Mark 8: 1–10. There is a great similarity between the two acounts: St. Mark's is somewhat more developed.

all their sick to the good Master, were so happy to be near Him, looking upon Him and listening to His divine words, that they could not leave Him. Thus it happened that finally they were without food and, what was more serious, without means of readily obtaining any, because the region where they had rejoined the Savior was almost uninhabited. His heart was moved at their plight. Calling to Him the Apostles, who were scattered in the crowd, He this time took the initiative and said to them: "I have compassion on the multitude, for behold they have now been with Me three days, and have nothing to eat. And if I shall send them away fasting to their home, they will faint in the way; for some of them came from afar off." If the mere sight of a crowd that came to hear Him and to implore His help aroused our Lord's compassion,[869] He was more deeply moved at feeling that those whom faith and love drew to Him were willing to endure some suffering thereby. So pleased were they to be near Him that they forgot their material needs. But He was unwilling to expose these good people to the fatigue of a long journey fasting, to go in search of food. Therefore He gathered the Apostles around Him and spoke to them as though asking their counsel, as though He wished them to suggest a means of feeding that multitude. He was, indeed, dealing with very imperfect counsellors. From their reply we can see that they were impressed especially by one thing, namely, the impossibility of supplying food for so many people in such a place. They answered: "Whence then should we have so many loaves in the desert, as to fill so great a multitude?" Their words enumerate the three chief difficulties of the situation: an enormous quantity of bread, in an uninhabited locality, for so large a number of people. They seem to be as much perplexed as if they had not, only a short time before, witnessed similar difficulties,

[869] Matt. 14:14; Mark 6:34.

which their Master had so easily overcome. How we wish they had given the answer that Jesus expected! But we must not blame them too severely. Perhaps they did not venture to suggest that He repeat the former miracle, because they were not aware of His intentions at the time.

The Savior, taking no notice of what might be called the banality of their reply, said to them: "How many loaves have you?" It did not take long to count them. "Seven," they replied, "and a few little fishes." This was the total of the available provisions. The rest of the episode took place as at the time of the former miracle. As directed by our Lord, the crowd sat down—not, this time, "upon the grass," which the burning sun of the Orient had long since dried up. Then Jesus gave thanks to God, blessed the loaves and the fishes, broke them and gave the pieces to the Apostles, who distributed them to the crowd. All ate and were sated. The disciples then filled seven baskets [870] with what was left. The number of those who ate was four thousand, "besides children and women." They must have been arranged in groups, so that it was easy to know their number approximately.

After the multitude had departed, Jesus and the Twelve went into the boat that He used when He was exercising His ministry in the vicinity of the lake.[871] They landed near a place which St. Matthew calls Magedan, and St. Mark Dalmanutha. This site has not yet been identified with certainty. St. Augustine, [872] like many modern authors, supposes that these two names, which are disconcerting at first sight, really designate the same district. It is not impossible that "Mage-

---

[870] In the Greek they are this time designated, not by the word κόρινοι, but by the noun σπυρίδες, which seems to refer to baskets of larger size, since it was in a σπύρις (Vulg., *sporta*) that St. Paul was put when he was let down from the wall at Damascus in order to escape the ambushes of the Jews. Cf. Acts 9: 25. See Fillion, *Atlas Archéologique de la Bible*, 2d ed., pl. XVII, figs. 4, 5, 6.

[871] Both Evangelists use the article: τὸ πλοῖον, *i. e.*, "the well-known boat."

[872] *De Consensu Evangel.*, II, 51.

dan" [873] is a copyist's error for "Magdala." [874] If this be so, we would be on well-known ground, on the western side of Lake Tiberias, and we would consider Dalmanutha as a hamlet close to Magdala. But this rests on a mere conjecture. At any rate, it seems certain that Jesus landed on the western shore of the lake.

The Savior's relentless enemies, the Pharisees, were constantly on the watch to lay snares for Him. We are not surprised, therefore, to see Him attacked by them soon after He landed. In the present instance they were accompanied, not by their usual friends, the Scribes or doctors of the law, but by the Sadducees, despite the fact that there was a marked hostility between the two parties.[875] But both sects treated Jesus as a foe; [876] and so it is not astonishing that they combined against Him.[877] As on a former occasion,[878] they asked Him for "a sign from heaven," a particularly striking miracle that would take place in the air above them and would decisively and beyond doubt prove the truth of the divine mission which He claimed to have.

Thus did they issue a sort of ultimatum to Him, but without being prepared to recognize His rights even should He gratify their desire. The purpose of these perfidious men was simply to "tempt" Him, as St. Mark expresses it,[879] that is, either to certify to His lack of power, or to have Him make a reply which would enable them to prefer charges against

---

[873] Or Μαγαδάν, according to various Greek manuscripts.

[874] Some manuscripts have this reading.

[875] See Vol. I, p. 190.

[876] The Sadducees had opposed Him from the very beginning of His ministry. (Cf. John 2: 18–22.)

[877] The Pharisees gave proof of great mobility in the alliances they formed against our Lord. We have seen them associated now with the disciples of John the Baptist (Mark 2: 18), and now with the Herodians (Mark 3: 6). In the present juncture they have entered upon a third alliance.

[878] Matt. 12: 38–40; Luke 11: 16, 29 f.

[879] We owe the details of this incident to the first two Evangelists: Matt. 16: 1–4; Mark 8: 11–13. St. Matthew is the more complete.

Him before the religious tribunals of the country. Jesus was not ignorant of their wile. And He grants them nothing but a second peremptory refusal. Sighing from the depth of His heart [880] because of their malice and unbelief, He first makes the same reply as before: "A wicked and adulterous generation seeketh after a sign. Amen I say to you, a sign shall not be given it, but the sign of Jonas the prophet," the wonderful and indubitable sign of Christ's Resurrection. He further confounds them by saying: "When it is evening, you say, it will be fair weather, for the sky is red. And in the morning: Today there will be a storm, for the sky is red and lowering. You know then how to discern the face of the sky; and can you not know the signs of the times?" [881]

The tempters had spoken of the heavens. Jesus spoke to them of the ability with which they knew how to predict rain or fair weather according to the state of the atmosphere, [882] a forecast that was not difficult. Then, in a tone of severe irony, He reproached these religious leaders of Israel for being unable to discern the many striking and important signs announcing the mightiest event in Jewish history, the coming of the Messias. Had not the scepter departed from Juda? Had not Daniel's "weeks" elapsed? Had not other undoubtedly

[880] As usual, it is St. Mark who mentions the Savior's inner feelings. In the Greek text the compound verb ἀναστενάξας intensifies the idea.

[881] This second part of our Lord's reply is lacking in a certain number of important manuscripts, as St. Jerome long ago pointed out in his commentary on this passage. Therefore several recent editions place it in brackets, as being doubtful. But a large number of Greek manuscripts (the Itala, the Vulgate, and other ancient versions) contain it; and it is hard to suppose it is not authentic. St. Luke (12: 54–56) quotes these same words of our Lord, but on a different occasion, and his text is too distinct from that of St. Matthew for us to regard the latter as having been taken from the former by some ignorant copyist. See Scrivener, *Introduction*, II, 326.

[882] The rabbis again and again engaged in forecasting the weather. The Talmud contains numerous rules, established by them for the purpose of pointing out to the farming population of Palestine the premonitory signs of good or bad weather. Cf. Lightfoot and Wetstein, *Horae Talmudicae, i. h. l.* With regard to the rule mentioned by our Lord, see also Pliny, *Hist. Nat.*, XVIII, 78.

Messianic prophecies been fulfilled? Had not the precursor
of the Christ appeared? Was not the Messianic expectancy
then universal among the Jews? What a telling blow there
was in that concession: You are good astronomers, and nothing else!

This was as much as the Pharisees and their Sadducean
allies deserved. Jesus, abruptly ending the interview and turning His back upon them, again entered the boat and crossed
the lake from Magedan to the northeast shore. During the
voyage His saddened thoughts quite naturally dwelt upon
the unworthy conduct of His enemies. Suddenly He said
to the Apostles: [883] "Take heed and beware of the leaven
of the Pharisees and Sadducees." [884] By this figurative expression, as St. Matthew explains further on, He meant the
dangerous doctrine and morals and the fatal example of
the two sects. In antiquity, leaven, because of the fermentation it sets up, was often regarded as a symbol and even as
an agent of corruption and putrefaction.[885] Hence the Mosaic
law strictly banned it from whatever was connected with divine worship.[886] With a like zeal Christ's disciples should
drive far away all unwholesome influence of their Master's
enemies.

But the Twelve took the Savior's words in a literal sense
and consequently made a curious blunder. The idea of leaven
suggested to their minds the idea of bread, and they remembered that, in the haste of their departure, they had forgotten
to provide themselves with bread. They were worried on this

[883] This other narrative we also owe to St. Matthew (16: 5–12) and St. Mark
(8: 14–21).

[884] According to St. Mark: "of the leaven of the Pharisees and of the leaven of
Herod." This amounts to about the same thing, because the Sadducee aristocracy
was very favorably inclined to the dynasty of the Herods. Sadducees and
Herodians had the same worldly tastes and the same skeptical tendencies. St. Luke
(12: 1) also quotes this warning of Christ, but on a different occasion.

[885] Cf. Wetstein, *Horae Talmudicae, i. h. l.;* Wünsche, *Neue Beiträge*, p. 193.

[886] See also 1 Cor. 5: 6; Gal. 5: 0.

account. "We have no bread," they said to one another. Jesus had but now miraculously fed thousands of people; yet there at His side, the Twelve were concerned over the matter of a bit of bread. And they supposed that their Master, apropos of their having forgotten to take bread, wished to admonish them about a matter that concerned merely their material welfare. This lack of faith and understanding deserved a rebuke, which was given at once and in justly severe language. "Why do you think within yourselves, O ye of little faith, for that you have no bread? Do you not yet know nor understand? Have you still your heart blinded? Having eyes, see you not? And having ears, hear you not? And do you not remember?"

The sacred narrative continues, first quoting Christ's words: "When I broke the five loaves among five thousand, how many baskets full of fragments took you up? They say to Him, Twelve. When also the seven loaves among four thousand, how many baskets of fragments took you up? And they say to Him, Seven. Why do you not understand that it was not concerning bread I said to you: Beware of the leaven of the Pharisees and Sadducees? How do you not yet understand?" Thus set on the right path, they understood. But their great fault lay in not reflecting upon what they saw and heard. They were often satisfied to be merely the happy witnesses of the Savior's life and miracles. This incident shows how greatly they still needed the Master's lessons, and throws light upon the method He used to train and enlighten them and to stir their slow understanding.

At Bethsaida Julias, where they landed, a blind man was brought to the Savior with the request "that He would touch him," to restore his sight. He does so by a series of acts that recall the curing of the deaf-mute.[887] Taking the blind man by the hand, He acted as his guide and led him outside the town, thus avoiding the gathering of a crowd. The Savior

---

[887] Here again St. Mark (8: 22–26) is our only source.

then placed a little saliva on the man's eyes and, imposing His hands on him, asked him "if he saw anything." The man looked up, after the manner of blind people, and replied, "I see men as it were trees, walking." To his still half-veiled eyes, the forms moving about nearby appeared vague and confused. His words prove that he was not blind from birth, but had become so by some mischance; otherwise it would have been impossible for him to make this comparison between men and trees. Jesus again laid His hands upon the man's eyes to complete his cure, which thereupon became so perfect that he saw all things clearly.[888] The Savior then sent him home, saying: "Go into thy house, and if thou enter into the town [of Bethsaida Julias], tell nobody." The account ends with this command, and does not say whether it was obeyed. Why had Jesus again made use of this exceptional method? That is His secret. It may well be that the interior dispositions of the blind man required this kind of treatment, and that his faith needed to be aroused. In any event, it would be ridiculous to think that the cure offered our Lord any special difficulties, for His miraculous power knew no bounds.

[888] The Greek text clearly describes the happy result of the miraculous cure, by means of three expressions having nice shades of distinction in their meanings: διεβλέψεν, ἀπεκατέστη, ἐνέβλεψεν. The first means "to see across"; the third, "to see to the interior of beings"; the second signifies that the organs returned to their normal state.

CHAPTER II

The Climax of the Savior's Public Life

WE now come to words and acts of the greatest consequence. Simon Peter's confession, his superb reward, the plain, direct announcement of Christ's Passion and Resurrection, His Transfiguration on the mountain, all these are extraordinary events even in a life like that of our Lord. That life, already so sublime, now rises to still higher spheres, before descending into what has been called the deep vale of suffering and humiliation. Henceforth Jesus is less engaged in the ministry of teaching the Jewish multitudes and is more rarely in contact with them; but He devotes His attention more to the little circle of His Apostles, to whom He is about to reveal the secret of His origin and mission. We now penetrate more and more deeply into the very heart of the gospel.

I. St. Peter's Confession

As we approach the famous episode usually called St. Peter's Confession, let us pause to contemplate the Savior's infinite wisdom, and the progressive steps by which He accomplished His great work of founding the Church. He began by gathering about Him the stray sheep of Israel; then He prepared shepherds for them by instituting the Apostolic College. But the fold must have a supreme ruler to take His place when He leaves the earth. He is now going to appoint this chief shepherd. By this same act He will be taking a decisive step in the founding and perpetuity of the Church, since He will choose a vicar, a visible representative, not only for a few years, but for the whole duration of this present world. We have, then, reached one of the culminating points of the gospel history. For a Catholic this event assumes supreme importance because it is the birth of the papacy. At this point we hear only a promise, like that concerning the Eucharist. But here, too, the fulfilment will not be long delayed, and Jesus, before ascending into Heaven, will plainly designate him and endue him with full powers.

We left our Lord and the Apostles at Bethsaida Julias, near the northern shore of Lake Tiberias. Thence they turned north, probably following the Jordan, and arrived at a point not far[889] from Cæsarea Philippi, after a constant climb[890] of about thirty miles. Cæsarea was formerly called Paneas, in honor of the god Pan, there being in that place a natural grotto (*Paneion*) which had long been a shrine of that god. When Herod the Great received this territory as a gift from Augustus, he promptly built, beside the spot dedicated to Pan, a white marble temple, consecrated to the worship of the Emperor,[891] with the result that one of the earliest religions, that of the god of nature, became associated with the most recent. Upon the death of King Herod, Paneas became part of the inheritance of the tetrarch Philip, who soon enlarged and beautified the city.[892] To flatter the Emperor, he named it Cæsarea, to which was then added the name of Philip himself, to prevent confusion between the new city and maritime Cæsarea (or Cæsarea of Palestine), the former Strabo's Tower, built on the Mediterranean shore between Jaffa and Mount Carmel. Of Cæsarea Philippi nothing remains to-day but ruins, near which there stands a little vil-

---

[889] St. Matthew: εἰς τὰ μέρη (Vulg., *in partes*). St. Mark: εἰς τὰς κώμας (Vulg., *in castella*). These two expressions designate the country about Caesarea.

[890] The difference in altitude between the two cities is about 1770 feet. See A. Legendre, *Carte de la Palestine Ancienne et Moderne.*

[891] Josephus, *Ant.,* XV, x, 3; *Bell Jud.,* I, xxi, 3.

[892] Josephus, *Ant.,* XVIII, ii, 1; *Bell Jud.,* III, iii, 1.

lage, called Banias, the ancient name having disappeared long since. The population of this whole district, which was situated at the extreme northern end of Palestine,[893] was mostly pagan.[894] But Jesus did not enter that region to exercise His usual ministry there. On the contrary, He was seeking solitude, to escape the ambuscades of His enemies and to labor peacefully in the training of His Apostles and to make important revelations to them, far from the crowds.

Nature has remained charming and majestic in this region. The site of Cæsarea is unique, combining the elements of greatness and beauty in an unusual degree. The city stood at the southern base of the mighty Hermon, which towered behind it, raising its snow-capped peak to a height of 9,000 feet. The abundant waters of the southernmost source of the Jordan, which issued from the rock in which the grotto of Pan was hollowed, spread a luxuriant vegetation on all sides: there you see a succession of groves, greensward, and cultivated fields.[895] It was a place where peace and calm reigned. In every way the spot was worthy of the sublime event about to be enacted there. All three Synoptics relate this episode, St. Luke here joining the other two.[896] But St. Matthew is the only one who sets it forth in its full amplitude.

As on other important occasions, such as just before choosing the Twelve, Jesus first prayed, entering into more direct communication with His heavenly Father,[897] and beseeching Him, as may clearly be inferred from the account, to illumine His disciples. He then resumed His journey and, on the

[893] The ancient city of Dan, which marked its northern limit, was located less than an hour's walk from Paneas.

[894] Josephus, *Vita*, 18.

[895] Robinson, *Palästina und die angrenzenden Länder*, III, 614. Cf. Stanley, *Sinai and Palestine*, new ed., p. 397; Tristram, *Land of Israel*, p. 581; G. A. Smith, *Historical Geography of Palestine*, p. 473.

[896] Matt. 16: 13–19; Mark 8: 27–29; Luke 9: 18–20.

[897] Luke 9: 18.

way,[898] He put this unexpected question to the Apostles: "Whom do men say that I, the Son of Man, am?" [899] In reality our Lord had no need of being informed on this point, because He knew thoroughly, both by His natural and His supernatural knowledge, what the people thought and said about Him. His purpose was to introduce another, much more essential question.

The Apostles' relations with the crowds that so often gathered around the Divine Master had long before made them acquainted with the different opinions that were current about Jesus. In connection with the circumstances of John the Baptist's martyrdom, we learned that most of these views circulated in the palace of the tetrarch Herod Antipas and in the ranks of the people. It was, therefore, easy to reply: "Some John the Baptist, and other some Elias, and others Jeremias, and others say that one of the former prophets is risen again." The Savior's lofty preaching, His numberless miracles of a kind never before heard of, the power that His least actions manifested or presupposed, all these together forced the mass of the Jewish people to recognize that He was comparable to the holiest and most illustrious personages of their history.

The disciples, in their reply, mention a name we have not heard before in this connection,—Jeremias. Especially since the episode related in the Second Book of Machabees,[900] this prophet was regarded as one of the most eminent protectors of the Jewish nation. Judas Machabeus, before beginning a decisive battle with the Syrian general Nicanor, had a vision in

---

[898] St. Mark (8: 27) explicitly mentions this detail: ἐν τῇ ὁδῷ (Vulg., in via).

[899] In the three accounts there is a slight variation in expression. The one we have just quoted is according to St. Matthew, as given by important Greek manuscripts, several ancient versions, and some of the Fathers. The authenticity of the pronoun "I" is not absolutely certain. In the Second Gospel we read: "Whom do men say that I am?" In the Third: "Whom do the people say that I am?"

[900] 2 Mach. 15: 13–16.

which there appeared to him a man "admirable for age and glory, and environed with great beauty and majesty." And in the vision Onias the High Priest said: "This is a lover of his brethren and of the people of Israel. This is he that prayeth much for the people and for all the holy city, Jeremias, the prophet of God." Jeremias then handed Judas a golden sword with which to strike the enemies of his people Israel.[901]

Jesus had, then, been highly esteemed and had been the object of great hopes. But it is sad to note that the Twelve, in their enumeration, did not connect the title of Messias with His name. Several Jews gave Him that title;[902] but in the case of many of them, faith in Him as the promised Liberator was not deep. Although, following His most brilliant miracles, the crowds acclaimed Him as the Christ, His reserve and His direct opposition to the popular preconceptions had cooled the enthusiasm. The open hostility and calumnies of His enemies had intensified that coldness. Thus the multitudes as a whole began to regard Him as only a precursor of the Christ.

The Savior said to the Apostles: "But whom do you say that I am?" They were His confidants, His intimate friends, who for years had seen Him at close range and knew Him as no one else could know Him outside their circle. What did they think of Him? What was their opinion of His nature and office? On this extremely important point, what was the result of their personal reflections and of their exchange of views among themselves? At this period each of the Twelve, in his inmost thoughts, must have formed a conviction as to Christ's origin and the character of His mission. The hour of trial was near, for them as for Him. Only a few months separated Jesus from His Passion and death,

[901] Cf. 4 Esdras (apocryphal) 2: 17 f., where God says to Esdras: "Fear not; to thy assistance I will send My servants Isaias and Jeremias."

[902] We have already had proof of this and we shall have it again. Cf. Matt 9: 27; 12: 23; 15: 22; John 7: 26–29; 9: 22, etc.

which would apparently attest the complete failure of His religious undertaking. He therefore wishes to know whether He can count upon them. He read their thought about Him, but He purposed gathering it from their own lips. It was a most solemn moment.

"What will Peter do in reply to this question?" says St. John Chrysostom.[903] When all are questioned, it is this impulsive leader of the Apostolic circle who replies. When Jesus asked them what was the opinion of the people, they all spoke. Now when He wishes to know their personal opinion, Peter comes to the fore, ahead of all the others, and says: "Thou art Christ, the Son of the living God." It is to be noted that Simon, though speaking in the name of all, is first concerned with expressing his own personal conviction. Otherwise our Lord would not have felicitated him separately and would not have said that he had spoken by virtue of an inspiration from Heaven. It was indeed from his ardent heart, from a soul full of faith, that came forth the enthusiastic reply: "Thou art Christ, the Son of the living God." [904]

His profession of faith could not have been more prompt or explicit or concise or forceful. It certainly goes farther than his words a short time previously under circumstances that were especially distressing for Jesus.[905] The pronoun placed at the beginning of the sentence, and the article inserted (in the Greek text) [906] before every word that can take the article, strongly accentuates the thought. Everything now becomes clear. Jesus is the "Christ," consequently the Messias, the center of Jewish history and of the history of the world, the universal Redeemer; that is His office, His mission. But,

---

[903] *Hom. in Matth., i. h. l.*

[904] St. Matthew has handed it down to us in its historical form. St. Mark and St. Luke abridge it. "Thou art the Christ," we read in the Second Gospel. In the Third: "[Thou art] the Christ of God."

[905] Page 503.

[906] Σὺ εἶ ὁ Χριστὸς ὁ υἱὸς τοῦ θεοῦ τοῦ ζῶντος.

under the influence of the Holy Ghost, Peter's faith rises much higher and shines in all its purity and beauty. The words, "Son of the living God," proclaim Jesus' origin and nature, that they both are truly divine. The two titles are here not at all synonymous.[907] The second title must be taken in the strict sense of the terms; of this there can be no doubt. If the words "Son of the living God" added nothing to the assertion, "Thou art Christ," and if consequently the Apostle had proclaimed merely his Master's Messianic character, what would have been surprising in his confession? He and the other members of the Apostolic College had known for a long time that Jesus was the Messias. John the Baptist had pointed Him out as such to a number of these Apostles,[908] who had at once accepted the statement and had recognized its truth.[909] No sooner had they joined the Savior permanently than they were convinced in every way that He was really the "Son of David," as He was often called. "Jesus' whole history would become incomprehensible if we did not admit this fact." [910] A revelation from Heaven was not absolutely necessary for Simon to affirm that Jesus was the Messias. The same cannot be said about Christ's divine nature. The Savior's intimate disciples might have sensed it when, after the miraculous calming of the tempest, they said: "Indeed Thou art the Son of God." [911] And in this same sense, Peter had said: "Thou art the Holy One of God." [912] They all were beginning to understand that Jesus was something more

---

[907] They were at times synonymous, as we see from various Gospel passages: Matt. 4:3, 6; "If Thou be the Son of God," the devil said to Christ; Mark 3:12: "Thou art the Son of God," the demoniacs cried out in His presence; John 1:49, the same words were addressed to our Lord by Nathanael, when he first met Him.

[908] John 1:35–37.

[909] John 1:41, 45, 49.

[910] Wohlenberg, *Das Evangelium des Markus ausgelegt*, p. 231.

[911] Matt. 14:33.

[912] John 6:70.

than human, that He was a being of a higher order. But at this moment, Peter's belief, which had, as it were, remained in a latent state, shines out marvelously under the effect of an illumination from Heaven. He says, "Thou art the Son of God"; the living God has begotten Thee, Thou dost participate in His nature. It might be said that this one sentence contains all the essential truths of Christianity. A living God who gives life, the plurality of divine persons, the Messianic character of Jesus, His divinity, His Incarnation—all these doctrines and the theological consequences contained in them, really flow from St. Peter's confession.

To this profession of faith, Jesus replies by a superb declaration which, after nineteen centuries, still produces its marvelous effects in the Christian Church. As we read it, we can almost hear the joyful tone with which it was uttered: "Blessed art thou, Simon Bar-Jona; because flesh and blood hath not revealed it to thee, but My Father who is in Heaven. And I say to thee: That thou art Peter; and upon this rock I will build My Church, and the gates of hell shall not prevail against it. And I will give to thee the keys of the Kingdom of Heaven. And whatsoever thou shalt bind upon earth, it shall be bound also in Heaven; and whatsoever thou shalt loose on earth, it shall be loosed also in Heaven."

The words of our Lord are in rhythm and cadence after the manner of the Orient; they are both simple and majestic. The form rises to the sublime height of the subject. Christian exegetes,[913] theologians,[914] and preachers [915] have thoroughly in-

---

[913] Particularly Maldonatus, in his commentary on this passage; Knabenbauer, *Commentar. in Evangel. sec. Matth.*, 2d ed., II, 48–72; Schanz, *Commentar über das Evangelium des hl. Matthäus*, pp. 375–381.

[914] Among others, Bellarmine, *Controvers. de Summo Pontif.*, lib. I, cap. 10–12; Franzelin, *Theses de Ecclesia Christi*, 1887, thes. 10–11; Palmieri, *De Summo Pontif.*, 3d ed., thes. 1–6; Tanquerey, *De Vera Religione, de Ecclesia*, 13th ed., pp. 426–444.

[915] Bossuet, "Sermon sur l'unité de l'Église" (*Œuvres*, Lachat ed., XI, 588–612); Monsabré, *Conférences de Notre-Dame*, Lent 1882, pp. 55–112, etc.

vestigated that subject from the earliest times of the Church and studied its doctrinal conclusions, on which the declarations of our great councils are based.[916]

Jesus began by warmly congratulating His disciple for so noble a profession of faith, which was made with a fine outburst of love. There is a solemnity in the use of the two names, "Simon Bar-Jona," the former being the one which the future Apostle received on the day of his circumcision, the latter being a patronymic [917] similar to many others mentioned by the Evangelists.[918] "Flesh and blood" clearly stand for earthly man considered in his various weaknesses, especially for human understanding left solely to its own powers and lights.[919] What the son of Jona happily expressed in such true terms, he did not learn through personal reflection; and it was not the fruit of any instruction which other men, likewise ignorant and limited, had communicated to him. Only the divine could reveal the divine; only the Father could manifest the Son,[920] since the latter had hidden Himself and, as it were, emptied Himself under the form of a servant,[921] and since His divinity, at rare intervals, allowed only a few rays of its light to emerge.

After the felicitation came the reward, introduced by these emphatic words: "And I say to thee." Simon had just confessed what he knew Jesus to be; the latter now informs the Apostle what he will be. "As My Father hath manifested My divinity to thee, so I will acquaint thee with thy own high

---

[916] Vatican Council, *Constitutio Dogmatica Prima de Ecclesia Christi,* cap. 1.

[917] Βαριωνᾶ (this is the form in the Greek) is a word transliterated from the Aramaic *bar Iona,* "son of Iona"; *Iona* is generally regarded as being an abbreviation of *Iohana,* the equivalent of the Hebrew *Iohanan,* "John." Cf. John 1:42. This was St. Jerome's opinion.

[918] Bartholomew, Bartimeus, Barabbas. In the Acts of the Apostles, Barjesus.

[919] This expression appears several times in the Bible: Ecclu. 14:19; I Cor. 15:50; Gal. 1:16. It occurs frequently in the Talmud and the Midrash.

[920] Cf. Matt. 11:27; I Cor. 12:3.

[921] Phil. 2:7.

rank." [922] Our Lord's language copies the Apostle's confession. The latter had said: "Thou art Christ, the Son of the living God." Jesus replies: "Thou art Peter," or rather, in the Aramaic idiom spoken by both of them, "Thou art Kepha." At His first meeting with the son of Jona, Christ had prophetically bestowed this characteristic name upon him.[923] He now confirms him in the possession of it, and at the same time indicates His purpose in so naming him. It was not in vain that He called him Kepha, "stone, rock," because Simon was to be the foundation stone on which would rest the sublime, mystical edifice which Christ had come to found. The metaphor was an expressive play on words. Our Lord, in the closing words of the Sermon on the Mount,[924] praised the wise man who built his house on a rock, so that it withstood all the assaults of the elements. And the Savior will build upon a solid, unshakable rock, because the structure, whose foundation He was laying at that very moment, was to last to the end of time.

We must here insert a brief explanation, by way of reply to a difficulty frequently raised by Protestants. Certain other passages in the New Testament [925] speak of Jesus Himself as the true foundation of the Church. St. Paul [926] and St. John [927] consider the twelve Apostles collectively as the Church's foundation. This being so, what becomes of St. Peter's privilege? The difficulty is easily solved. The Church is, in fact, built on several foundations: the Apostles, Peter, and Christ. Yet Peter is its foundation in a unique and very special sense. "If it is Christ who built the Church, He founded

---

[922] St. Leo, *Sermo in Anniv. Assumpt.*, III.

[923] John 1:42. See page 78.

[924] Matt. 7:24 f.

[925] I Cor. 3:11: "Other foundation no man can lay, but that which is laid, which is Christ Jesus." Cf. Eph. 2:20; I Pet. 2:4-8.

[926] Gal. 2:9; Eph. 2:20.

[927] Apoc. 21:14.

it on Peter; if it is Peter who built it, he founded it on Christ. Is there any contradiction in this? Can a house have a double foundation? No, if we mean a house of wood or stone; yes, if we are speaking of the Church, because it possesses a double character, inasmuch as it is the visible and spiritual society of believers. If it is Christ who built the Church, He must have built it as a visible edifice, upon a visible foundation, which is Peter, inasmuch as He Himself is enthroned in Heaven at the right hand of God. If it is Peter who built the Church, he must have built it on Christ; otherwise it would cease to be the Church of Christ." [928] Jesus is here speaking as the builder of His Church. As for the other Apostles, only in a secondary manner are they called the foundations and pillars of the Church, and they are rightly called so only on condition that they rest on the true foundation, which is Simon, son of Jona.

"I will build My Church." It is under these imposing circumstances that the Church of Jesus is directly named for the first time, and the hour could not have been better chosen. This name, which has become so famous, is derived from two Greek words,[929] which together mean "convoke." Hence it designates a public gathering or meeting; in this case, the meeting or assembly of all true disciples of the Savior, of all who accept His doctrinal and moral teaching; the realization of the Messianic Kingdom on earth. The term ἐκκλησία is employed only twice in the Gospel; [930] but it appears very often in the Acts of the Apostles and in St. Paul's Epistles.[931] The Church is the vast majestic edifice built by Jesus in God's honor, to house and save all men. It was, indeed, a glory

---

[928] P. Schegg, *Evangelium nach Matthäus*, 2d ed., 1863, *i. h. l.*

[929] Ἐκκλησία (ἐκ, "from," καλέω, "I call").

[930] In this passage and Matt. 18:17.

[931] More than twenty times in the Acts of the Apostles; more than sixty times in St. Paul's Epistles; about twenty-three times in the Apocalypse, etc.

for Peter to become its head, under the supreme direction of Christ.

Jesus in thought immediately sees, facing this temple, which is built on the rock, another structure, also strong and powerful, a menace to His Church. He designates it by a figurative expression as "the gates of Hades." [932] Among the Greeks, the word "Hades" designated the abode of the dead, which the ancients,[933] particularly the Hebrews,[934] represented as a subterranean citadel with solid gates, which opened to receive the souls of the departed, but which never opened to permit these souls to leave. The gates would wish to draw in the founders and the members of the Church. But Christ declares that they will not triumph in this moral strife. Kingdoms will crumble and nations disappear, but the Church will remain firm upon its rock. According to another interpretation, preferably adopted by the early commentators, the noun Hades in this passage stands for Hell properly so called, the domain of Satan and the bad angels. The gates of that frightful abode would thus be the infernal powers, constantly striving to overthrow the Church, joining forces with numerous allies whom they find among men. In both cases the idea is the same: Christ promises His Church, resting on the Prince of the Apostles as upon a visible foundation, a perpetual victory against the devil and his hosts. No hostile power will ever succeed in prevailing against it.

Jesus develops His promise by means of other characteristic figures. After making Simon Peter the foundation of His Church, He appoints him its steward with unlimited powers. It is for this reason He adds: "I will give to thee the keys of the Kingdom of Heaven." In all ages and in all countries the act of delivering to anyone the keys of a city, of a fortress, or

---

[932] Πυλαὶ ᾅδου, Vulg., portae inferi.

[933] Cf. Job 38:17; Cant. 8:6 f.; Ps. 106:18; Is. 38:10; Homer, Iliad, V, 646, etc.

[934] They called it Sheol.

of a house, has symbolized the granting of absolute authority to him over all that is contained in these various places. This metaphor is Biblical; [935] the Talmud likewise uses it.[936] In St. Peter's case, the "power of the keys" is therefore an emblem of the universal sway conferred on him over the Church of Christ, of which he is thereby constituted the supreme head.

By using a third figure, which is connected with the second as the latter is connected with the first, Jesus grants to His future vicar a veritable signature in blank and a universal jurisdiction. To make the words "bind" and "loose" designate merely the right of remitting or retaining sins is an unwarrantable restriction of their meaning. In the Talmudic writings these words often mean to forbid or to permit; [937] but even that is not broad enough, for Jesus set no limit to Peter's spiritual authority. The words "bind" and "loose" are here the emblem of an absolute power, of an unlimited doctrinal, legislative, and judicial power in the administration of the Church.[938] In saying, "Whatsoever thou shalt bind, whatsoever thou shalt loose," Jesus confided all His powers without exception and without restriction to him whom He chose for His successor and representative. Whatever Peter will decide, He ratifies in advance; God Himself will give His approval to it in Heaven.

True, we soon hear our Lord addressing similar words to the entire Apostolic College, saying: "Amen I say to you, whatsoever you shall bind upon earth, shall be bound also in heaven; and whatsoever you shall loose upon earth, shall be loosed also in heaven." [939] But it is evident that, in grant-

---

[935] Cf. Is. 22:22; Apoc. 1:18 and 3:7, where it is said that Jesus Himself is in possession of the keys of the abode of the dead.

[936] Cf. *Bab. Sanhed.*, 113, a.

[937] See the collections by Lightfoot, Wünsche, etc., *in h. l.*

[938] Diodorus of Sicily, I, 27, and Josephus, *Bell. Jud.*, I, v, 2, make frequent use of them in this sense.

[939] Matt. 18:18.

ing this extraordinary authority to the other Apostles, an authority required by the needs of the primitive Church, Christ does not make them equal to Peter, who had previously been constituted their supreme head. Just as He made them the foundation of the Church only in a secondary or relative manner, so too He does not bestow unlimited jurisdiction on them, as He does on His Vicar. Before being invested with their great powers, which ceased with them, they had been placed under the direction of a superior, who was to be for them what Jesus Himself had been.

It is, therefore, beyond doubt that the primacy of Peter follows from these divine words, which confer on him a priority of jurisdiction as well as of honor. By virtue of the Savior's magnificent promise, Peter will be, not only the firm rock supporting the edifice of the Church and assuring its perpetual duration, not only the all-powerful steward to whom the keys of this edifice are entrusted, but also the teacher who will infallibly instruct the members of the Messianic kingdom. "The words of Jesus Christ, who out of nothing makes whatsoever He pleases, gives this power to a mortal man." [940]

Those words of Christ, while referring directly to Simon Peter, reach beyond him. They apply to all his successors to the end of time, as the Catholic Church has always maintained and as the councils have defined.[941] The privilege conferred on Peter was not to stop with him, but was to pass to all the pontiffs succeeding him in the see of Rome. This power, which was created for the Church, must endure as long as the Church. "What has to serve as a support to an eternal Church can never have an end." [942] It is not a material edifice constructed once for all and then abandoned, but a living, spiritual edifice which is ceaselessly renewed and has constant

---

[940] Bossuet, "Discours sur l'Unité de l'Église, *loc. cit.*, p. 593.

[941] Vatican Council, *loc. cit.*

[942] Bossuet, *ibid.*, p. 594. Cf. Tanquerey, *op. cit.*, pp. 439-444. Appendix XXIV treats of the Protestant and Rationalist objections to the institution of the primacy

need of a spiritual foundation as living as itself. It is a sheep-
fold wherein the sheep cannot do without the attentive care
of a shepherd. It is a great family which constantly requires
the tender affection and wise guidance of a father. This foundation, this shepherd, this father is none other than the sovereign pontiff, who is called "Pope" because he exercises a paternal sovereignty.

Immediately after relating the episode of St. Peter's confession and the Savior's promise, which was its reward, the
three Synoptics [943] report an injunction which Jesus issued
to the Twelve in terms which stress its importance.[944] He
required of them, for the time being, absolute silence regarding what had just taken place; they must tell no one that He
was the Messias.

Apropos of similar prohibitions which the Savior frequently
addressed to the sick and to possessed persons cured by Him,
we have several times pointed out that the time was not suitable for making so important a revelation to the multitudes.
Their Messianic preconceptions were too gross and deep-
seated, their enthusiasm was still too worldly. What a contradiction there was between the worldly hopes which the mere
word "Messias" aroused in them, and the ideal of the Lord
Jesus! If He had been presented to them as the Christ, the
people would have immediately seized upon the occasion to
proclaim Him king, as they purposed doing not long before,[945]
without considering the evils which such an attempt would
have brought upon the country from the Romans, who were
so jealous of their absolute authority. The Apostles themselves were too much imbued with false ideas regarding the
true character of the Messias, for them to be able usefully
to speak to others about it. The Pharisees, the Scribes, and

---

[943] Matt. 16: 20; Mark 8: 30; Luke 9: 21.

[944] St. Mark and St. Luke here use the verb ἐπιτιμάω, Vulg., *comminatus est*.
St. Matthew speaks of a repeated command, διεστείλατο.

[945] John 6: 15.

the other numerous enemies of the Savior at the time, would not have failed to take advantage of so excellent a pretext for seizing Him before the time. From every point of view, there would be danger of compromising everything by undue haste.

It does not appear that Jesus ever presented Himself directly to the Galilean multitudes as the Messias, although His whole conduct showed Him to be the promised Redeemer. His reply to the messengers of John the Baptist was indirect, for He merely pointed to the facts, without drawing the evident conclusion. Except the Apostles, in the episode just described, the Evangelists mention only the Samaritan woman [946] and the man born blind [947] as persons to whom Jesus clearly revealed His Messianic dignity. And the Twelve, as St. Jerome remarks,[948] during their preaching tour of Galilee some time earlier, were limited by their Master's instructions to announce in general terms the near advent of the Messias, without saying that Jesus was personally the Christ. After His Resurrection and Ascension, every obstacle disappeared and the circumstances became, on the contrary, most favorable; the Apostles then could announce the glad tidings in their full extent, by proclaiming the Savior's name before the Sanhedrin as well as before the people. Meanwhile Jesus limited their zeal; whereas He reveals Himself to them, He habitually veils Himself in the presence of others.[949]

Another incident, which was rendered doubly dramatic by the contrast, followed St. Peter's profession of faith.[950] With-

[946] John 4: 26.

[947] John 9: 37.

[948] In his commentary on the First Gospel, i. h. l.

[949] More than once it has been very justly remarked that a prohibition of this sort is a very powerful guaranty for us of the historic character of the events which surround it. It could hardly occur to the mind of an author of fiction that Jesus, after openly accepting, with an outburst of joy, the title of Messias which St. Peter had just attributed to Him, would have at once required that the matter be kept secret. Cf. Plummer, *Commentary on the Gospel according to St. Matthew*, p. 231.

[950] Matt. 16: 21; Mark 8: 31 f.; Luke 9: 22.

out any transition, the Savior makes an altogether unexpected revelation to the Apostles. As St. Mark expresses it, "He began to teach them" [951] that "the Son of Man [*i. e.,* Jesus Himself as Messias] must go to Jerusalem and suffer many things and be rejected by the ancients and chief priests and Scribes, and be killed, and the third day rise again."

Once before, almost at the beginning of His public life,[952] our Lord had referred to His Passion. But He had then expressed Himself in enigmatic terms which were not fully understood until after the events occurred. In the present instance it was truly a new teaching that He began on that sorrowful subject; as St. Mark says, "He spoke the word openly." [953] This clear prophecy, brief as it is, sums up the whole tragedy as it took place in the council chamber of the Sanhedrin and on Calvary. Jerusalem would be the scene of its action; and it would subject the Son of Man to great humiliations [954] and many sufferings. Its chief instigator will be the supreme court of the Jews, the three classes of which are mentioned by name, as on other important occasions. Jesus will be condemned to undergo a violent death. Let us note the initial detail, "The Son of Man must," [955] which is emphasized by all three Evangelists. Christ's sufferings and ignominious death were a necessity according to the divine plan of redemption. These were also necessary by virtue of His office of Messias, as described by the inspired prophets.[956] Let us likewise note the simplicity and calmness with which Jesus mentions the sinister details of His Passion. In advance

---

[951] According to St. Matthew: "Jesus began to show to His disciples . . ."

[952] John 2:19; 3:14-16; Matt. 9:15 etc.

[953] Παρρησίᾳ (Vulg., *palam*): that is, clearly, without figures. John 7:4, this word is used in contrast to ἐν κρυπτῷ, "in secret"; John 16:25, in contrast to ἐν παροιμίαις, "in proverbs."

[954] The verb ἀποδοκιμασθῆναι (Vulg., *reprobari*), used by St. Mark and St. Luke, supposes a ballot (δοκιμασία), a vote by which a criminal trial is concluded.

[955] Δεῖ, *oportet*.

[956] Cf. Luke 13:33; 17:25; 22:37; 24:7, 44; John 3:14, etc.

He whole-heartedly submits to God's designs upon Him, and He could not have spoken with greater tranquillity, were it a question of some stranger being the victim. For His consolation and encouragement, He had the absolute assurance that His apparent failure would be only momentary, and that a brilliant victory would follow. This part of the prophecy is no less precise than the rest. Jesus knew that He would rise again "on the third day." [957]

Such was the beginning of the new teaching which the Divine Master gave to His Apostles. From this point onward the Evangelists frequently draw our attention to predictions of the same sort, which He repeats to the Apostles to impress upon them this idea which, as we shall see, entered their minds with such difficulty. It was to become an essential part of their education. Earlier they would have been unable to support this terrible announcement. But the time was perfectly chosen, since Jesus had just strengthened their faith in Him by accepting the title which Peter gave Him in the name of all of them. Moreover, they had to be prepared in advance for the dread trial that would come to them in their Master's death, which would happen under such conditions. For this reason He speaks to them so explicitly.[958]

A significant incident, related by St. Matthew and St. Mark,[959] vividly depicts the impression which the terrible prediction made upon the disciples, especially Simon. The vibrant, impulsive nature of the Prince of the Apostles started at this unforeseen blow. Taking Jesus familiarly by the hand or by His cloak,[960] Peter led him aside, so that his colleagues

---

[957] St. Matthew and St. Luke. St. Mark, with a slight shade of difference: "after three days." The two expressions amount to the same thing. Cf. Matt. 27: 63 f., where they are used synonymously, with reference to our Lord's resurrection.

[958] See Appendix XXV.

[959] Matt. 16: 22 f.; Mark 8: 32b–33.

[960] This is the meaning of the Greek word προσλαβόμενος, Vulg., *assumens, apprehendens.*

might not hear the reprimand which he intended. He then dared say to Him: "Lord, be it far from Thee. This shall not be unto Thee." [961] In his mind, as in that of all his fellow-Jews, it was utterly impossible that such a lot should be in store for the Messias, to whom, as they thought, every joy and glory were promised.

It was because Peter loved Jesus so dearly that he wished to remove every suffering from Him.[962] But the warmth of his affection and his natural vivacity had led him beyond bounds. Only a moment before, it was God who spoke by his mouth; now it is in "flesh and blood," from earthly thoughts and feelings that he draws his false wisdom. These words of his come not from Peter, the future foundation of the Church, but from Simon, son of Jona. Perhaps, if we take the Gospel accounts literally, he intended to show the Savior the reasons why "this" should not happen to him.[963] But he was given no time to say more. Christ, turning sharply,[964] and taking in with one look all the other Apostles, who shared but too well in the disposition of their leader, said to Peter with well-deserved severity: "Go behind Me, Satan; thou art a scandal unto Me, because thou hast no understanding [965] for the things that are of God, but the things that are of men." At the close of the temptation in the wilderness,[966] Jesus had dismissed the devil with similar words. Peter, like his fellow-countrymen, refused to accept or understand the *verbum crucis*,[967] and would gladly have turned Christ aside from the

[961] In the Greek, two negatives, placed before the second proposition, emphasize its meaning: οὐ μὴ ἔσται σοι τοῦτο.

[962] Venerable Bede, *i. h. l.*: "*Hoc autem amantis affectu et optantis dixit.*"

[963] In both accounts his reproach is introduced by the words: "Peter . . . began to rebuke Him."

[964] One of His familiar movements. Cf. Matt. 9: 22; Mark 5: 30; Luke 7: 9, 44; 9: 55; 10: 23; 14: 25; 22: 61; 23: 28; John 1: 38.

[965] According to the Greek: οὐ φρονεῖς. Cf. Rom. 8: 6 f. The Vulgate, *non sapis*, makes use of a different metaphor: "Thou hast no taste . . ."

[966] Matt. 4: 10.

[967] I Cor. 1: 18, 23.

faithful fulfilment of His mission. Was he not thus acting as a veritable tempter? [968] He spoke as a carnal man who does not acquiesce in God's designs, placing himself, so to speak, on the road to Calvary as a stumbling-block for his Master. He quite deserved this rebuke, which contrasts so strangely with the promise of the primacy.

Even in that remote district a considerable crowd had gathered about Jesus, though remaining at a respectful distance. The Master now called them to Him,[969] that He might impart to them one of the essential principles of the religion which He had come to found, and that He might in their presence deduce the practical conclusions which the Passion of the Messias presupposed. While these people might not be morally or intellectually capable of understanding that Christ must necessarily accomplish His work of salvation by a bloody immolation, at least they needed to know that, for His followers, no holiness or redemption is possible without self-renunciation, even, if need be, to the point of sacrificing life itself.

Addressing the multitude, which formed a circle around Him and the Apostles, Jesus said: "If any man will follow Me, let him deny himself and take up his cross and follow Me. For whosoever will save his life, shall lose it; and whosoever shall lose his life for My sake and the gospel, shall save it. For what shall it profit a man, if he gain the whole world and suffer the loss of his soul? Or what shall a man give in exchange for his soul? For he that shall be ashamed of Me and of My words, in this adulterous and sinful generation, the Son of Man also will be ashamed of him, when He shall come in the glory of His Father with the holy angels." [970]

---

[968] St. John Chrysostom has an eloquent development of this thought in his 54th *Hom. in Matth.*

[969] One of those lifelike details which we owe to St. Mark, 8:34. St. Luke (9:23a) also supposes that the Savior's discourse was addressed to others besides the Apostles. He introduces it by the words: "He said to all."

[970] Matt. 16:24-28; Mark 8:34-39; Luke 9:23-27. There is a striking resem-

These incisive and paradoxical sentences arrest the attention and call for reflection if one is to grasp their full import. Our Lord repeated them at different times, for we read them, somewhat modified, in several other places in the Gospels.[971] But, as has been said, "in this passage Jesus' thought is more fully and explicitly formulated." [972] Not long since we met the first abridgment.[973] In the present passage the thought is a little more developed. It indicates the three indispensable conditions for becoming a perfect disciple of the Messias. First, we must renounce not only all the goods of this world, as our Lord says later on,[974] but, what is more difficult, we must renounce ourselves and our own will; in other words, die to ourselves, according to St. Paul's forceful expression.[975] Secondly, we must carry our cross; this expression must have seemed very severe and terrible to those who heard it for the first time. St. Luke says also that this carrying of the cross must be daily, that is, perpetual. Thirdly, we must docilely follow Jesus on the way to Calvary.

The reader has doubtless remarked that the three aphorisms following the one we have just considered, are connected with it and with each other by the conjunction "for." In fact, all these sayings are closely related. The first introduces the second, which introduces the third, and this serves to introduce the fourth. The two intermediate sentences contain a play on words, after the manner of the Orient, turning upon the twofold meaning of the Greek noun which signifies both life and soul.[976] Sometimes a person loses his soul by determining to

blance here between the three narratives, as ordinarily happens when they quote the Savior's words, which, moreover, were easy to remember in the present case, so striking are the thoughts they express.

[971] Cf. Matt. 10 : 38 f. ; Luke 14 : 25–27 ; 17 : 33 ; John 12 : 25.

[972] Reuss, *Histoire Évangélique, Synopse*, p. 400.

[973] At the close of the instructions which our Lord gave His Apostles when sending them out to preach through Galilee (Matt. 10 : 38 f.).

[974] Luke 14 : 33.

[975] Gal. 2 : 19 f.

[976] Ψυχή, Vulg., *anima*.

save his bodily life at any price, even at the expense of duty. Better is it to sacrifice our life for Jesus and His sacred interests.[977] It is the best example of the principle that "he who loses wins." The Savior gives a proof of it. He supposes that some man, of unbridled ambition and desire for enjoyment, succeeds in making himself master of the whole world. But death will come upon him, and at one stroke he will lose his bodily life, his vast riches, and his soul, which will be everlastingly damned. By a just retaliation, the Son of Man, when He will exercise His judiciary power at the end of time, will "render to every man according to his works," as Jesus adds (according to the First Gospel); and He will treat His subjects, good and bad, as they treated Him.

With what solemnity Christ here speaks of His second coming! When He makes this final appearance, He will be clothed with three glories: His own personal glory, that of His Father, whose representative He will be at that judgment, and that of the angels who will form His brilliant court. But Christ passes rapidly over this scene, which He later pictures in detail.[978] From mention of His second coming, which will bring the present era to a close, He suddenly passes to an event of a different sort, which, as He explicitly says, many of those listening to Him were destined to behold with their own eyes. To designate the event, He employs a rather mysterious form of speech, which differs slightly in the three Synoptics and has been variously interpreted. As reported in the First Gospel, He said: "Amen I say to you, there are some of them that stand here, that shall not taste death,[979] till they see the Son of Man coming in His kingdom." The last portion is abridged in St. Mark's Gospel, where we read: "till they see the King-

[977] "For My sake and the gospel," we read in St. Mark's account.

[978] Matt. 25 : 31–46.

[979] "To taste death" is an expression which often appears under the pen of the rabbis. We find it also in John 8 : 52 and Heb. 2 : 9. It reflects the bitterness that is part of the passing away.

dom of God coming in power." In the Third Gospel it is still shorter: "till they see the Kingdom of God." Which of these three forms represents the language used by our Lord on that occasion? It is difficult to say; and the exegetes are not agreed on this point.

The general idea is clear: our Lord is speaking of a very important event that will manifest the Messias' power and, in a way, will constitute the act of His taking possession of His Kingdom. What will this event be? On this point the text itself furnishes two valuable data: many of those who were then about the Savior were to be witnesses of that imposing manifestation; and, so it seems, according to the words of the preceding context, this manifestation will have a judicial character. Hence Jesus could not have meant His Transfiguration, which occurred a few days later. He would not have referred to so proximate an event by saying that many of His hearers would be still living at the time.[980] Moreover, the mystery of the Transfiguration, nothwithstanding its importance and beauty, does not fully realize the idea of "the Kingdom of God coming in power" or of the Messias "coming in His Kingdom." The same may be said of our Lord's Resurrection and Ascension, and the descent of the Holy Ghost at Pentecost, although the text has sometimes been applied to those events. At first glance, it would seem more correct to say that Christ had in mind His second coming at the end of time. But many of His hearers were to be still living at the time of the prophesied event.[981]

In agreement with most modern commentators, we think that in this text our Lord is not referring to an appearance of

[980] Such was, however, the common opinion of the Fathers, and of the interpreters in the Middle Ages, in consequence of a forced connection between this prophecy and the episode related immediately after it.

[981] Further on we shall have to refute the error of the Rationalist critics who assert that Christ considered the end of this present world and the establishing of the Messianic kingdom as events very close at hand.

the Messias in person, but to a mystical coming, an historical judgment visibly accomplished by Him, although without His external presence. "Among the judicial acts performed by our Lord, there is none which seems to fulfil this prophecy better than the terrible destruction of the Jewish nation and of Jerusalem, its capital. Therein Jesus manifested Himself as a just and stern judge, thus beginning the series of dread decrees being carried out from His Resurrection to the last judgment. The destruction of Jerusalem by the Romans (A. D. 70) occurred only forty years after the date of the Savior's preaching; therefore quite a few of His listeners, besides the Apostle St. John, might easily have witnessed it." [982]

II. The Transfiguration [983]

Six days after this prophecy [984] there took place an episode of exceptional splendor, which is quite rightly considered the highest point of the Savior's public life. We refer to the mystery of the Transfiguration, which the three Synoptics relate with the most perfect harmony, while each of them points out a few particular details.[985] The important events which we discussed in the last few pages were, to some extent, a preparation for this mystery. Ever since Christ's first public appearance and up to this present point, we have observed a conspicuous and constantly increasing movement in success and glory for our divine Hero. From this same point of view we shall presently see the decline set in immediately after the Transfiguration. Christ's miracles will be less numerous, at least the Evangelists mention only six between the

---

[982] Fillion, *L'Évangile de S. Matthieu*, p. 332.

[983] See Appendix XXVI.

[984] This is the day indicated by St. Matthew and St. Mark. In St. Luke we read: "About eight days"; but the very wording of this phrase shows that the Evangelist did not intend to state a figure strictly exact. From the analogy of Mark 8:31, we may judge that the correct date here is probably the seventh day.

[985] Matt. 17:1-9; Mark 9:1-10; Luke 9:28-36.

Transfiguration and the Passion; His preaching will be less frequent; more than once He will clearly allude to His approaching death; habitually He will live in retirement with His intimate followers, devoting Himself almost entirely to their training.

The Fathers of the Church mention a twofold purpose of this glorious manifestation. For the Son of Man the Transfiguration was "a moment of repose after the long struggle He had so courageously sustained; and it was a foretaste of the glory and delights of Heaven, intended to comfort Him at the hour when His chalice becomes more bitter. It is noteworthy that this prodigy was immediately preceded and followed by a clear announcement of the Passion. Nor is it less remarkable that, in the midst of this imposing event, Christ's conversation with Moses and Elias was about the sufferings which He must soon undergo at Jerusalem. The Transfiguration consecrates Jesus to the cross and to death, as it also gives Him strength to undergo the humiliations and sorrows of Calvary." [986] Despite this brief gleam of glory, He will thereafter live in the shadow of the cross.

But this mystery has likewise a meaning and purpose for the Apostles who witness it. For them it will be a great consolation, following the terrible revelation which their Master had just made about the fate in store for Him in the near future.[987] Upon the "holy mount," as St. Peter calls it,[988] they will learn that their Master's death will not prevent His promises from being fully carried out and His Kingdom from being established in power, and that, after His Resurrection, He will eternally enjoy the glory with which they see Him clothed in a fleeting manner. His nation may reject Him; but

[986] Fillion, L'Évangile de S. Matthieu, p. 333.

[987] This is what St. Leo (Sermo XLIV) expresses with his usual forceful and elegant style: "In transfiguratione illud principaliter agebatur, ut de cordibus discipulorum scandalum crucis tolleretur."

[988] 2 Pet. 1:18.

more than ever He will be the Elect of God, and God will not forsake Him. For us, as for those blessed witnesses of Christ's Transfiguration, and as for the early Christians, this brilliant miracle is one of the most convincing proofs of His divine nature and mission.

It was fitting that this mystery should have witnesses. Jesus chose three from the members of the Apostolic College: Peter, James, and John. They were "the intimate among intimates," as St. John Chrysostom calls them, the close friends, the privileged disciples. To the exclusion of the other nine, they had been present at the raising to life of Jairus' daughter,[989] and we shall find them close to the august Victim at the time of His agony in Gethsemani.[990]

Jesus led them "up into a high mountain apart"; [991] but the Evangelists do not mention its name. What mountain was it? A weighty tradition, certainly earlier than the first half of the third century, since Origen mentions it,[992] gives Thabor the honor of being the scene of Christ's Transfiguration. St. Cyril of Jerusalem and St. Jerome adopt this view without hesitation,[993] as do Eusebius of Caesarea and the illustrious pilgrims of the following centuries (e. g., Arculf and St. Willibald), whose itineraries we possess. The shape of Mount Thabor is remarkably beautiful and contrasts with the monotonous character of the neighboring mountains. In this region, so filled with memories of Christ, it is not surprising that Thabor was considered the scene of the Transfiguration. It rises gracefully and symmetrically at the northeast corner of the extensive plain of Esdraelon. When viewed from the south or southeast, it appears like the segment of a sphere. It is almost

---

[989] Mark 5 : 37 ; Luke 8 : 51.

[990] Matt. 26 : 37 ; Mark 14 : 33.

[991] St. Mark emphasizes this detail by adding that they were apart "by themselves" with Christ in the secluded place chosen by Him.

[992] *In Ps.* 89 : 13. Cf. Pitra, *Analecta*, III, 163.

[993] St. Cyril, *Catech.*, XII, 16; St. Jerome, *Epist.*, XLVI and CVIII.

entirely separated from the other mountains of the vicinity, and is connected with the hills of Galilee only by a low ridge. Its height is not extraordinary, since it rises only 1300 feet above the surrounding plain, about 2000 feet above the Mediterranean, and 2560 feet above Lake Tiberias. But its isolation makes it appear higher than it really is. Its mass of chalky limestone is covered with rich soil. In the springtime its sides are clothed with thick green grass and with a great variety of trees and bushes (oaks of different kinds, mastics, carobs, and turpentine trees), many of which are evergreen. Most of these trees, however, do not grow to a great height. This verdure is in pleasing contrast with the bareness of the neighboring heights. It takes hardly more than an hour to climb to the top of Mount Thabor. At the summit is a level stretch of oblong shape, about 3200 feet long and 2000 feet in average width, which is mostly covered with ruins belonging to different periods of the Christian era.[994] The most notable are the remains of three churches erected in the sixth century in memory of the three tabernacles that St. Peter suggested should be set up; and there are ruins of several monasteries. Worthy of note also are the foundations of a fortification and intrenchments which Josephus, the celebrated Jewish historian, restored at the beginning of the revolt against Rome, when he was still an enthusiastic patriot.[995]

Since the middle of the nineteenth century, Mount Thabor, as the scene of our Lord's Transfiguration, has had a serious rival in Hermon, that other magnificent mountain of Palestine, more majestic even than Thabor. From most of the mountain heights of Palestine may be seen Hermon's enormous summit, covered with snow far into the summer. The

[994] See V. Guérin, *Description de la Palestine: Galilée*, I, 158–163; Chauvet and Isambert, *Syrie, Palestine*, pp. 446–449; B. Meistermann, *Le Mont Thabor, Notice Historique et Description*, 1900; *La Palestine, Guide Historique et Pratique*, by professors of Notre-Dame de France à Jérusalem, 2d ed., pp. 463–470.

[995] Josephus, *Ant.*, XIV, vi, 3; *Bell. Jud.*, I, viii, 7. See also Polybius, V, lxx, 6.

highest of its three bare peaks reaches an altitude of 9000 feet. From that point of vantage a wonderful view may be had in all directions,[996] especially northwest toward the Lebanon, northeast toward Damascus, its gardens and the desert beyond, east toward Hauran, southward over the Jordan valley, Lake Tiberias, Galilee, and Samaria, westward over Carmel and the Mediterranean as far as Tyre. Its splendors are less gentle and graceful than those of Thabor. For the purpose of offering the prayer that preceded the glory and holy joy accorded to His humanity, Jesus with His three companions had no need to make the long and laborious ascent to the principal summit. One of the many spurs of the mountain would have amply sufficed for His purpose.

But why has Thabor been abandoned for Hermon? Partly owing to an historical reason, but much more because of exegetical reasons. In our Lord's time, the summit of Thabor had a fortress and was therefore inhabited; Jesus would not have found there the solitude He sought. From the exegetical point of view it is alleged that the expression "a high mountain," which the Evangelists use to designate the mount of the Transfiguration, scarcely fits Thabor, since its summit can be reached in an hour's walk, whereas it would correctly apply to Hermon, which is the second highest mountain of Syria. The most impressive reason is the fact that all the incidents in the midst of which the Gospel narrative places the Transfiguration, took place in the neighborhood of Hermon; and the sacred writers make no mention of Jesus and the Apostles going elsewhere. At the time of St. Peter's confession [997] the Divine Master was near Caesarea Philippi, quite at the north of Palestine. Almost immediately after the Transfiguration,[998] the

[996] The panorama which can be viewed from the summit of Thabor is also one of great beauty. In a general way it resembles the view which we described when speaking of Nazareth (Vol. I, p. 372).

[997] Matt. 16: 13.

[998] Matt. 17: 21; Mark 9: 29.

Evangelists speak of His return to Galilee. But, in the interval, they do not mention any journey whatsoever. Would not this indicate that it was outside of Galilee, not far from ancient Paneas, that Jesus was transfigured? The six days that elapsed between the promise of the primacy and the Transfiguration would have been sufficient time to go from Caesarea to Thabor, for the journey can be made in three days. But, according to the view of many commentators, it is difficult to suppose that so considerable a journey would have been made without the Evangelists referring to it, especially at a period when they are so particular to note the smallest details of interest in the Savior's life." [999] These reasons are not without weight; but they are not decisive and tradition is of great value in solving this delicate question. Although the summit of Thabor was inhabited, solitary places were not wanting on its slopes; and we are not told that the Transfiguration took place on the top.

From this interesting but secondary question let us pass to the clear and full account of the mystery itself. Jesus, upon reaching the "holy mount," whichever one it was, gave His soul over to one of those fervent and mysterious prayers which the Evangelists, especially St. Luke, so often mention. Suddenly, "whilst He prayed," He became the object of a marvelous phenomenon, as it were God's reply to His prayer. His face was "transfigured"; [1] this expression means that His features, though not suddenly changing, were clothed in unusual beauty and brightness. In fact, it is in the face, the most mobile and intelligent part of the human body, that various sorts of transfigurations show themselves, which are produced by

[999] Fillion, *L'Évangile de S. Matthieu*, p. 335.

[1] Μετεμορφώθη, we read in the first two Gospels. St. Luke avoided using this expression, which his readers of pagan origin might have interpreted wrongly, because of the "metamorphoses" attributed to several divinities. He uses an expression of like significance, saying: "His countenance was altered." The word "transfigured" comes from the Vulgate translation: *transfiguratus est*.

joy, love, holiness, and intimate union with God. The face is then lighted up and transformed. Saints have sometimes been transfigured, in a way, on their deathbeds, while at prayer, at the moment of holy communion. The face of Moses, when he came down from the mountain after "the conversation of the Lord," was so resplendent that the Hebrews could not gaze upon it.[2]

In Christ's Transfiguration we have something more than the effulgence of a heavenly soul upon a human face, even something more than a reflection of the divinity transfiguring the features of a saint. It is the divine Logos Himself, momentarily laying aside the form of a servant, under which He humbly consented to hide Himself out of love for us, and putting on the form of the only begotten Son of the Father. Considering the event from this point of view, we might say, with St. Thomas Aquinas, that Christ's Transfiguration was much less a miracle than the temporary cessation of a habitual prodigy; for it was by virtue of a true miracle that the Savior veiled and hid the brightness with which His divine nature ceaselessly flooded His sacred humanity.

The Evangelists, by means of two special details, explain the meaning of the words "He was transfigured." While Christ's face "did shine as the sun," His garments became "white as the light," [3] with a whiteness, says St. Mark, which no fuller on earth can produce. The *candidati* of Rome, Athens, and Egypt wore linen tunics, the brightness of which was famous and vied with the whiteness of snow. But what was human skill compared with divine power? Moreover, the Savior's garments sparkled and, as it were, emitted flashes of light.[4]

All that is but a prelude to this glorious drama, made up

---

[2] Ex. 34 : 29.

[3] This is the authentic reading in the Greek. The Vulgate has: "white as snow."

[4] St. Mark: στίλβοντα, Vulg., *splendentia;* St. Luke: ἀξαστράπτων, Vulg., *refulgens.*

of three parts, each more sublime than the preceding.[5] We have just considered the first. Suddenly beside the transfigured Savior there appeared two majestic personages, also resplendent;[6] and they entered into conversation with Him. They were two additional witnesses of the mystery, sent by Heaven, as Peter and the sons of Zebedee had been led by Jesus. How did the disciples recognize them? Doubtless by a supernatural intuition or by some sign which we cannot determine. As the early Doctors remark,[7] these two heroes of Israel, both possessing so many titles to fame and so justly dear to the people of God, came to pay homage to the Messias as the Founder of the New Covenant: Moses in the name of the Law, Elias in the name of the prophets; Moses who had been the mediator of the institution of the theocracy, Elias who, more than any other, had contributed to its restoration during the evil days of its history.

Then occurred what at first seems more astonishing than their coming: namely, the subject of their conversation with Jesus. "They spoke of His departure, that He should accomplish in Jerusalem"; literally, His "going out."[8] But what is the meaning of this extraordinary phrase? St. Peter uses it in his Second Epistle[9] to designate death, which is likewise the sense of the expression in this passage; or rather, it includes the different scenes of the divine tragedy, the scenes through which Jesus must pass in leaving this world and returning to Heaven; consequently His Passion, Resurrection, and Ascension; but foremost and especially His Passion, which was, as we find repeated here,[10] a necessity according

---

[5] In St. Matthew's narrative, the beginning of the second and third is indicated by the particle ἰδού, ecce, so much used by this Evangelist.

[6] This detail we owe to St. Luke.

[7] Cf. Tertullian, *Adv. Marcion.*, IV, 22; St. Augustine, *Serm.*, CCXXXII.

[8] Τὴν ἔξοδον αὐτοῦ, Vulg., *excessum ejus.*

[9] 2 Pet. 1:15. Cf. Cicero, *De Republica*, II, 30.

[10] Ἤμελλεν, "He would have to." The Vulgate does not express this shade of meaning.

to the divine plan of redemption. What a remarkable fact it is that the cross and Calvary should cast their shadow upon the mount of the Transfiguration! In the very act of Christ's momentary glorification there was thus clearly associated the indication of the outrages and sufferings through which He must win His everlasting glory. "The Law and the Prophets," says St. Jerome, "announce Christ's Passion." [11] And let us note the use of the word "accomplish," [12] which, as usual, indicates that the events referred to take place in conformity with the prophetic oracles and the express will of God. Moses and Elias came, therefore, to confirm the Savior's recent prediction about His death, and to proclaim that His sorrowful Passion was in very truth the central point of the Law and the Prophets.

The Gospels do not state how long this conversation lasted. But at its close, when the two heavenly visitors were taking their leave of Jesus, Peter, who had been entranced by this sight, said in an outburst of feeling: "Rabbi,[13] it is good for us to be here; if Thou wilt, let us make here three tabernacles, one for Thee, and one for Moses, and one for Elias." In speaking thus, "he knew not what he said," as St. Mark and St. Luke remark. Forgetting the conditions of earthly existence and troubled by the splendor of the spectacle before his eyes, he wanted to protract for a long time those hours of holy delights, and, as a humble servant, he offered to erect, with his companions' assistance, three tents of branches, beneath which Jesus, Moses, and Elias might conveniently be accommodated for a longer stay. By way of somewhat excusing the Apostle, St. Mark says that the disciples were seized with fright, as happens in the presence of great supernatural man-

[11] *In Marc.*, 9:3.

[12] Ἡλήρουν, Vulg., *completurus erat.*

[13] St. Mark preserves this title, which was the one which the Apostle really used in addressing our Lord.

ifestations; and St. Luke states that for some time they had been heavy with sleep, although they were then awake.

While Peter was speaking thus, the scene again suddenly changed. A cloud, similar to those clouds which had at times symbolically manifested the divine presence in the first centuries of Israel's history,[14] enveloped Jesus and His two heavenly companions, after the manner of a veil. At the same time a voice from the cloud said: "This is My beloved Son, in whom I am well pleased: hear ye Him." [15] It was the voice of God the Father, again bearing witness to Jesus. It had greeted Him almost in the same terms at the time of His baptism. This time, in addition to the declaration made on the bank of the Jordan, there is a short exhortation, "Hear ye Him," which recalls the Messianic oracle addressed to Moses.[16] It clearly proclaims that Jesus is the supreme Lawgiver of the New Covenant; it is an unqualified approval of His teaching and commands all to obey Him as an all-powerful Master and infallible Teacher.

Upon seeing the Savior disappear in the cloud and hearing the divine voice, the three disciples were doubly frightened. Falling to the ground, they covered their faces with their hands, not daring to look about them. They were some time in this posture, when Jesus came to them, touched them gently, and said: "Arise, and fear not." Timidly looking about on all sides, they perceived that their Master was alone with them, in His ordinary appearance. The phenomenon of the Transfiguration had ended. But it remained indelibly imprinted on their minds, for St. John plainly alludes to it in the first lines

[14] Ex. 16: 10; 19: 9, 16; 24: 15 f.; 33: 8; 40: 32; Lev. 16: 2; Num. 11: 25; 3 Kings 8: 10, etc.

[15] These words, with slight differences, are quoted in all three accounts. Those just given are the ones in St. Matthew's Gospel. In St. Mark we read: "This is My most beloved Son: hear ye Him." In St. Luke: "This is My beloved Son: hear Him."

[16] Deut. 18: 15–19.

of his Gospel, when he says: "We saw His glory, the glory as it were of the only begotten of the Father." [17] And St. Peter, in his Second Epistle, sums up the principal details of the event, saying: "We have not by following artificial fables, made known to you the power and presence of our Lord Jesus Christ; but we were eyewitnesses of His greatness. For He received from God the Father, honor and glory; this voice coming down to Him from the excellent glory: This is My beloved Son, in whom I am well pleased; hear ye Him. And this voice we heard brought from Heaven, when we were with Him in the holy mount." [18]

As we have already observed in connection with certain humiliating mysteries in the Savior's life, "to His generous acts of self-abasement there often correspond, on the part of His heavenly Father, acts of glorification of which He was the object." [19] Scarcely has He openly consecrated Himself to suffering and death, when He is transfigured on the mountain. We shall again, farther on, witness divine acts of the same sort.[20]

While coming down from the mountain, Jesus issued a strict order to the three Apostles, an order which no longer surprises us after all the explanations that have been given of the necessity of the Messianic secret: "Tell the vision to no man, till the Son of Man is risen from the dead." [21] To no one: not even to the other members of the Apostolic College. The Divine Master knew that the witnesses of the mystery, exalted by the marvels they had just contemplated, would be eager to relate them to others: this would have contributed to the spread of the false ideas which were current about the Messias

[17] John 1 : 14.

[18] 2 Pet. 1 : 16–18.

[19] F. Godet, *Commentaire sur l'Évangile de S. Luc,* 2d ed., I, 536.

[20] See especially John 12 : 27 f.

[21] St. Luke omits this detail, as also the conversation between our Lord and the three disciples regarding the return of Elias. Cf. Matt. 17 : 9–13; Mark 9 : 8–12.

and to the production of a dangerous excitement among the crowds. After Christ's Resurrection no harm would be done by making such things known. Rather would it then be an advantage to disclose, in the interest of His cause, the great favors He had received from God. The Evangelists state that the Savior's order was faithfully obeyed. However, as St. Mark continues, the three Apostles, ever slow to believe and to understand, wondered what might be the meaning of the words, "till the Son of Man be risen from the dead." Evidently they were not wondering about the general fact of the resurrection of the dead, which was a very precise dogma of the Jewish creed; [22] their wonderment concerned the particular fact of Christ's Resurrection. Resurrection presupposes death; must the Messias, then, die like all other men? This idea had no little difficulty entering the minds of the disciples, especially after they had been privileged to contemplate Christ in so glorious a state.

Peter, James, and John did not dare question their Master on this point, for that would have been a direct manifestation that they doubted His word. But on the road they asked Him a question which was logically connected with the recent appearing of Elias: "Why then do the Pharisees and Scribes say that Elias must come first?" By "first" was meant "before the Messias," at least before His victorious manifestation. As explained above,[23] the return to the earth of the prophet Elias had always keenly interested the Jews, and the Talmud frequently reverts to this point, which is connected with a very clear prophecy of Malachias.[24] Elias was mysteriously

---

[22] Bousset, *Die Religion des Judentums,* pp. 280–288.

[23] Vol. I, pp. 251 f. Cf. Bousset, *op. cit.,* p. 220; Weber, *System der altssyna-gogalen palästinischen Theologie,* pp. 337–339.

[24] Mal. 4:5 f. Cf. Ecclu. 48:9 f. Modern Jews give scarcely less attention to Elias than did their ancestors. They are firmly confident that this holy personage constantly protects them and that, although invisible, he is present at their religious cermonies and their family fesivals. See Coypel, *Le Judaïsme,* pp. 102, 229; Stauben, *Scènes de la Vie Juive en Alsace,* p. 96.

taken away in a fiery chariot,[25] and thus far has miraculously escaped death, for God is reserving him for an important office which he will fill at the Messias' second coming. But at this time the Apostles were unable to distinguish between Christ's first and second coming. To their minds there was a contradiction between the scene they had just witnessed on the mountain and the Scribes' teaching about Elias. The Messias had made His appearance in the person of their Master: of that they were sure. The prophet had come and had greeted Him respectfully. But why did he at once disappear without fulfilling his office?

Jesus gave the disciples the enlightenment they desired. He answered them: "Elias indeed shall come and restore all things. But I say to you, that Elias is already come, and they knew him not, but have done unto him whatsoever they had a mind. So also the Son of Man shall suffer from them, as it is written of Him." These words of our Lord throw light on a point that had not been clear. He declares that there are two Eliases: the real Elias whom the Apostles had just beheld at the Transfiguration, and a mystical Elias, of whom the first will be the type. The prophet Elias will come again, as Malachias foretold, and he will labor for the moral regeneration of mankind at the end of time. The second Elias has already come; he is John the Baptist, of whom it was announced before his birth [26] that he would precede the Christ with the spirit and power of Elias. We have already seen with what strict fidelity he filled that office. Unfortunately the great mass of the Jews refused to recognize in him the envoy of Heaven, and his life ended in martyrdom. The words, "they have done unto him whatsoever they had a mind," are tragic in their simplicity. It will not be long before Jesus shares in the bloody fate of His precursor.

[25] 4 Kings 2 : 11.
[26] Luke 1 : 16 f.

This time, as St. Matthew remarks, the disciples understood the Master's words. They knew how they were to reconcile the sudden vanishing of Elias with the Messianic character of Jesus. But the Savior's allusion to His Passion probably escaped them; at any rate, they let it pass without comment.

St. Luke says it was not until the day after the Transfiguration that Jesus came down from the mountain.[27] By combining this detail with another furnished by the same Evangelist, that they "were heavy with sleep," some exegetes have supposed that the glorious mystery took place during the night. This opinion is probably correct; it is confirmed by the fact, also mentioned by St. Luke, that Jesus was transfigured "whilst He prayed." Several passages in the Gospel inform us that Christ frequently chose the quiet hours of the night to enter into closer communication with His Father, at the solemn moments of His life.[28]

III. Curing of a Young Lunatic; Second Announcement of the Passion; the Tax of the Didrachma

When our Lord rejoined those Apostles whom He had left the day before at the foot of Thabor or Hermon, He beheld a very different scene from that in which He had just been the glorious Hero. For a few moments on the mountain, earth became merged in Heaven. But upon descending into the vale of tears and suffering, Jesus again contemplated the desolating sight of the terrible consequences of sin. Our readers are, no doubt, familiar with the advantage Raphael took of this contrast in his wonderful painting of the Transfiguration. The upper part of the picture is devoted to the

27 Luke 9 : 37.
28 Cf. Mark 1 : 35; 6 : 46; 14 : 32; Luke 6 : 12 etc.

glorification of Jesus.[29] In the lower part we see the powerless Apostles and a mocking crowd, and in the center the possessed youth in a posture of violent agitation, with haggard, drawn, livid features in strong contrast to the beauty of the Savior's placid countenance.[30]

As Jesus came near, He saw the nine Apostles surrounded by a large multitude, and Scribes in discussion with them. The crowd at once perceived the Divine Master, in search of whom they had come to these remote regions. Disappointed at not finding Him, they were impatiently awaiting His return. At first glance we are surprised at St. Mark's description of what the crowd felt and what they did. He says: "All the people seeing Jesus, were astonished and struck with fear; and running to Him, they saluted Him." Are not these details contradictory? How are we to explain that extraordinary fright, so vividly giving way to an outburst of affection? By way of explanation, some have considered that it was due to surprise at the Savior's unexpected arrival. But this reason does not take sufficient account of St. Mark's using a very strong expression, indicating a veritable fright.[31] Is it not better to suppose, as many ancient and modern interpreters do, that on Christ's countenance some traces remained of the divine glory that had recently illumined it? It was not, of course,

[29] "Radiant figure of Christ, lighting up Thabor, suspended in midair and borne on the wing of God; then the three dazzled disciples, cast to the ground by the light emanating from the face and garments of the Son of Man, the glorious sight which only Elias and Moses could look upon . . . The head of Christ was the supreme effort of Raphael's genius. Having accomplished this, he never again touched a brush: at that hour death came upon him." Charles Blanc, *Histoire des Peintres, École Italienne: Raphael,* p. 31.

[30] The curing of the young "lunatic," as he was called, according to an expression used by St. Matthew (see below), is told by the three Synoptics: Matt. 17:14-17; Mark 9:16-26; Luke 9:37-44. St. Matthew gives us simply a brief sketch. But St. Mark depicts the details so dramatically that he must have heard them recounted by St. Peter. St. Luke is more ample than St. Matthew, but less complete than St. Mark.

[31] Ἐξεθαμβήθησαν. The Vulgate translates this Greek word by two distinct verbs: *Stupefactus est [populus] et expaverunt.*

a resplendence like that which shone from the face of Moses when he came down from Sinai,[32] because Jesus wished the mystery of His Transfiguration to remain hidden. At least it was a sort of effulgence which gave His features a more heavenly appearance, a new sight for those who were then looking upon Him.

In our Lord's presence a feeling of fear could not last long for those who loved Him. His kindness and affability soon gained the upper hand and drove away all fear. And so we see the multitude run to Him with touching familiarity. His arrival was most timely. Without paying any attention to the Scribes, He opened the conversation by asking: "What do you question about among you?" The answer was given by a man who came forward out of the crowd, knelt down before Jesus, and cried out in a voice made loud and vibrant by the strength of his feelings: [33] "Master, I beseech Thee, look upon my son, because he is my only one. I have brought my son to Thee, having a dumb spirit,[34] who, wheresoever he taketh him, dasheth him, and he foameth, and gnasheth with the teeth, and pineth away. And I spoke to Thy disciples to cast him out, and they could not."

It is impossible to misunderstand the situation. We have here an exact description, in popular terms, of a grievous case of epilepsy,[35] with diabolic possession added thereto. The poor father, when he did not find Jesus, begged the Apostles to deliver his son, for he no doubt knew that, during their

---

[32] Ex. 34: 29, 35.

[33] St. Matthew: ἐβόησεν, Vulg., *exclamavit*, "he cried out."

[34] *I. e.*, that makes him dumb; deaf also, as we learn further on in the narrative.

[35] All the symptoms are clearly indicated. Cf. Knur, *Christus Medicus?* p. 38. In ancient times, Celsus, a physician (*Med.*, III, 230, "*De morbo Comit.*," 3), gave this analogous diagnosis: "*Homo subito concidit, ex ore spumae moventur . . . interdum tamen, cum recens est* [*morbus*], *hominem consumit.*" To designate the disease, St. Matthew here uses the expression σεληνιάζετα (Vulg., *lunaticus est*), which in antiquity was employed to designate epilepsy and kindred morbid effects which were wholly or partly attributd to the influence of the moon, the periodic crises of the ailment coinciding more or less with the different phases of the moon.

preaching through Galilee, their exorcisms had been entirely successful.[36] They at once granted his request. But their efforts were fruitless because the devil victoriously resisted their commands. The Scribes, whom we find nearly always as spies in the midst of the crowd about the Savior, witnessed the scene and felt a malignant joy at the Apostles' failure. The Scribes at once entered into a public discussion with them before all the people present, drawing attention to their humiliating powerlessness, in order to discredit them, and their Master along with them. The disciples, of course, found themselves in a sad plight and were unable to make any reply.

But at this juncture Jesus arrived to cover their defeat. He first gives free rein to His indignation, saying: "O unbelieving and perverse generation, how long shall I be with you? how long shall I suffer you?" At whom was this just rebuke directed? In a general way at all who were there, for, on this occasion, the Scribes, the multitude, the father of the boy, and even the disciples (as Jesus will presently tell them in particular) had evinced more or less unbelief. Moreover, all those whom Jesus was then addressing were representative of the unbelieving mass of the Jewish people. These words certainly presuppose an anguish in Jesus' heart. Those severe epithets, that twice repeated "How long," [37] show a deep sadness, a sort of weariness, as though at times He wished that His task on earth were finished and that the hour were come for Him to return to Heaven, there to enjoy peace and rest, after so much annoyance and ingratitude from those whom He came to save at the price of so great sacrifices.

Conquering His grief, He said: "Bring hither thy son." The latter had remained some distance away, carefully guarded. When he was brought to the Savior, the devil

[36] Mark 6: 12 f.
[37] The Savior's *"Quousque tandem,"* it has been called (Swete, *The Gospel according to St. Mark,* p. 186).

showed his rage by a violent outburst, which Jesus tolerated for a few moments. The boy was thrown to the ground, where he rolled about and frothed at the mouth and was shaken by frightful convulsions.

Christ, with regal calmness, asked the boy's father: "How long time is it since this hath happened unto him?" Since Jesus knew all things, He asked this question, not as a physician might in seeking information about a patient, but as a friend, to show His interest in the afflicted father and to stir up his weak faith. The father replied: "From his infancy; and oftentimes hath he [the devil] cast him into the fire and into waters to destroy him.[38] But if Thou canst do anything, help us, having compassion on us." Although the evil was habitual, it had alternating periods of comparative calm and of frightful crises; during these latter all sort of perils menaced the unfortunate demoniac. "Help us, having compassion on us," said the father, speaking in the plural; for his son's affliction distressed him to the depth of his heart. We may well suppose that the words, "if Thou canst do anything," were uttered in a tone of great distress; but they testify to a great imperfection in the faith of the afflicted father. It may be that he had come full of confidence and that the disciples' failure had partly discouraged him. How we wish he might have said, like the leper, "If Thou wilt, Thou canst . . ."[39] He fell far short of reaching that height. In order to answer him more forcibly and to show him the imperfection of his disposition, Jesus makes use of some of the man's own words: "If Thou canst! [But] all things are possible to him that believeth."[40] The father of the boy was deeply moved and, bursting into

---

[38] Another physician of ancient times, Caelius Aurelianus, wrote, with reference to epilepsy (*De Morbo Comit.*, I, iv, 68): "*Alii . . . publicis in locis cadendo foedantur, adjunctis etiam externis periculis . . . loci causa praecipites dati, aut in flumina vel mare cadentes.*"

[39] Matt. 8:2.

[40] This reading is the more authentic, instead of, "If thou canst believe."

tears,[41] said: "I do believe, Lord; help my unbelief." This is an humble avowal and a touching prayer. In reality, he believed that Jesus was able to cure his son; but shadows of doubt crossed his mind, and he begged our Lord to dispel them and thus make his faith wholly conformable to His wishes.

This dramatic scene took place a little distance from the multitude. But as the crowd drew near in eager expectancy of what would happen and in a desire to miss none of the incident, Jesus hastened to perform the miracle, so as to divert from Himself the curious gaze of the people. In a threatening tone and in a voice of supreme authority which nothing has a right to resist, He issued this command to the evil spirit: "Deaf and dumb spirit, I command thee,[42] go out of him, and enter not any more into him." Being forced to obey, the devil, before taking flight, stirred up a last spasm in his victim, who uttered a piercing cry and fell down at the Savior's feet, motionless as a corpse. "He is dead," cried out many of the onlookers. But Jesus, taking the boy by the hand, raised him up and restored him to his father completely cured, as on a former occasion He had restored the son of the widow of Naim to his mother.

The witnesses of this miracle, says St. Luke, "were astonished at the mighty power of God, and all wondered at all the things He did." At that time, even more so than to-day, a cure effected under such circumstances, was regarded as an undeniable miracle. A physician of our own day writes: "We who endeavor to cure epilepsy by means of bromide, . . . we who are gratified, after treating a case for months or years, to see the intensity of the disease diminish, without being sure that we have prevented mental decadence, know what it means to cure an epileptic, and to do so in an instant." [43] We should

---

[41] This last detail is omitted by some manuscripts of the Second Gospel.

[42] In the Greek, the pronoun ἐγώ is very emphatic.

[43] Knur, *Christus Medicus?* p. 40.

also bear in mind that, in the present case, there was involved not only the curing of a physical ailment, but also the driving out of the devil, whose presence made the epilepsy more grievous and more cruel.

This twofold miracle had a little epilogue, simply mentioned by St. Mark and more fully related by St. Matthew.[44] Jesus entered a house nearby with His Apostles. They could not understand the reason for their failure, and in all simplicity asked the Savior: "Why could not we cast him out?" It did not occur to them that the Savior's rebuke to the "unbelieving and perverse generation" might also apply to them. Jesus discloses the true reason of their failure, because it was important for them to know it, so as not to expose themselves to other such defeats in the future. The Savior tells them: "It was because of your unbelief." [45] This does not mean that the disciples who tried to exorcise the possessed youth were unbelieving in the strict sense of the term; but they had not brought to that act that robust faith which, so to speak, snatches miracles from God. "For, amen I say to you, if you have faith [merely as great] as a grain of mustard-seed, you shall say to this mountain [Jesus here pointed to the Mount of the Transfiguration], remove from hence hither [another gesture by the Master], and it shall remove. And nothing shall be impossible to you. But this kind [of devil] is not cast out but by prayer and fasting."

Thus the Apostles learned the two reasons why they had not succeeded in curing the possessed youth. The first reason was the weakness of their faith. The second arose from the fact that the devil with whom they had been dealing belonged to a particularly powerful class of the infernal hierarchy; he was one of those who can be overcome only by recourse to prayer and fasting, to close union with God and penance, those

---

[44] Matt. 17:18-20; Mark 9:27 f.

[45] Some early documents wrongly changed the ἀπιστία to ὀλιγοπιστία ("little faith").

two means which communicate a superhuman power to the exorcist.

What an astonishing and magnificent promise Jesus makes to His followers, not only in this passage, but also in another one in the First Gospel![46] It is a most striking contrast between a mustard-seed [47] and a mountain like Thabor, or the much greater Hermon. But a lively faith is an all-powerful, irresistible lever. The annals of the early centuries of the Church show that such faith really accomplished wonders similar to that which the Savior just mentioned.[48] True, "it rarely makes use of this power which Jesus granted it, because it understands that the occasions when it ought prudently to exercise it, without seeming to tempt God, do not occur every day. It employs this power only under the influence of divine inspiration, and only real saints dare to use it. It has been well said that the Savior, in speaking thus, did not give to the first comer the right to upset the physical geography of the globe." [49] Aside from any metaphor or hyperbole it remains true that "nothing is impossible" to men of faith and prayer.

Our Lord soon left this region in which so many remarkable incidents had occurred. He continued to be accompanied by His twelve Apostles, to whose training He devoted Himself more and more, as St. Mark expressly says.[50] He made a rapid journey across Galilee, preferably following, as it seems, the less frequented roads.[51] As when He entered the regions of Tyre and Sidon, so, too, He now "would not that

---

[46] Matt. 21 : 21. See also Luke 17 : 6.

[47] See page 413.

[48] We allude especially to a well-known feature of the life of St. Gregory Thaumaturgus. Cf. Eusebius, *H. E.*, VII, 23; St. John Chrysostom, *Hom. in Matth.*, i. h. l.

[49] Fillion, *L'Évangile de S. Matthieu*, p. 344.

[50] "He taught His disciples." The use of the imperfect is very expressive.

[51] We can infer this from the verb παρεπορεύοντο (Vulg., *praetergradiebantur*), "to go hither and thither," which is the best authorized reading of the Greek text of this passage of St. Mark.

any man should know [His presence]." During these last months of His ministry, He more than ever lived in retirement. Aside from His visits to Jerusalem, we henceforth rarely find Him with the crowds, and even then only for brief moments.

It was in the course of these solitary journeys that He repeated to the Apostles the announcement of His Passion and death. "Do you," He said, emphasizing the pronoun, "put well into your ears [52] these words: The Son of Man shall be delivered into the hands of men, and they shall kill Him, and after that He is killed, He shall rise again the third day." The prediction is substantially the same as that which followed St. Peter's confession. But it enters less into detail, for there is no mention of Jerusalem or of the Sanhedrin. A special detail is stressed by all three Evangelists: "The Son of Man shall be delivered [53] into the hands of men," hands that will be horribly cruel to Him, hands which David had in his day so much reason to dread.[54] Delivered by whom? By the traitor Judas, by the Jewish authorities, by the thankless multitudes, who will loudly demand His death. It may possibly be, according to the view of some interpreters following Origen,[55] that Jesus' words referred chiefly to the eternal decrees of His heavenly Father, which had destined Him to die for our redemption.[56]

Will the Apostles this time understand the desolating news to which Jesus thought it necessary to accustom them? Yes, in a way; St. Matthew remarks that "they were troubled exceedingly," feeling that it forboded great sufferings for the

[52] This is the reading of the Greek text, in the expression by which St. Luke introduces the prophecy. It is a strong phrase, which is softened by the Vulgate: *Ponite vos in cordibus vestris.*

[53] The Second Gospel uses the present tense, "is delivered," so certain is the fact and now so near at hand.

[54] Ps. 30: 9.

[55] *Tract. in Matth., i. h. l.*

[56] Rom. 8: 32.

Master whom they loved so much. However, their state of mind remains the same as at Cæsarea Philippi. As St. Luke says, "they understood not this word, and it was hid from them, so that they perceived it not. And they were afraid to ask Him concerning this word." They were still blinded by their false ideas and their dreams about the Messianic kingdom, which they imagined as an institution of glory and happiness without a cloud. Jesus, on the contrary, in spite of the holy delights experienced during His Transfiguration, was not unmindful of the sorrowful way of Calvary, and He advanced toward it full of courage and fearlessness. But why did His disciples fear to question Him, as they had recently done after the curing of the young lunatic and on many other occasions? [57] Perhaps they instinctively dreaded to receive too precise and sorrowful enlightenment; or perhaps they did not wish to run the risk of paining Jesus, as Simon Peter had done at the time of the first announcement of the Passion. At least the lesson was not entirely lost on them. This holy seed, even though sown in unpromising soil, will finally germinate. Later on, in the bright light of the events, the Apostles recalled these exact predictions, and their faith in their Master and in His work became the more living.

St. Matthew alone relates an instructive little episode that occurred in Capharnaum [58] when Jesus returned there after an absence that seems to have been rather long. This incident fits well into the plan of the First Gospel, since it contains an excellent proof of Christ's Messianic character. Jesus had scarcely returned to the city, when the collectors of a special tax came to Peter, whom they had long known, and said to him: "Doth not your Master pay the didrachma?" The manner of the question shows that those who asked it were not the ordinary fiscal agents, demanding the tax in the name of

[57] Cf. Mark 4: 10; 7: 17; 10: 10, etc.
[58] Matt. 17: 23–26.

the tetrarch Antipas. The "publicans" would certainly have spoken in a different tone, and the Evangelist would probably have designated them by their usual name. Furthermore, the words, "pay the didrachma," would suffice to show that it was a question of a sacred tax imposed since the time of Moses upon every Israelite twenty years of age or more, to defray the expenses of worship, formerly in the tabernacle, then in the Temple at Jerusalem.[59] This tribute consisted of a half-shekel, a Jewish coin exactly equal to a didrachma (double drachma).[60] In our Lord's time, in places inhabited by Greek-speaking Jews,[61] it was usually designated by the specific name of "didrachma."

Without reflecting at all, Peter replied in the affirmative to the collector of the sacred tax. This presupposes that up to then Jesus had regularly paid this tribute, in conformity with the general principles affirmed by Him on various occasions.[62] But when the Divine Master, with the Twelve, had gone into the house where He lodged at Capharnaum,[63] He put this question to Peter: "What is thy opinion, Simon? The kings of the earth, of whom do they receive tribute or custom?[64] of their own children or of strangers?" And Peter answered: "Of strangers." The word "strangers" here stands for the subjects of a kingdom, as opposed to the members of the royal family. Jesus then drew the obvious conclusion: "Then the children are free," that is, exempt from paying tribute. Therefore the head of the Apostolic College had been too hasty in declaring that his Master would pay the sanctuary tax. He had for a moment forgotten that Jesus was "the

---

[59] Ex. 30: 13 f.; 4 Kings 12: 4; Neh. 10: 32 f.

[60] Josephus, *Ant.*, III, viii, 2, says that in his time the Jewish shekel equaled four Attic drachmas.

[61] Josephus, *Ant.*, XVIII, ix, 1; *Bell. Jud.*, VI, 6; *Dio Cassius*, LXVI, 7, 2.

[62] Cf. Matt. 3: 15; 5: 17; 8: 4, etc.

[63] In the Greek: εἰς τὴν οἰκίαν, with the article.

[64] The former of the two expressions refers to customs duties and tolls; the latter to personal taxes.

Christ, the Son of the living God," and that after having publicly accepted these titles, He was, by virtue of His double prerogative, free from the obligation of paying the sacred tax, which, in fact, was collected for His Father and for Himself. Nevertheless, since His word had been imprudently pledged by one of His own, Jesus consents to pay this tribute as formerly; He did not wish to cause scandal by having it thought He despised the Temple and its ceremonies. But He will procure the necessary amount by a miracle, thus protecting His dignity and His rights, which had been momentarily slighted. Jesus therefore said: "That we may not scandalize them, go to the sea, and cast in a hook, and that fish which shall first come up, take; and when thou hast opened its mouth, thou shalt find a stater.[65] Take that and give it to them for Me and thee." It was in the same spirit of obedience and with the same humility, "to fulfil all justice," that Jesus had come to John to be baptized. In this case, however, He purposes claiming His rights as Messias and Son of God; for the words clearly imply His Messianic character and divine origin.

Whether Peter carried out the order, St. Matthew does not say. But this is in keeping with the Evangelist's manner of writing. Instead of rounding out his accounts after the manner of St. Mark, he merely gives the essential details and leaves the rest to the understanding of his readers.[66] There is, of course, no doubt but that St. Peter promptly obeyed. It is also certain that Jesus intended to perform a real miracle. His order did not mean, as has been often said of late: "Go, catch enough fish so that their sale will amount to a stater, with which you will pay our sacred tax." [67] A certain

---

[65] A Greek silver coin, worth four drachmas or two didrachmas—sufficient to pay the Temple tax for two persons.

[66] Matt. 8: 1-4; 9: 2 (cf. Mark 2: 3 f.; Luke 5: 18 f.); 9: 10-13 (cf. Mark 2: 10-12); 11: 2-6 (cf. Luke 7: 18-23), etc.

[67] Evidently the Rationalists will accept no other interpretation.

candid Rationalist [68] justly says: "Unless we completely distort the Evangelist's account, we cannot succeed in removing the miracle." It would have been easy to take from the purse of the little community the necessary four drachmas; and, in fact, the tax of the other eleven Apostles had to be paid out of the community fund. But we have seen that Jesus, by miraculously procuring the money needed for His own tax and that of St. Peter, meant to attest His Messianic rights in a manner worthy of Him. That is why, in this single instance, He performed a miracle in His own behalf.[69]

IV. The Training of the Twelve

Several of the foregoing incidents show what defects the Apostles had even after being so long in the school of Christ. Their Master knew their imperfections better than anyone else, and unremittingly strove to correct them. More than ever, we must repeat, He now takes advantage of every opportunity to complete their religious and moral education. At this point we find several of His instructions grouped together. Were they given on a single occasion, in the way we see them assembled in the Synoptics' narratives, especially in the account by St. Matthew, who is here the most complete? This is not impossible. Yet some eminent commentators suppose the connection between many of them to be logical rather than chronological. In fact, it is sometimes rather difficult to establish the connection in a completely satisfactory man-

[68] E. Reuss, *Histoire Évangélique, Synopse,* p. 418.
[69] In memory of this incident, the name *Chromis Simonis* has been given to one kind of fish in the lake. See Lortet, *La Syrie d'Aujourd'hui,* p. 506. In order to deny the miracle, it has often been asserted that no fish of the lake could hold a stater in its mouth. Lortet, on the contrary, says that the *Chromis Petri* has "an enormous mouth, as compared with the size of its body," and that in the spring it carries in its mouth a large quantity of eggs and small fish.

ner.[70] The principal thought uniting them is the consideration of the duties of Christians to each other.

The first is a lesson of humility.[71] A few moments after the episode of the didrachma,[72] in the house at Capharnaum where He had entered, Jesus suddenly asked the Apostles this question: "What did you treat of in the way?" At the time of His recent journey, probably shortly before returning to Capharnaum, He had left them alone part of the way, while He himself walked ahead, absorbed in meditation and prayer. Now He wishes them to report the noisy discussion in which they had engaged at a certain point. He who saw "the thoughts of their heart" [73] was not ignorant of what had occurred; but, by this inquiry, He wished to turn their attention to what was imperfect in their conduct. St. Mark's statement that "they held their peace," is very eloquent. To the Master's question they could offer merely an embarrassed silence, not daring openly to acknowledge that they had discussed which of them would have the first place in Christ's earthly kingdom. A quarrel of ambition, rivalry, and precedence was engaging them, even while the Savior's cross was looming on the horizon! It is true that their preconceptions had been reawakened by several recent events, for example, the promise made to Simon, the special privilege granted three of them to accompany Jesus upon a mission that was kept secret, and also various sayings of their Master regarding the establishment of His Church.

They greatly needed a lesson in humility. To make it more striking, Jesus connected it with a charming symbol. Calling

---

[70] The Rationalists greatly exaggerate when they say that in this whole passage there is nothing more than a motley and wholly artificial composition (J. Weiss, *Die Schriften des N. T.*, p. 323).

[71] Matt. 18: 1–5; Mark 9: 32–36; Luke 9: 46–48.

[72] "At that hour," we read in most Greek manuscripts of the First Gospel, as in the Vulgate. The variant, "in that day," has but little warrant.

[73] This supernatural clairvoyance is often mentioned by the sacred writers. Cf. Mark 2: 8; 5: 30; John 2: 50; 6: 62; 13: 10 f.; 16: 19; Acts 1: 24, etc.

to Him a little child,[74] He took it by the hand and placed it
at His side in the place of honor. Then He sat down, took
this privileged child in His arms, and said: "Amen I say to
you, unless you be converted, and become as little children, you
shall not enter into the Kingdom of Heaven." Into what a singular error the Apostles had fallen! In a spirit of ambition they
had striven for the first place in the Kingdom of Christ, and
lo, they are threatened with being excluded from it unless
they return to better dispositions! According to the principle
announced by Jesus, true greatness does not consist in honors or glory, but in the attitude of humility which young children so well assume, instinctively conscious of their littleness.

The Savior develops His thought, saying: "Whosoever
therefore shall humble himself as this little child, he is the
greater in the Kingdom of Heaven. And he that shall receive
one such little child in My name, receiveth Me. For he that
is the lesser among you all, he is the greater. If any man desire
to be first, he shall be the last of all and the minister of all."
In this vivid and paradoxical form, Jesus declared the practical consequences of the principle He had just laid down. His
disciples must have been still more confounded, after hearing
these words, which condemned their ambitious thoughts and
settled their controversy in so unforeseen a manner. They
no doubt understood their Master was alluding not merely
to real children, whom He loved so much, but also to all simple, humble souls that are like them.[75] What honor Jesus
shows to "these little ones" by testifying that to receive them
kindly and to render them all the services that true charity
inspires, is to receive Him and to do good to Him! In a way,

---

[74] According to a tradition which goes back no further than the ninth century
and which offers no serious mark of authenticity, this child was the future St.
Ignatius of Antioch.

[75] This conclusion comes from the ensemble of the first four readings grouped
here. See in particular, especially in the Greek text, Matt. 18:5, 6, 10; Mark
9:37, 42.

it is also to receive God, His Father. It was hardly possible to give a stronger impulse to Christian humility to place itself at the feet of all and in the service of all. But Jesus would have it supernatural in the acts which it performs "in His name," [76] consequently for Him, to whom all "these little ones" belong.

The lesson of humility was followed by a lesson of tolerance, occasioned by a question of the beloved disciple.[77] John proposed a case of conscience to Jesus, apropos of a recent incident, in which he was probably the principal hero, with his brother James and perhaps a few other Apostles. "Master," he said, "we saw a certain man casting out devils in Thy name, and we forbade him, because he followeth not with us." Jesus had just recommended a kind reception done "in His name" to little ones and to the simple of heart. That expression may have recalled to John's mind the episode he mentioned. His delicate conscience was now troubled, for he feared having acted wrongly in showing himself so harsh.

Let us note in passing that the fact referred to has a very real importance in the Savior's life. Jesus' influence must have attained considerable proportions in Galilee, since men not reckoned among His intimate followers began of their own accord to make use of His name to drive out devils. The Apostles' conduct had been prompted by a spirit of zeal, lest His blessed name should be profaned by unauthorized people, who might place it at the service of superstition as a magical formula.[78] Did a feeling of jealousy increase the severity

---

[76] In the Greek text of the New Testament, this expressive phrase has several slight variations: ἐπὶ τῷ ὀνόματι (Matt. 18:5; 24:5; Mark 9:37; 13:6; Luke 9:48) ; ἐν τῷ ὀνόματι (Mark 9:38; Luke 9:49; John 14:13) ; εἰς τὸ ὄνομα Matt. 18:20; John 1:12; 2:23; Acts 8:16) ; ὑπὲρ τοῦ ὀνόματος (Acts 5:41; 9:16; 15:26) ; διὰ τὸ ὄνομα (Mark 13:13; John 15:21; Apoc. 2:3) ; ἕνεκεν τοῦ ὀνόματος (Matt. 19:29), etc. Cf. Geden, *Concordance,* pp. 696–698.

[77] This is the only place in the Synoptic Gospels where we see him taking an active part: Mark 9:37–40; Luke 9:49 f.

[78] This did actually happen later on. Cf. Acts 19:13.

of the prohibition which the Apostles addressed to him whom they looked upon as an intruder? This is not impossible. May they not have supposed that to them alone belonged the right of performing such exorcisms, by virtue of the powers which their Master had expressly conferred on them?

The Savior replied: "Do not forbid him. For there is no man that doth a miracle in My name, and can soon speak ill of Me. For he that is not against us is for us.[79] For whosoever shall give you to drink a cup of water in My name, because you belong to Christ, amen I say to you, he shall not lose his reward."

Without directly rebuking His disciples, who thought they were doing right and were taking up His defense, Jesus told them they were wrong and showed them that they had acted in a narrow-minded spirit in the case submitted to Him. He advised a broader conduct and more liberal feelings in the future. His decision was based on sound reasons. Inasmuch as the impromptu exorcist used the name of Christ to perform a good work, he showed his belief in the power of that name and a real confidence in Him who bore it. Hence, to a certain extent, he was a disciple, and there was no occasion to discourage such a helper, for it was hardly possible that he would pass much time in the enemy's camp. In the days of Moses, when Josue was informed that many of the Hebrews had begun to prophesy, Josue said to him: "My lord Moses, forbid them." But Moses, instead of following Josue's advice, said: "Why hast thou emulation for me? O that all the people might prophesy." [80] The great lawgiver thus gave a lesson like that of Jesus.[81]

[79] This is the correct reading of the passage of St. Mark. In St. Luke we read: "He that is not against you, is for you." The sense is the same, although expressed with a slight variation.

[80] Num. 11 : 27–29.

[81] We have already observed another saying of the Divine Master which, at first sight, seems to contradict this assertion, "He that is not against us is for us."

Our Lord, for the second time,[82] promised a great reward to whosoever, in a spirit of faith, would do a kindness to the "little ones" so dear to Him, though it were only by offering them a cup of cold water. In forceful language He now showed His displeasure towards all those who, by word or example, would commit the crime of leading those pure and delicate souls into evil.[83] He said: "He that shall scandalize one of these little ones that believe in Me, it were better for him that a millstone should be hanged about his neck and that he should be drowned in the depth of the sea." The Savior was referring to a particular kind of execution then in use in the Græco-Roman world; it consisted in throwing the condemned person into the sea. To make sure that the body would sink, a large stone was fastened to the person's neck.[84] The Jews ground their wheat by means of hand mills, made of two millstones that were turned one upon the other. But sometimes they also employed much larger millstones, which were turned by asses or horses.[85] These stones were, of course, of large size, and it was to them our Lord referred. Rather than cause the eternal loss of a soul, a frightful, cruel death would be better.

At the thought of the irreparable evils that would result from scandal, even in His Church, the Divine Master said: "Woe to the world because of scandals. For it must needs be that scandals come: but nevertheless woe to that man by whom the scandal cometh." His strong emotion still resounds in His words, in that double *Vae,* "Woe!" The first is a cry

Christ said then, according to St. Matthew (12:30) and St. Luke (11:23): "He that is not with Me, is against Me." But the contradiction is only apparent. The two propositions, in their absolute form, teach the same thing, namely, that it is not possible to remain neutral with regard to Christ. One must take sides either for or against Him.

[82] See Matt. 10:42.

[83] Matt. 18:6 f.; Mark 9:41.

[84] Suetonius, *Aug.,* 62.

[85] Some specimens of them have been discovered in Palestine, Greece, Italy, and elsewhere. See Fillion, *Atlas Archéologique de la Bible,* pl. XXI, figs. 1–3; pl. XLIII, figs. 1, 3, and Ovid, *Fast.,* VI, 318.

of compassion; the second contains a terrible threat. Scandal is necessary, not in an absolute way, but relatively, since the world is what it is, both corrupted and corrupting, with snares at every step on one's path. It is inevitable also because of the weakness and inclinations of our fallen nature. In this sense St. Paul speaks of the necessity of heresies.[86] But as this moral necessity leaves individual freewill intact, those who scandalize their brethren, especially children and such as are like them, are wholly responsible for their evil works.

Besides scandal "given," there is scandal "received," following the distinction made by theologians. Jesus therefore, to show how carefully a Christian should avoid the proximate occasions which might lead him into sin, adds: "If thy hand scandalize thee, cut it off; it is better for thee to enter into life, maimed, than having two hands to go into hell, into unquenchable fire, where their worm dieth not, and the fire is not extinguished. And if thy foot scandalize thee, cut it off. It is better for thee to enter lame into life everlasting, than having two feet, to be cast into the hell of unquenchable fire, where their worm dieth not, and the fire is not extinguished. And if thy eye scandalize thee, pluck it out. It is better for thee with one eye to enter into the Kingdom of God, than having two eyes, to be cast into the hell of fire, where their worm dieth not, and the fire is not extinguished." [87]

The Savior had already uttered these warnings in the Sermon on the Mount.[88] He repeats them here, but with developments and slight differences that make them even more impressive. In addition to the hand or eye which we should be ready heroically to cut off or pluck out if we fear it will commit evil deeds or will crave evil desires, He speaks of the foot, which may lead us to sin. As in the earlier passage, so here these organs of the human body figuratively stand for what-

[86] I Cor. 11 : 19.
[87] Matt. 18 : 8 f.; Mark 9 : 42–47. We quote the passage according to St. Mark.
[88] Matt. 5 : 29 f.

ever, within us or without, might seduce us and separate us from God. We must treat what gravely scandalizes us, however attached we may be to it and however necessary we may think it to be for us, as we treat gangrenous members, which we do not hesitate to sacrifice in order to save the whole body.

Upon reading this passage, we observe its rhythm and cadence, the parallelism between the bodily organs mentioned by Christ, the opposition between "life" or "life everlasting," which the blessed will enjoy with God after leaving this world, and "hell" or "the hell of unquenchable fire," destined for the damned.[89] The refrain which, in the Vulgate and in several ancient documents, terminates each of the Savior's terrible descriptions, "where their worm dieth not, and the fire is not extinguished," produces a most impressive effect. However, it is possible that it was pronounced only once, as a conclusion to the threat; important Greek manuscripts contain it only at the end of the paragraph about the eye. The expression is taken from the Book of Isaias.[90] The prophet, contemplating in spirit the punishment of Jehovah's enemies and seeing them like the dead that strew a battlefield, says: "They shall go out and see the carcasses of the men that have transgressed against Me: their worm shall not die, and their fire shall not be quenched; and they shall be a loathsome sight to all flesh." [91] This "unquenchable fire" is considered by the Fathers to be the eternal flames of hell, and the "worm that dieth not" an image of the remorse that forever tortures the damned.[92]

[89] We explained above the origin of the meaning of *gehenna*. See page 293.

[90] Is. 66: 24.

[91] Similar figurative expressions are to be found in Judith 16: 20 f., and Ecclu. 7: 19.

[92] In St. Mark, following our Lord's words regarding scandal, we read these additional lines: "For every one shall be salted with fire; and every victim shall be salted with salt. Salt is good. But if the salt become unsavory, wherewith will you season it? Have salt in you, and have peace among you." The Savior's thought is rather enigmatic in this passage; it has therefore received several interpretations.

Jesus still had at His side the little child who had served as a sort of model. The Savior passes from the consideration of scandal to a consideration of the value of souls. This lesson is recorded only by St. Matthew, in the following words of our Lord: "See that you despise not one of these little ones; for I say to you, that their angels in heaven always see the face of My Father who is in heaven. For the Son of Man is come to save that which was lost." [93] We should, therefore, highly esteem those whom God Himself honors by giving each of them, as perpetual guide and guardian, one of the glorious and blessed angels of His court, and whom the Messias, the Son of Man, so loved as to clothe Himself in their humble nature, that He might sacrifice Himself in order to save them.[94] Jesus' last thought in the passage just considered was that of the Son of Man bringing salvation to all mankind.[95] He then further explained the thought by one of His

See the commentaries of Knabenbauer, Schanz, Lagrange, and others. The first expression might mean that, since all men are guilty, all must in some way pass through fire: it will be through the fire of hell, if it is not through that of voluntary mortification which wards off sin and its occasions. We saw, at the beginning of the Sermon on the Mount (Matt. 5:13; cf. Luke 14:34), the words concerning salt that has lost it savor. The words "every victim shall be salted with salt," recall a divine command, Lev. 2:13 (cf. Ezech. 43:24), which required that the priests of Israel should put a little salt upon all liturgical offerings.

[93] Matt. 18:10-14.

[94] The latest critical editions of the Greek Text (Tischendorf, B. Weiss, Westcott and Hort, H. von Soden, Nestle, etc.) suppress the words "For the Son of man is come to save . . . ," which are omitted by important Greek manuscripts and by several of the Fathers. In this case, the passage is considered as being taken from Luke 19:10. But the words are found in many other manuscripts. It is difficult to reach an absolute decision in questions of this sort. To whatever opinion one inclines regarding the authenticity of this sentence, that which precedes it is quite rightly considered by exegetes and theologians as a *locus classicus* for the existence of guardian angels. Such was the view of the Fathers (see Knabenbauer, *Comment. in Evangelium S. Matthaei*, 2d ed., II, 121), as it was also of the Jews contemporary with our Lord. Cf. Acts 12:15; Bousset, *Die Religion des Judentums*, p. 317; Wünsche, *Neue Beiträge zur Erläuterung der Evangelien*, p. 212.

[95] "To save that which was lost" or which was threatened with being lost. These are truly golden words that might well be regarded as Christ's motto. Cf. Rom. 14:15; I Cor. 8:11, etc.

most famous parables, that of the lost sheep—a parable which vividly depicts the untiring devotedness of the Good Shepherd.[96] In the Third Gospel[97] it is found at a later point, in another group; it is not surprising that the Savior should have repeated it on different occasions. "What think you? If a man have an hundred sheep, and one of them should go astray, doth he not leave the ninety-nine in the mountains and go to seek that which is gone astray? And if it so be that he find it; Amen I say to you, he rejoiceth more for that, than for the ninety-nine that went not astray. Even so it is not the will of your Father, who is in heaven, that one of these little ones should perish."

This parable most clearly sets forth Christ's unselfish diligence in saving a single soul, even when it has strayed from Him through its own fault. No effort or fatigue is considered too great to recover such a soul. If He momentarily leaves the ninety-nine other sheep of His flock while He goes in search of the strayed one, it is not because He loves them less than the lost one; but He does not wish this one to perish. Moreover, He takes precautions that the rest of the flock shall run no risk during His short absence, and He leaves them in the plentiful pastures of the plain. There is, however, a cloud in the picture: "If it so be that he find it." That is by no means certain, especially in the application of the parable; the lost sheep stands for men endowed with free will, led on by their passions, and perhaps, in spite of all, persisting in their straying.

The rest of the Divine Master's discourse to the Apostles concerns love of one's neighbor, considered from two different points of view: forgiveness of injuries and fraternal correction. This twofold lesson is suited to Christians in general

[96] Matt. 18: 12–14.
[97] Luke 15: 3–7.

no less than to the Apostles. The first question [98] concerns
the way a disciple of the Messias should act when he has been
grievously and unjustly injured by another Christian. Christ
says: "If thy brother shall offend against thee, go, and rebuke
him between thee and him alone. If he shall hear thee, thou
shalt gain thy brother. And if he will not hear thee, take
with thee one or two more; that in the mouth of two or three
witnesses every word may stand. And if he will not hear them,
tell the Church. And if he will not hear the Church, let him
be to thee as the heathen and publican."

The rules here laid down by our Lord may be summed up
thus: great consideration for persons, lawful severity toward
their faults. The offended person is directed to adopt three
measures, which together form a sort of appeal to three courts
in succession, and end either in the guilty person's repentance
and amendment or else, if he remains obdurate to all fraternal
correction and official exhortation, in his excommunication.
Without discrediting itself and without imperilling its members, the Christian community could not keep in its bosom
a false brother who would refuse to obey lawful orders. It
will therefore treat him as the Jews treated pagans and publicans.[99] Those justly severe words presuppose that the Church
of Christ, from its very beginning, even while still a very
small community, will have and will thereafter always retain
the right to reject from its midst, as the Synagogue did,[100]
such members as it might judge unworthy. It was by virtue
of this principle that St. Paul pronounced sentence of excommunication against a Corinthian Christian who had committed
a grave offense.[101] Moreover, the sentence which the Church

[98] Matt. 18: 15–17.
[99] The Savior's language in this passage has a thoroughly Judaic coloring. Cf,
Matt. 5: 46 f.; 6: 7; 9: 10 f., etc.
[100] John 9: 34. Cf. Schürer, *Geschichte des jüdischen Volkes,* 3d ed., II, 434–436.
[101] 1 Cor. 5: 3–5.

may feel obliged to pronounce will be ratified by God in Heaven, as our Lord adds by conferring on the society founded by Him judicial powers like His own. "Amen I say to you, whatsoever you shall bind upon earth, shall be bound also in heaven; and whatsoever you shall loose upon earth, shall be loosed also in heaven." [102]

These unlimited powers, which concern both the external and the internal forum, the right to pronounce judicial sentence and to absolve from sins, are obviously not conferred upon the mass of the faithful, but upon their regularly constituted chiefs. Although the terms by which these powers are conferred resemble those which Jesus used in making Simon Peter the supreme head of the Church, yet it is likewise obvious that they confer only a jurisdiction subordinate to the authority of the supreme pastor.[103]

The Savior's promise then expands and communicates to the Christians themselves a veritable almighty power, through prayer in common in His name. "Again I say to you, that if two of you shall consent upon earth concerning any thing, whatsoever they shall ask, it shall be done to them by My Father who is in heaven. For where there are two or three gathered together in My name, there am I in the midst of them." [104]

Our Lord says, "Two or three," the smallest possible community; yet Jesus will be in their midst when they meet in His name,[105] for His greater glory; and as He will join in their prayers, His heavenly Father will be unable to refuse them.[106]

---

[102] Matt. 18:18.

[103] On this subject, see Knabenbauer, *Comment. in Evangelium S. Matthaei*, 2d ed., II, 129–132.

[104] Matt. 18:19 f.

[105] In the Greek, we have here: εἰς τὸ ὄνομα . . . , "for My name."

[106] According to the *Pirke Aboth*, III, 9, when ten Jews are gathered together to consider the law, God is in their midst.

At that moment Peter approached the Savior and, as the beloved disciple had done, proposed a case of conscience, which led to another lesson of great value for us, regarding forgiveness of injuries.[107] Fraternal correction presupposes in the person offended a great generosity of heart, since he must be ready to forget all the wrongs inflicted on him by his neighbor, if the latter acknowledges his fault and evinces his regret. But what should one do if the neighbor again and again repeats his offense? "Lord," St. Peter asked, with his usual frankness, "how often shall my brother offend against me, and I forgive him? Till seven times?" In such cases the rabbis of the time required only three successive pardons.[108] By more than doubling this figure, Simon Peter no doubt thought he was amply entering into the spirit of conciliation recommended by his Master. But this figure was far short of being sufficient, for Jesus answered: "I say not to thee, till seven times; but till seventy times seven times." [109] This means that a true disciple of Christ should pardon indefinitely, should never grow weary of forgiving.

What Jesus asserted in arithmetical terms, He presently taught in a little parable, saying: "Therefore is the Kingdom of Heaven likened to a king, who would take an account of his servants. And when he had begun to take the account, one was brought to him, that owed him ten thousand talents."

Ten thousand talents was an enormous sum, especially for those times. The talent was not a form of currency, but a money of account, used in financial calculations, as when we

[107] Matt. 18 : 21–35.

[108] *Bab. Ioma*, 86, 2. By virtue of their shabby exegesis they took as a basis for their decision the two passages, Job 33 : 29, and Amos 1 : 3, 6, 9.

[109] The Savior takes the number cited by Peter and multiplies it by ten; this product He again multiplies by seven, thus making 490. It has sometimes, but wrongly, been translated: "seventy-seven times." But in that case the numbers 70 and 7 would have been joined by the conjunction και.

speak of a hundred thousand francs or a million dollars.[110]
If the present text refers to the Attic talent, which was then
in general use throughout the Roman Empire and also in
Palestine, it was equal to about $1200, so that ten thousand
talents would correspond to twelve million dollars. The sum
would be twice this amount, if the Hebrew talent is meant. It
is therefore evident that those whom the king in the parable
called to him to render their accounts, were not ordinary servants, but ministers of state or great bankers, with whom he
had business dealings.

Let us continue the parable. "And as he had not wherewith
to pay it, his lord commanded that he should be sold, and his
wife and children and all that he had, and payment to be made.
But that servant falling down, besought him, saying: Have
patience with me, and I will pay thee all. And the lord of that
servant being moved with pity, let him go and forgave him
the debt. But when that servant was gone out, he found one
of his fellow-servants that owed him an hundred pence; and
laying hold of him, he throttled him, saying: Pay what thou
owest. And his fellow-servant falling down, besought him,
saying: Have patience with me, and I will pay thee all. And
he would not; but went and cast him into prison, till he paid
the debt."

The two scenes are very different from each other. In what
way could the first debtor have come to owe the king a sum
of twelve million dollars? By peculation perhaps, or crooked
financial operations. However, this matters little for the meaning of the parable. The more enormous the debt, the more insolvent was the debtor, and the more generous was the truly
royal munificence of the creditor, who, instead of punishing
his faithless servant in his person and family, as the Jewish

[110] The "talent" ($\tau\alpha\lambda\alpha\nu\tau\sigma\nu$, *talentum*) was originally a weight, equal to about 94
pounds. Considered from the viewpoint of money, there was a distinction between

law authorized,[111] was so moved by his servant's impassioned appeal. But following that incident, we share the monarch's indignation and approve his severity, when we see that servant whom he had treated with such generosity act so cruelly toward the fellow-servant who owed him only a hundred *denarii*—scarcely eighteen dollars. He deserved a punishment worthy of his offense. "Now his fellow-servants seeing what was done, were very much grieved, and they came and told their lord all that was done. Then his lord called him, and said to him: Thou wicked servant, I forgave thee all the debt, because thou besoughtest me. Shouldst not thou then have had compassion also on thy fellow-servant even as I had compassion on thee? And his lord being angry, delivered him to the torturers until he paid all the debt. So also shall My heavenly Father do to you, if you forgive not every one his brother from your hearts."

So clear is the application of the principal features of the parable that the Apostles had no need to ask Jesus for an explanation. The king is God. The servant owing ten thousand talents is man who has greatly offended God and thus contracted toward Him immense debts, which it was quite impossible for him to pay. But the heavenly Father, touched by his wretchedness, deigned to remit the entire debt. The second debtor is our neighbor. We often have towards one another more or less considerable credits; but, compared with what we owe to God, they are at most in the proportion of a hundred *denarii* to ten thousand talents. We are treated with great mercy by God; if we refuse to forgive our brethren the little

---

a talent of gold and a talent of silver. The latter, which is the one referred to in this parable, was divided into 6,000 drachmas, the drachma being equivalent to about 17 cents in our money.

[111] Lev. 25: 39-48; 4 Kings 4: 1. The Roman law was also very severe in such cases. Cf. Aulus Gellius, XX, 1, 4, 7.

debts which human frailty has led them to contract toward us, if we do not promptly and generously forgive their offenses, we shall deserve that the divine punishments fall upon us with a just severity.

APPENDICES

I. John the Baptist

Rationalist critics no longer compare the precursor, because of his mortified life and stern preaching, with a Mussulman dervish or a yogi of India.[112] Liberal theologians in general to-day better understand the person of John the Baptist and show more respect for him, although all of them reject as legendary the pages that St. Luke devotes to his birth.[113] They even attribute to him, as compared with Jesus, a moral influence that has no basis in the Gospel narrative and that he certainly did not exercise. According to these critics, not only was Jesus' entrance upon the scene a consequence and result of that of John,[114] but it was the latter who "cast into the soul of Him who was greater than himself the spark which set that soul aflame." [115] Another critic says that "the steadfast character of John . . . made a great impression upon Jesus, who was originally, we cannot doubt, of a tenderer character." [116] And we are told that Christ spent some time with him who is called His precursor and entered the ranks of the Baptist's disciples.[117] A day came, however, when Jesus de-

---

[112] This latter comparison, which is particularly shocking, is due to Ernest Renan, who prided himself on his delicacy (*Vie de Jésus,* 1863, p. 95).

[113] Says Neumann, *Jesus, wer er geschichtlich war,* p. 71: "We find therein clouds of embellishing legend."

[114] W. Hess, *Jesus von Nazareth in seiner geschichtlichen Lebensentwicklung,* p. 11.

[115] Heitmüller, *Jesus,* p. 91.

[116] O. Holtzmann, *Life of Jesus,* p. 134; T. Keim, *Geschichte Jesu von Nazara,* I, 526-528.

[117] Neumann, *op. cit.,* p. 79; Heitmüller, *op. cit.,* p. 93, etc.

cided to separate from John, for He did not agree with the latter's ideas on asceticism or with his way of understanding and preaching the coming of the Kingdom of God. Thenceforth He followed a separate life, but He retained the best of what He had learned from His cousin.[118]

We shall not refute these criticisms at length. That would be useless, because they are plainly contradicted by the very texts on which they are based. With perfect clearness the Evangelists set down the mutual relationship of John and Jesus; no one has a right to forsake these weighty authors in order to adopt imaginary hypotheses which falsify the historic truth. Jesus was the Messias, and John was His precursor. John had nothing to teach Jesus, and the Savior, when leaving John for the purpose of fulfilling His own supereminent office, did not criticize him in the least; the very contrary was true. But the Rationalist theory finds it worth while to exalt John at Christ's expense, as also to lower John's importance, by removing every trace of supernatural character from his ministry. One critic says that at first the Baptist had no idea of being the preacher of the Messias. He retired into the wilderness merely to live there alone with God and to await the coming of the Redeemer. But the extraordinary crowds that soon gathered about him created his vocation. "Like Isaias and Jeremias, he felt himself called";[119] which almost amounts to saying that he imagined that God Himself called him.

Not very long ago, the Liberal school commonly connected John the Baptist, as Jesus Himself,[120] with the sect of the Essenes, who had a colony in the desert of Engaddi near the Dead Sea. This opinion was advanced by the Jewish historian

[118] Stapfer, *Jésus avant son Ministère*, 2d ed., p. 145. Cf. A. Réville, *Jésus de Nazareth*, II, 11.
[119] J. Weiss, *Die Schriften des N. T.*, I, 225. Cf. O. Holtzmann, *op. cit.*, p. 116.
[120] See Vol. I, p. 185.

Graetz [121] and adopted by several Rationalists;[122] but it is almost entirely abandoned to-day.[123] It rests only on a few outward likenesses, such as austerity and purity of life, the practice of baptism, and a deeply religious spirit; against it are conspicuous differences. Before being surrounded by multitudes, John lived in solitude; the Essenes lived in community. They dressed in white; John's tunic was of coarse material. John was connected with the ancient Judaism and the great prophets of Israel; the Essenes stood almost entirely aloof from the practices of the Jewish religion.

II. Christ's Baptism by John the Baptist

The critics generally accept the historical reality of this episode, at least so far as concerns the ceremony of immersion in the Jordan. But they eliminate from the Gospel account, as later inventions, the supernatural manifestations, which form the most important part of it. The opening in the heavens, the descent of the Holy Ghost in the form of a dove, and the voice of the heavenly Father are phenomena which, we are told, could have existed only in Christ's "heated imagination"; [124] for the ceremony of His baptism had impressed Him most vividly. It was nothing more than an "inner vision," [125] which the Savior related to His disciples, and which the latter gradually translated into these external manifestations so as to make of them "a demonstrative miracle," [126]

[121] *Geschichte der Juden*, III, 268.

[122] Among others, by E. Renan, *Vie de Jésus*, p. 97.

[123] However, it has found a recent defender in the Jewish author of the article "Essenes," published in the *Jewish Encyclopedia*. Keim presents a learned refutation thereof in his *Geschichte Jesu*, I, 43.

[124] O. Holtzmann, *War Jesus Ekstatiker?* p. 41.

[125] A. Réville, *Jésus de Nazareth*, II, 8. Cf. W. Hess, *Jesus in seiner Lebensentwicklung*, p. 11, etc.

[126] A. Réville, *ibid.*; Hess, *op. cit.*, p. 11. Usener, in Cheyne's *Encyclopaedia Biblica*, III, cols. 3348 f., goes still farther. According to him, nothing particular happened then in Christ's soul. He even builds up a whole system on the subject: "When later on the conviction was reached that Jesus was the Messiah, . . .

whereas they are only "the figurative impression of the emotions that overflowed in Jesus' soul."

According to any honest interpretation of the Gospel documents, the three phenomena were external and sensible. St. Matthew and St. Mark [127] say explicitly that Jesus "saw" the heavens open and the Holy Ghost descend. And John the Baptist affirms [128] that with his own eyes he too saw this second manifestation. There is absolutely nothing to indicate that Christ and the Baptist were then in a visionary state; on the contrary, all the circumstances lead us to suppose that they were in a normal state of mind.[129]

We cannot help marveling at the attitude of those Rationalists who take seriously and regard as historic certain obviously legendary details, added by the apocryphal Gospels, such as the one which we cited above, namely, that Jesus came to John's baptism at the urging of His mother and brethren; yet details that possess every guaranty of authenticity are rejected by these same critics in a partisan spirit, solely because they are miraculous. Evidently they use a double set of weights and measures.

there was a desire to show that at the time of His baptism He received heaven's unction and verily became the Christ of God. Then was invented the heavenly voice heard by Jesus; then . . . the account of this prodigy was developed as we see it in Luke and Matthew. Still later, this was found insufficient, and the episode of Christ's thirteenth year was imagined (Luke 2:41–51). Finally, the better to prove that He was God, the Son of God, the narratives of the Infancy were created. Thus was born the story of the Nativity." *Invented, imagined, created:* we simply ask our readers on which side are found the invention, imagination, creation. Where are the proofs for Usener's assertions?

[127] Matt. 3:16; Mark 1:10.

[128] John 1:32: τεθέαμαι, "I beheld."

[129] According to Neumann, *Jesus, wer er geschichtlich war*, p. 72, there was not even any vision. The phenomena related by the Evangelists, he says, do not represent anything but "impressions" experienced by Jesus when He was living in the company of John the Baptist. The words, "Thou art My beloved Son," signify that at that period "the idea that God is a Father, that men are brethren, that the earth is a paternal house, became a certainty for Him." What would the Rationalist critics say if Christian exegetes were to indulge in like violence towards the texts?

In the matter of our Lord's baptism, Strauss [130] offers a particularly odious objection. We are told that Jesus, by submitting to this ceremony, made a public avowal of the guilt which He shared with other men, and that He considered His immersion in the Jordan as a means of obtaining pardon for His sins. Nowadays nobody ventures to repeat this sacrilegious assertion except perhaps in a mitigated form. This is what Neumann does when he says: "If we consider this event [the baptism] with eyes that have not been spoiled by the theologians, we see that Jesus showed thereby that an inner transformation was a condition of salvation for every human soul. And from that hour He wished to serve God with increased fervor and a new vigor. . . . Surely, He had no need of a break with the past, as did Paul, Augustine, and Luther [!]. His piety and purity were the natural fragrance of the soul of a hero whom God had blessed. But this does not imply a feeling of being without fault or an entire self-complacency. . . . Nothing that is human must be foreign to a child of men." [131]

We forestalled this objection by saying that it was for our sins that Jesus willed to take the blame and burden, by receiving baptism at the hands of His precursor. As to Himself personally, in the words of a Protestant theologian,[132] "if any one feature particularly characterizes His life and distinguishes it from all others, it is the absence of any remorse or need of pardon." [133]

Those critics whose specialty it is to discover everywhere in the Gospels, features taken from the pagan religions of the period, allege a parallel passage from the legend of Buddha. The parents of the Indian god one day wished to

---

[130] *Das Leben Jesu kritisch bearbeitet*, 1835, I, 371–374.

[131] *Jesus, wer er geschichtlich war*, p. 75. Cf. Giran, *Jésus de Nazareth*, p. 64.

[132] F. Godet, *Commentaire sur l'Évangile de S. Luc*, 2d ed., I, 236.

[133] As we said above and as we shall have occasion to repeat, Christ's holiness was absolute.

bring him to the temple. At first he hesitated, for he felt himself to be superior to all the other gods. In the end he consented, that he might bend to the existing customs. "The
crowd went wild," he said, "and encompassed me with homage
and with the greatest reverence; gods and men united in saying: He alone is God." [134] But so vague is the resemblance
that other critics, even among the advanced Liberals, think
it impossible to take this pretended parallelism into account; [135]
and, of course, they are quite right.

Most of the Rationalist critics recognize, as we do, that
Christ's baptism was of very special importance in His life
and was "one of the greatest turning-points in the world's
development." [136] They vie with one another in saying that
in receiving this baptism the Savior, "who was already the
Son of God through the inner consciousness of His union
with the heavenly Father, had the supreme intention of His
providential mission, and that He felt Himself to be the Son
of God, the Messias promised to Israel." [137] We shall return
to this subject later.

III. Christ's Temptation

The temptation of Christ, say the Rationalist critics, was
a subjective though very intense struggle, and the only place
where it occurred was in His soul. The Evangelists narrate
the incident as if it had an external reality. But they were
mistaken, and the error is due to tradition, "the natural tendency of which has been, in this as in other instances, to transform into an objective scene and material fact what was es-

---

[134] Van den Burgh van Eysinga, *Indische Einflüsse auf evangelische Erzählungen*, p. 29.

[135] Cf. C. Clemen, *Religionsgeschichtliche Erklärung des N. T.*, pp. 245, 247;
J. Weiss, *Die Schriften des N. T.*, I, 281.

[136] O. Holtzmann, *Life of Jesus*, p. 137.

[137] Loisy, *Les Évangiles Synoptiques*, I, 406–409.

pecially, and we might say solely, an internal phenomenon which a historian should not attempt to describe." [138]

Need we repeat that such an interpretation is arbitrary? For our Lord's temptation, as for His baptism and all the other events of His life, tradition has faithfully handed down the truth. The so-called "tendencies" have no existence except in the mind of the critics, who have imagined them as an argument easy to expound, but impossible to prove. We will, therefore, adhere to the testimony of the Evangelists, who clearly intend, as even our adversaries acknowledge,[139] to recount a real, tangible event.

The sacred writers could have learned the details of the temptation only from our Lord's own lips: St. Matthew and St. John in a direct manner; St. Mark and St. Luke indirectly, but most surely. How, then, did they and the tradition they represent fall into the error with which they are charged? A desperate answer is sometimes given to this question. We are told that Jesus simply spoke to His disciples about temptation in general and the best way of resisting it; He then introduced Himself on the scene, to add more force to His exhortation; or this latter was given in the form of a parable.[140] In either case, His hearers would have strangely misunderstood, giving substance to what was only an image, and introducing this complex temptation into their Master's life, as though it were a personal experience. The expedient is too clumsy.

The critics have searched elsewhere. They preferably adopt St. Mark's account, in which the episode is very condensed and the miraculous element reduced to the presence of the tempting devil and the angels; and they regard St. Mark's version as the only authentic one, on the ground that

[138] Loisy, *ibid.*
[139] Loisy, *op. cit.*, I, 418.
[140] P. W. Schmidt, *Das Leben Jesu ausgelegt*, pp. 244-246, etc.

it "certainly represents the primitive theme, which was subsequently elaborated by the imagination of pious Christians." [141] We have already seen that St. Mark's account has by no means the significance which they are pleased to give it. It is extremely brief, because the Evangelist did not choose to enter into details; and on account of its brevity, the account is obscure. Consequently we have to supplement it by the two other narratives.

The critics speak of "tendencies," "imagination," "dogmatic reflections." But is it likely, unless the event were real, that the early Christians would have dared to subject the Messias, the Son of God, for whom they cherished such great love and respect, to the humiliating trial of a temptation; would they have put Him into the hands of Satan? [142] Moreover, how could popular legend have invented out of the whole cloth an account which many Rationalist critics [143] no less than Christian exegetes [144] admire for its exquisite art, its perfect psychology, its fine gradation, and its delicate restraint? In particular, Christ's replies to Satan are remarkably appropriate to the devil's suggestions; throughout the episode Christ appears in a light entirely worthy of Him.

In spite of all the difficulties they raise against the historical character of the Savior's temptation, the critics admit that the Gospel pages relating it contain at least "a kernel of truth." Jesus was tempted in the desert: not however, with the outward display described by St. Matthew and St. Luke, and not in a vision, as erroneously thought by Origen, Theodore of Mopsuestia, and other ancient and modern commentators, but in a purely psychological manner. And the critics deem themselves able, after these many centuries, to recon-

[141] A. Réville, *Jésus de Nazareth*, II, 13.
[142] Cf. O. Holtzmann, *War Jesus Ekstatiker?* p. 48.
[143] J. Weiss, *Die Schriften des N. T.*, I, 231; O. Holtzmann, *Life of Jesus*, p. 154.
[144] T. Zahn, *Das Evangelium des Matthäus ausgelegt*, I, 148.

struct all the phases of this psychological process, which are far more complicated than the details in the sacred narratives of the episode. It was a terrible "crisis" for Jesus, so we are told; for "at that time His whole being was tempest-tossed." [145] His soul experienced "inner dramas," which are described for us at endless length, in pages that quickly become tiresome.[146] The critics charge the Evangelists with having overmuch materialized the facts; the critics themselves spiritualize the facts to excess, suppressing Satan and his dialogue with the Savior, the pinnacle of the Temple, the high mountain, and the angels. They leave us only Jesus face to face with Himself in the wilderness.

Let us do them the justice to say that they have grasped the general character of the temptation. For them, as for us, it was strictly Messianic.[147] But what errors are to be found in their psychological elucubrations about the feelings Jesus must have experienced! How poorly they judge, and into what exaggerations they fall! Since no devil exists, our Lord's temptation came from His own spirit, which urged Him to realize the picture of that glorious, political, conquering, entirely human Messias, whom most of His countrymen were expecting. "After the great divine voice filled His soul,[148] nature born of the dust rose up against that voice, and had to be fought and conquered to the last atom." [149] He was now aware that He was the Savior, the Christ, and that God had conferred the holy anointment upon Him. Having been changed into a new man by baptism, He felt an irresistible desire to seek refuge . . . for a while in the desert. He needed to draw up His plan of action. He wanted to be alone with

---

[145] Neumann, *Jesus*, p. 81.

[146] Cf. Stapfer, *Jésus-Christ avant son Ministère*, pp. 163–167.

[147] Loisy, *op. cit.*, p. 423: "These temptations are not those which can reach all men . . . No one but Christ could have been tempted in this manner."

[148] Immediately after the baptism.

[149] Bousset, *Jesus*, p. 5.

His heavenly Father. He was resolved to hurl Himself into the strife with a view to the preparation for the Kingdom; but how . . . and with what weapons? This was not yet clear in His mind, and . . . He seems to have feared being led to confuse the interests of His personal greatness with the interests of God's cause." [150]

The office of Messias, to which Jesus now thought Himself called, was for Him "a leap into the unknown"; whence He experienced a violent excitation of mind [151] and real temptations. "Whatever human respect, vainglory, and imperfections there were in Him, struggled with the vigor of a robust man against what was pure and holy in Him, and these latter elements predominated. . . . Often there was danger lest He mix earthly elements with what was holy." [152]

We trust the reader will pardon us for so many citations, which fundamentally express the same thought, slightly varied according to the more or less advanced Rationalism of their authors. They will help to point out how much is false, arbitrary, and irreverent in Rationalist psychology. The reading of the Gospels suffices to show its emptiness and inanity. Certainly the temptation did not have its source in the Savior's soul, in His inner dispositions: that was impossible. It came entirely from without, from the devil. Those perplexing conversations which Jesus is supposed to have held with Himself in the desert, those endles reveries, those discussions about the Messianic ideal never happened. The devil came to Him and proposed that He fail in His duty; but He triumphed over those perfidious suggestions, in the way related by St.

---

[150] A. Réville, *Jésus de Nazareth*, II, 12. Cf. Loisy, *Les Évangiles Synoptiques,* I, 408; O. Holtzmann, *Life of Jesus,* p. 145; P. W. Schmidt, *Geschichte Jesu ausgelegt,* p. 59, etc.

[151] J. Weiss, *Die Schriften des N. T.,* I, 68.

[152] Frenssen, *Der Heiland,* p. 26.

Matthew and St. Luke: there is no need of searching further, for here only is the truth to be found.[153]

We must expect to find what Rationalists regard as the two chief factors of the Gospel accounts: elements taken from the Old Testament and from various pagan mythologies. Dr. H. J. Holtzmann [154] has been the principal advocate of the thesis that the whole account was composed by the aid of several Old Testament passages joined together. The forty days' fast, says Holtzmann, has its type in the fasts of Moses and Elias, which lasted exactly the same number of days,[155] and in Israel's forty years' wandering in the desert. The trials through which the Hebrews passed during that hard period served as a model for Christ's real temptation. We are also told that the Jewish people at that time received the name of children of God.[156] And the critics further allege the second psalm and its celebrated passages: "Thou art my son, this day have I begotten thee. . . . I will give thee the Gentiles of the earth for thy possession." Lastly, they say that Jesus took from Deuteronomy the three replies which He made to Satan.[157] But what artist was there clever enough to construct, from these composite elements an account of such perfection? Nor must we forget that the primitive Church would never have thought of creating an incident unfavorable to its Founder.

As for the mythological interpretation, several Rationalist critics repudiate it no less than we. This explanation "must be set aside as useless and unlikely," says Loisy.[158] Albert Ré-

[153] Guignebert, *Manuel d'Histoire Ancienne du Christianisme*, p. 179, reduces Jesus' temptation to its simplest expression: a retreat of some duration in a desert place, in order to recollect Himself and "to try His vocation by abstinence."
[154] *Hand-Commentar zum N. T., Die Synoptiker*, 3d ed., pp. 45-48.
[155] Ex. 34: 28; 3 Kings 19: 8.
[156] Ex. 8: 5.
[157] See pages 56-63.
[158] *Les Évangiles Synoptiques*, I, 427.

ville,[159] however, attributes a mythological character to the wild beasts mentioned by St. Mark, and the angels spoken of by all three Synoptics. Among the pagan features that are put forward as having served as models for the temptation of Christ, we note the temptation of Buddha, that of Zarathustra, and that of Hercules "between the two ways." [160] "Parallels" have been sought even in the Babylonian religion.[161] Clemen strongly protests against these hypotheses, in a special work which he devotes to the attempts at mythological interpretation of the Gospels.[162] We have no need to insist further, so patent is it that such explanations are impossible.

IV. John the Baptist's Testimony as Recorded in the Fourth Gospel

Doctor Bousset says: "John did not directly announce that Jesus was the Messias, as Christian tradition claims. He prophesied a Messias who would come with a winnowing fan in his hand, with the fire of judgment. Jesus presents Himself in an altogether different manner from that which John expected on the Messias' part." [163] These words might surprise us, after the accounts we have read above, if we did not know that their author does not grant any historic authority to the Fourth Gospel.

Other critics of the same school try to justify this view by adding that the precursor necessarily shared the Messianic notions of his contemporaries and that consequently it was impossible for him to regard Christ as the Savior of the world, a fortiori as the Son of God.

---

[159] Jésus de Nazareth, II, 14.

[160] Cf. Van den Bergh van Eysinga, op. cit., pp. 30–41; Gunkel, Zum religionsgeschichtlichen Verständnis des N. T., p. 94.

[161] Jeremias, Babylonisches im N. T., p. 94.

[162] Religionsgeschichtl. Erklärung des N. T., p. 246.

[163] Jesus, p. 4.

That supposition is wholly false. In sketching his portrait of the Messias, John the Baptist had documents which could not lead him into error, for they consisted of the ancient prophecies, the authenticity of which is acknowledged by the critics. Many of those prophecies clearly predicted the divinity of the future Liberator,[164] the redemption to be wrought by Him, and the universal character of that redemption.[165] Furthermore, the Synoptics record the Baptist's protestations against the narrow, selfish particularism of the Jews of that time, who affirmed that the pagans would have no share in the Messianic redemption.

V. Christ's Meeting with Nicodemus

Most of the Rationalist critics deny the historical character of Christ's meeting with Nicodemus. Nicodemus, they say, was a fictitious personage, symbolizing "the imperfect believers who were willing to recognize in Jesus a teacher sent from God, but to whom the proposal of the spiritual gospel seemed at first an insoluble enigma." [166] And the whole episode, we are told, was intended to prove that Christianity had its early followers not only in the lower classes, among the ignorant, the publicans, and sinners, but also in the higher social circles. In proof of these assertions we are reminded that Nicodemus is nowhere mentioned by the Synoptics, that he promptly disappears from the scene without it being known what became of him or what profit he derived from his interview with the Savior, and lastly that Jesus "could not,"

---

164 Cf. Ps. 2:7; 109:3 (according to the Septuagint and the Vulgate) ; Is. 9:6 etc.

165 Especially Is. chaps. 52–53.

166 Loisy, Le Quatrième Évangile, p. 303. See also H. J. Holtzmann, Evangelium des Johannes, 2d ed., p. 70; Jean Réville, Le Quatrième Évangile p. 142; W. Bauer, Das Johannesevangelium, p. 38, etc.

if He wished to be understood by Nicodemus, have spoken to him of Christian baptism or of His death on the cross.

But the silence of the Synoptic Gospels signifies nothing, since one of St. John's purposes in writing his Gospel was precisely to supplement them. Though we are not at once informed what was the result of the interview, the Evangelist clearly indicates it later on in his narrative.[167] Christian baptism had been already announced to the Jewish crowds by the precursor; there was, therefore, nothing to hinder Jesus from speaking of it to a doctor of Israel, just as He had a right to reveal to him in advance the mystery of His death. Our adversaries' arguments thus collapse one after the other. Moreover, it is evident that the Evangelist intended to recount a real event, to present a real person to his readers. This he shows, first by the short introduction, in which he indicates Nicodemus' name, as also the occasion and purpose of his coming to Christ. These various details would be quite useless if he were treating of a legendary person. At that time, among the lawyers, Pharisees, and other religious leaders of Israel, there certainly were men who were attracted by Christ's person, miracles, and teaching, but who dared not show that attraction publicly on account of the hostile sentiments of their colleagues. The person and conduct of Nicodemus, as described by St. John, are in no way improbable.[168]

VI. Christ's Meeting with the Samaritan Woman

The critics assert that the account of Christ's meeting with the Samaritan woman, taken as a whole, is "a literary creation of the Evangelist"; it is conceded that "certain traces of Jesus' life and teaching may have found their way into the narrative," although it is impossible to point them out specif-

---

[167] Cf. John 7 : 50–52; 19 : 39–42.
[168] See Lepin, *Valeur Historique du Quatrième Évangile*, II, pp. 8–14.

ically.[169] The Evangelist had no idea of recounting a historical event; he wished, in the form of an allegory, to describe the wholly spiritual character of the religion of Jesus, to show that it is independent of any local or national boundaries. Many modern Rationalist authors enter into details about the pretended allegory. The Samaritan woman is not a real person, but a figure of her people, whose form of worship was half-pagan with a mixture of Mosaic elements. The five lawful husbands correspond to the five divinities who, according to the Bible,[170] were transplanted from Babylon to Samaria in the eighth century before Christ, to replace the Israelites of the kingdom of the ten tribes, who had been put to death or led into captivity. The unlawful husband symbolizes Jehovah, whom the Samaritans had partly adopted as their God, thus cheating their other divinities. And this is what it is proposed to substitute for the charming scene which St. John relates! We might also mention that, in the Biblical text to which the critics refer, there is question, not of five, but of seven alien peoples.

As the reader may easily note, nothing in the whole episode of the Samaritan woman indicates that we are in the presence of an allegory. Jesus' journey across Samaria on His way back to Galilee, His noonday stop at Jacob's well, in conformity with Eastern custom, to take a little rest and food, the arrival of the woman to replenish her water supply, the progress of the dialogue and its ending, the disciples' astonishment, our Lord's stay at Sychar and the people's conversion, all are clearly historical facts. And the reader may also observe

---

[169] W. Bauer, *Das Johannesevangelium erklärt*, p. 50; Heitmüller, *Die Schriften des N. T.*, II, 225; Loisy, *Le Quatrième Évangile*, p. 369; H. J. Holtzmann, *Evangelium des Johannes*, 2d ed., pp. 83–85; Jean Réville, *Le Quatrième Évangile*, p. 155, etc. Renan had already sacrificed the whole episode on the pretext that it was a piece of Apostolic theology (*Vie de Jésus*, p. 229, note 1). See an excellent refutation in Lepin, *La Valeur Historique du Quatrième Évangile*, II, 14–29.

[170] 4 Kings 17: 24–33.

the precision of the chronological details ("It was about the sixth hour"; Jesus remained "two days" at Sychar) and the exactness of the topographical description which we mentioned above. The writer of an allegory would hardly have attained this perfection, and would scarcely have been concerned to do so. The critics are unwilling to acknowledge that Jesus revealed Himself as the Messias at so early a date to the Samaritan woman and her compatriots. And the ideas He sets forth to His different hearers are considered too lofty. But the Synoptics also show us that at an early date Jesus manifests His Messianic character to a few privileged persons; probably He explained to the Samaritan woman, as He did to Nicodemus, the thoughts that were beyond her grasp.

As we might expect, the Rationalist critics call upon mythology to furnish them an argument to reinforce their position.[171] They particularly mention the following: "One day Ananda, the servant of Sakyamuni [Buddha], after journeying for a long time through the country, met a Matangi maiden, that is, one belonging to the tribe of the Chandalas; she was drawing water, and he asked her for a drink. But the maiden, fearing to defile him by her touch, informed him that she was born in the Matanga caste,[172] and that she was not allowed to come near a monk. Ananda answered her: Sister, I do not ask you your caste or family; I ask only for water, if you will give me some." [173] What does this prove? The meeting at a well of a maiden coming to draw water and of a thirsty traveler is a common happening in all times and countries,[174] and the resemblances between the two accounts

---

[171] See Van den Bergh van Eysinga, *Indische Einflüsse auf evangel. Erzählungen,* pp. 49–53.

[172] The caste which was regarded as the vilest of all.

[173] This passage is taken from the *Divyavadana,* fol. 217, a. It is cited by Burnouf, *Introduction à l'Histoire du Bouddhisme Indien,* 1884, I, 205.

[174] See, in Lortet, *La Syrie d'Aujourd'hui,* p. 18, the very interesting account of a meeting of the same sort near Jacob's well.

are too vague to justify the supposition that one is taken from the other. What relation is there between Buddha's favorite disciple and Jesus, between the Indian maiden and the Samaritan woman? How would the Evangelist, with these data, of which he certainly had no knowledge, have succeeded in composing an account that transports us into such different spheres? [175]

VII. The Kingdom of Heaven

Contemporary Rationalists are right in recognizing that the Kingdom of Heaven is a central and essential idea in Jesus' teaching, and they make it the subject of deep study.[176] Unhappily their dogmatic preconceptions accompany them in the investigation of this question as in the case of every other one, and they transform the inquiry into a basis for attacks upon the Savior's person and doctrine. Their arguments have their source in three principal errors: (1) that Jesus shared all the errors of the Jews of His time about the nature of that kingdom; (2) that His ideas were considerably modified and transformed on this point in the course of His public life; and (3) that He supposed that the coming of the divine rule would take place during His own lifetime in the form of a world-wide catastrophe. The examination of this last objection will be more appropriate when we come to the consideration of the Savior's eschatological discourse.[177] At

[175] C. Clemen, *Religionsgeschichtliche Erklärung der Evangelien*, p. 279, absolutely rejects any notion of a text or idea taken thus.

[176] See especially: Baldensperger, *Die messianischapokalyptischen Hoffnungen*, 1888, 3d ed., 1903; J. Weiss, *Die Predigt Jesu vom Reiche Gottes*, 2d ed., 1900; Titius, *Die Lehre Jesu vom Reiche Gottes*, 1895; Schnedermann, *Jesu Verkündigung und Lehre vom Reiche Gottes*, 1893; L. Paul, *Die Vorstellung vom Messias und vom Gottesreich bei den Synoptikern*, 1895; Bousset, "Das Reich Gottes in der Predigt Jesu," in the *Theolog. Rundschau*, October and November, 1902; B. Duhm, *Das kommende Reich Gottes*, 1910; H. J. Holtzmann, *Lehrbuch der neutestamentlichen Theologie*, 2d ed., II, 248–295.

[177] Matt. chaps. 24 and 25; Mark chap. 13; Luke chap. 21.

this point, therefore, we will reply only to the other two. But can it truly be said that "it is hard to know what Jesus means by those traditional words," [178] the Kingdom of Heaven, and the Kingdom of God? We acknowledge that this expression is somewhat complex, because the heavenly Kingdom is presented under different aspects in the Gospels. But whether we analyze, one after the other, the texts containing it, or whether we consider them in groups, and then all of them as a whole, we see that they develop a concept which is nowise lacking in clearness. To understand Jesus' thought, it is sufficient to make, as the best authors do, a distinction between the different phases of the establishment of the Kingdom, not to insist at any price upon placing at the beginning what is reserved for the end, and to ascribe to each saying its natural meaning. It is the Rationalists themselves who, by their preconceived theories, often give the texts in question a sense which they do not have. Moreover, the many serious contradictions between their particular theories are a proof of the weakness of their method.

1. Let us return to the first objection. It is stated as follows in all its crudity: "Here, too, Jesus adopted the popular ideas, and spoke of eating and drinking, of sitting at table with Abraham, of resting in the bosom of Abraham, and of other material things [to be enjoyed in the Kingdom of Heaven]. And certainly He expected a transformation by which sickness, especially demoniac possession, would forever disappear, and suffering, wretchedness, and death would be eliminated." [179] The author from whom we quote these words is willing to admit that Jesus did not completely agree with His fellow-Jews in this order of ideas, and that He did not believe in those wonderful vines, each of which was to produce ten thousand bunches, each containing one thousand

[178] Guignebert, *Manuel d'Histoire Ancienne du Christianisme*, p. 212.
[179] H. Weinel, *Jesus im XIX. Jahrhundert*, 2d ed., p. 94.

grapes, which would contain one thousand quarts of wine apiece. Says another Liberal theologian: "Jesus certainly considered the new wine to be drunk in the Kingdom of Heaven as being no less material than that which He then [at the Last Supper] beheld in the chalice before Him." [180] Upon reading such things, one is tempted to question whether those who wrote them were speaking seriously. How could Jesus, whose superior intelligence they do not deny, have accepted such gross beliefs? Is it not evident that, in the passages to which they refer and in other similar ones, He employs, like the ancient prophets, a figurative and thoroughly Oriental manner of speaking, which no one would think of interpreting literally, unless in the hope of finding therein a weapon with which to attack Him?

The critics are equally mistaken in declaring that our Lord, like His fellow-countrymen, "thought of a political reëstablishment" of Israel, and in saying that this hope, "as well as the disappearance of sickness and death, necessarily belonged to the idea which He had of the future." [181] This assertion is most certainly incorrect, and the Savior's whole conduct and all His words protest against it. The kingdom founded and organized by Him "was not of this world"; it had nothing earthly or political about it. As even many Rationalists attest, what distinguished Christ's teaching on this point is the essentially religious and moral character of the kingdom, the coming of which He so zealously preached.

2. According to Baldensperger,[182] we should distinguish three phases in Christ's idea of the Kingdom of Heaven. First, He regarded it as a thing of the future, floating, so to speak, between heaven and earth, in accord with the apocalyptical conceptions of the time. Later on, it seemed to Him that it

[180] O. Holtzmann, *War Jesus Ekstatiker?* p. 63. See also A. Meyer, *Die moderne Forschung über die Geschichte des Urchristentums*, p. 74.

[181] J. Weiss, *op. cit.*, 2d ed., p. 123.

[182] *Op. cit.*, p. 546.

was already present, but in a spiritual state, and that it existed interiorly in the souls of the just. He then returned to His first view and attributed, according to the accepted expression, a wholly *transcendent* nature to the Kingdom of Heaven, which thus would really belong to Heaven, not to earth. Such was, we are told, the "development of Jesus' thought" upon this special point. And these critics also tell us that, at the beginning of His public life, our Lord intended the Kingdom of God only for the Jews, to the exclusion of all other peoples, and that He decided to enlarge its bounds and open it to the pagans only after having sorrowfully observed the opposition of most of His fellow-countrymen. But read and reread the Gospels attentively: you will not find a single line to sanction the hypothesis of such an evolution. Moreover, "modifications so extremely radical . . . during a comparatively short interval, would be hardly explicable from the psychological point of view." [183] This opinion is, therefore, being more and more abandoned, after having prevailed for a while among Liberal theologians.

VIII. Christ's Messianic Consciousness

In the minds of the critics, the question of Christ's Messianic consciousness constitutes one of the most difficult problems in the life of the Savior.[184] They must take to themselves the responsibility for this difficulty, because they have created it out of the whole cloth, and while refusing to credit the Gospel data, have plunged into arbitrary conjectures, incapable of furnishing a satisfactory solution.

I. Many of these false critics, belonging to the radical wing of the Liberal school, flatly assert that Jesus never believed

---

[183] H. von Soden, *Die wichtigsten Fragen im Leben Jesu*, p. 76. Likewise H. Monnier, *La Mission Historique de Jésus*, p. 220: "There was no evolution in the idea of the Kingdom of God."

[184] Wellhausen, *Einleitung in die drei ersten Evangelien*, pp. 89–94.

that He was the Messias. It was His disciples, they tell us, then the early Christians of Judaism, who decreed that title for Him, when they began to suppose His Resurrection. The French Protestant Colani maintained that thesis in his book *Jésus et les Croyances Messianiques de son Temps.*[185] Another Protestant theologian, Maurice Vernes, adopts the same conclusion and even goes beyond it, because, according to him, "it is not certain that Jesus believed in the coming of a personal Messias." [186] From that time, this audacious denial has continued to find enthusiastic supporters.[187] Let us see with what ease they accept the consequences of their theory. Says one of them: [188] "We should sacrifice nothing if we had to renounce Christ's Messianic character." Other critics, with rather broader ideas, have better understood the disastrous nature of these consequences, and Schweitzer is right when he says: "If Jesus is not regarded as the Messias, it is the death-blow to the Christian faith." [189] In fact, without a "Christ" to whom it can be closely connected, a religion calling itself "Christian" would be veritable nonsense.

This theory is so extreme, so manifestly false, that most Liberal theologians have repudiated it. It can be proved only by "applying to the Gospel texts a too subjective criti-

[185] Second edition, 1864.

[186] *Histoire des Idées Messianiques, depuis Alexandre le Grand jusqu'à l'Empereur Hadrien,* 1874, p. 174.

[187] Among others, Wellhausen, *op. cit.;* J. Martineau, *Seat of Authority in Religion,* 1890, p. 31; Volkmar, *Jesus Nazarenus,* p. 104, and especially Wrede, *Das Messiasgeheimnis in den Evangelien,* 1901 (see particularly pp. 221 f., 226 f.) ; E. Havet, *Le Christianisme et ses Origines,* 1881, IV, 15 f., 75.

[188] R. Steck, in the *Protestant. Monatsschrift,* 1903, p. 91. Paul Wernle, *Die Anfänge unserer Religion,* 2d ed., p. 32, adds ironically: "Thanks be to God, Jesus was quite something else and something greater than the Messiah." What was He, then? A religious reformer. Harnack, who believes in the Savior's Messianic consciousness, makes this rather strange remark (*Das Wesen des Christentums,* 1903, p. 81) : "Being non-Jewish, we do not understand what that dignity [of Messiah] signifies nor what extent or height it possessed." Yet Harnack must know the Old Testament and the Gospels, where this title is explained and developed in every form.

[189] *Von Reimarus zu Wrede,* p. vi.

cism." [190] Thus Albert Réville thought it proper "to persist in the opinion that Jesus received and accepted the title of Messias at a definite moment of Gospel history." [191] We see no need to return to the proofs that we have given of this incontestable fact. It will suffice to quote the following summary from another Liberal theologian: [192] "The baptism, the story of the temptation, Peter's confession, . . . the prophecies relative to the Passion and Resurrection, the request of the sons of Zebedee, the Messianic entry into Jerusalem, the parable of the dishonest husbandmen, the trial before the Sanhedrin and before Pilate, the sign bearing the reason for Jesus' death, all these and many other details would have to be eliminated from the life of Christ if we would claim that He was not conscious of being the Messias."

Certain advanced critics have gone still farther. They tell us that Jesus, while not considering Himself to be the Christ, at one point in His public life and under the pressure of circumstances, allowed this notion to be entertained by His followers, who looked upon Him as the expected Messias, and He simply "conformed" to the rôle. But the Savior's noble and honest character, the uprightness and modesty of His conduct loudly protest against so odious a hypothesis, which we will examine no further.

2. Those critics who for the most part admit what they call Christ's Messianic consciousness are, however, far from avoiding every error on this important subject. In conformity with their false principles, they recognize no supernatural character in the title and office of Messias, which, as Harnack informs us, they treat as a vague Jewish concept of small importance. We have no occasion to follow them upon this

[190] A. Sabatier, article "Jésus-Christ" in Lichtenberger's *Encyclopédie des Sciences Religieuses*, Vol. VII.

[191] *Jésus de Nazareth*, II, 185.

[192] O. Holtzmann, *Das Messiasbewusstsein Jesu und seine neueste Bestreitung*, 1902, p. 11. Cf. A. Schlatter, *Der Zweifel an der Messianität Jesu*, 1907.

ground, for the whole Bible contradicts them. But we will briefly consider their manner of explaining how Jesus came to look upon Himself as the Messias. They find themselves in an embarrassing situation, because they partly reject the Gospel documents and, deprived of any solid basis, are obliged to solve the question by means of endless psychological analyses, which are plainly contradicted by history and reason. Nothing would be more curious, if it were not so sad, than their attempt to reconstruct by this *a priori* psychology, the inner labor which, according to them, took place in Jesus' soul during the last years of His hidden life, and even, some of them say, during a considerable part of His public life. The whole thing is dramatized and set forth in detail, quite as though they had witnessed those inner discussions, those painful doubts, those struggles *pro* and *con* that are suposed to have taken place in the Savior's mind.[193]

These are baseless hypotheses. Harnack frankly acknowledges that "never shall we know the inner phases through which Jesus passed" to reach His belief that He was the Messias.[194] Burkitt, alluding to these psychological investigations, quite rightly says they are futile because what is certain is that our Gospels are very far from being a sort of psychological novel with Jesus Christ for the hero.[195] The novel has been composed by the critics.

Many of them, however, are so confident of their theory that they point out two successive steps in "the connection of ideas and experiences"; and this connection led Jesus to consider Himself the Messias.[196] He is supposed to have been persuaded, first, that He had closer relations with God than

---

[193] See particularly Stapfer, *Jésus-Christ avant son Ministère*, 2d ed., pp. 93–96, 146–150. With regard to Christ's intellectual and moral growth, we have already given some specimens of this psychology of a sentimental sort.

[194] *Wesen des Christentums*, p. 36 of the French translation.

[195] *The Gospel History and its Transmission*, p. 77.

[196] A. Réville, *Jésus de Nazareth*, II, 186.

other men, and that He was a son of God in a unique way, although there is no question of anything more than a moral sonship. From this thought, with the idea of the Kingdom of Heaven as a transition, He gradually passed to the certainty of being called to found that Kingdom personally as the Messias. His thought, therefore, evolved little by little until it reached that point.

Once again we repeat that all this is mere speculation without any genuine foundation, because, as one Rationalist critic admits, "the Gospels do not really contain the evidence of an evolution taking place in the Savior's consciousness and in His manner of appreciating the rôle assigned to Him by Providence." [197] We have distinguished two clearly marked periods in our Lord's manifestation to others of His Messianic office. But His personal conviction on this point never underwent any change. Where do we see any evidence that He passed through such changes and that at times He was "a problem to Himself," a problem that He succeeded in solving "only by force of reflections"? [198] All this is purely imaginary.

Those Liberal theologians who believe in the Savior's Messianic consciousness, as indicated above, find themselves faced by another difficulty, which they are at great pains to solve. At what period in His life did Jesus become convinced that He was the Messias? On this point also great differences of opinion prevail among the critics; nor could it be otherwise, since everything in their reasoning is personal and arbitrary. The opinion of most of them to-day is that our Lord's Messianic consciousness dated from His baptism and the revelation (which they regard as purely internal and subjective) that accompanied it. Theodore Keim says it was the baptism at the hands of John "which placed on Jesus' shoulders the duty of devoting the full measure of His powers to the King-

[197] Loisy, *Les Évangiles Synoptiques*, I, 212.
[198] O. Frommel, *Die Poesie der Evangelien*, p. 149.

dom of God, to the service of God and of justice." [199] It was then that the light fully illumined Him and the "Messianic thought" took entire possession of Him. And H. J. Holtzmann says that "for Jesus the baptism was God's answer to the preoccupations of His soul and above all to this question: Why am I on earth? . . . He had been expecting the Messias, and lo, He was Himself the Messias." [200]

A smaller number of critics fix upon some later date as the time when Jesus became fully conscious of possessing the Messianic dignity. Some connect it with St. Peter's confession; others, such as Strauss, place it a little earlier. According to them, if the baptism "determined an interior crisis in Jesus, from which He emerged as a new man, He did not yet consider Himself the Messias." [201] J. Weiss [202] has a special theory on this point: Jesus, during His public life, merely supposed that He was destined to become the Messias later on, when His glory would shine in all its fulness; but He did not suppose He was already the Messias.

We shall not refute these various allegations in detail. That has already been done, since the Evangelists, whose clear and precise thought we have summed up, inform us that Jesus was the Messias from His birth and that He directly or indirectly declared Himself such on numerous occasions. "According to the Gospel history," says Keim, "there is no doubt but Jesus more or less proclaimed Himself as the Messias" [203] from the hour when He began His ministry. His baptism and the epi-

---

[199] *Geschichte Jesu von Nazara*, I, 545.

[200] *Das messianische Bewusstsein Jesu*, p. 33. See also his *Lehrbuch der neutestam. Theologie*, 2d ed., I, 338; Harnack, *Wesen des Christentums*, p. 88; Wendt, *Lehre Jesu*, 2d ed., pp. 97, 260, 413; Bousset, *War Jesus Ekstatiker?* p. 35; H. von Soden, *Die wichtigsten Fragen im Leben Jesu*, 2d ed., pp. 73 f., 99: f.; Loisy, *Les Évangiles Synoptiques*, I, 468.

[201] Guignebert, *Manuel*, p. 173. Cf. E. Klostermann, *Matthäus*, p. 173; Neumann, *Jesus, wer er geschichtlich war*, p. 78: P. W. Schmidt, *Das Leven Jesu ausgelegt*, p. 165; A. Réville, *Jésus de Nazareth*, II, 188–190; 201, etc.

[202] *Die Predigt Jesu vom Reiche Gottes*, 2d ed., 1900.

[203] *Op. cit.*, I, 347–349.

sode at Caesarea were certainly culminating points in His life; but they taught Him nothing, nor did they confer anything on Him in the matter of His office. Let us again note the variations and the contradictions of our adversaries about a question which is a matter of capital importance. These disagreements prove the weakness or rather falsity of those subversive theories, which are mutually self-destructive.

3. But does not the "Messianic secret," about which there has been so much ado, favor the Rationalist hypotheses regarding the late period when the Savior is said to have definitely considered Himself the promised Messias? Most certainly not; for this secret is greatly exaggerated, and from it conclusions are drawn that are utterly opposite to historic fact. Wrede, in particular, has acquired a rather unenviable reputation for himself on this point. "Evidently he has been hypnotised by his theory of the Messianic secret." [204] He and his followers imagine they see this secret everywhere. They rely preferably upon St. Mark's Gospel, where it stands out more conspicuously, and they decline to put faith in the assertions of St. Matthew and St. Luke, who cite the Savior's Messianic declarations long before St. Peter's confession. Have not those two biographers of Jesus the same right to our confidence as has the author of the Second Gospel? [205]

We have said enough by way of explanation of the reasons for the Messianic secret. The Savior's special rôle was one of those pearls that must not be given to the unworthy, who would surely have profaned them. As we have already remarked, if Jesus had revealed Himself as the Christ immediately and indiscriminately to all, His work would have run the risk of being seriously compromised, on account of the false popular hopes. The Jewish nation by and large was nowise prepared to profit by a knowledge of this secret. In due

[204] H. Monnier, *La Mission Historique de Jésus*, p. 52.

[205] It is true that for some time past the critics have sworn only by St. Mark, at the expense of the other two Synoptics.

time the Savior would hide nothing of His vocation, which, moreover, was manifested with sufficient clearness by His preaching, by His miracles, and by His whole conduct. Men of good will were hardly deceived about it. Jesus allowed no opportunity to pass to correct whatever was mistaken in the Messianic notions of the people and to replace them by the true ideal. Thus are explained His reticence toward some, His frank avowal to others, according to circumstances. The Messianic secret, honestly interpreted, had no other cause or significance.[206]

Furthermore, the Savior's reserve in this matter was in conformity with His whole manner of acting, so gentle and modest. This is what St. Matthew remarks[207] when he applies to the Savior a certain Old Testament prophecy:[208] "Many followed Him, and He healed them all. And He charged them that they should not make Him known. That it might be fulfilled which was spoken by Isaias the prophet, saying: Behold my servant whom I have chosen. . . . He shall not contend nor cry out, neither shall any man hear his voice in the streets." He never wished to force Himself upon His hearers' faith by any manner of violence, but suavely endeavored to arouse their intelligent, spontaneous adherence. And it was fitting that the Kingdom of Heaven should first be announced throughout the land and should begin to be founded, before the Messias, who was its King, should officially present Himself to receive the homage of His subjects.

4. Apropos of the expression, "Son of Man," the Rational-

---

[206] Albert Réville recognizes it, *Jésus de Nazareth*, II, 201: "There was too great a distance between the Messiah that He [Jesus] was and wished to be, and the Messiah that the Jews expected, for Him to be able, without moral violence, abruptly to claim such a dignity, at the risk of being misunderstood and of provoking political disturbances diametrically contrary to the end He hoped to attain."

[207] Matt. 12: 15–21.

[208] Is. 42: 1–4.

ist critics have published numerous works;[209] but, as they wrote them with preconceived ideas, they have generally attained only negative results. It may at least be said that they drew attention to this title, which had been too little studied, and thus had a share in placing it in the light. We will now point out three principal errors into which they have fallen.

The first concerns the meaning of the expression. Since the language which our Lord spoke was Aramaic, it was natural to investigate what was the form corresponding to the words "Son of Man" in that tongue. Philologists are almost all agreed that it is to be found in the expression *bar nacha* or *bar enacha*. [210] As to the meaning attributed to this title in Jesus' time, there are two contradictory opinions. The Liberal critics, *e. g.,* Lietzmann [211] and Wellhausen, [212] see in it only "the most colorless and indeterminate designation of a human person," equivalent to the noun "man," or the simple pronoun "I." And they say that in Greek the phrase *bar nacha,* if it existed at all, would have had to be translated simply by "man," and not by "son of man," supposing that *bar* ("son") is in this phrase a pleonasm, *bar nacha* and *nacha* being synonymous terms. But Dalman, who of contemporary linguists is most familiar with the Aramaic idiom, protests against this conclusion.[213] Why would the Greek translator of St. Matthew's Gospel have habitually rendered *bar nacha* by "son of man" if that expresion did not differ in meaning from "man"? Others have protested from a general point of view.

[209] Cf. Lietzmann, *Der Menschensohn, Beiträge zur neutestamentl. Theologie,* 1896; Wellhausen, "Der Menschensohn," in the *Skizzen und Vorarbeiten,* pp. 187–215; Fiebig, *Der Menschensohn, Jesu Selbstbezeichnung,* 1901; Edwin A. Abbott, *The Son of Man, Contributions to the Study of the Thought of Jesus,* 1912; H. J. Holtzmann, *Lehrbuch der neutestam. Theologie,* 2d ed., I, 313–335, etc.

[210] See Dalman, *Worte Jesu,* pp. 191–193; Tillmann, *Der Menschensohn,* pp. 60–64.

[211] *Op. cit.,* p. 38.

[212] *Israelitische und jüdische Geschichte,* 2d ed., p. 346, note. See also A. Meyer, *Die Muttersprache Jesu,* pp. 91–101, 140–149.

[213] *Op. cit.,* pp. 191–197. Cf. Tillmann, *loc. cit.*

As Albert Réville forcibly says, "We cannot accept the ridiculous supposition that Jesus wished simply to call Himself the 'man'." [214] "Son of man" is certainly an unusual expression, which must have had its *raison d' être*. It exactly corresponds to *bar enach* of Daniel's prophecy, from which it was taken,[215] and it was wonderfully well suited to the purpose which Jesus intended in using it. In several Gospel texts where we meet it, we would obtain a very banal meaning were we to translate it simply by the word "man." [216] Although it is true that in many passages it is equivalent to the first person singular pronoun, why does it so often replace that pronoun? The following instance is particularly significant. In St. Mark we read: "He said to them: The Sabbath was made for man, and not man for the Sabbath. Therefore the Son of Man is Lord of the Sabbath also." [217] Here we have juxtaposed, or rather contrasted with each other, these two expressions, "man" and "Son of Man." Evidently they have not an identical meaning.

As this citation proves, it is an error to claim that Jesus did not attach a Messianic sense to the phrase "Son of Man." [218] We have amply demonstrated that He employed it in this precise sense, although He made use of it to attenuate His Messianic claims for a while. Renan, in spite of his prejudices, says that "it seems the expression 'Son of Man' can be understood only in the Messianic sense." [219] After a painstaking examination of all Gospel texts containing the expression, Tillmann rightly concludes: "The Messianic meaning is the only

[214] *Jésus de Nazareth,* II, 291.

[215] Dan. 7 : 13.

[216] Let it suffice to cite, by way of example, Mark 2 : 10 (and the parallel passages in Matthew and Luke) : "That you may know that the Son of Man hath power on earth to forgive sins"; Luke 12 : 10 : "Whosoever speaketh a word against the Son of Man, it shall be forgiven him."

[217] Mark 2 : 27 f.

[218] Maurice Vernes, *Histoire des Idées Messianiques,* p. 187; J. Martineau, *Seat of Authority.* p. 339, etc.

[219] *Vie de Jésus,* p. 197. Likewise A. Loisy, *Les Évangiles Synoptiques,* I, 243.

one that furnishes a sufficient explanation" [220] of all these texts.

A third error, as serious as the first, consists in saying that Jesus never made use of this term.[221] This is a strange assertion, when we recall that the Evangelists quote it ninety times. Other critics, therefore, somewhat moderate the form of this assertion. They say: "In most cases the use of this term belongs to the Gospel revisers. . . . Its use by Jesus Himself seems probable only in a very limited measure." [222] It is true that here or there the Evangelists may have substituted the phrase "Son of Man" for the first personal pronoun, or vice versa. We have evidence of this in the following comparison between a saying of Christ as quoted by St. Matthew and as quoted by St. Luke.[223] In the First Gospel we read: "Blessed are ye when they shall revile you . . . for My sake"; in the Third Gospel, "for the Son of Man's sake." But instances of this sort are rare and exceptional; only by the use of violence do they yield the conclusions just cited.

5. Liberal theologians deceive themselves and proceed contrary to the historical documents, when they treat the question of the Savior's "programme." [224] They maintain that Jesus was very slow to work out His plan of action, that He was undecided on many occasions because He was surprised by favorable or unfavorable events, and that He was obliged to alter His projects and His method under the influence of events. At first He foresaw merely rapid success. Only gradually, in contact with men and things, did He comprehend that He was advancing to a complete disaster. This He perceived,

---

[220] *Der Menschensohn,* p. 117.

[221] Volkmar, *Jesus Nazarenus,* p. 193; Brandt, *Die evangelische Geschichte,* pp. 562–568; E. Carpenter, *The First Three Gospels,* pp. 372–388; Lietzmann, *op. cit.,* p. 85; Wellhausen, *Das Evangelium Marci,* pp. 66–69; etc.

[222] Loisy, *op. cit.,* I, 243. Cf. Bousset, *Jesus,* p. 92; *Religion des Judentums,* pp. 248–254 etc.

[223] Matt. 5: 11; Luke 6: 22. Cf. Matt. 16: 13; Mark 8: 27.

[224] They are the ones who first used this term.

although there were moments, as at Gethesemani, when He hoped He could escape death. It would be tiresome to enumerate all the affirmations of the critics on this subject, especially as we have a reliable summary of them, contained in the following words of an Anglican theologian, whose views are usually rather Liberal: "The dogmatic conception that Jesus knew the end [of His career] from the beginning, and gave mechanical fulfilment to a prearranged plan, is not only untrue to facts, but destroys the whole moral worth and significance of the divine life." [225]

To speak thus, one must evidently see in our Lord nothing more than an ordinary man, a man not very intelligent, but full of illusions, rushing ahead haphazard, allowing himself to be at the mercy of events, foreseeing nothing and planning nothing. And one must entirely reject every supernatural idea. We admire Lebrun's charming canvas which depicts the Savior with the features of a young man looking toward Heaven, where He constantly seeks the will of God; His lips seem to be pronouncing these words of the Gospel, which are painted on the picture: *"Quae placita sunt ei facio semper."* [226] But this admiration is poorly founded, say the Rationalists. To obey like Jesus, is, to their mind, a manner of acting that has no moral value.

Let us now return to the principal objection, namely, that Jesus had no programme, or that He had to change His plans frequently and was the unwitting victim of events. We have already demonstrated the contrary, basing our proof upon the most reliable documents. In opposition to our thesis, only assertions are advanced, or recourse is had again to psychological analyses, which prove nothing, because they are purely imaginary. It is evident that, throughout His public life, Jesus was aware that He had a very definite work to perform, al-

---

[225] E. F. Scott, in Hastings' *Dictionary of Christ*, II, 369.
[226] John 8:29: "I do always the things that please Him [God]."

ways making use of means well suited to His purpose. He advances straight ahead, voluntarily bending to the divine will, familiar with its smallest details, knowing full well all that was going to happen to Him, and adhering whole-heartedly to the designs of Providence. Throughout His life, particularly in His active ministry, there prevailed a perfect unity that came from the clearness and the ideal execution of His programme. It is because His plan was never absent from His mind that He dominated all the events, that He did not permit Himself to be disturbed by any of them and was subject to no human influence. Neither His relatives nor His Apostles nor the friendly multitudes nor His enemies could make Him deviate from His path. The proof that He was not surprised by being partly thwarted or by His death, is that He several times foretold these events to the Apostles.

IX. The Choosing of the Apostles

Most of the Rationalist critics express doubt about the institution of the Apostolic College. They tell us that Jesus never intended to surround Himself by a limited number of intimate disciples to whom He purposed entrusting a special mission. A few of His followers, at their own request, were permitted to accompany Him for a more or less considerable time while He was preaching; only after His death did "Christian theology" surround Him with the College of the Twelve. Wellhausen says: "One may question whether the Apostles belong to the life of Jesus, whether He chose them, and *a fortiori* whether He sent them to preach the gospel. . . . Most probably the Apostles belong only to the beginning of the history of the Church. Yet they may have been Jesus' companions at the Last Supper and may thus have become the executors of His last will." [227] And J. Weiss says: "It is hardly credible

---

[227] *Einleitung in die Evangelien,* p. 112.

that the group of the Twelve was founded by so formal an act." [228]

What reasons are brought forward in opposition to the plain and constant Gospel tradition, which is confirmed by the Acts of the Apostles and the Epistles of St. Paul? The New Testament lists do not agree "as to the names of the Twelve." But there is no disagreement; at least, it is merely apparent,[229] and comes from the fact that some of the Apostles had two different names, as a careful comparison of the four lists shows. The critics also allege, as a reason, the number "twelve," which, they say, awakens suspicions against it as a symbolic number and because "it is not evident that Jesus attached such importance to details of this sort." [230]

It is true that with the Hebrews the number twelve was symbolic, and it was precisely in memory of the twelve patriarchs who had been the founders of the Jewish people that the Savior gathered twelve Apostles about Him; but we are unable to see in what way that circumstance weakens the authenticity of the account. The scene related by St. Mark and St. Luke has not "the dubious character" which the critics attribute to it in order to rid themselves of an institution which is inconvenient for their theory that our Lord never contemplated the founding of a Church. Its every detail argues in favor of its reality.

The choosing of Judas as a member of the Apostolic College has given rise to more serious objections. Strauss,[231] and many of his followers after him,[232] solve the difficulty by making the traitor a mythical or legendary personage. But, although the Gospels furnish but few details about Judas,

---

[228] *Die Schriften des N. T.*, I, 91. See also W. Bousset, *Jesus*, p. 29; A. Neumann, *Jesus, wer er geschichtlich war*, p. 108.

[229] Bousset, *loc. cit.*

[230] Bousset, *ibid.* According to Jeremias, *Babylonisches im Neuen Testament*, p. 87, this number alludes to the signs of the zodiac!

[231] *Leben Jesu*, sec. 130; *Neues Leben*, sec. 90.

[232] Cf. G. Marquardt, *Der Verrat des Judas Ischarioth, eine Sage*, 1900.

their portrait of him is too concrete, too living, to be merely a creation of the imagination.[233] Even Doctor Brandt, who has gone rather far in denials in the matter of the Gospels, condemns this opinion.[234] In its justification, some have claimed [235] that the betrayal was superfluous. But this assertion is refuted by St. Luke's statement: "The chief priests and the Scribes sought how they might put Jesus to death; but they feared the people." [236] Therefore they needed someone to come to their aid for the arrest of Him whom they had condemned in advance.[237]

Several contemporary Rationalists, while not denying the historical existence of Judas, have fallen into other serious errors about him. Some of these critics try to exculpate him almost entirely. According to Ernest Renan,[238] "the remembrance of horror which the folly or the wickedness of this man has left in the Christian tradition has doubtless given rise to some exaggeration on this point. . . . The peculiar hatred John [the Evangelist] manifests towards Judas confirms this hypothesis. . . . Without denying that Judas of Kerioth may have contributed to the arrest of His Master, we still believe that the curses with which he is loaded are somewhat unjust. There was, perhaps, in his deed more awkwardness than perversity. . . . If the foolish desire for a few pieces of silver turned the head of poor Judas, he does not seem to have lost the moral sentiment completely, since when he had seen the consequences of his fault he repented, and, it is said, committed suicide." To show the falseness of this rea-

[233] See Fairbairn, *Studies in the Life of Christ*, p. 264. His image is presented to us "as if fresh from the sculptor's chisel."

[234] *Die evangelische Geschichte*, pp. 12–14.

[235] Cf. P. W. Schmidt, *Geschichte Jesu erläutert*, p. 300.

[236] Luke 22: 2.

[237] Cf. Matt. 26: 4, and Mark 14: 1, where the members of the Sanhedrin, before making their agreement with Judas, "sought how they might by some wile lay hold" on the Savior.

[238] *Vie de Jésus*, 1863, pp. 380–382.

soning, it will suffice to recall the traitor's going of his own accord to the chief priests and his infamous proposal: "What will you give me, and I will deliver Him unto you?" [239] Is the use of such language the effect of "awkwardness" or of "perversity"? The answer to this question leaves no room for doubt. And many Rationalist critics express it in no less severe terms than do orthodox writers: "By his conduct toward the purest and noblest human figure that has ever appeared in the clear light of history, Judas has become for us the type of the most criminal of sinners." [240] "Judas' treason has remained, in the opinion of Christianity, the type of all misdeeds of this sort; it is an object of disgust and horror." [241]

Judas has found advocates in another camp. We are assured that he did not have the hateful intention which the Evangelists and Christian tradition attribute to him, but, on the contrary, thought he was rendering a veritable service to his Master by seeming to betray Him. De Quincy developed this theory,[242] and various critics have adopted it. The following are its chief features. Judas was not less devoted to Christ than were the other Apostles, and he felt an earnest desire to hasten the hour of His triumph. At length, seeing that his Master was delaying the public proclamation of His Messianic office, Judas resorted to the expedient of an apparent betrayal, that he might thus oblige Jesus to declare Himself. Judas did not doubt that the Savior would have recourse to His miraculous powers to win a brilliant victory over His enemies. Under these conditions he was sadly mistaken; but we can blame him only for allowing himself to be misled by an exalted enthusiasm.—Need we say that this sort of defense has not the least basis in the Gospel documents, which, on the contrary, most explicitly contradict it? Judas himself

[239] Matt. 26 : 15.
[240] A. Neumann, *Jesus, wer er geschichtlich war*, p. 175.
[241] A. Réville, *Jésus de Nazareth*, II, 342.
[242] *Works*, VI, 21–25.

gave his act the only name it deserves, when he said to the priests: "I have sinned in betraying innocent blood." [243] And if he had no other motives than those which are so curiously credited to him, Jesus would not have stigmatized his treason in such forcible terms.[244] Réville is therefore quite right in declaring that this "explanation lacks all likelihood," [245] and that "Judas' conduct, from the day when he conferred with the chiefs of the Sanhedrin, betokens a cold, cunning spirit, a man possessing sufficient self-control to deceive Jesus [246] up to the last moment."

To endeavor to exonerate Judas from all treachery and infamy, is labor lost. But attempts have been made to attenuate his guilt as much as possible. To that end, the critics have sought, not in the Gospels, but in psychological possibilities, for what must have gradually led one of the Twelve to betray his Master. In a word, it was disillusion. Judas never believed with utter certainty in Jesus' Messianic character,[247] or else, after believing for a while, he lost the faith. It is supposed, despite the contrary evidence of the documents, that he joined the group of intimate disciples rather late and that, after conceiving the finest hopes about Jesus, from whom he personally expected great favors, he allowed himself to fall into the practice of deceit, then to feelings of hatred and vengeance, in consequence of that disappointment. Not only did Jesus not fulfil the magnificent prospects which He had made to glow before the eyes of His followers, but He ceased performing numerous miracles; He no longer drew the people; He was no longer able to withstand His enemies. The latter were more and more getting the upper hand, and it was becoming clear that this false Messias would soon fall into their power and

[243] Matt. 27 : 4.
[244] Matt. 26 : 20–25.
[245] *Jésus de Nazareth,* II, 344.
[246] Or at least to attempt to deceive Him.
[247] O. Holtzmann, *Life of Jesus,* p. 447.

come to a miserable end. Those who were known to be more closely associated with Him would evidently share in the danger. It was, therefore, necessary to act quickly and to win the favor of the Jewish authorities, at the same time obtaining, as the price of the betrayal, whatever sum they would be willing to give. In a general way, such are the feelings that are supposed to have succeeded one another in Judas' soul, finally making a traitor of him.[248]

Oscar Holtzmann [249] acknowledges that these are merely conjectures and that their reality is not proved by the historical documents. "For it certainly is remarkable that after preaching repentance and the Kingdom of Heaven in the name of Jesus, after subsequently sharing in all the privations of his Master's wanderings in heathen territory, and finally after even venturing upon the perilous journey to Jerusalem, he should in the end have betrayed his Master there." [250] If Judas' treason is a very real psychological problem, why should we not be willing to solve it by means of the Gospel data, which are unquestionably authentic and, despite their brevity, suffice for an explanation. It is useless to go to so much trouble seeking elsewhere what cannot be found. It requires a violent handling of the texts to eliminate the sordid avarice of Judas and to maintain that a motive of jealousy lay at the basis of the accusation which the Fourth Gospel makes against him. To say that John was jealous of Judas is silly.

While striving to free the traitor from blame, the Rationalists sometimes charge Jesus with part of the responsibility for Judas' crime. "If it was true, as tradition says, that Jesus was

[248] See A. Réville, *Jésus de Nazareth,* II, 345; W. Brandt, *Die evangelische Geschichte und der Ursprung des Christentums,* pp. 484–487; J. Weiss, *Die Schriften des N. T.,* I, 92; O. Holtzmann, *Leben Jesu,* p. 351; T. Keim, *Geschichte Jesu,* III, 247; W. Hess, *Jesus von Nazareth in seiner geschichtlichl. Lebensentwicklung,* p. 101; A. Neumann, *op. cit.,* p. 175, etc. Each of these authors sets forth the theory with slight individual differences.

[249] *Op. cit.,* p. 449.

[250] O. Holtzmann, *op. cit.,* p. 448.

aware of this treason in advance, and that He did nothing to prevent it, even furnishing Judas, through the apparent confidence He continued to show him, the means with which to perpetrate the betrayal, . . . we are tempted to ask ourselves whether Judas, a base instrument of the divine plan, deserves the curses that are heaped on his memory." Albert Réville [251] quite rightly does not insist on this objection and attaches only secondary importance to it, although he states it in language which is almost blasphemous. Jesus did everything He could to save the wretched Apostle. The latter enjoyed all the graces needed to remain a faithful disciple, in spite of his temptation. He alone was responsible for his terrible fall and his eternal damnation.

But was not our Lord deceived in admitting this unworthy follower into the circle of His Apostles? The Rationalist critics commonly say that He was. "How could Jesus, who knew men's hearts, be deceived about this disciple?" [252] "Among the Twelve a Judas was able to slip in; Jesus was deceived as to his character, unless we prefer to say that His skill as an educator failed in this case." [253] The traitor, we are told, entered the Apostolic College at a rather late date, and of his own accord; hence the Savior had not time to know him.—No, Jesus was not deceived about Judas; He foresaw the betrayal from the very beginning, and He disclosed it early.[254] His skill as an educator failed in this case, it is true: divine grace is but too often witness to such failures. As for Judas' Apostolic election, that occurred at the same time as the choosing of the other Apostles, and the Divine Master was fully responsible for it.

[251] *Jésus de Nazareth,* II, 342.

[252] P. W. Schmidt, *Das Leben Jesu erläutert,* p. 363.

[253] J. Ninck, *Jesus als Charakter,* p. 111. Likewise A. Neumann, *Jesus, wer er geschichtlich war,* p. 108, and many others.

[254] John 6: 71 f.

X. The Sermon on the Mount

Rationalist critics generally show, at least in theory, great admiration for this discourse, and they praise it sincerely. However, it does not escape their spirit of opposition, which leaves no page of the Gospels intact.

1. Many of them say this sermon was never delivered by the Savior, but was composed entirely, though perhaps not directly, by the two Evangelists who record it, or at least by the authors of the documents from which they copied it.[255] Yet a large number of them admit that most of the sayings quoted in it by St. Matthew and St. Luke really belong to Jesus, who spoke them on various occasions.[256] But the discourse as a whole is "a free composition," "an anthology of aphorisms," which were grouped, as we now read them in the two accounts, especially in St. Matthew's, about the beginning of the Christian era, to make a sort of Manual of Piety, a collection of rules of conduct.

We have said that perhaps St. Matthew, here and there in the discourse, added a few thoughts which were spoken at other times, and we remarked that St. Luke certainly abridges the sermon. But there is nothing to justify the supposition that we have here only a "compilation." [257] Such a hypothesis fails utterly to account for the respect which the Evangelists and the first Christian generations cherished to-

---

[255] With various slight differences, such is the thought also of the following: Weizsäcker, *Apostolische Geschichte*, 2d ed., p. 380; P. W. Schmiedel in Cheyne's *Encyclopedia Biblica*, II, col. 1886; H. J. Holtzmann, *Die Synoptiker*, p. 99; Jülicher, *Einleitung in das N. T.*, 3d ed., p. 232; Heinrici, *Bergpredigt*, I, 39; E. Klostermann, *Matthäus*, p. 179; Loisy, *Les Évangiles Synoptiques*, I, 535.

[256] Loisy, *op. cit.*, p. 535: The elements of the sermon are "nearly all taken from the most authentic tradition."

[257] Loisy, *op. cit.*, p. 536. Without any sound reason this same author adds: "The actual form of this passage indicates a work of successive composition and does not represent simply Christ's words."

ward historic truth, particularly when it concerned the life of the Divine Master. Furthermore, the Sermon on the Mount, as recorded in St. Matthew's Gospel, exactly corresponds to what we might expect from Jesus at that period of His ministry. His disciples had become numerous, and friendly crowds from all directions were gathered about Him. What would be more natural than for Him to give them a summary of His teaching and to sketch the ideal that should be realized by all who desired to acquire citizenship in the Kingdom of Heaven? And who, except Christ alone, would have been able to create a literary composition of such unity and beauty, advancing from point to point so truly and naturally, with its thoughts so connected, forming an inimitable entity? [258] The Rationalist hypothesis is therefore *a priori* improbable. And it is based on no solid reasons.[259]

2. In general the Rationalists have as much aversion for dogma as they have for miracles. We see them striving with all their might against both these elements in the Gospels. Some of them avow that the (so-called) absence of dogma in the Sermon on the Mount is one of the chief reasons why they have a special fondness for that example of our Lord's eloquence. Stier quite properly replies to them: "You Rationalists, who so gladly listen to the moral teaching in the *Oratio montana,* should not be deaf to the dogma which it contains." [260] In fact, doctrinal ideas are far from being entirely absent.

With this error we may connect that of Harnack and other critics, who treat the Sermon on the Mount as though it contained the whole substance of Christianity, and who, in

[258] Some critics are, so to speak, scandalized at this unity. But, as one of them declares, "Jesus never spoke without giving a clear sequence and connection to His thoughts. The view that His sentences and reasonings came from His lips without such sequence," is contrary to the truth. W. Hess, *Jesus von Nazareth in seiner geschichtl. Lebensentwicklung,* p. 24.

[259] See Plummer, *Commentary on the Gospel according to St. Matthew,* p. 56.

[260] Stier, *Die Reden des Herrn Jesu, i. h. l.*

consequence of this false assumption, regard all later developments, whether contained in other portions of the Gospels or in other parts of the New Testament or in tradition, as not belonging to the essence of Jesus' teaching.[261] But how do these critics know that the Savior intended to condense within these few pages all the doctrinal and moral teaching that He brought to mankind? Inserted therein are to be found especially rules of conduct suited to His disciples; but on this point, as in the matter of Christian doctrine, He notably supplements His teaching on many other occasions.

3. Other Rationalists attack the authenticity of one of the most important passages in the Sermon, that in which Jesus expressly declares that He came, not to destroy the Jewish Law, but to fulfil and perfect it.[262] Says Loisy: [263] "Did Jesus have occasion thus to define His attitude toward the Law? He did not have to do so, nor did He do so systematically and scholastically, as in the present discourse, by first enunciating a universal principle, and then enumerating various applications in accordance with that principle." [264] In refutation of this opinion, we will not say, as a certain other critic does,[265] that Jesus "never intended to separate from Judaism and to found a new religion," that He "wished merely to infuse a new spirit into the existing forms" of the Jewish religion, and that consequently there was no reason against His publicly proclaiming His respect for everything which constituted the religion of Judaism. But this is merely to fall into another error. Loisy felt the weakness of his opinion and abandoned

[261] Cf. Harnack, *Wesen des Christentums*, 1903, *passim*.

[262] Matt. 5 : 17–20.

[263] *Les Évangiles Synoptiques*, I, 563.

[264] See the same view in Wernle, *Die Anfänge unserer Religion*, 2. ed., p. 59. Marcion, that great foe of Judaism, affirmed that the actual wording of the text in question was due to a falsification by the Jews. According to him, its primitive form was: "Think you that I am come to fulfil the Law? . . . I am come to destroy, not to fulfil." Cf. St. Isidore of Pelusium, *Epist.*, I, 371; Origen, *Contra Celsum*, II, 15.

[265] W. Hess, *Jesus von Nazareth*, II, 25.

it, acknowledging that the Savior may well have enunciated the principle here in question. And we will add, as our chief argument in this place as in so many other places, that the authenticity of this whole passage of the First Gospel is too well attested by textual criticism for anything to be advanced against it except arbitrary preoccupations.[266]

4. We must now set forth at greater length an objection which in our day is often made by Jewish writers, and in which many Protestant theologians have joined. It concerns the origin of the Sermon on the Mount, which they say is almost exclusively connected with the Old Testament writings and to an even greater extent with rabbinical literature. Whole volumes have been written by Jews to prove this thesis,[267] not to speak of articles in dictionaries [268] and reviews, as well as isolated statements. A few quotations will show how far these claims of Jews and others have gone. Rabbi A. Geiger [269] says that "Jesus was a Pharisee, who walked in the footsteps of Hillel" [270] and "did not express a single new thought." Rodrigues announces in his preface [271] that his aim is "to demonstrate, for those who are not afraid of the light, that what is called Christian morality is nothing other than Jewish moral-

---

[266] Hence we may judge the value of H. J. Holtzmann's assertion, *Neutestament. Theologie,* 1st ed., I, 152, that to attempt to prove the authenticity of Matt. 15:17 f., is "undertaking to square the circle."

[267] Suffice it to mention the following: Salvador, *Jésus-Christ et sa Doctrine,* 2 vols., 1864; J. Cohen, *Les Déicides: Examen de la Vie de Jésus et des Développements de l'Église Chrétienne dans leurs rapports avec le Judaïsme,* 1864; H. Rodrigues, *Les Origines du Sermon sur la Montagne,* 1868; E. Schreiber, *Die Principien des Judentums verglichen mit denen des Christentums,* 1877; E. Banamozegh, *Morale Juive et Morale Chrétienne,* 1878; Friedemann, *Jüdische Moral und christl. Staat,* 1894; Nork, *Rabbinische Quellen und Parallelen zu neutestam. Schriftstellen,* 1899; G. Friedländer, *The Jewish Sources of the Sermon on the Mount,* 1911. A much more extensive bibliography will be found in Bischoff's work, which we will mention presently. (See note 276 *infra.*)

[268] For example, in Hamburger's *Real-Encyklopädie für Bibel und Talmud,* 4 vols., 1884–1892, and in the *Jewish Encyclopedia.*

[269] Cited by F. Delitzsch, *Jesus und Hillel,* 2d ed., p. 7.

[270] E. Renan appropriated this assertion.

[271] *Op. cit.,* p. 1.

ity." He quotes [272] these words of Munk,[273] a fellow-Jew: "Surprise is sometimes expressed at the small effect produced in Jerusalem by the Sermon on the Mount. How could it have been otherwise? The Sermon on the Mount *coursed the streets of Jerusalem* [274] long before it was pronounced." And he says further: "It is a very easy matter to reconstruct this sermon with documents anterior to its time." The work of Benamozegh, the "preaching rabbi," abounds in shallow, declamatory statements. Therein you will find headings such as these: "Pretended superiority [of Christian moral teaching] over Judaism; absurdity of this hypothesis, its impiety; weaknesses and difficulties of Christian moral teaching." Another rabbi, E. Schreiber, writes that "the Sermon on the Mount is a collection of passages from the Talmud." [275]

Christian savants familiar with rabbinical literature [276] have dealt with this pretentious language as it deserves. No one thinks of denying that there is a blood relationship between Jesus' moral teaching and that of the Old Testament, between the rules of conduct proposed by Him and those that can be read in certain places in the books of Moses, the Psalms, the Prophets, and the hagiographies. Jesus Himself publicly affirmed this similarity. And it is a patent fact that numerous precepts contained in the Sermon on the Mount have, if not their equivalent, at least their basis in the Old Law. And yet, what a difference! In the one case, we have the seed and the root, in the other, we have the plant in all its growth, with its foliage and blossoms and fruit. Moreover, the moral beauties which are to be found isolated in the Old Testament writ-

---

[272] *Ibid.*, p. 11.

[273] A Jewish scholar who lived in the nineteenth century.

[274] Rodrigues himself italicizes these words.

[275] *Op. cit.*, p. 10.

[276] Especially Edersheim (a Rabbi converted to Anglicanism), *Life and Times of Jesus the Messiah*, I, 524–541, and still more E. Bischoff, *Jesus und die Rabbinen, Jesu Bergpredigt in ihrer Unabhängigkeit vom Rabbinismus dargestellt*, 1905. See also F. Delitzsch, *op. cit.*

ings are here grouped in a unique way, Jesus having gathered them into a body of doctrine unparalleled anywhere else. If it were true that Jesus added nothing to the moral teaching of the Law and the Prophets, how are we to explain the enthusiastic admiration with which His countrymen welcomed His preaching? We must insist upon this point, that Jesus transformed and transfigured the Jewish moral teaching, supplementing it by new and more perfect precepts and by drawing His disciples' attention to the spirit and import of the divine commandments, since previously attention had been directed too much to the mere letter, as the Scribes had been satisfied with insisting on external obedience.

As for the Talmud, a considerable amount of good will would be needed to consider it even remotely as the source of the Sermon on the Mount and of the morality preached by our Lord. True, you may find, scattered through the interminable tractates that compose it, some specks of gold; we refer to a few moral precepts that resemble such or such of our Lord's sayings. There were, of course, good rabbis, with noble, pious souls, and it would be a matter of astonishment if, nourished on the Bible, they had not expressed some fine thoughts. We quoted several of them in connection with the Sermon we are now considering, and we compared them with those of Jesus. The following belong to the same category.[277] Some rabbis said that not a single letter must be taken away from the text of the Mosaic Law.[278] Others made, as did Jesus, a distinction between the "heavy" (more important) precepts and the "light" or less important precepts. Rabbi Chanina (in the third century of our era) said: "There are three who go down to hell: he who does wrong with the wife of another; he who insults his neighbor in public; and he who calls his

---

[277] Bischoff, *op. cit.,* mentions several others, all related to the Sermon on the Mount.
[278] *Shemoth R.,* 6.

neighbor by an opprobrious name." [279] According to Rabbi Huna, "for the just, their Yes is yes, their No is no." [280] In the words of another rabbi, "Whoever has a loaf of bread in his basket and says: What shall I eat to-morrow? is a man of little faith." [281] To Rabbi Tarphon (end of the first century) is attributed the following: "If anyone should say to another: Take out the splinter that is in thy eye, the other would reply: Take out the beam that is in thy own eye." [282]

The originality of the Lord's Prayer is strongly contested. Hamburger [283] says that "each phrase in it is to be found in the prayers and instructions of the Jewish rabbis which have been consigned to the Talmud; this whole prayer, therefore, has its home on Jewish soil." In proof of this assertion, there are alleged, independent of unconnected phrases, collected in the writings of the rabbis, the following petitions, contained in the Kaddish and the Shemone Esre, Jewish prayers which we have already mentioned: "May His [God's] sublime name become great and hallowed in the world. . . . May He let His royal domination have sway during our life and our days. . . . Hear the prayers and the desires of the house of Israel.[284] Thou art holy and Thy name is terrible. . . . Pardon us, our Father, . . . and deliver us because of Thy name . . . , and fill the world with the treasures of Thy goodness, and be Thou King over us, Lord, but in grace and mercy." [285]

We do not deny these more or less real, more or less vague resemblances. They may impress readers who are not acquainted with the rabbinical literature as a whole, and who judge it only by quotations of this sort. But these citations are valueless for proving that the Sermon on the Mount is

279 *Baba mezia*, 29, a. Cf. Matt. 5:22.
280 *Ruth R.*, III, 18. Cf. Matt. 5:37.
281 *Sota*, 42, b. Cf. Matt. 6:25.
282 *Arachin*, 16, b. Cf. Matt. 7:3-5.
283 *Op. cit.*, III, 55.
284 Taken from the *Kaddish*.
285 From the *Shemone Esre*.

devoid of originality and that Jesus derived its ideas from the rabbis. Moreover, the question is not whether the Talmud contains moral precepts of good quality, but whether, even by uniting in a single composition all that is best in the Talmud, we would succeed in reproducing the unique masterpiece recorded by St. Matthew. Where, in all the Jewish writings, are we to find sayings comparable with the Beatitudes, the Pater Noster, Jesus' words about detachment from the goods of this world and trust in God? Nowhere can they be found.

Let us go to the bottom of the question. First we will say that the resemblances between the Sermon on the Mount and the rabbinical writings can be easily explained without supposing any borrowing by our Lord. Even should it be demonstrated that Jesus used figurative expressions, popular ideas, or proverbial sayings which were found on the lips of such or such a rabbi previous to Him, it would still be quite uncritical to conclude that He was dependent upon the rabbis. "Whoever wishes to be understood by the people must speak the language of the people; and when he has grown up in a definite environment, he uses, even unconsciously, the language of that environment." [286] It would therefore be natural that Jesus, without taking anything from the Jewish doctors, should at times be in agreement with them in the religious and moral domain.

Since those who claim for the rabbis a proprietorship over most of the texts in the Sermon on the Mount, do so with such presumption, let us point out their extreme exaggerations and their total want of scientific method. They boast that the Talmud contains the whole Gospel, and that all the Savior's moral instructions were taken from the early Jewish doctors. The Christian scholars whose names we have mentioned, men well versed in Talmudic literature, have taken up the gage and have carefully studied the texts that are

---

[286] Bischoff, *Jesus und die Rabbinen,* p. 4.

said to have served as sources for Jesus' thoughts. What is the result of those patient researches? They reveal the most deplorable lack of weight. Often these protagonists of the Talmud, in translating the rabbis' sayings from which it is said that Jesus borrowed, deliberately or unconsciously stress the likeness between those sayings and the Gospel text, in such a way as to make the scales incline in favor of the rabbis. Although the Talmud is made up of very unlike parts, which in their final form date from several different centuries, it is considered in its *ensemble* as if all its portions were anterior to the Gospels; rabbis are quoted without any regard to the period when they lived. By procedures of this sort, the proofs are totally falsified and, for the most part, lose their force. In this way, Nork, Hamburger, Friedmann, and others represent Jesus as taking sayings from rabbis of the fourth century of our era, and even from writings of the Middle Ages.[287] By so doing they may succeed in throwing dust into the eyes of the ignorant; but they destroy their thesis with their own hands.

In short, there is not a single instance where it can be said that Jesus, in the Sermon on the Mount or elsewhere, is dependent on the Talmud. Between Christ and the rabbis there exist the most profound differences. Jesus bases His moral teaching on that of the Old Law; He owes absolutely nothing to the Talmud.[288]

5. Some critics, stressing the details which we mentioned when we were explaining the principle "I am not come to destroy [the Law], but to fulfil," attribute to Jesus two differ-

[287] See Bischoff, *loc. cit.,* p. 3; Kittel, *Jesus und die Rabbinen,* pp. 4–6; Dalman, *Die Worte Jesu,* p. 62.

[288] "The first and most obvious, perhaps, also, most superficial thought, is that which brings this teaching of Christ into comparison . . . with the best of the wisdom and piety of the Jewish sages, as preserved in rabbinic writings." But there is an "essential difference, or rather contrariety in spirit and substance, not only when viewed as a whole, but in almost each of its individual parts." (Edersheim, *Life and Times of Jesus,* I, 524.)

ent attitudes toward the Mosaic legislation. J. Weiss [289] says that at bottom, according to the totality of His words and conduct, Jesus was full of respect for the Jewish Law; but— we marvel at this comparison—just as Luther "wished to be and remained a faithful child of his Church, although he had long since published propositions that threatened to shatter the system of the Middle Ages," so, too, the Savior "thought Himself rooted in the soil of His fatherland, although His spirit had long since led Him into new regions." Dr. Pfleiderer [290] writes that Jesus, as it were, "unawares" and led on by the heat of His strife with the Pharisees, uttered words the true import of which was not only to suppress abuses, but to abolish the Law itself.

Others, like A. Neumann,[291] mark out several different periods in the attitude of Jesus toward the Law. First His purpose was to perfect it internally: in place of the letter, He substituted the religion of the spirit. Then, after the manner of the ancient prophets, He placed the moral commandments of the Law in the foreground and relegated to the background the ceremonial part. Lastly, He directly attacked the Law, at first not knowingly, but later on with full intent. "At the beginning it must have been hard for Him to forsake, bit by bit, what ever since boyhood He had looked upon as the expression of God's will." Nevertheless, "on this point Jesus never reached a clearly avowed decision. . . . It was St. Paul who declared that the Jewish Law is void and valueless, and that it is impossible to fulfil it." [292]

These are all arbitrary hypotheses, with no foundation but the apparently different attitude which the Savior took to-

---

[289] *Die Schriften des N. T.,* I, 248.

[290] *Die Entstehung des Christentums.* See also Wellhausen, *Einleitung in die Evangelien,* p. 113.

[291] *Jesus, wer er geschichtlich war,* pp. 140–142.

[292] E. Klostermann, *Jesus Stellung zum Alten Testam.,* 1904, p. 25, speaks in the same strain.

ward the Old Law. We have already given a sufficient explanation of these variations. His position regarding the Jewish Law was never contradictory or "paradoxical." [293] In the Sermon on the Mount, at the head of those details wherein He takes the attitude of a reformer of the Law, when He enunciated the principle, "I am not come to destroy . . . ," He was aware that those details were not in contradiction with the principle. Indeed He did not destroy; but it was impossible for the Mosaic legislation not to evolve in His hands and in the hands of the Apostles. Yet that evolution was always a development, a transfiguration. Evidently the juridical and constitutional laws, which had in mind the segregated existence of the Jewish nation, were not destined to endure permanently; the same may be said of most of the ceremonial regulations. The prophets had zealously striven to perfect the Law of Sinai; Jesus, too, and much better than they. Thanks to Him, the Old Law still exists and exercises its full power in the Christian Church, but in a final, supereminent form, as our risen body will be distinct from our mortal body, while not ceasing to be identical with it.

XI. Christ's Eloquence

The following appreciation of our Lord's eloquence is by Adolph Harnack.[294] "Jesus taught that it is no profit to gain the whole world if the soul suffer harm, and yet He kept a friendly feeling for every living thing. . . . His sayings, usually set in comparisons and proverbs, express all the shades of human speech and the whole gamut of feelings. He employs the sternest accents of impassioned denunciation and wrathful feeling and irony, although these tones must have been the exception. Mourning and tears, laughter and dancing,

---

[293] W. Bousset, *Jesus*, p. 65, uses this epithet.
[294] *Das Wesen des Christentums*, 1903, p. 23.

riches and poverty, hunger and thirst, health and sickness, children's playing and the politics of state, . . . an inn and the payment for lodging, weddings and funerals, the luxurious dress of the living and the tombs of the dead, . . . the vinedresser in the vineyard and the idle workers in the marketplace, the shepherd looking for his lost sheep, the pearl merchant, . . . the housewife's anxiety on account of the flour, the leaven, or the lost drachma, the widow's plea before the merciless judge, . . . the intellectual relations of teachers and pupils, . . . the glamor of royalty, the ambition of the powerful, the innocence of children, the ready alacrity of servants—all these figures appear in the Savior's discourses and make them dramatic. The supernatural world in which Jesus lived did not destroy the present world for Him, but led Him wholly to God."

XII. The Curing of the Centurion's Servant Wrongly Identified with the Curing of the Son of the Royal Officer [295]

The identification of these two miracles goes back to early centuries. St. Irenaeus seems to have held it,[296] unless he accidentally wrote "son of the centurion" in place of "son of the royal officer." Other early authors adopted this view, as we are informed by Origen and St. John Chrysostom, who reject it without hesitation.[297] Many Rationalist critics also favor it; this does not greatly surprise us, for they are pleased to find in the Gospels as many "doublets" as possible, hoping thus more easily to place the sacred writers in contradiction with one another. But in the texts with which we are here concerned, except for the fact that in both accounts the cure

[295] John 4 : 46–54.
[296] *Adv. Haer.*, II, xxii, 3.
[297] In their commentaries, *i. h. l.*

was effected at a distance, nearly everything is different. In the one case we· have a pagan soldier, in the other, a Jewish civil officer; in one case Capharnaum, in the other, Cana; in the one case a paralyzed slave, in the other, a son suffering from fever; in one case a man whose humility keeps him from receiving Jesus into his house, in the other, a man who urges Jesus to accompany him to Capharnaum; in one case admirable faith, in the other, a faith that is at first imperfect; in one case a pagan whom Jesus holds up as an example to the Jews, in the other, a Jew whose deed furnishes our Lord occasion to criticize His countrymen. Under these circumstances the identity cannot be admitted.[298]

XIII. The Savior's Miracles

For a long time past the Gospel miracles have been a battlefield for out-and-out Rationalists, and even for a large number of Liberal Protestants who acknowledge the reality of Christ's miracles in principle, but almost at once turn against them by the wholly false interpretations they give them.

The most advanced contemporary Rationalists, who deny *a priori* the existence or even the possibility of the miraculous in general, of course reject *in toto* the historical character of the miracles which the Evangelists attribute to our Lord. Dr. Pfleiderer [299] sums up their idea, when he expresses the hope that in the near future all miracles, especially those recorded in the Gospels, will be relegated from the realm of facts to that of art, and that they will pass from the pages of history to the stained-glass windows of cathedrals and will there remain; in other words, that they will still be an

[298] See Godet, *Commentaire sur l'Évangile de S. Luc,* 2d ed., I, 423; T. Zahn, *Das Evangelium des Johannes ausgelegt,* 2d ed., p. 268.

[299] *Geschichte der Religionsphilosophie von Spinoza bis zur Gegenwart,* 3d ed., 1893, p. 62.

object of esthetic pleasure, but will no longer have a right to demand that we believe in them. Before Pfleiderer, Reimarus, Paulus, Strauss, Ferdinand Baur, Renan, and others,[300] and contemporary with him Holtzmann, Harnack, Bousset, J. Weiss, and Soltau,[301] to mention only a few, all maintain the same thesis, which they endeavor to establish by all sorts of sophisms.

These writers quite well comprehended that if they succeeded in destroying, or even shaking, the authority of Christ's miracles, it would be much easier for them to make a breach in the rest of the Christian edifice. Their schemes have varied, discrediting and upsetting one another, but their purpose has remained the same, namely, to remove every supernatural element from the Gospels, and to prove that, although Jesus was a remarkable personage, we must give up the notion that He was a miracle-worker.

Reimarus (1694–1768) accused the Savior's disciples of having fraudulently invented His miracles, in connivance with Him, so as more easily to succeed in having Him pass as the Messias. Paulus (1761–1851) explained all the Gospel miracles in a purely natural way, maintaining that the sacred writers did not intend to relate a single really miraculous event. Strauss (1808–1874) undertook to make out that they were "myths," legendary creations formed in the early Church. Ferdinand Christian Baur (1792–1860) attributed to the Gospels certain "tendencies," by virtue of which our Lord's miracles would be fictitious in varying degrees. Recent Rationalist critics, not finding any new ideas to propose, have resorted to eclecticism, taking from their predecessors a few shreds of their theories and combining them. This negative

---

[300] See Fillion, *Les Étapes du Rationalisme,* pp. 9–180, and *Les Miracles de Notre-Seigneur,* I, 74–60; F. Vigouroux, *La Sainte Bible et les Critiques Contemporains,* 5th ed., Vol. V, *passim.*

[301] Cf. Fillion, *Les Étapes du Rationalisme,* pp. 181–190; *Les Miracles de Notre-Seigneur,* I, 81–96.

theology, "having been won to its dogmatic [and arbitrary] ideas, twists and turns as though in a circle from which it is unable to emerge." [302] We hardly need to add that it is a vicious circle.

What characterizes most of these authors is the boldness of their assertions. The following lines of Ernest Havet (1813–1889) [303] show us without any circumlocution what is the inner thought of many unbelieving theologians and exegetes. "The first obligation imposed on us by the Rationalist principle, which is the foundation of all criticism, is to eliminate the supernatural from the life of Christ. This at a single stroke removes from the Gospels what are called the miracles. Paralytics and lepers cured instantly, the deaf, the dumb, and men born blind who suddenly recover their hearing or speech or sight, by a mere touch or word of Jesus, in all this there is clearly no reality. Not only did Jesus do nothing of this sort, but I make bold to add that it was not possible for such to be believed of Him while He was still alive. It was only at a distance and long afterwards that such things were imagined. Inasmuch as criticism declines to believe in accounts of miracles, it has no need to advance proofs in support of its denials: what is related is false, simply because what is related could not be." [304]

This system of audacious negation is easy, but is it scientific? Most certainly not. It is a begging of the question, and nothing more; the modern critics will not succeed any better than did the ancient Rationalists in proving the impossibility of miracles in general; [305] nor will they succeed in proving the falsity of the Gospel miracles. We will confine ourselves

[302] F. Bovon, *Théologie du N. T.*, 2d ed., I, 298.

[303] *Revue des Deux Mondes*, April 1, 1881, p. 587.

[304] "Jesus was not able to perform miracles; no man is capable of doing so," wrote Dr. H. Schaefer, *Jesus in psychiatrischer Betrachtung*, 1910, p. 54.

[305] On the nature, possibility, and reality of miracles, see the theologians and particularly L. Gondal, *Le Miracle*, 1905.

to this second point. Yet we must note that the most recent Liberal critics, such as Holtzmann, Harnack, J. Weiss, W. Bousset, and their disciples, although regarding the Savior's most brilliant miracles as pure legends—for example, the miracles of power over inanimate nature, and the raising of the dead—are willing to regard as historical most of His marvelous cures; but only on condition that they be explained by a purely natural influence which Jesus exercised over the sick, owing to His will power, His art of suggestion, and the supreme confidence which the sick had in Him. We will examine this opinion separately.

We said above that fear of the miraculous has obsessed numerous Protestant theologians of the orthodox school, who accept the Savior's miracles, but who often do so with barely concealed reluctance, or with an undue restriction of the part of the supernatural. One of them says: "Tradition may have exaggerated: the eyewitnesses themselves may have been deceived, taking for a miracle what was not one." [306] Fairbairn affirms that "miracles, once regarded as the great bulwark of the Christian faith, are now regarded as its greatest burden," [307] since "they are more embarrassing than useful to Christian faith." [308]

But let us proceed in order, considering those Rationalist objections that ought to be discussed by themselves. The others have already been refuted in our general discussion of the Savior's miracles.

I. One group of objections refers to the Gospel accounts

[306] Beth, *Die Wunder Jesu,* 1905, p. 28.

[307] *Studies in the Life of Christ,* p. 149.

[308] Dr. Forsith, London *Quarterly Review,* July 1909, in an article entitled "Evidential Value of Miracles." See also F. Barth, *Die Hauptprobleme des Lebens Jesu,* 2d ed., pp. 106–146; W. Sanday, *The Criticism of the Fourth Gospel,* 1905, pp. 169–182. Warschauer (*Jesus: Seven Questions,* 1908, p. 178) says: "Not only is the power to perform miracles not essential to the greatness of our Lord, but the emphasis placed upon the miraculous element has obscured His true greatness more than any other single cause."

considered in themselves. Among the Rationalists who deny
the existence of the supernatural, are some who push their
theory to its ultimate consequences, making assertions like
the following: "Accounts in which miracles figure are not
historic in the modern and scientific sense of that term." [309]
But just as Huxley, despite his unbelief, said that the denial
of the possibility of miracles seemed to him as unjustifiable
as speculative atheism,[310] so it is just to regard as superficial [311] and opposed to genuine criticism the opinion we have
mentioned. The leaders of Liberal Protestantism also protest
against it again and again. "To reject documents as utterly
unserviceable or to assign them to a later period, because
they contain accounts of miracles, arises from a prejudice. . . . We have no right to hide behind the Gospel miracles in order to escape from the Gospel." This reasoning by
Harnack [312] is impregnable. We are pleased to quote the words
of a contemporary apologist: "The whole question of the
Gospel miracles may be reduced to a single point: Are they
sufficiently attested? Is the book relating them the work of
witnesses close enough to the events so that we may not doubt
their exactness, and sufficiently worthy of credence so that
we may not accuse them of imposture?" [313] The Evangelists
and their writings wonderfully meet these two requirements.

The Rationalists are resolved, all reason to the contrary notwithstanding, to eliminate the miraculous element from the
life of Christ. Sometimes they presuppose, without other foundation than their arbitrary desire, the existence of a primitive

[309] Cheyne's *Encyclopedia Biblica*, IV, col. 535. Ernest Renan also went very
far along this easy road. "It is not because I was previously convinced that the
Evangelists do not merit absolute credence that I reject the miracles related by
them. Rather is it because they relate miracles that I say: The Gospels are
legends; they may contain history, but certainly not everything therein is historical." (*Vie de Jésus*, 13th ed., p. vi.)

[310] *The Spectator*, February 10, 1866.

[311] F. Nolloth, *The Historic Personality of Christ*, p. 19.

[312] *Das Wesen des Christentums*, p. 6.

[313] De Broglie, *Problèmes et Conclusions de l'Histoire des Religions*, p. 344.

Gospel which is considered the "kernel" of all the others and from which the supernatural element was totally absent. But the history of the sacred text is opposed to this hypothesis no less than is the ecclesiastical tradition. Nowhere is the least trace of "a Gospel without miracles" to be discovered. Even the *Logia,* about which there has been so much ado,[314] contains many miracles. Furthermore, St. Mark's Gospel, which many modern Rationalists regard as the prototype of St. Matthew's and St. Luke's, is distinguished by such an accumulation of the miraculous element that it has been called the "book of miracles." [315]

Especially numerous are the attacks against the pages of the Fourth Gospel which recount mostly new miracles. These are said to be "miracles of ostentation," "works of art," which have "not at all the aspect of real events." [316] All this is likewise pure assertion. Besides the general arguments proving the authenticity and credibility of St. John's accounts,[317] including the miracles, we should note that the supernatural element in the Fourth Gospel is of the same sort as in the Synoptics, and the miracles of Christ are therein described with such precision and accompanied by such minute details and conclusive proofs [318] that they show the Evangelist to be a trustworthy witness.[319]

It is true that the narratives of the Evangelists, both when referring to the Savior's miracles and when mentioning the other events of His life, ordinarily present variants, and Rationalism takes advantage of this fact to point to what

[314] See Vol. I, pp. 484 ff.

[315] Fillion, *Les Miracles de Notre-Seigneur,* I, 30.

[316] J. Wellhausen, *Einleitung in die Evangelien,* p. 377; A. Bruce, *The Miraculous Element in the Gospels,* p. 151; K. Furrer, *Beiträge über das Leben Jesu Christi,* p. 189, etc.

[317] We again refer the reader to an excellent study by Lepin, entitled *La Valeur Historique du Quatrième Évangile.*

[318] Cardinal Wiseman, *op. cit.,* p. 94.

[319] Cf. John 19:38; 21:24.

it is pleased to call contradiction, and therefore falsity. Aside from two events which we shall study in their proper chronological place—the curing of the demoniacs of Gerasa [320] and that of the blind men of Jericho [321]—wherein the divergence is very marked on a special point, the variants are but *nuances,* happy additions, due to more complete information possessed by one or other of the narrators. Was it necessary that the same incidents should be related in exactly the same terms by the four Evangelists? The Rationalists seek to draw from these variants an argument against the Gospels. Are they not, on the contrary, an additional proof of the Evangelists' independence and love for the truth?

Other objections are derived from the person of Jesus and from the attitude falsely attributed to Him with regard to His own miracles. Nowadays no one would venture openly to return to Reimarus' theory and charge the Savior with a calculated connivance with what is called the superstitious notions of His countrymen; even less would anyone accuse Him of having taken advantage of the public's good faith to pass for a miracle-worker. Sometimes complicated explanations are offered, which imply that on several occasions Jesus made concessions to popular superstitions so as to assure the success of His work. Ernest Renan thus ends a long tirade full of errors: "Jesus' miracles were a violence done to Him by His age, a connivance wrung from Him by a passing need." [322] This serious accusation falls of itself in the presence of the holiness and sincerity and nobility of the Savior's whole being. We reject it with just indignation.

Most Rationalists, while not going so far as Renan and his like, reject at least the miracles performed upon inanimate nature, called miracles of ostentation, for, say these critics,

---

[320] Matt. 8:28. Cf. Mark 5:2; Luke 8:27.
[321] Matt. 20:30. Cf. Mark 10:46; Luke 18:35.
[322] *Vie de Jésus,* 1863, p. 268.

such miracles would be at variance with Christ's sober and modest tastes, as also with His refusal to comply with the requests of Satan, the Scribes, and the Pharisees, that He perform acts of dazzling brilliance. Moreover, even when commanding the forces of nature or when raising the dead, He never abandoned His customary reserve and simplicity. Lastly, these miracles, precisely because they were more remarkable, served the better to prove His divine mission.

The foes of the Gospel miracles stress the repugnance which they say the Savior felt for the rôle of miracle-worker and assert that He attached but little importance to His miracles. "Did He not say, by way of blame and reproach: 'Unless you see signs and wonders, you believe not'? He who spoke thus cannot have thought that belief in His miracles was the true or only means of attaining to a knowledge of His person and mission." [323] It is a simple matter to answer this objection. Certainly our Lord did not encourage a very imperfect faith that had as its only basis the wonderful side of His ministry; but He denied neither the usefulness nor the necessity nor the probative force of His miracles, since He performed a great number of them precisely to lead His countrymen to believe in Him. [324] Many of His words prove that He performed His miracles of His own volition, that He considered them manifestations which gave rise to obligations on the part of men toward Him and which gave Him a right to their belief in Him. [325] His reply to the Baptist's messengers, [326] His cursing of the cities which refused to believe in Him despite the "works of power" which they had wit-

---

[323] Harnack, *Das Wesen des Christentums*, p. 19. Cf. Strauss, *Leben Jesu*, II, 94; Renan, *Vie de Jésus*, p. 264; Schenkel, *Das Charakterbild Jesu*, p. 52, etc.

[324] At the proper place we explained the silence which our Lord frequently imposed upon the devils that He drove out of persons possessed and upon the sick whom He cured. From this it cannot be concluded that the divine Miracle-worker performed these miraculous cures reluctantly.

[325] A. Bruce, *The Miraculous Element in the Gospels*, p. 250.

[326] Matt. 11 : 2–6; Luke 7 : 19–23.

nessed,[327] the discourse in which He refuted the charge that
He performed His miracles with the aid of Satan [328]—all
these words of His, and others besides, are so many proofs
of the spontaneity with which He filled the office of miracle-
worker.

To rid themselves of the Gospel miracles, modern Rationalists commonly employ another kind of fallacy. They tell us
that these miracles were largely the creation of the unre-
flecting enthusiasm of the first disciples and the credulousness of the early Church, so eager to glorify Jesus, though
somewhat tardily, and to make His humiliating end forgotten
by the splendor of the deeds performed by Him during His
public life. "On the gilded background of the marvelous,"
they say, "Christianity painted the simple image of Jesus"; [329]
His miracles "are a glowing crown which the poetic faith of
the early Christians placed upon His brow." [330]

We will sum up our reply in a few propositions: (1) The
bitterest enemies of our Lord believed in the reality of His
miracles. How would it have been possible, under their watchful eyes, falsely to make out that Jesus was a miracle-worker?
(2) If it is true that the early Christians invented the Savior's
miracles, how is it that they did not attribute a single one to
His infancy or hidden life? Because they were unwilling to
become false witnesses in their Master's cause, whether for
that period or for any later one. (3) The popularity of Jesus,
which was so prompt and universal in Palestine from the
beginning of His ministry, is a fact which no one has seriously
attempted to deny. It remains inexplicable without His many
miracles. On the contrary, the miraculous power with which
His biographers clothe Him from the time of His public
appearance, accounts for the enthusiasm of the crowds for

[327] Matt. 11:20-24.
[328] Matt. 12:25-35; Mark 3:23-30; Luke 11:17-23.
[329] W. Bousset, *Jesus*, p. 15.
[330] *Ibid.*, p. 5.

Him; whence it follows that it is not a tardy invention of the early Christians. (4) Faith in a superhuman, supernatural Christ, who arose from the dead and ascended to heaven, in whose name the Apostles themselves performed miracles, is as clear and strong in St. Paul's Epistles,[331] written before the year 58, as in the four canonical Gospels. It is therefore as contemporary as possible with Jesus.

By what right do the critics attribute to the members of the early Church an eager and credulous imagination, ever in quest of legendary miracles, in order to adorn the Savior's life with a posthumous crown? A study of the fairly plentiful literature going back to the beginnings of the Church leaves us with a quite opposite impression, for it shows us disciples who are slow to credit miracles performed in their very presence, Evangelists who recount them with a calmness bordering on apparent indifference, Apostles who are so opposed to novelty that they vigorously attack it at its first appearance.[332] Hence "impartial historical science is obliged to recognize the miracles of early Christian times as real facts." [333]

The wonderful deeds claimed by several religions of antiquity on behalf of their founders or heroes have given birth to another class of general objections to the Savior's miracles.[334] To-day scarcely any importance is attached to the many wonders that are said to have occurred in the footsteps of Buddha, and that form an odd accumuation of ridiculous, extravagant events, patently legendary; nor to those credited to Apollonius of Tyana, according to the mostly fabulous and

---

[331] Cf. 1 Cor. 12:4-11, etc.

[332] This fact is witnessed by several New Testament passages. Cf. Acts 20:30; Gal. 1:6 f.; 1 Tim. 4:1-3; 6:3-5, 20 f.; 2 Tim. 3:1-9, 14; 2 Pet. 2:1-19; 1 John 4:1-16; Jude 17 f.; Apoc. 2:14 f., etc.

[333] Von Gerdtell, *Die urchristlichen Wunder*, p. 16.

[334] Recently these miracles or pretended miracles of Greek and Roman paganism have been collected and published in special works. See R. Lembert, *Der Wunderglaube bei Römern und Griechen*, 1905; R. Reitzenstein, *Hellenische Wundererzählungen*, 1906; O. Weinisch, *Antike Heilungswunder*, 1909.

theatrical account of Philostrates;[335] even less to those fraudulently attributed to Mohammed.[336] In those which Suetonius
and Tacitus [337] relate about Emperor Vespasian, Strauss believes he has found a more solid weapon for attacking the
reality of Christ's miracles; he is scandalized that anybody
accepts the latter as historic, while rejecting the former as
fabulous.[338] But Tacitus is careful to say that the marvels
referred to, the curing of a blind man and of a paralytic (which
we accept only hypothetically) may have taken place *ope hu-
mana*. As to Æsculapius, who is the so-called offspring of
Apollo and a human mother, and who was said to have received
from his father the unlimited power to cure every kind of
disease, if his reputed miracles seem, in a few rare cases, to
have a preternatural character,[339] which was, however, the
work of the devil, they are evidently not miraculous.

The early Christian apologists discuss this question of
the pseudo-miracles of paganism. They draw attention to
the essential differences between those marvels and the Savior's miracles: in the case of the former, at least so far
as the prodigies attributed to various pagan personages may
be regarded as real, we have the coöperation of Satan, the
use of magical formulas and superstitious practices, the vainglory and pride of the so-called miracle-workers; in the case
of the Savior's miracles, we have His divine power, the ease
and simplicity with which He performs even His most stu-
pendous deeds, which always have the lofty purpose of doing

[335] "No one gives credence to the Life of Apollonius of Tyana, because it was
written long after the hero's time and under the conditions of a pure romance."
E. Renan, *Vie de Jésus,* 1863, p. 15. See also, by the same author, *Les Évangiles
et la Seconde Génération Chrétienne,* p. 408, and Vacant-Mangenot's *Dictionnaire
de Théologie,* I, cols. 1508–1511.

[336] Cf. Gondal, *Islamisme et Christianisme,* 1906, p. 70; L. von Gerdtell, *Die
urchristlichen Wunder,* p. 63.

[337] Suetonius, *De Vita Caesarum,* VIII, 7; Tacitus, *Hist.,* IV, 81.

[338] *Nouvelle Vie de Jésus* (French trans.), II, 66.

[339] See an interesting study by Professor Mangenot in the *Revue du Clergé
Français,* August 15, September 1 and 15, 1917, and December 1 and 15, 1918.

good to men and making them better.[340] These considerations have lost none of their value. And we should note, from the standpoint of literary criticism, how poorly authenticated are most of the events, supernatural or natural, which are advanced in opposition to the Gospel miracles.[341] Such being the case, it matters little whether the extremely conglomerate paganism then prevailing in the Roman Empire believed in miracles with astonishing readiness and imputed them to emperors, heroes, and other eminent men. The miracles of our Lord Jesus Christ belong to an entirely different category and are as truly historical as they are fully accredited.[342]

We will close this part of our apologetic and polemical study on the miracles in the Gospels, by saying that they "form such an important portion of the plan of Christ that every system that would seek to regard them as the integral product of His disciples' imagination or of a subsequent epoch, . . . leaves us a Christ as mythical as Hercules."[343] A Jesus stripped of His miracles would certainly not be He who founded the Christian Church and who went about doing good.

II. The Rationalists are not satisfied with attacking our Lord's miracles as a whole, but raise special difficulties against each of the classes into which we have divided them.

1. The miracles of power (in contradistinction to miracles of mercy) are condemned *in toto* or so explained that they

---

[340] Cf. St. Justin, *Apol.*, I, 30; Origen, *Contra Celsum*, I, 6, 60, 68; II, 48 f.; Pseudo-Clement, *Hom.*, II, 34; Arnobius, I, 43 f. 48, etc.

[341] "Outside of Christianity certain supernatural facts may be met with; but these facts are either not very striking or only poorly attested . . . In another direction, in certain religions we find the claim of very extensive display of a supernatural power. Such are the accounts regarding Zoroaster and Sakya Muni (another name for Buddha). But this brings us into the domain of pure legend, without any solid historical basis." (Abbé de Broglie, *op. cit.*, p. 342.)

[342] On the miracles of paganism as compared with those of the Gospels, see De Bonniot, *Le Miracle et ses Contrefaçons*, 5th ed., 1895, pp. 119–215; E. Mangenot, *Les Évangiles Synoptiques*, pp. 181–225; Fillion, *Les Miracles de Notre-Seigneur*, I, 120–129. The pretended miracles of the rabbis have been collected by P. Fiebig, in his work, *Jüdische Wundergeschichten des neutestam. Zeitalters*, 1911.

[343] Hastings' *Dictionary of the Bible*, II, 390.

retain not the least supernatural character. Those mentioned by the Evangelists are nine in number: the changing of the water into wine, the two multiplications of loaves, the two miraculous draughts of fishes, the sudden calming of the tempest on the lake, Christ's walking on the water, the didrachma in the fish's mouth, the cursing of the fig tree. The critics declare them impossible and futile, opposed to the ideal which Jesus intended with respect to His miraculous powers. These three assertions are unfounded. Why should inanimate nature offer the Savior any greater resistance than the human body? But He cured the most inveterate sufferings of the latter. Do not our bodies form part of nature? Such miracles were by no means futile, because, like the others, they were intended to prove Christ's divine mission, to show His goodness, to arouse faith.

On what ground are these facts rejected? Their attestation is as complete as could be desired. They are to be found in all four Gospels, in St. John's as well as in the Synoptics, and they are scattered through every period of our Lord's public life. Therefore, whoever does not reject all the Gospel miracles on principle, should admit the reality of those composing this important category. It is precisely because those miracles so plainly testify to the Savior's almighty power, that the Rationalists deny their historical character. But it was impossible for the numerous witnesses of these miracles to be mistaken about them. Let us note further that on various occasions even Christ's enemies asked Him to give them a "sign" performed in the upper regions of the air;[344] consequently to perform miracles of this sort. Therefore, they thought Him powerful enough to do so.

The childish and ridiculous explanations which Rationalist criticism gives of the miracles of this class, are in themselves their own refutation. Who will admit, for example, that the

[344] Matt. 12: 38; Luke 11: 16, etc.

facts as reported are greatly exaggerated, that they are mere symbols, that at times they are somewhat shocking,[345] that they are myths pure and simple, materialized parables (the barren fig tree), poetic conceptions (the walking on the water)?[346] In another work we have set forth and refuted all these strange theories in detail.[347]

2. Supernatural cures occupy a preponderant place among the Gospel miracles. According to several statements by the sacred writers,[348] they would certainly amount to hundreds, perhaps thousands,[349] if separately enumerated. There is nothing surprising in this fact, because they were in perfect harmony both with the office of the Messias, and with Jesus' loving, sympathetic nature, which moved Him to compassion for the sick and infirm,[350] then so numerous and so neglected in Palestine. The gravest and most deep-seated diseases were instantly and completely cured at His word or touch.[351] There was no transition between sickness and full health, no slow convalescence: the flesh of lepers became healthy in the twinkling of an eye, those suffering from fever at once left their beds and took up their usual labors, paralytics walked away, carrying their beds. And all these facts are attested in a way to satisfy the most exacting reader.

[345] A. Loisy, *Les Évangiles Synoptiques*, I, 272: "Is there not something rather shocking in the supposition that Jesus changed water into wine so as to allow those at the festive table to drink more?" *Ibid.*, p. 284: "The changing of water into wine signifies the replacing of the water of the Law by the wine of the Gospel."

[346] Giran, *Jésus de Nazareth*, p. 87, note.

[347] Fillion, *Les Miracles de Notre-Seigneur*, II, 14–18, 24–27, 31–34, 40 f., 45–47, 50 f., 55–57, 64–66, 70–72.

[348] Matt. 4:23 f.; 8:16 f.; 14:35; 15:30 f.; 21:14; Mark 1:32–34; 3:10; 6:51–56; Luke 4:40; 5:17; 6:18 f.; 9:11, etc.

[349] This is admitted by several Rationalist interpreters; among others Ewald and O. Holtzmann.

[350] Matt. 8:16 f.

[351] Keim, *Geschichte Jesu von Nazara*, II, 153, acknowledges that "the Gospels regularly represent the effect of the Savior's word or touch as immediate, as real and not at all illusory."

Yet the Rationalists still deny, refusing to yield to the evidence, although they are, of course, constrained to make a few vague concessions to the truth and on this point to modify their system. They no longer venture to reject *en masse,* as they formerly did, the historic character of these cures, which are too well attested to be reasonably regarded as the invention of the early Church. One of them writes as follows: "Judged by the methods of criticism, the ministry of healing rests upon as solid historic ground as the best accredited parts of the Savior's teaching." [352] It necessarily forms an integral portion of the "irreducible residue" which the most intransigent criticism accepts as real. "In most cases, Jesus' curative act is so interwoven with undoubtedly authentic words, that it is impossible to separate these two elements. His popularity bears witness that the ministry of healing was a very notable fact in His life." Our Lord certainly "performed wonderful cures, and evidently a very large number of them." [353] This is now admitted by most Rationalists. In this sense they are pleased to call Him "Wonderful Doctor," "Wonderful Physician," [354] on condition that these titles be not given any supernatural significance. And they sometimes add, by way of expressing their thought more exactly, that at that time "every wise man was a physician" and, as "the popular practice of medicine was flourishing in all its forms," it is not surprising that Jesus concerned Himself about diseases after the manner of a physician, and that He

---

[352] P. W. Schmiedel in Cheyne's *Encyclopedia Biblica,* II, col. 2445. Cf. Weizsäcker, *Untersuchungen über die evangelische Geschichte,* 2d ed., p. 231. See also Sanday, *Outlines of the Life of Christ,* pp. 105–109.

[353] Traub, *Die Wunder im N. T.,* p. 41. Cf. J. Weiss, *Die Schriften des N. T.,* I, 112; P. Wernle, *Die Anfänge unserer Religion,* 2d ed., p. xiii; A. Neumann, *Jesus, wer er geschichtlich war,* p. 100, etc.

[354] *Wunderdoktor, Wunderarzt.* Sometimes they add that Jesus was at first surprised at these cures and that therein He saw a sign of His Messianic vocation. Others, on the contrary, say that He was "a physician in spite of Himself," and that this rôle was always a burden to Him.

performed "merely natural" [355] cures. Taking a detail from the ultra-Rationalist Paulus, these critics even say that Jesus "did not disdain to employ the customary remedies of His time." [356]

But this sort of explanation is so evidently false that even many Rationalists protest against it. "The Gospel narrative," they say, "does not describe the cures wrought by Jesus as something natural, that is, as the method of a physician who uses remedies adapted to the diseases." [357] In curing the sick, Jesus made use of no intermediary, no instrument, no vegetable or mineral medicine, He employed no formula of words, magical or otherwise. No one will seriously offer the objection that in two cases,[358] when restoring sight to the blind, He placed a little saliva on their eyes, because that certainly was not an effective remedy.

Though accepting the historical character of the cures performed by the Savior, the Liberal theologians of whom we have just been speaking refuse to consider them as miraculous events. To explain them in a purely natural way, "they have adopted a very subtle and apparently clever theory, which they base on pathological phenomena which have had a great vogue in our day and which have been the subject of special studies by celebrated physicians. Granted, they say, that Jesus was not an ordinary physician; that He was far ahead of the healing art as it existed in His time, anticipating a therapeutic method which, thanks to modern psychology, has now become the possession of all. His cures were psychical cures, attributable simply to moral influence, to suggestion, to hypnotism. They were, therefore, in no way miraculous, since they were produced by means similar to those now employed in

[355] J. Weiss, op. cit., p. 44.

[356] P. Wernle, op. cit., p. 65.

[357] Weizsäcker, Untersuchungen, p. 236; T. Keim, Geschichte Jesu, II, 157; Bousset, Jesus, p. 23, etc.

[358] Mark 8:23; John 9:6. See also Mark 8:23.

hospitals and clinics where nervous diseases are treated." [359]
This is what we hear repeated by the leaders of the modern
Rationalist party and their disciples. Bousset says: "We may
well apply the epithet 'psychical' to Christ's therapeutical
method. He transmitted so powerful a shock to the forces of
the inner life that they acted from within outwardly upon the
bodily life. He was able to awaken in the sick and suffering
an absolute confidence in Himself as the envoy of God. Thus
His curative methods are perfectly understandable from the
psychological point of view," [360] and for this reason, they
lose their whole miraculous character in the eyes of Rationalists.

The disciples surpass their masters in gratuitous assertions
and misleading insinuations, intended to give a semblance of
truth to their thesis. One of them says: "We may suppose that
Jesus was a person gifted with a dominating intellectual power,
an imposing figure, a commanding voice. We will then understand many things." [361] Another of them, on the contrary,
connects Christ's medical influence with His great gentleness.
"We learn that Jesus cured many sick people. Who could deny
it? We ought, as vividly as possible, picture this simple fact to
ourselves: He had in Him the complete peace of God; upon
His face shone holy, unselfish love, pure goodness; from His
whole being radiated a heavenly peace; and He, who bore in
Himself the peace of God as no other ever bore it, stood in
the midst of a race that was extremely agitated. The people
of His time with feverish impatience were expecting the coming of a Messias. Long hope and daily expectancy had shaken
the nerves of thousands of persons, and provoked a great
amount of pathological phenomena." [362] We can surmise the

[359] Fillion, *Les Miracles de Notre-Seigneur*, II, 91.
[360] *Jesus*, p. 23. See also Pfleiderer, *Die Entstehung des Christentums*, p. 18;
H. Schaefer, M. D., *Jesus in psychiatrischer Beleuchtung*, pp. 58–68.
[361] O. Schmiedel, *Die Hauptprobleme der Leben-Jesu-Forschung*, 2d ed., p. 44.
[362] K. Furrer, *Vorträge über das Leben Jesu Christi*, p. 126.

rest: Jesus cured a number of these nervous cases by suggestion, by quieting their nerves through His own suavity.[363]

But where was it ascertained that Christ had an imposing presence and a commanding voice? In what documentary source do we read that Palestine in our Lord's time was a sort of vast Salpetrière, full of hysterical people? And through what extraordinary coincidence did it happen that all the sick people with whom Christ had dealings were afflicted with nervous diseases? True, the Messianic expectancy was then very keen; but no one can prove that it brought about thousands of cases of the pathological ailments which these critics talk about.

We do not deny that in various instances Jesus began by arousing the faith of those who asked, or to whom He wished spontaneously to grant, a supernatural cure. "Do you believe that I can do this unto you?" He asked the two blind men who were imploring Him to restore their sight; and upon their answering in the affirmative, He said: "According to your faith, be it done unto you." [364] "If thou canst believe, all things are possible to him that believeth," He said to the father of the young lunatic.[365] The faith of the sick or of those who brought them to Him greatly moved the heart of the divine Miracle-worker,[366] who several times declared that their faith had coöperated in their cure.[367] On the other hand, the

---

[363] Renan, *Vie* (populaire) *de Jésus*, p. 178, proclaims this easy theory: "The presence of a man of superior type, treating a sick person with gentleness and by some outward signs giving assurance of his restoration to health, is frequently a decisive remedy. Who would venture to say that in many a case, outside quite well defined lesions, the contact with a charming person is not worth as much as all the resources of a pharmacy? The pleasure of seeing such a one brings about a cure. Such a person gives what he can, a smile, a hope, and this is not in vain." These are clever words, which prove nothing.

[364] Matt. 9: 28 f.

[365] Mark 9: 22. See also Luke 8: 50; John 6: 35; 11: 26.

[366] Cf. Matt. 8: 5–10; 9: 2; 15: 22–28; Mark 5: 28.

[367] Matt. 9: 22 f.; Luke 18: 41 f., etc.

absence or imperfection of that faith grieved His soul [368] and
to some extent prevented Him from giving free reign to
His supernatural activity.[369] Was it not just and fitting that
He should miraculously grant the blessing of health only to
those who showed themselves worthy of it by their belief in
His divine mission?

The Rationalist critics claim to see, in this special circumstance, a confirmation of their contention regarding the extraordinary cures which they are forced to admit as real. According to them, those cures were caused by what they call
"the dynamic of faith." They say that "earnest faith, in this
matter being identical with suggestion, can cure all nervous
diseases and can occasion a temporary amelioration in diseases
of every kind. . . . The Evangelists' accounts of miraculous
cures are the naïve and exaggerated expression of events that
used to be mysterious, but that are now quite explicable.
Hence there is really nothing miraculous in them. It would
be possible to cite multitudes of similar cures, effected either
by hypnotism or by suggestion." [370]

To refute these assertions with greater authority and to
prove that the cures performed by the Savior have nothing in
common with those brought about through the intermediary
of suggestion and hypnotism, we will take our stand on the
testimony of competent and unbiased physicians.[371] Our adversaries are satisfied with vague general assertions. They
offer us "a number of quite commonplace allusions to the
power of mind over body, and we find a complacent conviction . . . to the effect that a certain class of disorders which

368 Matt. 14: 31; Luke 8: 25; John 4: 48, etc.
369 Matt. 13: 58; Mark 6: 5 f.
370 Giran, *Jésus de Nazareth*, p. 85.
371 R. J. Ryle, in the *Hibbert Journal*, April, 1907, pp. 572 ff., published a very
substantial article entitled, "The Neurotic Theory of the Miracles of Healing."
See also K. Knur, *Christus Medicus?*

are vaguely alluded to as 'nervous' are promptly curable by emotional methods. But we do not find any recognition of the fact that only a small portion of the diseases to which human flesh is heir are nervous diseases: and that of nervous diseases, again, only a very small and unimportant group admit of cure in this way." [372] The Rationalists make great pretense, but they have not delved beneath the surface of the question.

First they forget, or they never knew, that with two or three exceptions [373] the diseases cured by our Lord did not belong to the "very small and unimportant group" of those which are susceptible of being treated by what is called moral therapeutics. What connection is there between psychotherapy and leprosy, blindness, fever from which the patient is at the point of death, dropsy, deafness, dumbness, a bleeding wound? Surely no such connection exists, especially if it be a question of suddenly and completely banishing these various ailments.

Secondly, the method used by Christ in effecting His miraculous cures sets them quite apart from that of suggesters or hypnotists. Faith does indeed play a part therein; but there is no relation between it and the methods of moral therapeutics. It was not faith that cured; faith was only a condition. In a small and very irreligious work [374] Dr. Charcot says that for the exercise of faith-healing we need special subjects and special diseases, those which are cases of the influence of mind over body. Ryle remarks: "We do not find reason to believe that the works of healing [in the Gospels] were instances of faith-healing. The cases are too numerous, and they are not of the sort among which we look for cures of the faith-healing kind." [375]

---

[372] Ryle, *loc. cit.*, p. 575.

[373] We refer to the cases of paralysis mentioned by the Synoptics: Matt. 9: 1-8 and parallel passages; John 5: 1-9. See also Matt. 12: 9-14 and parallel texts.

[374] *La Foi qui guérit*, p. 37.

[375] *Ibid.*, p. 583.

Thirdly, the most competent specialists in nervous diseases and psychotherapy honestly acknowledge that "the suggestion treatment is very often powerless to cure cases of this sort, especially when the ailment is an old one, and when the nervous system has contracted the invincible habit of the ailment," [376] or when the long duration of the pathological nervous state has produced organic lesions.[377] Furthermore, "it must be said that the results obtained are temporary; suggestion can restore the function, provided the lesion has not yet definitely destroyed it, and provided the functional disturbance is only an organic trouble independent of the lesion; suggestion does not check the organic progress of the disease; frequently it only produces a transitory improvement, . . . and a time comes when suggestion can no longer accomplish anything in the case." [378] Such is the teaching of independent and experienced physicians. Therefore if Jesus had used only moral therapeutics, He would have met with frequent failure, which would soon have become widely known, whereas He always met with success, whatever the character and previous duration of the diseases.

Such, in brief, is the present theory of the Rationalist critics with regard to the cures performed by our Lord. They admit the reality of a great number of them, but they take pains to eliminate the miraculous element. They fall into other specific errors when they consider each cure separately. In some cases they minimize the nature of the disease as much as possible; in other cases they question the extent and duration of the cure; again, on the ground that certain dieases, such as tuberculosis, typhus, and diphtheria, are not mentioned by the Evangelists, they conclude that the Savior's healing power was imperfect; in still other cases they claim, with no reason

[376] Dr. Bernheim, *Hypnotisme, Suggestion,* 1st ed., p. 393.
[377] *Ibid.,* p. 325.
[378] *Ibid.,* p. 355.

but their own ill-will, that the early Church transformed certain figurative expressions of the Savior [379] into miraculous cures; others reject, as obvious exaggerations, cures *en masse* and cures performed at a distance. It is easy to see that these are vain sophisms, which a fair-minded reading of the Gospels refutes. [380]

3. The curing of demoniacs.—Rationalists of all classes energetically deny the reality of diabolical possession and, consequently, of the supernatural delivery of possessed persons by our Lord. The Evangelists, as all the Jews of that time, the Fathers of the Church, and all orthodox Christians have attributed certain phenomena to diabolical possession. But, according to the Rationalist critics, these phenomena were purely material, and were owing to insanity, epilepsy, hysteria, in short to nervous diseases which Jesus cured by natural methods, without performing any real miracles. Bousset, [381] summing up the thought of his predecessors, [382] says: "The demoniacs we recognize, with the plainest evidence, as insane persons," over whom Jesus possessed "an extraordinary influence"; and Albert Réville [383] tells us that this influence was by means of "moral therapeutics as much as, or more than, physical therapeutics." The Savior was, then, only a "wonderful doctor," nothing else. Eminent but unbelieving physicians have unfortunately adopted this theory, and have likewise been willing to see in diabolical possession only a

[379] For example, the words: "They that are in health need not a physician, but they that are ill," Matt. 9 : 12; "If the blind lead the blind, both fall into the pit," Matt. 15 : 14. But how can these clear and simple sayings, which are not connected with any miracle in the Gospel narratives, be altered into false cures?

[380] We have refuted them in our work, *Les Miracles de Notre-Seigneur*, II, 104–235.

[381] *Jesus*, p. 24 f.

[382] Especially that of Strauss, *Leben Jesu*, II, 5–21; K. Hase, *Geschichte Jesu*, 2d ed., II, 436–443; Renan, *Vie de Jésus*, pp. 261–264.

[383] *Jésus de Nazareth*, II, 77. See also Harnack, *Wesen des Christentums*, p. 37; H. J. Holtzmann, *Die Synoptiker*, 2d ed., p. 73; J. Weiss, *Die Schriften des N. T.*, I, 72–75; A. Loisy, *Les Évangiles Synoptiques*, I, 207, etc.

"pathological state," in which "major hysteria" played the chief part, "under most varied forms."[384]

The frequent association of some natural disease with diabolical possession has given the Rationalists occasion to deny the reality of that supernatural condition. But possession was not always accompanied by some real disease. Moreover, many of the effects which the Evangelists mention in the case of demoniacs cannot be classed among those which are the result of an ordinary disease or infirmity. Which is the disease that enables a patient to break iron chains?[385] What disease, after afflicting a man for a long time and just as it is about to disappear, violently hurls him to the ground so that he appears to be lifeless?[386] The Savior's biographers never mistake possessed persons for sick people. On the contrary, they clearly distinguish between these two categories of human sufferers, and they speak of demoniacs separately, as forming a special, well-marked class.[387] In no instance do they suppose that all diseases and infirmities were caused by devils. The critics, by way of objection, say that the Jews of that time had fallen into superstitious beliefs and practices about Satan, the bad angels, and exorcisms for driving them out.[388] But there are essential differences between the demonology of the Gospels and that of contemporary Judaism, between the method used by Jesus for driving out devils, and the method of Jewish exorcists.

According to the Gospel accounts, it is evident that the Savior believed in the personal existence of devils and in their power, with God's permission, to seize upon certain men,

[384] Charcot and Rechet, *Les Démoniaques dans l'Art*, pp. vi and 136.
[385] Mark 5 : 3 f.
[386] Mark 9 : 25.
[387] Cf. Matt. 4 : 24; Mark 1 : 32; Luke 4 : 40 f.; 6 : 18.
[388] On this point, see Josephus, *Ant.*, VIII, ii, 2; *Bell. Jud.*, VII, vi, 3; the Talmud, tractates *Shabbath*, 14, 3, and *Abodah zarah*, 12, 2; W. Bousset, *Die Religion des Judentums im neutestam. Zeitalter*, pp. 331–333; L. Blau, *Das altjüdische Zauberwesen*, 1898.

by the phenomenon called "possession." When Jesus is shown freeing the demoniacs, it is not the latter whom He threatens and whom He drives out with authority.[389] Like the sacred writers, He, too, makes an explicit distinction between possessed persons and the sick.[390] When His enemies accuse Him of holding from Satan the power that enabled Him to drive out the devils, His irresistibly forceful apology is based on the reality of the evil spirits and of possessions.[391] An eminent English exegete says: "If the demons were not there, and demoniacal possession is a superstition, we must choose between three hypotheses. (1) Jesus did not employ this method of healing those who were believed to be possessed, but the Evangelists have erroneously attributed it to Him. (2) Jesus did employ this method and went through the form of casting out demons, although He knew that there were no demons there to be cast out. (3) Jesus did employ this method and went through the form of casting out demons, because in this matter He shared the erroneous belief of His contemporaries." [392] As none of these hypotheses is tenable, we must say that at that time in Palestine there really were many possessed persons and that Jesus freed some of them by His miraculous power.[393]

4. Miraculous resurrections.—The Gospels contain specific mention of only three cases of this sort. According to the most probable chronological order, they are: the resurrection of the widow's son at Naim; [394] that of Jairus' daughter; [395] and that

[389] Matt. 8:32; Mark 1:25; 5:13; 9:24; Luke 4:35; 8:29–32, etc.

[390] Luke 13:32 is especially clear: "Behold, I cast out devils, and do cures . . ."

[391] Matt. 12:26–28; Mark 3:23–27; Luke 11:18–22.

[392] A. Plummer, *A Critical and Exegetical Commentary on the Gospel according to St. Luke*, p. 136.

[393] For the refutation of the rationalist errors relative to each of the seven special cases of expulsion related in the Gospels, see our work, *Les Miracles de Notre-Seigneur*, II, 262–310; F. Vigouroux, *Les Livres Saints et la Critique Rationaliste*, 5th ed., V, 386–395.

[394] Luke 7:11–17.

[395] Matt. 9:23–26; Mark 5:35–48; Luke 8:49–56.

of Lazarus.[396] This class of miracles contains the most brilliant manifestation of the Savior's power. It shows Him to be the true "Prince of life." [397] We are, therefore, not surprised that the Rationalists, and those who take their watchword from them in matters of exegesis or theology, absolutely deny the truth of the Gospel narrative in these cases.

First, they state a general reason: the resurrection of the dead is in itself impossible. This is the opinion, not only of the most advanced Rationalists, but also of most critics who call themselves Liberal.[398] One of them says: "This class of miracles surpasses anything that can be imagined or that can be historically admitted." [399] We have no occasion to repeat here the philosophical and theological arguments proving the possibility of the resurrection of the dead. We will say nothing of the numerous similar facts of an undeniable historic character, but will merely offer, in opposition to the Rationalist assertion, the three cases related by the Evangelists. But we must again repeat that these writers are conscientious, well-informed historians, who recount what they saw with their own eyes (St. Matthew and St. John), or what they received from the most trustworthy witnesses (St. Mark and St. Luke). An eminent member of the medical profession says that "for a physician who attentively considers the facts, Christ's curing of the sick is of such a nature that only a little step separates it from the raising of the dead. We receive the impression that here is the Master of life and death." [400] This little step was an easy one for Christ's almighty power.

But the Rationalists, both ancient and modern, go further and claim that from the texts of the Gospel we must hold that,

---

[396] John 11: 1-44.
[397] Acts 3: 15, according to the Greek text.
[398] Among others, Harnack, Holtzmann, J. Weiss, Schmiedel, Loisy.
[399] R. Otto, *Das Leben und Wirken Jesu*, p. 34. Cf. Keim, *Geschichte Jesu*, II, 470.
[400] K. Knur, M. D., *Christus Medicus?* p. 74.

in the three cases cited by the Evangelists, death was only apparent and not real, and that the deceased were merely in a state of more or less prolonged lethargy. Following Renan, the more recent critics insist upon the need of an official statement, proving that the death and resurrection were real. Professor O. Holtzmann, speaking of the resurrection of Jairus' daughter, says: "Here again we lack an accurate medical account of the disease, apparent death, and return to life." [401] But are physicians the only ones competent to testify as to a case of death? Jesus did say, upon entering the room where the dead girl's body was lying: "The girl is not dead, but sleepeth," [402] as He also said to His Apostles, when word was brought to Him of Lazarus' death: "Lazarus our friend sleepeth; but I go that I may awake him out of sleep." [403] Nevertheless, it is evident that the words were simply a euphemism, well suited to the occasion, since He was at once going to call the girl and Lazarus back to life. The girl's death was so manifest that the people who were present, when they heard the Savior's words, "laughed Him to scorn"; St. Luke, who as a physician is careful about details, adds that the people did this, "knowing that she was dead." [404] In the case of Lazarus, we have the protesting words of his sister Martha: "Lord, by this time he stinketh, for he is now of four days." [405] Nor can there be any doubt as to a real death in the case of the widow's son. Would it not be strange that Jesus should have had to do only with persons apparently dead in these three cases of resurrection? If those to whom He is supposed to have restored life were merely in a state of catalepsy, it must be said that He was wonderfully served by chance,

[401] *Life of Jesus*, p. 273.
[402] Matt. 9:24.
[403] John 11:11-13.
[404] Luke 8:53.
[405] John 11:39.

since He was so fortunate in the choice of these persons to be raised to life.[406]

We quote Doctor Knur's words, which draw attention to other impossibilities in the Rationalist theory. She says: "It is highly improbable that, in the resurrection of the dead as effected by Christ, we have cases of apparent death. A lethargy that is mistaken for death and that, by means of a simple spoken word, is suddenly changed into a complete cure, is not to be found in the experience of physicians. . . . Even in the most complete lethargy, the heart still beats, although very feebly; breathing continues, although in a very light manner; the stiffness of the members may simulate the *rigor mortis,* but the wetness and coldness of the body are lacking (the bodily temperature often rises above normal). Furthermore, in most cases, isolated indications of life are observed by those present: the moving of the eyelids, a change in the direction of the patient's look, etc. We should also remark that a complete lethargy develops only gradually." [407] Therefore so gross a mistake was not possible in the cases related by the Evangelists.

St. Irenaeus [408] drew the attention of his fellow-Christians to the fact that, in these three miracles of resurrection, our Lord's power was shown with increasing intensity. He raises to life a girl who had just been stricken by death; then a young man who was being borne to the cemetery; lastly a full-grown man, who had been buried for several days. The critics

[406] The following reflection by the rationalist Zeller (a disciple of Ferdinand Christian Baur) retains its full value: "To admit this hypothesis [of a lethargy], you must be able to believe that, in the short space of time embraced within the Gospel history, there was five times repeated—three times in the Gospels and twice in the Acts of the Apostles (Acts 9: 36–42 and 20: 6–12)—this same circumstance, this same remarkable chance of a lethargy which, though remaining unperceived by all those who had to do with the corpse, yielded at the first word of the divine envoy and gave occasion for belief in a real resurrection."

[407] Knur, *Christus Medicus?* p. 72.

[408] *Adv. Haer.,* V, xiii, 1.

use this circumstance as a basis for their assertion that the accounts have been falsified and exaggerated and the miracles enlarged. The resurrection of Jairus' daughter, they say,[409] is "in the positive degree"; that of the widow's son, "in the comparative"; that of Lazarus, "in the superlative." This gradation is said to be deliberate and systematic; consequently it is not to be trusted. But the objection is groundless, because the sacred writers make no reference to this symmetry; and St. Luke, who is the only one to relate two of these resurrection miracles, speaks of the widow's son before mentioning the daughter of Jairus. Consequently he had no idea of indicating a progressive series.

The four Evangelists in these instances are as simple and objective as they are everywhere else, apparently no more moved at the sight of the dead brought back to life than they are in the presence of the sick people restored to health. Besides this testimony we have that of the earliest ecclesiastical tradition, which is of priceless value to us. The earliest Fathers or apologists, such as Quadratus, Papias, St. Justin, and Origen, mention as a most firm belief of the Christians of their day that Jesus had raised several persons from the dead; they even affirm that some of these persons were still alive at the beginning of the second century.[410] This testimony supplements and guarantees that of the Gospels.[411]

XIV. The Reasons for the Embassy from John the Baptist to Jesus

Tertullian goes far astray on this point: but curious and erroneous views often disfigure his best treatises. On the ques-

[409] H. J. Holtzmann, *Die Synoptiker*, 2d ed., p. 158.

[410] See Eusebius, *H. E.*, IV, 3; St. Justin, *Dial. cum Tryph.*, 69; Origen, *Contra Celsum*, 2, 18; Harnack, *Texte und Untersuchungen*, Vol. V, Part II, p. 70.

[411] For a more detailed refutation of the Rationalist errors regarding our Lord's raising of the dead, see Fillion, *Les Miracles de Notre-Seigneur*, II, 335–392.

tion now before us, he declares that, after the descent of the
Holy Ghost upon Jesus at the time of His baptism, that same
Spirit, which theretofore had guided and enlightened the pre-
cursor, left him and reserved all His gifts for the Messias.
Thus abandoned to his own lights, John was shaken in His be-
lief about Jesus.[412]

In recent times, under various forms, it has likewise been
held that the Baptist had real doubts about our Lord's Messianic character. We are told that the holiest persons in the
Bible passed through hours of discouragement and even of
weakness. Why should the Baptist be exempted? A long and
trying stay in the prison of Machaerus had gradually diminished his strength. Beset by countless perplexities about his
own office and that of Jesus, in a moment of distress he feared
that his cousin was not really the Christ. Then it was that, in
an attempt to reassure himself, he deputed two of his disciples to go to Jesus and obtain a clear explanation from Him.
But all this is mere psychological romance, which the sacred
texts upset, instead of furnishing any basis for it. Jesus
plainly declared that John was not a reed easily shaken; the
Baptist did not change his mind about the Messias.

The Evangelists themselves refute H. J. Holtzmann,[413] J.
Weiss,[414] and others[415] who invent the following theory to
explain the question which the Baptist's messengers ask Jesus.
The step taken by John was not at all the result of any doubt
in his mind; on the contrary, it marked the beginning of faith
in his cousin's Messianic character. In his prison cell, he was
awaiting news of the results produced by his personal ministry; and lo, of a sudden he learns that Jesus, who had been
baptized by him, was performing wonderful miracles. There-

[412] *De Baptismo*, 10; *Contra Marcion.*, IV, 18.
[413] *Die Synoptiker*, 3d ed., p. 66.
[414] *Die Schriften des N. T.*, I, 291.
[415] Notably Loisy, *Les Évangiles Synoptiques*, I, 660, and A. Réville, *Jésus de
Nazareth*, II, 114.

upon he entertains great hopes about this miracle-worker so clearly blessed by God; thinking that Jesus might indeed be the Messias, he sends two of his disciples to question Him on this point. But that was merely a hope, a strong suspicion; we shall never know what was John's final judgment about Jesus.—This whole theory is mere psychology. Do not St. Matthew and St. John tell us that at the very moment when the precursor baptized Jesus, he clearly recognized Him as the Messias?[416] This may be granted, Loisy replies; but St. Matthew "actually forgets" what he wrote above, and in this passage "conforms to another document which had come to his hands." It is a very poor hypothesis that needs to resort to such "proofs."

Without going so far as that, some Protestant exegetes think they have discovered in the situation described by St. Matthew and St. Luke, the indications, if not of a formal doubt that crept into the precursor's mind about Jesus' office, at least a certain dissatisfaction or impatience. John continued to look upon Him as the Christ; but he took the liberty of passing judgment on Jesus' conduct and thought the Savior was filling His high office too mildly. Why did He not openly declare who He was? Why did He not at once found His kingdom, after the manner indicated by John himself, that is, by the condemnation and punishment of the wicked?[417] The Baptist, by putting this question to Jesus, intended simply to stimulate Him and accelerate His advance.—Although this opinion is more moderate, it must be rejected like the two preceding ones, and for the same reasons. Against it are the Gospel accounts, which nowhere mention the least sign of impatience in the precursor's soul, nor, a fortiori, any indication of disapproval touching the Savior's conduct. And those same

[416] Matt. 3: 13-15; John 1: 29-34.
[417] Cf. K. Hase, *Geschichte Jesu*, 2d ed., p. 388; Godet, *Comment. sur l'Évangile de S. Luc*, I, 430; Plummer, *op. cit.*, p. 160.

narratives always show the Baptist as very humble, effacing himself before Him whom he did not for a moment cease to regard as the mystical Bridegroom, and considering himself as only the friend of the Bridegroom. The various feelings attributed to John in order to explain his embassy are without any foundation in fact and make it incomprehensible rather than clarify it.

XV. The Two Anointings of Jesus: by the Sinful Woman and by Mary, the Sister of Lazarus

From the earliest periods attempts have been made to identify the two anointings. Against this view Origen expressed legitimate protests,[418] which were later repeated by St. John Chrysostom.[419] In our day the identification has still some defenders, especially among the Rationalists. To weaken the historical character of the Gospels by showing that they often distort the facts, these critics seek to increase the number of what they call "doublets," that is, the repetition of the same episodes in a form arbitrarily or unconsciously altered. Thus it is that H. J. Holtzmann accuses St. Luke, who does not relate the anointing by Mary, of inventing that by the sinful woman, by changing the scene related in the other three Gospels: [420] that he did so for an ideal purpose, to contrast with an act performed by a legally pure person (Mary of Bethania) in a legally impure house (that of Simon the leper), the act of an impure woman (the sinful woman) in a pure house (that of Simon the Pharisee). And so St. Luke is said to have further emphasized Christ's kindness to repentant sinners: this is a well-known characteristic feature of the Third Gospel. The strange theory is as gratuitous as it is complex.

[418] *Tractat. in Matth.*, XXXV.
[419] *Hom. in Joan.*, LX.
[420] Matt. 26:6-13; Mark 14:3-9; John 12:1-11.

If we examine the two incidents more closely, we shall see that everything is opposed to their identification. They offer certain resemblances which consist of the three following details: during a meal, which took place in the home of a Jew named Simon, a woman poured a precious ointment upon Jesus and then dried His feet with her hair. All the other details are different in the two incidents, as ancient and modern commentators alike point out. The dates are not the same: in the Third Gospel, the Savior's public life has not yet advanced very far; in the other accounts, it is at its close. The places are not the same: in one case, a city of Galilee; in the other, Bethania, close to Jerusalem. And there are many further differences. In the one case, a sinful woman of ill-fame, testifying her thanksgiving to Jesus because of His part in her conversion; in the other case, a young woman who belonged to a respectable family, for a long time past beloved by the Savior. In the one case, an anointing of the feet only, accompanied by tears and kisses; in the other case, an anointing of the head first, then of the feet. In one case, Jesus tells the woman of her forgiveness; in the other, He prophesies that Mary's act will be made known throughout the world. In one case, some are shocked because of the pardon granted by our Lord; but no one protests, as Judas does at Bethania, against the so-called waste of the ointment. Although both anointings took place at the home of a Jew called Simon, this coincidence is not at all surprising, since that name was then one of the commonest in Palestine; [421] moreover, the two hosts are distinguished from each other, one being called a Pharisee, the other, a leper. And the repetition of an anointing of this sort is *in se* not unlikely; it would be natural that the first of them, being widely reported, might occasion the second, on the part

---

[421] The New Testament mentions more than ten persons of this name; Josephus refers to at least twenty. Cf. Zahn, *Das Evangelium des Lucas ausgelegt*, p. 335, note 36.

of a holy friend of Jesus. For these reasons, which might easily be further developed, we must regard both events as historic and quite distinct.[422]

XVI. Christ Regarded as a Fanatic, as a Madman

Without entering into obnoxious details, we cannot fail to mention here, since our plan is partly apologetical and polemical, certain comparatively recent works whose authors have of their own accord repeated, with developments and an attempt to justify it, the insult ἐξέστη addressed to Jesus. In these pitiful writings, the authors are not ashamed to consider the Divine Master, not merely as an extreme enthusiast or fanatic from the religious point of view, as an "ecstatic," that is, a sort of *"illuminatus,"* a more or less misled dreamer,[423] but also as a madman, a common fool, who should have received the treatment accorded to the insane.[424] These books, of course, aroused the contempt and disgust which they deserved; the Liberal theologians were not the slowest in refuting them.[425] It is none the less true that they are a sad indication of the times in which we live.[426]

XVII. The Visit of Mary and the "Brethren"

Those Rationalist critics, being the majority of them, who are pleased to represent Jesus as having early had misunder-

---

[422] See Lagrange in the *Revue Biblique,* 1912, pp. 481–504.

[423] O. Holtzmann, *War Jesus Ekstatiker?* 1903; J. Baumann, *Die Gemütsart Jesu . . . erkenntlich gemacht,* 1908.

[424] J. Soury, *Jésus et les Évangiles,* 2d ed., 1878; Dr. de Looster, *Jesus Christus vom Standpunkt des Psychiaters,* 1905; E. Rasmussen, *Jesus: eine vergleichende psychopathologische Studie,* 1905.

[425] Among the best replies, we cite those of a Catholic professor, Philipp Kneib, *Moderne Leben-Jesu-Forschung unter dem Einflusse der Psychiatrie,* 1908; a Protestant minister, H. Werner, *Die psychische Gesundheit Jesu,* 1909; and a Rationalist physician, Dr. H. Schäfer, *Jesus in psychiatrischer Beleuchtung,* 1910.

[426] See our *Étapes du Rationalisme,* pp. 243 f., 257 f.

standings with His kinsfolk, even with His mother, seize upon this episode and its preliminaries, such as related by the three Synoptics, in the hope of finding therein a basis for their contention and with the purpose of attacking the filial veneration which the Catholic Church has always paid to the Blessed Virgin. They cite three texts for use against us. The first records the steps taken by those whom St. Mark calls οἱ παρ αὐτοῦ to seize Jesus by force, on the pretext that He was mad (ἐξέστη). The second text consists of the Savior's reply to the woman who had declared His mother to be blessed: "Yea rather, blessed are they who hear the word of God, and keep it." [427] The third text comprises the words which close the episode: "Who is My mother, and who are My brethren? . . . Whosoever shall do the will of My Father, that is in heaven, he is My brother and sister and mother." Although the natural and honest interpretation that we have already given these texts refutes the Rationalist objections, let us examine the latter more closely, to show that they are groundless.

Oscar Holtzmann sums them up in comparatively moderate terms: [428] "They [our Lord's mother and brethren] had heard in Nazareth of His ever-increasing activity. At an earlier date they were, we may suppose, annoyed that Jesus, when He left John [the Baptist], did not return home and resume His handicraft. They may indeed have been gratified with the great success of His preaching, perhaps also with His work of healing; but when He caused offence and ill-will by forgiving sins, by associating with outcasts, by disregarding pious customs, and, still, worse, by openly scorning the Law, we can easily understand that His family suffered by it and were ready to believe that Jesus had taken leave of his senses (ὅτι ἐξέστη, Mark 3: 20 f.). . . . What form the further discussion between Him and His family took, we do not know.

[427] Luke 11 : 27 f.
[428] *Life of Jesus*, p. 248.

But what we can say with certainty is that Jesus did not at the time go with them to Nazareth (Mark 3: 31–53), and that neither His mother nor His brethren nor His sisters attached themselves to His following during His lifetime. It sounds like repudiation when, in answer to the blessing pronounced upon His mother (Luke 11: 27: 'Blessed is the womb that bare Thee, and the breasts which Thou didst suck'), Jesus utters the solemn words, 'Yea, rather, blessed are they that hear God's word and keep it.' " [429]

What errors these lines contain! But let us reply in order. (1) The critics pretend to identify the Savior's mother and brethren with those who had come to seize Him as a man suffering hallucinations, as a madman.[430] Yet St. Mark's account is most explicitly opposed to this hypothesis. He mentions, as coming to Jesus one after the other, three different groups: that of the Scribes and Pharisees, whom the Divine Master reduced to silence after their hateful calumny; the group which is represented by the expression οἱ παρ' αὐτοῦ; and that consisting of our Lord's mother and brethren. We have a very clear idea of this third group. The same is not true of the second, because, as we said in connection with this incident when describing it in its proper place in the narrative, the phrase οἱ παρ' αὐτοῦ is a bit vague and may apply equally well to kinsmen, whether closely or distantly related, and to simple disciples. It matters little, however.

The essential point here is that the Evangelist completely separates them from our Lord's mother and brethren. He distinguishes them by different appellations. The former he shows arriving at the beginning of the episode, the others at its close; the former coming to seize Him, the others merely

---

[429] In his short work, *War Jesus Ekstatiker?* p. 122, the same author repeats this opinion, but with much less moderation. See also P. W. Schmidt, *Die Geschichte Jesu erzählt*, p. 81; A. Réville, *Jésus de Nazareth*, II, 110.

[430] A rather large number of more or less orthodox Protestants make this same identification, although with reservations, as we note below.

asking to speak with Him: a whole interlude [431] separates them in the narrative. What right has anyone to unite them in one and the same group? Since the two groups are so distant, it is evident that the critics lay a most unjust accusation upon the mother of Christ, since they associate her with the violent measures of the second group and with the gratuitous insult contained in their absurd supposition: "He is become mad." "According to what we otherwise know of Mary, we must absolutely deny that she placed herself in any way whatsoever in opposition to Jesus." [432] If anyone will read the Gospels carefully and impartially, he will perceive not the slightest trace of doubt on her part regarding the nature and mission of her Son, or of any coolness on Jesus' part toward her. [433] After all the revelations she had received, especially her miraculous conception, how could the Blessed Virgin for a single moment have been undecided about her Son? That she was troubled or disquieted when she thought Him menaced by powerful enemies, that she wished to inform herself of the situation, to comfort and reassure herself by having a loving interview with Him, is self-evident, for her heart was that of the fondest of mothers. But it would be unjust to attribute the least imperfection to her step. The Gospel accounts do not sanction it.

(2) There has been equal bias and injustice in the interpretation of Christ's words, "Who is My mother, and who are My brethren? Whosoever shall do the will of My Father, that is in heaven, he is My brother and sister and mother." These words are called "harsh" and "stern," as if they meant: "I no longer have any relatives; I know neither mother nor brethren according to nature." [434] We are told that Jesus' soul was "so completely filled with the importance of His mission

[431] Christ's apologetic discourse (Mark 3 : 23–30).
[432] Wohlenberg, *Das Evangelium des Markus ausgelegt,* p. 110.
[433] B. Weiss, *Leben Jesu,* II, 99.
[434] J. Weiss, *Die Schriften des N. T.,* I, 97.

that it no longer had room for feeling any affectionate interest with regard to His kindred." [435] Another critic writes:
"We here see how Jesus turned aside from His relatives. Because of His prophetic vocation, He separates from His family. But His vocation is not the only reason for this abandonment. He would not have turned from His own, if they had
fulfilled God's will. But Jesus did not reckon His mother and
brethren among those who do God's will. Here again we are
confirmed in the thought that the mother of Jesus was one of
those who did not believe in Him." [436] Where does anyone see
this? What are the premises that justify such a conclusion?

It is only with great repugnance that we cite these assertions, which for us are veritable blasphemies both toward the
Son and toward His mother. But they show how far party
spirit and religious antipathy go with a large number of
contemporary Rationalists. And those declarations are given
out as "results" acquired by science! To Mary are attributed
unmotherly feelings toward Jesus; to Jesus, most harsh declarations to His mother. However, the words in question do
not astonish anyone who has studied the Savior's habitual
teaching and recalls the attitude He always had toward His
mother. The feelings which He expressed in the Temple at
Jerusalem while yet a boy, and at the wedding feast at Cana
as a grown man, are heard again here. In the exercise of His
office, the will of God holds first place, above all other things;
He will not heed any suggestions, even the holiest, of human
nature. His words ring with the same accents as when He
said: "I must be about My Father's business"; to Him it belongs to regulate whatever concerns My ministry. Where in
these words is there evidence that He intended to wound or
humiliate His mother and His near relatives? In the words
of a certain Rationalist, who is by no means devoted to the

---

[435] *Ibid.*
[436] Petersen, *Die wunderbare Geburt des Heilandes,* p. 5.

Blessed Virgin, "It is absurd to conclude from these words that Jesus took no account of family duty." [437]

(3) We must look at the question from the point of view of our Lord's relations, as Messias, toward God, if we are to understand the Savior's reply to the woman who spoke such warm praises of His mother. That woman in the crowd certainly had not the least idea of the heavenly, superhuman character of Mary's maternity. It was a mother congratulating a mother; and the felicitations could not have been better placed. Jesus, in His reply, does not deny their truth; when He corrects them, He does so to make them clearer and still more beautiful. Hence the Church introduces into her liturgy the words, *"Beatus venter qui te portavit, et beata ubera quae suxisti,"* which are to be understood especially in the lofty sense given them by our Lord, who always strove to make His hearers practice the *Sursum corda.* But assuredly, in speaking thus, He had no intention of prophetically condemning what is sometimes falsely and stupidly called "the Mariolatry of Catholics." [438]

XVIII. The Parables

I. Most Rationalists to-day admire the Gospel parables and praise them from a literary point of view and from the standpoint of their spiritual application.[439] But in recent years several erroneous assertions have been made about them.

In passing, we mention the curious view of a few extreme radical critics, who have the audacity to deny the authenticity of the Savior's parables,[440] and who attribute their

[437] A. Réville, *Jésus de Nazareth,* II, 110.

[438] On the questions treated in this Appendix, see the excellent remarks of Dr. B. Bartmann, *Christus ein Gegner des Marienkultus?* pp. 95–122.

[439] Except, however, as will be said below, with regard to certain "eschatological" parables and their descriptions of the end of the world.

[440] Among others, Arthur Drews, who goes so far as to maintain that Jesus Christ never existed. See our *Étapes du Rationalisme,* pp. 322–350.

composition to the early Church. Even in the Liberal school of exegesis and theology protests are made against such an assertion, which violates the most firmly established laws of literary and historical criticism. As may be easily demonstrated, the parables "are to be counted among the most secure and best preserved elements that we possess in the discourses of Jesus"; [441] "they undoubtedly go back to Jesus Himself." It is true that many Liberal theologians suppose that the Evangelists have done some "retouching," with regard to the parables, as well as other parts of the Savior's life; but this theory never has been and never will be proved. [442] Weinel has no justification for declaring that "we can say but little as to the form of Jesus' parables, and this little we must say with much wariness, because both the oral and the written tradition altered the form of the accounts in several ways." [443] On the contrary, the Evangelists have handed down the parables most faithfully, without presuming to add anything. Moreover, it was not a difficult matter to preserve them, so deeply were they impressed upon the memory on account of their great beauty and originality and their dramatic details. No one questions the authenticity of the rabbinical parables, although they were not committed to writing until about two hundred years after Christ and had previously been preserved only by passing from mouth to mouth. Why should we treat otherwise the Savior's parables, which were incorporated in the Gospels thirty years, at the most, after they had been spoken? And do they not fit in perfectly with all we know of our Lord's life and character? It has even been said that they are inimitable and that the Divine Master alone was able to compose them. [444]

[441] Jülicher, *Die Gleichnisreden Jesu*, I, 24. Cf. H. J. Holtzmann, *Die Synoptiker*, 3d ed., p. 70.

[442] See what has been said respecting the authenticity of the Gospels in general and the honesty of their authors, *supra*, Vol. I, p. 35–78.

[443] *Die Gleichnisse Jesu*, 3d ed., p. 77.

[444] Cf. Giebig, *Die Gleichnisreden Jesu*, p. 277.

II. Jülicher is the author of a theory which, despite its arbitrary character and the weakness of its logic, has won many followers in the Rationalist school.[445] He sums up its chief tenets in the following words: "The Evangelists have mistaken notions about the nature and purpose of the parables. They completely fail to grasp the reason for this kind of teaching." [446] The accusation is then developed on the two points complained of. "The idea which the Evangelists have of the nature of the parables is not tenable. The parables are not λόγοι σκοτεινοί (dark discourses) that are always in need of a special λύσις (explanation). If we find them somewhat obscure, the fault is with their imperfect, fragmentary transmission. A perfectly recorded parable does not require a single word of interpretation; it cannot even tolerate such explanation, since everything in it is clear and manifest." [447] The reason why, according to the Evangelists (particularly St. Mark) Jesus for a time made exclusive use of this form of preaching, is (the critics tell us) simply "monstrous." [448] It is "a fatal theory," [449] for "it is impossible that Jesus spoke in parables with the intention of not being understood by a single one of His hearers." [450] A Paul of Tarsus might have had such a notion, but not Jesus; [451] in vain did opposition rise up against Him, "His language was no more altered than was His heart."

Whence, then, came so serious a mistake on the part of the Evangelists? After the Savior's death, it was noted that the parabolic element formed a very considerable part of His preaching, and there was an effort to find reasons for this fact. Although the parable is itself very clear, the contrary

[445] It is set forth in *Die Gleichnisreden Jesu*, 2 vols., 1899.
[446] *Op. cit.*, I, 24.
[447] *Ibid.*, p. 117.
[448] Page 133.
[449] Page 132.
[450] Page 143.
[451] Page 144.

was asserted, namely, that it was more obscure than ordinary speech. And that obscurity was increased by interpolations which Jesus never thought of giving, since He would have judged them useless.

Such, in its most salient points, is the theory of Jülicher and several other critics.[452] Before refuting it directly, we wish to remind the reader that the assertion that early Christian tradition took the liberty of seriously altering the Savior's preaching, is a pure invention. This fact is sufficiently demonstrated at the beginning of this work. We will now reply to the two objections.

1. "It is a fundamental error . . . to declare that parables, properly so called, are in themselves quite clear. . . . It is not true to say that a parable can never be enigmatic and is never in need of interpretation." These words are quoted from Fiebig's work,[453] which he wrote largely as a refutation of Jülicher's theory. It is, indeed, undeniable that in itself all figurative language is obscure, if we have no indication enabling us to understand its import and if the subject to be illumined is but imperfectly known or not actually identified. Thus, although the parable which Nathan proposed to David, after the latter's twofold crime,[454] possesses the greatest clearness for us, the king understood its meaning only when the prophet applied it directly to him, by his terrible: *"Tu es ille vir."* In every comparison we find the same sort of phenomenon: the figure conceals even while it impresses and attracts and explains. This is what we have called the two facets or aspects of the parable.

Certainly some of the parables in the Gospels are easier to

---

[452] We mention particularly H. J. Holtzmann, *Die Synoptiker,* 3d ed., pp. 70–77; A. Loisy, *Les Évangiles Synoptiques,* I, 743, and *Études Évangéliques,* pp. 1–121 ("Les Parables de l'Évangile"); J. Weiss, *Die Schriften des N. T.,* I, 100; O. Frommel, *Die Poesie des Evangeliums Jesu,* pp. 54–57.

[453] *Gleichnisreden Jesu,* p. 128.

[454] 2 Kings 12: 1–4.

understand than others: for example, those of the lost sheep, of the prodigal son, of the dishonest steward. Yet it must be acknowledged that, even in their case, the particular lesson which Jesus implied by them became evident only because He set us on the path of their interpretation. Among the disciples and Apostles there were some very intelligent men, yet they did not always grasp the parables at first sight. They, too, had to be set on the path. It cannot be too often repeated, that "the parable has this double property, to impress the truth deeply in the mind of him who is able to grasp it under the image with which it is clothed, and to veil it from the eyes of a slothful or inattentive listener, whose mind does not seek to penetrate the covering which envelops it." [455]

The critics are guilty of a curious exaggeration when they claim that a parable, by its very nature, excludes all obscurity. But their theory needed to be bolstered, and they have advanced this proof, which is certainly false, for the simple reason that the "Gospel parable . . . treats of supernatural truths, which are inaccessible to the human mind." [456]

2. Another exaggeration is to found in the statement that the Evangelists say that the Savior chose this new form of teaching purposely so as not to be understood and so as to prevent the great mass of Jews from being saved. So far as Jesus was concerned, it was a new kind of preaching: the sacred writers draw attention to this fact, which at first occasioned a feeling of surprise in the Apostles and the principal disciples. [457] But in agreement with most Christian commentators, we recognize that we should not excessively press the meaning of the words, "without parable He did not speak unto them," for these words seem to be somewhat hyperbolic. At any rate, they refer only to a limited period of our Lord's ministry. To some extent we should here give the word

[455] Godet, *Comment. sur l'Évangile de S. Luc*, 2d ed., I, 452.
[456] Lagrange, *Revue Biblique*, 1910, p. 19.
[457] Cf. Matt. 13: 10, 34; Mark 4: 34.

"parable" the general significance of figurative speech.

But this is not the difficult point of the Rationalists' second objection. That point is Jesus' own application of Isaias' prophecy to His teaching in the form of parables. For what reason did the Divine Master, at a particular period of His public life, use this sort of preaching, which He Himself says is less easy to be understood? Did he really intend not to be understood? Did He thus wish to close the path of salvation to most of His hearers? Were we obliged to answer these questions in the affirmative, then might our adversaries justly call this opinion "monstrous." St. John Chrysostom said: "If Jesus did not wish the Jews to hear and be saved, He should have remained silent and not have spoken in parables." [458] This remark is quite true and has often been repeated. Yet the penal character of the new form of teaching is too clearly marked by Jesus Himself and by His first biographers, and too justly accepted by most Catholic [459] and orthodox Protestant [460] interpreters, for it to be possibly eliminated. It must therefore be explained, as in fact it is, in a reasonable and satisfactory manner.[461]

We have no intention of denying that the change of method which Jesus adopted for His preaching, and the comparative obscurity with which He encompassed His doctrine for a while and before certain listeners, were something deliberate and intentional, but entirely justified. The Divine Master adopted this measure only after being morally constrained to do so by an increase of hostility on the part of His enemies

[458] *Hom. in Matth.,* XIII, 4–5.

[459] Maldonatus shows remarkable firmness on this point.

[460] To cite merely a few of the latest and best known, we mention Keil, Godet, Plummer, Swete, and Zahn.

[461] See the commentaries (in particular that of Knabenbauer, *In Evang. sec. Matth.,* I, 116 f.) and also the articles by Durand ("Pourquoi Jésus a-t-il parlé en Paraboles?" in the *Études,* 1906, Vol. CXVI), by Prat ("Nature et but des Paraboles" (*ibid.,* Vol. CXXXV, pp. 198–213), and by Lagrange ("Le but des Paraboles d'après l'Évangile de S. Marc," *Revue Biblique,* 1910, pp. 5–36).

and the beginning of indifference on the part of the multitudes. Thus it was that Isaias' prophecy, having first been
fulfilled in his own time and in his own person, was more sorrowfully realized in the person of Christ. But, just as Isaias
did not, for that reason, cease to be a sign both of salvation
and of reprobation, with all the more reason was the same
true in the case of Christ. God is free in the bestowal of His
gifts and graces. By what right do they complain who do not
profit thereby or who abuse those gifts, if God withdraws
those graces from them? That is what happened when our
Lord, by means of the parables, placed a veil upon the truth,
the light of which was contemned by many. St. John and St.
Paul [462] in like manner apply Isaias' prophecy to their coreligionists, and this unanimity of the Evangelists and the Doctor of the Gentiles is certainly striking. And they quote it,
without making any explanation of the difficult problem regarding the reconciling of human free will with predestination. They merely recall that God gives more to some than to
others. Would He not act thus, when those to whom He had
shown Himself infinitely generous have become unworthy of
His favors? What Jesus and the sacred writers severely express, "is the logical consequence, the natural outcome of the
fact mentioned, and not something strictly final." [463] We have
not, in the words of the present passage, an expression of "an
absolute decree of the divine will, taking away in advance
every hope of conversion, but the prophetic announcement of
an effective blindness," if the persons concerned do not return
to better dispositions. Therefore, to see in these texts, as do
the Rationalist critics, an irrevocable sentence of reprobation,
would be to distort their meaning, because the Savior did not
for a moment forget that He had come on earth to bring life,
not eternal death.

462 John 12: 37–40; Acts 28: 26 f.
463 Prat, *loc. cit.*, p. 211.

In St. Mark's account we note a most important reservation: "With many such parables He spoke to them the word, *according as they were able to hear.*" [464] If Jesus accommodated Himself to the understanding of His hearers, He did so because He wished to be understood by all. Mercy therefore combined with the penal character. The Savior's frequent appeals for attention, while He was speaking in parables,[465] are also to be observed here. No one speaks thus to an audience if He desires not to be understood by them.

The critics, therefore, are not justified in saying that parables are by themselves always clear, or in asserting that the Evangelists attributed to them a purpose irreconcilable with Christ's ministry, or in claiming that they have come down to us only after undergoing serious modifications which wholly changed their spirit.

XIX. The Calming of the Tempest, the Demoniacs of Gergesa, the Woman with a Flow of Blood, the Daughter of Jairus, as Viewed by the Rationalist Critics

We indicated above, in the case of each category of Gospel miracles, what are the latest and most usual objections of Rationalism, and what are the principles that aid us in refuting those objections. Consequently we have no need to concern ourselves with Liberal criticism in connection with the Savior's miracles considered individually. But we have just studied a series of remarkably brilliant miracles, and it will be useful to acquaint the reader with the thought of modern Rationalists about them.

1. Strauss frankly confesses [466] that the Evangelists consider the calming of the tempest a great miracle. But H. J. Holtzmann [467] regards it as a miracle "surpassing all we can

---

[464] Mark 4:33.
[465] Matt. 13:9; 15:10; Mark 4:3, 9; 7:14.
[466] *Vie de Jésus* (Littré's trans.), II, 189.
[467] *Die Synoptiker,* 3d ed., p. 74.

imagine," inasmuch at "neither wind nor waves become calm in deference to a moral command which they do not hear," [468] a miracle which the Rationalists do not admit really occurred. With them we, too, believe that wind and waves are creatures utterly unsubmissive to human commands. Yet, if the command comes from God, or from His representative whom He has furnished with all His powers, they are forced to obey.

Some time ago the critics commonly relegated the whole account of this miracle to the domain of legend. It was one of those "sailors' yarns," one of the "fishermen's tales," which abound along the coasts of seas and lakes. To-day a large number of Liberal theologians, while still considering as legendary those details which are of a supernatural character, acknowledge that the narrative may have a historical basis. "There was in reality some scene in which Jesus revived His disciples' weakened courage, and which left upon them an impression that He made the wild elements, as well as the devils, obey Him." [469] A notable portion of the Rationalist school declares that in the command "Be still," addressed to irrational objects, "there can be nothing surprising, for the man who says he believed that a word spoken in firm faith could cast a mountain into the sea." [470]

The author just quoted seems to experience an awkward difficulty, for he adds that "the only wonderful circumstance is that the lake actually did become calmer," and that, on this point, we have no reason to distrust the Evangelists, especially St. Mark, whose account is so dramatic. But a Rationalist is never long puzzled when there is question of denying the existence of a miracle. "Coincidences of this sort can happen. . . . It was not Jesus' command that ended the tempest; the regular course of things may well have calmed the water shortly after the command given by Jesus." This was cer-

[468] A. Réville, *ibid.*, II, 203.
[469] A. Réville, *ibid.*
[470] O. Holtzmann, *Life of Jesus*, p. 269.

tainly a fortunate stroke of good luck. But how are we to explain the immediate subsidence of the waves? This, we are told, is a legendary detail which belongs to the circle of stories due "to the supernatural nimbus which gradually enveloped the person of Jesus to the eyes of His disciples and transfigured it." [471]

Such are the best arguments which Rationalism has been able to invent against the reality of the miracle and the truthfulness of the narrative. Rationalism is constantly driven to fortify itself in a partial, subjective proof, which is incapable of withstanding an honest examination of the facts. The historical kernel of this miracle is supposed to be merely some saying of Christ relative to the power of faith, a saying that was subsequently transformed into a miracle. But we ask for the proof. It would be more logical, although quite as false, to look upon the whole account as nothing more than an allegory,[472] made up by means of various Old Testament passages, in which we see God commanding the stormy waves and making them obey.[473] Attempts are made to justify this view by citing the fact that this incident is often applied to the bark of the Church tossed on the waves of the world. But it should be noted that the application was begotten by the miracle; it did not give birth to the miracle.

2. The freeing of the demoniacs of Gadara (or Gergesa), as recounted by the Synoptics, is perhaps the one Gospel miracle that is most objectionable to the Rationalists. Strauss [474] sought to rid himself of it by ironically calling it a "fine specimen" (*Prachtstück*), and pretended that such a miracle was destructive of faith, even in those interpreters who had the largest amount of it. More recently, H. J. Holtzmann speaks of it as "the most bizarre of the miraculous

---

[471] Réville, *loc. cit.*
[472] H. J. Holtzmann, *Die Synoptiker*, p. 74.
[473] Cf. Ps. 17:16; 103:6 f.; 105:9; Nah. 1:4, etc.
[474] *Leben Jesu*, II, 25-40.

stories." [475] Loisy, who often takes Holtzmann as his guide, writes: "The account contains the most curious and remarkable of the miracles attributed to Jesus. It is like a popular tale," [476] and reveals the mentality of the Evangelists, who easily believed in the impossible, when there was question of the Savior. The possessed men of Gergesa were violently insane men, whom Jesus succeeded in quieting.

Catholic exegetes are in agreement with the Rationalists on this last point. But they believe that, in the present case, the madness was caused by a veritable demoniacal possession. Precisely from that circumstance arose certain extraordinary phenomena which the Evangelists mention, particularly the madmen's superhuman strength. Regardless of what the Rationalists say, neither Jesus nor the Apostles who witnessed the event, nor the Evangelists could be mistaken as to the nature of an affliction which was then only too well known in Palestine. We have the strict truth presented to us by the Synoptics in their three accounts.

What the Rationalists and many so-called orthodox Protestants are especially unwilling to admit is the entering of the devils into the swine. How stoutly they protest! "In the marvelous there are limits beyond which one may not go without unbecomingness. . . . To reconstruct whatever historical reality lies beneath this legendary account is quite impossible." It is "an inadmissible fact." [477] The fashion nowadays is to find almost everywhere, through the most supernatural elements of the Gospels, the famous "historic kernel"; hence these critics have reduced the miracle at Gergesa to its strictest expression. It all happened in a simple and natural way. The two madmen (for, we are told, they were that, and nothing more), in the final crisis, occasioned by their conversation with Jesus, hurled themselves upon the

[475] *Die Synoptiker,* 3d ed., p. 75.
[476] *Les Évangiles Synoptiques,* I, 799.
[477] Réville, *Jésus de Nazareth,* II, 497, 499.

herd of swine, and the latter became frightened and cast themselves *en masse* into the lake.[478]

Harnack, who is never short of hypotheses, holds that at first it had been supposed that the devils went out of the two possessed men in the form of swine; then the story was changed and developed, until it was believed that the devils, upon leaving the demoniacs, seized the swine, as our present Gospels relate.[479] But if we ask for proofs, none are forthcoming, save the alleged impossibility of the account as we now have it. But criticism has not stopped on so fine a pathway. In imitation of Dr. Volkmar, it sees in the Gergesa miracle a Jewish joke, perpetrated on pagans of shameless morals, of whom the pigs were the emblem.[480] The critics have gone even farther than this, giving the whole account an allegorical interpretation which one would hardly dream of. Herein we have the history of St. Paul, summed up in its four chief stages: his hatred of Christianity, his inner struggle, his conversion, and his mission among the pagans.[481] Albert Réville says with reference to this miracle: "The whole thing finds our minds absolutely recalcitrant." [482] As emphatically as we can, we repeat those same words in the presence of these theories, which have no basis or *raison d'être* except hatred for the supernatural, and which are far more difficult to admit than the most brilliant of the miracles.

As to the alleged impossibility of diabolical possession in the case of swine, an Anglican theologian of great weight makes the following remarks: "Can beings which are purely

---

[478] J. Weiss, *Die Schriften des N. T.*, I, 109 f. This is now the thesis commonly maintained by the so-callel liberal theologians.

[479] *Zeitschrift f. d. Neue Testament*, 1907, p. 162.

[480] "The idea of a humorous allegory about the devils may have occurred to the mind of the Evangelists." Loisy, *Les Évangiles Synoptiques*, I, 800. Cfr. P. W. Schmidt, *Die Geschichte Jesu ausgelegt*, p. 280; Réville, *Jésus de Nazareth*, II, 499, etc.

[481] O. Schmiedel, *Die Hauptprobleme der Leben Jesu-Forschung*, 2d ed., pp. 114–119.

[482] *Op. cit.*, II, 497.

spiritual enter and influence beings which are purely animal? How can we justify the destruction of the swine . . . ? On the first of these two questions our ignorance is so great that we do not even know whether there is a difficulty. Who can explain how mind acts upon matter, or matter upon mind? Yet the fact is as certain as that mind acts upon mind or that matter acts upon matter. There is nothing in experience to forbid us from believing that evil spirits could act upon brute beasts; and science admits that it has 'no *a priori* objection to offer' to such an hypothesis." [483] We fully subscribe to this judgment.

3. According to the Rationalists, the curing of the woman with a flow of blood was manifestly a case of auto-suggestion.[484] But physicians protest [485] that "this kind of hemorrhage is not cured by suggestion," and that its cure, when taking place in a natural manner, requires considerable time. The Rationalists pretend to be shocked at what they call the magical or magnetic character of this miracle. They say that "in the present case, Jesus' miraculous power became like a constantly charged electric battery," [486] which was discharged without the miracle-worker being aware of the fact. These assertions are but so many groundless errors; for we cannot for a moment suppose that the healing force issued from the Savior without the full consent of His will. There is nothing in the language of St. Mark and St. Luke to make us think that such an emanation of His power was without His knowledge. As adequately proved by His question, "Who hath touched My garments?" Jesus was not unaware of the smallest detail of what had just happened and He knew full well that an im-

---

[483] A. Plummer, *Commentary on the Gospel according to St. Luke*, p. 228.

[484] J. Weiss, *Die Schriften des N. T.*, p. 112; O. Holtzmann, *Life of Jesus*, p. 273, etc.

[485] K. Knur, M. D., *Christus Medicus?* p. 45. Cf. Ryle, *Hibbert Journal*, April 1907, p. 582.

[486] K. Hase, *Geschichte Jesu*, p. 547.

mediate cure had been the consequence of the woman's act of faith.

It is in order to be better understood that the two Evangelists, here and in another passage of the same sort,[487] make use of an expression which, if taken too literally, would seem to materialize the facts. We have already [488] drawn attention to the terms by which St. Mark notes an essential difference between the physical feeling experienced by the woman at the moment of her cure and the purely intellectual knowledge which Jesus had of the event. In speaking of the "virtue" that "went out" from the Savior, the Evangelist was not thinking of a magical or magnetic force, but of the divine power by which Christ performed His miracles. St. Mark habitually employs plastic, picturesque expressions; hence the language in the present passage. It is simple and clear, provided we do not give it a meaning which it does not possess.

4. We have only a few words to say about the raising to life of Jairus' daughter, because in connection therewith the Rationalists merely repeat the general objection which they make in connection with all three cases of this kind. Her death was not real, but simply apparent; Jesus therefore only drew the girl out of a lethargic swoon, which, according to H. J. Holtzmann,[489] was connected with the critical age which she had just reached. Rationalist writers and even some Protestant theologians who usually repudiate Liberal doctrines, take literally the statement of our Lord when He entered Jairus' home: "The damsel is not dead, but sleepeth." Strauss seizes the opportunity to tell them their explanation is "utterly wretched," [490] inasmuch as it contradicts the texts while claim-

---

[487] Luke 6:19: "All the multitude sought to touch Him, for virtue went out from Him, and healed all."

[488] Page 443.

[489] *Die Synoptiker*, p. 75. He does not say on what he bases this conjecture. Cf. P. W. Schmidt, *Geschichte Jesu erläutert*, p. 260.

[490] *Leben Jesu*, II, 171–173.

ing to interpret them. True, he forthwith rejects the event as mythical and legendary. We have given Jesus' words their true significance, which, in all three accounts, cannot be subject to any doubt, since the people of the household and those who had seen the child "well knew that she was dead." Professor Oscar Holtzmann,[491] imitating the procedure to which Ernest Renan resorted, demands "an accurate medical account of the form of the disease—apparent death, and return to life." And he says: "All that we can assert is that if the event had happened amongst us, no physician would have admitted afterwards that death had already taken place."

But this report does exist in the three narratives, as plain and clear as possible, although it does not come from a contemporary physician. The difference between such a lethargy and a disease terminating in death was familiar to the girl's parents, their relatives, friends, and servants, as well as to physicians.[492] Let us hold to the texts of the Evangelists; they are the best guides.

XX. The Multiplication of Loaves

We cite the objections of Rationalist or Liberal theologians only on account of the special importance of this miracle. We will group them under three heads. They are so weak that, for their refutation, it is almost enough to state them.

1. We are told that we have to do simply with something taken from the Old Testament. In accord with the lofty idea which the early Christians had of Jesus, He must not be inferior to any of the great personages of the Jewish theocracy. Moses, however, gave manna to the Hebrews in the desert (Ex. 16: 13–36); Eliseus once miraculously fed a hundred

---

[491] Life of Jesus, p. 273.

[492] A. Bruce, The Miraculous Element in the Gospels, 5th ed., p. 199. Cf. E. Reuss, Histoire Évangélique, Synopse, p. 342.

men with twenty loaves (4 Kings 4: 42–44).[493] But what relation does the manna bear to the multiplication of the loaves? Eliseus' miracle is, it is true, of the same nature; nevertheless it is remarkably surpassed by that of the Savior, and the analogy between the two events is merely fortuitous, not to mention that considerable differences exist between them, as to the number of the loaves, the number of those who were fed, and the fishes, of which there is no question in Eliseus' miracle.

2. The whole episode is to be traced to a natural incident which has been embellished [494] and transformed by Christian tradition. What is that incident? On this point the critics give free rein to their imagination and invent hypotheses as varied as they are arbitrary. For example, the crowd, eager to hear Jesus preaching, so economized in using their provisions as to make them last longer; thus we have merely an extraordinary case of moderation.[495] Or again, in imitation of Jesus, who generously shared the provisions of His little community with those persons in the crowd who had eaten theirs, the rich, who were abundantly supplied with food, gave a notable portion of it to those who were without any. In this way nobody had to suffer from hunger.—To these baseless conjectures we reply, in the words of Traub, a theologian belonging to the extreme Liberal school: "The account purports to set forth a miracle, and any interpretation which seeks to suppress this miracle contradicts the meaning of the story." [496] If everything took place in a natural manner, how did the crowd see in the incident a miracle of the first class, to such an extent that they wanted to proclaim the Miracle-worker at once as their Mes-

---

[493] H. J. Holtzmann, *Die Synoptiker*, 3d ed., p. 79; Soltau, *Hat Jesus Wunder gethan?* p. 32; E. Klostermann, *Markus*, p. 53, etc.

[494] O. Holtzmann, *Life of Jesus*, p. 287.

[495] E. Renan, *Vie de Jésus*, p. 492. Cf. Réville, *Jésus de Nazareth*, II, 71.

[496] *Das Wunder im N. T.*, p. 64. It is true that Traub then proceeds to treat the fact as a legend.

sias-King? How were the Apostles themselves so absurdly misled? We should note, moreover, that two of them wrote Gospels which relate the multiplication of loaves.

3. The external details of the so-called miracle should be interpreted ideally: Jesus fed the crowd with the nourishment of His doctrine. All the rest is the work of legend.[497] According to some critics, this legend was based on one of the Savior's parables, or simply on a recommendation to the rich, that they share their superfluity with the needy. Whether parable or recommendation, in passing from mouth to mouth it became a miraculous event.—What proofs are offered for these curious assertions? None. Zahn is therefore quite right in saying that "it is a waste of time to refute the sorry attempts that have been made" [498] to suppress the great miracle which the Evangelists here relate. In accordance with the principles of sound criticism, it is impossible to eliminate this account of a miracle—an account vouched for, as it is, by the four Evangelists, so that we possess a fourfold guaranty in the matter. So striking is this fact, and so lifelike and so marked with veracity are the details in the different accounts, that many Rationalist critics [499] have felt themselves obliged to admit, to some extent, the existence of an historical basis.[500] But what basis? They themselves do not know. But a miracle is there, and on account of the miracle they reject the whole episode.

XXI. The Promise of the Eucharist

The promise of the Eucharist is so clearly contained in the second half of the sixth chapter of the Gospel according to St.

[497] Keim, *Geschichte Jesu,* II, 432, etc.

[498] *Das Evangelium des Johannes ausgelegt,* p. 320.

[499] *E. g.,* J. Weiss, *Die Schriften des N. T.,* I, 120.

[500] Dr. Barth tells us, *Die Hauptprobleme des Lebens Jesu,* 2d ed., p. 138, that "there occurred something which stirred the crowd to the highest pitch"; but this "something" remains quite indefinite for him.

John [501] that a large number of Protestant and Rationalist theologians have, on this point, not hesitated to adopt the almost unanimous opinion of the Fathers and of Catholic interpreters. The chief objection offered by orthodox or Liberal Protestants who reject this view is that, if Jesus in His discourse at Capharnaum had the Eucharist in mind, He could not possibly have been understood. But the very facts may be left to refute this objection, since the Savior was really understood by most of His hearers, at least in what formed the essential point of His thought, the eating of His flesh and blood. The error of those who thereupon withdrew from Him, because they formed a material and crude idea of His promise, concerned only the manner in which the promise would be realized. It was not necessary that Jesus should make complete revelations on this subject the first time He spoke of it. With regard to the Eucharist, He acted in the same manner as He did in the case of the Sacrament of Baptism: He laid the foundation on which He would build in due time. Nicodemus was unable to grasp the full significance of Christ's words, "Unless a man be born again of water and the Holy Ghost, he cannot enter the Kingdom of God"; [502] yet those words contain in germ the Sacrament of Baptism. In the present case we have, much more than in germ, the Sacrament of the Eucharist with its wonderful consequences.

It is objected that the author of the Fourth Gospel does not mention the Eucharist elsewhere. This is true; he entirely omits the details of the Last Supper which refer to the Eucharist, because the three other Gospel narratives had adequately made them known. But he compensates for this omission by inserting in his Gospel the promise of the Eucharist. Albert Réville acknowledges that in this discourse of Christ, "the Evangelist alludes to the idea expressed by the ceremony

[501] Beginning with verse 48, according to most commentators; according to others it does not begin until verse 51.

[502] John 3 : 5.

which was already long established in the Christian Church when he wrote his book." [503]

Jesus had, on the previous day, miraculously multiplied the loaves and had generously played the part of a merciful father; this action was in the nature of a prelude to the Eucharistic banquet, in which He shows Himself still greater and more generous. "The early Christians were so impressed by the close analogy of the two events that, until the sixth century, when their painters wished to figure the Eucharist, they depicted, not the Last Supper, but the multiplication of the loaves, and they placed before the table at which Christ was seated, the fishes and the baskets full of fragments of bread gathered up by the Apostles.[504] The Fathers [505] also mention this striking relationship." [506]

XXII. St. Peter's Two Professions of Faith

What we have just heard at Capharnaum is a worthy preface to what St. Peter soon afterwards proclaims, on a more solemn occasion, in terms that are still more explicit and complete.[507] Those critics, generally Protestant or Rationalist, are wrong who attempt to identify the two declarations, as though the author of the Fourth Gospel had taken from the Synoptics and slightly altered what he mentions as being made after our Lord's discourse in the synagogue at Capharnaum.[508] Despite the similarity of the Apostle's two "confessions," the differences in the matter of place, time, content, and form are

[503] *Jésus de Nazareth*, II, 512.

[504] Martigny, *Dictionnaire des Antiquités Chrétiennes*, new ed., 1877, pp. 289-291; J. Wilpert, *Fractio Panis*, 1895.

[505] Origen, *Hom. in Matth.*, X, 25; St. John Chrysostom, *Hom. in Matth.*, XLIX, 3, etc.

[506] Fillion, *Les Miracles de Notre-Seigneur*, I, 28.

[507] Matt. 16: 16.

[508] Cf. H. J. Holtzmann, *Evangelium, Briefe und Offenbarung des Johannes*, 2d ed., p. 116; W. Bauer, *Das Johannesevangelium*, p. 76; Loisy, *Le Quatrième Évangile*, p. 477, etc.

too notable for us to regard them as a single one. The first took place at Capharnaum; the other, near Caesarea Philippi, at the foot of Mount Hermon, seemingly a few months after the promise of the Eucharist. The first acknowledges Jesus to be the Holy One of God, the Messias; the second calls Him the Son of the living God, which means much more. Although both were elicited by a question of the Savior's, the two questions are not at all the same. Simon Peter, in his first answer, speaks rather in the name of all the Apostles; his second profession of faith is more personal.[509] Moreover, the Rationalists make a purely arbitrary assertion when they accuse St. John of composing his Gospel by taking incidents from the Synoptics, combining and arranging them according to an artificial plan.

XXIII. The Two Multiplications of Loaves

"The Rationalist critics do not bother to attack the second of these miracles in its minor details or to offer curious explanations for the purpose of destroying its supernatural character. They simply deny its historical reality. If we are to take their word for it, there was only one multiplication of loaves, or rather, only one historical incident which served as a basis for this false, miraculous interpretation. In consequence of a confusion that early crept into the documents used by the editors of the Gospels, this incident was later duplicated. Thus we have two different versions of one and same legend, of one and the same myth, etc." [510]

As we said above, when discussing the accounts in St. Matthew's Gospel and in St. Mark's, striking resemblances

[509] See Lepin, *La Valeur Historique du Quatrième Évangile*, II, 30–42; T. Zahn, *Das Evangelium des Johannes ausgelegt*, p. 367, n. 18.

[510] Fillion, *Les Miracles de Notre-Seigneur*, II, 31. This is the common opinion of Rationalist interpreters, such as Renan, Keim, H. J. Holtzmann, J. Weiss, Loisy, E. Klostermann, etc.

are to be observed between the two events. It could hardly be otherwise, since exactly the same reason prompted our Lord to perform the same miracle twice in succession. Furthermore, the two miracles, when closely examined, are found to differ on a great number of points, as St. Jerome indicated.[511] In the case of the second miracle, the crowd had been following Jesus for three days; in the other case, they had met Him only a few hours before. In the second case, Christ Himself takes the initiative; in the other case, the disciples are the first to intervene. In the second case, there are four thousand men who are fed with seven loaves; in the other case, there are five loaves and five thousand men. In the second case, after the crowd had been filled, seven baskets of fragments are gathered up instead of twelve, and the baskets are not called by the same name. The date is not the same, for the two episodes are separated by a considerable time. The place of the miracles also differs, for in the second case Jesus is no longer northeast of the lake, near Bethsaida Julias, but in the territory of Decapolis. The final result is likewise different, for after the first multiplication of loaves the enthusiastic crowd wishes to proclaim Christ king, and He is forced to prevent a demonstration contrary to His Messianic office, by sending His Apostles away as quickly as possible and to "flee" to the mountain; in the second case, He is able to embark peacefully and return to the western shore of the lake. And Jesus Himself plainly makes a distinction between the two events, when He questions His disciples after the second episode. A mistake regarding such simple matters of fact was impossible for conscientious historians, one of whom (St. Matthew) had been an eyewitness of both miracles, and the other (St. Mark) received his account from the Prince of the Apostles, who was an eyewitness. St. Luke omits all mention of the second incident; but he also omits

[511] In his commentary on St. Matthew's Gospel, 15 : 32–35.

many others, which did not enter into his plan, without such events thereby having their historic validity impugned.

XXIV. The Promise of the Primacy

On the question of St. Peter's primacy, the Catholic ex-egete must face not only the Rationalists, but also orthodox Protestants. Although these latter accept the authenticity of our Lord's promise to Peter and although they apply it to the Apostle almost as we do, yet they refuse to believe that it concerns the perpetual institution of the papacy in the Church or, consequently, that it concerns the successors of Peter in the Roman See.

1. According to the Rationalists, Christ's words, by which He replied to St. Peter's profession of faith, are not even authentic. "This passage (Matth. 16: 17–19) must be con-sidered as a particular expression of the First Evangelist and probably of the Judeo-Christian environment in which he lived, with a view to which he wrote his Gospel." [512] Just as the Evangelist obtained his own special Christology from Peter, so did he place on Jesus' lips a reply that glorified the Apostle, whom he also strives to exalt on several occasions,[513] by virtue of a "tendency to partiality," for the purpose of contrasting him with Paul.[514] Hence it was the early Church that imagined this episode. "Peter was venerated as the first of the Apostles; it was therefore naturally supposed that he must have been the first to believe [in Jesus]." [515] Or we have here an embellishment of the account of Simon's first inter-view with the Savior.[516] On any hypothesis, the words in

---

[512] Réville, *Jésus de Nazareth,* II, 506.

[513] Loisy, *Les Évangiles Synoptiques,* II, 6 f.

[514] J. Weiss, *Die Schriften des N. T.,* I, 320. Cf. Guignebert, *La Primauté de Pierre,* 1910, p. 65.

[515] J. Weiss, *ibid.,* p. 319.

[516] Spitta, *Streitfragen der Geschichte Jesu,* p. 122. Cf. John 1: 41–45.

question were "introduced into a setting which did not contain them originally." [517] They are not and cannot be authentic: such is the almost unanimous verdict of the Rationalists. [518]

In reply let us first present an incontestable proof: all the Greek manuscripts and early versions contain the text which these critics so lightly and arbitrarily repudiate, solely because it contradicts their preconceived ideas. If this promise by the Savior had been fraudulently inserted at a later period, as is asserted, and not before the second half of the second century, [519] how could it have been thus received without protest everywhere? For we have other witnesses besides the manuscripts and versions. Although the Christian literature of the second century is comparatively meager, it furnishes a proof that Jesus' words were known very early in the different quarters of the Christian world. At the date mentioned, St. Justin [520] wrote that the Savior had given one of His disciples, called Simon, the surname Peter, because, owing to a revelation, that disciple had confessed Him to be the Son of God. The allusion to the episode at Caesarea, as recorded by St. Matthew, is obvious. The Clementine Homilies [521] and Tertullian [522] are also undeniable witnesses of the authenticity of the text. The same may be said of Tatian, whose *Diatessaron,* composed in the second century, mentions Christ's promise to Simon Peter. It seems to be considerably abridged, if the form in which St. Ephrem quotes it is exact: "Thou art Peter, and the gates of hell shall not overcome thee." But the essential is there; [523] and we should bear

[517] Réville, *op. cit.,* p. 499.
[518] See among others, H. J. Holtzmann, *Die Synoptiker,* 3d ed., p. 258; P. W. Schmidt, *Die Geschichte Jesu erläutert,* p. 320; Bousset, *Jesus,* p. 83.
[519] A. Resch, *Ausserkanonische Parallelen,* II, 19; H. J. Holtzmann, *Die Synoptiker,* 3d ed., p. 259; J. Weiss, *op. cit.,* p. 320; Guignebert, *op. cit.,* etc.
[520] *Dial. cum Tryph.,* 100.
[521] *Hom.,* III, 72.
[522] *Ad Scorpiac.,* 10.
[523] Cf. Zahn, *Forschungen,* I, 163.

in mind that the *Diatessaron* is in the nature of a condensation of the four Gospels. Origen comes a little later. But he quotes our Lord's words just as we read them in the Gospel. Origen, who was engaged scientifically in the textual criticism of the Sacred Books, would not have failed to protest if he had known that the words were a tardy "intercalation." We would be pleased to read this passage in the writings of St. Irenaeus; but he had no occasion to mention it. Yet it is possible that the words *"fundati super petram,"* in his treatise against the heresies of his time,[524] are a reminiscence of the *"tu es Petrus. . . ."*

The assertion that the celebrated text is not authentic and does not go back beyond the second century is "more than audacious," as a most competent modern scholar says.[525] How can anyone say that "the criticism of the texts does not allow us to attach a historical value" [526] to the verses we are here considering? It is objected that neither St. Mark's nor St. Luke's Gospel contains them. This fact, especially in the case of St. Mark, whose Gospel in general sets forth St. Peter's preaching, as early Doctors tell us, would be a serious difficulty if these two Evangelists had purposed recounting all the Savior's words and deeds. But it is certain that such was not their plan. We should therefore not require of them, in the present instance any more than in other cases, what it was not their intention to give us. St. Mark's silence attracted the attention of Victor of Antioch, the earliest commentator of the Second Gospel, and he seems to have indicated its true reason. He says: "Matthew set forth this passage with more exactness . . . ; for Mark, fearing lest he seem to say something by way of pleasing Peter, his master, merely gives an abridgment, and omits the more complete explana-

[524] *Adv. Haer.*, III, xxiv, 2 (cf. IV, xxi, 3). See Batiffol, *L'Église Naissante*, p. 255, n. 4.
[525] T. Zahn, *Das Evangelium des Matthäus ausgelegt*, p. 538, n. 65.
[526] Réville, *Jésus de Nazareth*, II, 501.

tion of the incident." [527] Eusebius of Caesarea is still more explicit: "Mark did not himself hear what was said by Christ, and Peter did not judge it well to repeat with his own lips what Christ had said about him." [528] If this be so, it was St. Peter's humility that was responsible for his disciple's silence. St. Mark and St. Luke preferred to note, in the scene near Caesarea, the fact that Jesus had then been clearly acknowledged as the Messias by the Apostolic College. We should add that the four Evangelists, without exception, mention the surname of Peter, given to Simon by our Lord, and that Christ's promise to His Apostle furnishes the only key to it.

There is another objection, which we refuted when discussing this text in its proper place in the narrative. It is enunciated by Albert Réville as follows: Christ's so-called promise to Simon is contradicted "by Paul's teaching (1 Cor. 9: 10-11), where Christ is said to be the only foundation that can be laid, and also by the Apocalypse (21: 14), which speaks of the twelve Apostles as the foundation stones of the new Jerusalem, but not a unique foundation superior to the others." [529] To this Loisy replies: "No doubt the other Apostles also, and all the faithful, are stones of the sacred building; but the foundation stone on which the house of God rests is that which the Savior established, Simon Peter." [530]

But Loisy does not long remain in agreement with Catholic interpreters. Along with Rationalist Protestants, he rejects the authenticity of Matthew 16: 16-19, on the ground that it was possible to speak of the Church only when the Church existed,[531] that is, according to him, following the

[527] *In Marc.*, VIII, 29.
[528] *Demonstr. Evang.*, III, 5.
[529] *Jésus de Nazareth*, II, 522.
[530] *Les Évangiles Synoptiques*, II, 8.
[531] *Op. cit.*, p. 9.

fruitful preaching of St. Paul and the other early Christian missionaries. Albert Réville voices the same opinion: "As Jesus did not form a church, He could not have instituted an ecclesiastical hierarchy." [532]

In reply to this objection it will suffice to say that the Rationalist assertion goes quite against the Gospel history, and reveals a complete misunderstanding of the Savior's work. The Jewish nation had for a long time formed the Church of Jehovah; but it showed itself unfaithful to its God by rejecting the Messias. For this reason Jesus had to establish on new foundations, as the prophets had previously foretold, a new Israel, more perfect than the old. When we study the Gospel without preconceived notions, we see that the thought of founding the Christian Church was always in the forefront of Jesus' mind. In fact, He instituted it in germ at the beginning of His active ministry, by gathering about Him His Apostles and a number of regularly designated disciples. All those who adhered to Him as to the promised Messias increased this little society, and it was right that at this period of His life He should take measures to assure its organization. Here again a Rationalist critic lends us assistance. Oscar Holtzmann [533] says: "In this moment [the moment of Peter's confession] Christianity was a realized fact. It consisted of a society (church) which had separated from Judaism and was now grouped about a new ideal; and in the faith that they had the Messiah amongst them, the members of this society had absorbed the glad sureness of victory which belonged to Judaism." In another place [534] he says: "In now calling His little band of followers His

---

[532] *Op. cit.,* II, 506. Cf. Wellhausen, *Das Evangelium Matthaei,* p. 84. J. Weiss, *Die Schriften des N. T.,* I, 320, after affirming that "it is unlikely that Jesus designated the society of His disciples by the name of Church," admits it is possible that He used that expression.

[533] *Life of Jesus,* p. 324.

[534] *Ibid.,* p. 327.

'church' (ἐκκλησία)—the same band which, in the words of comfort addressed by Him to the disciples, in Luke 12: 32 He calls τὸ μικρὸν ποίμνιον—Jesus is using a quite appropriate term. The title of ἐκκλησία confers upon the community, as far as externals are concerned, the succession to the Old Testament congregation of God, which in the Septuagint is described by this term; as the community of the Messiah, it has a right to this suggestion."

In favor of the authenticity of the Savior's promise we have the right to allege the language in which it is clothed. The words themselves and the many figurative expressions employed are perfectly suited to the period. Bar-Jona, flesh and blood, the gates of the abode of the dead, to bind and to loose: these phrases are all characteristic of the Aramaic of that time, the language which our Lord spoke. It is quite true that "Christ's joyous response to Peter's confession bears the stamp of originality in every phrase." [535] We confess that it is hard to understand how writers sometimes [536] assert that they scarcely recognize in the text which we are considering, "the habitual manner of speech of the Son of Man."

We would never come to an end if we were to mention all the details on which the Rationalist school relies to condemn the *"Tu es Petrus"* as a subsequent interpolation. But there is one detail which we cannot omit. The proof that these words do not belong to Jesus or His time is, we are told, that "they breathe the spirit of an altogether different period, . . . the spirit of the Catholic Church in formation"; and "for this reason the Church of Rome raised these words aloft on its banner." [537] They are said to contain "the first manifestation of the consciousness that the Roman Church

[535] Plummer, *An Exegetical Commentary on the Gospel according to St. Matthew*, p. 227.
[536] Réville, *Jésus de Nazareth*, II, 505.
[537] J. Weiss. *Die Schriften des N. T.*, I, 320.

felt of its predominance," [538] or, what amounts to the same thing, "a projection of Roman claims into Matthew's text." But another Rationalist very justly declares that this opinion encounters "gross difficulties," so gross that he fails to see in Christ's reply to His Apostle "a textual alteration issuing from the Church of Rome." [539] He is right, because that Church existed only in germ and owes its glorious and legitimate preëminence to the Savior's promise.

In short, the Rationalist theory regarding the *"Tu es Petrus"* is worthless. Many of those who hold it have so little confidence in it that they are disposed to admit that the passage (Matthew 16: 17–19) is to a certain extent historic, having as its basis some saying of Jesus that has not come down to us.[540]

2. Orthodox Protestants to-day study this text more calmly than did their predecessors of the past, and the Rationalist theologians. It is a pleasure to observe that often the interpretation they give it and the application they make of it to St. Peter hardly differ from those of Catholic commentators and theologians. This is very natural, since the meaning of Christ's words is so clear and evident and since it follows that they bestow on St. Peter a primacy, not only of honor, but also of authority and jurisdiction among the Apostles. What is no less evident is the perpetual confirmation of this sense by the Gospel accounts and by the Acts of the Apostles. We have no room here to develop this proof; but it is undeniable that, even while Jesus was still alive, Peter held the first place among the Twelve. *"Primus Simon, qui dicitur Petrus"*: these words, which we read in St. Matthew's Gospel [541] at the beginning of the list of the Twelve, possess a striking reality through our Lord's whole public life. Every-

538 H. J. Holtzmann, *Die Synoptiker*, p. 259.
539 Guignebert, *La Primauté de Pierre*, p. 65.
540 Cf. H. Wendt, *Die Lehre Jesu*, 2d ed., p. 153; Guignebert, *loc. cit.*
541 Matt. 10; 2

where Peter occupies the first place, in the beginning as a simple disciple, then as a member of the Apostolic College. Everywhere he is accorded the place of honor, everywhere he is shown to be aware of his high office. The Greek phrase οἱ περὶ Πέτρον (literally, "those about Peter"), by which the Evangelists sometimes designate the others,[542] is very eloquent.

The same fact appears even more conspicuously after the Savior's death, especially in the first ten chapters of the Acts of the Apostles. "Peter is the first to act on every occasion: he is the first to preach the faith of his Master Jesus Christ, the first to confirm it by miracles, the first to convert the Jews, the first to baptize Gentiles, the first to speak to the assemblies, whether there be question of filling a vacancy in the Apostolic College or of settling the early matters of discipline or of quieting disagreements; the whole Church, pastors and faithful, hear him respectfully, obey his orders, grieve and pray for him continually when he is persecuted, everywhere name him the first and look upon him as the head of the Apostolic College, over which he presides and which he directs. Even Paul, the great Paul who was taught by Jesus Christ, felt himself obliged to seek from Peter the confirmation of his sacred ministry."[543]

In explaining Christ's words to Peter, orthodox Protestants are now generally in agreement with us on the essential points, at least so far as those words concern the Prince of the Apostles directly and personally. One of the most eminent of them, Professor Zahn, acknowledges that formerly, in the school which he represents, "verses 17–19 were wrongly interpreted or their meaning weakened, or doubts were raised as to their historical character, out of fear of

[542] Mark 1 : 36; Luke 8 : 45.

[543] Monsabré, *Conférences de Notre-Dame de Paris,* Lent 1882, p. 63. Cf. Hugueny, *Critique et Catholique,* 1, 76; W. Bauer, *Das Leben Jesu im Zeitalter der neutestam. Apokryphen,* p. 456.

the conclusions which the Catholics draw from them." [544]

Some of those interpretations were indeed very curious. For example, in our Lord's declaration, "Upon this rock I will build My Church," the word "this" was applied, not to the Apostle, but to Christ, who is supposed to have pointed to Himself as He pronounced it. The modern Rationalists are at one with us in condemning this "unfair interpretation," as they quite rightly call it.[545] A more subtle explanation, which might appeal to the sanction of several Fathers of the Church, applies the Savior's promise directly only to Peter's faith, independently of his person. The most illustrious of our Doctors of the first centuries (such as Origen, St. Cyril of Alexandria, St. John Chrysostom, St. Ambrose, St. Hilary, St. Jerome, and St. Augustine [546]) are wont to say, in a mystical sense and by a sort of accommodation, that Jesus built His Church not only on the faith of the Prince of the Apostles, but also on that of all the other members of the Apostolic College, and on that of all Christians in general. This last feature shows that these early Doctors, in speaking thus, were not intending to give a literal and doctrinal explanation of our Lord's words, but were interpreting them in a broad sense. In other places in their writings they show their true thought, and that thought, clearly affirmed,[547] is that Jesus established Peter as the foundation of His Church, conferring on him a primacy both of honor and of jurisdiction over the entire Church and even over the other Apostles. It is, therefore, not merely "as confessing his faith, and also as confessing it on behalf of the Twelve," [548] that Simon Peter

---

[544] *Das Evangelium des Matthäus ausgelegt*, p. 546.

[545] Cf. H. J. Holtzmann, *Zeitschrift für wissenschaftliche Theologie*, 1878, p. 115.

[546] Knabenbauer quotes some of their texts in his *Comment. in Evangel. sec. Matth.*, 2d ed., II, 59. See also Palmieri, *De Romano Pontifice*, 1877, p. 246.

[547] For the citations, we again refer the reader to the scholarly commentary by Maldonatus and to the theologians.

[548] Plummer, *op. cit.*, p. 229.

is made the foundation of the Church of Christ, but in a personal, individual way.[549]

Most orthodox Protestants join with us in declaring that at Caesarea our Lord made Peter the head of the Apostolic College; but they will not admit what they call the "Roman consequences" of the words then spoken by Christ. They hold that Christ had in mind only Simon Peter, and not his eventual successors. Moreover, they say, Peter did not found the Christian center at Rome and was not its bishop; perhaps he never even came to Rome.

On this last point, Protestant theologians have acknowledged that the denial has exceeded just bounds, so evident are the proofs of St. Peter's sojourn in the capital of the Roman Empire. But they firmly decline to admit that the pontiffs who have occupied the see of Peter at Rome have been his lawful successors. This is not the proper place, however, to demonstrate the contrary thesis, which historical facts suffice to establish most conclusively.[550] If Christ's promise is not to have a perpetual effect, what becomes of the foundation of the Church to the end of time? Who would be its head? Who would maintain its dogmas, its moral teaching, and the hierarchy with which an organized society cannot dispense? The popes have nobly filled the office entrusted to them, to govern the Church after St. Peter; and they have safeguarded its unity as well as its perpetuity. We see what

[549] Loisy, *Les Évangiles Synoptiques,* II, 7, is here in agreement with Catholic exegesis. He says: "It really is not necessary to prove that Christ's words are addressed to Simon . . . who was to be and was the foundation stone of the Church, and that they do not exclusively concern Simon's faith or the faith of all those who might have the same faith as he; still less can the rock here spoken of be Christ Himself. Such interpretations may have been proposed by ancient commentators with a view to a moral application and mentioned by Protestant exegesis for polemical purposes, but . . . these are merely subtle distinctions which do violence to the text. Christ's words envisage Peter's rôle in the founding of the Church."

[550] Cf. Hugueny, *Critique et Catholique,* I, 120–125; Duchesne, *Histoire Ancienne de l'Église,* and *Églises Séparées, passim.*

has become of the religion of Christ in countries that have separated from the head established by Him. How can we believe that an institution which has been the salvation of the Church of Christ rests, in the last analysis, on a false interpretation of one of His sayings, or upon a surreptitious insertion of a saying which He never uttered?

XXV. Jesus' Prophecies About His Passion, Death, and Resurrection

In very clear and precise language, as recorded in the first three Gospels, Christ announced the humiliating and sorrowful fate in store for Him at Jerusalem in the near future. That prediction He repeated several times and added to it; for the thought of His bloody sacrifice was thenceforth, so to speak, the element in which His soul lived. It is true that He rarely mentions His Passion without also referring to its glorious ending, His Resurrection on the third day. When we read the Gospels, without any ulterior design, as we follow the progress of events, we are not surprised at these prophecies; there is no sound reason for questioning their authenticity. But they belong to the supernatural sphere, and those critics who have taken upon themselves the task of attacking the supernatural wherever they meet it, have not failed to deny the reality of these prophecies.[551]

According to most Rationalists of the middle of the last century, Jesus never thought He would meet with a serious failure. At that period of His ministry, He was planning, we are assured, to go to Jerusalem and there establish His kingdom, and He did not doubt that the whole thing would succeed. Recent critics treat this false assertion as it deserves. Thus Albert Réville says: "It is natural to admit that after

---

[551] Celsus long ago made them the object of his criticism. Cf. Origen, *Contra Celsum*, II, 13, 16, 18–20, 45, 54 f.

the Baptist's martyrdom, Jesus, being exposed to the wrath of a fanatical party, seeing the ranks of His followers thinning out, and having of necessity decided to brave the perilous chances of shifting the strife to the very heart of Judaism, was haunted by sinister forebodings. He was entering upon a combat that might end with His being crushed. To this possibility he resigned Himself in advance, not without an inner trepidation, that of truly courageous souls who triumph over the repugnances of the living flesh, because they feel them keenly." [552] The thought is expressed in language that is impregnated with Rationalism. But in a general way it is true, in the sense that Jesus could, even from a purely human standpoint, perceive the perils that were piling up over His head. Under such conditions, "His uprightness would not let Him permit His disciples to indulge in dreams of greatness so easily engendered by the very name of Messias. He had to warn them that His Messianic career would certainly be quite the opposite of a road of triumph." [553] Réville and the Liberal theologians who belong to the same school as he,[554] to some extent admit the historical character of these prophecies of Christ, because, if understood in the Rationalist fashion, there was nothing supernatural about them and because, taken as a whole, they seem quite probable.

But we have a double complaint against these critics. First, they have no right to exclude the supernatural element from the Synoptics' account, since it forms an essential part of that narrative. It is plain that the three Evangelists attribute to Jesus, at this point and in other like passages, a superhuman knowledge of the events foretold by Him. Liberal theologians fall into another flagrant error when, to eliminate the super-

---

[552] *Jésus de Nazareth,* II, 210.

[553] *Jésus de Nazareth,* II, p. 211.

[554] Among others, J. Weiss, *Die Schriften des N. T.,* I, 137; O. Holtzmann, *Life of Jesus,* p. 332; P. W. Schmidt, *Das Leben Jesu erläutert,* p. 321.

natural, they reduce the Savior's prophecy to its simplest terms by suppressing all the details which give it so much force and clearness. Jesus, they say, "could not have used" the expression "carry his cross," because "it would have had no meaning for His hearers." "He neither foresaw nor predicted things in those precise terms with that miraculous clairvoyance." [555] It is Christian tradition that "has substituted an impossible divination of the future for that fear which foresees danger, without being able to know its precise form." [556] But, say the Rationalists, was it not necessary, in the interest of Christ's glory, to think and say, after His Resurrection was believed and His titles of Messias and Son of God fully admitted, to suppose and loudly affirm that "the catastrophe [the Passion] with all its ignominies and pains and horrible ending, had been perfectly foreseen, accepted in advance, and expressly foretold by the great Victim of persecution?" [557] Jesus merely assured His disciples that, whatever might happen, even though He should succumb in the strife He was going to enter, a triumph was sure to follow within a short time. Christ's words were embellished and on His lips were placed the details we have read and are yet to read concerning His death and Resurrection. Those details were easily selected, since "they were taken from the subsequent history." [558]

Thus it is that at every step the Liberal critics alter and distort the Gospel facts, upon the most futile pretexts and often with no reason except that of their negative principles. With what do they replace those facts as related in the Gospel? With wholly arbitrary hypotheses, utterly devoid of historical foundation, and in flagrant contradiction with his-

[555] A. Réville, *op. cit.*, p. 210.
[556] *Ibid.*, p. 212.
[557] *Ibid.*, p. 213.
[558] J. Weiss, *op. cit.*, I, 137; P. W. Schmidt, *Leben Jesu erläutert*, p. 321; Loisy, *Les Évangiles Synoptiques*, II, 18, etc.

tory, such as related by honest men who were perfectly informed.

We are told "it would be inconceivable that the ulterior events had taken the Apostles unawares, if Jesus had spoken of those events as clearly and emphatically as the accounts would give us to understand." [559] To this objection Lagrange replies as follows: [560] "It is quite natural that the Apostles should have been surprised by the arrest, condemnation, and execution of Jesus, at the time when they were close to the realization of their hopes. Perhaps they regarded the Master's words merely as the baseless presentiment of an event that was irreconcilable with the opinion they had of the Messias. It is even more natural that the crucifixion should have ruined their projects and endangered their faith," even though they had been forewarned. If at intervals they perceived the danger that threatened Jesus,[561] their confidence promptly returned; and Christ's triumphal entry into Jerusalem completely reassured them.

XXVI. The Transfiguration

Reimarus, Paulus, Baur, and Strauss consign to the region of historical falsification, myth, and legend, an event which, by its very nature, is far above human possibilities. But if the accounts are studied without dogmatic preoccupations, they offer such remarkably strong guaranties of the reality of that event [562] that it has not been possible for critics to retain an absolutely negative stand. Between the three Evangelists who narrate the Transfiguration, there is perfect harmony, as also a certain independence, which is

---

[559] Loisy, *loc cit.* A. Réville, *Jésus de Nazareth,* II, 205, note, says: "We see by the sequel that the Apostles did not expect such a catastrophe."

[560] Lagrange, *L'Évangile selon S. Marc,* p. 208.

[561] Cf. John 11:8, 16.

[562] A. S. Martin in Hastings' *Dictionary of Christ and the Gospels,* II, 742.

a guaranty of their truthfulness as historians. Numerous details of utmost exactness testify to the objective reality of the miracle. The date and place of its occurrence, its witnesses, Jesus' prayer, the effects produced upon His features and garments, the appearance of the two heavenly visitors and the subject of their conversation, Peter's candid remark, the cloud, the divine voice, the fright and the joy of the three disciples, the sudden ceasing of the miraculous phenomenon, the prohibition which Christ imposed on the three Apostles, the conversation about Elias as they came down from the mountain: all these lifelike details prove that the episode was not invented. It is futile for the critics to allege the silence of the Fourth Gospel, since its author purposed supplementing the Synoptics and did not feel obliged to repeat most of the events which they had recorded with sufficient fulness. Furthermore, as a certain Rationalist says, "if we examine attentively, we will find the essence of the Transfiguration in the Fourth Gospel. Carefully read the passage in John 12: 23–25; there you will find, closely connected with one another, the chief elements of the Synoptics' account." [563] And does not St. Peter relate this glorious mystery in abridged form? [564]

Such being the case, recent Liberal theologians feel obliged to alter the basis of their attitude. The greater part of them no longer unqualifiedly deny the historic truth of our Lord's Transfiguration, although, in their usual manner, they strip it of all its miraculous elements, extracting from it an historical substratum which is false and ridiculous. What is the "nucleus" of the episode? It is simply this, that Jesus climbed Mount Hermon or one of its spurs with three of His disciples, and that something extraordinary occurred up

---

[563] E. Reuss, *Histoire Évangélique, Synopse,* p. 409.

[564] It is true that modern critics reject the authenticity of the Second Epistle of St. Peter.

there. As to what really took place, there is a great variety of opinions. Some suppose a sudden storm: the lightning illumined our Lord's face and garments; the thunder took the place of the voice of God.[565] Others, with equal seriousness, imagine some combination or other of luminous reverberations, with the snow of Mount Hermon as the starting point.[566] We have no hesitation in calling these explanations contemptible. They seek to revive Paulus' method of natural interpretation of miracles,[567] a method that went out of style long ago.

The most advanced critics to-day generally abandon these crude solutions and endeavor to find an explanation which will enable them to emerge more creditably from the difficulty in which this mystery places them. The word "vision," by which Jesus Himself designated the phenomenon of His Transfiguration,[568] serves as a pretext for a theory that is often adopted. It all happened in a vision, in the imagination of the Apostles, who had been greatly stirred by Peter's confession and Christ's acceptance of the title of Messias.[569] A number of variations have been composed on this simple theme. Loisy says: "With considerable probability we may suppose that the Transfiguration was originally an apparition of the risen Christ, a vision in Peter's imagination" [570] —a visionary apparition of course. The same author even goes into some detail: "The Transfiguration is really an apocalyptical scene; it is symbolic, like the visions of the apocalypses, and was first conceived as a vision." Most certainly

---

[565] It is a sad surprise to see Spitta, ordinarily more serious and reserved, have recourse to such a subterfuge (*Zeitschrift für wissenschaftliche Theologie*, 53d year, 2d fasc., p. 97).

[566] Volter, *Das Bekenntnis des Petrus und die Verklärung auf dem Berge*, 1911, p. 47.

[567] See Fillion, *Les Étapes du Rationalisme*, pp. 35–44.

[568] Matt. 17:9: τὸ ὅραμα (Vulg., *visionem*).

[569] H. J. Holtzmann, *Die Synoptiker*, 3d ed., p. 85.

[570] *Les Évangiles Synoptiques*, II, 39.

it was not; not a vision in the sense intended by these critics, not a vision to which no external phenomenon corresponded; but an objective fact, with all the circumstances occurring in reality, in the manner related by the Evangelists. St. Matthew's account of it receives its true interpretation on this point from St. Mark's version: Jesus commanded the three Apostles to tell no one "what things they had seen." [571] And those three could have seen only real events.

But does not St. Luke say that they "were heavy with sleep"? He does say so, and this fact is a proof of the truthfulness of his account. He adds that they overcame their drowsiness; [572] at any rate, they were quite awake during the three parts of the glorious mystery, and, as the small details of the account prove, they noted exactly what was taking place about them.

As Reuss says, "It is impossible not to see that the three Evangelists place this event in the number of historic facts." [573] They are not the ones who imagined it; nor did tradition, with a view to glorifying our Lord afterwards. How did the idea originate? Was not Christ's Resurrection enough to prove His divinity? The Transfiguration itself is mysterious indeed; but it had a very lofty purpose, and we feel there is nothing artificial in the accounts of it that have come down to us.

[571] Mark 9:8: ἃ εἶδον (Vulg., *quae vidissent*).

[572] This meaning can be given to the Greek word διαγρηγορήσαντες. It can also be translated as it is in the Vulgate: *evigilantes*, "waking."

[573] *Histoire Évangelique*, p. 406. In the same way, A. Réville, *Jésus de Nazareth*, II, 206.

END OF VOLUME TWO